Children's Literature Review

volume 4

Children's Literature Review

Excerpts from Reviews,
Criticism, and Commentary
on Books for Children

Gerard J. Senick
Editor

Gale Research Company
Book Tower
Detroit, Michigan 48226

STAFF

Gerard J. Senick, *Editor*

Jeanne A. Gough, Susan Miller Harig and Melissa Reiff Hug, *Assistant Editors*

Phyllis Carmel Mendelson, *Contributing Editor*

Carolyn Bancroft, *Production Supervisor*
Lizbeth A. Purdy, *Production Coordinator*

Linda M. Pugliese, *Manuscript Coordinator*
Donna Craft, *Manuscript Assistant*

Robert J. Elster, Jr., *Research Coordinator*
Anne Marie Dadah, Jeannine Schiffman Davidson, Kathleen Gensley, Robert J. Hill,
James A. MacEachern, Carol Angela Thomas, *Research Assistants*

Cherie D. Abbey, Frank James Borovsky, Denise B. Grove, Serita Lanette Lockard,
Marie M. Mazur, Denise Michlewicz, Gloria Anne Williams, *Editorial Assistants*

L. Elizabeth Hardin, *Permissions Supervisor*
Filomena Sgambati, *Permissions Coordinator*
Patricia A. Seefelt, *Photo and Illustrations Permissions*
Anna Maria DiNello, Janice M. Mach, Mary P. McGrane, Susan D. Nobles, *Permissions Assistants*
Margaret Chamberlain and Joan B. Weber, *Permissions Clerks*

Cover design by Arthur Chartow

Copyright © 1982 by Gale Research Company

Library of Congress Catalog Card Number 75-34953
ISBN 0-8103-0080-X
ISSN 0362-4145

The Library of Congress has cataloged the first printing
of this serial as follows:

Children's literature review.   1976-
Detroit, Gale Research.

(1)v.   29 cm.   semiannual.

Key title: Children's literature review, ISSN 0362-4145

1. Children's literature—History and criticism—Periodicals.
2. Children's literature—Book reviews—Periodicals.

PN1009.A1C5139   028.52   76-643301
                    MARC-S

Library of Congress   76   Serial

CONTENTS

Authors included in Volume 4

PREFACE

Walter de la Mare has said that "only the rarest kind of best of anything can be good enough for the young." The editors of *Children's Literature Review* enthusiastically endorse this belief. Accordingly, *CLR* has been designed and published to assist those entrusted with the selection of reading materials for children in making those selections wisely.

Each biannual volume contains selected excerpts from published criticism on the literary works of approximately twenty-five authors and author/illustrators who create books for children from preschool to junior high age. The author list for each volume of *CLR* is compiled to represent a variety of genres—including picture books, fiction, nonfiction, poetry, and drama—and is international in scope. Since the majority of authors covered by *CLR* are living and continue to write, it is necessary to update their entries periodically. Future volumes of *CLR* will include criticism on the new works of authors covered in earlier volumes as well as covering the entire careers of authors new to the series.

Organization of the Book

An author section consists of the following elements: author heading, bio-critical introduction, author's commentary and general commentary (when available), title entries, and bibliographical citations.

• The *author heading* consists of the name under which the author is most frequently published and the author's birth and death dates. If an author writes consistently under a pseudonym, the pseudonym will be listed in the author heading and the real name given in parentheses on the first line of the bio-critical introduction. Uncertainty as to a birth or death date is indicated by a question mark.

• The *bio-critical introduction* contains background information designed to introduce the reader to an author. These introductions typically begin with a phrase describing the author's nationality and the genres in which he or she writes. The text of the introduction presents an overview of the author's themes and styles, biographical facts, a summary of the critical response to the author's works, major awards and prizes, and, in most cases, cross references to other biographical and critical reference books published by Gale Research Company. These books include *Contemporary Authors, Contemporary Literary Criticism, Something about the Author,* and *Yesterday's Authors of Books for Children.*

• The *author's commentary* presents background material written by the author being profiled. This commentary may cover a specific work or several works, or discuss the reasons why an author writes.

• *General commentary* consists of critical excerpts from articles that consider more than one work by the author being profiled.

• *Title entries* consist of critical excerpts on the author's individual works, arranged chronologically. They generally include two to six reviews per title, depending on the stature of the book and the amount of criticism it has generated. Not every title published by the author is represented. The editors select titles which reflect the author's variety of genres and subjects as well as the most important books by the author. Thus, the reader is provided with a record of the author's literary development.

• A complete *bibliographical citation* designed to facilitate the location of the original article or book follows each piece of criticism. An asterisk following a citation indicates that the essay or book contains information on more than one author.

Each volume of *CLR* contains cumulative indexes to authors, titles, and critics. An appendix is also included in volume 4 which lists the sources from which material has been reprinted in this volume. It does not, however, list every book or periodical consulted for the volume.

New Features

With the publication of *CLR*, volume 4, several changes have been made to the series. Many of these changes were made at the suggestion of users.

CLR will now be published biannually rather than annually.

Bio-critical introductions now provide more information on the author; each contains from two to four full paragraphs, rather than the single paragraph style of previous volumes.

When available, photographs of the author are now included.

Authors who write primarily for a young adult audience will no longer be represented in the *CLR* series in order to expand coverage of creators of books for a pre-junior high audience. Coverage of young adult writers can now be found in *Contemporary Literary Criticism* volumes on Young Adult Literature.

An effort has been made to reprint criticism from sources which represent the full scope of a work's publication history—from the year of its initial publication to current references.

If an author has retold folktales or legends with what critics consider to be a special originality (e.g., Wanda Gág's *Tales from Grimm* or Tomie de Paola's *The Clown of God*), criticism is included on these adaptations.

Title entries are now arranged chronologically according to the work's first publication. Publication information follows the title headings in parentheses. The U.S. publication date of each work is listed first:

KING OF THE WIND (1948)

This format also applies to a foreign work published simultaneously in the United States and its country of origin. If the work was published in a different year in its country of origin it appears as:

EMIL AND THE DETECTIVES (1930; German edition, 1928)

If the work has not yet been published in the United States, we list the year it first appeared in its country of origin:

THE TROUBLE WITH DONOVAN CROFT (British edition, 1974)

If a book has been published under an alternate title, this information is also included in parentheses:

WHEN I WAS A BOY (1961; German edition, 1956(?); British edition, 1959, as *When I Was a Little Boy*)

Titles by authors being profiled in *CLR* are now highlighted in boldface within the text for easier access by researchers. When available, first names are added to surnames of figures in literature, history, and fine arts that are used by critics as comparisons to *CLR* authors.

Other Citations, a feature in previous volumes of *CLR*, has been discontinued with this volume. Since title entries now average two to six reviews, the editors feel that the most significant criticism has been covered.

Illustrations by authors who illustrate their own works are now featured in *CLR*. Each entry on author/illustrators contains from two to six illustrations. An effort has been made to select illustrations which are mentioned in the criticism and to place each illustration as close as possible to its critical reference. Each illustration is accompanied by a caption identifying the work in which the illustration originally appeared. An acknowledgments section giving credit to copyright holders of illustrations follows the preface.

Acknowledgments

The editors wish to thank the copyright holders of the excerpts included in this volume, the permissions managers of many book and magazine publishing companies for assisting us in locating copyright holders, and Henrietta Epstein for her editorial assistance. We are also grateful to the staffs of the Kresge Library at Wayne State University, the libraries of the University of Michigan, and the Detroit Public Library; we extend a special thanks to Gloria Sniderman, curator of the Ramsey Collection, Wayne State University.

Suggestions Are Welcome

If readers wish to suggest authors they are particularly anxious to have covered in upcoming volumes, or if they have other suggestions, they are cordially invited to write the editors.

AUTHORS FORTHCOMING IN *CLR*

CLR, volume 5, will include criticism on a number of authors not previously listed and will also feature criticism of authors included in earlier volumes.

Lloyd Alexander (American author of fiction and fantasy)—This acclaimed creator of the mythical world of Prydain won the 1982 American Book Award for *Westmark* and recently published its sequel, *The Kestrel.*

Jeanne Bendick (American author/illustrator of nonfiction)—She is a prolific science education writer known for the skillful simplicity with which she explains educational topics and for her lively, humorous illustrations.

Margaret Wise Brown (American author of picture books and poetry)—A pioneer in the use of sensory awareness in children's literature, she is the author of such favorites as *The Runaway Bunny, The Friendly Book,* and *Goodnight, Moon.*

Lucille Clifton (Black American author of fiction and poetry)—One of the most popular writers on the black experience, she reinforces the importance of developing a positive self-image in works such as the *Everett Anderson* series.

Carlo Collodi (Italian author of fiction and nonfiction)—His *The Adventures of Pinocchio* recently celebrated its centennial as a classic book for children.

Maria Gripe (Swedish author of fiction)—An international award-winner, Gripe treats her characters with depth and sensitivity in such books as *Hugo and Josephine, The Glassblower's Daughter,* and the *Elvis* series.

Arnold Lobel (American author/illustrator of picture books, fiction, and nonfiction)—He is especially popular for his easy-to-read *Frog and Toad* books and was awarded the 1981 Caldecott Medal for *Fables.*

Mary Norton (British author of fiction and plays)—Her magical *Borrowers* series is considered classic fantasy and continues to captivate readers.

Joan Phipson (Australian author of fiction)—In her latest novel, *A Tide Flowing,* this distinguished writer once again portrays the individual's need for acceptance.

Thomas Rockwell (American author of picture books, fiction, and nonfiction)—His popular novel *How to Eat Fried Worms* has been selected by children as the winner of several awards.

Shel Silverstein (American poet, author/illustrator, and songwriter)—His humorous self-illustrated poetry collections have made Silverstein a favorite with children. His collection of poetry, *A Light in the Attic,* has been a national best-seller.

Chris Van Allsburg (American author/illustrator)—Winner of the 1982 Caldecott Medal for *Jumanji,* this new author is noted for his unusual illustrations and the elements of fantasy that characterize his works.

Nancy Willard (American poet and author of picture books and fiction)—Willard's *A Visit to William Blake's Inn* won the 1982 Newbery Medal, becoming the first book of poetry to receive this award.

ACKNOWLEDGMENTS

are made to the following publishers, authors, and artists for their kind permission to reproduce copyrighted material.

Addison-Wesley Publishing Company, Inc. Illustration by Harvey Weiss from *Clay, Wood, and Wire: A How-To-Do-It Book of Sculpture* by Harvey Weiss. Copyright © 1957 by Harvey Weiss./ Illustration by Harvey Weiss from *Paint, Brush, and Palette* by Harvey Weiss. Copyright © 1966 by Harvey Weiss. Both by permission of Addison-Wesley Publishing Company, Reading, MA.

Coward, McCann & Geoghegan, Inc. Illustrations by Wanda Gág from *Millions of Cats* by Wanda Gág. Copyright 1928 by Coward-McCann, Inc.; renewed © 1956./ Illustration by Wanda Gág from *The Funny Thing* by Wanda Gág. Copyright 1929 by Coward-McCann, Inc.; renewed © 1957./ Illustration by Wanda Gág from *Snippy and Snappy* by Wanda Gág. Copyright 1934 by Coward-McCann, Inc.; renewed © 1959./ Illustration by Wanda Gág from *The ABC Bunny* by Wanda Gág. Copyright 1933; renewed © 1961 by Wanda Gág./ Illustration by Wanda Gág from *Nothing At All* by Wanda Gág. Copyright 1941 by Coward-McCann, Inc.; renewed © 1969. All reprinted by permission of Coward, McCann & Geoghegan, Inc.

Thomas Y. Crowell Publishers. Illustration by Harvey Weiss from *The Gadget Book* by Harvey Weiss. Copyright © 1971 by Harvey Weiss. Reprinted by permission of Thomas Y. Crowell Publishers.

Dodd, Mead & Company, Inc. Illustration by Manus Pinkwater from *Blue Moose* by Manus Pinkwater. Copyright © 1975 by Manus Pinkwater./ Illustration by Manus Pinkwater from *Wingman* by Manus Pinkwater. Copyright © 1975 by Manus Pinkwater./ Illustration by D. Manus Pinkwater from *Lizard Music* by D. Manus Pinkwater. Copyright © 1976 by Manus Pinkwater. All reprinted by permission of Dodd, Mead & Company, Inc.

Harcourt Brace Jovanovich, Inc. Illustration by Laurence Pringle from *Dinosaurs and Their World* by Laurence Pringle. Copyright © 1968 by Laurence Pringle./ Illustration by Tomie de Paola from *Helga's Dowry: A Troll Love Story* by Tomie de Paola. Copyright © 1977 by Tomie de Paola./ Illustration by Tomie de Paola from *The Clown of God* by Tomie de Paola. Copyright © 1978 by Tomie de Paola. All reproduced by permission of Harcourt Brace Jovanovich, Inc.

Harper & Row, Publishers, Inc. Illustration by Karla Kuskin from *All Sizes of Noises* by Karla Kuskin. Copyright © 1962 by Karla Kuskin./ Illustration by Karla Kuskin from *Watson, the Smartest Dog in the U.S.A.* by Karla Kuskin. Copyright © 1968 by Karla Kuskin. Both reprinted by permission of Harriet Wasserman Literary Agency./ Illustration by Karla Kuskin from *Any Me I Want To Be* by Karla Kuskin. Copyright © 1972 by Karla Kuskin. Reprinted by permission of Harper & Row, Publishers, Inc.

Holt, Rinehart and Winston, Publishers. Illustration by Elizabeth Enright from *Kintu: A Congo Adventure* by Elizabeth Enright. Copyright 1935, © 1963 by Elizabeth Enright Gillham./ Illustration by Elizabeth Enright from *Thimble Summer* by Elizabeth Enright. Copyright 1938, © 1966 by Elizabeth Enright Gillham./ Illustration by Elizabeth Enright from *The Sea Is All Around* by Elizabeth Enright. Copyright 1940 by Elizabeth Enright Gillham./ Illustration by Elizabeth Enright from *The Saturdays* by Elizabeth Enright. Copyright © 1969 by Robert M. Gillham. All reproduced by permission of Holt, Rinehart and Winston, Publishers.

Houghton Mifflin Company. Illustration by Karla Kuskin from *A Boy Had a Mother Who Bought Him a Hat* by Karla Kuskin. Copyright © 1976 by Karla Kuskin. Reprinted by permission of Houghton Mifflin Company.

Macmillan Publishing Co., Inc. Illustration by M. Sasek from *This Is Paris* by M. Sasek. © 1959 by Miroslav Sasek./ Illustration by M. Sasek from *This Is New York* by M. Sasek. © 1960, 1973 by Miroslav Sasek./ Illustration by M. Sasek from *This Is Edinburgh* by M. Sasek. © 1961 by Miroslav Sasek./ Illustration by M. Sasek from *This Is San Francisco* by M. Sasek. © 1962, 1973 by Miroslav Sasek./ Illustration by Laurence Pringle from *Ecology: Science of Survival* by Laurence Pringle. Copyright © 1971 by Laurence Pringle. All reprinted with permission of Macmillan Publishing Co., Inc.

Prentice-Hall, Inc. Illustration by Tomie de Paola from *"Charlie Needs a Cloak"* by Tomie de Paola. © 1973 by Thomas de Paola./ Illustration by Tomie de Paola from *Strega Nona: An Old Tale* by Tomie de Paola. © 1975 by Tomie de Paola. Both reprinted by permission of Prentice-Hall, Inc., Englewood Cliffs, New Jersey 07632.

Bernard Ashley

1935-

British author of fiction for children. Ashley is recognized as one of the most promising writers of realistic fiction for children approaching adolescence. His books are about becoming aware of the difficulties of life and learning to surmount them. They reflect his understanding that growing up is often unpleasant and that life can be terrifying, painful, and even dangerous for children. Ashley's young protagonists encounter conflicts at home and at school, with their peers and among adults; often they must make difficult choices to endure their situations. The fact that these choices are sometimes morally and socially painful and their resolutions not always happy are aspects that add to the credibility of Ashley's works.

All of Ashley's books are set in contemporary working-class England. Underscoring the narratives are unsentimental portraits of race and class discrimination and the effect of environment on children's behavior. Early in his career, Ashley was occasionally criticized for concentrating on the social aspects of his characters' circumstances at the expense of effective storytelling. However, his recent works are praised for successfully interweaving serious themes and character studies with exciting, suspenseful plots. Much of Ashley's professional life has been spent as a teacher and headmaster in multiracial schools, and his use of these children as characters and his observations of their speech, problems, and feelings reflect this experience. Although American readers are sometimes confused by the Cockney dialect and other Briticisms in Ashley's language, his works are credited for their skillful construction, honesty, and sensitivity toward children in trouble. Ashley received the Children's Rights Workshop Other Award in 1976 for *The Trouble with Donovan Croft* and was commended for the 1979 Carnegie Medal for *A Kind of Wild Justice*. (See also *Contemporary Authors*, Vols. 93-96.)

Courtesy of Bernard Ashley

AUTHOR'S COMMENTARY

Children from unhappy homes, children who are being "pushed", children who dislike some aspect of school life or who are at odds with other children, they are all living under long-term stresses which are not always apparent to others, even to the experts. At the same time, those who seek to help these children may often be doing so from their own stressful situations. So children's behaviour can appear odd and anti-social, their abilities can be underestimated, and confrontation (or boiling) point can be reached too soon because it is not always easy to be sensitive to the signs.

The Bullock Report (1975) says that, in addition to the safety-valve of second-hand experiencing, one of the values of literature is the assurance books can give to the young reader that others have similar thoughts and problems to his own. I do hope this theory is rooted in fact. As adults we discover there is no comfort like knowing that our family problems are not unique—for even if that knowledge cannot solve our problem it helps us to feel better about having them—and I would like to think that some children, somewhere, whose stresses may not even have been guessed at, can draw comfort from fictional parallels. Equally importantly, I hope their supporting adults can be informed by the same literature, their eyes opened to the possibilities of stress existing through similarities in factual and fictional behaviour.

The educational system contains a high proportion of built-in stresses of one sort and another—the whole business of examination and the awaiting of results, the changing of schools and classes, the pressure to read and to compute—and we must constantly ask ourselves how unacceptable stresses can be relieved. This goes for the social services and the legal system, too. In *Terry On The Fence* Terry spent "twenty-odd nights tossing and turning, and twenty-odd uncertain, bad-tempered days" waiting for an impending juvenile court appearance. Obviously I knew this could happen when I wrote it, but I was made aware of the comparative lenity of Terry's fictional situation when a worse example of needless stress occurred recently. Two of my pupils who were involved in a break-in at the school waited over two full months for a juvenile court appearance, and when they did appear the case was put back for a further three weeks because home and school reports on the children had not been sought. Meanwhile, a visible change had occurred in the older boy (10). He had become arrogant, anti-authority and unco-operative, and he had changed from a misguided participant to a tough law-breaker. I am sure this was due to the effect of stress. Isn't it only to be expected that for a child to survive such lengthy apprehension he should tell himself that none of us matters—the court, the police, the school?

I very much hope books *can* help children with problems. But let's make no mistake about it, whatever value literature may have in this sort of way, the most important thing about books must always be the pleasure they can give. The Bullock Report concluded: "We can sum up by saying that whatever else the pupil takes away from his experience of literature in school he should have learned to see it as a source of pleasure, as something that will continue to be a part of his life". If story books fail to provide that unclassifiable something called pleasure, both for author and for reader, then they have failed as fiction and are of dubious value as anything else. Once any other criteria are employed—no matter how worthy—the author saddles himself, or is saddled by others, with a responsibility towards a narrowed readership of children with similar problems or social backgrounds to those of his characters.

Because my two books have been "working class" and set in and around junior schools I seem to be expected by some to peg the writing to a level thought suitable for "these sorts of children". I find this view muddled and condescending. As one of my sons remarked on reading such a review, "He must think we're all thick around here." Good readers at my school in East London (who can cope with [Richard Adams's] *Watership Down*—and, incidentally, I don't know of any rabbits who can, so what price identification?) will, I have been told, find *Terry On The Fence* too difficult because it probes beneath surface characterisation and relationships. . . . No, books are for everyone who feels tempted to pick them up, for anyone who might get pleasure from them. How successful, in any terms, are books which create situations in order that children might come to terms with them? The acid test, I suppose, is how one feels inclined to catalogue them. When they are as happily placed on the reference shelf under "Adoption", "Divorce" and "Death" as they are alphabetically under author, then they have already proclaimed their failure as fiction. A need exists, for instance, for more books which reflect the multi-racial nature of society, for children who are under the stress of just being black, but if such books emerge other than because their writers have pleasure-giving stories to tell, then they will be as spurious as the worst offerings of the old religious press. A writer with a Purpose will fare no better than the over-devout teacher telling a story in Assembly. No hymn book slams closed as loudly as the young mind when the moral is reached. (p. 10)

Bernard Ashley, "Children under Stress," in Books for Your Children *(© Books for Your Children 1976), Vol. 11, No. 3, Summer, 1976, pp. 10-11.*

THE TROUBLE WITH DONOVAN CROFT   (British edition, 1974)

This is a remarkable book, sympathetic yet unsentimental, curiously convincing. The central theme is the relationship between a bewildered young Jamaican boy, Donovan Croft, and an extrovert English boy of the same age, Keith Chapman. Donovan has disconcertingly lost his power of speech through the double shock of his mother apparently deserting him, and his equally beloved father inexplicably sending him to a foster home. Keith unaware of these complications, looks forward to his foster brother's arrival with some apprehension. . . . For some while there is no change in Donovan's state. Whatever the Chapman family do fails to rouse him from his abject misery. The change in Keith, meanwhile, is rapid. His amazed

mother watches him develop (wholly convincingly) into a companion for Donovan aware of each change in mood, each degree of misery, and anxious to protect him from the contempt and active unkindness of others. As a result, Keith is deserted and ridiculed by his previous friends, two realistic characters called Tony and Dave.

The family atmosphere is absolutely authentic. . . .

Equally authentic and equally succinctly expressed are the descriptions of life at school and the behaviour and reactions of staff and pupils. One recognised the school secretary, hurrying away to her office, a converted stock cupboard, which the headmaster has to share when the psychologist . . . comes to interview Donovan in the only quiet place in school, the headmaster's study. . . . The description of Mr. Roper's reactions are brilliant in their evocativeness and economy of language. Mr. Henry, the boys' form master, is equally sharply defined, always angered by staff meetings, military in his bearing and language, wholly unable to understand Donovan's predicament. (p. 61)

Mr. Ashley has a keen ear for dialogue, and one of the pleasures of this book is the subtle style which conveys the staccato speech of Mr. Henry ('All right! Up straight and concentrate') then changes to echo the hauntingly rhythmic phrases of the Jamaican father 'We go to football, him and me, every home game we go to Park Lane') or the crude and limited phrases of Mrs. Parsons accurately reflecting her unimaginative and limited philosophy ('Go on; you bloody little wog!'). It is tempting to quote at length in an attempt to give the flavour of this book, and a hint of its variety, but it is more sensible to urge others to read it too. *The Trouble with Donovan Croft* has rare quality. (pp. 61-2)

Barbara Sherrard-Smith, "Reviews: 'The Trouble with Donovan Croft'," in Children's Book Review *(© 1974 Five Owls Press Ltd.; all rights reserved), Vol. 4, No. 2, Summer, 1974, pp. 61-2.*

[*The trouble with Donovan Croft* presents] a rather improbable situation, while not impossible, and at times the story is a bit sentimental; it seems odd, for example, that the other West Indians in the multi-racial school don't take a hand. The author knows schools, teachers and their anxieties and prejudices, and he catches successfully the flavour of the old inner city school. But the children who would be capable of reading this book would be older than the characters and consequently less interested in them.

J. Medway, "Eleven to Fifteen: 'The Trouble with Donovan Croft'," in The School Librarian, *Vol. 22, No. 3, September, 1974, p. 342.*

Children's books have come a long way since the days of [Maria L. Charlesworth's] *Ministering Children* and its like. Yet, while we may shy in theory from the notion of "improving tales for the young", in practice the line is often all too finely drawn between a novel and a tract.

This is especially true where so-called "social problems" are concerned. A touch of the welfare will keep creeping in. The trouble with *The Trouble with Donovan Croft* is just that it is so very worthy. Bernard Ashley's absorption in the case-history of a West Indian boy and his white foster-family leads him to forget that what he is writing is supposed to be a novel. Individual scenes, especially between the two boys, Donovan and his foster-brother, Keith, can be well and sensitively done, but too many of the characters, adults and children, are stereotypes performing mechanical actions with only the crudest sketches of motivation. This is a book about children written entirely from an adult point of view, showing what children's lives look like, not what it feels like to be part of them. Children reading it are likely to be both bored and suspicious.

"Lives against the Odds," in The Times Literary Supplement *(© Times Newspapers Ltd. (London) 1974; reproduced from* The Times Literary Supplement *by permission), No. 3785, September 20, 1974, p. 1006.**

[*The Trouble with Donovan Croft*] is most seriously about feeling, sympathy, loyalty: Mr Ashley has a marvellous ear for the way children speak, though he is less effective in trying to record their thoughts.

Audrey Laski, "Audrey Laski on Paperbacks: 'The Trouble with Donovan Croft'," in The Times Educational Supplement *(© Times Newspapers Ltd. (London) 1977; reproduced from* The Times Educational Supplement *by permission), No. 3261, December 9, 1977, p. 21.*

TERRY ON THE FENCE (1977; British edition, 1975)

A close, deliberate style fits the continuous narrative form of *Terry on the fence,* the story of two or three days in which a lad from a stable if quarrelsome home is suddenly thrust into a world of violence, stupidity and deprivation and forced to realise that nothing will ever seem simple any more. . . . With a careful enumeration of detail the author builds a picture of Terry's environment, both home and school, occasionally extending his view to other characters—the overworked, conscientious headmaster, the caretaker, Les's smart, demanding mother—but always coming back to what Terry sees, does, thinks and feels. . . . There are no tricks in the author's repertoire. What he wants us to know and remember about his young hero is delivered simply and directly. (pp. 2737-38)

Where there was almost too much documentation in *The trouble with Donovan Croft,* in this second book Bernard Ashley has *selected* his evidence, the important situations and the dialogue and descriptions that contribute to them. Everything in the book works for the story and towards the analysis of a boy's awakening to an uncomfortable world of decisions and compulsions. (p. 2738)

Margery Fisher, "A Change of Heart," in her Growing Point, *Vol. 14, No. 5, November, 1975, pp. 2737-38.**

[*Terry on the Fence* is] a masterly presentation of the sort of dilemma that could face any school kid. . . . The book's interest lies in the reactions of Terry to the gang-leader, Les, beginning in fear and hatred and ending in something like protectiveness. Les is a terrifying and at the same time pathetic juvenile villain, arousing the sort of mixed feelings that are perhaps the most useful things a child's book can build on.

Roger Gellert, "True Grit," in New Statesman *(©1975 The Statesman & Nation Publishing Co. Ltd.), Vol. 90, No. 2329, November 7, 1975, p. 587.*

[*Terry on the Fence*'s] moral issues are anything but clear-cut, . . . and the theme is developed with subtlety and a kind of robust humour. The escalation of Terry's misfortunes is entirely convincing. The story ends in the only possible way, in a

juvenile court, but the author has avoided a morally facile conclusion.

Patricia Craig, "Young Readers: 'Terry on the Fence'" (© copyright Patricia Craig 1975; reprinted with permission), in Books and Bookmen, *Vol. 21, No. 3, December, 1975, p. 66.*

[*Terry on the fence*] is absorbing and excellently written. I like particularly Mr Ashley's description of a disadvantaged housing estate: '. . . an untidy urban flower-bed, where babies were the annuals and the law did the weeding.' The most remarkable achievement, however, is the deep insight into and convincing portrayal of the special relationship which can develop spontaneously between kidnappers and hostages such as has been a phenomenon of recent real-life parallel situations, and this raises the book from the level of a good yarn to that of a perceptive and penetrating study in child psychology. Very strongly recommended. (pp. 45-6)

Robert Bell, "Eleven to Fifteen: 'Terry on the Fence'," in The School Librarian, *Vol. 24, No. 1, March, 1976, pp. 45-6.*

The awful pressure of being forced into evil by physical stress, discovery, and shame are dramatized in a perceptive book whose only drawback might be an unappealing format and the burden of British colloquialisms. . . .

Carved on the reader's mind are sobering conclusions: morals often depend on what's held over us, truth doesn't always open doors of understanding, and trust in fellow man is the touchstone of human survival.

Hildagarde Gray, "Young People's Books: 'Terry on the Fence'," in Best Sellers *(copyright © 1977 Helen Dwight Reid Educational Foundation), Vol. 39, No. 2, May, 1977, p. 43.*

ALL MY MEN (1979; British edition, 1977)

[*All My Men*] is less of a social tract than *The Trouble with Donovan Croft* and *Terry on the Fence,* but Mr Ashley knows children, and if as a writer he gives the impression that he knows them from outside and above, from the stance of an understanding headmaster, he also knows that kids will prefer the sort of ending he gives to *All My Men,* with everything neatly sorted out, the bully routed, the hero vindicated. Mr Ashley has a good story to tell and sets real problems for Paul to face. Anyone who still mutters about schooldays being the happiest days of your life might do well to ponder some of the appalling situations. . . .

Bernard Ashley's mistake, it seems to me, is that he is not content to tell a good story in his straightforward pedestrian prose. He would like to be a more literary writer than he is. . . . He sometimes overwrites. For instance, it is "dark stains of effort in the sun" which soak the shirts, not sweat; and the same fault can even lead to misunderstanding, as when Paul's father breathes "the shallow signs of unconscious exhaustion"; for a moment the reader may well think he has been knocked unconscious rather than that he is merely asleep.

In his quest for realism, Mr Ashley scatters exclamations with a will: Blast! Hell! Thank God! Hell! God, he was jumpy! And there is no doubt at all that many readers will enjoy this highly documented school story, and recognize its truth to their own knowledge of the world.

Ann Thwaite, "Warts and All," in The Times Literary Supplement *(© Times Newspapers Ltd. (London) 1977; reproduced from* The Times Literary Supplement *by permission), No. 3943, October 21, 1977, p. 1247.**

Every novelist has the arduous, if satisfying, job of creating scenes through which his characters can gradually take on substance for the reader. Bernard Ashley has placed his young hero in the classroom, at home, in Arthur's house, on the disused airfield, in the shop, driving his plot forward with no sense of strain or disunity, using dialogue when it is needed but relying most of the time on a direct, practical narrative through which he can describe action or follow out, plausibly, Paul's growing doubts and eventual decisions. (pp. 3220-21)

Margery Fisher, "Defensive Measures," in her Growing Point, *Vol. 16, No. 6, December, 1977, pp. 3220-21.**

Bernard Ashley catches nicely the atmosphere of new housing estates on the London fringe. Paul and his parents leave the familiar scenes of East London and seek their fortune . . . in Eastfleet. Paul, who has been the faithful lieutenant of the cock of his school, is troubled to find that Billy Richardson will have none of him—or at least will tolerate him only on payment. Paul has a brief tussle with his conscience and then succumbs. Only the love of a good woman, Lorraine who giggles, saves him.

This is the kind of book which many teachers and librarians have asked for, an honest picture of ordinary life, overdrawn only a little in order to sustain interest. It poses real problems and offers acceptable solutions. The adult characters are not too convincing, but Paul and Billy and the others have the authentic colouring.

"For Children from Ten to Fourteen: 'All My Men'," in The Junior Bookshelf, *Vol. 41, No. 6, December, 1977, p. 345.*

Terry on the fence, the author's last novel, excellent as it is, is surpassed by this one, his best to date. There have been a good many less than satisfactory attempts by children's writers to produce convincing stories about 'ordinary' children from 'ordinary' backgrounds at 'ordinary' schools. Indeed, many have been very damp squibs, but Mr Ashley has established himself firmly among the few who are pre-eminent in this field.

Young Paul's parents have moved from London to one of the less attractive of the Medway towns, and he is a new boy at the local school. At first it seems all-important to him to be accepted by the gang element, and he goes to great lengths to placate the school bully, even allowing himself to be led into deception and dishonesty. After a time, however, he becomes involved, rather reluctantly to begin with, in a project on the history of the locality, and he becomes so absorbed in and affected by this that the values of the bully and his gang are seen in all their hollowness.

There is a moral in this, of course, and one which cannot be too often stressed, but so excellent are the plot and the writing, and so great the author's skill, that young readers will not be aware that they are being given a lesson in ethics, though they will be very much the better for it. Very highly recommended.

Robert Bell, "Eleven to Fifteen: 'All My Men'," in The School Librarian, *Vol. 25, No. 4, December, 1977, p. 363.*

A KIND OF WILD JUSTICE   (1979)

*A **Kind of Wild Justice*** borrows its title from Francis Bacon's essay on revenge. That is what the book is about: Ronnie Webster's revenge on the world for what it has done to him. . . . The book is pretty convincing evidence for those of us (not just soft-hearted social workers) who believe that kids get into trouble not because of original sin but because of what has been done to them and left undone. . . .

It is a good story, complex but not difficult to follow, and surprisingly convincing most of the time, except perhaps for the language. Not even Bernard Ashley can convey the stream of consciousness that flows through the head of an inarticulate and illiterate kid like Ronnie. Still, it will do, and many children from quite different backgrounds will feel a stab of sympathy and identification with Ronnie.

Ann Thwaite, "No Easy Answers," in The Times Literary Supplement *(© Times Newspapers Ltd. (London) 1978; reproduced from* The Times Literary Supplement *by permission), No. 4000, December 1, 1978, p. 1394.**

Bernard Ashley takes a stride forward with this remarkable novel, taking the story of contemporary city life just about as far as some readers will be prepared to follow. This is tough, realistic writing, totally unsentimental, shatteringly honest. (p. 45)

I hope children will read this book. Thank goodness, it reflects the real life of a minority of children, but it has wider implications. Read as a thriller it is highly successful, with many exciting moments, a well-paced narrative and a little humour. Above all it is an honest book, one which rejects easy solutions to very big problems, and this surely is a quality which all children recognise and respect. (p. 46)

"For Children from Ten to Fourteen: 'A Kind of Wild Justice'," in The Junior Bookshelf, *Vol. 43, No. 1, February, 1979, pp. 45-6.*

Unfortunately, the British setting and Cockney slang make this inaccessible to all but the very good readers. For those who can overcome these difficulties, this is an exciting story, full of insights into the prejudices of race and class in England today. Ashley is especially adept at depicting Ronnie's fear of the printed word and his street-smart methods of avoiding print.

Nelda Mohr, "Older Readers: 'A Kind of Wild Justice'," in Children's Book Review Service *(copyright © 1979 Children's Book Review Service Inc.), Vol. 7, No. 9, April, 1979, p. 86.*

How [Ronnie] manages to get his father out of jail and to take revenge on the Bradshaws makes compelling reading. The British terms, particularly in dialogue, may deter some readers, but once they become swept up in the fast paced twists of plot, they will ignore what they can't understand in haste to discover what happens. (p. 65)

Kathy Piehl, "Book Reviews: 'A Kind of Wild Justice'," in School Library Journal *(reprinted from the April, 1979 issue of* School Library Journal, *published by R. R. Bowker Co./A Xerox Corporation; copyright © 1979), Vol. 25, No. 8, April, 1979, pp. 65-6.*

The suspense-filled novel integrates a variety of narrative techniques into a single entity, relentlessly probing the various subcultures of the East End—from that of the newly arrived Pakistanis to the gin-soaked, thrill-seeking lifestyle of Ronnie's parents. As in a [Alfred] Hitchcock movie, the tension is created through skillful use of details to develop characters, setting, and plot. The narrative utilizes street argot, thus enabling the reader to perceive events through the haunted eyes of the hunted and intensifying the sense of urgency and terror. Although some of the slang may be unfamiliar to an American audience, the structure, pace, and style of the story raise it above the standard thriller.

> Mary M. Burns, "Stories for Older Readers," in The Horn Book Magazine (copyright © 1979 by The Horn Book, Inc., Boston), Vol. LV, No. 3, June, 1979, p. 306.*

Bernard Ashley is an author to look out for, each new book is better than his last, and in *A Kind Of Wild Justice* we surely have a prize winner. Ronnie lives in the East End of London under the shadow of the Bradshaw brothers, who have threatened to break his back if Steve, his father, does not help them with their next job. Torn in two by divided loyalties, betrayed by his own mother, Ronnie strives to achieve some kind of balance and morality amongst it all. That he fails occasionally only heightens the readers' respect for this boy whose life has had no stability, no understanding of ordinary family loyalties.

There must be many thousands of Ronnies smoking in school lavatories and hanging around street corners. I wish that all their teachers and social workers could read this perceptive book for the insight it gives into just how difficult the Ronnies of this world find ordinary living. Like Miss Lessor the reader longs for Ronnie to make just the hint of progress in learning to read, but knowing the turmoil of his mind, the uncertainty of his resolve, there is just no chance that he will have the will, let alone the wit, to apply himself. This is a major novel, not sad but full of hope.

It is very readable for older children who may or may not live in a multi-racial area very like Ronnie's. Illegal immigration is a secondary theme. Through Ronnie's eyes we see the problems facing an Indian immigrant family. Most young people will have problems, hopefully not as great as Ronnie's but which will need the same courage to solve them.

> Anne Wood, "A Child of the Present," in Books for Your Children (© Books for Your Children 1979), Vol. 14, No. 4, Autumn, 1979, p. 9.

BREAK IN THE SUN   (1980)

Bernard Ashley has gone from strength to strength since *The Trouble with Donovan Croft*. . . . The early books, written as they were with impeccable sympathy and carefully accurate detail (Tuf shoes, scampi and chips, stainless steel Parker), sometimes seem too neatly formulated. Now his books show an ease, a more relaxed approach that smacks less of the social worker's casebook.

Patsy Bligh, the girl in the new book *Break in the Sun,* is a problem child; and her problem is one that has never before, I think, been raised in children's fiction. She is a bed-wetter. . . .

The boy in the book, Kenny Granger, also has his problems. Every day he wakes up to another day of being fat. Kenny reluctantly finds himself accompanying [Patsy's layabout stepfather] Eddie Green on his search for Patsy and somehow,

almost convincingly, their journey together releases and changes both of them, so that at the final denouement, with Patsy threatening to jump from the big dipper in Margate's Dreamland, Green rises to the occasion. Life is still a muddle (the story has no more cheerful message), but there is no reason to give up.

> Ann Thwaite, "Contemporary Fables," in The Times Literary Supplement (© Times Newspapers Ltd. (London) 1980; reproduced from The Times Literary Supplement by permission), No. 4034, July 18, 1980, p. 807.*

Bernard Ashley understands how children work. In *Break in the Sun* both Patsy, on the run from a brutal and brutish stepfather, and Kenny, a boy trapped in a mountain of fat, are brought alive for the reader with great skill and perception. The adults, unfortunately, are less rounded and less convincing. . . .

[The story] is written with a throbbing immediacy which undeniably grips the reader, and the thoughts and fears of Patsy and Kenny are explored in impressive depth. The plot, however, is scarcely credible, and neither the actors nor the children's mothers rise much beyond caricature; Eddie is powerfully drawn, but his return to humanity is still somewhat glib. The mechanics of Patsy's flight are similarly convenient rather than realistic: no group of adults, however feckless, would take an unknown child on an acting tour on the strength of the vague note which Patsy produces.

Bernard Ashley's previous books have relied for their effect on realism of character, setting and language, and *Break in the Sun*'s value is diminished by the extent to which that realism is undermined in the story and in the depiction of the adults. As a study of children under severe emotional stress, *Break in the Sun* stands with *The Trouble with Donovan Croft* and *All My Men*; as a novel, it does not. It has, however, enough of the tough, pacy, no-nonsense style of Ashley's earlier work to hold its intended audience.

> "Throbbing Immediacy," in The Times Educational Supplement (© Times Newspapers Ltd. (London) 1980; reproduced from The Times Educational Supplement by permission), No. 3348, August 15, 1980, p. 20.

Patsy's escape from a spiteful stepfather and her overworked mother did not interest the sixth graders who tried to read the book. . . . Patsy's adventures with a theater group are well told. Her dreams of a safe past and a bright future are credible. The efforts of Fat Kenny, Patsy's friend, to help Patsy and bring her back home result in a profound change in his personality. He helps Patsy's stepfather gain insight into Patsy's problems at home. All this should have made good reading. Too bad it didn't.

> Barbara Baker, "Older Readers: 'Break in the Sun'," in Children's Book Review Service (copyright © 1981 Children's Book Review Service Inc.), Vol. 9, No. 6, Winter, 1981, p. 45.

Tension and suspense are inherent in the linear structure of one familiar plotline, the journey—it may be a quest, a picaresque wandering or, as in *Break in the sun*, an escape. . . . The story has the ingredients of adventure—varied scenes, suspense, apt timing, strongly marked characters. But the adventure formula is broadened by a second purpose. Alongside the action—rehearsing, train journeys, a wayside camp, police interviews—a running commentary, in its way a kind of private dialogue, reveals what each of the characters feels and thinks. The reader is aware how the actions of one individual affect another, in an interaction both physical and emotional. (pp. 3844-45)

> *Margery Fisher, "Approaches to Adventure," in her* Growing Point, *Vol. 19, No. 6, March, 1981, pp. 3844-45.**

The author . . . creates a suspenseful plot alternating between desperate runaway Patsy and her determined pursuers. At first glance, the main characters (Patsy, despite all her vitality and imagination; Kenny, her schoolmate, a fat loner; and boorish Eddie Green) appear to be losers and victims. As events rapidly unfold, it becomes apparent they are survivors against odds. These lives, with their depth, tangibility and growth, involve readers to an unusual extent. Other characters also come to life in deft strokes. Not all readers are willing to leave the shores of the familiar, but those who venture into Ashley's world will find it convincing in its detail as well as interesting in its novelty.

> *Helen Gregory, "Junior High Up: 'Break in the Sun',"* in School Library Journal *(reprinted from the March, 1981 issue of* School Library Journal, *published by R. R. Bowker Co./A Xerox Corporation; copyright © 1981), Vol. 27, No. 7, March, 1981, p. 154.*

DINNER LADIES DON'T COUNT (1981)

Dinner Ladies Don't Count is a hard knotty story of Jason at school "in a hump". . . . This book breathes the air of the primary school. Sensitive without being sentimental, it hints of social issues that do not need stating and identifies the feelings of the ragamuffin well.

> *Peter Fanning, "Tin Can Treasure,"* in The Times Educational Supplement *(© Times Newspapers Ltd. (London) 1981; reproduced from* The Times Educational Supplement *by permission), No. 3376, March 6, 1981, p. 29.*

[*Dinner Ladies Don't Count*] has some universal qualities but is weak in its focus: Jason behaves badly, is accused of doing something of which he's innocent, proves his innocence—and that's the end of the book. . . . [The] story is adequately told, certainly perceptive in expressing the stubborn hostility of an unhappy child but less clear in depicting the teacher, whose soft question, "Oh, Jason! Why, love?" when he spoils another child's work has been preceded by her saying "You're a nasty, naughty little boy, and none of us wants you in our room, do we, children?" The dinner lady of the title is a staff member who, despite Jason's dismissal of her as unimportant, is the one adult who gets Jason to talk about why he is miserable and defiant.

> *Zena Sutherland, "New Titles for Children and Young People: 'Dinner Ladies Don't Count',"* in Bulletin of the Center for Children's Books *(reprinted by permission of The University of Chicago Press; © 1981 by The University of Chicago), Vol. 35, No. 1, September, 1981, p. 4.*

I'M TRYING TO TELL YOU (British edition, 1981)

Bernard Ashley is becoming an important chronicler of the proletarian scene, but this is one of his slighter efforts, four little pictures of days in the lives of the children of Saffin Street School. It is of course a multi-racial school, and Mr. Ashley has a keen ear for the authentic cadences of Pakistan, the West Indies and places nearer home. Nothing much happens: the wedding car goes to the wrong church, Lenny doesn't pinch the postal order, Sir has a new car—but not so new after all, and so on. In their brevity, their concern with everyday things, their uncrowded pages, the stories may appeal to older children who are still finding reading difficult. The rest romp through them with gusto.

> *"For Children from Ten to Fourteen: 'I'm Trying to Tell You',"* in The Junior Bookshelf, *Vol. 45, No. 4, August, 1981, p. 155.*

Jean de Brunhoff

1899-1937

Laurent de Brunhoff

1925-

Photograph by Schall: courtesy of Random House, Inc.

Wide World Photos

French father and son author/illustrators for children. Both de Brunhoffs share credit for the beloved character of Babar, the elephant king: Jean for creating Babar and establishing his history and personality, and Laurent for keeping him contemporary. *The Story of Babar the Little Elephant* developed out of the spontaneous stories de Brunhoff and his wife, Cecil, told their children. Initially written and illustrated solely for family enjoyment, the book was immediately successful for its natural characterizations, colorful, detailed illustrations, and the excitement and warmth of its text. De Brunhoff introduced several continuing characters throughout seven books, including Babar's benefactress The Old Lady (the only human of any note), his wife, Queen Celeste, their children Pom, Flora, and Alexander, Zephir the monkey, and several officials of the kingdom of Celesteville. It was thought Babar's adventures were over when de Brunhoff died in 1937, but ten years later his oldest son wrote and illustrated *Babar's Cousin: That Rascal Arthur,* and the series has continued ever since.

Laurent de Brunhoff's Babar books met with the same immediate popularity as those of his father. While most critics were pleased with the transition, noting little difference in the writing and drawing styles, some pointed out that Laurent was not his father's equal and that his works lacked the crispness and distinctive storytelling ability that characterized the earlier books. Nonetheless, Laurent has continued to create new situations for Babar. He has expanded Babar's realm of experience by having him travel to such exotic places as America and Outer Space and dabble in gardening, cooking, and other hobbies. Some critics claim that Laurent is too prolific—the Babar stories now number in the twenties—and that Babar has lost his original charm. They also argue that recent collections of short stories and the introduction of Babar to television have diminished his appeal. However, the tales are still considered classic anthropomorphic animal stories and are consistent favorites with children. Laurent has also created original characters, most of them animals; his characterizations are said to be more childlike than those of the Babar stories, and his illustrations for these works range from elaborate, surrealistic pieces to simple lines and subtle colors. These books fare better critically than de Brunhoff's Babar stories since reviewers are more appreciative of his talents in the works that are totally his own conception.

The early Babar books were unique in several ways, the most obvious being their physical size—they were originally published as large, oversize volumes with the text printed in cursive writing and illustrations often spread over two pages. This format was deemed highly responsible for the fascination children had with the books—they were literally able to immerse themselves in them and could follow the stories easily through the large pictures. Many adults asked by their children to read *The Story of Babar* aloud were shocked by the frankness of the violent death of Babar's mother. Some critics felt this was an overly mature element to include in a work for young children and feared it would be disturbing to them, but most children accepted it without distress. Adult readers were often fascinated by the structure of Babar's kingdom and its political ramifications, and the stories are often subjects for cultural and sociological discussions.

Current Babar books are published in a standard size, but their appeal has not waned with children. It is felt that Jean de Brunhoff's creation will last since his stories are invested with enthusiasm, wisdom, affection, and the knowledge of what pleases children; Laurent has not measurably changed this philosophy and has added his own attributes to the series as well. *The Story of Babar* was selected for the Lewis Carroll Shelf Award in 1959, and Laurent de Brunhoff was awarded the New York Times Choice of Best Illustrated Books of the Year for *Babar's Fair* in 1956. (See also *Contemporary Authors*, Vols. 73-76.)

GENERAL COMMENTARY

When the creator of the Babar books, M. Jean de Brunhoff, died not long ago, the world lost Edward Lear's closest neighbour. If de Brunhoff was not quite so great a man it was because he was not quite so fancy-free. But he had that power of careful observation that allowed him again and again to hit on ideas so simple and obvious that nobody has thought of them in just that way before, though everybody wishes they had. And they are all ideas that children want to be told about. He never digs slyly at grown-ups, or remarks in a clever-clever way what sillies they are; but he treats them as of great importance, and whenever he makes them speak (they are usually grown-up elephants) they say something characteristic and weighty. The adult talk is, indeed, highly educative to parents who are out to improve themselves, for it consists almost entirely of clichés of the kind likely to strike the ears of children. Here are some examples. (Simple) "The refreshments were delicious. What a glorious day! The time passed only too quickly!" (Pompous) "I had the greatest difficulty last year in arranging an even distribution of toys." (Phrase-book style, parent conscious of the presence of foreigners) "Good morning, Lady Whale. I am Babar the King of the elephants, and this is my wife, Celeste. We have had a balloon accident."

Examined as a continuous and connected comment on life, Babar would let one down, perhaps. . . . What, for instance, is one to make of Celesteville, city created by elephants for elephants, but as far as lagging humans are concerned entirely a city of the future? . . . Is this a comment on our poor efforts in the present, or is it a plan for the future? And to what capital

(Moscow or Berlin—surely not Paris or London) are we to look for practical details? The elephants, having built their model city, discover that they experience precisely the same number of joys and misfortunes in it as they did before they thought of its existence. It is the parrots that have the final word, repeating over and over again with their parrot voices, "Come and see Celesteville, most beautiful of towns!"

In most books for children you (and especially children) can feel the author thinking up incidents, and filling them out as much as possible. In the Babar world, as in the Peter Rabbit world of old, you are allowed a look in now and again, but there is obviously a lot going on you do not hear about at all, because the animals have such very busy lives. This can easily be told from the pictures, where there is often a lot going on that the author does not bother to mention in the text.

As an artist de Brunhoff may easily live longer than some of the men who influenced him. His trees after Dufy and his ballet-decor flames take part in a life as active as that of the elephants who live with them. Not much that was worth while in European art of the last thirty years escaped the attention of this observant artist; and the Douanier Rousseau, Picasso, Matisse and Chagall are only a few of the artists who are echoed without being imitated in colour or form. There was evidently nothing too good or too complicated or too highbrow for him to use in his own way. Nor was it only the good art of the present that he rifled so brilliantly. In *Babar the King* there is a big double-page picture of the awful spirits of Misfortune and Despair fleeing before the elephant hordes of Happiness that combines the didactic, sermon-like quality and the simple colourfulness of early church wall-paintings. De Brunhoff could use anything and everything.

John Piper, "Babar the Elephant," in The Spectator *(© 1940 by* The Spectator; *reprinted by permission of* The Spectator), *No. 5867, December 6, 1940, p. 611.*

Everything about [*The Story of Babar*] was revolutionary, from its glacine jacket, sparkling over its gay red cover, to its sheer physical size. Its large pages caught everyone's attention. Many said it was too large, cumbersome, unwieldly, impossible for a child to manipulate alone, etc., etc. But the reception it met with, at the hands of every child who had the luck to encounter it, soon robbed those critics of their argument. (p. 49)

Soon, of course, people said, *"If big picture books are the order of the day, let us all do big picture books!"* A fair number appeared, and more were designed, but most of them served only to demonstrate the rarity of such talent as de Brunhoff's.

What always struck me first and most vitally about his work was its benevolence, expressed in the smooth curves of his figures, in the clear tones of his colours, in the open simplicity of his designs. There were no jagged flashes of fear, no unexplained darknesses to threaten, no niggling meaningless gestures to disturb and disrupt. He never roused that uneasy excitement which so often betrays the secret fear which a child cannot, even though willing, find words to express. Moreover, his humour is innocent of all mockery and malice. Indeed, the benevolence permeating everything he did must, I feel sure, have been fundamental in the personality of the man himself.

Yes, benevolence is the first note he strikes, but two other qualities come almost as quickly to my mind: his inventiveness, and his understanding of human nature.

Right from the very first page of the first Babar book these qualities are evident and striking, and play their part in winning the appreciation of the very young.

Recall the opening scene in **The Story of Babar,** where the baby elephant and his mother are resting in the shade of the trees, and the first few lines of the text tell, very simply, all a child wants to know about them. It says:

> "In the Great Forest a little elephant was born. His name was Babar. His mother loved him dearly, and used to rock him to sleep with her trunk, singing to him softly the while."

Elephant or human baby, the implication of all-embracing motherly love, and of childish trust in the same: and there, within the limits of childish experience, in the simplest terms, is a description of unshadowed bliss.

On the next page de Brunhoff carries us to a playground where thirty-one little elephants and two monkeys are disporting themselves in and around a lake—and almost every one of them is worth a child's particular attention. This is by no means the most typical example of the artist's inventiveness, but it will serve, since it leaves so much for the child to find out for himself by sheer intelligent observation.

It is by virtue of his humanity that de Brunhoff understands so well the shape and style of adventure which provokes a child's imagination to lively action, and that also may be instanced from the first Babar book, though it is found consistently all through the series. Recall the giving of a purse—an apparently limitless purse—to Babar and allowing him to go shopping alone. The incident with the lift, too, is peculiarly satisfying, for most children will enter into his feelings when he succeeds in going up and down in it ten times without stopping, and will sympathize wholeheartedly with him when the liftboy stops him and is heard to say, *"Sir, this is not a toy!"*

There is fun behind, and fun sparkling through every detail of Babar's experiences, and when it bursts out into occasional slapstick comedy, it is always of the kind children most enjoy—as, for example, the morning exercises with the little old lady, or the grand device in **Babar's Travels** for the defeat of the rhinos.

De Brunhoff creates an atmosphere which is spacious and leisurely. The adult may want to hurry on from page to page, urging the child "to see what happens next." But, unmolested, the child will most probably follow the intention of the artist, and pursue with questing forefinger, the activities going on in each corner and section of the picture.

There is one episode in the first Babar book which has caused much shaking of heads—and, indeed, I myself always feel a little shock when I come across it unexpectedly, and see the little hunter with his gun, and Babar's mother lying there, dead.

Perhaps in the past we have been so safe that it has been too easy to shake our heads and say disparagingly of such scenes—and this is not an unusual one in French books for children: *"Oh, the French are like that!"* That may be so—and with reason. But now that we have learned from the fringes of experience that death may actually drop down suddenly, wantonly and devastatingly, out of a clear sky, on to even an English child's mother, I wonder whether our own outlook may not change a little? I fancy many of our children, with that curious and completely unreflective realism of theirs, may not accept that death scene as "just the way of the world" as

From The Story of Babar, the Little Elephant, *written and illustrated by Jean de Brunhoff.*

the good old fairy tales have it, and as perhaps the French children always did, being more familiar with the general situation. Perhaps even this scene may have something to do with the artist's intimate knowledge of the mind of a child which accepts unquestioningly the fate of the grandmother, as long as Little Red Riding Hood is safe. It is certainly notable that he has kept the human values of that picture so lightly balanced that there is little stress of emotion, no sadism, nothing morbid, only a sad fact, simply portrayed.

Further, I maintain that plunge where you will into any of the Babar books, you will never have to look far for signs of his benevolence, and for that insight, that accurate recalling of childish experience in its real-life dimensions, and the exact terms of a child's reactions to it. Those big pictures, full and varied and suggestive, stir up memory, natural curiosity, and longings both satisfied and otherwise. Even adults, coming on the picture of Father Christmas's workshop, for example, will surely find themselves obliged to linger over it, examining the detail, and speculating on hidden contents or possible issues, unstated in the text. Surely only those who have green cheese in place of a heart, can fail to feel curiosity as to the contents of all those promising stores of sacks and boxes? The child who is free from adult pressure, fear of criticism, and spared the self-consciousness of knowing itself watched, will find a whole omnibus book of stories to be discovered, one by one, as the full intention of each section of each picture is comprehended. And part of the great success of these books lies in that private appeal to the reader to explore for herself, to seek and to unravel, the whole full story which the artist has painted there. Who has eyes to see let him see.

There is, of course, too, in all the Babar books, the good wholesome taste of nursery morality. It is borne in on the reader that one must be kind and considerate: one must not be selfish: people should help one another—that people do, in fact, help one another—and that, if these standards are neglected, life cannot go on happily. Witness, on the one hand, the burning down of Cornelius's house in *Babar the King,* and all the attendant disasters, with Babar's subsequent nightmare in which he saw very clearly the cause of all the trouble. And witness, on the other hand, the successful outcome of Babar's painstaking quest for Father Christmas.

Unquestionably, one man's whole genius went to the making of these books; his whole artistic skill, the full weight and strength of his personality, and all the wit and wisdom of his adult mind. (pp. 49-53)

Eleanor Graham, ''The Genius of de Brunhoff: The Creator of the Babar Books,'' in The Junior Bookshelf, *Vol. 5, No. 2, January, 1941, pp. 49-55.*

It is adult rather than childish preference which from time to time awards a classic accolade to particular characters in nursery literature. Two generations back it was Alice and Peter Rabbit, then, save our souls, Winnie-the-Pooh, and today Babar. What is it that the adults find so remarkable? Why does Babar reign among the immortals?

Perhaps it is simply the author's prophetic insight into French politics: Babar, born c. 1933, is a long-nosed gentleman who returns to his devastated country in the midst of a disastrous war against the rhinoceroses; under his paternal rule as *Général-Président* the elephants achieve unheard-of prosperity; Babar, like his human counterpart, now travels in a Citröen DS19 and leads a genteel bourgeois existence in a country château remote from the turmoil of Celesteville politics.

Or should we look for Freudian symbolism? Any overdressed European male must surely derive considerable exhibitionist delight from seeing himself displayed as an elephant, whichever end you approach the matter. And no doubt there are all sorts of other possibilities as far-fetched or as obvious as you will.

But let us consider some matters of fact. The Old Lady (La Vieille Dame) recurs in all the stories. She is a direct link with mundane reality and she is the only human character of any consequence. The others such as Fernando, a circus owner, a nameless sea captain, sundry Arabs and Africans etc. make only brief appearances, usually in crowd scenes. The Old Lady has no personal name. In the earlier (Jean de Brunhoff) books the geography is a nice blend of North Africa and Southern or even Central France. Real places are never mentioned by name, but the pictures imply that it is just a short scamper from darkest Africa to the banks of the Seine. A later (Laurent de Brunhoff) volume jumbles up Arabs and kangaroos. This seems to me a mistake; it is the wrong kind of inconsistency.

Babar himself is a thoroughly civilized elephant who sleeps in a bed, reads the newspaper, drives a car, and so on. To wear no clothes is a mark of savagery. This is a characteristic both of pre-Babar elephants and of post-Babar black men ('savages'). The increasing opulence of the elephant ruling class—the consequences no doubt of an oil strike in the South Sahara—has regularly been marked by the ever-increasing complexity of their human attire.

Elephant society is strictly on a par with that of men, and intermingles with it directly without evoking astonishment on the part of either the elephants or the humans. This land of the elephants is merely a different country, as England is to France. Other animals occupy further countries in a similar way, but it is not the case that *all* animal species are elevated to an identical para-human status. There is a definite hierarchy. Rhinos, though unpleasant fellows, are as civilized as elephants; they fight on equal terms, and an elephant airline employs a rhino as pilot. Likewise Zephir, the monkey playmate of the younger elephants, has a monkey land of his own complete with a monkey fiancée, Princess Isabel. But the other animals, which are humanized in the sense that they attend parties and generally participate in Celesteville high jinks, all seem to be on a slightly lower plane—Asiatics as against Europeans perhaps? A Michelin guide to Babar's zoology would run something like this:

★★★★ CIVILIZED RULERS:
    White Men, Elephants, Rhinoceroses, Monkeys

★★★ SERVILE COLONIAL POPULATIONS:
    Black Men, Dromedaries, Hippopotamuses, Kangaroos

★★ HUMANIZED ANIMALS (appearing only occasionally and then as individuals):
    Lion, Tiger, Giraffe, Deer, Tortoise, Mouse, Porcupine, Lizard. Various exotic birds (e.g. Flamingo, Ibis, Pelican, Marabout)

★ WILD BEASTS (hostile to elephants as they would be to man):
    Crocodile, Snake

DOMESTIC ANIMALS

Domestic animals, e.g. horses, cows, sheep, goats, pigs, frequently appear in the pictures but never as 'characters' in the story; they remain domestic animals quite devoid of human qualities. Animals which rate as pets for humans (i.e. cats and dogs) are eliminated altogether with one exception: when Babar goes in search of Father Christmas—a sort of fantasy within a fantasy—he is accompanied by a talking dog (which is rather surprisingly called Duck).

The allocation of names in Babar's world has a definite pattern. The Old Lady, the only 'real' human, has no name. Babar's closest associates, that is those who are closest to being human, have names appropriate to real humans or to pets: Babar, Celeste, Pom, Flora, Alexander, Arthur, Zephir, Isabel, Eleanor (a mermaid), Cornelius.

Beyond this there is a list of Celesteville elephants who have 'real' occupations but fanciful names. . . . The names of the rhinos are rather similar: Rataxes, Pamir, Baribarbottom. Likewise the minor characters associated with Zephir: Huc and Aristobel are monkeys; Aunt Crustadel and Polomoche are 'monsters' which look like nursery toys, and it is never stated whose aunt they are. None of the three-, two-, or one-star animals have personal names except the tortoise, who on one occasion is called Martha.

It will be seen that Babar's world is very urban. The humanized animals and birds are those one might meet in a zoo, behind bars. The list of professions suggests the atmosphere of a small-town street.

The naming pattern has the effect of setting up class discriminations even within the category of four-star animals. The reader is coerced into making a self-identification with one or the other of the members of Babar's own household; the rest of the universe of humanized animals is then ranged round about in categories of inferior status.

The ethnographers provide us with other evidence concerning Babar's ideas of social class. Though Babar is elected as 'King', he is not an hereditary aristocrat. There is no suggestion that he is a relative of the previous monarch who died from eating a poisonous mushroom. Nor do any of Babar's associates carry hereditary titles such as Count; they are all Mr and Mrs plain and simple. True, Babar has covered the walls of his new château with portraits of sixteenth-century 'ancestors', but this is obviously a completely fake piece of snobbery. Further evidence of class sensitivity may be seen in the fact that Babar marries his cousin Celeste, and that the only other elephant outsider with whom the family has intimate relations is another cousin, Arthur. When Babar and Celeste amuse themselves in the Celesteville Garden of Pleasure they play tennis with Mr and Mrs Pilophage, Pilophage being a military officer. In the same context, General Cornelius plays bowls with a sort of intellectual élite: Fandango the scholar, Podula the sculptor, Capoulosse the doctor. But Babar does not associate with tradesmen.

All this is as it should be. It is important that the comfortable bourgeois adult readers should not have their basic assumptions about social relationships in any way disturbed. Babar has the prejudices of a middle class *colon* of the 1930s.

I have a theory about all this. I think that Babar appeals to adults because the fantasy is so carefully contrived, so fully under control. In the ordinary way we tend to categorize living creatures in terms of social distance, depending upon the degree of remoteness from 'myself', thus:

1	2	3	4
ME VERY NEAR	NEAR	FAR	VERY FAR
very tame	tame	wild	very wild
	domestic	familiar	unfamiliar
pets	animals	wild animals	wild animals
inedible	edible	some edible	inedible
family	neighbours	strangers	total strangers
members			savages
		some	not
incest	marriageable	marriageable	marriageable

The categories of animals and humans falling into columns 1 and 4 are both abnormal and sacred, and the sacredness is in both cases marked by the taboo on edibility and sex relations.

This I admit is a complicated matter. The English have tended to accept biblical injunctions so that all meat-eating creatures and creeping things are inedible, also horses. But the French eat snails and frogs and horse. In Canton the restaurants serve up dog and snake as delicacies. . . . But the point is that eating and sex are both matters of social convention and in all cases there is a 'very near' and a 'very far' category, *both* of which are alike inedible and sexually illegitimate.

I find it significant that almost all the humanized beasts in the Babar books belong to column 4, whereas surely the child's natural interests must lie in columns 1 and 2? Children's books in which the leading characters are humanized pets and humanized domestic animals are published with great regularity but seem to have no staying power—this can only be because the adults disapprove. But why? Might not the explanation be something like this:

For the child, fantasy is obvious. The category distinction real/unreal (true/false) is vague and unimportant; For the adult it is crucial. And in the adult's painfully constructed image of the real world the categories which are very close—those relating to the parts and excretions of the body—to family relations, to pets and familiar creatures—are the basic discriminations which serve as a rather shaky foundation for a vast superstructure of precisely defined linguistic concepts. As we get older the uncertainty of these early discriminations becomes a source of great anxiety, sex and excretion become 'obscene', they are loaded with a taboo which infects even Chanticleer and the harmless pussycat. Small wonder then that the adult finds this kind of country uncomfortable. We may blandly assure ourselves that we thoroughly approve of childish fantasy, but at the same time we want to be quite sure that the real and the unreal never get muddled up in our own imagination. Alice can do what she likes on the other side of the looking-glass or down the rabbit hole, but not too close please, not too close. If you want to see a real elephant go to the zoo: I don't want any of Mr [Eugene] Ionesco's rhinoceroses around here if you please. (pp. 176-82)

Edmund Leach, "Babar's Civilization Analysed," in New Society *(© New Society), Vol. 1, No. 12, pp. 16-17, December 20, 1962 (and reprinted in* Only Connect: Readings on Children's Literature, *edited by Sheila Egoff, G. T. Stubbs, and L. F. Ashley, Oxford University Press, Canadian Branch, 1969, pp. 176-82).*

Edmund Leach has analysed Babar the elephant's carefully constructed world [see excerpt above], and there is no doubt that this cohesion gives the books much of their adult satisfaction. But the earlier Babar stories have much more to offer: they are a primer in power politics.

In the first of his key books, *The Story of Babar,* Jean de Brunhoff described a do-it-yourself *coup d'état.* Babar is born into a primitive, matriarchal, child-centred community, which has no defined economic system and is ruled by a monarch chosen by the elders and elected by acclamation.

Babar himself left this society—its primitiveness is stressed by the nakedness of its members—and went to the west, where he was educated and made lasting contacts with capitalist elements, represented in the books by the "very rich Old Lady," who "gave him everything he wanted."

The mechanism of the plot is left implicit. Arthur and Celeste, two cousins of Babar—they are still naked, unlike Babar himself who is now dressed in the height of western fashion—race into town, where they too are bought clothes. Their haste is not explained in the book, except by the sinister coincidence . . . of the King of the Elephants dying of poison. Babar makes rapid preparations to return to his country, while Cornelius, his future chief minister, arranges the election procedure, timing it to coincide with Babar's sensational return . . . in a motor car, representing western technology.

Cornelius played his part "in his quavering voice," a defect that is significantly never mentioned again. "My dear friends, we must have a new king . . . Why not choose Babar?" And, although Babar has been out of the country since childhood, his election is stampeded through the bewildered "electors".

Cornelius is quickly rewarded for his part ("You have such good ideas I shall make you a general"), and is given a hat to mark his elevation to the power group. The later emphasis in the story on this hat can only be explained by its significance as a symbol of power. A Royal Wedding—Babar has conveniently become engaged to Celeste "on our journey in the car"—is immediately staged further to seduce the population and to persuade neighbouring powers to recognise the new regime.

The second book, *Babar's Travels,* shows the establishment of his position as the result of a rather specious military success. Babar had begun his reign in a surprising way by setting off for his honeymoon in a balloon. Undoubtedly the real reason for this trip to the west was to reestablish contact with western capitalists and to raise support for his government.

His account of his travels is so patently incredible that one can only conclude that it was invented for publicity purposes for a childlike people. In any event Babar returns to the scene of a war in his country with the Old Lady herself, on this occasion in an aeroplar.e, symbolising an even more sophisticated technology. He quickly wins a battle by an imaginative but unheroic trick that nevertheless establishes him as a "great general." His primitive, still naked people are treated to a victory celebration, which features certain rewards for the Old Lady (mineral resources?) for extremely vaguely defined services rendered. (She had "been so kind to them . . .") the power group of Babar, Queen Celeste, cousin Arthur, the Old Lady, Cornelius and a foreign favourite "Babar's friend Zephir" (a monkey) is now complete.

In the third Jean de Brunhoff story, *Babar the King,* Babar digs in. Characteristically, he establishes a new city, Celesteville. This turns out to be an unimaginatively planned city with rows of identical houses, rising up to the juxtaposed Orwellian Palaces of Work and Pleasure, flanked by the large houses of Babar and the Old Lady. There is no opposition to this project. ("'Hear, hear' cried the elephants, raising their trunks in the air"—clearly a fascist salute.)

Any criticism is silenced by the timely arrival of loads of foreign luxury consumer goods ("dresses, hats, silks, paint boxes, drums, tins of peaches, feathers, racquets . . ."). The existing inhabitants are persuaded off the site by another Orwellian ploy of a parrot claque chanting: "Come and see Celesteville, most beautiful of towns." To convince his people of their emergence as a power, all are now given clothes, hitherto the prerogative of the ruling group. A national anthem, incomprehensible to all, is produced by Cornelius as "The Old Song of the Mammoths," and this is sung by a specially rehearsed children's choir.

Socially a lot is made of a sort of Owenite idea of the equality of labour, but this very rapidly develops into a privileged hierarchy on the one side and uniformed gardeners and cooks on the other. Babar significantly plays tennis with Pilophage, a general, while the intellectuals form a bowls clique. The theatre becomes the social apex with ludicrously full evening dress worn for what appear to be Molière. Nothing could be more alien to this primitive people.

After a year another of the huge non-events is staged—this one being to commemorate the founding of the city, which is to be celebrated by a May Day type parade. The workers are marched past in their gaudy fancy dresses, while one notices that in only a year a powerful military element has appeared, both in the parade in their elite uniforms and lining the route. Babar has developed his personality cult to the extent of sitting on a mechanical horse.

Towards the end of this book one of the great mysteries of the saga occurs. Both Cornelius, who paved the way for Babar's

accession, and the Old Lady, who financed it, are victims of simultaneous "accidents," on both occasions in the presence of Babar or the Court group. Ironically Babar's efficient hospital and fire services save both victims, and some sort of *rapprochement* is reached in the grounds of the hospital. The humourless Babar tries to explain this setback to his bid for sole power in terms of a mystical dream, hurriedly producing a rather unpolished new bromide: "Let us work and play with a will and we shall always be happy."

In the last of the mainstream books, *Babar at Home,* we see the system fully operative, and Babar a conservative father figure. Babar and Celeste are anxious for an heir—they in fact produce triplets—as the dictatorship is to be made permanent by transformation into a hereditary monarchy. The babies wear baby crowns in some pictures. A proclamation for the happy event is made by the army. (Drums; and the people "running up in great numbers listened respectfully.") The arrivals are announced by gun salutes fired by the King's Artillery in the Fort of St John, which has mysteriously appeared to dominate Celesteville. Soldiers are now a common sight on the roads.

The whole book deals with the problems of raising the heirs safely, since they have become essential to the survival of the dynasty. As Babar says frankly to Celeste, "I don't know what we should do without them."

The political substructure of the story is as pointed as that in [George Orwell's] *Animal Farm,* with perhaps a higher degree of universality. The whole machinery of dictatorship is here: the capitalist-backed coup, the nationalist trimmings, the deception of the people by status symbols, the reality of military backing and the inner power struggles. The entire system is secured by a carefully developed personality cult of omniscience, justice and kindness. Brunhoff wrote these books in the 1930s, and his Babar is surely a parody reaction to the peculiar political climate in France and Europe at the time. Leach attributed some of the appeal of these books to adults to their prophetic powers. General Charles [de Gaulle] may well be the French mass's wish-fulfilment for a Babar.

The books now republished are not fundamental to the epic. Jean de Brunhoff's *Babar's Friend Zephir* is at least a fringe statement. It sees Babar's state beginning to push its own ideology out to a more primitive neighbour, just as Babar himself was a product of the west. But even in the monkey state the social structure is carefully observed and the military power structure is immediately interesting. But even Jean de Brunhoff may have worked out true Babar vein—*Babar and Father Christmas* . . . has little further to offer. The books by the younger Laurent de Brunhoff merely use Babar as a cuddly nursery figure in two fairly charming but empty little tales. They really have nothing to do with the main statement. (pp. 179-83)

> *Patrick Richardson, "Teach Your Baby to Rule," in* New Society *(© New Society), March 10, 1966 (and reprinted in* Suitable for Children? Controversies in Children's Literature, *edited by Nicholas Tucker, University of California Press, 1976, pp. 179-83).*

[The flavour of the Babar stories] seems almost aromatically French. A kindly colonialism, with scarcely a vestige of anti-pachyderm prejudice, pervades the original half dozen. A lovable Old Lady, presumably some kind of millionaire crank, supplies the pocket money which allows the runaway immigrant to be educated and outfitted in the most chic style. There is a funny, and touching, scene where he leans on the mantelpiece in his snappy green suit enthralling the pallid, metropolitan, human intellectuals with his tales of life in the underprivileged empire. Class, if not species, bias remains a mild threat—having mislaid their crowns in a honeymoon accident (*Babar's Travels*) the couple lose their regal rank and are exhibited in a circus.

There is no denying the pictorial vividness evaporates in the jump across the generations. Brunhoff Jr cannot command that opulent, yet somehow economical, line which gives some of the earlier set-pieces—a holiday balloon hovering over an idyllic coast-line or the almost invisible nightingale on the window of Zephir's darkened room in Monkey Town—an Oriental, timeless, charm. Nor does he possess the ability to keep the narrative shuttling so that a short, straight-forward story seems to its audience long and too complex.

But children do not, as sentimental historians of the *genre* delude themselves, always love the highest when they see it. My listeners' two favourites are one from the father (*Babar and Father Christmas*) and one from the son (*Babar's Castle*). I think I understand their attraction—a variation in pace so that a full-page drawing full of fascinating detail is succeeded by a simple collection of strip-cartoon boxes, and a delight in showing cross-sections of this fantasy world with all the hidden secrets of Father Christmas's underground palace, or the subterranean passage beneath Babar's country mansion, laid bare to the curious infant eye.

I dread to count how many times now I have read my way aloud through all but one of the entire set. (What has happened to *Babar's Visit to Bird Island*?) Yet the saccharine which collects on the tongue after prolonged exposure to other children's favourites has still not destroyed my palate. (pp. 603-04)

Alan Brien, "If You Love Elephants," in New Statesman (© *1967 The Statesman & Nation Publishing Co. Ltd.), Vol. 74, No. 1912, November 3, 1967, pp. 603-04.*

Babar first saw the light of day in 1931, a time when it was regarded as progressive to show children animals as they actually are in real life. Cats wearing little pointed caps and hares in leather breeches were abhorred, however much unprincipled children might take delight in them in secret. And then, in the middle of all these admittedly well-meaning and most necessary efforts, there suddenly stomped in this elephant Babar. (p. 195)

This Babar, mad for civilization, is something of an anachronism in our world-weary time; at the same time, however, he is a wonderfully inspiring example. For as an elephant he approaches the achievements of civilization with all the innocence of an animal. Those children who take such delight in the adventures of an enterprising elephant partake without realizing it in the evolution of an ideal society.

As a young elephant, Babar is directed to a human city and is adopted by an old lady with a pointed nose, herself an uncommon enough figure in a children's book. Throughout all the books she simply remains '*la vieille dame*' and she represents the positive aspect of humanity. After turning her great awkward visitor from the primeval forest into a well-dressed and upright future king, she assists him to return to the land of the elephants. Later on he brings her to his own country and it is she who gives fresh heart to him at a time when his state is taking on too much of the character of a self-satisfied welfare-state. This is the occasion . . . when Babar is visited by nightmares. After they have finally been dispelled by the triumphant

elephant angels it is the old lady who adjures the king: '*Travaillons avec gaieté et nous continuerons d'être heureux.*'

This is only a single incident in the story. People have not often made the attempt of sneaking political ideas into books for such young children. Eric Kästner and Jella Lepman tried it out with some success in their *Konferenz der Tiere* [*The Animals' Conference*] (1949), but without Brunhoff's air of wide-eyed innocence. Political didacticism is so neatly camouflaged in his books that it goes unnoticed in the welter of comic and exciting incidents which unfold themselves before the child's eyes in huge, expressive pictures.

The artistic value of these pictures is a high one. Turn, for instance, to pages 6 and 7 of *Le voyage de Babar* [*The Travels of Babar*], where the balloon journey of the royal bride and her bridegroom is set out. The whole thing is reminiscent of a fine Japanese woodcut; and if one considers pages 16 to 19 in the same volume, preferably with a child beside one, then one can only marvel at the artistic daring with which such elementary things as water and isolation and the arrival of the rescuing ship are presented. An extreme directness of language, such as is usually only achieved by children, is here united with an artistic perfection which was and is rarely found not only in children's books but also in modern graphic art. In this Brunhoff has been a guiding and an animating influence and even if his early death has prevented his genius from creating other works in a similar vein, it is certain that many fine children's books of the present day would never have appeared if these books of his had not shown the way—even down to the excellence of their printing. (pp. 195-96)

[Jean de Brunhoff's] life is inseparable from his books. For although these stories were mostly written in the mountains of Switzerland and although they deal with elephants living in the wastes of Africa, they are entirely French in the fullest and finest meaning of the word. They contain all the lovable aspects of the world of France, translated to a world of animals—a fact which doubles their success with children, who like humanized animals more than anything. You have only to walk with the elephants in their pleasure-grounds—the Versailles of this animal state—or visit their theatre with its bejewelled audience and its caryatids in the form of sculptured elephants; you have only to listen while little Arthur, the king's nephew, and Zéphir the monkey play Mozart trios with the old lady at the piano, the royal couple watching them with wonderment and then afterwards sending them to the '*pâtissier*' to choose as many cakes as they like; or you have only to go fishing with Babar, or riding on a round-about, or taking the salute at a parade, in all these manifold aspects he remains a French *père de famille* whose company it is always a pleasure to share.

'*La vieille dame*' is a sublime and, as I have already said, a singular figure in children's literature. Her delicate and fragile appearance is enormously effective beside that of the huge, fat elephants and it is the climax of the series when she is almost killed by a snake-bite. It is the moment when the demons appear to Babar, . . . and it is followed by one of the most moving pictures when the little white-haired lady in her dressing-gown comes from the 'hospital' to greet her king and his chief-minister Cornelius with open arms.

The other character to delight children so much is Zéphir the little monkey. He belongs to the old lady, but often appears separately. One volume, *Les vacances de Zéphir* [*Zephir's Holidays*], is devoted solely to him. No child is likely to forget quickly the monkey colony with its tree-houses. Or again the night scene at the bedroom window, although drawn with an economical and expressive poetry, might well lapse into sentimentality on the arrival of the nightingale. But the text ensures that this remains a children's picture-book, for when Zéphir hears the nightingale singing, we are told: *Joyeux il se lève, court à la fenêtre et s'écrie: "Salut mon vieux!"*'

This book also contains the scene with the little mermaid Eléonore, whom he catches in his net and then lets go again. Both pictures and text are full of especially happy inspirations and there are moments (particularly this one) which have a genuine fairy-tale ring to them. The little mermaid Eléonore is only a tiny 'extra' among all the characters who people these books so abundantly, but she is a portent of the fresh imaginative powers that the artist Jean de Brunhoff might have been able to exercise if he had been spared to devote himself to the things of this world.

This he could not do, but it is perhaps timely to bear in mind here the phenomenon, unusual today, of a son continuing the work of his father.

We scarcely dared believe our eyes when, in 1946, from a hungry Paris there appeared a new Babar book: *Babar et ce coquin d'Arthur* [*Babar and His Cousin: That Rascal Arthur*]— a story which right from the start has Arthur for its *'enfant terrible'*.

It was obvious that there would be indications of weakness in the work of the twenty-year-old son of the painter and naturally these weaknesses are present. Consider the boldness and the painterly freedom with which Brunhoff *père* represented nature in, say, the trees, or the waves of the sea, or the attitudes of the animals (as an example of which you need only study the pictures on the middle pages of *Babar en famille* [*Babar and His Children*]**,** when little Alexandre falls into the squirrel's tree, and then compare them with the somewhat conventional trees and, above all, the general lack of landscape in *Babar et ce coquin d'Arthur*). The numerous weaknesses which such a comparison showed in the son were not eradicated when *Pique-Nique chez Babar* [*Babar's Picnic*] appeared three years later— a volume which still fell short of his father's perfection.

Nevertheless, *Babar et ce coquin d'Arthur* quickly became one of my own son's special favourites. If the young Parisian's trees had somewhat the appearance of stage-property, he still had a mastery over the world of vehicles and indeed invented some which are a particular delight to all children. The railway . . . of *Babar et ce coquin d'Arthur* is unforgettable, with the children travelling in a special train on wires above the train with the adults in. All the scenes with aircraft and parachute jumps in them are marvellously observed and the little forest track is quite charming with the monkeys jumping down on to it from the trees. It is still almost a boy's heart here, letting itself go with boyish dreams, but the result still lacks a quality which gives the first five volumes an almost indescribable magic for us grown-ups. Perhaps it was the gaiety of the dying painter, who lived so close to sadness, coupled with the tenderness of the young husband who put all his best into a simple children's book.

Children are not worried about that. Laurent the son gave them much pleasure in continuing his father's work with so much of his own fancy. It is therefore the more regrettable that the books by the son have proliferated to such an extent that they threaten to overwhelm the so much more delicate and poetic work of the father. This inventive young man would surely do better to turn his talents to some new subject.

From Babar's Cousin: That Rascal Arthur, *written and illustrated by Laurent de Brunhoff.*

The sagas of Babar, king of the elephants, will belong to the daily fare of the nursery for many generations to come, even though perhaps not to the same degree everywhere. The heart of every child nurtures seeds of good and evil and certain barbaric books and magazines, however harmless their appearance, have the quality of fostering the evil seeds. But only the good shall grow under Babar's majestic rule. (pp. 198-200)

> *Bettina Hürlimann, "Jean de Brunhoff," in her* Three Centuries of Children's Books in Europe, *translated and edited by Brian W. Alderson (English translation © Oxford University Press 1967; reprinted by permission), Oxford University Press, Oxford, 1967, pp. 195-200.*

Yesterday's heroes are open to as much confusion: think of Alice, seen in splendid isolation. Peter Rabbit, useful but parochial, Amerliaranne, better, Babar . . . superb. Surely anyone brought up ′on the Babar books can instantly recall the pictures: Babar's breathless arrival in the provincial town, his first meeting with the old lady, every detail of his splendid shopping spree. [Marcel] Proust can write his volumes, but [the] single picture of Babar, Arthur and Celeste guzzling éclairs *chez le pâtissier* is worth as much. What a satisfying hero Babar is; he is not specially clever, or good, but his common sense is equal to any situation. Whether he is arranging his wedding, saving Alexander from a crocodile or looking for

Father Christmas, he always behaves in exactly the way he should: model patriarch, husband, father.

"Elephant Social History," in The Times Literary Supplement *(© Times Newspapers Ltd. (London) 1969; reproduced from* The Times Literary Supplement *by permission), No. 3513, June 26, 1969, p. 695.*

[Except] for the characters of Dr. Seuss, there are few inhabitants of picture books which have more loyal fans [than Babar]. This is due in part to the basic incongruity of an elephant driving a small car, bathing in a bathtub, doing setting-up exercises, wearing shoes with spats, and so on. It can perhaps be attributed also to the identification children feel when Babar engages in such childlike amusements as riding a department store elevator up and down ten times and being scolded: "Elevators are not toys." But in addition to these qualities, there is a fantastic mixture of animal and human traits in each character, and the author does not shy away from emotional kinds of experience. A great variety of life revolves around Babar as he grows up, grieves over the death of his mother, runs away to the city and then comes home again, is crowned king of the jungle, marries, goes on his honeymoon in a balloon, raises a family, and takes care of all his relatives and the citizens of his realm. . . .

Besides the range of emotions, there is an overriding sense of warmth in the Babar stories. . . .

Something must be said about the style of the Babar stories also, for they are told in such a matter-of-fact tone that incidents

When all is ready in the cave, the children invite Babar, Celeste and their friends to a tea party. with the help of the Old Lady, they prepare a fine feast with lots of cakes. Arthur, the greedy little fellow, takes a whole plate of eclairs all for himself!

From Babar and the Professor, *written and illustrated by Laurent de Brunhoff.*

sound credible and even serious. But at the same time, this appearance of nonchalance makes Babar very comical. . . . [Directness of language in the books] has the effect of speeding up the action, and listeners are left a little bit breathless when the stories end.

The popularity of Babar can be explained in these terms, but the devotion that some children feel for him is still somewhat mystifying. For them his place is somehow never usurped by any other picture-book character.

Donnarae MacCann and Olga Richard, "Outstanding Narrative Writers: Jean de Brunhoff (1899-1937)," in their The Child's First Books: A Critical Study of Pictures and Texts *(copyright © 1973 by Donnarae MacCann and Olga Richard; reprinted by permission of The H. W. Wilson Company), Wilson, 1973, p. 101.*

If you turn the world into Elephant Land rather than Dog Land or Cat Land, there has to be some sort of human compromise if anything is to take place outside the Jungle. Elephants are not pets. They are large and noble or menacing, strange and undomestic, and like dragons they have to be tamed and reduced—which explains the childlike Babar, adopted baby and 'friend' of that useful character, the Old Lady, who plays Mr Brownlow to his Oliver Twist. Babar exists in a perpetual, infantile middle age. The simple colourful illustrations of the de Brunhoffs, father and son, make the appeal of this device quite clear; Babar does what most small children would like to do—joins in the adult world on a child's terms, and gets away with it. There is no one to tell him not to. He can wear grown-up clothes, ride up and down in the lift, go fishing, drive a car, marry Celeste and become King of the Jungle all because his real self is hidden behind an animal hide and he is neither child nor adult but a bit of both. . . . (p. 274)

Margaret Blount, "Where There Are No People," in her Animal Land: The Creatures of Children's Fiction *(reprinted by permission of Georges Borchardt Inc.; copyright © 1974 by Margaret Ingle-Finch) William Morrow & Company, Inc., 1975, pp. 267-83.**

While [Laurent de Brunhoff] has faithfully copied the style, characters and structure of his father's stories, the pictures show harder colour and a less imaginative handling of detail, and something of Babar's benevolent nature has been lost as he has become a kind of tourist whose travels (to Bird Island, to America and into Space) are described in a somewhat trite chronicle style. Then, too, the sly satire in the early books, the unobtrusive social nuances seen in Babar's conventional middle-class clothes and behaviour, the architectural style of Celesteville and so on, have been smoothed out as Babar has moved from the Great Forest into other spheres. His equable personality has triumphed over these changes, but is not so well preserved in the miniature books in which the longer stories have been telescoped into texts whose curtness is scarcely supported by modifications of the original illustrations. (p. 35)

Margery Fisher, "Who's Who in Children's Books: Babar the Elephant," in her Who's Who in Children's Books: A Treasury of the Familiar Characters of Childhood *(copyright © 1975 by Margery Fisher; reprinted by permission), Holt, Rinehart and Winston, Weidenfeld & Nicolson, 1975, pp. 33-5.*

[The Babar stories of Jean de Brunhoff] rightly rank with the Beatrix Potter books as the best ever made for very young children. Everyone who has read these books remembers two vivid moments in *The Story of Babar,* one in which Babar's mother is killed by a cruel hunter while Babar is riding on her back, the other in which the King of the Elephants eats a poisonous mushroom, turns green, and dies. Taken in isolation these moments seem [piercing and frightening], and since many do thus isolate these moments, ignoring or forgetting de Brunhoff's context, it is perhaps better to begin with a somewhat quieter, though no less typical sequence, from *The Travels of Babar.* On their honeymoon, King Babar and Queen Celeste are rescued from a cannibals' island by a whale, who then puts them down on a reef, chases after some fish, and forgets to come back. They are rescued by a huge ocean liner, but the elephants' relief quickly turns to frustration and anger when the captain of the ship not only won't let them go ashore but puts them in the stables instead. . . . Celeste then offers the advice often associated with the name of Uncle Tom: "It is the captain. Let us be good, and he may set us free." Babar, who could smash locks and tear the stables to bits quite easily, agrees, and on the next page we see only their large and seemingly defiant posteriors as they stand in the straw as though they were donkeys. But as reward for their acquiescence Babar and Celeste are sold to an animal trainer in a circus, which is just as humiliating as the stables, since of course they need no training and are no less smart and much more regal than the human beings who control them. But Celeste still counsels patience: "We won't stay in the circus long; we will get back to our own country and see Cornelius and little Arthur again." On the next page we are switched back to the elephant country where Arthur is exploding a firecracker on the tail of an old rhino, and Cornelius is unable to pacify the rhino, who then threatens war.

It is a sequence more somber than anything in Dr. Seuss, more destructive and apparently more cynical. Each of the rescues raises false hopes: the whale is pleasant but forgetful, the captain is greedy, the animal trainer is foolish and arrogant, Celeste is naive not to know these things, Babar is powerless while his country is getting ready for war. Every move that seems not to instruct us in cynicism is soon undercut. We do not need, thus, to dwell on the very troubling moments when Babar's mother is shot or when the king dies from eating a bad mushroom to see that de Brunhoff despairs that life is ever more than momentarily free of trouble, or that hoping does much good, or that, especially when dealing with people, we can ever know whom to trust or what to expect. He shows us misfortunes of a kind seldom found in children's books: betrayal, desertion, and cruelty, as we have seen, adventurousness and curiosity punished, capricious weather, house fires, nightmares, homesickness. De Brunhoff's tone in the presence of these events is impassive and accepting.

My rendering of de Brunhoff, however, falsifies the effect of his books. He does deal relentlessly with many unpleasant facts of life, but he is nowhere near as gloomy, or as gothic, or as like Edward Gorey, as I have implied. The major reason for this is that there is no register inside the stories to carry the burdens of the pain and sorrow, no invitation to imagine ourselves inside these terrible situations, though of course we must be very attentive to them from the outside. The impassivity that seems for a moment like indifference also assures us that this moment will pass, that there is nothing extraordinary about a cannibal attack, or a whale forgetting to come back after a meal of fish. When Babar returns home to lead the elephants in battle against the rhinoceroses, de Brunhoff says "King Babar was a great general" in exactly the same tone in which

he says "It was a great misfortune" when Babar's predecessor eats the bad mushroom As he uses them, words like "happy," "cruel," "great," "poison," "choke," "play," and "help" are all robbed of their capacity to excite or alarm. Nor do we have a narrative proposition to guide or offer power; de Brunhoff's stories are episodic, one thing after another, the task not being to get somewhere in particular, but to dwell slowly on a single moment, even to linger, and then to move on, thereby gaining all the equilibrium we need to juxtapose and eventually to reconcile disparate attitudes and possibilities.

All this, though, seems beyond even the instinctive comprehension of a child; at least none of this that I see now can I remember seeing forty years ago. I was, I know, almost totally absorbed with the pictures, which I stared at as I did no others. Part of their glory is that de Brunhoff thinks of so many wonderful things for elephants to do, especially with their trunks, that human beings can't do because they have no trunks, and that elephants don't do because they have no interest in playing tennis, watering flower beds, holding chalk, pulling naughty monkeys out of vats of vanilla cream. But there is more than that. I stared at that picture of the chef hauling the monkey Zephir out of the vanilla cream because, in effect, I was allowed to. There are V's drawn on the chef's brows to show his anger, but no one in the picture is frightened or even alarmed. Zephir is forlorn and a mess, no more, and the last sentence on the page has Celeste taking Zephir away to wash him. On the next page we are at a garden party at the Palace of Pleasure. The pictures don't register the feelings a reader of the text alone might be expected to have, so one is freed by de Brunhoff's somber equilibrium because it released him into playfulness in the pictures. If Dr. Seuss fights dragons by walking between their legs, de Brunhoff fights his by staring at them, by insisting he knows the limits of the dragons' power, since even the most shocking moments will last no longer than the most satisfying ones: both take no longer than two facing pages.

I could not say as a child how all this was done, but could receive "Look at the pictures" as the essential message of the text and not get the wrong message at all. It is no accident that my happiest moments of reading aloud to my children were with the Babar books. I could watch the child stare at the pictures, solemn but never frightened, amused but never laughing, and derive my own pleasure from the way the apparently skimpy text released us both into enjoying the pictures. De Brunhoff allies child and adult so that each can arrive at the same place by a somewhat different route. With Dr. Seuss my adult pleasure is only a replica of my childhood pleasure; with de Brunhoff the two pleasures are somewhat different, since I do see more in his books than I did as a child, but they are never in conflict with each other. (pp. 12-15)

Roger Sale, "Introduction: Child Reading and Man Reading," in his Fairy Tales and After: From Snow White to E. B. White *(copyright © 1978 by the President and Fellows of Harvard College; excerpted by permission), Cambridge, Mass.: Harvard University Press, 1978, pp. 1-22.*

Babar's escape to Paris, when he fled the jungle in 1931, was not, alas, via Brooklyn. If he had come my way, how I would have welcomed that little orphaned elephant and smothered him with affection. What a pity he didn't visit my house; some of that gentle spirit, those sensible ways, might have rubbed off on a child whose childhood was largely governed by ungoverned emotions. When I did make his acquaintance, as a young artist in the early 1950s, it was too late. By then, raised on a diet of Sturm und Drang, I inwardly condemned the Babar books for what I considered an overly reasoned approach to life: typically French, I said then. About this last judgment I was right, but not in my negative inference. So although I admired the whole series of books, their Gallic tone, which I interpreted as aloofness, continued to rankle. And while I loved the Babars, I loved them purely for their graphic splendor.

After all, the French, at the turn of the century, had practically reinvented the illustrated book. Along with the work of André Hellé, Edy Legrand, Boutet de Monvel, Felix Vallotton, and Pierre Bonnard, de Brunhoff shared a freedom and charm, a freshness of vision that captivates and takes the breath away. . . .

Jean de Brunhoff was a master of this form. Between 1931 and 1937 he completed a body of work that forever changed the face of the illustrated book. (p. 7)

My early indifference to de Brunhoff's writing was, in retrospect, a curious and significant blind spot. I was busy then, furiously learning what a picture book was and, more to the point, what it could be. . . . This was in the 1950s. I was then a green recruit fresh from the analyst's couch and woe betide the work that failed to loudly signal its Freudian allegiance. With a convert's proverbial fervor I rushed pell-mell into the very heart of what I considered Babar's unresolved problem: his mother's death, of course.

I never quite got over that death. It was a landmark experience for me in children's literature. The ease and remarkable calm with which de Brunhoff blighted the life of his baby elephant numbed me. That sublimely happy babyhood lost, after only two full pages, and then, as in a nightmare (and too much like life), Babar, cruelly and arbitrarily deprived of his loving mother, runs wildly out of babyhood (the innocent jungle) and into cozy, amnesia-inducing society (Paris, only blocks away from that jungle). It is there that he feverishly embraces adulthood, culture, manners, any surface, to hide the hideous trauma of that useless death. Or so it seemed to me then. Why, I wondered, give us a mother's death and then deprive us of a fulsome wallowing in its gory psychological repercussions? Why not, in fact, go back and find another less volatile reason for Babar to flee the jungle? Easy enough solution, thought I. In summation, I judged this death to be a gratuitously punishing touch, an issue raised and bewilderingly passed over. Simply, I missed the point. It took years of further exposure to the work of many different artists, my own redefinition of the picture book form, and much growing up to complete my appreciation of Babar. Now, from a distance of more than thirty years, Babar is at the very heart of my conception of what turns a picture book into a work of art. The graphics are tightly linked to the deceptively loose prose-poetry style that is astonishing in its ease of expression. The pictures, rather than merely echoing the text, enrich and expand Babar's world. (pp. 8, 11)

[Ordered] tight-knit feeling of family is the very essence of Babar. (p. 11)

Jean de Brunhoff, it seems, had to be oblique. Perhaps he knew, instinctively, what I was to learn, that this was the best way to reach and teach children. Beneath the pure fun, the originality of style, and the vivacity of imagination is a serious and touching theme: a father writing to his sons and voicing his natural concern for their welfare, for their lives. At the end of *Babar and His Children,* King Babar says, "Truly it is not easy to bring up a family." And truly it is this hard wisdom that lies at the heart of the books. Why was this such a vital issue in the creation of Babar? In the early 1930s Jean de

Brunhoff contracted tuberculosis. . . . That Jean had intimations of death must be true. That he was a loving, generous-spirited man is true too. We see it in his work. And, in my many conversations with Laurent, it has been clear that Jean never communicated to his children the private fears and regrets he surely had. He died in 1937. Laurent was twelve at the time and Thierry, the youngest, was not yet three. Jean's bequest to his family, and the world, shines from the books that rushed from his pen at the extraordinary rate of almost one a year between 1931 and 1937. These contain, in [Bettina] Hürlimann's words, "glimpses of things dear to the de Brunhoff family as the background for a father's affectionate counsel"— his counsel on coming of age with grace and kindness, on weathering the inevitable storms of life.

The devotion to family and the circumstances of life that produced Babar must account for the special power and honest sentiment that is the very core of the books. This also helps to explain the balanced emotional climate that is never allowed to go out of control. And here I come back to my first appraisal of Babar, but in a new, most sympathetic light. These books are so traditionally French, filled with what might be considered old-fashioned ideas of manhood, womanhood, and manners. But there is always an underlying emphasis on developing a child's (an elephant child's) personal freedom and individuality through self-control. Not self-control in the repressive sense but defined rather as the awareness of choices of behavior, the awareness that some choices are better than others. "Do you see how in this life one must never be discouraged?" says *la Vieille Dame.* "Let's work hard and cheerfully and we'll continue to be happy." . . . In *Babar the King* a perfectly wonderful day suddenly turns into a nightmare. Babar is nearly overwhelmed by the arbitrary nature of disaster. But he is comforted by his dream, or vision, of graceful, winged elephants chasing Misfortune away from Celesteville and bringing back Happiness. Then he feels "ever so much better." . . . He understands that it takes patience, with himself, and perseverance to be happy. It is an earned state of health.

My favorite among Jean's books, *The Travels of Babar,* is full of alarming and very amusing twists of fate. For the one and only time in all the books Babar loses his fine balance and has a good old temper tantrum. He is brought out of it by Celeste. The two alternately comfort each other in times of stress. Here they resolve many crises and, with the good *Vieille Dame* in tow, rush to the mountains "to enjoy the fresh air and try a little skiing." At this point the book stops short so we can study, at leisure, the stupendous double spread of Babar, Celeste, and *la Vieille Dame* calmly gliding down the Swiss slopes. . . . It is a picture filled with intense concentration, yet soft with the sensuous pleasure of this favorite de Brunhoff sport.

Scale is crucial to de Brunhoff's pictures. Those first editions of Babar have an undiminished splendor with their huge, delectable formats and grand, spacious compositions. They are as pleasing to the eye and as totally original as anything coming out of that fine and rare period of French art. These early editions fell victim to the high cost of production and have been out of print for years. Children, sadly, can no longer "climb into" a Babar book.

No one before, and very few since, has utilized the double-spread illustration to such dazzling, dramatic effect. When Babar and Celeste are taken prisoner, there is a spectacular circus scene. The handsome red arch that denotes the arena floor is also a perfect symbol of their glittering confinement.

This is a tour de force of composition and a perfect example of de Brunhoff's sly sense of counterpoint. There is no doubt that the artist is enjoying himself immensely. He has even placed himself in the scene, the young man sitting in the audience pedantically measuring Celeste for a portrait with his outstretched thumb and pencil. . . . The line of text below the picture is so simple that the art absolutely "blooms" above the words. One can hear Babar's trumpet music. But these books are full of music, both literally and figuratively. The ravishing theatre picture in *Babar the King* . . . , with every element of architecture fancifully elephantized, is accompanied (at least for me) by the most delicious harpsichord music, Rameau perhaps. And where the grand parade scene from the same book . . . is set to a joyous march, Berlioz would be wonderfully suitable. The pictures, by the way, actually move rhythmically in step if you keep your eye on those stolid elephant feet, all thumpingly clumping to the same measure. Color, costume, high comedy mixed with touching solemnity, blend into a characteristic composition that appears ingeniously simple on the surface but is, in fact, extravagantly complex. This is one of my favorite Babar pictures. And it makes a superb psychological point. The celebration catches Babar, and all of Celesteville, at the very peak of happiness and security. Immediately following, and in a series of swift, comic book style squares, shockingly unlike the grandeur of the previous picture, we see the deterioration of that happiness: the near death of *la Vieille Dame* from snakebite. The composition falls apart and only comes together again in the double spread of Babar's vision . . . and, not surprisingly, at the very end when we are treated to a small version of that selfsame parade. (pp. 11-12, 14-15)

The little known *Babar and His Children* is the most moving of the series. How happy Babar is to be the father of three little elephants! He knows well how to love his babies. After all, his own brief childhood was graced with the most intense and happy mother's love. And like all wise elephants, Babar does not forget. He never forgets *la Vieille Dame* and he never forgets his mother. "He often stands at the window, thinking sadly of his childhood, and cries when he remembers his mother." Although Babar finds a wonderful second mother in *la Vieille Dame*, this does not erase his early loss. That permeates all the books, but it is never allowed to overwhelm or destroy Babar's self-confidence. It is living that concerns and delights de Brunhoff. He recognizes death as inseparable from the fixed order of things and is never obsessed with it.

At this point I cannot resist quoting Laurent on the death of the old elephant king in *The Story of Babar.* "I do not want to be cynical," he said, "but he dies for the purpose of the plot, to make room for Babar! It is also done in a way to show death as a natural thing." How similar to the death of Babar's mother. How like de Brunhoff's own death, a natural occurrence moving the plot along.

The precious sense of reason that at first struck me as lack of feeling now moves and excites me. Babar "the very good little elephant" deserves his kingdom. He is noble, certainly, and it is by proving this inner worth that he gains his position in life. But de Brunhoff's lessons are suggested in a tone at once so right and humorous, so engaging, that they are irresistible. The grace and graphic charm are almost sufficient by themselves, but to deny the message is to deny the full weight of Jean de Brunhoff's genius. I would like to carry this thought a bit further because it seems to me that Laurent de Brunhoff's Babars are both a continuation of the order his father be-

queathed and an answering letter back from son to father. A letter brimming with health and pleasure, confirming all those father's fondest hopes. (p. 15)

Maurice Sendak, "Homage to Babar on His 50th Birthday" (copyright © 1981 by Maurice Sendak; reprinted by permission of Random House, Inc.), in Babar's Anniversary Album: 6 Favorite Stories *by Jean and Laurent de Brunhoff, Random House, 1981, pp. 7-15.*

THE STORY OF BABAR, THE LITTLE ELEPHANT (1933; French edition, 1931)

It is practically impossible to report on "The Story of Babar" without stating that 50,000 Frenchmen can't be wrong—this being the number of papas who brought the book home to Bébé. . . .

It is a delightful, happy book, taking the place of the funnies in colored supplements, with the striking difference that it is funny.

May Lamberton Becker, "Books for Young People: 'The Story of Babar, the Little Elephant'," in New York Herald Tribune Books *(© I.H.T. Corporation; reprinted by permission), October 29, 1933, p. 9.*

"Babar the Elephant" by Jean de Brunhoff is a most spectacular book translated from the French. It is gay and amusing, sophisticated yet childlike—just the kind of book that fathers enjoy as much as small boys.

Alice Dalgliesh, "Picture Books: 'Babar the Elephant'," in The Saturday Review of Literature *(copyright © 1933 by* Saturday Review; *all rights reserved; reprinted by permission), Vol. X, No. 18, November 18, 1933, p. 279.*

[*The Story of Babar*] has a French orderly and logical progression and is told with a judicious and witty minimum of words.

The novelty of the idea and the freshness with which Jean de Brunhoff develops the theme compels a child's interest. The affable charm of Babar's character makes him his friend. The impossible and absurd adjustments to city life which the little elephant undertakes with imperturbable poise are taken in faith by little children. In imagination they accompany him in his enjoyment of civilized amenities, as well as when he is at home in the Great Forest. Babar is given human characteristics as well as human clothing, yet he remains essentially an elephant, and after his brief excursion into human society, his instinctive return to his own kind is inevitable.

Jean de Brunhoff has drawn the pictures in bright, primary colors which contrast pleasurably with the elephant-gray of Babar and his elephant friends. The flat surface suggests a poster-like form which yet achieves a three-dimensional effect in the drawing of the characters so that we can see Babar advancing with the utmost naturalness into the life of the city. As we turn from one picture to another we become aware of the illustrator's care for the page itself, fitting the picture into it, alternating picture with text to produce a complementary balance. This balance reveals Brunhoff's feeling for over-all design—a superior quality in any picture book. In *The Story of Babar* there is a significant mingling of the real world and fantasia which suggests a libretto for a children's comic opera in the French mood. (pp. 124-25)

Lillian H. Smith, "Picture Books," in her The Un-reluctant Years: A Critical Approach to Children's Literature (reprinted by permission; copyright © 1953, 1981 by the American Library Association), American Library Association, 1953, pp. 114-29.*

[Jean de Brunhoff's] wit is of a particularly delightful kind, with a warmth that has made Babar one of the best loved of animal characters. Perhaps children are not entirely aware of the happy joke of Babar's apotheosis as the perfect bourgeois gentleman, complete with spats, bowler hat and bow tie, and they may have found the old lady's instinctive knowledge that "he was longing for a smart suit" a good deal less natural than the glee with which the young elephant and his cousins Arthur and Celeste get through platefuls of "delicious cakes" after they too have been suitably and respectably clad. Again, for children the end of this first story has a satisfying ring quite outside satire, as the young orphan, finding his own land in confusion after the King's death (from eating a bad mushroom), is chosen to rule over the elephants because "he has lived among men and learned much". How obvious it is, to adults and children alike, that when the happy pair return from their honeymoon trip in the "glorious yellow balloon" they will rule wisely and well, but how gratifying it is too to remember that there are more exciting adventures in store for the couple before they settle down to regal domesticity.

Jean de Brunhoff's humanisation of Babar and his friends is as tactful and undistorting in line and colour as it is in words. His art can compass tenderness (in the affecting picture of young Babar weeping over his mother's body and in the prancing of the newly married couple when "everyone danced merrily"); it can present satisfying colour patterns, as in the picture of Babar and the old lady packing his trunk or in the simple composition of the coronation scene; it can verge on the ridiculous (for example, when we see Babar and his hostess doing their morning exercises together) and can express contentment (in the view of Babar as an after-dinner raconteur, for instance). The relaxed air of the pictures comes from precisely organised detail and an obvious enjoyment of subject and characters which is one of the many reasons why these seminal picture-story books have a long life ahead of them as well as behind them. In the past forty years many artists have tried to imitate the Babar formula: it remains inimitable. (pp. 3082-83)

Margery Fisher, "An Old Favourite: 'The Story of Babar'," in her Growing Point, Vol. 15, No. 9, April, 1977, pp. 3082-83.

THE TRAVELS OF BABAR   (1934; French edition, 1932)

The tale has the sweet reasonableness of its predecessor. Granting the existence of a little elephant who walks on his hind legs, wears clothes and talks French, this is the way he would act. It will be remembered by all Babar addicts that on his return to the jungle he was made king in recognition of his superiority gained through travel. It will thus be no matter of surprise that he should start off again with his consort Celeste, that his return should be delayed by a series of circumstances of an unusual nature, and that he should be on hand for the last page, lovely and serene as ever. It might seem unnecessary for a book whose pictures alone could hold a foreign audience to put so much art into the telling of a story, but that is the way with the best picture books. . . . With each season the spread of Babar's influence will increase.

May Lamberton Becker, "Those Paris Pigs; Babar; and Six Plummers," in New York Herald Tribune Books (© I.H.T. Corporation; reprinted by permission), November 11, 1934, p. 9.*

If you love elephants, you will love Babar and Celeste. If you have never loved elephants you will love them now. If you who are grown-up have never been fascinated by a picture-book before, then this is the one which will fascinate you. If you who are a child do not take these enchanting people to your heart; if you do not spend delightful hours making sure that no detail of their adventures has escaped you: then you deserve to wear gloves and be kept off wet grass for the rest of your life.

I can say no more. I salute M. de Brunhoff. I am at his feet.

A. A. Milne, "Introduction," The Travels of Babar by Jean de Brunhoff, 1936.

BABAR THE KING   (1935; French edition, 1933)

Of course one of the gems of the season is the latest Babar book. . . . [The] pictures are as gorgeous as ever. The French author of the immortal saga of Babar is, of course, Jean de Brunhoff, and the Babar books . . . have become contemporary classics.

William Rose Benét, "The Children's Bookshop: 'Babar the King'," in The Saturday Review of Literature (copyright © 1935 by Saturday Review; all rights reserved; reprinted by permission), Vol. XIII, No. 3, November 16, 1935, p. 27.

King Babar and his consort, Celeste, now established as adored rulers of the country of the elephants, have made peace with the rhinoceros, and induced their friend, the old lady, to remain with them, accompanied by her monkey, Zephir. They have no capital city, and Babar, who has traveled, means to build Celesteville on the best foreign models but without the deplorable features of human towns. So the Caravans come in with everything needful for the work and the city comes up under your eyes in huge and brilliant pages, till at last it stands complete on a double-page spread. This stood open on my desk all the summer the book came out in French; it was my own dream city, in which I would like to live and work, and because there are none such as yet I find it hard to work in any city.

Trouble comes fast for a while after that. The old lady is bitten by a snake, fire breaks out, and the crown on Babar's head lies uneasily. But all comes out well. "Do you see," says the old lady a week later, "how in this life one must never be discouraged? The vicious snake didn't kill me, and Cornelius is completely recovered. Let's work hard and cheerfully and we'll continue to be happy." If this be moral, make the most of it; we could do with more of it than we have been getting lately. . . .

Let us hope that the serene sunset with which Babar's adventures close will prove a weather breeder so we will have more adventures later.

Idella Purnell, "Animals from a World of Fancy and Fable," in New York Herald Tribune Books (© I.H.T. Corporation; reprinted by permission), November 17, 1935, p. 8.*

From Babar the King, *written and illustrated by Jean de Brunhoff.*

BABAR AND HIS CHILDREN   (1938; British edition as *Babar at Home*)

There is more genius in the Babar books than in any other books for the youngest reader that have appeared for many years. As each new volume has been published I have wondered which I like best. With *Babar's Friend Zephir* I confess to have been a little disappointed. It was mainly about monkeys which do not lend themselves quite so well to the lovingly comic treatment of M. de Brunhoff.

In *Babar At Home* we return to Celesteville and to the news, duly proclaimed, that the Royal Household is expecting a happy event and that it will be announced by the firing of a cannon. The firing of three cannon gives rise to puzzled speculation, but all is well and three little elephants, Flora, Pom and Alexander, have arrived to gladden the hearts of Babar and his subjects. Alexander is more precocious and enterprising than the others and the book is largely concerned with certain thrilling incidents in which he is involved.

Readers will agree with me, I think, that *Babar At Home* is at least as good as its predecessors and it will bring home to us again what a debt we owe to M. de Brunhoff and what a loss we have sustained by his death.

> *"Reviews: 'Babar and His Children',"* in The Junior Bookshelf, *Vol. 3, No. 1, October, 1938, p. 39.*

There is not so much plot as in the Babar just before this, and more of the detail dear to little folks: the elephant babies are washed and fed and get into all sorts of scrapes as they grow older, and Babar says to Celeste on a blissful last page, "Truly it is not easy to bring up a family—but how nice the babies

are! I wouldn't know how to get along without them any more." And neither would we.

> *May Lamberton Becker, "Books for Young Children: 'Babar and His Children',"* in New York Herald Tribune Books *(© I.H.T. Corporation; reprinted by permission), November 13, 1938, p. 9.*

Jean de Brunhoff is dead but happily Babar still lives. The latest chronicle of that beloved elephant family is gay as ever in dress, and particularly entertaining in story. . . . The adventures of the triplets through infancy and early childhood afford opportunity for an amusing little tale which the pictures, with their clever drawing and clear and lovely color, adorn delightfully. A book to covet for the youngsters.

> *Rosemary Carr Benét, "The Children's Bookshop: 'Babar and His Children',"* in The Saturday Review of Literature *(copyright © 1938 by* Saturday Review; *all rights reserved; reprinted by permission), Vol. XIX, No. 4, November 19, 1938, p. 18.*

BABAR AND FATHER CHRISTMAS   (1940; French edition, 1939)

It is very fitting that the tales of one of the friendliest and most lovable of the picture-book animals should include a Christmas story. . . .

Childlike, gently humorous and convincing in its logical detail, **"Babar and Father Christmas"** will take its place in childish hearts with Jean de Brunhoff's other much-loved books.

> *Anne T. Eaton, "Babar Returns,"* in The New York Times Book Review *(© 1940 by The New York Times*

Company; reprinted by permission), December 1, 1940, p. 10.

[Jean de Brunhoff] is dead. And sadly, the new and last Babar book is not as good as the others. It is about Babar going in search of Father Christmas so that he can persuade him to come to his own country to distribute presents. The colour (partly on account of so much snow) looks a little washed out, after the blue seas with whales, the great black ships with three red funnels, and the battle scenes, circus scenes and theatre scenes that we have been used to. The writing is slightly washed out too, in spite of some sentences with the authentic ring. There is no "excellent soup" in it, as there is in so many of the others, no nightingale that sings "Troulala! Tiou—tiou—tiou! Tidi! Tidi!" and there are fewer really expressive back views of elephants. (If de Brunhoff wanted to be really expressive about an elephant's feelings he usually drew a back view.) There is, however, in the new volume one excellent scene in which Father Christmas gives Babar a magic costume.

John Piper, "Babar the Elephant," in The Spectator *(© 1940 by* The Spectator; *reprinted by permission of* The Spectator), *No. 5867, December 6, 1940, p. 611.*

Babar and Father Christmas ought to be given to every child from three to seven, and can absolutely be counted on to delight him. If it is not the best of the Babar books it is well up to standard, and introduces some delightful new characters. The pictures are as pretty as ever, and made even more gay by an unusually winning Father Christmas, while the narrative style, direct and graphic in the tradition of [Daniel] Defoe, is a model to all. There are various ways of treating the animal heroes of children's books. Babar's very great charm is partly human and partly elephantine, and he potters round his garden or rides

From Babar and Father Christmas, *written and illustrated by Jean de Brunhoff.*

a bicycle in his familiar green suit like an elderly Victorian gentleman. (p. 588)

Francis Bird, "Babar and Others," in The New Statesman & Nation *(© 1940 The Statesman & Nation Publishing Co. Ltd.), Vol. XX, No. 511, December 7, 1940, pp. 587-88.**

BABAR'S COUSIN: THAT RASCAL ARTHUR   (1948; French edition, 1947)

When teenagers of today were in their cribs **"The Story of Babar"** came out of France and captured in record time for a picture book the nurseries of the world. Jean de Brunhoff gave little children a creature of their dreams, something between the real baby elephant they all adore and the flannel one they all embrace. . . . Seven beautiful big books were completed— and then no more. Too soon. Jean de Brunhoff left the world. To the children of the world he had left Babar.

But now—can we believe our eyes?—Babar comes back. On the same immense pages, wide enough to take in seas, shores and parachute drops, in the same colors, comes dear Babar in a new book. His companions, his children come, too—Zephir the monkey, the baby elephants Pom, Flora and Alexander, even a glimpse of "the old lady" waving good by as they set off for the seaside. There fat little Cousin Arthur takes over; his talent for getting into trouble is surpassed only by his luck in getting out of it. . . .

Look once more at the cover. Where once you read Jean de Brunhoff, what you now read is Laurent de Brunhoff. Fronting the first page, in the same gentle script of the first books, are the words: "Dedicated to the memory of my father." His son, artist and author, too, has taken up the story in his father's spirit. I suppose, if I tried, I might find something in this book that wasn't quite so good as the others, but I am too grateful to try. Little children, with good reason, will be just as grateful.

May Lamberton Becker, "Books for Young People: 'Babar's Cousin: That Rascal Arthur'," in New York Herald Tribune Weekly Book Review *(© I.H.T. Corporation; reprinted by permission), November 14, 1948, p. 6.*

The new Babar book by the son of Jean de Brunhoff is as full of entertainment as if the famous elephant's adventures had never been interrupted. The fascinating details of the large pictures are just as absorbing as those in the earlier books. . . . Seldom do we find the continuation of a series by another hand so completely successful.

Alice M. Jordan, "New Books for Christmas : 'Babar's Cousin'," in The Horn Book Magazine *(copyrighted, 1948, by The Horn Book, Inc., Boston), Vol. XXIV, No. 6, November-December, 1948, p. 452.*

Laurent de Brunhoff in providing this new story-picture book in the tradition of his father's genius has succeeded well in giving us a book that, at any rate in the necessarily cursory examination permitted in a review, might well have been by the creator of Babar. The physical appearance of the book, its size, illustrations and text in script, (so difficult for small English children to read) is like its predecessors, and the pleasing little story of Arthur's latest escapade is in the same strain. . . . I feel that it will be accepted by its young readers as authentic de Brunhoff.

"Picture Books: 'Babar and That Rascal Arthur'," in The Junior Bookshelf, *Vol. 12, No. 4, December, 1948, p. 178.*

BABAR'S PICNIC **(1949; British edition published as *Picnic at Babar's*)**

Let it be admitted at once that [***Picnic at Babar's***] is disappointing. Any young reader making with this volume his first introduction to the famous Babar may be forgiven if he fails to experience the joy that the earlier Babar books always give. The plain truth is that Laurent de Brunhoff has none of the genius of his father. Jean's claim to the unique position he holds is partly the result of an extraordinarily close relationship between story and pictures. His stories have great simplicity yet possess warmth and completeness. They move gently onwards to a logical and satisfying conclusion. Laurent, in his efforts to achieve the simplicity of his father's style has achieved merely scrappiness and mediocrity. He is more successful in his pictures but even in these we miss the rich imagination and quiet humour that the earlier volumes possessed. A comparison I was able to make between these and the present one convinced me that Laurent should now strike out in a line of his own. (pp. 194-95)

"Picture Books: 'Picnic at Babar's'," in The Junior Bookshelf, *Vol. 14, No. 5, November, 1950, pp. 194-95.*

BABAR'S VISIT TO BIRD ISLAND **(1952)**

It is impossible for an admirer of Babar to be completely detached about a new book of his adventures. Perhaps a more objective eye will detect a certain clutter in some of these pictures, but to an old friend this seems a mere quibble, for the majority are as gay and brilliantly designed as ever. Certainly the elephant king retains his Olympian imperturbability; his queen Celeste, the three children, and that rascal Arthur are still rotundly appealing. It is great fun to watch them all disporting themselves on Bird Island swanking about in feather cloaks—watching an ostrich race, riding bird-back over the sea—with that bland, matter-of-fact air which makes good nonsense convincing.

Ellen Lewis Buell, "The Elephant King," in The New York Times *(© 1952 by The New York Times Company; reprinted by permission), November 2, 1952, p. 24.*

[The] spring has gone out of the elephant family and the latest Babar isn't so happy a sequel. One is grateful to Laurent de Brunhoff for prolonging the series—he gave up his career as an abstract painter, it appears, to carry on his father's invention—but a sense of effort is evident. Is this how Babar would behave? how Arthur would talk? The new story is on the dull side, and the design of the big pictures a bit of a mess. But it is by the high standards of its series that it disappoints.

Janet Adam Smith, "Christmas Books: Picture Books," in The New Statesman & Nation *(© 1952 The Statesman & Nation Publishing Co. Ltd.), Vol. XLIV, No. 1134, November 29, 1952, p. 650.**

This is the best example to date of neo-Babarism, partly because the artist is less obviously modelling his style on his father's, partly because the pictures are, comparisons apart, good, and partly because one is no longer shocked at the im-

propriety of carrying on the Babar books after the death of their creator. ***Babar's visit to Bird Island*** is charmingly drawn, with that loving attention to active detail which has always distinguished the series, but the story lacks some of the intense seriousness of the original.

"The New Books: 'Babar's Visit to Bird Island'," in The Junior Bookshelf, *Vol. 16, No. 5, December, 1952, p. 265.*

BABAR'S FAIR **(1954)**

The complete insouciance and artlessness with which the Babar books are written and illustrated, continues to fascinate. Here the people of Celesteville, in a project spearheaded by King Babar, have a fair to which all the animals from the surrounding territories are invited as participants too. They go through their motions a little like UN delegates on holiday and, being very human, endear themselves to us the more.

"Juvenile Supplement: Books to Read Aloud," in Virginia Kirkus' Service, *Vol. XXIV, No. 19, October 1, 1956, p. 750.*

"Babar's Fair" is well named. The new book about Jean de Brunhoff's utterly captivating elephant family is a map of Celesteville Fair. Each page shows a different attraction with guests and the famous family of Babar the King, Queen Celeste, the triplets, Arthur and Zephir enjoying themselves thoroughly. . . . Babar fans will enjoy the amusing details in the pictures. . . .

Laurent de Brunhoff has been faithful to his father's genius but one wonders if he might not offer us some original work of his own outside of the Babar tradition. There is promise of this in the double spread showing the evening spectacle at the Fair which is quite different from the rest in feeling and style.

Margaret Sherwood Libby, "Books for Boys and Girls: 'Babar's Fair'," in New York Herald Tribune Book Review *(© I.H.T. Corporation; reprinted by permission), November 25, 1956, p. 12.*

BABAR AND THE PROFESSOR **(1957; French edition, 1956)**

There are some delightful new developments in **"Babar and the Professor,"** notably exploration of an underground river and the construction of a paddle-wheel steamer, possessing among other things a piquant combination bar and library. In a fairly long story that rambles in the customary Babar manner, touching on the day-by-day doings in the elephant city of Celesteville, we read of a visit of the Old Lady, her brother Professor Grifaton (specialist in butterflies, caves and boars, apparently) and his two grandchildren, Nadine and Colin. These two little human children, half the size of the elephant triplets, are a welcome, if temporary, addition to the Celesteville group, inspiring a picnic, a costume party and the cave investigation. Among the bright drawings the children will see their old friends, except Zephir, in a variety of charming poses. We especially enjoy the sight of Arthur at a cave picnic gloating over a plate of five éclairs (three chocolate, two coffee), Babar sitting at ease, his knees crossed, his crown on his head and a letter nonchalantly held in his trunk, and some handsome double-page spreads of the cave in a more eerie style, very effective as contrast to the elephant characters who peer at the wonders by the light of their flashlights.

Margaret S. Libby, "Beguiling Animals in Handsome Pictures," in New York Herald Tribune Book Review (© I.H.T. Corporation; reprinted by permission), November 17, 1957, p. 4.*

SERAFINA THE GIRAFFE   (1961)

Laurent de Brunhoff has shown in so many pictures in the sequels to his father's famous Babar books that he had some gay ideas of his own not precisely in keeping with the Babar tradition that we are delighted to have him branch out for himself with a totally new character, and a heroine at that, Serafina the giraffe. The book is like the Babar books in size, in the abundant use of effective flat clear colors (here, a beautiful pinkish orange, bright yellows and greens and a dark greenish ochre) and in using a handsome script for the text. As this use of script is attractive on the page and easy for the grownup to read, we like it, although it is a slight deterrent for the child, not yet at home in reading, when he tries to read it to himself. The story is the ever-popular one of a birthday party, a birthday party for Serafina's grandmother. Like all children, Serafina and her friends, Patrick the rabbit, Hugo the kangaroo, Beryl the frog and Ernest the crocodile get into some difficulties when they try to do the preparations alone. Jungle sightseeing, quarrels and inattention delay the making of the banana-flour cake until aid comes from the elegant Lady Rhinoceros, and all ends happily. Slight, of course, but with decorative imaginative drawings and the reassuring sense of family happiness, no matter how exotic the locale which makes all the de Brunhoff books favorites.

Margaret Sherwood Libby, "Books for Boys and Girls: 'Serafina the Giraffe'," in Lively Arts and Book Review (© I.H.T. Corporation; reprinted by permission), March 5, 1961, p. 35.

For the sake of Babar we all read anything by a de Brunhoff, but this gives us the right, I think, to compare subsequent stories (even with different characters) with the original masterpieces. Serafina is a dim character beside Babar or Zephir and her adventures with her friends . . . and with kindly Lady Rhinoceros are of slight interest. Nostalgic echoes (the train, the monkey houses, the car) fail to compensate for crude pictures and a general inconsequence of story; and what, Babar-fans may ask, is a kangaroo doing in Africa?

Margery Fisher, "Picture/Story Books: 'Serafina the Giraffe'," in her Growing Point, Vol. 4, No. 1, May, 1965, p. 524.

Brunhoff is a magic name, and the familiar orange and green covers raise high hopes; sad to relate *Serafina* is a poor, wilting thing and her outing with granny giraffe a dull affair. Serafina's head gets stuck in a rabbit hole, a frog breaks a leg, a crocodile gets a wounded nose, but it is all badly drawn and crudely coloured; better to stay with Babar.

"Accent on Pictures," in The Times Literary Supplement (© Times Newspapers Ltd. (London) 1965; reproduced from The Times Literary Supplement by permission), No. 3303, June 17, 1965, p. 506.*

BABAR'S CASTLE   (1962; French edition, 1961)

Another Babar book, which makes one wonder if it isn't past time to call a halt to the series. The illustrations are not as good as the earlier ones, though the paintings and the tapestry on the castle walls are well done. Babar fans will mourn the change from cursive writing to hand lettering, which makes the book seem more prosaic.

Laurie Dudley, "Children's and Young People's Libraries," in School Library Journal, an appendix to Library Journal (reprinted from the October, 1962 issue of School Library Journal, published by R. R. Bowker Co./A Xerox Corporation; copyright © 1962), Vol. 9, No. 2, October, 1962, p. 178.

After the war, Laurent de Brunhoff, Jean's son, inherited [Babar's kingdom] and did some Babar books of his own. The code of morals, the old sobrieties, lapsed, as has the apt copperplate in which the stories were once set down. Laurent's elephants lack the lovely wobbling sinuosity of the originals. His earlier books were lively enough, a chronicle of pranks and plights, but I can't say I admire his recent *Babar's Castle.* The colours are harsh; the elephants are made to look funny, lapped in loony armour; Celesteville does not lend itself to cute castles and grandeur. The horns of Disneyland are blowing. Laurent always avoids the real disasters of the old series, where fires break out and burn people, where fathers are beside themselves with grief. In Jean's books the quaint civic and domestic round is described with love, and with morsels of good advice. Laurent's coldish compilations will never help any little girl to retort, as one I know did, to her father's complaint about the sheer *business* of bringing up children: 'But as Babar said, I don't know what we should do without them.'

Karl Miller, "Welfare King," in New Statesman (© 1962 The Statesman & Nation Publishing Co. Ltd.), Vol. 64, No. 1652, November 9, 1962, p. 670.

Anyone confessing to *nostalgie de Babar* will be amazed and delighted to find that the king of elephants has been brought back to life by Jean de Brunhoff's son, Laurent. Not a day older, Babar, Queen Céleste and the family decide to move, and in *Babar's Castle* are seen exploring their new home. . . . Babar (always the sensationalist) has a new motor car and a splendid motor mower; and the pictures are as fresh and gay as ever. (p. 904)

"Eyecatchers Designed to Please the Youngest," in The Times Literary Supplement (© Times Newspapers Ltd. (London) 1962; reproduced from The Times Literary Supplement by permission), No. 3169, November 23, 1962, pp. 904-05.*

BABAR'S FRENCH LESSONS   (1963)

The fashion for disguising lesson-books is not new, but I wonder how much use a French vocabulary is when it offers (as most of this kind do) a fairly random selection of nouns, verbs and phrases. Anyhow, here is Babar, with his family, going through the day (breakfast, bicycle ride, birthday party, visit to seaside, bedtime) to give the opportunity for mixing French words (printed in blue) with a simple English text. I feel a little sad to see this shadow Babar (compare the breakfast, for instance, with that meal in the old lady's house so many years ago); but for those who like learning this way, a pleasant picture-book.

Margery Fisher, "Picture/Story Books: 'Babar's French Lessons'," in her Growing Point, Vol. 4, No. 5, November, 1965, p. 604.

There is no nonsense . . . about Laurent de Brunhoff's ***Babar's French Lessons***. . . . 'I am Babar, King of the elephants and I want to give you French lessons. Would you like that? Very well.' Babar in his green suit, bow tie, and yellow crown has been an irresistible favourite with English children for so long that they eagerly follow him, the Old Lady, that rascal Arthur and the mischievous monkey Zéphir on expeditions into the garden, the country—and French vocabulary. A great deal of thought and care has gone into the preparation of this book and a clever production device ensures that the child knows exactly which portion of an English sentence is being translated into French.

> *Elaine Moss, "Hands across the Sea: 'Babar's French Lessons',"* in The Spectator *(© 1965 by* The Spectator; *reprinted by permission of* The Spectator*), No. 7168, November 12, 1965, p. 627.*

Some sort of bilingualism is found in Laurent de Brunhoff's ***Babar's French Lessons*** or alternatively, ***Les Leçons de Français de Babar.*** The publishers claim in the short foreword that "Babar knows what boys and girls like" and there is some substance in the claim. But for whom is the book intended? It is a hotch-potch of French and English, disconcerting and bewildering. One could perhaps imagine the almost monolingual parent of a persistent child deriving some despairing solace from it; the vocabulary is concrete and mercifully free from whimsy; but no child who has had sensible lessons in French should need the intrusive English. Nevertheless, without the English, this book could play a part in the intelligent learning of French, and might thus be a little cheaper.

> *"Beginning in the Primary School: 'Babar's French Lessons',"* in The Times Literary Supplement *(© Times Newspapers Ltd. (London) 1965; reproduced from* The Times Literary Supplement *by permission), No. 3328, December 9, 1965, p. 1154.*

BABAR COMES TO AMERICA (1965)

Babar has been no passing fancy for my household. We believed him. We took him seriously. His gentle, prudent, slightly priggish elephant soul was very dear to us. But now I have spent over a week with his newest adventure, and I am unable to get around my dismay. It has occurred to me that I may be merely possessive about my own Babar, vintage 1956, and therefore not sympathetic to what came later. So I have read other recent Babars by de Brunhoff *fils*, and they are as captivating as the original books by his father Jean. It is just this current one, about Babar's visit to America, that irks me, oppresses me, and has baffled my loyalties.

Perhaps part of the trouble is that Babar has left France, or that segment of elephant country which seems to lie about 50 miles southwest of the *Tour Eiffel*. Perhaps, like a good *brie*, Babar is at his best at home. At least in his earlier books, he did things and was himself: built a city, fought a war with rhinos, organized a fair. Here in America, he is reduced to a mildly dazed onlooker. It is as though he were implanted on a 6,000 mile conveyor belt that runs from New York to Los Angeles and back. Babar stands still and all the American cliches pass by. In Manhattan he encounters rude bus drivers, raucous street noise, dust in his eyes, and brand names (Hilton, Coke, Pepsi, 7-Up, V-8 etc.). For food, there is a drugstore and a Japanese restaurant, and when he looks for a certain store that has been recommended to him, he finds a skyscraper going up in its place. As he moves west, it gets worse: supermarkets,

superhighways, forests of telegraph poles, oil derricks, portable TV, drive-in-movies; neon signs. A half hour in the office of the Harvard Lampoon is as close to any civilized life as he gets.

Now all of these elements are certainly part of America. The hardiest chauvinist couldn't deny it—might even be proud of it. In one corner of my dismay, I keep wondering if Babar's creator can possibly have intended this book to flatter just such readers, at the same time, of course, that, in its European editions, exactly the same elements will gratify equally superficial anti-Americans. But a visitor as intelligent and cultivated and just as Babar owes it to himself to look for our best as well as our most crapulous and notorious aspects. After all, there are noisy traffic jams along the *Quai Mégisserie* in Paris, but there are also bookstalls.

Why, then, instead of a room at the Hilton, where he looks out on construction cranes, didn't Babar take a room at the Chelsea, where he might have heard a very indigenous American composer, Virgil Thomson, composing upstairs? Instead of a Detroit auto plant, why not the Bronx Botanical Gardens? Instead of a drive-in movie, why not the Unicorn Tapestry, or the orchards of Oregon instead of Chicago's State Street, or New York's Lincoln Center instead of Disneyland?

Am I being a snob? I don't think so. In the first place, when he is at home, Babar appears to lead a civilized life. Celesteville has gardens and portrait painters and a beautiful theater, and Babar's friends play chamber music and read books and eat well. Why not look for comparable values here? In the second place, the America Babar sees is a superficial half-truth. There is a flavor and way of life to be found here which Babar almost entirely ignores.

Worst of all, considering what he sees, Babar keeps inexplicably smiling, and on the last page, he even sails away full of "wonderful memories." But the America he visited was a nightmare, so I must conclude either that Babar is very ingenuous indeed—in fact a fool—or that he is a liar, and that his whole trip was "sponsored," perhaps even by some of those brand names (none of the *other* Babar books I've ever read used brand names).

But I decline to do either. It will be simpler just to drop this particular Babar from my private canon, and in fact to pretend that he never left Celesteville in the first place.

> *Robert Phelps, "Travel Stickers on His Trunk," in* Book Week—New York Herald Tribune *(© 1965, The Washington Post), October 31, 1965, p. 2.*

This latest addition to the series begun by Jean de Brunhoff and now continued by his son isn't really a story, but, as my oldest son says, "more of a funny travelogue." Babar tours America, following, I suspect, much the same route as his biographer's family took on a recent visit. It's a pretty upper-middle-class tour. . . . But Chicago, New York, Washington, Disneyland, and the Grand Canyon are included too; the pictures are lively and colorful, and it's a fine book to read aloud to children who like Babar and have been to some of these places.

> *Alison Lurie, "Books for Children: 'Babar Comes to America'," in* The New York Review of Books *(reprinted by permission of the author), Vol. V, No. 9, December 9, 1965, p. 38.*

Not only does Babar go to America, he loses his identity there. No longer is he the benign ruler of a kingdom in French African territory—he has become an expatriate rubberneck doing a "Sasek" tour of the United States. There is no story; the pictures are poor in quality; the charm, flavour, the originality of the old Babar books is entirely lost. Alas for the (absent) old lady, poor Celeste, and what a pale shadow of that rascal Arthur! It is a sad, sad day for the elephants.

> *E.D.M., "Picture Books: 'Babar Goes to America'," in* Children's Book News *(copyright © 1969 by Baker Book Services Ltd.), Vol. 4, No. 5, September-October, 1969, p. 249.*

BABAR LOSES HIS CROWN   (1967)

This latest episode comes in a new don't-wait-for-mother, read-it-yourself format, and parents who enjoyed Babar as much as their offspring are the first losers; next are the youngsters who absorbed a little piquancy along with the plot. There's not much plot here anyhow—just a quick tour of Paris on the trail of the man with the moustache who picked up the suitcase containing Babar's crown. The views of Paris from the Eiffel Tower, of a traffic jam at the Etoile, are pleasant, and the elephants are as endearing as ever, but the story is too rudimentary for first

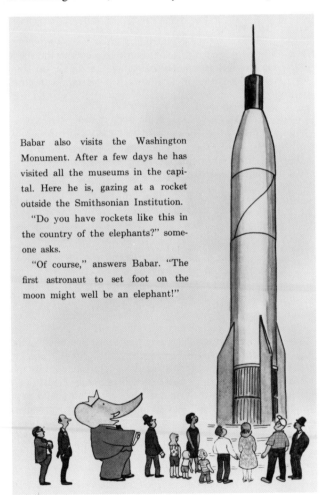

Babar also visits the Washington Monument. After a few days he has visited all the museums in the capital. Here he is, gazing at a rocket outside the Smithsonian Institution.

"Do you have rockets like this in the country of the elephants?" someone asks.

"Of course," answers Babar. "The first astronaut to set foot on the moon might well be an elephant!"

From Babar Comes to America, *written and illustrated by Laurent de Brunhoff.*

graders (and the telling too constricted for effective reading aloud). Maybe for early learners to read to their superseded parents?

> *"Easy Reading: 'Babar Loses His Crown'," in* Kirkus Service *(copyright © 1967 Virginia Kirkus' Service, Inc.), Vol. XXXV, No. 15, August 1, 1967, p. 1045.*

Keep one eye on the Man with the Mustache; the scoundrel has made off with the suitcase containing Babar's crown. Out of the other eye see the wonders of Paris from Metro to Eiffel Tower. It's all first-class: the trip, the adventure, the meeting with the affable elephant family, a longtime childhood favorite.

> *"Easy Reading for Beginners: 'Babar Loses His Crown'," in* The New York Times Book Review, *Part II (© 1967 by The New York Times Company; reprinted by permission), November 5, 1967, p. 60.*

BABAR'S CHILDHOOD, BABAR AND THE OLD LADY, BABAR'S CORONATION (LITTLE BABAR BOOKS)   (British edition, 1969)

The degradation of Babar is complete. The growing unease felt in previous years that there were too many Babar books and that more inevitably meant worse is now justified. 1969 has seen the final wrecking of a great creation—and such is the affection engendered by the Babar of Brunhoff *père* that it is difficult to escape from feelings of profound bitterness and anger at what has happened to him in the hands of Brunhoff *fils*.

Of the two groups of books under review [**Babar Goes Visiting** and **Babar Learns to Drive** comprise the second group] the **Little Babar Books** are the more repulsive, chiefly because there is still discernible inside them the spirit of the original Babar. They are in fact based upon the first book ever, **The Story of Babar,** (although this is nowhere acknowledged) and each 'little' book proffers what the publishers hope will be seen as a self-contained chunk of the story—the three books . . . adding up to the ordinary single volume. . . .

But of course they don't add up to it at all. Quite apart from their wholly unsatisfactory fragmentation of the original, the **Little Babar Books** have corrupted every feature in it that was of value: the classic organization of its pages (which have already been sadly modified once), the delicacy of its line and colour, the unaffectedness of its text. Bits have been added or removed to help the new tripartite division, so that we now get sloppy drawings of Babar's mother giving him his bottle and telling him 'wonderful stories' and we lose such gorgeous sketches as that of Arthur and Celeste being berated by their respective *mamans*.

'The Adventures of Babar on Television' contribute to his destruction in another way. Where **'The Little Babar Books'** gave us poverty, these give us gloss. Every page has its quota of colour photographs taken from the television production and these are accompanied by texts of unbelievable banality and tedium.

No doubt the shareholders of Associated Book Publishers are enjoying the prospect of an almost infinite extension of these series, which because of their fundamental vulgarity will doubtless have a wide popular success. Among the toadstools of Toyland too there will be infinite rejoicing; for Noddy and Big Ears, so recently joined by Rosemary Garland's Pooh, have won a new recruit.

B.W.A., "Picture Books: 'Babar Goes Visiting' and 'Babar Learns to Drive'," in Children's Book News *(copyright © 1970 by Baker Book Services Ltd.), Vol. 5, No. 1, January-February, 1970, p. 21.*

BABAR'S TRUNK (1969; includes *Babar at the Seashore, Babar Goes on a Picnic, Babar Goes Skiing, Babar the Gardener;* **British edition as** *Little Babar Books,* **including** *Babar at the Seaside, Babar in the Snow, Babar's Day Out, Babar the Gardener*)

The latest four titles in the **'Little Babar Books'** bring the total in this unnecessary series to fourteen. Other suitable adjectives are: inadequate, irritating and cheaply produced. Inadequate because all the magic of the detailed, action-packed, colourful pictures of the earlier, larger editions is lost. It is, to say the least, irritating to see this lovable children's favourite reduced to no more than a commercialised pot-boiler (beware Peter Rabbit!) and the production adds nothing to the publisher's high reputation. Unlike the first titles issued, these latest four have the saving grace of being new. However, even the author has, I think, found difficulty with the miniaturising process for the writing is rather stinted; the short sentences barely adequate to describe the pictures, which would seem to be their only function. Very little is left to the child's imagination. As in *Babar the Gardener* where tulips are in bloom at the same time as cherries are being picked, there is for me a similar anachronism between Babar, King of the Elephants, 1934 style and the **'Little Babar Books',** 1971. The two just don't go together! One can only regret the appearance of this series at a time when, more than ever before, the awareness of quality in children's book writing, illustration and production is being pursued wherever children's books are discussed. (pp. 50-1)

E. Hudson, "Reviews: 'Babar's Trunk'," in Children's Book Review *(© 1971 by Five Owls Press Ltd.; all rights reserved), Vol. 1, No. 2, April, 1971, pp. 50-1.*

BABAR'S BIRTHDAY SURPRISE (1970)

[In *Babar's Birthday Surprise*] the plot thickens around just the kind of civilized problem that Arthur, Celeste and their colleagues can handle: how to keep King Babar from finding out that they've cut a massive birthday statue of him in a nearby mountain. The inexplicable charm of the Babar stories is that they can be read with equal pleasure by kids who have barely heard of Paris and francophile parents.

"For the Young: 'Babar's Birthday Surprise'," in Time *(copyright 1970 Time Inc.; all rights reserved; reprinted by permission from* Time*), Vol. 96, No. 25, December 21, 1970, p. 68.*

Babar, the benign despot of the elephants, is once again seen basking in the affection and admiration of his family and subjects. How many families could be so sure that the most successful birthday present for their head would be a colossal statue of himself carved in a mountainside? But Babar continues likable as well as all-powerful, a living contradiction of Lord Acton's assertion, and if this book does not break any new ground it does nothing to disappoint the expectations of addicts.

"More Picture Books: 'Babar's Birthday Surprise'," in The Times Literary Supplement *(© Times Newspapers Ltd. (London) 1971; reproduced from* The Times Literary Supplement *by permission), No. 3634, October 22, 1971, p. 1343.*

The land of the elephants has long since lost its original magic, and the business of this particular story's plot scarcely compensates for the charm of the early books although it is one of the gayest for some time.

Jeff Jackson, "Picture Books: 'Babar's Birthday Surprise'," in Children's Book Review *(© 1972 Five Owls Press Ltd.; all rights reserved), Vol. 2, No. 1, February, 1972, p. 8.*

BABAR VISITS ANOTHER PLANET (1972)

No doubt Babar has some old friends who happily revisit him under any circumstances, but most will be disappointed by the blobby pastel pictures and uninspired text of this latest of the popular elephant's adventures. Kidnapped via rocket by creatures who "look like elephants but yet they're not elephants," Babar, Celeste, and the children visit a floating city that hangs in the air (from large red balloons) above a soft, mucky planet. . . . Little of Babar's old ingenuousness and few of the endearing incongruities of his condition are recaptured here; indeed, the depicted space town with its silly looking inhabitants resembles a 2nd-class Seussy Disneyland more than the jungle Celesteville we remember.

"Picture Books: 'Babar Visits Another Planet'," in Kirkus Reviews *(copyright © 1972 The Kirkus Service, Inc.), Vol. XL, No. 19, October 1, 1972, p. 1139.*

When Laurent de Brunhoff took up his late father's business in 1946, it was not as it might be for you or me or the sons of B. Altman, because the de Brunhoff business was Babar, that urbane and exemplary elephant. Babar is 43, but he doesn't look it. He wears the same-size suit (he never did have a waist line), and he was gray to begin with, naturally. He, his family, Zephir the monkey, and the Old Lady have remained amazingly unchanged from their first adventure in *The Story of Babar* . . . to their current appearance in *Babar Visits Another Planet*. The world that provides a backdrop for their continuing saga has altered, the handwriting used in the early books has been replaced by type (it is not as attractive but is more legible for young eyes), and, oh yes, the author-illustrator has changed. When Laurent de Brunhoff picked up his father's pen, he also took over the paternal style. (pp. 67-8)

It cannot be easy to write and draw in another man's style, no matter how well you know it. M. de Brunhoff II is obviously talented, but his expression is a little like artistic ventriloquism. We admire books for their originality in saying something new or something old in a new way. Therefore I find it hard to look at this latest *Babar* completely without prejudice. Perhaps this is why, although the outward appearances are faithful to the original pattern, the spirit seems to be flagging. Due partly to differences in palette and reproduction (more modern but less interesting), the art is not as fresh and bright as in the early books. In those the overall design was less cluttered, and there was more of a stylish simplicity that is particularly European.

From the beginning the story line has dealt with pleasant details of bourgeois elephant life told in the present tense. It has been easy for children to understand, to identify with, and to laugh at. There are nice touches in *Babar Visits Another Planet*. A spread of the city held up by orange balloons and floating over the odd, sticky surface of the planet ("Maybe this planet is made of caramel," Arthur says) is gay and wonderfully detailed. There are the natives of this strange world who look surprisingly like pin-headed, curly-eared elephants. And there are, too, those literate flourishes that seem to be a *spécialité du maison* Brunhoff: "Babar would very much like to replace his lost shoe . . . but he is very disappointed. None of them are large enough for him. He decides to take off his remaining shoe, and walk about in his socks. 'It will be more elegant,' he says.''

The story rambles too much, and many of the pictures are undistinguished. The bloom is gone, but after some 40 years and nearly 20 books why not? Perhaps Laurent de Brunhoff could let us hear his own voice in his next book, and Babar might be allowed to rest on his laurels, or whatever it is elephants rest on. (p. 68)

> *Karla Kuskin, "Books for Children: 'Babar Visits Another Planet'," in* Saturday Review of Education, *Vol. 1, No. 3, March 10, 1973, pp. 67-8.*

BONHOMME AND THE HUGE BEAST (1974)

As pictured, Emilie's squiggly friend Bonhomme falls somewhere between a blob of glup and Casper the friendly ghost. Emilie herself is sketched in a mode one step up from stick figures, and de Brunhoff's deliberately naive present tense narration similarly resembles what a kid herself might do—or an improvising grownup at her bedside. The subject and the structure follow suit for this is simply about how Emilie and Bonhomme tell each other pointless little ministories when Bonhomme sleeps over, and then how the two go off—by foot and then borne by an accommodating cloud—to a Seussy pink house on a mountain top where they meet their inventions: a silly, fringed purple saurian, a giant frog with a jam jar, and a stone horse who falls and breaks but is quickly put together again. That's all and though there's no telling what kind of matter-of-factly told nonsense preschoolers will take to, you won't miss another Babar if you pass this by.

> *"Picture Books: 'Bonhomme and the Huge Beast',"" in* Kirkus Reviews *(copyright © 1974 The Kirkus Service, Inc.), Vol. XLII, No. 24, December 15, 1974, p. 1298.*

There's no sparkle in this flat fantasy in which Emilie and her imaginary friend Bonhomme amuse each other by telling stories and go looking for the strange beast Randolphe. . . . Multicolor pastel illustrations in de Brunhoff's familiar style give an otherwise bland offering a friendly boost.

> *Joan Reamer, "The Book Review: 'Bonhomme and the Huge Beast'," in* School Library Journal *(reprinted from the January, 1975 issue of* School Library Journal, *published by R. R. Bowker Co./A Xerox Corporation; copyright © 1975), Vol. 21, No. 5, January, 1975, p. 38.*

BABAR AND THE WULLY-WULLY (1975)

A family of elephants and their monkey friend find something called a Wully-Wully and adopt it as a pet. Then at a picnic the Wully-Wully is stolen away by a rhinoceros king and when one of the little elephants goes to the rhino city to rescue it he is caught and put in jail, and must be rescued in turn by the monkey. Surely no one but a de Brunhoff could get away with such a plot, but no doubt de Brunhoff will—not only for old acquaintance's sake but, too, for the surprises when it seems all has been resolved: first the rhinos thunder through Celeste-

ville and recapture the Wully-Wully, and then as both sides prepare for war there's a more redeeming switch with little Flora elephant visiting the rhino king and persuading him to set the disputed Wully-Wully free to go where he wishes.

> *"Picture Books: 'Babar and the Wully-Wully'," in* Kirkus Reviews *(copyright © 1975 The Kirkus Service, Inc.), Vol. XLII, No. 19, October 1, 1975, p. 1120.*

Kidnapped by Rataxes and taken to rhino country where it is kept imprisoned in a cage, the Wully-Wully becomes the object of great dispute. Babar's daughter Flora does the mediating and gets the credit for settling the argument by allowing the Wully-Wully to roam freely. But, the plot is only mildly involving and obviously didactic.

> *Corinne Camarata, "The Book Review: 'Babar and the Wully-Wully'," in* School Library Journal *(reprinted from the April, 1976 issue of* School Library Journal, *published by R. R. Bowker Co./A Xerox Corporation; copyright ©1976), Vol. 22, No. 8, April, 1976, p. 60.*

BABAR'S MYSTERY (1978)

[*Babar's Mystery*] finds the resort of Celesteville-on-the-Sea plagued by a series of thefts. . . . Young Arthur eventually cracks the case. . . . If this was about anyone but Babar, librarians would definitely want to pass. Yet regardless of the choppy writing and rambling plot, de Brunhoff's latest offering will be in demand by young listeners who never seem to tire of these books crammed with colorful cartoons.

> *Drew Stevenson, "Mystery and Suspense: 'Babar's Mystery'," in* School Library Journal *(reprinted from the December, 1978 issue of* School Library Journal, *published by R. R. Bowker Co./A Xerox Corporation; copyright © 1978), Vol. 25, No. 4, December, 1978, p. 67.*

Television-reared children will probably appreciate the light parody of stereotyped thrillers but if they have inherited early Babar books they may also join their parents and grand-parents in comparisons that will not favour Laurent de Brunhoff's artwork, heavier and cruder than that of his father as the jokes are somewhat more obvious.

> *Margery Fisher, "Picture/Story Books: 'Babar's Mystery'," in her* Growing Point, *Vol. 18, No. 2, July, 1979, p. 3552.*

Here are some memories for the middle-aged. There cannot be many children's book heroes as old as Babar and still going strong. Strong? Well, perhaps not. He was never the same after Jean de Brunhoff died. Laurent has plenty of filial piety and he can draw elephants in his sleep, but he lacks the inimitable delicacy of touch which made the original Babar books such world-beaters. The pictures in *Babar's Mystery* are good enough, but the story is a poor thing, badly put together, unfunny and unconvincing. It would be churlish to be less than welcoming to so courteous an elephant, but we are welcoming a memory rather than a current achievement.

> *"The New Books: 'Babar's Mystery'," in* The Junior Bookshelf, *Vol. 43, No. 4, August, 1979, p. 194.*

THE ONE PIG WITH HORNS (1979)

Laurent de Brunhoff's **"The One Pig with Horns"** . . . is bursting with hostile manic energy: The author of many Babar books has blown his cool on this excursion far from bourgeois Celesteville and has plunged into an R. D. Laing fable about a furious, grotesque pig who keeps exploding with rage and literally losing his head; it comes off, weeps, is up a tree—all very gross, even the deliberately sloppy, violent illustrations (as shapeless and undisciplined as the Babar pictures are neatly detailed and buttoned up). Back to the elephants, please; pigs and nightmares aren't your forte.

> *Harold C.K. Rice, "The Picture Books: 'The One Pig with Horns'," in* The New York Times Book Review (© *1967 by The New York Times Company; reprinted by permission), April 29, 1979, p. 29.*

This book is *very* surrealistic, making use of fantastic and incongruous imagery by unnatural juxtapositions and combinations both in the writing and the artwork. Initially, I did not like *The One Pig with Horns* and felt children would not either. But the book grows on you. The more I read it, the more I feel children could understand it. A very interesting book— "Curiouser and curiouser." Well worth looking at.

> *Barbara S. Worth, "Picture Books: 'The One Pig with Horns'," in* Children's Book Review Service *(copyright © 1979 Children's Book Review Service Inc.), Vol. 7, No. 11, June, 1979, p. 101.*

Susan Cooper

1935-

British author of fiction and nonfiction for children and adults. Cooper blends the backgrounds of Arthurian and Welsh myths and legends with realistic, contemporary figures and concepts in her fantasy quintet *The Dark Is Rising,* **which includes** *Over Sea, Under Stone, The Dark Is Rising, Greenwitch, The Grey King,* **and** *Silver on the Tree.* **The ongoing characters are Simon, Jane, and Barney, their mysterious uncle Merriman Lyon (the wizard Merlin), and Will Stanton, who is introduced in the second book as the vital link between the present and the ancient past. The ageless battle between good and evil is the underlying theme of these works: the children's struggles with the Dark Ones, which include basic ingredients of the great legendary contests such as sorcery, mystical tokens, demons, and omens, prepare the protagonists for the conflicts which will continue throughout their lives in the natural world.**

The style and structure of these works has prompted comparisons with the fantasies of C. S. Lewis and J.R.R. Tolkien, under whom Cooper studied at Oxford. She uses England and Wales as the setting for her series, and it is generally agreed that her intimacy with the people, places, and customs of these areas contributes to its success. While Cooper has been applauded for her ability to build and sustain an interesting level of intrigue, critics mention an occasional failure to thoroughly explain the causes behind particular resolutions. However, reviewers consistently note her natural dialogue and the skill with which she meshes the daily lives of the characters with their fantastic adventures.

In addition to high fantasy, Cooper has written a realistic novel and a light fantasy for younger children. *Dawn of Fear* **relates the actions and reactions of a group of children in London during the Blitz of World War II. This autobiographical work is considered a realistic portrayal of how war and its destruction affects children, and although it is set in a more familiar period than** *The Dark Is Rising,* **the ominous struggle of the dark against the light is equally present.** *Jethro and the Jumbie* **was prompted by Cooper's vacations in the Virgin Islands and details the antics of a young boy and a gnomelike spectre.**

Cooper's capacity for substantial entertainment is evident from the critical and popular acclaim awarded her work. She is respected as a writer who has invented engaging characters, sustained a fascinating serial storyline, and explored the standard conflict of good versus evil with originality. In 1970 *Dawn of Fear* **was included in the Horn Book Honor List and was an A.L.A. Notable Children's Book.** *The Dark Is Rising* **was awarded the Boston Globe-Horn Book Award in 1973 and was the Newbery Award Honor Book for 1974. In 1976** *The Grey King* **received the Newbery Award and the Tir na n-Og Award for a children's book dealing with a Welsh subject, and was commended for the Carnegie Medal in the same year. (See also** *Contemporary Authors,* **Vols. 29-32, and** *Something about the Author,* **Vol. 4.)**

GENERAL COMMENTARY

Maybe there is scope for some research into the effects of World War II on adults today writing children's books. Cer-

Photograph by Zoë Dominic F.R.P.S.

tainly there has been a spate of books recalling the sorrowful experiences of evacuees and refugees but none of them conjure up the sheer physical fear that ripples through the pages of Susan Cooper's work.

Her book *Dawn of Fear* . . . is a largely autobiographical account of life for a child in Buckinghamshire during the war—the disturbed nights crowded in air raid shelters during the worst of the Blitz, the stunned effect of the loss in a bombing raid of a real friend with whom one had played war games. Susan Cooper always chooses boys as her main characters, but Will, hero of *The Dark Is Rising,* is no ordinary boy. He is the last of the Old Ones, servants of the Light, dedicated to saving the world from domination by the force of evil, which calls itself the Dark, and Susan Cooper is very aware of the effect the stark contrast between good and evil as presented to children in World War II has had on her attitudes. . . .

Each book is deliberately set in a specific season, Lammas, Christmas, Midsummer, Hallowe'en. She does not believe in God though does acknowledge the abstract forces of good and evil; but one senses that the books live so strongly under her hand that she has an overwhelming feeling of being taken over by her theme. The power is so strong that it seems to embarrass her by its hold. She did admit that certain places where terrible events had taken place for example could exude for her an almost tangible atmosphere of evil.

All her novels are set in parts of Britain she knows well and where she spent her first eighteen years, Buckinghamshire, Cornwall where she spent holidays, and North Wales where her grandmother was born. All of these places are haunted by the Old Ways ancient tracks, Bronze Age barrows and Iron Age forts and these with all their mystic associations are the springs of Susan Cooper's inspiration. She admits that she is still frightened of the dark and that her books are in part a conscious attempt to present fear in real terms. . . .

There is nothing original about Susan Cooper's sources. She lists the Mabinogion, *The God of The Witches* by M. Murray, *The White Goddess* by Robert Graves (*the* book she would choose to take to a desert island) and *The Golden Bough* by [Sir James] Fraser. They have all been used before by writers such as Alan Garner for example "the one genius amongst us" in Susan Cooper's words. Nevertheless Susan Cooper herself has constructed a major work in her sequence of novels which increase in imaginative force and power as they develop.

> *Anne Wood, "Adventure," in* Books for Your Children *(© Books for Your Children 1976), Vol. 11, No. 2, Spring, 1976, p. 9.*

Susan Cooper is one of the small and very select company of writers who—somehow, somewhere—have been touched by magic; the gift of creation is theirs, the power to bring to life for ordinary mortals "the best of symbolic high fantasy." Where does such a gift originate? How is it manifested? These are questions never wholly answerable since they lead back to the ultimate mystery of birth, but they are intensely interesting to pursue, and the pursuit is infinitely rewarding though never concluded. The impact of Susan Cooper's writing . . . sends one off on this pursuit, to seek answers to the unanswerable, to gain insight and treasure along the way. (pp. 367-68)

Her years as a writer . . . have given Susan Cooper a sure command of the English language. She uses it as a fine instrument to achieve her purpose. But the deep, subconscious well-springs from which her true creation comes are not subject to command. Susan likens the sense of revelation that comes at moments of imaginative breakthrough to Will Stanton's opening the great carved doors on the snowy hillside that led him into the vast hall where he first met Merriman Lyon and the Lady in *The Dark Is Rising*. (p. 371)

Music and song, old tales and legends, prose and poetry, theater and reality, imagination and intellect, power and control, a strong sense of place and people both past and present—all are part of the magic that has touched Susan Cooper. She is undismayed by the challenge of crossing borders old and new, physical and metaphysical. Her journeys add great luster to the world of literature. (p. 372)

> *Margaret K. McElderry, "Susan Cooper," in* The Horn Book Magazine *(copyright © 1976 by the Horn Book, Inc., Boston), Vol. LII, No. 4, August, 1976, pp. 367-72.*

Cooper has made increasing use of legend and folklore with each book in [*The Dark Is Rising*] series. Since we have accepted these elements in the stories previously, we are willing to immerse ourselves more deeply as the tale progresses. Setting is important in all of these stories, providing an atmosphere in which old tales naturally come true. Characterization is vivid, especially of the three children and Will Stanton, and

there is much action, described in rich, meaning-laden language. (p. 221)

> *Zena Sutherland, Dianne L. Monson, and May Hill Arbuthnot, "Modern Fantasy," in their* Children and Books *(copyright © 1947, 1957, 1964, 1972, 1977, 1981 by Scott, Foresman and Company; reprinted by permission), sixth edition, Scott, Foresman, 1981, pp. 213-54.**

OVER SEA, UNDER STONE   (1966; British edition, 1965)

For those who like stories of children involved in a complicated investigation into an antiquarian mystery, pitting their wits against unscrupulous adults, this is very good value, and not only in terms of length. The story of the Holy Grail is still one of the most mystic in tone among the many off-shoots of legend surviving in these legend-saturated islands, and one finds it not too difficult to believe that the children's opponents in this case are members of a vaguely-defined sect whose passion is "evil" rather than mere intellectual curiosity. Their mentor, the famed and unfathomable Great-Uncle Merry, representing the persistent forces of good, plays an observer's part which is not altogether convincing, since his exceptional powers of antiquarian detection would obviously have simplified the whole affair, but if one accepts the powers of evil—as one almost does—one must accept him as well. Setting the story in Cornwall not only provides the appropriate physical background but by long tradition contains the necessary associations of the legends on which the investigation and eventual discoveries are based. It is not everyone's book but it is undeniably well written. Perhaps there is at times too much of the cat-and-mouse technique in the plot but at a certain level this also is acceptable. (p. 216)

> *"For Children from Ten to Fourteen: 'Over Sea, Under Stone',"* in The Junior Bookshelf, *Vol. 29, No. 4, August, 1965, p. 216.*

Over Sea, Under Stone suffers a little, I think, from its lack of a consistent everyday background against which its fantasy can take wings. There is a strain of mysticism in the book which seems to me exaggerated: though the story starts in an ordinary family, it soon takes on a magic atmosphere which blurs reality and almost gets out of hand. This is a contest of good and evil taking place on two levels. First, on the level of everyday life, where Simon, Jane and Barney, staying in Cornwall with Great-Uncle Merry, are involved with a group of unpleasant people—including a dark-visaged man masquerading as the parson. This group goes back a long way in its iniquity, seeking to overwhelm the world with evil just as earlier exemplars did when Arthur died and England was plunged into chaos. The children have found an old map in the attic which, riddling though it is, may well guide them (and does eventually) to no less an object than the Grail. Here is a symbol that should mean something to most readers, just as the fragment of sword in the stone should; and those whose imagination responds to the mystery and magic of the Arthurian legends will appreciate the overtones of this story, the seriousness of the contest, and the identity, guessed at some stage in the story, of Great-Uncle Merry. To other children it will be read as an adventure story, well told, with cleverly managed clues, dangerous encounters, chase, disguise and all the rest. It is in the carry-over from flesh and blood people to Enemies of the Good that I feel the book lacks coherence, and besides, there is so much weight given to the moral and mystical aspect of the contest that it would be difficult, if not impossible, to invent any ending that would not be an anti-climax. In short, perhaps this is a book with a theme too big for itself, but it is a fascinating book to read and it has considerable literary quality. (p. 555)

> *Margery Fisher, "Arthurian Echoes," in her* Growing Point, *Vol. 4, No. 3, September, 1965, pp. 554-55.**

[The plot of *Over Sea, Under Stone*] sounds very much the mixture as before, but Susan Cooper has woven into the story elements of the Arthurian Legend, created an atmosphere of crackling tension, and invested the characters of Great-Uncle Merry and Mr. Hastings with such an aura of power for good and evil that the tale is lifted well above the common run.

The children are credible and their adventures shift so cunningly from the plausible to the legendary as to be totally absorbing. There is pace, suspense and mystery, and the final scene on the jagged rocks amid an incoming tide is a feast for any imaginative twelve- or thirteen-year-old. The ending hints at a possible sequel—I shall look forward to it. (p. 358)

> *C.E.J. Smith, "Book Reviews: 'Over Sea, Under Stone'," in* The School Librarian and School Library Review, *Vol. 13, No. 3, December, 1965, p. 358.*

[*Over Sea, Under Stone*] . . . that's the cryptic route followed in this story which starts as a typical juvenile mystery/adventure but then turns out to be a morality tale. . . . The story, which starts slowly, becomes more compelling as the supernatural starts to take over, although the mystic powers never reach the terrifying proportions they should have, and the ending, necessarily ambiguous, seems uncomfortably contrived. The theme of good and evil in violent opposition is always a forceful one, but beyond this book's capacity. (p. 301)

> *"Eight to Eleven—Fiction: 'Over Sea, Under Stone'," in* Virginia Kirkus' Service *(copyright © 1966 Virginia Kirkus' Service, Inc.), Vol. XXXIV, No. 6, March 15, 1966, p. 301*

After eleven years in print, the first volume of Susan Cooper's projected five-part sequence is enjoying a brisk readership on its own merits. What, in a period replete with well-written fantasy, gives this book such life?

First, Susan Cooper is a superb storyteller who uses all the instruments available to her—plot, character, setting, language—to create an atmosphere of expectant tension which propels the reader as well as the action. Her knowledge of folklore and archaeology adds dimension to the setting, enhancing the mystery and the otherworldliness.

Second, there is the clearly drawn line between good and evil—with occasional ambiguities for the sake of suspense. One knows immediately which characters to cheer for; but whether their strength will be sufficient to overcome the enemy is in doubt until the very end. This is the stuff of melodrama, to be sure; but it is also the underlying theme of the entire series, the struggle between good and evil. (p. 522)

A third life-giving ingredient is the verisimilitude with which the relationships among the three children are drawn. Like most siblings, they bicker and tease, are alternately companionable or querulous, but unite when confronted by the enemy. Their conversation is in the language of real children; their enthusiasm and their fears are real and contagious. . . .

Only Jane strikes a momentary sour note. Cautious and proper, careful to carry a clean handkerchief and follow parental rules, she is clearly a prefeminist character. One might wish that she were less inclined to be fastidious and to quaver anxiously when danger threatens. Yet even here, the author's sense of balance triumphs: Jane is as good as her brothers at following clues and solving riddles, and the boys, in their turn, are not ashamed to acknowledge their own fears.

Perhaps it is just this balance which holds the whole tale together so effectively. Susan Cooper seems to know just which note to strike at any moment; whether to excite or to soothe, to tease or to fill with awe. And we respond, with her characters, to an experience which, because it is so real, we cannot forget. (p. 523)

> *Dudley Brown Carlson, "A Second Look: 'Over Sea, Under Stone'," in* The Horn Book Magazine *(copyright © 1976 by the Horn Book, Inc., Boston), Vol. LII, No. 5, October, 1976, pp. 522-23.*

DAWN OF FEAR (1970)

The gifted author of **"Over Sea, Under Stone"** has brought her insight and writing skills to creating another remarkable story, with one of the most apt and illustrative titles of the year. Because, as the reader is drawn irresistibly into the life of a small boy who lives in the English countryside during World War II, he, along with the boy, experiences a dawn of fear, as England is bombed by the Nazis. . . . The frenzied efforts by a gang of neighborhood bullies to save treasures from destruction by bombs turn a story about boys into a moving chronicle of despair and of courage.

> *"Children's Books: 'Dawn of Fear'," in* Publishers Weekly *(reprinted from the August 31, 1970 issue of* Publishers Weekly, *published by R. R. Bowker Company, a Xerox company; copyright © 1970 by Xerox Corporation), Vol. 198, No. 9, August 31, 1970, p. 279.*

There were three surprises for me in this novel. First, that we still get World War II stories with tea and drippings and nature-in-blossom. Second, that without suspense or drama, **"Dawn of Fear"** was well-written. Third, that at its conclusion the author didn't shy from realistic facts and emotions. . . .

A story in which recent history plays so little havoc with its principals and their ordinary ways of life makes war an adventure, not a tragedy. Miss Cooper needed more drama, more tension and less old-fashioned "Boys Life" narrative to create a memorable book.

> *John Neufeld, "Ages 9 to 12: 'Dawn of Fear'," in* The New York Times Book Review *(© 1970 by The New York Times Company; reprinted by permission), November 8, 1970, p. 28.*

It is a convention of children's book reviewing that one does not usually notice the books one has not liked. If, therefore, I mention Susan Cooper's *Dawn of Fear* . . . unfavourably, it is not just for the sake of doing so but because I want to warn parents and libraries against it. It is a well-written, 'realistic' tale about a group of boys living on a housing estate during the Second World War. So far so good—and had the author limited her horrors to death from bombs *or* to really vicious gang warfare *or* to tormenting an animal I might well have felt that this was a praiseworthy study of a serious theme which children ought to recognise. But the combination of all three seems to me phoney, gratuitously nasty and fundamentally pointless. This is not real life, it is Straw Dogs. (p. 760)

> Gillian Tindall, ''Younger Fiction: 'Dreams to Sell','' in New Statesman (© 1972 The Statesman & Nation Publishing Co. Ltd.), Vol. 83, No. 2150, June 2, 1972, p. 760.

[*Dawn of Fear*] tells how a Thames Valley schoolboy, delighting in ''dogfights'', longing for the excitement of an incendiary, learns the meaning of fear and human suffering. It is beautifully done. . . .

Susan Cooper really makes her young readers face the facts. War is not just a matter of battlefield heroics, of life-sized Action Men. It is a matter of innocent ordinary people dying. Peter, Derek's best friend, is killed in an air-raid. It is unusual these days to find death in a children's book—though not as startling as it would have been a few years ago. Certainly it is still surprising to find the death of a main child character in a book for junior school children. Some parents and teachers will not welcome *Dawn of Fear* for this reason. Let them go on enjoying their games a little longer, such people might say. But with so much death on our television screens blunting our children's sensitivity, it is surely good that they can weep over Peter's death, as other children wept, at other times, over the deaths of Paul Dombey, Beth and Froggy's little brother.

> ''Man's Inhumanity to Man,'' in The Times Literary Supplement (© Times Newspapers Ltd. (London) 1972; reproduced from The Times Literary Supplement by permission), No. 3672, July 14, 1972, p. 803.*

There are three main threads in the tale: one is the realistic notion that the minor ''gang'' warfare which is always a feature among urban children of school age continues irrespective of the general situation; through the involvement of adult allies in their private war they begin to learn the meaning of grown-up hatred which perhaps gives them some idea of how deeply adults now in uniform have come to be involved in a conflict which they did not seek; finally, in the actual ''dawn of fear'', when a friend and his family and their schoolmistress are wiped out by a direct hit, things are never to be the same again.

American comment has described the book as ''an uncommon kind of war story focussing largely on the emotions of sharply individual boys'', a verdict which, though incomplete, is fair enough. If you can imagine a pilot programme for a juvenile ''Dad's Army'' and then imagine the reverse of the coin you have some idea of what *Dawn of Fear* is about. To date I have not come across a book which makes anything like the same impression.

> ''For Children from Ten to Fourteen: 'Dawn of Fear','' in The Junior Bookshelf, Vol. 36, No. 4, August, 1972, p. 241.

Susan Cooper's *Dawn of Fear* develops the interesting idea of a local squabble between rival gangs taking place beneath the German bombing of London. . . . But much of the conflict between the gangs is poorly motivated, not deeply explored, and it descends on occasion to the banality of mud-slinging (literally). A fussy concern for trivial details of where fences lie and how they may best be circumvented, including a secret map of various landmarks, does little to redeem this rather commonplace book. (p. 73)

> David L. James, ''Recent World-War II Fiction: A Survey,'' in Children's literature in education (© 1977 Agathon Press, Inc.; reprinted by permission of the publisher), Vol. 8, No. 2 (Summer), 1977, pp. 71-9.*

THE DARK IS RISING   (1973)

[In *The Dark Is Rising*] seventh son of a seventh son Will Stanton comes of age—great unknowable age—on his eleventh birthday and begins reuniting the six signs which will have the power to stave off the rising Dark. . . . Though Cooper labels Good and Evil with a humorless certainty which even C. S. Lewis couldn't fault, the pell-mell introduction of omens, bad spirits and eclectic magic seems aimed chiefly at engendering breathless bewilderment. We never did figure out the lessons of the six elemental signs which Will wears attached to his belt, but we're promised three more chances to get it all straightened out (though at the present pace, the end of the series seems to be approaching rather more slowly than Armageddon). To be fair, connoisseurs of metaphysical fantasy will find this satisfyingly complex and dramatically accomplished—while recognizing that, even by the standards of the genre, the symbolism is overextended.

> ''Younger Fiction: 'The Dark Is Rising','' in Kirkus Reviews (copyright © 1973 The Kirkus Service, Inc.), Vol. XLI, No. 6, March 15, 1973, p. 315.

This is a muscular fantasy. Characters bounce through time, transcendental yo-yos. **''The Dark Is Rising''** houses a mail-order gift catalogue of magical equipment: six secret signs that must be collected (circles quartered, looking, I judge, like so many jeweled hot cross buns); rings, doorways without walls, grotesque carnival heads; a Manichean world conflict between the dark and the light. The book will thrill children. It thrilled me—and I presume that speaks more for Susan Cooper's craft than for my somewhat arrested development.

It is a book particularly for children second-bested by their families: those children to whom parental affection comes divided or diluted. Susan Cooper strip mines a dependable emotion: child power. An 11-year-old, youngest of many, learns that he is an Ancient One with immense authority. All children imagine at some time that they are protectors, not dependents. A father to one's father: Oedipus complexes worked off by supernatural proxy. **''The Dark Is Rising''** gives protein nourishment to that profound hunger in our most disadvantaged class: the pre-teens. Its two worlds are parallel, interpenetrable only at a few recondite places. In one Will Stanton is least; in the other he is supreme. The teasing requirements of secrecy thwart a hot need for revelation. The reader child will want Will's elders to acknowledge his power; will want to rebut their grown-up, disbelieving condescension. It's a reliable device.

''The Dark Is Rising'' suffers from generic defects. Science fiction, detective fiction, fantasy—all are more relishable at their beginnings than at their conclusions. The initial, delicious injection of weird events into commonplace life cannot be recaptured. . . . In **''The Dark Is Rising''** a first eerie raven attack is worth—in emotive wattage—the entire frantic panoply Susan Cooper calls up at the end. A kind of inflation is intrinsic to the genre. Horrors must appear in a geometrical progression of horribleness. Every climactic attack of the Dark Ones has to be made super climactic in the ensuing chapter. I sensed some straining at the denouement. But a monstrous snow storm is used superbly to join worlds together: to provision the story with terrors on both levels of reality.

The writing is robust, but noticeably better out of human time than at the Stanton hearth: as if the author's style, too, had experienced a salutary, magical translation. The housekeeping style tends to be somewhat saccharine and red cheeked. The fantastic style is virile and, for all its paraphernalia, spare. Susan Cooper's vocabulary is athletic; the complications are dense. Her book seems to have been prepared for a special small age group: those who can read with fluency and attention, but who haven't yet been afflicted by adolescent cynicism.

The author doesn't set up as a casuist. Fine by me. The forces of light and dark are roughly good and bad, but the morality is indefinite, motiveless: they struggle because it has always been their lot to struggle. Will Stanton is a nice boy, yet he comes to his great inheritance not by virtue, but rather by some Crypto-Calvinist theory of the Elect. With a single exception, free will is not pertinent. Consequently the plot winds down with a sort of mechanical determinism. You never doubt: the forces of light are fated to win and even the exciting close calls appear a part of ritual. Susan Cooper meant, I think, to write an entertainment, not much more than that. She has succeeded. **"The Dark Is Rising"** affords thunderous good fun.

> *D. Keith Mano, " 'The Dark Is Rising'," in* The New York Times Book Review *(© 1973 by The New York Times Company; reprinted by permission), April 22, 1973, p. 8.*

With a cosmic struggle between good and evil as her subject Susan Cooper invites comparison with Tolkien, and survives the comparison remarkably well. She lacks the leisurely lyricism of Tolkien's landscapes, and his humour. But she gains in spine chilling immediacy by setting her scene in an ordinary English village. Susan Cooper is a brilliant writer, with an intense and powerful style at her command; she can call up both the good and evil supernatural with flesh-creeping vividness. A weird and ghostly beauty shines about the manifestations of the power of the signs. This book deserves to be judged by the highest standards, and by those standards it is not unflawed.

Some of the villagers are actors in the metaphysical drama as well as their humdrum everyday selves, while others serve the enemy on the enchanted level, and yet others live through it all without noticing anything except the weather. This leads to some difficult shifts of key which are not always quite plausible. More seriously, the richness and heterogeneity of the source material the author has drawn upon is positively mind-boggling. The hunting of the "wren" is there, and Herne the Hunter; the Celtic tree mythology and a ship burial, not to mention an emended inscription from the Alfred Jewel, and so on and on; nearly every page has a concept or image drawn from some mythology. Such powerful and ancient images carry a reverberation whether or not they are placed and understood, but here they seem harder to join into a total pattern, a meaningful new texture of the author's own, than are the six signs to join on Will's belt. This book, however, is the second in a projected sequence of five . . . ; when all can be read together perhaps a satisfying synthesis will triumphantly emerge.

> *"Imaginary Kingdoms," in* The Times Literary Supplement *(© Times Newspapers Ltd. (London) 1973; reproduced from* The Times Literary Supplement *by permission), No. 3719, June 15, 1973, p. 685.*

[A British excursion into fantasy which] is exceptional by any standards, is Susan Cooper's **The Dark Is Rising.** This story opens in an everyday milieu with ordinary enough circumstances, but then it grips the reader. . . . Omens and symbols of the quest, scenes of otherworld peril and impending disaster for the village impel the reader through a . . . children's book which is clear, convincing and satisfying in its development. As in all the best of symbolic high fantasy, analogies for our times may be found, but the young reader will first of all— and chiefly—enjoy the superb storytelling.

> *Virginia Haviland, "A Child's Garden of Ghosts, Poltergeists and Werewolves," in* Book World—The Washington Post *(copyright © 1973 The Washington Post Company), July 8, 1973, p. 13.*

With its ingenious plot and superbly natural expression, **The Dark is Rising** captures and holds one's imagination, almost as if the magic forces within the story were themselves reaching out to spellbind the reader. Susan Cooper has stepped forward from the simple plot and imitative style of **Over Sea, Under Stone** to give us a book which . . . approaches the heights of Tolkien's *Lord of the Rings,* though her style owes little to [it], except perhaps for its rich quality.

> *S. William Alderson, "Reviews: 'The Dark Is Rising'," in* Children's Book Review *(© 1973 Five Owls Press Ltd.; all rights reserved), Vol. 3, No. 4, September, 1973, p. 112.*

Susan Cooper, like Ursula Le Guin in her fantasy *A Wizard of Earthsea,* combines a magnificent gift for story telling with a poetic style which swirls the reader deep into the scenes she describes and into the sense that there is far more mystery to life that most twentieth century adults can accept. . . . Anyone who fears that they or their children are becoming rigidly sensible should buy this book to enrich imagination and recover wonderment. (p. 131)

> *Sally Emerson, "Reviews: 'The Dark Is Rising'" (© copyright Sally Emerson 1973; reprinted with permission), in* Books and Bookmen, *Vol. 19, No. 1, October, 1973, pp. 130-31.*

GREENWITCH (1974)

Four aspects trouble me about this book. First, it seems a lack of resourcefulness to again engage the children in the recovery of an object they have already spent a book in the pursuit of as though the Greenwich material was not sufficient and must be filled out. Second, the grail was stolen when the forces of Light were off their guard, and was recovered when the Dark was "preoccupied, for a time"—a pair of too easy conveniences. Third, Will, present throughout, is not really needed, which is a structural weakness. Fourth, with more discipline of language, particularly in the descriptive passages, and her obsessive repetition of the word "great," Susan Cooper's imaginative use of the Greenwitch as a force of Wild Magic, neither of the Light nor of the Dark, would have come through with greater power and dignity.

> *Eleanor Cameron, "Other Worlds, Other Times: 'Greenwitch'," in* The New York Times Book Review *(© 1974 by The New York Times Company; reprinted by permission), May 5, 1974, p. 43.*

Greenwitch is the middle story in a sequence of five books; it can be read as complete in itself, but it contains references backwards to the material of the earlier books, and presumably forwards to the stories yet to come. Final judgment must therefore wait till the sequence is complete. . . . [It] is obvious that a five-volume sequence is a very ambitious project; it asks to be judged by the highest standards, especially as it belongs to a genre, the fantasy-epic, in which some of the finest children's books have been written.

Much in this book is very good; Miss Cooper is deeply moved, and moving, when she writes of the release of the forces of nature in a supernatural form—the shape of tree, called the Greenwitch, the spirit of the depths of the sea, the working of ancient spells; all these are powerfully and beautifully evoked, in passages which pass A. E. Housman's famous test for poetry—that it should make the scalp tingle, should raise gooseflesh. Unfortunately the books cannot win unqualified praise, because harnessed with the successful set pieces are banal passages; standard children's book children whose triteness subtracts all belief from their grand magical roles; dreadfully corny villagers; and some elements in the plot—ransom notes for kidnapped dogs, treasure stolen from the local museum—would be more at home in a very different kind of children's book. The degree of irritation and disappointment felt at these lapses is some measure of the talent of the rest; when Miss Cooper manages to knit her material into a single organic whole her achievement will be great.

> *"Supernatural Forms,"* in The Times Literary Supplement (© *Times Newspapers Ltd. (London) 1974; reproduced from* The Times Literary Supplement *by permission), No. 3774, July 5, 1974, p. 721.**

In her attempts to combine the principal characters from both the preceding volumes, Susan Cooper has tried to reconcile two incompatible temperaments, the superficial and immature Drews and the profound Will Stanton, and to manage too many important figures. As a result, no central character emerges: Will is out of the way most of the time due to friction between himself and the Drews; Jane has an influence on the outcome, but not an active one; the brothers merely fill in the gaps.

In addition, the author has re-introduced the Wild Magic only hinted at in the Wild Hunt of *The Dark is Rising,* but has not, I feel, explored it as fully as she might have done, due to her lack of concentration on a single active figure. Overall, the book lacks the driving force behind *The Dark is Rising* and tends to be rather patchy, with a poorer style close to that of *Over Sea, Under Stone.* My enthusiasm having been somewhat dampened, I look forward with mixed feelings to the fourth book in the series.

> *S. William Alderson, "Reviews: 'Greenwitch',"* in Children's Book Review (© *1974 Five Owls Press Ltd.; all rights reserved), Vol. IV, No. 3, Autumn, 1974, p. 105.*

[In *Greenwitch*] there are some wonderful things. First, there are adults who act like mature, autonomous individuals rather than Parents. Further, in this English book there are Americans who don't sound like composites of [actor James] Cagney and Little Lulu. Then there are children—intelligent, sensitive, humorous, quirky children—who not only act and react but grow within themselves. There is also evil, called the Dark—fine, solid, nasty evil we can get our teeth into, and how welcome that is in these days of moral ambiguity. . . . There are, too, a setting in Cornwall that goes beyond quaint cottages and clotted cream into living landscape, an Irish setter, a cosmically important quest, and an appalling storm. Best of all, there is

mythology that transcends the equation of ancient with weird to introduce the Greenwitch, a vaguely human form made of branches, "an interesting Cornish village custom," whose powerful amorality, possessiveness, and even pathos are a unique reminder of what myth is all about. For perhaps every book of fantasy, with its elements of magic and mighty deeds, is a myth. But it is a myth for our time, and it must be as significant for us as the tales of Oedipus, Beowulf, and Gilgamesh were for their contemporaries. Anything less is just *maugas* in the *flets.* (p. 611)

> *Georgess McHargue, "Leaping into Fantasy,"* in American Libraries (reprinted by permission of the American Library Association; copyright © 1974 by the American Library Association), Vol. 5, No. 11, December, 1974, pp. 610-11.**

I didn't entirely share the enthusiasm for Susan Cooper's **The Dark is Rising,** second in a five-novel sequence. (The first, **Over Sea, Under Stone,** I've not yet managed to read.) An enormous matter of conflict between forces of Dark and Light, it didn't solve, I thought, the problem of making us at ease with a boyish hero who is also (if I understand the metaphysics of it) rather older than time. . . .

Greenwitch is the third in the series, and, for me, a far more successful book. It clings tighter round a single magical emergency, and a single setting. . . . We don't have to worry so much as in the previous book about Will being a boy only when he's not being some fantastic ancient wizard. The excitement is very real, there are passages of strangely thrilling beauty. I hope the two remaining novels are of this tauter kind, and give us equally little room for anxiety about Susan Cooper's attempts to marry ordinary reality and extraordinary magical drama.

> *Edward Blishen, "Young Readers: 'Greenwitch'"* (© *copyright Edward Blishen 1975; reprinted with permission), in Books and Bookmen, Vol. 21, No. 4, January, 1975, p. 74.*

Compared with the intricacies of **The Dark is rising, Greenwitch** is relatively short and compact and both setting and situation recall the more simplistic adventure of **Over sea, under stone,** for the emissaries of the dark make the change from everyday to other-world behaviour in the same stated and unimpressive way and even Will, a character who has shown to be open to enchantments and beliefs in his first adventure, has caught in this new book something of the bounce and normality of the Drews. All the same, the book does contain the terror and the mystery which the theme demands, and they come from the ancient, traditional figure of the Greenwitch and the strange sympathy that sensitive Jane feels for it. (p. 2555)

Fantasies like this depend most of all on the sheer power of the writing, on the literary synthesis between the sunlit world of here and now and the dark, misty otherwhere from which evil comes. The synthesis is less strong in this new book and the effect less consistent than in the other two books of the five so far published. None the less, it is a compelling story and it is all the more tantalising to have to wait for the two succeeding books which have been promised. (p. 2556)

> *Margery Fisher, "Sources for Fantasy: 'Greenwitch',"* in her Growing Point, Vol. 13, No. 7, January, 1975, pp. 2555-56.

THE GREY KING (1975)

It is useless to try to recreate the subtleties of Susan Cooper's plotting and language. Enough to say that this volume, like those preceding it, is brimful of mythic elements and is beautifully told. There are clues along the way for those who are up on their lore; Celtic sacred king identified with the raven, and Cooper's Bran is called the raven boy. The dog, Cafall, inherits his name from King Arthur's favorite hound, Cavall, and in fact this Bran turns out to be a son of Arthur brought out of prehistory by his mother Guinevere, the lost Gwen of this novel.

Obviously, Cooper's central problem with her series, and this volume in particular—since we all know something about King Arthur—is to render believable an ancient mode at work in modern times. . . . A lesser imagist simply could not carry it off. In this era of instant reporting, the Dark rises—and falls and rises again—right before our eyes in tangible places and forms. (p. 10)

> *Natalie Babbitt, "For Young Readers: 'The Grey King',"* in The New York Times Book Review *(© 1975 by The New York Times Company; reprinted by permission), September 28, 1975, pp. 10, 12.*

Although Will and the Grey King are the major protagonists, the struggle between good and evil is extended through local folklore and is reflected in the long-standing antagonism between Bran's stepfather, Owen Davies, and the half-crazed Caradog Pritchard. It is only with the disclosure of Bran's true identity that Will fully grasps the significance of that antagonism. Freshly conceived, richly sustained, the multi-dimensional narrative adroitly interweaves traditional motifs with everyday realities so that cosmic conflict is interpreted in human terms. So well-crafted that it stands as an entity in itself, [*The Grey King*] . . . is nevertheless strengthened by its relationship to the preceding volumes—as the individual legends within the Arthurian cycles take on deeper significance in the context of the whole. A spellbinding tour de force.

> *Mary M. Burns, "Stories for the Middle Readers: 'The Grey King',"* in The Horn Book Magazine *(copyright ©1975 by the Horn Book, Inc., Boston), Vol. LI, No. 5, October, 1975, p. 461.*

The fascination of the book lies in its double reality, the plain life of the Welsh sheepmen shadowed and given a sense of destiny by the parallel world of High Magic. The warm-hearted English Will of *The Dark Is Rising* . . . is lost in *The Grey King,* overwhelmed by his role as instrument of fate. But even without the depth of character development, this is a finely constructed contribution to the high fantasy genre. . . . (pp. 104-05)

> *Shirley M. Wilton, "The Book Review: 'The Grey King',"* in School Library Journal *(reprinted from the October, 1975 issue of* School Library Journal, *published by R. R. Bowker Co./A Xerox Corporation; copyright © 1975), Vol. 22, No. 2, October, 1975, pp. 104-05.*

In all Susan Cooper's fantasies the real and the supernatural are meshed together by the force of her narrative. To believe in the truth and depth of the conflict she is chronicling is not a matter of intellectual acceptance nor of any recognition of moral right and wrong. Ultimately the force behind these books is a very primitive one; imagination and style together force the reader to recognise the elements of weather and of landscape

in an almost animistic way, to apprehend rather than to understand the argument. The Matter of Britain, as Susan Cooper uses it, is seen to grow out of the land itself. This is an exciting narrative, with sharp characterisation and briskly drawn scenes of village and farm life, and the mystery of Bran's identity introduces a very human tale of love and hate. In this way fantasy performs its task of irradiating the life we know with the life we are now and then called upon to imagine.

> *Margery Fisher, "Darkness against Light," in her* Growing Point, *Vol. 14, No. 6, December, 1975, p. 2773.*

Susan Cooper is a widely acclaimed writer, and the earlier volumes in this sequence have been reviewed as important books. Necessarily so; whether good or bad, a scheme which involves the synthesis of five separate books, and a reworking of material from the Arthurian cycle is clearly on the grand scale, and invites comparisons with other and famous names in what one might almost call the Oxford movement in children's books—C. S. Lewis, J.R.R. Tolkien, Alan Garner being all, like Susan Cooper, products of the Oxford English school. Only a provisional judgement on the sequence as a whole or any of its parts can be made till the final volume is published; the books already available vary in weight and forcefulness, and if there is an organic and cumulative plot running through all five, it is of an episodic kind, or is still to be made clear.

What can be judged now is the quality of Susan Cooper's writing. This has real weaknesses. Though the grand conflict of the Light and the Dark reminds us of J.R.R. Tolkien, Susan Cooper, like Alan Garner, pats her enchantments into a real, not an imagined world and in conveying the real world in which the servants of the Light play humdrum roles there is a desultory quality, a descent into banality in which the precious credulity of the reader leaks away. This flaw is less marked in *The Grey King* than in earlier volumes, but it is still there. It is not the contemporary surface of her subject that interests this writer.

This said, however, it can also be said that Susan Cooper commands, to a rare degree, the power to thrill the reader, to produce a particular tremor of excitement and fear, in response not only to Arthurian magic—the fulfillment of prophecies, the return of the great Rex Quondam, the finding and using of talismans of great force, and suchlike—but rather to haunted places, to landscape deeply embedded in ancient fable, to a sense of secret forces breaking through. Because of these merits one should wholeheartedly recommend this book. In spite of its flaws it has authentic evocative power.

> *Jill Paton Walsh, "Evoking Dark Powers," in* The Times Literary Supplement *(© Times Newspapers Ltd. (London) 1975; reproduced from* The Times Literary Supplement *by permission), No. 3847, December 5, 1975, p. 1457.*

SILVER ON THE TREE (1977)

Miss Cooper is a master of effects, and in this book she pulls out all the stops. The flesh-creeping sense of shift between present and past, or of danger in seemingly peaceful landscapes is brilliantly evoked, and there are marvellous visions—as of a drowned City rising from beneath the sea. Like the climax of an orchestral piece we hear every note from the early volumes here struck repeatedly.

But, alas, the coherence, the sense of the meaning of the conflict, which one has been hoping this book would lend to the whole sequence does not emerge.

At a moment of crisis in **"Silver on the Tree"** we are told: "The *Afanc* roared and screamed and thrashed; its noise was terrifying. But gradually now they began to realise that it was no more than noise; that in spite of the creature's horrifying bulk, it seemed to have power only to utter threats. It was nightmare, but no more than that."

This, it seems, is always true of The Dark. Though it is infinitely sinister, it wins no victories. But it is not clear in this finale *why* The Light succeeds.

> *Jill Paton Walsh, "Magical Mysteries and Romance for Pre-teens," in* The Christian Science Monitor *(reprinted by permission from* The Christian Science Monitor; © 1977 The Christian Science Publishing Society; all rights reserved), November 2, 1977, p. B-2.*

In the triumphant conclusion to *The Dark Is Rising* sequence the author has produced a tour de force. The many strands from the four previous books are interwoven in a masterly fashion. . . . The story is filled with terror and beauty; the complexities of gaining the weapons required to combat the final rising of the Dark lead to disparate, striking episodes, such as the horrifying pursuit of Bran and Will by a skeleton horse and the haunting adventure in the Lost Land, which is willingly sacrificed for the Light. Vignettes remain with the reader: Will's close, loving family; the horrible encounter with the bigot Mr. Moore; Bran's farewell to Arthur as he chooses mortal life and the bonds of human affection. The distinguishing characteristic of the sequence is not so much the style of writing, superb and clear though it is, but the underlying conception of the books, deeply rooted in myth and legend yet perfectly intermeshed with daily reality. So ably has the author blended the fantasy with the concerns of humanity, that in the magnificent finale an ordinary, decent human being under stress, not an Old One, provides the means to the ultimate weapon against the Dark. (pp. 660-61)

> *Ann A. Flowers, "Stories for Intermediate Readers: 'Silver on the Tree'," in* The Horn Book Magazine *(copyright © 1977 by the Horn Book, Inc., Boston), Vol. 53, No. 6, December, 1977, pp. 660-61.*

Cooper's fifth book is not so much the story of Will Stanton's final duties as the last of the Old Ones nor of the three Drew children and their Uncle Merriman (or Merlin). The human figures are there to be led, played upon, directed to their separate destinies in the last confrontation between the Light and the Dark; but central to the complex plot is the workings of High Magic itself. Individually, the events test credulity, but so skillfully is the tale told and the last spell woven that magic trains rushing through time, lost lands, mirror mazes, skeleton horses, and a tree whose silver fruit will determine the victory of good or evil seem not only plausible but necessary. Cooper maintains a masterly control over the complex strands of her story sweeping readers along on a fantastic journey. It is an experience not to be missed and, for Cooper fans, a fitting wrap-up to the unfolding saga.

> *Shirley Wilton, "The Book Review: 'Silver on the Tree'," in* School Library Journal *(reprinted from the December, 1977 issue of* School Library Journal, *published by R. R. Bowker C./A Xerox Corporation;*

copyright © 1977), Vol. 24, No. 4, December, 1977, p. 48.

In Susan Cooper's *Silver on the Tree* (which though the final book in a series of five can stand, I think, in its own right) the powers of light confront for the last time the powers of dark, with the aid of five children. The narrative lacks some of the urgency of the earlier volumes, *The Dark is Rising* in particular, reaching its climax magnificently, but rather too early, in the sequence in the Lost Land. Nevertheless Susan Cooper has sustained her creation remarkably, even venturing—pretty successfully—into new territory for her, with episodes set in earlier stages of Welsh and English history. The force and flexibility of her imagination remain in no doubt at all. In which lies the puzzle: that the writing can be so rich sometimes, so thin elsewhere, on the human level especially, passion and subtlety reserved mainly for the landscapes on the one hand, her supernatural magic lantern show on the other.

Of course she has learnt by now to minimize her failings. The Drew family is much less crudely shown than in the first book. Yet still one is reminded of the staple plot of the children's book; children defeating the crooks where the adults have failed to do so. This is perhaps why too, for all the author's marvellous evoking of atmosphere, her forces of good and evil remain ultimately stereotyped, the more so if you compare them with the much more intriguing ambiguities in Ursula Le Guin's trilogy on similar themes. In human and magic terms alike the only moment of real human conviction lies in the description of the King of the Lost Land, endlessly brooding that he has spent all his creative powers on one magnificent creation; the description of his fear is so felt and strong you realize how much you miss just that elsewhere.

But then, presumably, his is Susan Cooper's own dilemma. Where can she go now, after this extraordinary if limited achievement? Perhaps she herself has indicated her answer. Just as in her book we are told the battleground must shift to the human world, can she too now, at last, shift her gaze from the complexities of magic to the equally fascinating and not so wholly unrelated complexities of men?

> *Penelope Farmer, "Shades of Magic," in* The Times Literary Supplement *(© Times Newspapers Ltd. (London) 1977; reproduced from* The Times Literary Supplement *by permission), No. 3949, December 2, 1977, p. 1409.*

The final, summarising volume of Susan Cooper's five-book sequence was bound to be weighty. Perhaps it is almost too much so—not in style, for the prose is, as always, crystal clear, incisive and pictorial, but in the accumulation of its elements, each evoking a different response. Here are analogues to the Fisher King of Celtic myth and the concept of the Drowned Land, here are trees, lamps, weapons used with symbolic overtones, here are dark riders reminiscent of Tolkien and intermittent Arthurian echoes, some medieval in type and others more ancient. The same richness was better balanced in **"The Dark is rising"** (still, for me, the most impressive of the five books), though there are moments in this new book of the most piercing poetic terror, for example on the fantastic train journey when Bronwen Reynolds reveals her true self. Bran and Will Stanton attract to themselves a certain authority from the imagery and tension of their part in the adventure, but Uncle Merry's three seekers have never quite outgrown the hearty extrovert approach of **"Over Sea, under Stone"** and Jane's part in this fifth book seems especially flat after her intuitive moments in **"Greenwitch"**. Compared with the work of Tolkien and Ursula Le Guin, Susan Cooper's extended fantasy adventure seems uneven in quality and emphasis, but if it has not succeeded in making a satisfactorily united impression, it has given readers many moments of startled awareness and now that it is complete it deserves more deliberate consideration as a whole.

> *Margery Fisher, "Dual Worlds: 'Silver on the Tree',"*
> *in her* Growing Point, *Vol. 16, No. 8, March, 1978,*
> *p. 3277.*

It is early days to assess the importance of [**'The Dark Is Rising'**] as a whole, but doubtless many critical studies will be made in due course. For me the work, and this book in particular, falls short of *The Hobbit* and the Narnia chronicles because, although it surpasses the one in range and the other in consistency, it fails to achieve the ultimate conviction. This reader at least retained throughout an independent critical judgment and, even in the most thrilling moments, never surrendered to the compulsion of the narrative. This may well be my fault, as it is my loss.

One of the difficulties lies in accepting that apparently very ordinary children have a special destiny. This is the major obstacle to the acceptance of Narnia. Four at least of the Six who have the duty of holding back the Dark do not seem up to the task. Time switches too, although handled skilfully enough, are not always easy to swallow. Where Miss Cooper excels is in the management of setting. About half of the action takes place in and around one small locality on the southern edge of Snowdonia, and the landscape and the essential Welshness are vital factors in the story. The writer captures the smell of the countryside. There is a lovely chapter called **'Sunrise'** in which Jane, in one still moment between crises, walks on the sands of Aberdyfi in the golden light of dawn when "each shell had its own dark clear shadow", and Miss Cooper shows how fine her observation is and her ability to convey its tingling reality. Perhaps, now that the Dark has been put finally to flight, she will pursue this aspect of her art.

Meanwhile, here, crafted by the hand of a master, is a story of the ageless battle of good and evil, a book in one of the great traditions of children's literature and destined, perhaps, to become one of the high peaks of that tradition. (pp. 99-100)

> *"For Children from Ten to Fourteen: 'Silver on the*
> *Tree',"* in The Junior Bookshelf, *Vol. 42, No. 2,*
> *April, 1978, pp. 99-100.*

JETHRO AND THE JUMBIE (1979)

[Playfulness and warmth] pervade Cooper's first story for younger children. . . . Jethro's big brother had promised he would take the boy fishing when he was eight; now brother Thomas says that Jethro is too small, too weak. Furious, Jethro storms off, despite warnings from friends, on the trail where the jumbies, the spirits of the dead, live. And he meets a jumbie. Refusing to believe, Jethro says, "You is just a figment of the imagination," and when the jumbie takes horrendous forms to frighten him, it says, "You not raised right, child. You don' have respect." This humorous treatment works beautifully to lift the story, so that it is more than a boy-meets-ghost incident, and it is used to further the action . . . rather than being incidental to it. The writing is light, but it's polished.

> *Zena Sutherland, "New Titles for Children and Young*
> *People: 'Jethro and the Jumbie',"* in Bulletin of the
> Center for Children's Books *(reprinted by permission*
> *of The University of Chicago Press; © 1980 by The*
> *University of Chicago), Vol. 33, No. 5, January,*
> *1980, p. 91.*

Cooper uses the melodic dialect of the British Virgin Islands to enhance the story of a spirited boy and a boyish spirit. . . . Everything is understandable, and island terms are explained easily in context except for the name-calling ". . . pot of gundi!" We could guess, but it would be nice to be certain.

> *Helen Gregory, "The Book Review: 'Jethro and the*
> *Jumbie',"* in School Library Journal *(reprinted from*
> *the February, 1980 issue of* School Library Journal,
> *published by R. R. Bowker Co./A Xerox Corporation;*
> *copyright © 1980), Vol. 26, No. 6, February, 1980,*
> *p. 44.*

On the jacket flap Cooper says that she wanted to remind children of the "music and vitality of regional language." The idiomatic speech and other regional touches give the well-made little story some color, though like the jumbie it lacks the fullness of life that would convince you it's real.

> *"Picture Books: 'Jethro and the Jumbie,"* in Kirkus
> Reviews *(copyright © 1980 The Kirkus Service, Inc.),*
> *Vol. XLVIII, No. 3, February 1, 1980, p. 120.*

Real boys and girls are surprisingly rare animals in books that appear for young children. And stories about them that capture the range and depth of young children's emotions and thinking are astonishingly rare.

Susan Cooper's **Jethro and the Jumbie** . . . is a winner on both scores. . . .

It's a lovely story, dealing comfortably with beliefs and terrors. And it has the added bonus that West Indian English is used, quite naturally, in a compelling tale that all children—British English or Asian English or West Indian English—can relate to.

> *Virginia Makins, "Blithe Spirits,"* in The Times Ed-
> ucational Supplement *(© Times Newspapers Ltd.*
> *(London) 1980; reproduced from* The Times Edu-
> cational Supplement *by permission), No. 3340, June*
> *20, 1980, p. 44.*

Tomie de Paola

1934-

(Real name Thomas Anthony de Paola) American author/illustrator and illustrator of picture books, folktales, and fiction for children. De Paola is currently among the most popular and prolific creators of picture books. His varied works consist of retellings of religious and ethnic folktales, realistic fiction, and concept books which combine fiction with educational topics. During de Paola's early career he painted murals for Catholic churches and monastaries; this experience and his upbringing and childhood memories contribute to the character of his books.

The illustrations in de Paola's early works were usually well-received, but the fanciful storylines were often thought superficial. De Paola decided to bring more honesty and personal depth into his picture books after experiencing psychotherapy. The result was realistic fiction that blended his youthful and cultural experiences. His first book of this type, *Nana Upstairs and Nana Downstairs,* deals with Tommy's relationship with his great-grandmother and with her death; it is credited for presenting old age and dying in simple and affectionate terms. De Paola refers to this book and *Oliver Button Is a Sissy* as his autobiographies.

De Paola's utilization of his ethnic and religious background is especially evident in his retold tales, which most critics appreciate for their vitality, humor, and lack of sentimentality. *Strega Nona,* a picture book based on the cooking witch of Italian folklore, established de Paola internationally. It exemplifies the use of his Italian and Catholic influences in both choice of tale and illustration and receives praise for the humor and expressions of its characters, a warm, soft use of color, and its authentic representation of a Mediterranean village. Another retold tale in which these elements are present is *The Clown of God,* which is especially noted for its originality and sensitivity. Critics commend de Paola's moving rendition of this French religious legend and are impressed with his illustrations, which reflect the backgrounds of the Italian Renaissance.

De Paola is the creator of several works that blend information and humorous fiction. *Andy (That's My Name)* focuses on simple word play and is credited for reaching the youngest of readers with an entertaining learning activity. *"Charlie Needs a Cloak,"* his most successful book in this category, is praised for providing advanced concepts in an uncomplicated text and for illustrations which add comic action and amusing subplots. De Paola's light-hearted approach to this type of book can be attributed to his experiences as an art teacher and an illustrator of elementary school text books and his dissatisfaction with their ability to make learning enjoyable. Although de Paola's concept books are occasionally criticized for presenting information through forced, encyclopedic dialogue, most of them receive positive reviews.

De Paola's books are admired by critics and enjoyed by many children. His popularity suggests the achievement of his goal to create books that are both personally satisfying and appealing to children. He has said: "I don't really know why children respond to my work. My guess is only that it is simple and honest. My pictures spring from an emotional place inside

myself." De Paola has received selections for the American Institute of Graphic Arts exhibit of outstanding children's books in 1970 for *The Journey of a Kiss* and in 1979 for *Helga's Dowry,* received Children's Book Showcase selections in 1975 for *"Charlie Needs a Cloak"* and the Art Books for Children Award in 1975 for *"Charlie Needs a Cloak"* and in 1977 for *Strega Nona,* the Caldecott Honor Book Award in 1976 for *Strega Nona,* and the Nakamore Prize (Japan) in 1978 for *Strega Nona.* He received the 1981 Kerlan Award for recognition of singular attainments in the creation of children's literature. He has also received many awards as an artist and as a children's book illustrator and many of his works have been named notable books by the American Library Association and as classroom choices by the International Reading Association. (See also *Contemporary Authors,* Vol. 49, *Contemporary Authors, New Revision Series,* Vol. 2, *Something about the Author,* Vol. 11)

AUTHOR'S COMMENTARY

Illustrating and writing books for children seems to me, to be a profession very involved with dreams. A dream that I expressed as a child, that when I grew up I would write and draw pictures for books; a dream that people I've never met would get to know me a little better; a dream that the invisible world could be made visible and even a dream that I could somehow touch others' lives.

But dreams are more often than not, grounded in hard reality. The making of books is indeed one of the hardest realities of my life. Deadlines, late hours, negative reviews, production problems, artistic problems—these are only a few. But I wouldn't have it any other way. Books are my life.

Since each book is unique, each book has its own unique problems. First of all is choice. As an illustrator, it is fairly easy to choose which manuscripts I will do. I rely on an *"inner voice"* that says *"yes, that will be a challenge or fun or stretch me as an artist."* But ultimately it is the story that dictates and I must rely on my own judgement. I still find writing difficult and I rely heavily on editorial feedback—that objective point of view—exactly what am I trying to say. I try *not* to get set ideas about the pictures until the text is written and edited. Naturally it is a big temptation to let the pictures dictate the book and, of course, I feel, this would be a mistake. Even in wordless-picture books, I write a type of "film-script." I do believe that even a book with minimal text does rely on the STORY. Once the story-line is good and strong (and hopefully appealing) then I can let my pictures not only illustrate the text but amplify it, add to it, and sometimes include a sub-plot told only through the pictures. This, of course, is extremely important in a picture-book. My personal definition for a picture-book (as opposed to an illustrated story-book) is that the very young child who may not even know how to decipher words can indeed read the book by actually "reading the pictures."

Reading the pictures, that's an interesting phrase. I find, that quite often adults will read the text *only,* flipping the pages as soon as the words are finished instead of lingering over the pictures. In several of my earlier books, I have seen teachers surprised that the children they were presenting the books to, saw things that they didn't. It is a question of not "savouring" the pictures, not looking for more than the text relates.

Another problem is the visual style of a book. Sometimes a text will absolutely dictate style, but occasionally visual style and even characterization of the cast, can be open. It is like a play. I immediately think of Shakespeare's plays—"Midsummer Night's Dream" in particular. I have seen productions of "Dream" done "authentically" as it would have been presented at the Globe Theatre in Shakespeare's time—"historically" as it would have taken place at the time of the period of the play itself—"romantically," a visual fairy-tale complete with [Felix] Mendelssohn's music and Robert Helpmann and Moira Shearer flying up into the sky at the end and several years ago, the innovative production of Peter Brooks.

The other very important problem that I must solve is choice of material. I totally rely on personal interest. The idea, even in retelling an old tale, must (to use a very American phrase) "grab me." Sometimes it can become close to an obsession. *Clown of God* . . . , for instance, was a tale I loved as a child. I did my first draft of that tale many years ago. It wasn't very good. It didn't have the impact of the original Anatole France version. So I began to research it. I found that Anatole France himself, retold an old legend. More search.

Finally, I found the root-tale. Then, in the tradition of the story-teller, I took that root-tale, which is very sparse and told the story from my own point of view—just as Anatole France had. My retelling has a great deal to do with a haunting image of a very strong Romanesque Madonna and Child, the child holding not an apple, not an orb, but a mysterious golden ball.

Also, the growing conviction I have, that the greatest gift anyone can give is the gift of oneself, coupled with the fact that quite often in contemporary society the old are ignored, ridiculed and pushed aside by the public are important in my retelling.

I try to stay open to ideas. Children often ask me where I get my ideas. I tell them that I get them everywhere. It's a question of being open, receptive—like an empty cup. Of course, not every idea is a good one. The boring ones usually quietly go away. . . . The idea for my *The Knight and the Dragon* . . . actually came from a poster I myself did for the American Library Association to promote reading. I was looking at the poster which had been on my studio wall for months when suddenly the kernel of the idea came—Something that rings true for me—something worthy to share with children.

Then there is that ever constant fear that no ideas will come! Well, I have a personal solution to that. I have been able to line up books into the future—just in case I run out. Then I have time to get the old brain and heart going. The important thing is the heart. An idea for me must be "heart-felt"— something that rings true for me—something worthy to share with children.

"Children" is the important word. Many beautiful books are being produced that are NOT for children. I certainly don't say that they don't deserve to exist. And I am adamant about not writing or drawing down to children, but quite often I see beautifully illustrated books that children cannot relate to because they are too sophisticated visually. They rely on previous, and sometimes educated, visual experiences. Adults love them, but they are visually inaccessible to children. I certainly believe in offering new visual forms to children, but I just as firmly believe that as a children's book artist part of my duty is to draw children into that new experience, not shove it down their throats. And it MUST be the best work I can do at the moment.

On the other end of the spectrum are books that are visual sentimentality rather than true visual sentiment. As I see it, sentimentality is the watering-down, sugaring-up or romanticization of real feeling—a feeling about a feeling. Sentiment is sharing the feeling itself. I'm not surprised when people tell me they cry at the end of *Clown of God.* I cannot read the text or look at the pictures without those feelings myself. The feelings of hope, success, failure, desolation, death and the final triumph were very present in me when I created the book. I believe that children appreciate my desire to share these feelings with them.

It's a dream of mine that one of my books, any book, any picture, will touch the heart of some individual child and change that child's life for the better. I don't even have to know about it. I hope it's not a far-fetched dream. Meanwhile, I'll keep working, doing the best I'm capable of. (pp. 2-3)

Tomie de Paola, "Involved with Dreams," in Books for Your Children *(© Books for Your Children 1980), Vol. 15, No. 3, Summer, 1980, pp. 2-3.*

GENERAL COMMENTARY

Can there be a higher honor for a creator of children's books than to be selected by children as a favorite? In 1978, children across the U.S. chose four of Tomie de Paola's works among their favorites. No other creator of children's books in 1978 was given such an honor.

The evidence is clear. Tomie de Paola is one of the most popular creators of picture books for children in America today. Now that the children have spoken, it's time for us educators to take our cue from de Paola's popularity and bring his creations into our libraries and classrooms.

Tomie de Paola's work is at its best when he both illustrates and writes a picture book. (p. 264)

De Paola's books fall into three general categories: informational books, folktales, and twentieth century fiction that blends fantasy and realism.

De Paola's informational books couple humor with accurate information, incorporated into a fictional story line. He successfully breaks the rule that says information is clouded if it is presented through fiction.

The Quicksand Book . . . is, on one level, the story of Jungle Girl sinking in quicksand as Jungle Boy (an authority on quicksand) and the animals look on. It is also the story of how quicksand is created and what to do when you find yourself in it. The most obvious extending activity is provided in the book itself. It lists directions on how children can make quicksand and watch as objects placed on top stay put or sink depending on the amount of water forced into the sand. The book is an ideal tool for teaching youngsters how to read charts and diagrams as well as how to follow directions. . . . (p. 264)

[*"Charlie Needs a Cloak"*] is a fine introduction to clothmaking. At the end of the book, de Paola lists six words pertaining to clothmaking and defines each. Also, since all four seasons of the year are depicted, the book invites a comparison between its pictures and the pictures of the four seasons in de Paola's *Four Stories for Four Seasons*. . . .

Teachers and students alike enjoy *The Popcorn Book*. . . . It starts out with two youngsters getting ready to pop some corn and becoming intrigued with what popcorn is, where it comes from and how it pops. De Paola blends facts with ancient Indian legends about little demons in the kernels who get so mad when they get hot that they blow up. On the last page the author provides two special recipes. A popular activity is to pop corn according to both recipes and write down the differences between the two, thus incorporating many reading and language arts skills.

As the title implies, *The Cloud Book* . . . introduces the ten most common types of clouds. But the book goes far beyond the science text approach. It includes Indian folklore about clouds and introduces the myth of Hermes stealing the sun cattle, which are really clouds. No book about clouds would be complete without some mention of creating imaginary pictures out of cloud shapes. Identifying particular clouds can be even more fun if students are allowed to create pictures as they look at them. Since some folklore dealing with clouds is presented, the book would fit in well with a unit on American folklore. (p. 265)

Another book by de Paola that is not strictly informational yet appears to belong in this category is *Andy: That's My Name*. . . . Primary grade youngsters enjoy this tale about little Andy, who pulls a wagon that contains big cardboard cut-out letters that spell ANDY. When his friends see the name, they begin to play with the letters and form 15 different words using ANDY as a base. The phonograms found in this book can help young readers learn the importance of word families in an interesting way. Students can experiment with other phonograms and surely they'll look with new interest at their own names, hoping to find other words there. The book provides lessons in reading and spelling, and Andy's reaction to his friends provides a lesson in human relations.

Perhaps more attention has been paid to de Paola's illustrated, retold folktales than to all of his other work. The books in this category represent some of the most beautiful picture storybooks available today. These editions of folktales also provide the classroom teacher with a myriad of activities that help to create better readers and to develop in children a strong foundation in literature and an appreciation of fine picture books. . . . (pp. 265-66)

[*Strega Nona*] is de Paola's Caldecott Honor Book. It is a traditional tale set in Italy. Many people know this story as ''The Magic Cooking Pot.'' The pot produces food for the person who knows the correct chant, and keeps on producing it until it is given a special signal to stop. The pot is owned by Strega Nona (Grandmother Witch) and it is Big Anthony, her curious houseboy, who, not knowing how to stop the magic pot, turns the little Italian town into a disaster area about to be engulfed by pasta.

Strega Nona deserves comparison with *The Clown of God*. *Strega Nona* has a good deal more humor in it and the artist's use of bright color suggests the lighthearted tone. (p. 266)

The final book in this category [*Helga's Dowry: A Troll Love Story*] is not really a retelling of a folktale but rather a new story based on Norse folklore. . . . Helga is a lovely, poor troll possessing no dowry. In the story, she earns a dowry and finds a willing suitor, the king of trolls. Helga is one of the strongest, most ambitious, most resourceful female characters in modern picture storybooks. . . . Finally, children will enjoy finding the tiny hearts de Paola sprinkles here and there in this and all his books.

A book that bridges the gap between de Paola's folktales and his modern fiction picture books is *When Everyone Was Fast Asleep*. . . . In this story, two children are roused from their sleep by Token, the Fog Maiden's mysterious cat. During their night of flying, they meet trolls, a king and queen, and a sand serpent, among others. As dawn comes closer, the children are picked up by the Fog Maiden, tucked into bed, and kissed asleep.

The colors in this book are soft and dreamlike, compared to the vibrant *Strega Nona* illustrations. A comparison with [Maurice] Sendak's *In the Night Kitchen* (1970) is interesting since both are based on what happens at night when most people are asleep. De Paola includes in this book some familiar characters from his other books. Children can find characters from *The Clown of God* and *Helga's Dowry*, as well as from one of de Paola's most humorous books, *Bill and Pete*.

Bill and Pete . . . is about a crocodile and his talking toothbrush. William Everett, the crocodile, is about to enter school, so his mother takes him to the store to select a toothbrush. He chooses a talking bird. Elementary youngsters will enjoy this idea of a talking bird toothbrush, and some research into the Egyptian plover reveals that these birds do, in fact, act as ''toothbrushes'' for crocodiles.

William Everett has trouble spelling his name because of all the letters in it. Pete, his toothbrush, helps by telling William to spell his name as Bill. A lesson in nicknames is perfect here. Where does the term nickname come from? Are there times when nicknames shouldn't or can't be used? What are common nicknames for Robert, Elizabeth, Richard and so forth? (pp. 266-67)

Students interested in ecology and the environment will like de Paola's **Michael Bird-Boy**. . . . Michael lived in the country where it was bright and clear. One day a dark cloud came over and everything turned dirty and the flowers wilted. Michael went to the city and found a factory causing the great black cloud. The factory produced artificial honey syrup for pancakes. Michael suggested that producing real honey with bees would be better and it would eliminate the black cloud. Boss Lady liked Michael's idea, so he sent her some bees and the black cloud disappeared. The country became clear again and everyone got to eat fine, natural honey.

This book is informational in that it describes the honey making process. As a story on pollution, it belongs in a unit with [Virginia Lee] Burton's *The Little House* (1942) and [Bill] Peet's *The Wump World* (1970). . . . **Michael Bird-Boy** tackles the question of real versus artificial and, as such, suggests a comparison with Hans Christian Andersen's *The Nightingale*. There's also a lesson here on good nutrition and eating habits.

Eating plays an important part in de Paola's work. His first textless book, **Pancakes for Breakfast** . . . follows the main character as she begins to make a stack of pancakes but runs out of eggs, then milk, then butter, then syrup. At her farm she collects all of these fresh ingredients, but when she returns home after getting the syrup, her dog and cat have made a feast of the other ingredients. The books lends itself to teaching story sequence, following directions, and is an introduction to the origin of certain foods. Youngsters can tell their own version of this story in a language experience lesson.

De Paola's Italian background is most obvious in **Watch Out for the Chicken Feet in Your Soup**. . . . Joey, who looks very much like de Paola, takes his friend, Eugene, to meet his old-fashioned Italian grandmother. Joey is embarrassed by his grandmother's actions and constant offering of food. Eugene is anything but embarrassed and thinks Joey's grandmother, who serves real chicken feet in her soup, is wonderful. He helps her make bread dolls while Joey pouts. In the end, Joey gets the most beautiful bread doll and realizes just how lucky he is to have such a special grandmother.

On the last page of the book, the author provides directions for making bread dolls. The recipe is a lesson in traditional ethnic foods as well as in the importance of a cultural heritage. This book encourages youngsters to overcome the embarrassment of the old ways and instead realize the value of tradition and heritage.

De Paola's grandmother is also a central character in **Nana Upstairs and Nana Downstairs**. . . . Tommy's great grandmother and grandmother live in the same house. His great grandmother lives upstairs, hence, Nana Upstairs. One day his great grandmother dies and several years later his grandmother dies. This book concerns itself with Tommy's adjustment to their deaths. (pp. 267-68)

Children who have been exposed to other de Paola books will recognize the Tommy in this book as the author himself. They'll also see the grandmother from **Chicken Feet**. This recognition of an author in his own works may spark a search, comparing a picture of de Paola with similar looking characters in his books. . . .

De Paola's informational books, his folktales, and his books that blend fantasy and realism all combine humor with inter-

esting characterization and intriguing story line. Elementary youngsters select his books as their favorites. Certainly the books are primarily for entertainment, but teachers should be doubly pleased because each provides fuel for interesting learning activities. (p. 268)

> *Richard F. Abrahamson and Marilyn Colvin, ''Tomie de Paola: Children's Choice,'' (copyright 1979 by the International Reading Association, Inc.; reprinted with permission of the International Reading Association and Richard F. Abrahamson and Marilyn Colvin), in The Reading Teacher, Vol. 33, No. 3, December, 1979, pp. 264-69.*

There is no rule that says that nonfiction can't be funny. Starting with **The Cloud Book**, Tomie de Paola sets out to prove that we can laugh *with* (not *at*) science. A factual account of different kinds of clouds ends up with funny sayings about clouds and a ridiculous story, all illustrated in his own inimitable style. In **The Quicksand Book**, he really hits his stride with a mad tall tale in dialogue that somehow manages to tell us all the important scientific facts about quicksand. We can't help laughing as he gets more and more absurd in his imaginative playing around with a ridiculous yet revealing situation. No didacticism laid on here.

In these books, style becomes an essential ingredient of the author's approach to the subject matter. The best nonfiction for children is neither didactic in tone, nor dry and dusty in language and pattern. Such books are a literary experience rather than a school assignment. (pp. 8-9)

> *Betty Bacon, ''The Art of Nonfiction,'' in Children's literature in education (© 1981, Agathon Press, Inc.; reprinted by permission of the publisher), Vol. 12, No. 1 (Spring), 1981, pp. 8-9.*

THE WONDERFUL DRAGON OF TIMLIN (1966)

A pleasant, undistinguished picture-story about a young princess, a page, and a bright pink misunderstood dragon with long curly eyelashes. The pictures are drawn in mustard and various shades of pink and red. Little girls who adore dragons and princesses will probably enjoy this.

> *Ann Currah, ''Brief Mention: 'The Wonderful Dragon of Timlin','' in School Library Journal, an appendix to Library Journal (reprinted from the May, 1966 issue of School Library Journal, published by R. R. Bowker Co./A Xerox Corporation; copyright © 1966), Vol. 12, No. 9, May, 1966, p. 178.*

The Wonderful Dragon of Timlin . . . is a tale a bit above ordinary. Tomie de Paola sets his story in a mythical kingdom with a princess and page and a reluctant dragon. The happy ending and marriage after an initial banishment revolve around the dragon's remarkable fire-breathing skills. The illustrations use tints of red and yellow inside thin black lines and are somewhat childlike—in keeping with the naivete of the text. But I wish it was a girl dragon because "he" looks so effeminate.

> *Kenneth Marantz, ''A Potpourri of Color and Merriment,'' in Chicago Tribune Books Today, May 8, 1966, p. 9A.**

JOE AND THE SNOW   (1968)

What's fun about Joe is that he *never* has too much snow—not even when his wished-for snowstorm lasts for five days and nights, depositing enough for two hundred snowmen and burying the house except for the chimney; not even when the melting snow becomes an inland sea (like the grouchy old man warned) and Joe and his animal friends have to hoist a sail. When the water has receded Joe starts to think again SNOW, SNOW, SNOW. At the start Joe's housemate Martin, a dog with more than a pipe-smoking kinship to Professor Higgins, seems an intrusion (as do cat Alexander and rabbit Philip), but it's Martin/Higgins whose quick-thinking (because "I read a lot") saves the house from floating away. As a story it's no more than a flurry, but amusingly conceived and drawn.

> *"Picture Books: 'Joe and the Snow',"* in Kirkus Service *(copyright © 1968 The Kirkus Service, Inc.), Vol. XXXVI, No. 21, November 1, 1968, p. 1212.*

A topical (if it snows in your part of the country), cheerful little anecdote of a story—a snow-filled blue and white fantasy—this record of what happens when a small boy thinks snow, which will entertain other snowbound small boys.

> *"P. W. Forecasts: 'Joe and the Snow',"* in Publishers Weekly *(reprinted from the December 2, 1968 issue of* Publishers Weekly, *published by R. R. Bowker Company, a Xerox company; copyright © 1968 by Xerox Corporation), Vol. 194, No. 23, December 2, 1968, p. 37.*

PARKER PIG, ESQUIRE   (1969)

Parker Pig should brighten up your January, for as Tomie de Paola tells and illustrates his story, he is the kind of friendly, warmhearted character you'd like to have for a neighbor. You'll enjoy your visit to his nice old house. . . .

> *"Children's Books: 'Parker Pig Esquire',"* in Publishers Weekly *(reprinted from the January 19, 1970 issue of* Publishers Weekly, *published by R. R. Bowker Company, a Xerox company; copyright © 1970 by Xerox Corporation), Vol. 197, No. 3, January 19, 1970, p. 81.*

Four very human animals (three from London, one from America) visit their friend Parker Pig, Esquire, who has a house in Yorkshire. They try—successfully—to change their host's slightly messy way of life; then, surprised to discover that they had more fun when Parker was being himself, they urge him back to his old life style. Unfortunately, the obvious moral lesson is one which would probably benefit more mothers than young readers, who seldom seem to be too tidy. However, the illustrations are bright and sprightly, and the text is easy enough for newly independent readers.

> *Alice D. Ehlet, "The Book Review: 'Parker Pig, Esquire',"* in School Library Journal, *an appendix to* Library Journal *(reprinted from the May, 1970 issue of* School Library Journal, *published by R. R. Bowker Co./A Xerox Corporation; copyright © 1970), Vol. 16, No. 9, May, 1970, p. 58.*

THE MONSTERS' BALL   (1970)

Successful monsters are very individual and do not bear a too distinct resemblance to a readily recognizable creature. Tomie de Paola's *The Monsters' Ball* . . . is more like a carnival freak show with monsters too twistedly human to be funny. It features a group of bored weirdies who throw a ball which ends in a brawl. So much for that.

> *Ingeborg Boudreau, "From Three-Toed Glisson Glop to Six-Eyed Galaplop,"* in The New York Times Book Review, Part II *(© 1970 by The New York Times Company; reprinted by permission), May 24, 1970, p. 47.**

Children do love monsters, and the characters in *The Monsters' Ball* are amusing to look at, but the book's success ends here. The text is primarily adult in tone, and it has neither humor nor point. Let the children stick to [Maurice Sendak's] *Where the Wild Things Are.*

> *Joan M. Eaton, "The Book Review: 'The Monsters' Ball',"* in School Library Journal, *an appendix to* Library Journal *(reprinted from the December, 1970 issue of* School Library Journal, *published by R. R. Bowker Co./A Xerox Corporation; copyright © 1970), Vol. 17, No. 4, December, 1970, p. 81.*

NANA UPSTAIRS AND NANA DOWNSTAIRS   (1973)

A little boy's Sunday visits to his grandmother . . . are recalled with low keyed affection in simple words and subdued pink and beige pictures. . . . Particulars such as Tommy and Nana Upstairs chatting and eating candy while tied to their chairs (Nana so she won't fall out, Tommy just for fun) help to vivify the memories and modulate the mood.

> *"Picture Books: 'Nana Upstairs and Nana Downstairs',"* in Kirkus Reviews *(copyright © 1973 The Kirkus Service, Inc.), Vol. XLI, No. 11, June 1, 1973, p. 596.*

[After Nana Upstairs dies] the book gets a little soupy, with falling stars representing kisses from heaven and both Nanas eventually becoming "Nana Upstairs," but none of this will offend. The charcoal drawings, filled with pink, rose and tan tints, depict a 1940-ish grandmotherly house and people; the print is large and clear on light beige paper; and each page . . . is appealingly framed. Children will want to hear this again and again, as they puzzle over what it means to be young and old and very old and, finally, to die.

> *Melinda Schroeder, "The Book Review: 'Nana Upstairs and Nana Downstairs',"* in School Library Journal, *an appendix to* Library Journal *(reprinted from the September, 1973 issue of* School Library Journal, *published by R. R. Bowker Co./A Xerox Corporation; copyright © 1973), Vol. 20, No. 1, September, 1973, p. 56.*

This is one of the best of the several stories for very young children that shows the love between a child and a grandparent, and pictures the child's adjustment to death. Like [Max] Lundgren's *Matt's Grandfather*, this stresses the affinity between the very young and the very old; unlike any of the other stories, it includes a great-grandmother as well as a grandmother. . . . The book gives a tender—but not overly sentimental—picture of the child's relationships with his grandmothers, the quiet tone given relief by touches of humor—as when Tommy sees his older grandmother tied into a chair to enjoy a rare time of being out of bed, and he wants to be tied in, too. (pp. 24-5)

> *Zena Sutherland, "New Titles for Children and Young People: 'Nana Upstairs and Nana Downstairs',"* in

Bulletin of the Center for Children's Books *(reprinted by permission of The University of Chicago Press; © 1973 by The University of Chicago), Vol. 27, No. 2, October, 1973, pp. 24-5.*

While [Sam] Cornish leaves no doubt as to the love and respect within the family [in *Grandmother's Pictures*], there is not the same warmth and affection evident in Tomie de Paola's *Nana Upstairs and Nana Downstairs*. De Paola presents, very simply, the realities of aging in a story which not only could be understood by the pre-schooler, but also could be read by seven year-olds. He reinforces the conviction that the infirmities which so often accompany old age are a fact of life which need not be feared, ridiculed, or hidden. It is refreshing to see the young child look forward to his visits to his great-grandmother. . . . His older brother does not have quite the same attitude and we see the younger child . . . rise to the defence of the elderly. To [him] there is a definite beauty in being old. (pp. 38-9)

> *Janet Dobbins, "Aging and Death in Children's Books: 'Nana Upstairs and Nana Downstairs'," in* The World of Children's Books *(© 1978 Jon C. Stott), Vol. III, No. 1, Spring, 1978, pp. 38-9.*

ANDY (THAT'S MY NAME) (1973)

Even though the other kids won't let little Andy play, he is assured of his importance when they all start playing around with his name. . . . All the words in the book (except those that they make) are spoken by the children in comic-style bubbles, the pictures are as unpretentiously witty as the concept, and we so rarely see either a pre-pre-primer or an ego-building parable with any style at all that we'd like to give *Andy* a boost. (pp. 879-80)

> *"Picture Book: 'Andy (That's My Name)'," in* Kirkus Reviews *(copyright © 1973 The Kirkus Service,*

From Nana Upstairs & Nana Downstairs, *written and illustrated by Tomie de Paola.*

Inc.), Vol. XLI, No. 16, August 15, 1973, pp. 879-80.

[*Andy (That's My Name)*] gives us a rugged little individual. . . . "I may be little," he says, "BUT . . . I'm very important!"

For any child who is just learning to read, this book offers a challenge as well as a much needed pat-on-the-back.

> *Deborah Komaiko, "Andy (That's My Name)," in* The Christian Science Monitor *(reprinted by permission from* The Christian Science Monitor; *© 1973 The Christian Science Publishing Society; all rights reserved), November 7, 1973, p. B2.*

"CHARLIE NEEDS A CLOAK" (1973)

Charlie, a shepherd, needs a cloak and so, in the spring, he sets about shearing his sheep, washing and carding the wool and spinning it into yarn. . . . That's all, but pink-smocked, contentedly industrious Charlie and the unobtrusive antics of his sheep and mouse add a comfortable glow to the simple summary of a process that will be new to preschoolers.

> *"Picture Books: 'Charlie Needs a Cloak'," in* Kirkus Reviews *(copyright © 1974 The Kirkus Service, Inc.), Vol. XLII, No. 3, February 1, 1974, p. 104.*

Charlie, the shepherd, needs a new cloak; so, he shears his sheep; washes, cards, and spins the wool; dries and weaves the yarn; cuts and sews the cloth—all with the help of one woolly, black-faced sheep, who gets woollier on each doublespread. As a subplot, the story features the activities of a rather acquisitive, bourgeois mouse, who takes advantage of Charlie's preoccupation and carries away various desirables—scissors, soap, candles—to store in a tree stump. But strange are the ways of mice, men, and sheep; for when Charlie finally bedecks himself in his new cloak, his woolly friend faithfully nibbles away at the new creation. The drawings, which show the sheep and mouse cavorting in house and field, have been executed in muted tones and simple lines—each doublespread uncomplex and uncluttered in composition. Books written to teach children facts seldom can stand on their own artistic integrity; but the instruction in this story simply highlights a delightful piece of light entertainment. (pp. 138-39)

> *Anita Silvey, "Early Spring Booklist: 'Charlie Needs a Cloak'," in* The Horn Book Magazine *(copyright © 1974 by the Horn Book, Inc., Boston), Vol. L, No. 2, April, 1974, pp. 138-39.*

The text is minimal, the story will give children an idea of the processes of handwork required to make cloth, but the story alone is static. What it needs, and gets from the illustrations, are action and lightness.

> *Karla Kuskin, "Picture Books: 'Charlie Needs a Cloak'," in* The New York Times Book Review *(© 1974 by The New York Times Company; reprinted by permission), May 5, 1974, p. 47.*

For the child who would like to know how to make a new red cloak (the old one being worn out) starting with the sheep **"Charlie Needs a Cloak"** . . . will be indispensable. Charlie is a shepherd and this book shows, step by step, how he shears, cards, spins, dyes, weaves and sews himself a new cloak. Words and pictures are entertaining. One tiny cavil: the glos-

Charlie wanted a red cloak, so he picked some pokeweed berries during the late summer, and boiled them over a fire.

Then Charlie dyed the yarn red in the berry juice.

From "Charlie Needs a Cloak", *written and illustrated by Tomie de Paola.*

sary identifies "Weave— to twist thread into cloth." It's clear that Charlie knows better than that.

> *Zena Sutherland, "New Titles for Children and Young People: 'Charlie Needs a Cloak'," in* Bulletin of the Center for Children's Books *(reprinted by permission of The University of Chicago Press; © by The University of Chicago), Vol. 27, No. 10, June, 1974, p. 156.*

WATCH OUT FOR THE CHICKEN FEET IN YOUR SOUP (1974)

Tomie de Paola appends a recipe for the bread dolls which he remembers from his own grandmother's kitchen, and both his cozy pictures and his simple text (which is all dialogue and almost entirely made up of the expansive grandma's fond fussing) glow with a genuine warmth that other visitors of whatever background can't help sharing.

> *"Picture Books: 'Watch Out for the Chicken Feet in Your Soup'," in* Kirkus Reviews *(copyright © 1974 The Kirkus Service, Inc.), Vol. XLII, No. 19, October 1, 1974, p. 1057.*

The author-illustrator tells us in an afterword to his exuberant story that he had an old-fashioned grandmother, just like Joey, the boy in the book. . . . She's the heart and soul of the ma-

ternal symbol: "I give you something nice to eat. *Zuppa*, nice chicken soup . . . spaghetti. Mangia!" A grand time is had by all and mothers of any nationality will appreciate the recipe for grandma's bread dolls . . . , a sure winner.

> *"Watch Out for the Chicken Feet in Your Soup," in* Publishers Weekly *(reprinted from the October 7, 1974 issue of* Publishers Weekly, *published by R. R. Bowker Company, a Xerox company; copyright © 1974 by Xerox Corporation), Vol. 206, No. 15, October 7, 1974, p. 64.*

Even children of Italian descent may not be familiar with the vocabulary, e.g., *ragazzi* (little boys), *caro* (dear), *mangia* (eat), etc. The food-obsessed (Italian, Jewish, etc.) grandmother has become a humorless cliché, and de Paola's tasteless stereotyping is hard to stomach. (pp. 46-47)

> *Leah Deland Stenson, "The Book Review: 'Watch Out for the Chicken Feet in Your Soup'," in* School Library Journal, *an appendix to* Library Journal *(reprinted from the November, 1974 issue of* School Library Journal, *published by R. R. Bowker Co./A Xerox Corporation; copyright © 1974), Vol. 21, No. 3, November, 1974, pp. 46-7.*

STREGA NONA: AN OLD TALE   (1975)

De Paola's illustrations aptly capture the whimsy of this ancient tale. And while his simple line drawings clearly reveal the agony and ecstasy of pasta power, the muted colors create just the right ambiance for a quaint Mediterranean village.

> *Norma Malina Feld, "For Younger Readers: 'Good Pasta and Bad Rumors',"* in The New York Times Book Review *(© 1975 by The New York Times Company; reprinted by permission), August 31, 1975, p. 8.**

The illustrator has given new vitality to the magic cooking pot theme. . . . The pictures for the well-told story show the houses and streets of an Italian town and the brightly costumed townspeople with droll expressions. Erratic in the quality of his work, the artist has, in his latest venture, chosen an excellent story to illustrate in warm, mellow color, making an appealing, successful picture book. (pp. 458-59)

> *Anita Silvey, "Fall Booklist: 'Strega Nona: An Old Tale',"* in The Horn Book Magazine *(copyright © 1975 by the Horn Book, Inc., Boston), Vol. LI, No. 5, October, 1975, pp. 458-59.*

[Tomie de Paola] has used soft colors, simple line, and medieval costume and architecture in his spaciously composed, humorous pictures. The tale of Strega Nona ("Grandmother Witch") is told in modest but fluent style, and the familiar theme of a self-filling magical object is used to good effect. Strega Nona's pasta pot, her helper Anthony has secretly noted, produces pasta when the right verse is said, stops at another verse; what Anthony carelessly ignores is the fact that Strega Nona also blows three kisses to the pot. Having boasted to the townspeople that he can produce pasta galore, Anthony says the magic verse when Strega Nona is away. Predictable, funny result: Anthony doesn't know how to stem the tide, and a river of pasta flows through the town. Strega Nona returns and saves the day, and she suggests a poetically just punishment instead of the vengeful hanging Anthony's neighbors propose: the poor lad has to eat all the pasta he's evoked—an ending children will probably enjoy tremendously.

> *Zena Sutherland, "New Titles for Children and Young People: 'Strega Nona: An Old Tale',"* in Bulletin of the Center for Children's Books *(reprinted by permission of The University of Chicago Press; © 1975 by The University of Chicago), Vol. 29, No. 3, November, 1975, p. 42.*

MICHAEL BIRD-BOY   (1975)

Warm, delicate watercolor illustrations in soft pastels highlight the story. . . . In the spirit of sex equality, de Paola makes the factory manager a "Boss-Lady" and has Michael bake her a honey cake. Why Michael wears a bird suit and lives on his own isn't made clear, however, and the forced introduction of a topical theme makes this fantasy disjointed and less effective than the author/illustrator's previous picture books.

> *Judith S. Kronick, "Book Reviews: 'Michael Bird-Boy',"* in School Library Journal *(reprinted from the September, 1975 issue of* School Library Journal, *published by R. R. Bowker Co./A Xerox Corporation; copyright © 1975), Vol. 22, No. 1, September, 1975, p. 79.*

Investigating the cause of sudden darkness, a boy/bird finds a factory making "Genuine Shoo-Fly Artificial Honey Syrup" and demonstrates to the proprietor the advantages of the more natural methods employed by bees. Subdued, subtly varied colour animates pleasantly odd pictures in a mildly Sendakian style which suits the quiet fantasy of the story. (p. 2859)

> *Margery Fisher, "A Child and a Dream,"* in her Growing Point, *Vol. 14, No. 9, April, 1976, pp. 2857-59.*

THE CLOUD BOOK: WORDS AND PICTURES   (1975)

An inviting and low-keyed introduction. . . . The treatment is simple enough to be understood by youngest cloud gazers; the tone is informative yet playful in the manner of the author's ***"Charlie Needs a Cloak"***. . . . De Paola's familiar softly colored illustrations with their plump figures complete the joyful mood that [Kazuo] Niizaka's *Clouds* (Addisonian Press, 1975) tried unsuccessfully to create. The skillful blend of fun and information makes this book a great success.

> *Diane Holzheimer, "The Book Review: 'The Cloud Book',"* in School Library Journal *(reprinted from the November, 1975 issue of* School Library Journal, *published by R. R. Bowker Co./A Xerox Corporation; copyright © 1975), Vol. 22, No. 3, November, 1975, p. 44.*

This very elementary introduction to common cloud types utilizes simple text and colored line drawings. . . . The chief value of the book will be to increase the curiosity of young children about clouds and their physical significance. It should not be considered to be an adequate introduction to cloud types for children whose interests lie in identifying real cloud types. (pp. 38-9)

> *William H. Long, "Pure Science: 'The Cloud Book: Words and Pictures',"* in Science Books & Films *(copyright ©1976 by the American Association for the Advancement of Science), Vol. XII, No. 1, May, 1976, pp. 38-9.*

I would have given this book a rating of Excellent [rather than Fair] but for one thing: the last three pages. In an effort to put something on every page of the signature, an absolutely dreadful "Cloud Story" showing a cloud coming into a room, knocking over a bottle and going out the window was included. It is misleading and altogether useless. Perhaps the purchaser could tear out the pages—then the book is indeed excellent. A few blank pages could have given the child reader a place to draw pictures of clouds he sees in the sky. (pp. 15-16)

> *John D. Stackpole, "Children's Science Book Review: 'The Cloud Book',"* in Appraisal: Science Books for Young People *(copyright © 1976 by the Children's Science Book Review Committee), Vol. 9, No. 1, Winter, 1976, pp. 15-16.*

WHEN EVERYONE WAS FAST ASLEEP   (1976)

"When everyone was fast asleep, the Fog Maiden sent Token to wake us up." And though Token is not identified, as befits the dreamy mood, you'll have no trouble spotting the oversized, pale blue cat's face filling the window, luring you, and the two nightgowned children, outdoors. . . . De Paola's unassuming, childlike manner proves a charming antidote to the

From Strega Nona: An Old Tale, *written and illustrated by Tomie de Paola.*

airiness such fancies might assume in other hands. Drift along. . . . It's a soothing, dulcet reverie.

> "Picture Books: 'When Everyone Was Fast Asleep'," in Kirkus Reviews (copyright © 1976 The Kirkus Service, Inc.), Vol. XLIV, No. 14, July 15, 1976, p. 789.

Creamy pastel shades fit the spirit of a consistently believable fantasy about a magic night in the lives of a little boy and girl. . . . A sense of fun as well as of dreaminess pervades the story, especially when the friends arrive at a palace to take part in a gala performance. The huge cat, Token, dominates the scenes even though he's in the background, up to the end where the kindly Fog Maiden takes the children home and tucks them into bed with a tender kiss.

> "Children's Books: 'When Everyone Was Fast Asleep'," in Publishers Weekly (reprinted from the July 19, 1976 issue of Publishers Weekly, published by R. R. Bowker Company, a Xerox company; copyright © 1976 by Xerox Corporation), Vol. 210, No. 3, July 19, 1976, p. 132.

A whimsical excursion into a child's dream world. There are no shadows or lurking demons here—only gentle animals and friendly trolls. . . . Illustrated in de Paola's trademark style, the simple, pleasant text is conveniently printed in very large letters—a boon for beginning readers; however, this nighttime dream sequence seems decidedly pale next to [Janice May] Udry's The Moon Jumpers (Harper, 1959) or [Elinor] Horowitz's When the Sky Is Like Lace (Lippincott, 1975).

> Cynthia Percak Infantino, "Book Reviews: 'When Everyone Was Fast Asleep'," in School Library Journal (reprinted from the October, 1976 issue of School Library Journal, published by R. R. Bowker Co./A Xerox Corporation; copyright © 1976), Vol. 23, No. 2, October, 1976, p. 96.

THINGS TO MAKE AND DO FOR VALENTINE'S DAY (1976)

A cheerful and pleasant book of typical Valentine's Day activities. . . . None of the ideas is especially remarkable or unique, but the presentation is attractive and this can be enjoyed by holiday celebrants of early elementary age.

> Phyllis Ingram, "Book Reviews: 'Things to Make and Do for Valentine's Day'," in School Library Journal (reprinted from the October, 1976 issue of School Library Journal, published by R. R. Bowker Co./A Xerox Corporation; copyright © 1976), Vol. 23, No. 2, October, 1976, p. 96.

Hearts are trumps in a gathering of information about and ideas for the celebration of Valentine's Day. Presented in a simple text with full-color explanatory illustrations executed as amusingly elegant cartoons, the book includes explicit directions for printing greeting cards as well as instructions for games, recipes, and crafts. For those more skilled with words and word play, a sampling of tongue twisters, jokes, and riddles—all with a Valentine motif—is provided. An appealing resource for young party givers and Valentine enthusiasts. (pp. 36-7)

Mary M. Burns, "Late Winter Booklist: 'Things to Make and Do for Valentine's Day'," in The Horn Book Magazine *(copyright © 1977 by the Horn Book, Inc., Boston), Vol. LIII, No. 1, February, 1977, pp. 36-7.*

THE QUICKSAND BOOK (1977)

[As in *Clouds* and *"Charlie Needs a Cloak"*] de Paola again uses a picture-book format to present basic science information in an utterly appealing, humorous way. . . . Very funny and very sensible in the calm survival procedures suggested.

Michele Woggon, "The Book Review: 'The Quicksand Book'," in School Library Journal *(reprinted from the April, 1977 issue of* School Library Journal, *published by R. R. Bowker Co./A Xerox Corporation; copyright © 1977), Vol. 23, No. 8, April, 1977, p. 54.*

By the time this damsel in distress is finally rescued, young readers will be as knowledgeable as she is, and they'll cheer as she takes a most satisfying revenge on her pedantic savior.

Joyce Milton, "Children's Books: 'The Quicksand Book'," in The New York Times Book Review *(© 1977 by The New York Times Company; reprinted by permission), September 18, 1977, p. 42.*

Tomie de Paola has always had a talent for making his informational books entertaining and amusing as well as accurate. His latest is called *The Quicksand Book* and it follows in this tradition. There can be no surprise about the subject of the book—the title is perfectly clear. The surprise is in the manner of presentation. . . . [The inclusion of Jungle Girl sinking in quicksand] is a clever approach to the presentation of the information of the story, for not only do we get the facts, but also we laugh at the foolishness of Jungle Boy who is so engrossed in his pedantry that he doesn't seem to notice his companion is sinking deeper and deeper into the quicksand. As in de Paola's other books, there is much humorous byplay in the illustrations. While Jungle Boy pontificates, his pet ape is setting a table, complete with linen, and preparing a very elegant tea. From out of the foliage an assortment of jungle animals look on, mystified at the strange sights. And at the end, our own academic hero, having rescued Jungle Girl, falls himself into the quicksand, a victim of his own pride!

Jon C. Stott, "The Best Picture Books, Our Baker's Dozen: 'The Quicksand Book'," in The World of Children's Books *(© 1977 Jon C. Stott), Vol. II, No. 2, Fall, 1977, p. 14.*

He's done it again! De Paola has created the perfect combination of learning and fun. . . . Every page has jungle creatures, lots of colorful details, and appealing leading characters to look at.

Elizabeth Gillis, "The Quicksand Book," in Appraisal: Science Books for Young People *(copyright © 1978 by the Children's Science Book Review Committee), Vol. 11, No. 1, Winter, 1978, p. 20.*

FOUR STORIES FOR FOUR SEASONS (1977)

[Master Dog, Missy Cat, Mistress Pig, and Mister Frog] . . . mince and gush their way through four inconsequential tales. They take a spill while rowing ("Are you all right, Kitty dear?"); they all plant gardens and admire each other's ("You must tell me your secret". . . . "I'm so pleased you like it"), though Dog's turns out to be a bone garden; "Piggy Sweet" has a dinner party but "samples" all the food away while her guests wait to be served ("Oh Piggy dear, don't cry"); and Frog wakes from a "tiny nap" just in time to experience Christmas, which he usually sleeps through ("Oh Froggy, you would love it!"). But whatever humor was intended doesn't surface in all this simpering small talk—and the pictures are just stock de Paola.

"Picture Books: 'Four Stories for Four Seasons'," in Kirkus Reviews *(copyright © 1977 The Kirkus Service, Inc.), Vol. XLV, No. 14, July 15, 1977, p. 724.*

[The natty, timid Master Dog of Mr. de Paola's **"Four Stories for Four Seasons"** is an appealing canine] but he barely emerges as a personality in these weak, overly whimsical tales. The book is pretty: de Paola uses soft, clear colors and the pages are bordered with seasonal flowers and leaves. And in **"Winter,"** there is a welcome note of wryness. If Mister Frog bears a faint resemblance to an archetypal [Arnold] Lobelian cousin, his stupefied reaction to the three small Santas of **"Winter"** is a comic delight on its own.

Jennifer Dunning, "Hard Winter's Work," in The New York Times Book Review *(© 1977 by The New York Times Company; reprinted by permission), November 13, 1977, pp. 42, 45.**

De Paola's *Four Stories for Four Seasons* . . . traces the experiences of four animal friends during each season. The title, however, is something of a misnomer since the adventures are more like rather impoverished anecdotes than well-shaped stories. Only the Winter chapter, in which Mister Frog tries to avoid hibernating so that he can experience Christmas, has any semblance of shape and meaningful conflict and action. The poverty of de Paola's inventions are readily apparent when the Summer chapter, in which the animals decide to plant gardens, is compared with a similar but better story in Arnold Lobel's *Frog and Toad Together* (New York. Harper and Row, 1972). Lobel's story has action which reveals interesting personalities. De Paola's anecdote merely describes: it is static and dull. Compounding this problem is dialogue which is more than ordinarily awkward because de Paola repeatedly insists on having all four characters speak. (p. 8)

Raymond E. Jones, "Easy Reader, Literature and Reading Matter for the Beginning Reader: 'Four Stories for Four Seasons'," in The World of Children's Books *(© 1978 Jon C. Stott), Vol. III, No. 1, Spring, 1978, pp. 7-8.*

HELGA'S DOWRY: A TROLL LOVE STORY (1977)

It isn't every day such a character [as Helga] comes along. Beside Helga's good sense and humor, the ideological pieties of "genderless" children's books pale.

Helga, "the loveliest troll in three parishes," has had the misfortune to grow up too poor to have a dowry. (Mr. de Paola's inspiration often comes from faculty-meeting doodles. "A troll appeared on the doodle pad," Mr. de Paola recalled. "I thought, 'Gee, must be a troll story inside me.' So I did a lot of research on trolls and found the women are condemned to wander the face of the earth if they have no dowry.") (p. 42)

Even the most confirmed of female doll-cradlers and their brothers are likely to feel a stab of kinship at the following exchange between Helga and a mysterious rich man: ''I'll make you a bargain, then,'' said Helga. ''If I can clear those trees, all in a week, will you give *me* the land they're on?'' ''Madam, you're a woman!'' exclaimed the man. ''So what!'' said Helga. (pp. 42, 45)

Mr. de Paola's illustrations are as yeasty as the story. Full of comic detail, they have the same almost glaze-clear bright colors as his illustrations for **"Strega Nona"**. . . . The gingerbread page-borders add an extra fairy-tale element. (p. 45)

> *Jennifer Dunning, ''Hard Winter's Work,'' in* The New York Times Book Review *(© 1977 by The New York Times Company; reprinted by permission), November 13, 1977, pp. 42, 45.**

Most of the fun is in Helga's magical despatch of loot-producing tasks (35 cows in return for doing an enormous laundry by sundown) and in the blatant ugliness of lovely Helga and handsome Lars; the pictures are in Tomie de Paola's usual rustic-peasant style, and the text has, despite a tinge of contrivance, a structure that is within the folktale tradition.

> *Zena Sutherland, ''New Titles for Children and Young People: 'Helga's Dowry: A Troll Love Story','' in* Bulletin of the Center for Children's Books *(reprinted by permission of The University of Chicago Press; © 1977 by The University of Chicago), Vol. 31, No. 4, December, 1977, p. 59.*

From Helga's Dowry: A Troll Love Story, *written and illustrated by Tomie de Paola.*

PANCAKES FOR BREAKFAST   (1978)

In his usual comfy drawings and, this time, no words, de Paola shows a farm woman getting up and getting dressed and, propping up the recipe for all to see, proceeding to make pancakes—from scratch. . . . A final scene at the neighbors', whose pancake breakfast she more or less appropriates, provides the necessary if uninspired pickup ending. This is no special feast for the audience, but it's an easily palatable reminder that our food is not created at the supermarket—and the built-in anticipation of the project's outcome should help to keep the pages turning.

> *''Picture Books: 'Pancakes for Breakfast','' in* Kirkus Reviews *(copyright © 1978 The Kirkus Service, Inc.), Vol. XLVI, No. 7, April 1, 1978, p. 366.*

In his first textless book, imaginative de Paola offers proof that appealingly detailed, colorful paintings can speak louder than words. In her attractive home in the snow-covered New England countryside, an elderly widow awakens with visions of pancakes dancing in her head. As her dog and cat watch interestedly, she gathers ingredients for a breakfast feast in her cozy kitchen. She discovers during the mixing however, that she has run out of essentials and—donning bonnet and shawl—ventures out to fetch milk from her cow, eggs from obliging hens and syrup from a neighbor. Back home, she finds that the dog and cat have dumped the other ingredients on the floor. But readers who think the lady isn't going to get her pancakes have a surprise waiting. The thoughtful artist includes his heroine's recipe for the taste treat.

> *''Children's Books: 'Pancakes for Breakfast','' in* Publishers Weekly *(reprinted from the May 29, 1978 issue of* Publishers Weekly, *published by R. R. Bowker Company, a Xerox company; copyright © 1978 by Xerox Corporation), Vol. 213, No. 22, May 29, 1978, p. 51.*

In this wordless picture book, Tomie de Paola's little old lady, round and solid as a homemade doughnut, encounters problems in fixing pancakes for her breakfast. . . . Solution: Invite yourself to the neighbors' for breakfast. Mr. de Paola's renditions of a New England farm kitchen, in tans, mauves and brick reds, are cozily appealing, if a little static in their pacing.

> *Georgess McHargue, ''Children's Books: 'Pancakes for Breakfast','' in* The New York Times Book Review *(© 1979 by The New York Times Company; reprinted by permission), January 28, 1979, p. 25.*

THE POPCORN BOOK   (1978)

A pair of twins conversing in a comic-strip format tells facts about popcorn in this brief book. While one boy makes popcorn, the other reads encyclopedia information, which is illustrated in lively balloons above the children's heads. . . . There is no information about popcorn as a plant or about its cultivation. This is an amusing book for any young popcorn lover.

> *Katharine C. Payne, ''Agriculture: 'The Popcorn Book','' in* Science Books & Films *(copyright © 1979 by the American Association for the Advancement of Science), Vol. XV, No. 1, May, 1979, p. 43.*

The total science content of the book is contained in the statement that ''When the kernel is heated, the moisture turns to steam and the heart gets bigger until the shell bursts with a ''pop.'' The book is not devoted to an exploration of this statement, but to a general account of popcorn. But even as such and account it is deficient. The format and illustrations are clearly designed with young children in mind. What are such children to make of "Today, Americans use 500,000,000 pounds of popcorn each year. Thirty percent is eaten at movies, circuses, ball games, and county fairs. Ten percent is saved for seed and sold to other countries. But 60 percent is popped right at home." They are unlikely to be able to read the massive number, not to speak of percent calculations. The illustrations are delightful, but the text is very poor.

> *Lazar Goldberg, "The Popcorn Book," in* Appraisal: Science Books for Young People *(copyright © 1979 by the Children's Science Book Review Committee), Vol. 12, No. 1, Winter, 1979, pp. 8-9.*

THE CLOWN OF GOD: AN OLD STORY (1978)

This is in the limited tradition of the believers' tale, less impressive to outsiders; but it's easy to be enticed by de Paola's early, pastel street scenes, and when the miracles comes along his unprepossessing figures and warm familiarity help cut the piety. (pp. 1013-14)

> *"Picture Books: 'The Clown of God'," in* Kirkus Reviews *(copyright © 1978 The Kirkus Service, Inc.), Vol. XLVI, No. 18, September 15, 1978, pp. 1013-14.*

De Paola's double-page paintings have drama and movement (Giovanni ages 50 years in the turn of a page) if not depth, but the sentimental story of an artist's rise and fall is more for book creators than young readers.

> *Pamela D. Pollack, "Christmas Books '78, a Mixed Bag: 'The Clown of God'," in* School Library Journal *(reprinted from the October, 1978 issue of* School Library Journal, *published by R. R. Bowker Co./A Xerox Corporation; copyright © 1978), Vol. 25, No. 2, October, 1978, p. 113.*

The full-color pictures with subtle tonal modulations are an integral part of the design of the luminous pages full of movement and vitality. The Italianate aspects of the setting are beautifully realized—the countryside, the clothing of the people, the gondoliers, the slightly anachronistic reference to commedia dell'arte, and especially the architecture, in which the rounded arch is used not as a cliché but as a motif. The artist's statement is unquestionable; the work has surely been a labor of love. (p. 628)

> *Ethel L. Heins, "Early Winter Booklist: 'The Clown of God: An Old Story'," in* The Horn Book Magazine *(copyright © 1978 by The Horn Book, Inc., Boston), Vol. LIV, No. 6, December, 1978, pp. 627-28.*

Here the old story of a juggler's rise and fall and final miraculous performance before a statue of the Virgin and Child is presented with enough verbal energy and momentum to complement the splendid pictures, which are decorative in the best sense and filled with sub-Milton Glaser allusions to great Italian Renaissance paintings. These illustrations make the backgrounds of all those glorious portraits and altar pieces come alive; one recognizes faces from Piero della Francesca and many others in the crowds surrounding the juggler. But unlike so many picture books these days, this allusive art is not a self-indulgence but a spur to the artist's invention. Children wholly innocent of the Renaissance background will respond to the clear shapes and colors and to the generous scale of the images. This is one of the finest picture books of the year. (p. 93)

> *Harold C. K. Rice, "Good Looking," in* The New York Times Book Review *(© 1978 by The New York Times Company; reprinted by permission), December 10, 1978, pp. 72-3, 93.**

[*The Clown of God* is] a Renaissance version of *Godspell*. There are flat, pastel shades of the Quattrocento and a tale that blends myth with the glory of God. Less easy to shrug off along with the Christmas wrapping paper, this Christian tale about suffering and joy has a straightforward no-nonsense charm: and all manner of things shall be well.

> *Peter Fanning, "Kisses Colder than Ice," in* The Times Educational Supplement *(© Times Newspapers Ltd. (London) 1979; reproduced from* The Times Educational Supplement *by permission), No. 3311, November 23, 1979, p. 31.**

BILL AND PETE (1978)

If de Paola punched a time clock, he would earn millions in overtime. One of the hardest working and most popular author-illustrators proves in his latest that he can imbue anthropomorphs with the same appeal that his little humans boast. Near the Nile River, long ago, William Everett Crocodile chooses Pete the plover for his toothbrush, and they become friends as well. . . . Then, the Bad Guy (a human trapper) captures Bill

From The Clown of God: An Old Story, *written and illustrated by Tomie de Paola.*

and plans to make a suitcase of him. The solution to that problem is heady fun. The entertaining story is illustrated by de Paola's inimitable cartoons, in yummy pastels.

> *"Children's Books: 'Bill and Pete',"* in Publishers Weekly *(reprinted from the October 23, 1978 issue of* Publishers Weekly, *published by R. R. Bowker Company, a Xerox company; copyright © 1978 by Xerox Corporation), Vol. 214, No. 17, October 23, 1978, p. 61.*

[In **"Bill and Pete"**] a gifted, often facile artist—playing with a crocodile, a bird who serves as his toothbrush and a splendidly slimy crocodile-hunting Bad Guy—gives us bright Egyptian colors (yellow-green, pink, lavender and blue) and energetic cartoon forms; but without a narrative with at least some of the wit and brio of the illustrations, the reader's interest flags. (p. 73.)

> *Harold C. K. Rice, "Good Looking," in* The New York Times Book Review *(© 1978 by The New York Times Company; reprinted by permission), December 10, 1978, pp. 72-3, 93.**

SONGS OF THE FOG MAIDEN (1979)

The Fog Maiden who took the children on a dreamy outing **When Everyone Was Fast Asleep** . . . is reduced here to wandering about her Day Garden and Night Garden singing insipid little songs. . . . And the Fog Maiden's blue cat Token, a teasingly mysterious presence in his first appearance, outdoes his mistress in saccharin vapidity when the two leave to visit the earth: "I see children dreaming, fast asleep, / Till the stars begin to fade. / I watch, and protect my sweet dear friends / So they'll never be afraid." De Paola's sprightly cover promises a light, daytime version of the earlier book, but to the extent that **When Everyone** . . . succeeded it was by leaving such sappiness out.

> *"Picture Books: 'Songs of the Fog Maiden'," in* Kirkus Reviews *(copyright © 1979 The Kirkus Service, Inc.), Vol. XLVII, No. 6, March 15, 1979, p. 322.*

The illustrations for these "songs of innocence" are full of evocative textures, shapes, and colors so pleasing to the eye and the senses that they create a fantasy world all their own. In fact, their visual poetry completely upstages the poetry contained in the impressionistic story of the Fog Maiden who returns to her garden every day and offers a series of songs. De Paola's feelings are in the right place, but his language gets lost in repetitiveness, clichés, and highly predictable images. His verbal music is soft and gentle, but there is too little melody and drama to move the songs beyond being soporific chants. This would work as a lullabye book for very young children, but grade schoolers had trouble sitting still for it.

> *John Cech, "Picture Books: 'Songs of the Fog Maiden'," in* Children's Book Review Service *(copyright © 1979 Children's Book Review Service Inc.), Vol. 7, No. 9, April, 1979, p. 81.*

BIG ANTHONY AND THE MAGIC RING (1979)

Tomie de Paola's **"Big Anthony and the Magic Ring"** . . . is a knock-about slapstick folk tale set in early Renaissance Calabria. A goofy adolescent farm boy, who cleans the slops and tends the sheep of a shlumpy country witch, steals her magic ring and transforms himself into the John Travolta of the village dance. But his success is overwhelming: He's soon pursued by the disconcertingly predatory amorous local ladies, and is rescued by the witch in the knick of time. Though there's a disconcertingly misogynistic undertone to this farce, the comic energy and always professional, cartoon-Renaissance de Paola draftsmanship makes this one of the more entertaining picture books of the season.

> *Harold C. K. Rice, "Picture Books: 'Big Anthony and the Magic Ring'," in* The New York Times Book Review *(©1979 by The New York Times Company; reprinted by permission), April 29, 1979, p. 47.*

The magic of spring frames this funny tale illustrated with caricatures that in their earthiness seem to magnify its rollicking folk tale quality. Kids old enough to know what Night Life is, and the ancient meaning of spring for lovers, will find Big Anthony's predicament hilarious. Sexist, yes. But lots of fun anyway.

> *Marjorie Lewis, "Book Review: 'Big Anthony and the Magic Ring'," in* School Library Journal *(reprinted from the May, 1979 issue of* School Library Journal, *published by R. R. Bowker Co./A Xerox Corporation; copyright ©1979), Vol. 25, No. 9, May, 1979, p. 50.*

In a rerun of the popular **Strega Nona** . . . Big Anthony borrows not a magic pasta pot but a magic ring from his witch employer. . . . It's a good formula and it still works, but—repetition aside—this hasn't the delightful touches of **Strega Nona**.

> *"Picture Books: 'Big Anthony and the Magic Ring'," in* Kirkus Reviews *(copyright © 1979 The Kirkus Service, Inc.), Vol. XLVII, No. 10, May 15, 1979, p. 572.*

OLIVER BUTTON IS A SISSY (1979)

Oliver's father rudely shoos him out to play ball when he finds him playing paper dolls and dress-up instead, but, strangely, when Oliver demonstrates his dancing talent his parents buy him shiny new tap shoes and send him to Ms. Leah's Dancing School (all girl, as pictured) "for the exercise." The other boys continue to tease Oliver and when he doesn't win the talent contest he expects worse—only to find that his performance alone has prompted them to change the word "sissy" in the graffiti that gives the book its title to "star." De Paola "admits that a lot of Oliver Button's problems" were his— but we doubt that his vindication came so early and easy.

> *"Picture Books: 'Oliver Button Is a Sissy'," in* Kirkus Reviews *(copyright © 1979 The Kirkus Service, Inc.), Vol. XLVII, No. 12, June 15, 1979, p. 683.*

This is a gentle story that shows that it is all right to do nontraditional activities. The soft-colored, uncluttered illustrations lend themselves to story hours for small groups. The creative pen and brush of Tomie de Paola have produced another highly recommended and satisfying title for his growing audience.

> *Lee Beasley, "Picture Books: 'Oliver Button Is a Sissy'," in* Children's Book Review Service *(copyright © 1979 Children's Book Review Service Inc.), Vol. 7, No. 14, August, 1979, p. 132.*

There is a good balance between the simple text (usually one or two lines per page) and the expressive pictures which feature humorous characters in contemporary dress. De Paola cleverly achieves a whole range of color using only three—black, cinnamon brown, and turquoise—and sets up some exciting visual rhythms. All in all, an attractive little book that might offer reassurance to those readers who will identify with Oliver, as well as good counsel for their parents and teachers. Let's hope, however, that the story doesn't cause some as yet undefined sensitive soul to be branded.

> *Marilyn R. Singer, "Book Reviews: 'Oliver Button Is a Sissy'," in* School Library Journal *(reprinted from the October, 1979, issue of* School Library Journal, *published by R. R. Bowker Co./A Xerox Corporation; copyright © 1979), Vol. 26, No. 2, October, 1979, p. 138.*

FLICKS (1979)

Tomie de Paola pops up as an illustrator and author more than anyone else in the children's field. You just can't keep that man away from the drawing board. His **"Flicks"** . . . is a series of panels—"silent movies"—on time-worn themes: the bad tooth and the doorknob, blowing out the birthday candles, the skates and the pillow tied to your bottom, the new baby in the house and putting off sleep. They are merely pleasant for adults, but we must remember that a time-worn theme can be riotously new to a 5-year-old.

> *William Cole, "Children's Book: 'Flicks'," in* The New York Times Book Review *(© 1979 by The New York Times Company; reprinted by permission), October 21, 1979, p. 52.*

The vignettes are drawn up as moving pictures, and since it's a tribute to the old-timers, they're in black and white (pencil). The pink background isn't necessary. While these are silent pictures, the dedication is to stars of the talkies: Mae West, Shirley Temple and Mickey Mouse. No matter. These simple visuals will appeal to the youngest.

> *Helen Gregory, "Book Reviews: 'Flicks'," in* School Library Journal *(reprinted from the November, 1979 issue of* School Library Journal, *published by R. R. Bowker Co./A Xerox Corporation; copyright © 1979), Vol. 26, No. 3, November, 1979, p. 64.*

Shoring up his reputation as an author-illustrator as original as he is prolific, de Paola's latest should outdraw weekend TV cartoon shows. A haughty usher is at his post where a silent-movie audience, a gaggle of de Paola's instantly recognizable moppets, file by. . . . Every reel is a success, as proved by the audience's enthusiastic reception.

> *"Picture Books: 'Flicks'," in* Publishers Weekly *(reprinted from the November 19, 1979 issue of* Publishers Weekly, *published by R. R. Bowker Company, a Xerox company; copyright © 1979 by Xerox Corporation), Vol. 216, No. 21, November 19, 1979, p. 78.*

THE KIDS' CAT BOOK (1979)

Granny Twinkle is giving away kittens and tries to help Patrick decide which one to take. She describes characteristics of each breed, relates interesting bits of cat history, and gives some pointers on cat care. Patrick finally decides what to do, but his parents do not agree with him. The illustrations add great touches of humor and show cats being cats everywhere. All

those who have new kittens will find useful information. Those who do not have a kitten may want one after reading this.

> *Annette C. Blank, "Picture Books: 'The Kids' Cat Book'," in* Children's Book Review Service *(copyright © 1979 Children's Book Review Service Inc.), Vol. 8, No. 3, November, 1979, p. 21.*

Patrick goes to get a free kitten from Granny Twinkle (a sprightly dame in a lavender pants suit) and gets not only a kitten but a free lesson. . . . Although I generally prefer informational books without fictional frameworks, this could be a welcome addition to the library of the budding ailurophile. The *very* young reader may be somewhat bemused by the illustration of cats in "all different colors," including fuchsia and chartreuse, but I suspect that is just Mr. de Paola's little dig at his own two cats, who are pictured with him on the back flap of the jacket and who, he avers, "taught him everything he knows about cats, book illustration, cooking, and catching moles."

> *Georgess McHargue, "Children's Books: 'The Kids' Cat Book'," in* The New York Times Book Review *(© 1979 by The New York Times Company; reprinted by permission), December 23, 1979, p. 16.*

THE LADY OF GUADALUPE (1980)

This book recounts the legend of the Lady of Guadalupe, patron saint of Mexico, who appeared in 1531 to a poor, Christian Aztec named Juan Diego. The story is a simply told and well-developed narrative. The accompanying pencil, ink, and watercolor illustrations in soft, muted tones are appealing and appropriate. A publisher's note relates Mr. de Paola's lifelong interest in the legend and attests to the faithfulness of his version of the story to Mexican folklore, and to the accuracy of the drawings of sixteenth-century Mexican dress and architecture. A fine addition to the nonfiction section on Christian religion.

> *Glenda Broughton, "Younger Readers: 'The Lady of Guadalupe'," in* Children's Book Review Service *(copyright © 1980 Children's Book Review Service Inc.), Vol. 8, No. 9, April, 1980, p. 83.*

["**The Lady of Guadalupe**" is] a good story with a satisfying ending, simply told and illustrated in a style that is pleasant, if rather too pallid, static and unemotional to convey the folk art or landscape of Mexico. With its pretty imagery and humble hero, the story is one that non-Catholics can also enjoy on the level of folktale (indeed, the essentials of the entire story are familiar to folklorists). The tale is also available in a Spanish edition.

> *Georgess McHargue, "Children's Books: 'The Lady of Guadalupe'," in* The New York Times Book Review *(© 1980 by The New York Times Company; reprinted by permission), June 15, 1980, p. 21.*

The legend of the Lady of Guadalupe, patron saint of Mexico, is one of the most popular and appealing traditional religious stories of the Western hemisphere. At the great shrine a four-hundred-year-old *tilma* is imprinted with the image of a woman dressed as an Aztec princess. According to the author's note, the portrait has a particular fascination for artists, who have tried unsuccessfully over the years to duplicate its coloring and technique; and this sense of appreciation and reverence infuses the familiar story with fresh vitality. The text is commendably restrained, conversational but not sentimental. The handsome

While the book may lead children to think that all those who suffer a stroke improve, and while it's not quite believable that no other person gives therapeutic assistance to the old man, it's still a satisfying story of one kind of family love. (pp. 168-69)

> Zena Sutherland, "New Titles for Children and Young People: 'Now One Foot, Now the Other'," in Bulletin of the Center for Children's Books *(reprinted by permission of The University of Chicago Press;* © *1981 by The University of Chicago), Vol. 34, No. 9, May, 1981, pp. 168-69.*

De Paola has applied to this more subtle problem the same sensitivity he demonstrated in both text and pictures in **Nana Upstairs and Nana Downstairs**. . . . Explanations are forthright and appropriate to readers' level of understanding. The tone is gentle and low-key and the illustrations are, as usual, first-rate. (pp. 105-06)

> Karen Harris, "Book Reviews: 'Now One Foot, Now the Other'," in School Library Journal *(reprinted from the September, 1981 issue of* School Library Journal, *published by R. R. Bowker Co./A Xerox Corporation; copyright* © *1981), Vol. 28, No.1, September, 1981, pp. 105-06.*

Like its companion piece, **"Nana Upstairs and Nana Downstairs,"** this is a big and difficult story compressed into a small and simple story. Mr. de Paola is able somehow to leave nothing out—not even the horror of Bob's first efforts to speak after his stroke—and yet present a warm and positive picture of the power of love.

To be sure, Bobby is an unusual child. A number of us have gone through the experience of living with a grandparent who has been knocked out of kilter by a stroke. It is not a happy experience. I recall, with shame, my own strong desire to be somewhere else. This reaction is probably the norm, but norms are by no means necessarily attractive. Perhaps this "little" story will help other children to see past their distress into actions that are useful and more satisfying all the way around, even if they are not all as successful as Bobby's.

The illustrations are exactly right. In calm browns and blues, with figures that are just realistic enough, they reinforce the straightforward tone of the prose. Mr. de Paola is very good with color; he knows how to use its subtle messages. Even the single addition of skin tones would have tipped the work off-balance. As it stands—and it stands with admirable steadiness—it is a handsome book with pleasingly large type and a sturdy, square format. Not all-occasion reading, but there is a place for it—a sad place that perhaps it can make a little brighter.

> Natalie Babbitt, "Children's Books: 'Now One Foot, Now the Other'," in The New York Times Book Review *(*© *1981 by The New York Times Company; reprinted by permission), September 20, 1981, p. 30.*

FIN M'COUL: THE GIANT OF KNOCKMANY HILL (1981)

Fin M'Coul comes alive through Tomie de Paola's comic illustrating and retelling of his tale. You can almost hear Fin's Irish brogue as you read the story. It is interesting to note that Fin's strength comes not from his size, but rather from his wife's clever schemes. De Paola has certainly added another winner to his collection of fairy tales, one that is sure to be a favorite in any folktale collection.

> Fellis L. Jordon, "Picture Books: 'Fin M'Coul: The Giant of Knockmany Hill'," in Children's Book Review Service *(copyright* © *1981 Children's Book Review Service Inc.), Vol. 9, No. 10, May, 1981, p. 81.*

Children of picture book age won't mind that Tomie de Paola's retelling of the mythic confrontation between two of Ireland's favorite heroes doesn't feel very Irish or very heroic. The author/artist, known for a number of imaginative books, has opted here for a domestic comedy, populated by giants, dimwitted and dopey-looking.

The situation is funny: For all his size and power, good giant Fin is terrified of being beaten to a pulp by bad, even bigger giant Cucullin, but he's saved by his clever wife Oonagh. . . . The proceedings are suitably silly, and it's satisfying to watch Cucullin's own stupidity do him in once he mistakes huge, redhaired Fin—disguised in frilly pink nightie and lace cap and squashed into a cradle—as a real baby.

The book is a large, comfortable size, but unfortunately the pictures have been enclosed inside half-page frames, which makes the visual world feel crowded. The giants' giant-size doesn't quite register—they seem cramped, rather than huge—while the slapstick action lacks enough open space to generate the off-the-wall energy this approach really calls for. Still, scenes of mighty Fin done up as a baby are a giggle.

> Elaine Edelman, "Children's Books: 'Fin M'Coul: The Giant of Knockmany Hill'," in The New York Times Book Review *(*© *1981 by The New York Times Company; reprinted by permission), May 24, 1981, p. 18.*

The story of Cucullin and Fin M'Coul is presented in quite a different way. The action comes in packed half-page pictures, on which the giant forms of the protagonists are squashed, giving just the right scale to each scene. The accompanying text is framed with Celtic motifs. Much as we may admire the sheer cleverness of the book it is the humour that lives longest in the mind. This is the perfect version of the immemorial theme of the triumph of cunning over force, and Mr. de Paola tells it for all it is worth. There are some lovely moments: Fin busy building the Giants' Causeway, his lovely wife Oonagh unflappable in the face of danger, Fin as an improbable baby in his enormous cradle, and in each domestic scene three minute leprachauns, a sheep and a cat unobtrusively busy in a corner of the picture. Very good stuff this. It can scarcely fail to delight today's tough and rumbustious kids.

> "The New Books: 'Fin M'Coul: The Giant of Knockmany Hill'," in The Junior Bookshelf, *Vol. 45, No. 4, August, 1981, p. 144.*

Elizabeth Enright

1909-1968

American author/illustrator of fiction for children, short story writer for adults, and critic. Enright is recognized as an outstanding contributor to the genres of realistic fiction and fantasy for children. She is often called the American counterpart to the nineteenth century writer E. Nesbit for her successful creation of imaginative, relevant, and well-written books. Enright presents the state of childhood as a secure and happy one—her children come from families where relationships among all members, regardless of age, are based on love and mutual support. Although Enright's works do not exclude the pain and conflicts of childhood, they stress its joys in language often praised for its beauty and clarity. The accuracy of her dialogue and the appeal of her characterizations have also been noted, and her books are among those determined to have lasting value.

Perhaps Enright's most popular characters are the Melendy family, four motherless children of varying ages who live in New York City with their father and housekeeper. Introduced in *The Saturdays*, the Melendys return in three sequels which show the growing individuality and maturity of each child while underscoring the importance of the family unit. Enright created the Melendys to do all the things she had wanted to accomplish while growing up; Randy, the middle child who wants to be a dancer and an artist, is Enright's characterization of herself. Enright's parents were illustrators, and they instilled in her a strong love of art and literature, especially of classic children's books and their illustrations. She wrote the text of her first book, *Kintu: A Congo Adventure*, around some pictures she had drawn, and discovered "the phenomenon in writing—the way memories came back fresh and unexpected." She eventually gave up illustration to concentrate solely on writing.

To create her next work, *Thimble Summer*, Enright drew on her experiences from a summer spent on her uncle's farm during a drought and from the stories her mother and grandmother told about their childhoods. Her perceptive depiction of Garnet and her evocation of Midwestern country life were called exceptional; the book won the Newbery Medal in 1939. Fascination with the natural world is also present in *Gone-Away Lake* and *Return to Gone-Away*. The excitement in discovering the old lake and forgotten mansion and the comfortable relationship between young and old characters are considered especially appealing in both works.

Although she included elements of fantasy in her earlier fiction, Enright did not write her first complete book in this genre until near the end of her career. Her last two works are seen as successful combinations of fairy-tale tradition and original invention. In *Tatsinda*, Enright creates a world that is solid and consistent, yet delicate and enchanting; she also makes some subtle points about prejudice and greed. Several critics feel that *Tatsinda* contains some of Enright's finest writing. *Zeee* is less profound, but features an irascible, memorable title character. Despite occasional objections to precious dialogue and contrived plotting, critical reception of Enright's works is usually positive. She is regarded as one of the few writers for children who could express herself to them in a natural, sensitive, and literate way. The fact that her books remain favorites suggests that she satisfies her audience's need for both entertainment and substance in their literature. (See also *Contemporary Authors*, Vols. 61-64; obituary, Vols. 25-28, rev. ed.; *Something about the Author*, Vol. 9.)

AUTHOR'S COMMENTARY

What vivifies the sense of reality in fiction begins in the vast domain of one's own experience and observation. I use the word vast because even for those who lead the quietest lives this domain is far larger and less used than we ever dream. Everything that has happened to us or been observed by us is recorded and stored in that enormous unseen territory. Parts of it, of course, are hidden from us by ourselves forever, but other parts return to view mysteriously when needed, or even without bidding. (p. 165)

One of the phenomena we discover in writing for children is that in returning to the trail we trod in our earliest days much of that far region is revealed to us by details that infer the whole. We turn inward to see the landscape, and faces of dolls, forgotten for scores of years, look out at us—their names come back to us, even the smell of the glue that held their wigs together. Weather comes back to us—the way the wind made weeping noises in the porch screen and the rain wrote cuneiform symbols on that screen, always running down in joints and elbows, never straight or curving. Sounds come back to us—a meadow lark calls and there we are in early morning, all the grasses blazed and tufted. The milkman's horse stamps and jingles and smells wonderful, and the milkman offers us a ride. Looking inward we remember that was bliss. Or at another time we relive for an instant the almost physical feeling of boredom that could suddenly attack us, making us want to howl or hit someone. Or we remember the wild, unreasoning happiness of certain evenings that caused us to career around the garden like a dog let out, shouting for nothing except the excellence of shouting.

These things come back and we know them again and use them, and if we use them well the book seems real because in essence, if not in fact, what happens in the book has roots in what *was* real.

The highest accolade a child can pay a book is to say: "I felt just as if it was happening to me." And all of us can remember with the child this first revealing, altogether fascinating sense of identification, of being at once oneself and someone else: that third person whose adventures, in nearly every case, far transcended ours in glamour and excitement. The third-person part was important. (pp. 165-66)

[For] the most part reality seemed realer in the third-person books.

When we speak of reality I feel that we mean less that which is current, factual, a part of known life, than that which is universal in the personality, action, and reaction of the characters, whether they are people, animals, or even objects. (p. 166)

Perhaps it would be helpful for me, as a practitioner of realistic fiction for children, to try to be a little more specific about how I proceed, how I deal with stories of current children, with current mores—children who live in our time, use our colloquialisms, know and explore a familiar world. The children of these stories are not too good and not too bad. Perhaps they are always a *little* more reasonable and ingenious than live children are apt to be, but on the whole one tries to make them seem real, and in the imagination they do seem real, often taking matters into their own hands and changing the trend of the story. Indeed it is desirable that they should do so.

They are, of course, edited, as all fiction characters are edited. Their conversations are to the point; in the tales about them, as in tales about adults, they cannot be allowed all the ragtag slack of daily life, all the humdrum comings and goings and yawnings and coughings and desultory chatter.

As a friend of mine once remarked in a moment of profound insight: "Life is so daily!"

Since it does not have to be like that in books, the characters are edited to some extent because they must be. They are not, however, edited to fit the plot. If one conceives of them as real they will, as I have said, take on a life of their own and out of that life—or rather, those interreacting lives—the plot is built, just as it is in living itself. Of course, like the characters, their living is edited too. It is apt to be kinder than the real thing; also neater, more just, and more exciting. Things turn out well in the end. But, unlike life, the end of the story comes at the high point. We do not have to go on with these people through high school, college, marriage, mortgage payments, child rearing, money worries, dental problems, old age, death, or any of the rest of it. It is our privilege to leave them in their happiness forever: another of the joys in writing about them.

Nevertheless the life of our characters must be believable while it lasts, and it will be if *they* are. There are many ways to make this happen. One is to have some children of your own around the house. Listen to what they have to say (you won't have any trouble) and you will learn a lot. First you learn the current slang. For another thing you will discover how fresh the language of an observant child can be. (pp. 168-69)

[A] child uses language without resort to cliché. The cliché does not yet exist for him. He describes as he sees, and that is what we must try to do and what we ought to do for the rest of our lives, whether we write or talk: treat language as though it were our own, a perpetually new and valued means of conveying to others our reaction and experience. But alas we seldom do. Among the best work of our current adult authors we still find the man whose brows "shoot up in surprise" and who has a muscle that twitches in his cheek when he is under stress.

But it is the children, mistakenly believed by many to be the easiest audience to write for, who are most often insulted by the use of cliché: they of all people, for whom language should be as scrupulously exact and germane to the material as one can possibly make it!

And here we come to the use of detail. Most children are fascinated by it in illustration and, when freshly presented, in their reading. I suppose this is in part because a child begins to perceive life through details. He is too young for generalities; they simply do not exist for him. In infancy he examines his own fist for minutes at a time, learns his mother's face, dis-

covers his toes, the bells of his rattle, and so on. He learns piece by piece, each piece a bit of the larger mosaic of which later on he will see the pattern or a part of it. Probably no one ever sees it whole. (pp. 169-70)

In presenting detail, then, how can we make it fresh and recognizable? One way that works, and why that is I do not quite know, is the use of simile: the describing of something in terms of something else to make it more vivid to the imagination.

For instance: Delphinium buds look like blue tadpoles. Commas look like polliwogs. . . .

But of course the use of simile is only one tool to make a scene sharp, though it is a useful, incisive one. And there are others, but the most important one is the true wish to convey, to make credible.

All of this is the sum of what I think to be the means of creating believable characters in a believable story: first our own experience remembered; then the observation of children themselves and the respect for their vision of life, still not smudged or overlaid with the dust of repetition. Then the inward view: the deeper remembering—*not* so that one writes autobiography per se, but so that one regains a partial sense of that first naked clarity of response to things, people, situations, and surroundings. We will find in this recovered sharpening of sense that not only early memories but early wishes are revived. Did we wish for brothers and sisters when we had none? Or to live in the country instead of the city? Or to find a treasure or a jewel when all we ever found was safety pins and pennies? Now we have a chance to grant our wishes: another joy.

So one reaches the conclusion that there are four things: observation and experience are the blood and bone, while wish and memory are the mind and heart that make book children real. (p. 170)

Elizabeth Enright, "Realism in Children's Literature," in The Horn Book Magazine *(copyright © 1967, by The Horn Book, Inc., Boston), Vol. XLIII, No. 2, April, 1967, pp. 165-70.*

GENERAL COMMENTARY

There is one type of story where [children being on their own] is essential, the story about the solitary child, where everything and everybody else becomes background, to be seen through her eyes. We are concerned here with the poetry of living, a single, private affair. Among the riotous family chronicles of Elizabeth Enright, two books stand out for their concentration of atmosphere. *Thimble Summer* is the story of a few months in the life of Garnet Linden, a nine-year-old girl on a farm in the Middle West. Garnet is not a recluse. She works in the harvest field, she goes to a country fair, she helps in the house and the farmyard. All the same, the book is a record of private pleasures, of an enchanted summer. Here is a child seeing familiar surroundings with the fresh vision of her age. In *The Sea Is All Around*, Mab Kendall opens sharp eyes and ears to an unfamiliar world, an island she is visiting off the New England coast, with the noise of the sea, the oddness of the people, the delight of new objects, all to discover. This kind of story cannot be written to order. It must come from a mind recollecting in tranquillity the joys of childhood. (p. 270)

Margery Fisher, "Little Birds in Their Nests Agree," in her Intent Upon Reading: A Critical Appraisal of Modern Fiction for Children *(copyright © 1961 by Margery Fisher), Hodder & Stoughton Children's*

Books (formerly Brockhampton Press), 1961, pp. 270-96.*

Throughout my reading of [Elizabeth Enright's books], I have often thought of Katherine Mansfield (who, however, published nothing for children): of how both women wrote short stories but no novels, though they tried; and of how both had such an uncanny understanding of the "febrile, evanescent moments of inner childhood" [Meindert DeJong], of children's odd, quirky thinking (which Richard Hughes has called mad), of their unpredictable reactions, extraordinary imaginings, their moods and obscure longings. It is as if these writers were themselves children but possessing, miraculously, the ability to put into words the life of childhood in a way no child ever can, in prose that stretches the imagination and lengthens and intensifies one's sight. Then, too, I felt as I read, there was something else: an indefinable echo—an imagery, was it? a particular way of seeing?—that reminded me of Mansfield. "The duck took matters more calmly, warping herself sideways, like a little ferryboat . . . ," Elizabeth Enright observes in *Gone-Away Lake.*

But do I mean that I sense in this imagery Elizabeth Enright speaking in Mansfield's voice? No, never that. Only that I kept noticing in her prose the same precise, ironic wit, the same wonderful sense of the absurd. . . . Like Katherine Mansfield she delights in the comic aspects of life and of human beings, their qualities and idiosyncrasies. . . . She, too, has an equal purity and sharpness of observation which only poets and the child-eyed have. (p. 642)

[Each] writer—both Mansfield and Enright—created out of her own spiritual world, out of her own private sensibilities and ways of reacting. Because of Elizabeth Enright's more positive philosophy of life, at least as shown in her writing, we never find in her short stories [for adults] the black bitterness and cynicism that lie beneath Katherine Mansfield's "Je Ne Parle Pas Français." . . . Certainly, in most of Elizabeth Enright's work, there is a positive rather than a negative confrontation to be felt, no matter with what irony and clarity of insight she views the human condition.

There is, of course, given this clarity, more than one kind of cruelty depicted in her work for adults. . . . But this element is, for the most part, left out of her books for children. It is true that Mark Herron's cousin, Oren Meeker, with whom Mark lives in the Melendy book, *Then There Were Five,* is a cold and villainous man who cares nothing for the boy; that Mark would have been shot at or unmercifully beaten had Oren and his drinking companions discovered Mark spying on them and listening to their plans for him; and that Oren dies in a drunken stupor in a fire of his own making. It is true that there is evil and planned cruelty in Miss Enright's fairy tale, *Tatsinda;* but there is traditionally more often the depiction of overt cruelty and evil in this form of literature which children have taken for their own than there is in their realistic literature, and the author was writing wholly inside the tradition.

It is fascinating, and could be instructive for those who wish to write for children, to note the echoing that rings back and forth between certain scenes in Elizabeth Enright's short stories and in her books for children, scenes in which the same, or almost the same happening is used but which, though written with equal artistry in both cases, reveal a change in implication, in tone, in the reverberation of mood in the children's book. In *Then There Were Five* there are two especially perfect chapters, V and VII, both belonging to young Oliver, one having

to do with his passion for moths and the other with his passion for fishing. Apparently simple as they are as far as action is concerned, quite without struggle or crisis (at least in the present, we must say of Chapter VII), they are nevertheless so conceived, so shaped, and so written that they linger on in the mind because of the intensity of the author's seeing, because of the completeness of her empathy with Oliver. (pp. 643-45)

[In the] author's children's books the adult protagonists, with the exception of Oren Meeker, do not direct children's lives through either tyranny or bullying, nor through the imposition of those social niceties by which Curtis's grandmother ruled him [in the adult short story **"The House by the River"**]. In the Melendy books, the children's mother is dead, their father is away on government business, and Cuffy, the housekeeper, maintains a kind of order by means of affectionate, often exasperated, firmness. In the Gone-Away books, though there is evasion and secrets are kept, parents and uncles and aunts are loving, but firm when it comes to chores; put up with the usual amount of noise and dirt produced by furiously energetic children; and join with them in the last of *Gone-Away Lake* and throughout the whole of *Return to Gone-Away* in the carrying out of a mutually satisfying project. There can be little doubt that Elizabeth Enright had a belief about family life which included the conviction that children have a need not only for hours of unplanned privacy, but for spiritual buttressing with the kind of family love that directs lightly but with assurance. (pp. 646-47)

Elizabeth Enright was never inclined to present the kind of reality that would introduce into her children's books psychosis, sadism, hatred between parents and children, horror, and death—with the one exception of Oren Meeker's—although these are a part of the lives of many children and although most children are well aware of the brutalities of humankind as well as of the brutalities resulting from the mindless movements of fate. It might be said that such a writer, bringing to bear those awarenesses and experiences of childhood she portrayed with such insight in her short stories, could have given us a powerful children's book quite different from and possibly more valuable, more "needful," than any she ever wrote. (p. 648)

I do not know what, exactly, Elizabeth Enright would have answered to this, but I suspect that she would have declared a writer does his best work in any field of literature only when he writes, not at the response of a need from the outside, but out of the compulsions and requirements of his own being. Nevertheless it is true, as J. B. Priestley has pointed out, that "The writer of genius cannot help responding to the innermost needs of his age; he sees and reports what in its depths it asks him to see and report." And for almost all gifted and sensitive writers, inner and outer needs are very often synonymous. Elizabeth Enright's fairy tale, *Tatsinda,* is about discrimination and greed, two deeply rooted evils of our time that may yet defeat us; it was published in 1963 but it is interesting to note that we find the first hint of it near the end of *Then There Were Five,* so that apparently it had been brewing for at least ten years. (p. 649)

[Perhaps] there existed in Elizabeth Enright a conviction about the family which can freely respect both individuality and privacy: a conviction having to do with communion between old and young. Mab, in *The Sea Is All Around,* during a period of unhappy withdrawal, temporarily rejects old Yancey Bates, who owns a Curiosity Shop filled with relics of the New England past and who tells her one engrossing story after another concerning the objects she picks up and questions him about. But after the winter is over and she has found friends her own age, one knows she will go back for other stories and, more deeply perhaps, for the sense of security and comfort his shop and personality bestow. In *Thimble Summer,* there are Mr. Freebody and the Zangles, all of whom have a special feeling for Garnet, and it is Citronella's great-grandmother, Mrs. Eberhardt, who tells Garnet and Citronella stories of her own childhood in Wisconsin. There is Mrs. Oliphant in the Melendy books who is the children's close friend and, of course, Jasper Titus, Oliver's companion, who is just as young as he in so many ways. . . . As for old Tanda-nan, Tatsinda's friend and mentor, she is far more than simply a good fairy or a good magician in the traditional sense; she is a real personality, her unique qualities carrying her beyond the traditional fairy-tale protagonist. When you come to think of it, there is not one of Elizabeth Enright's children's books (with the exception of *Zeee*) in which there is not a fruitful and satisfying relationship between young and old.

She must greatly have loved and valued the past, a loving and valuing which is implicit in these relationships between young and old, in the storytelling, and in the fact that the Melendys, and then the Jarmans and the Blakes in the Gone-Away books, all find big old comfortable houses in the country to live in. She must have felt very strongly a sense of the past and its power for good, and believed that this is another thing children need to be given in a society which she spoke of as being sick as long ago as 1939 in her Newbery Acceptance speech. I think she believed that in the rootless, swiftly changing cities—where everything old is being destroyed and built over; where families never stay in one house for long, sometimes for less than a year, and very often exist in box-like compartments in huge modern buildings utterly lacking in either character or atmosphere; and where grandparents, no longer living close by, have no opportunity to tell children of their own childhoods—a sense of the past is being lost and with it that invaluable sense of continuity which can be so strangely potent and fortifying, and the lack of which, so destructive. (pp. 650-51)

．　．　．　．　．

[Though] Elizabeth Enright lived in New York almost all her life and many of her stories for adults are New York stories, only one of her children's books, *The Saturdays* . . . has a city background. . . . It is the country—real, deep country—that thereafter becomes Elizabeth Enright's "place," affording her far more potency than the city ever could in bringing to all her senses and to her writing, not mere background, but a full, vibrant awareness of the natural world. Possibly remembering the joy with which she evoked Wisconsin countryside and country people in *Thimble Summer* . . . she realized that if she was to do her best work she must go back to the country again. *The Saturdays* was a fine book containing fresh story material, and the qualities of each Melendy child unfold with quiet sureness. Yet, for me, it is not so good as the succeeding Melendy books, nor does it compare with the two Gone-Away books. It is revealing that a city episode in *The Four-Story Mistake*—the winning by Mona, the oldest Melendy child, of a role in a continuing radio play, which would be a glamorous happening in any teen-ager's life—seems almost artificial, a catering to audience, when one compares it with the quiet childhood truth of those two chapters of Oliver's . . . in *Then There Were Five;* indeed, when one compares it with any of the country happenings in the other books. (p. 27)

[We] come upon a certain description which closes one of her finest short stories, **"Borrowed Summer"**—the picture of "a river with a mane of mists, hills ten miles across a valley, all the different kinds of green, the revelatory tones of sunrise and the enormous phantoms of aurora borealis." And we realize that for Elizabeth Enright, too, this country had given her, as it had her poor nonhero, "the intimate knowledge of a loved time and place," and "a memory which included birds, weeds, vegetables, animals, and human love and work and leisure." It is all of these things, intensely felt and remembered, which have gone into making the richness of her children's books. (p. 28)

Children would not especially note the fact that in her books for them (as in her work for adults) she was capable of handling with striking success either realism or fantasy as well as a number of different kinds of structures: the plotted story, as in *Spiderweb for Two* and *Tatsinda;* the linked incident tale, such as *Thimble Summer, The Sea Is All Around,* and all of the Melendy books except *Spiderweb;* and the linked incidents in which plot is lightly woven throughout, as in both Gone-Away books. Nor will they realize how these books have been lifted above the superficial, the ephemeral—in which one hangs on from page to page simply to find out what happens next—into the universal, the timeless, because of Elizabeth Enright's extraordinary ability to hear and see and smell, and to communicate with freshness and originality of phrase each of her perceptions. But children's continuing love of her books, generation after generation, testifies to the fact that they are responding wholeheartedly to that ability of hers to take notice with her entire being.

Few children would be consciously aware of the artistry in the dialogue that goes on among Elizabeth Enright's child characters: her unfailing fidelity in these conversations to the sound of childhood, her remarkable gift of capturing both the overt humor that compels her child reader to burst into laughter as well as the subtle, implied humor, growing out of both character and situation, that warms him deep inside, though why he cannot tell or would not stop to think. As for adults, we recall how perfectly the conversational tone of Minnehaha Cheever and her brother Tarquin places them in precisely that era when the old Gone-Away mansions were new and in that social milieu of which these mansions were symbols, but it is a tone tempered by the couple's own naturalness, humanity, and a kindliness always lighted with humor. (pp. 28-9)

Because the essence of any creator gets back into the system through the work he has left, it comforts me that the essence of Elizabeth Enright as an artist and as a human being will get back year after year through the children, whose minds and imaginations are fresh and hungry and eager. (p. 30)

Eleanor Cameron, "The Art of Elizabeth Enright," in The Horn Book Magazine *(copyright © 1969, 1970 by The Horn Book, Inc., Boston), Vol. XLV, No. 6, December, 1969 and Vol. XLVI, No. 1, February, 1970, pp. 641-51; 26-30.*

The Melendy children have individual voices and a communal voice as members of a united, if argumentative, family. . . .

Though the freedom of the countryside has been somewhat curtailed since the Melendys began their fictional lives, and a dollar and a half would finance little enough nowadays, the fresh, lively chatter of the books has not dated. Elizabeth Enright brings the Melendys to life through their appearance, their likes and dislikes and the way they change as they grow older, and has given them substance by a domestic background that does much to explain their warm-hearted, rackety, intelligent attitude to life. (p. 224)

> *Margery Fisher, "Who's Who in Children's Books: The Melendys," in her* Who's Who in Children's Books: A Treasury of the Familiar Characters of Childhood *(copyright © 1975 by Margery Fisher; reprinted by permission), Holt, Rinehart and Winston, Weidenfeld & Nicolson, 1975, pp. 223-24.*

KINTU: A CONGO ADVENTURE   (1935)

In its own way this is as pretty a piece of bookmaking . . . as I have seen this long while. Kintu is a chief's son, a small boy whose one trouble is that he is afraid of the jungle, something highly inconvenient in view of his future. . . . [In] the end Kintu spends the night in a tree and has to kill a leopard that tries to share it with him. In the morning he wakes to find himself not in the least afraid of his surroundings. The tribe celebrates both his return and his unexpected glory as a hunter, and that, said Kintu in effect, is that.

This is neatly told, in just enough words; the pictures, both small and full-page, are in bright colors and the blackest of black, very brisk and tidy. A sly humor plays over both text and illustrations, and a sort of moral, good for children of lighter complexion, dodges among the branches. The book will last, I think; it is worth keeping for its looks and its naive wisdom.

> *May Lamberton Becker, "Books for Young People: 'Kintu: A Congo Adventure'," in* New York Herald Tribune Books *(© I.H.T. Corporation; reprinted by permission), November 17, 1935, p. 29.*

The style is simple and direct and the incidents well suited to children's interests. It would seem, however, that boys and girls old enough to enjoy Kintu's adventures might prefer pictures that really illustrated the text. The story is straightforward and realistic, but in her drawings Elizabeth Enright has not taken her characters or her audience seriously, with the result that the pictures seem to belong in a book for children much younger than those to whom the story itself will appeal.

> *Anne T. Eaton, "Children's Books: 'Kintu: A Congo Adventure'," in* The New York Times Book Review *(© 1935 by The New York Times Company; reprinted by permission), November 17, 1935, p. 31.*

THIMBLE SUMMER   (1938)

This is a story for 8 to 11 year-old children of the sort for which there is a constant demand; one of everyday life among contemporary children, yet it is in no sense a made-to-order book. Rather it seems to have sprung spontaneously from the author's own happy experience of life on a Middle Western farm, and in its expression of a child's awareness of the small delights of living it approaches in spirit Elizabeth Coatsworth's lovely "Alice-All-by-Herself."

If Garnet believed that the particularly happy Summer described here was the result of finding a silver thimble in mud-flats of the creek, it is scarcely necessary to point the moral that much of her joy came from her own responsive and adventurous nature. At any rate, the tension and discouragement of long weeks of drought was broken that night. . . . There were friendly visits with the neighbors; a small adventure with

From Kintu: A Congo Adventure, *written and illustrated by Elizabeth Enright.*

her friend Citronella; and the kind of stories which placid grandmothers like to spin about their own childhood.

There is the flavor of real life in this story, expressed with charm and humor. The author's illustrations, both the line drawings and those in clear, bright colors, are unusual in style, and possess an attractive quality of quaintness.

> *"The New Books for Younger Readers," in* The New York Times Book Review *(© 1938 by The New York Times Company; reprinted by permission), August 21, 1938, p. 10.**

Garnet is bound to entertain all who meet her. Younger boys and girls will like her modern looks at once in her gay and adventurous pictures. High school boys and girls may easily pick her up, have a good laugh and remark, "Some kid."

> *"Browsing among the New Books," in* The Christian Science Monitor *(reprinted by permission from* The Christian Science Monitor; *© 1938 The Christian Science Publishing Society; all rights reserved), August 25, 1938, p. 6.**

Now and again people ask me what book to send to a child in some other country—usually England—to represent the best we have to offer, in our own characteristic way, to children of that age. For the rest of the year at least I shall tell such people to get **"Thimble Summer"** for the discriminating age of eight-to-ten. I would be glad to have our own eight-year-olds generally provided with it.

Garnet Linden was halfway between nine and ten when the long drought broke on their farm, solid and sleepy at the bend of the Wisconsin road. When that day and that storm were over, and "it almost seemed as if she could hear roots deep in the wet earth drinking and coming to life again," but one of ten good chapters has passed, but there can be no doubt that the book is the real thing. The great power of being able to make a reader feel and smell and touch as well as hear and see, has made itself evident. . . .

From Thimble Summer, *written and illustrated by Elizabeth Enright.*

Garnet is one with whom the fates co-operate; they like her; so will any one. They will like her hen Brunnhilde, and her pig, and her best friend, Citronella Hauser, and the dime store and the country fair and the mysterious stranger.

And if they know anything about balance and beauty in book-making they will be happy with those line drawings, lucent end papers in color, and lively and youthful full-page color plates, and especially with the way they all hold together to make a harmonious book. I read it first on a ship full of tired, apprehensive adults; it gave me brief contact with youth and happiness. We can do with plenty of such contacts this year. I am glad that this Wisconsin summer comes to the winter of our discontent.

> *"Books for Young People: 'Thimble Summer',"* in The New York Herald Tribune Books *(© I.H.T. Corporation; reprinted by permission), October 2, 1938, p. 6.*

At first sight [**Thimble Summer**] seems like a trans-Atlantic Enid Blyton, but there is a punch and precision in the writing, a sensuous and imaginative use of detail, which give it a more lasting value. The characters, dialogue and small-town rural atmosphere are all significantly real—but the book is no feminine *Tom Sawyer* either, and some readers may find a slight sense of contrivance and the lack of a fully integrating story.

> *Jerome Hanratty, "'Thimble Summer'"* (© Granada Publishing Limited 1960; reprinted by permission of the author), in The Use of English, *Vol. XII, No. 1, Autumn, 1960, p. 66.*

[American writers during the 'thirties could be] most beautifully simple, particularly when they wrote . . . of their own rural and small-town life. Elizabeth Enright's Garnet in *Thimble Summer* . . . was as American as Huck Finn. There was a fine frankness and spiritual toughness in a story which grew naturally without an invention on the author's part. (p. 80)

> *Marcus Crouch, "Renaissance," in his* Treasure Seekers and Borrowers: Children's Books in Britain 1900-1960 *(© Marcus Crouch, 1962), The Library Association, 1962, pp. 55-86.**

Thimble Summer by Elizabeth Enright reveals the author's insights into the concerns of childhood and the characters who share these concerns in a beautiful real-life drama that sings with the joy and contentment of a little girl whose roots sink deep into a well-loved farm home. . . . *Thimble Summer* underscores the dignity of family life on a Midwestern farm. . . . [The story's events] entertain the reader greatly with their humor, excitement, and delightful characterization. (p. 378)

> *Constantine Georgiou, "Realism in Children's Literature," in his* Children and Their Literature *(© 1969; reprinted by permission of Prentice-Hall, Inc., Englewood Cliffs, New Jersey 07632), Prentice-Hall, 1969, pp. 359-412.**

THE SEA IS ALL AROUND (1940)

From the moment when Mab . . . exchanges with her aunt at the railway station one of those deaf-and-dumb farewells that go on through glass till trains draw out, her experiences are those of an alert American child receptive to influences of nature and interested in doings of man. With simple sincerity, Mab's world is carried into the consciousness of a reader. A young reader takes it for granted; this is a lively, lovable account of a little girl's winter on an island off the New England coast, as "Thimble Summer" was of its season in the Middle West. Little girls happily share it. Older readers, however, will share with them her intuitive sense of the beauty of America. It is something we need just now.

It has a personality. It opens gently, like the night-blooming cereus the neighbors gather to watch, an event in the life of the community. It leaves a sense that after the print stops, the story will go on, a child's life on an island of peace.

A child gets, through Mab, a sense of the goodness and gayety of New England winters; of their round of nature and festivals; of school and friendship and the enveloping kindness people show a child far from home. It is told as it happens; pictures do much of the telling. Some are spirited black-and-white, but a large proportion is in color, wind-blown and free. On the title-page an oil lamp stands for much in island life. The book itself is full of light.

> *May Lamberton Becker, "Books for Young People: 'The Sea Is All Around'," in* New York Herald Tribune Books *(© I.H.T. Corporation; reprinted by permission), November 10, 1940, p. 12.*

["**The Sea Is All Around**"] is fifteen hundred miles removed in scene from "**Thimble Summer**," but it has the same sensitive appreciation which makes a kind of magic out of the everyday things of a little girl's world.

Like Garnet, Mab is a Middle Westerner, and loving her sun-warmed creeks and rolling hills, is just as ready to discover the salty delights of Pokenick, an island off the New England

From The Sea Is All Around, *written and illustrated by Elizabeth Enright.*

coast which bears a strong resemblance to Nantucket. . . . [Here] Mab learned to know the shady streets of old houses, the windy sweep of the moors, the loveliness of the marshes in the sudden New England Spring. As Mab comes to know them the reader knows them too in all their overtones, so sharply are the impressions made in exactly the right words. Lovely as the writing is, this is not a precious book. There is for Mab, a spirited and inquisitive and none too patient little girl, always something doing, . . . and the whole adds up, with its understanding of people as well as place, into a worthy successor to **"Thimble Summer."**

> *E.L.B., "New England," in* The New York Times Book Review *(© 1940 by The New York Times Company; reprinted by permission), November 10, 1940, p. 32.*

["The Sea Is All Around"] will endear itself to girls. . . .

In an enchanting way the author lets us travel with Mab, seeing through her eyes the strange and wonderful things on that journey [from Iowa to the island of Pokenick] which was crowded with a vast and bewildering number of impressions. The events which occur during those first winter days after her arrival on the island and the many that follow are dramatically told and you won't want to miss a word.

> *Florence Bethune Sloan, "Gaily We Parade!" in* The Christian Science Monitor *(reprinted by permission from* The Christian Science Monitor; *© 1940 The Christian Science Publishing Society; all rights reserved), November 11, 1940, p. 16.*

THE SATURDAYS (1941)

One is hard put to it to analyze the special charm which characterizes Elizabeth Enright's books, but it seems to be chiefly derived from her quick eye for the unexpected, the amusing and the beautiful in what might be just ordinary experiences, and from her own joyous sense of living. These qualities are abundantly illustrated in this story. . . .

The Melendys, being resourceful children, pool their small allowances so that each one during the Winter can have one Saturday afternoon a month to do exactly what he or she wants to do. What they manage to see and do on $1.60 apiece is amazing. There is one Saturday at the opera, a spree in Central Park, a gossipy interlude in a beauty parlor, interspersed with the domestic affairs of an amusing and unpredictable household. Our own vote for the best Saturday goes to Oliver, very level-headed for a 6-year-old, and his unsanctioned but gloriously successful afternoon at the circus; but the whole series of adventures makes a highly diverting tale of the interests and the dear desires of childhood.

> *E.L.B., "A Gay Family," in* The New York Times Book Review *(© 1941 by The New York Times Company; reprinted by permission), November 2, 1941, p. 31.*

The four Melendy children of this book . . . are the intelligent, independent, creative sort of kids every mother would like to think her own are. Their scheme to pool resources and get more out of city Saturday afternoons should make pleasant reading for children who like stories of family life and don't wince at the thought of going to an art exhibit or the opera.

> *K.S.W., "Books for Children: 'The Saturdays'," in* The New Yorker *(© 1941, copyright renewed © 1968, by The New Yorker Magazine, Inc.), Vol. XVII, No. 43, December 6, 1941, p. 116.*

"The Saturdays" . . . is one of our favorites. We believe young people will enjoy the exploits of the four Melendys. . . . [The story] is told with naturalness and rare understanding of young moderns. The series of good times that resulted as each took a Saturday, spent the money, did exactly as she or he wished was fun for the participants, and reading about them is good entertainment.

> *Florence Bethune Sloan, "For Young People," in* The Christian Science Monitor *(reprinted by permission from* The Christian Science Monitor; *© 1942 The Christian Science Publishing Society; all rights reserved), January 8, 1942, p. 15.*

In *The Saturdays* . . . a rather superficial sort of unity is contributed by having each child in the family choose how he will use their pooled resources on a given Saturday in New York City; but because the inclinations of each of the children begin to be discernible early and continue to unfold and exhibit themselves, the book has the additional unity of these developing attitudes. (pp. 137-38)

> *James Steel Smith, "Sense and Sensibility in Children's Literature: Part 1, Sense," in his* A Critical

Approach to Children's Literature *(copyright © 1967 by McGraw-Hill, Inc.; used with permission of McGraw-Hill Book Company), McGraw-Hill, 1967, pp. 125-71.**

The Saturdays satisfies each of the three requirements of regional literature [the region must enter constructively into the story as the instigator of plot; it must be both about and of the country, reflecting in some fashion the essential qualities of the land; finally, it must place the setting and the story in contemporary terms, giving the reader the sense that the events being related are part of a greater sweep of human history]. The diverse offerings of New York, which Miss Enright knows from her own childhood, provide the impetus for the plot. . . . In addition, the setting is totally a part of the characters' lives. The city provides the Metropolitan Opera and Carnegie Hall to satisfy young Rush's yearning for [Johann Sebastian] Bach and [(Wilhelm) Richard] Wagner; it provides Madison Square Garden to satisfy six-year-old Oliver's hankering for the circus; and it provides art galleries to exhibit the French Impressionist paintings that so deeply move Miranda. The Melendys are children, to be sure, but they are also urban children, accustomed to adapting their lives and activities to what the city offers. The reader sees them as persons, and he sees how the city has made its mark upon them.

Even as ***The Saturdays*** delineates the city as ecosphere, it supplies a sense of the world outside of the city. The Melendy children know that their well-being depends upon their father's maintaining his competence as an economist, and they tolerate his frequent absences on professional duties. They learn, through their elderly friend Mrs. Oliphant, of the remorseless coming of old age, and its consequences. And they learn, indeed are constantly aware, that the world is at war. Their father warns them against a too-idealized view of mankind, remarking that 'Sometimes I think the Golden Age must have been the Age of Reptiles,' and the well-lighted New York skyline reminds them that Europe under the Blitz is another world indeed. The book, in short, is all that a regional novel ought to be. Drawing upon her own consciousness of the complex contradictions of the present, Miss Enright gives to her readers the same sense of place and time that the authors of more rural works give, but does so within the boundaries of the contemporary city and the contemporary world. (pp. 63-4)

> *Fred Erisman, "Regionalism in American Children's Literature" (originally presented at a symposium for Special Collections of the Children's Services Division of the American Library Association on May 14-15, 1976), in* Society & Children's Literature, *edited by James H. Fraser (copyright © 1978 by Simmons College; reprinted by permission of David R. Godine, Publisher, Inc.) 1978, pp. 53-76.**

THE FOUR-STORY MISTAKE (1942)

Here is one of the year's books that ten-year-olds may confidently recommend to their parents, after they have found for themselves what fun it is. It is one of those family stories like those of Kenneth Grahame, where children rely on each other, as in real life, for special gifts each one possesses. One is a born musician, another means to act, the interests of the other two are all their own, yet they live as an orchestra plays, each his own instrument but the same music. When they move to the country you see that the Four-Story Mistake is a house whose cupola perches over three stories because the builder's funds gave out at that point. It is a house full of possibili-

From The Saturdays, *written and illustrated by Elizabeth Enright.*

ties. . . . When somebody gives them an alligator, keep your eye on it, for it will turn up in hilarious places. Laugh with them at their family entertainment, believe in the extraordinary ease with which they make money—is romance to have no rights?—and if you are grown-up, relax and let yourself be carried along with this living spring of childhood. . . .

To think there are grown-ups who don't know about books like this!

> *May Lamberton Becker, "Books for Young People: 'The Four-Story Mistake'," in* New York Herald Tribune Books, *November 15, 1942, p. 7.*

["**The Four-Story Mistake**" contains realistic,] modern, surprising occurrences written in an amusing, up-to-the-minute idiom.

Special because of its uncontrived, carefree humor and its modern appeal to everyone.

> *Leo Lerman, "Six Special Books: 'The Four-Story Mistake'," in* The Saturday Review of Literature *(copyright © 1942, copyright renewed © 1970, by Saturday Review; all rights reserved; reprinted by permission), Vol. XXV, No. 49, December 5, 1942, p. 60.*

THEN THERE WERE FIVE (1944)

Hundreds of American boys and girls will remember the four Melendy children—Mona, Rush, Randy, and Oliver. They are the ones that made such good stories of **"The Saturdays"** and **"The Four-Story Mistake."** . . . [In **"Then There Were Five"**] they find Mark Herron who becomes in the end the fifth of the Melendys. . . . Mark's whole relationship to the Melendy family and their final acceptance of him show a fine sense of values. So many stories for young people in these last years have had a conscious concern with democracy and with class and race prejudice. There is no such concern here. Mark is weighed first by the children, then by their father for what he is in himself. They do not discuss him; they test him. And he meets the test every time. Perhaps the outstanding character in this new chronicle of the Melendy family is Oliver. There is insight and some beautiful writing in the chapter where he sees the lunar moth. . . . In his relationship with Mr. Titus, too, Oliver is delightful. . . . As you finish this story you can almost hear the children say: "That is a good book!"

> *M.G.D., "The Melendy Family," in* The Saturday Review of Literature *(copyright © 1944, copyright renewed © 1971, by* Saturday Review; *all rights reserved; reprinted by permission), Vol. XXVII, No. 39, September 23, 1944, p. 28.*

It is hard for one who has lived through **"The Saturdays"** with the Melendys and helped them settle into **"The Four-Story Mistake"** to say anything really new about those four brothers and sisters. Admiration and affection are now taken for granted and the best news is that they are still very much themselves, only more so, for these children really grow in their various interests. . . .

The Melendys certainly have a talent for fun and, being sensitive youngsters as well, their everyday adventures are shot through with that sharp perception of experience which makes for vitality in fiction.

> *Ellen Lewis Buell, "A Talent for Fun," in* The New York Times Book Review *(© 1944 by The New York Times Company; reprinted by permission), October 8, 1944, p. 24.*

The Melendy family . . . not only takes the hurdle at which so many fall—third volume in a series—but shows every sign of going right on running. At least I hope they will, and believe the hope shared by a crowd of children growing in numbers with each book.

For the Melendy children's adventures, close enough to everyday life to convince children they really happen, happen to children only extraordinary enough to make them more stimulating, more romantic than what takes place in most families—more like what children wish would happen. . . .

The children carry on fairly familiar activities, but these do not take an altogether familiar turn. A salvage drive impelled by a "talent for trash," Mona's dealings with Shakespeare and Randy's with the ballet—for example, her appearance on the lawn in a bathing suit as Helen of Troy with an iron deer as Trojan Horse; the unpredictable part played by citronella in one of the wilder experiences; the trouble Mona had with canning—this and much more goes on in a whirl of natural talk. They do not make bright speeches, but just keep talking like real children, only not always what you expect them to say—any more than real children do. . . . As usual, the pictures

decorate as well as illustrate; it is a joyous book, shining with summer.

> *May Lamberton Becker, "New Books to Be Remembered," in* New York Herald Tribune Weekly Book Review, *November 12, 1944, p. 8.**

SPIDERWEB FOR TWO: A MELENDY MAZE (1951)

Meeting the Melendy family in any of their four books is pure joy for ten to twelve year olds and adults alike. . . . [In **"Spiderweb for Two: A Melendy Maze"** the youngest two] are matching their considerable wits against those of the rest of the family. Each new search brings new adventure, indoors and out, humorous or exciting. The non-material prize at the end is very satisfactory.

Thank goodness, these Melendys make no bones about having brains. They know lots of books, remember their history and much poetry, and treasure up the words of interesting people like Cuff. The result is a literate family whose talk and "clues" too, are shot through with intelligence worn gaily and naturally. The author's brilliant observation of, and probably remembrance of, childhood, makes every page a delight.

> *Louise S. Bechtel, "American Families, Then and Now," in* New York Herald Tribune Book Review *(© I.H.T. Corporation; reprinted by permission), November 11, 1951, p. 10.**

When the three older Melendy children go away to school for the first time they leave behind them the clues for a nine-month-long treasure hunt so that the two younger members of the family will not be lonesome while they are gone. Randy and Oliver . . . progress from clue to clue through the fall, winter and spring to a jubilant and unexpected ending. . . .

In this fourth chronicle, Elizabeth Enright gives evidence again of her rare ability to create real children in real situations and to write about their relationships with humor and distinction.

> *Eulalie Steinmetz, "Treasure Hunt," in* The New York Times Book Review *(© 1951 by The New York Times Company; reprinted by permission), November 11, 1951, p. 30.*

Another book about the Melendy family is an event for children between ten and fourteen, and though [*Spiderweb for Two*] is in some ways more of a tour de force than the others, its fun is just as spirited and spontaneous.

> *"Picture Books: 'Spiderweb for Two'," in* The New Yorker *(© 1951 by The New Yorker Magazine, Inc.), Vol. XXVII, No. 42, December 1, 1951, p. 176.*

GONE-AWAY LAKE (1957)

This is a book for homes, for families to laugh over together. Libraries will need many copies, for seldom do we have distinguished writing combined with so much immediate appeal for children. They'll love Foster, whose main interests are "outer space and inner pie," Portia with new braces on her teeth, making her look "just like the front of a Buick," and Julian, an "emotionable" boy, excited over butterflies and garnets. . . . Everyone, young and old, will be charmed by the way Elizabeth Enright's delightful style has endowed **"Gone-Away Lake"** with the glow of the land of Sleeping Beauty.

Margaret Sherwood Libby, "The Three 1957 Prize Books," in New York Herald Tribune Book Review *(© I.H.T. Corporation; reprinted by permission), May 12, 1957, p. 6.**

This is the kind of book in which nothing very dramatic happens (except when Portia's little brother is mired in the swamp) and possibly the conventional reader may prefer more of a plot. Yet there is here a constant feeling of excitement, of anticipation of the next discovery and of satisfaction. And, as readers of **"The Melendy Family"** and **"Thimble Summer"** know, Miss Enright can create a scene, describe a person and record a conversation with a brilliance and a humor that make it seem as if it were happening right this minute.

Ellen Lewis Buell, "Summer of Discovery," in The New York Times Book Review *(© 1957 by The New York Times Company; reprinted by permission), May 15, 1957, p. 36.*

The most interesting story I have read [this season] is Elizabeth Enright's *Gone-Away Lake* . . . , which has far more body and bones than many novels contain. The characters all live in the book, and I found old and young equally fascinating. There is lovely feeling for nature throughout and a fine sense of humor. Although Miss Enright has already had the Newbery Medal, this book might make her eligible again next year. . . . (pp. 207-08)

Anne Carroll Moore, "The Three Owls Notebook," in The Horn Book Magazine *(copyright © 1957 by The Horn Book, Inc., Boston), Vol. XXXIII, No. 3, June, 1957, pp. 206-08.**

One of the freshest of books to appear in many years, [*Gone-Away Lake*] is a mingling of summer fun, a feeling for nature and humorous situations with strongly individualized characters of widely separated generations, and an original setting and plot. . . . Genuine humor, originality, and life are enduring qualities. (p. 571)

Ruth Hill Viguers, "Experiences to Share," in A Critical History of Children's Literature *by Cornelia Meigs, Anne Thaxter Eaton, Elizabeth Nesbitt, and Ruth Hill Viguers, edited by Cornelia Meigs (reprinted with permission of Macmillan Publishing Co., Inc.; copyright © 1953, 1969 by Macmillan Publishing Co., Inc.), revised edition, Macmillan, 1969, pp. 567-600.**

RETURN TO GONE-AWAY (1961)

All the genial characters of the first book are present [in **"Return to Gone-Away"**], especially Julian the future scientist, Davey, a very contemporary small boy, old Mrs. Cheever and her brother, old Mr. Pindar Payton, plus assorted children, dogs, cats, and Uncle Sam, the goat. The cheerful events include discoveries of treasure in the attic, a note inside a suit of armor, and, finally, a hidden safe. Although the book contains less true adventure than **"Gone-Away Lake"** and leans somewhat too heavily on catalogues of all the findings in the old mansion, even these details are in fine contrast to the kind of world where too many houses are exactly like other houses, and people are as exactly like other people as they can make themselves. Here all is individualized, and told with Miss Enright's good-humored knowledge of human beings, especially children, in a prose that is quick, accurate, witty and poetic.

Marjorie Fischer, "At Villa Caprice," in The New York Times Book Review *(© 1961 by The New York Times Company; reprinted by permission), May 14, 1961, p. 20.*

As any good sequel should, this one carries the same humor, the warm, yet detached air of seeing its characters and happenings whole, and the good style one has come to expect from this author. Writing is marred only by too many parentheses and children's cuteness. . . . [This story] would interest families for reading aloud and independent readers whether or not they've read **"Gone-Away Lake."**

Peggy Sullivan, "Grades 3-6: 'Return to Gone-Away'," in Library Journal *(reprinted from* Library Journal, *June 15, 1961; published by R. R. Bowker Co. (a Xerox company); copyright © 1961 by Xerox Corporation), Vol. 86, No. 12, June 15, 1961, p. 2356.*

It is a visit to a very small but very real-seeming world that Elizabeth Enright offers the 8-12's in [**"Return to Gone-Away"**]. The sense of being gathered into a charming family circle for a happy summer more than compensates for the lack of dramatic plot. The Blake family moves to the country to a house that might be any child's dream house. . . . And the book is equally full of stories about olden days, neighbors and, to the delight of reading aloud adults, sudden small descriptions—Andy's new teeth, for instance, appear as "two tiny scallopings of white just showing at the gum."

Pamela Marsh, "Widening Horizons for Children: 'Return to Gone-Away'," in The Christian Science Monitor *(reprinted by permission from* The Christian Science Monitor; *© 1961 The Christian Science Publishing Society; all rights reserved), September 7, 1961, p. 7.*

TATSINDA (1963)

Usually original fairy tales come from across the ocean, but [*Tatsinda*] is an indigenous one with originality and good writing (what else from this author?). It reminds me a little of [George Macdonald's] *The Princess and the Goblin,* yet it is entirely different.

Tatsinda lived in the kingdom of Tatrajan, where the people all had names that began with Ta, and the animals had names that began with Ti, like the racing Tidwell. There are complications for an adult as Tatrajinni names begin to build up, but children, who like secret languages, will probably take this in their stride.

The greatest complication was that all the Tatrajinni had glittering white hair, and their eyes were a cool, greenish blue. They were sorry for Tatsinda because her hair was golden, and her eyes were brown. The Gadblangs, who lived on the other side of the wall of mist, were a menace; but in the end Tatsinda and Prince Tackatan overcame all dangers, were married, and had children of their own, with suitably mixed eye and hair color. . . . There is now no word in the language that means war, no word that means hate except in children's games, and no one ever comes to trouble them again. It sounds like Utopia— and our children will wish it could be their world. Perhaps the fairy tale has gone back to its original purpose, but let us not dream too much. All adversaries do not vanish in a puff of smoke.

Alice Dalgliesh, "Spring Books for Young People," in Saturday Review (copyright © 1963 by Saturday Review; all rights reserved; reprinted by permission), Vol. XLVI, No. 19, May 11, 1963, p. 50.*

Although Elizabeth Enright has invented new twists in the fairy-tale plot and written poetically, with delightfully original details, she has retained the age-old reassuring atmosphere of the old tales. From the beginning young readers will feel that while there is a brave prince like Tackatan and a resourceful maiden like Tatsinda in the mountain kingdom of Tatrajan, good will triumph over evil, though not without a struggle. . . .

Though readers can happily anticipate the outcome, every detail of the struggle and of this kingdom, "queer, curious, beautiful—different," is fascinating. . . . This slender book is a treasure to go on your shelf of favorites to read and reread for the imaginative detail, the style and the truths about greed and conformity tactfully but firmly emphasized.

"Honor Books," in Books—New York Herald Tribune (© I.H.T. Corporation; reprinted by permission), May 12, 1963, p. 3.

["Tatsinda"] is delightfully feminine. Little girls will love this tale of a golden-haired girl who lives in Tatrajan, a fascinating land. . . . Miss Enright makes some implications about the profit motive and racial bias but none of this is tedious. The whole book is charmingly written, technically skillful and highly inventive.

Jane Cobb, "A Time to Talk of Men in Space, of Princesses and Mops," in The New York Times Book Review (© 1963 by The New York Times Company; reprinted by permission), May 12, 1963, p. 18.*

A new fairy world is created in this story. . . . There is much here to delight imaginative children: the careful descriptions of the Tatrajanni, their homes, their customs, their animals, their wonderful names . . . and the romance and magic of the story. . . . A beautiful, many-faceted story.

Ruth Hill Viguers, "Folk Tales, Legends, and Fanciful Stories," in The Horn Book Magazine (copyright © 1963, by The Horn Book, Inc., Boston), Vol. XXXIX, No. 4, August, 1963, p. 382.*

[Elizabeth Enright's Tatsinda] is a work of great imagination. . . . Not only does she write with vividness and grace, but in her world of the Tatrajanni, all is unheard of. Its creator puts toe to ground only at those points which admit that the Tatrajanni are human creatures, that what are not humans are animals and birds, and that what grows out of the earth are plants. Otherwise she is airborne on her own fancy. And in addition to setting herself the problem of inventing a world utterly unlike our own, she works freely and apparently with the greatest ease within the idea that the names of all human Tatrajanni begin with Ta and the names of all animals with ti. It is as if, out of pure joyous daring, she gave herself this extra hurdle, yet never once is the reader made to feel that someone is inventing, making a desperate effort to think of sufficiently astonishing names and ways and appearances. None of her creatures . . . seem to have been thought up but to have evolved naturally out of the very nature of this strange, high, beautiful world. (p. 199)

It is a country which somehow recalls Elinor Wylie's poetry, with its crystal and filigree and mother-of-pearl, and the telling of it as well, delicate but firm, fastidious and subtle. Her world may not have the breadth and depth of [J.R.R.] Tolkien's, nor the richness of implication of [Walter] de la Mare's. Yet one rests secure in the assurance that Elizabeth Enright accomplished precisely what she set out to do, and her accomplishment is perfect of its kind. (p. 200)

Eleanor Cameron, "A Country of the Mind," in her The Green and Burning Tree: On the Writing and Enjoyment of Children's Books (© 1962, 1964, 1966, 1969 by Eleanor Cameron; reprinted by permission of Little, Brown and Company in association with The Atlantic Monthly Press), Atlantic-Little, Brown, 1969, pp. 163-202.*

ZEEE (1965)

Zeee was a bad fairy, and she hated people. That in itself makes a refreshing start to a story, for many children's books drip with sweetness. . . .

Zeee hates people because they are always taking the various houses she has moved into for uses of their own. We follow the fairy's harrowing adventures until there comes along a little girl who can see her and believes in her. After that things change. Zeee changes, too. I cannot fall for that bit about Pandora and Hope, but children won't be critical of it.

Alice Dalgliesh, "An April Shower to Share," in Saturday Review (copyright © 1965 by Saturday Review; all rights reserved; reprinted with permission), Vol. XLVIII, No. 17, April 24, 1965, p. 45.*

Pretty, prickly-tempered Zeee, the tiny, bumblebee-sized fairy who dwells in Elizabeth Enright's tale, sparkles with personality. . . .

A harmony of fantasy and reality hold the enchantment here. Miss Enright has gracefully spun threads of imagination, elegant words, wit and inventive detail into a fragile, feminine miniature world. The beautiful blithesomeness of "Zeee" slips slightly into sentimentality near the story's end, but the comments on friendship are firmly sensible.

Margaret F. O'Connell, "Books for the Young Readers: 'Zeee'," in The New York Times Book Review (© 1965 by The New York Times Company; reprinted by permission), June 13, 1965, p. 24.

Although this story does not have the depth or the enchantment of Tatsinda, Miss Enright continues to tread lightly but with sure footing through fairyland. Adults may see satire in Zeee's observations of adults and their offspring. Children, too, will find them funny and recognize their substance.

Patricia H. Allen, "Grades 3-6: 'Zeee'," in Library Journal (reprinted from Library Journal, June 15, 1965; published by R. R. Bowker Co. (a Xerox company); copyright © 1965 by Xerox Corporation), Vol. 90, No. 12, June 15, 1965, p. 2883.

Wanda Gág

1893-1946

American author/illustrator of picture books, translator and adapter of folktales for children, and author of nonfiction for adults. When Wanda Gág created *Millions of Cats* in 1928, she awed the children's book audience with her ability to create a picture book which combined artistic talent with an equally adept old-world technique for storytelling. Her four succeeding picture books share the quality illustrations and skillful language construction of her first book, but each retains its distinction. Gág is also noted for contributing to the folklore genre with her translations of the fairy tales of the Brothers Grimm.

Gág grew up in New Ulm, Minnesota, a secluded town populated by immigrants from Yugoslavia, Bohemia, Austria, and Hungary. Gág spoke only German until she started school. She heard folktales daily in their traditional peasant style and was impressed by the importance of sound in the effect of these stories. Her talents were bred and nurtured in a rare home environment presided over by two imaginative and artistic parents who encouraged their children to excel in music, art, and writing. From an early eage Gág followed her handyman father and watched in silence as he created pictures during his free time. He never became a professional artist; before he died, however, he gave her the words which helped her to act on her right to pursue an art career even under severe financial and social pressures: "What papa couldn't do, Wanda will have to finish." Gág became the head of her family at the age of fifteen. She began using her skills to bring money into the household by drawing postcards, calendars, and drugstore posters, by painting lampshades, and by writing and illustrating magazine articles. When their mother died after a long illness, the Gág children decided that each of them would complete high school despite financial hardships. After the last of her six siblings received a high school diploma Gág quit her job as a commercial artist and concentrated exclusively on her art techniques.

Gág's first exhibition established her as one of the most original artists in America. She was recognized for her ability to capture the nuances of her environment, household scenes, and the surrounding countryside with new vitality. Children's book editor Ernestine Evans saw Gág's potential as an illustrator after attending one of her art exhibits. When Evans arranged a meeting with her, Gág brought a story with her from a box of rejected works. This was *Millions of Cats,* which won Gág immediate success. She utilized her artistic styles and techniques to create its illustrations, which were, like her paintings, done entirely in black and white. Concerning the translation from artist to illustrator at a time when children's book illustration was not considered serious art, Gág stated that she intended to do her best in all of her art work whether for adults or children. "I strive to make [my illustrations] warmly human, imaginative, or humorous—not coldly decorative—and to make them so clear that a three-year-old can recognize the main objects in them."

Gág told and retold the story of *Millions of Cats* to the children she knew, gradually developing it into the version recited by parents and children ever since. Although Gág used this same technique with several of her books, notably *Snippy and Snappy* and *The Funny Thing,* some critics feel that *Millions of Cats* is her best picture book and is unequalled by her succeeding works. They admire *Nothing at All,* Gág's only book in color, for her drawings of an invisible dog and his gradual appearance; they appreciate *ABC Bunny* for its unique combination of alphabet book and story, and for its realistic, expressive rabbit.

Gág's ability to capture and recreate the personality of traditional folklore is displayed in her renderings of the Grimm tales. She used exact translations when they kept the flavor of the original story, and reworked the language in the areas of the tales that would lose their freshness in a literal translation. Unlike the Grimms, whose purpose was to preserve oral history, Gág stressed the intrinsic character of the folktales. Since she brought her European sensibility to these tales and underscored their entertainment value, many reviewers feel that her versions of them are a major achievement. She is also specifically credited for preserving the Märchen of her childhood, *Gone Is Gone:*

or, The Story of a Man Who Wanted to Do Housework, **a tale which she told completely from memory since she felt it was inaccurately represented in other sources. It is generally agreed that Gág used her background and personal vision to create works that continue to appeal to children for their rhythm, their lively, expressive pictures, and their simple peasant humor. She received the Newbery Honor Book Award for** *Millions of Cats* **in 1929 and for** *ABC Bunny* **in 1934, the Caldecott Honor Book Award for** *Snow White and the Seven Dwarfs* **in 1939 and for** *Nothing at All* **in 1942, the Lewis Carrol Shelf Award for** *Millions of Cats* **in 1958, and the Kerlan Award for recongnition of singular attainments in the creation of children's literature in 1977. (See also** *Yesterday's Authors of Books for Children,* **Vol. 1.)**

AUTHOR'S COMMENTARY

Some of my pictures are drawn from my imagination, but I also make many sketches from life and the objects about me. To children who are interested in becoming artists, I would like to say: Draw the things about you, not only people and animals, flowers, and so on, but also the very ordinary things, such as chairs, stoves, woodpiles, frying pans, smoke stacks. Almost anything is beautiful and *drawable.* . . .

I am often asked whether I draw from actual models or from my imagination. I do both, of course, but practically all of my animal characters are based on sketches of living models. For example, in *Millions of Cats,* I used two little kittens, Snoopy and Snookie, for models, making a great many action sketches of them. . . . In preparation for *The ABC Bunny,* I studied dozens of rabbits from which I finally selected a little snub-nosed one for my hero. For fairy stories, of course, one naturally draws from imagination, but even here there is a basis of years of observation of the real things about me—not to forget also considerable research into the authentic costumes and customs of the past. (p. 205)

> *Wanda Gág, "Letters from Children to Wanda Gág,"* in The Horn Book Magazine *(copyrighted, 1947, by The Horn Book, Inc., Boston), Vol. XXIII, No. 3, May-June, 1947, pp. 199-205.*

GENERAL COMMENTARY

In Wanda Gág's own tales today there are quaint reminders of earlier, Old World story-telling. The books, of course, are chiefly pictures, running up and down and across the words, which have their own magic, too. Kindly gnome-like little old men, stocky kindly little old women, homely cottage interiors, bring to mind all our associations with the Brothers Grimm. *Millions of Cats* is a slim, delicious volume first recounted to a group of child friends who clamored for a story. On its pages you really do seem to see millions of cats, actually acres of stalking feet and stuck-up tails. The artist made a business of living with two cats in order to draw her millions. The second animal book is all about *The Funny Thing,* who is not an animal at all, but an horrific creature of Miss Gág's fancy, who has a cruel habit of eating dolls, until, as the narrative proceeds, he is persuaded to a diet of jumjills instead. *Snippy and Snappy* records the escapade of two little field mice who wander too far from home. One unforgettable page depicts the two petrified with fear on a strange doorstep. The open doorspace looms high as the sky above them, and is absolutely black. Only two tiny field mice looking into a limitless black unknown, but if one of us older ones looks across some small reader's shoulder at that illustration, we shall find ourselves suddenly becoming

grave, just a little awed, perhaps. This is only a child's picture book, but such a picture can evoke even for an adult stark mystery. Wanda Gág is herself at play when she makes her books for children, but even to them she is giving the best of her inimitable art. (pp. 9-10)

> *Winifred Kirkland and Frances Kirkland, "Wanda Gág, Who Followed Her Own Way," in their* Girls Who Became Artists *(reprinted by permission of Harper & Row, Publishers, Inc.), Harper, 1934, pp. 1-12.*

Beauty at the heart of all life is the keynote to the work of Wanda Gág and the source of its power, whether expressed in one of her memorable prints or in an intimate picture of the home of the very old man in *Millions of Cats.* Clear memory of her own happy childhood and a kinship with all children made her respect their intelligence, and gave them at once ease and joy in her company.

With as sure an instinct for the right word for the ear as for the right line for the eye, Wanda Gág became quite unconsciously a regenerative force in the field of children's books. . . . She heartily disliked the word juvenile and "thought it was a crime to give the public bad pictures, even though they demanded it." She could not be persuaded to do anything against her own conviction. When asked to do "more machinery that looks like dinosaurs," she replied, "Why should I? I did that because it amused me. . . . But one cannot laugh and laugh at the same joke."

Wise Wanda Gág! The comic strip beckoned to her in vain. But the dearly loved Märchen of her childhood set up a claim that would not be denied. Wanda Gág's *Tales from Grimm, Snow White and the Seven Dwarfs* and *More Tales from Grimm* are a rare gift to the children of our time. The old tales reaching far back into man's past have come alive again in this fresh,

From Snippy and Snappy, *written and illustrated by Wanda Gág.*

free translation with pictorial interpretations which children will read as eagerly as the words of the story.

The *Horn Book* is deeply grateful for the life and work of Wanda Gág—for the rhythm and balance, the wisdom, the wonder, the gift of laughter, and the warm feeling of security so precious to childhood, which are a veritable part of the artist and her books.

Anne Carroll Moore, "Art for Life's Sake," in The Horn Book Magazine (copyrighted, 1947, by The Horn Book, Inc., Boston), Vol. XXIII, No. 3, May, 1947, p. 157.

All I knew about Wanda Gág were her pictures. I had seen them at exhibitions and reproduced in magazines. They were beautiful, and very simple, and full of the wonder of common things. They excited more senses than one. I always wanted to reach out and touch them. It was this that made me sure that if the new publishing house of Coward-McCann was going to enlist America's artists in the service of children, Wanda should head the list. An appointment was made to see her, and I set out for the Weyhe Gallery. (p. 182)

What I found was an artist, and a storyteller as well. Stories with pictures, stories without pictures. She was an old hand with them, as entertainer and comforter and exhorter of a whole family of little Gágs. And more than that, as was plain when, years afterward, she dedicated *Gone Is Gone* "To My Peasant Ancestors," she had inherited a wonder-bin of tales to begin with. She had the hang of setting a scene and putting her characters in motion, of sharing what she remembered, and inventing surprises. . . . [When] we had in the office the marvelous manuscript of *Millions of Cats*, I hugged myself, as children all over the country have been doing ever since for nearly twenty years. But the bits she told me that first day— shyly, but directly, in answer to questions, never piling it on, but making you see New Ulm by words, and the table with the children eating supper and governing each other with "Eat fair!"—were proof that she was a writer.

> Tell me where is fancy bred
> Or in the heart or in the head?

I suppose "fancy" there means love. But with Art it is as mystifying. Too many children's books are fancies from the tops of not very good heads, and more are too full of heart with hardly any head concerned. Not so any of Wanda's tales, the ones she invented herself, or the ones she carefully chose to translate and rewrite from those gathered, in cottage and forest by the Brothers Grimm, which represented the experience and wishes and dreams of generations of hard-working peasants, so few of whom could read or write, so many of whom were dependent on oral relation for what there was to remember of the past.

Wanda's style in telling stories, a very conscious and conscientious style, gained immensely from the old patterns which were often half song and half story, handed on to be retold and remembered. She used devices like repetition and cunning simple rhyme well. "They followed it over this and that, and over things both round and flat, and over things both small and tall." See, even I can remember that from *Snippy and Snappy*. . . . This is a minor touch of art and very pleasurable, and sometimes only noticeable when you discover from some young Patsy or Jossie that it tickles them, or when you vaguely miss the easy sway in the sentences of some other little book the children have brought you on a rainy day.

I always liked the moral note in Wanda's stories. Oh, no moral sticking out like a sore thumb, or even one wrapped in a cracker, but there, all the same, to cheer a body into being good rather than "bad." There is a universal moral in telling your child or your neighbor or yourself to go on and on and try harder, and I always enjoyed the part in *Nothing at All* where it says: "But do you think he sat down and cried? Oh no, he had a plan."

Her care about format was part of her writing and drawing. She wanted to squeeze the last possibility of communication out of each story. I wanted the shape of *Millions of Cats* to be the same as [William] Nicolson's *Clever Bill*, which was both small book and large one, a wide page and yet not "big merchandise." She agreed to that, for it suited her notion of the old man journeying home. . . . Everything was done to make the story as simple as possible and as clear. She was painstaking in her choice of words, and there was a sort of sureness about the stories, however surprising they were, as if they had already stood the test of time and were by way of being classics. This is most true of *Millions of Cats*. It was, from the beginning, as sure-fire as *The Three Bears*, another story written by a known author, that has a sort of patina—as if it had been handed down by your Grandmother, who got it from hers or dear knows where. . . . (pp. 182-84)

The Funny Thing I liked much less than *Millions of Cats*, but I learned from it that neither I nor the public had a storyteller to deal with who meant to pander to us or repeat herself; and after *Snippy and Snappy* and the *ABC Bunny*, it was a pleasure to see the same skill used on different characters and in new forms.

Perhaps I am wrong, but in herself, and in her stories, or so it seemed to me, there was never any pattern of humor in the conventional sense. When she decided to be, in part, an editor herself and select certain of the old folk stories for retelling, there was an impish humor in her selections. She was always aware of the political and social issues in the world around her. I do not think I am imagining that she often found in some of the oldest stories much that was slyly apropos to high policy in Washington and grim struggles in farm and factory. Read **"Clever Elsie"** again, one of the stories in *Tales from Grimm*. "There was a man. He had a daughter who always tried to use her brains as much as possible and so she was called Clever Elsie." I still think the story appealed to her because she thought that less brains, maybe, and more common sense, and a little less exploitation of crises and imagined crises might be wiser politics. As an editor, she had a sense of spoof; and it amused her that old sense, like old wine, was so good in the flasks.

When she simplified stories, she was an ideal barber. She cared for the shape of an old tale's head. She never fussed up curls. She brushed out the natural wave. Styles might change and local historical customs confuse. Some such bits she snipped out. The old story itself she never changed. She respected the past in the sense that she recognized lasting values. Stories were for use. And by use she meant the sharing of experience, and her art lay in making the sharing so very entertaining and so simply put that there was meaning and rhythm for the widest possible audience. Her ear was as concerned as her eye in relating a story. And if you as reader could bring your own experience, you were welcome to write "between the lines" as you read. Which is, isn't it, what all the enduring classics do for an audience? (pp. 185-86)

Ernestine Evans, "Wanda Gág as Writer," in The Horn Book Magazine (copyrighted, 1947, by The

And they began to quarrel.

From Millions of Cats, *written and illustrated by Wanda Gág.*

Horn Book, Inc., Boston), Vol. XXIII, No. 3, May-June, 1947, pp. 182-93.

Wanda Gág's work always hit you with its simplicity and sincerity of content and its freshness and originality of vision. As we saw more of her lithographs and wood-engravings, and learned a few things of her Mid-Western background, her family heritage and the difficulties of her struggle for a minimum economic base on which to carry on her creative work, the roots of those qualities of simplicity, sincerity and originality became pretty clear. Here was a completely integrated individual, who had an intense but highly rational relationship with the world about her, whose work was an affirmation of the basic good of that experience. You got the feeling that here was an artist whose complete motivation was a sharing of experience, and that is a much rarer thing than it may seem.

The transition from prints to books is a very natural one, for as far as artists are concerned there is a close relationship between the two historically, technically and ideologically. Wanda Gág was one of the first in this country to demonstrate this kinship in her own work. Her *Millions of Cats* was an extension into the field of children's books of those same qualities of freshness and simplicity that distinguished her work in the field of prints. At that time it was still a little heretical for an artist whose reputation was grounded in what critics call one of the "fine arts" to work seriously and without pretentious

apology in the field of illustration for children. The children of America, of course, are immeasurably richer because of what Wanda Gág brought them within the covers of her books. It is somewhat less generally recognized that the field of book illustration is today a far better thing than it was precisely because there were artists like Wanda Gág who were anxious to work in books with the same basic seriousness of approach and concern for what we lamely call "art values" that are so often presumed to be the exclusive concern of the "fine" artist who has no goal save self-expression.

I think the evidence all indicates that the outstanding quality of Wanda Gág, both as an artist and as a person, was that of social motivation, in its best and deepest sense. Her art was something to be shared by others, and though she was so quiet and unassuming you might find it hard to get to know her, her feelings toward people were warm and grounded in a very basic sympathy. Despite the great success that her books brought her, her spiritual home was always among those, both artists and laymen, who were pushed around by circumstance and less than well treated by a world that in our lifetime has too often seemed patterned more for the strong and ruthless than for those who, to put it a bit obliquely, believe that cats and trees and old spinning wheels are pretty important in the scheme of things. (pp. 195-96)

Artists will remember Wanda Gág as one who knew, probably instinctively, what human and artistic values were necessary for real progress. Her work, in both prints and books, was an affirmation of those values; and for that reason, I suspect, what she did in too short a lifetime will live and have meaning for generations yet unborn. (p. 197)

Lynd Ward, "Wanda Gág, Fellow-Artist," in The Horn Book Magazine *(copyrighted, 1947, by The Horn Book, Inc., Boston), Vol. XXIII, No. 3, May-June, 1947, pp. 194-97.*

The flowering of the many talents of Wanda Gág bear mute witness to the grim struggle which a determined, courageous wisp of a girl successfully conquered. Had she not been able to find "beauty amidst poverty" the world would indeed be the lesser. (p. 347)

Throughout all of her work Wanda Gág shows the influence of the sturdy and resourceful quality of peasant thinking, feeling, and living. Her roundish, very old man in thick serviceable shoes, and the very old woman clad in apron and scarf tied round her head in *Millions of Cats* are examples of this Old World influence.

As an enthusiastic admirer of Wanda Gág, I am by no means alone. I am, in fact, in excellent company. New groups of children each year discover for the first time the inimitable folk-tale quality of *Millions of Cats*. . . . The spontaneous response of young children to the problem the very old man faces as he attempts to choose just the right cat for his wife is a cherished memory in many households. (p. 348)

The strength and tenderness which Wanda Gág portrays in the illustrations, together with the living folk-tale quality of the text combine to make *Millions of Cats* a picture-story book of distinction. It is irresistible in its appeal to young children. They have bestowed upon it the same joyous approval they so lavishly accord to such favorites as [Beatrix Potter's] *Peter Rabbit* and *Mother Goose*. Children respond wholeheartedly to the good story that the author is telling. They identify with the dilemma in which the very old man finds himself. They sympathize with the thin and scraggly cat too homely even to fight. They sense the up and down rhythmic quality and the atmosphere of domesticity of both text and illustrations as the very old man traverses rolling hills and winding roads in his search. The author has produced a picture-story book of gentle and humorous quality, a story so happily concluded that it establishes a solid and honest relationship with each successive young reader. In this sense it is timeless and will go alongside other timeless classics on nursery shelves everywhere. (pp. 348-49)

One looking at the drawings for *Millions of Cats* might imagine that "All Creation," the author's country home, was literally overrun with cats. Such, however, was not the case. Snoopy and Snookie were the only two there. Wanda Gág's earlier training in quick action sketching enabled her to catch these two household pets in the alluringly natural and endearing poses found on many pages of *Millions of Cats*. On one page they are drinking the pond dry. On another, they are denuding the once green hills of every blade of grass. On another, the most remarkable of all, I think, they are scratching each other's eyes out in the quarrel to decide which one is the prettiest. In this drawing even the very old man and the very old woman are so frightened that they have taken to their heels and are about to take shelter inside the "nice clean house with flowers all around it except where the door was."

Millions of Cats has yet another claim to distinction. It is the first truly American picture book done by an American artist-author. Up until this time . . . American children had had to content themselves with English picture books. Perhaps but for the urge to drive herself forward, born of a need to make ends meet, Wanda might never have resurrected this story from the "Rejection Box" where it had resided along with others for quite some considerable length of time. (p. 349)

Tucked neatly on many a library shelf along with the volume already mentioned, young readers may discover **The Funny Thing**. . . . Here again a quality of Old Worldliness shines through both text and illustrations. (p. 350)

I have watched five and six year olds almost instinctively count the ingredients on Bobo's kitchen table. Nor was a careful craftsman like Wanda Gág to be found amiss in her drawing. Not one single one of [the] fifteen cheeses or of the seven nut cakes or five seed puddings is missing. They are all easily visible and waiting for children gleefully to count.

Another well loved, if not so widely read, volume is **Snippy and Snappy**. . . . As is characteristic of the author-artist's works, **Snippy and Snappy** surges with aliveness. The remarkable degree of intensive reality of two little field mice who live in a cozy nook in a hay field causes children to breathe the breath of life into each. What child could fail to enter wholeheartedly into the reality of the text as it describes Father Mouse reading an evening newspaper just small enough for him to hold easily while Mother Mouse contentedly knits jackets for her family. . . .

To add to this descriptive text Wanda Gág enhances children's delight with this homey scene by her clean, clear portrayal of it in black and white drawings. Each drawing captures perfectly the feelings of each mouse character in relation to his surroundings. Such art is directly communicative to young readers. Both physically and psychologically it is part and parcel of the whole—one incomplete without the other.

Here as in her other stories for young children are those characteristic rhythmical passages which delight young readers. . . .

In a world where adult concepts often outrun children's understanding, the experience of a five year old finding himself "in the know" as it were with the mice being the uninformed victim of circumstances, is basically delightful.

Nor should the quick action drawings of these adorable mice go unnoticed. Only the artist's careful observation and quick action sketches of these shy creatures as they come close to her sheltered secluded countryside home, "All Creation," could produce such graphic and lovable creatures. They cry real tears—a copious amount. They dance gaily as their graceful long tails flow out behind them. Their beady eyes grow beadier as they shyly stand in wonder before the mouse trap and listen to father say:

> With a snip and a snap
> and a trip and a trap—
> and that's the end of little mousie.

All in all, teachers everywhere might well turn to this slender volume for beginning reading material. It has artistic charm and literary substance upon which children may feast. . . .

[In **ABC Bunny**] Wanda Gág's rhythmic text, supplemented by brilliantly decorative lithographs, accords this volume an enviable place among ABC books for children for all time. (pp. 351-52)

Both text and drawings have an easy sweep and swing. . . . (p. 352)

[In *Gone Is Gone*] the author-artist has placed her distinctly original stamp upon both text and pictures. Two sturdy neighbors living in a small Minnesota town were the inspiration for Fritzl and Liesi, the principal characters in *Gone Is Gone.*

Wanda Gág's *Nothing At All* . . . finds its roots in the author's early interest in gnomes, fairies, and magic charms. Her faith in invisible beings and their power to live is easily discernible in this story of three small dogs. Far and away the invisible one is the captivating hero of this tale. . . .

The author-artist wastes no words in her story telling. Each of the dogs, in their pointed, curly, and round kennels respectively, are skillfully etched in direct and straightforward text. And who, except this artist, would decide to portray the invisibility of Nothing-at-all as a small white ball trekking over the long, long road. . . .

Nothing-at-all became separated from his two companions. This event brought about the necessity of finding some way for Nothing-at-all to become visible. With the aid of Jackdaw's knowledge of magic, acquired by reading incantations in *A Book of Magic,* Nothing-at-all gradually becomes "Something-thingy" instead of "Nothingy." Simplicity and directness of text convey all of this magic effectively. . . . [At] each successive whirl and swirl and twirl "Nothing-at-all" becomes "Something-after-all" and is happily reunited with his long lost brothers. . . . What more soul satisfying conclusion to a story could any young child desire? Although *Millions of Cats* is my favorite, to this book I also accord its full measure of praise. (p. 353)

Now he took a big bowl, into which he put:
     seven nut cakes
     five seed puddings
     two cabbage salads
     and fifteen little cheeses.
He mixed them with a spoon and rolled
them into little round balls.
These little balls were jum-jills.

From The Funny Thing, *written and illustrated by Wanda Gág.*

Doing her own free translation of Grimm she has left for the enjoyment of untold generations of children "**Tales from Grimm,**" . . . "**More Tales from Grimm**" . . . and "**Three Gay Tales from Grimm.**" . . . All three volumes are illustrated with her characteristic black and white drawings so charmingly unhorrifying that to think of changing them is to ruin the artistic essence of each collection. The witch in **Hansel and Gretel,** the dragon in **The Dragon and His Grandmother,** and Cinderella's wicked stepsisters are pleasingly ugly but never terrifyingly so. Gág portrays a playfulness of quality in Grimm's "near gory" characters. (pp. 353-54)

Into each book this author-artist has poured the best of her rich talents. Nothing less than the best would suffice. Her work possesses both simplicity in idea and truthfulness in art. Each book lives as all original works of art must live. Readers invariably catch the joy-in-the-doing which Wanda Gág brought to these truly creative pieces of work. (p. 354)

Beatrice J. Hurley, "Wanda Gág—Artist, Author," in Elementary English *(copyright © 1955 by the National Council of Teachers of English; reprinted by permission of the publisher and the author), Vol. XXXII, No. 6, October, 1955, pp. 347-54.*

At last Wanda Gág's last (posthumous) book has reached us. Most of them had English editions within a year or two, but we have waited fifteen years for **More Tales from Grimm.** It was worth waiting for. A few of the drawings show signs of hasty treatment, but the book as a whole crowns most fittingly a rich and productive life. (p. 51)

It was natural that Wanda should turn to painting and drawing, and natural too that, after a period of uneasy experiment, she should find for herself a style which was completely personal and firmly founded in peasant traditions. And when she came to write, first brief rhythmic texts for her own picture-books, then free versions of ancient fairy-tales, she matched her drawings most miraculously with a prose which was innocent, flexible and full of the rough music of country speech.

Millions of Cats, which came to England in 1929, was the first and is still the best of her original work. It shows her characteristic qualities admirably, the sturdy, uncompromising black-and-whites in the woodcut manner—although so far as I know she did not make woodcuts—the conscious yet naive stylisation, particularly the careful design of each page (more correctly each opening) in which elongated landscapes stride along between banks of hand-written text. The words are simple and fitting and the passage of the story is marked by the lovely rhythmic refrain "Hundreds of cats . . ." which every right-minded child quickly gets by heart and chants with satisfaction at its mounting splendour. It is notably a book conceived and executed as a whole. Not everyone may like the style—happily a great many children do—but the book is beyond criticism; it is impossible to alter a word or a line without destroying its inner harmony.

I have always thought *Snippy and Snappy* . . . a little lacking in creative energy. The materials are much like those of *Millions of Cats:* the pattern-making in design and phrase, the rhythms, the repetitions are all there; but they seem tired and lacking in spontaneity. Perhaps the real trouble is that Wanda Gág, unlike Beatrix Potter, had not sufficient first-hand acquaintance with mice; her hero and heroine, to my mind, are deficient in personality.

Nothing At All . . . is much better. It was, I believe, her only work—apart from the frontispiece of *Gone Is Gone*—in colour.

The story is highly original. . . . How Nothing-at-all finally gets a shape is the theme of an enchanting story, told with drawings and words of a sweet simplicity. Not many artists would choose to draw an invisible hero; Wanda Gág's charming dog is pleasing at every stage of his emergence. . . . (pp. 51-2)

In her version of [*Gone Is Gone*] Wanda Gág caught exactly the cadences of ordinary speech. It is one of the best of all stories to tell aloud and one of those which must be told "just-so." The drawings have an irresistible innocence. Is there any picture more idyllic than the one in which Fritzl is churning while little Kinndli plays moo-cow among the daisies? (p. 52)

In bulk and in importance Wanda Gág's major achievement lies in her versions of Grimm's tales, contained in four books: [*Tales from Grimm, Snow White and the Seven Dwarfs, Three Gay Tales from Grimm*, and *More Tales from Grimm*]. . . . (pp. 52-3)

Wanda Gág's *Snow White* is not in her best vein. The year of publication is significant, for this was the year of Disney's first major cartoon film, and the Wanda Gág version was hurried out to remind children of the real nature of dwarfs, princesses and wicked queens. The whole production showed signs of haste and Wanda Gág's drawings were over-full of those clichés which come in handy when inspiration flags.

What makes Wanda Gág the most successful of all interpreters of Grimm is her fundamental lack of sophistication. The best of her predecessors, [George] Cruickshank and [Walter] Crane among the artists, Edgar Taylor and Margaret Hunt among translators, were products of an urban civilisation, separated by an unknown number of generations from their peasant ancestors. Wanda-chen in childhood had heard all around her the authentic accents of the German forests, just as the Grimm brothers had heard them, with this difference, that Wanda Gág identified herself with the stories, while for Jakob and Wilhelm they were sources to be studied objectively. What comes out most clearly from the Wanda Gág tales is the intense inward glow of love which she felt for them.

The introduction to *Tales from Grimm* contains a very fine appreciation of the qualities of *Märchen* and of the artist's approach to her task. She approached it with affection but without an exaggerated reverence, knowing that the texts which the brothers Grimm left were the raw materials for ethnological and linguistic studies and not works of art. The tales were often muddled, with incomplete fragments or alternative versions confusing the line of the story. Wanda Gág brought an expert surgery to the tales to reveal their basic shape, while keeping the essential atmosphere of each tale. Her method is seen at its most simple in "**The Fisherman and his Wife**," to my mind the finest of all folk-tales. The original is in dialect, and she alone of all the translators kept the feeling of dialect, not by

The fourth day, after Nothing-at-all had whirled and twirled and swirled and repeated his busy-dizzy chant, the jackdaw came and said, "You are certainly working hard at your magic task. That black tail-tip is a beauty, I must say!"

The little dog was so pleased that he wagged his tail wildly, and although the *tail* was still invisible, its black tip showed the wagging plainly enough. The jackdaw laughed at this and then disappeared.

From Nothing At All, *written and illustrated by Wanda Gág.*

the use of archaic or obscure words but by masterly control of a very simple colloquial style. (p. 53)

The superiority of Wanda Gág's version can be followed throughout this superb tale. Compare her fisherman's wife's complaint "Listen, man, the hut is much too small" with Lucy Crane's "Look here, husband, the cottage is really too confined!"

The fisherman's call to the magic fish is a stumbling block to all translators. How is one to retain its incantatory quality, and its sense, and have a rhyme which the fisherman can shout against the howling wind and the roaring sea. Wanda Gág's last line "Does not want my way of life" is an inadequate rendering of "Will nich so as ik woll will," but, avoiding Mrs. Lucas's "Prythees" and Lucy Crane's "tiresome wife," she retains the strange, unquestionably magical first line which had haunted her childhood: "Manntje, Manntje, Timpe Te," and so shared its music with generations of English and American children.

It is tempting to continue the comparison. What becomes ever increasingly clear is that Wanda Gág's touch rarely fails her, that she finds for each German original a parallel rather than a translation, and that she keeps the tone of the original successfully because the tone is one in which she herself grew and which she inherited.

The title of her second Grimm book is significant. She brings out continually the gaiety of Grimm and not the grimness which, in the popular view, is their main characteristic. There are harsh touches—Snow White's step-mother dances out her wicked life in red-hot dancing shoes—but these always satisfy a child's (or a peasant's) sense of rough justice. What Wanda Gág delights in most are the sharp simple story-telling, the naive literalism—like the bear in **"Snow White and Rose Red"** whose bearishness is literally only skin-deep—above all the good-humoured fun poked at human folly and stupidity. These preferences guided her choice of material; they also governed her selection of viewpoint and detail in her drawings and the rightness of each crystal-clear word in her versions. In the three books of Grimm tales we have the pure spring-water of folktale, not the flat "pop" which children are too often given in substitute. (pp. 54-5)

> *Marcus S. Crouch, "Through Peasant Eyes," in* The Junior Bookshelf, *Vol. 26, No. 2, March, 1962, pp. 51-5.*

In the introduction to her *Tales from Grimm,* Wanda has said that it wasn't until 1932, when she was doing a Hansel and Gretel drawing, that the old *Märchen* magic gripped her again as it had done in her childhood so that she was compelled to begin the long work which preceded her translations from Grimm. But surely it was her little German *Märchenbuch* which brought her, several years before *Tales from Grimm,* into the world of children's literature with her first publication. For what is *Millions of Cats,* in spirit at least, but a real honest-to-goodness *Märchen*—a fable, a folk tale—sounding for all the world, with its special rhythms and repetitions, as if it had been handed down from generation to generation of storytellers, smoothed and polished and perfected a bit more with each retelling until each word was in its right and unchangeable place. Only it happens to have been made up out of whole cloth in our own time by one for whom "the magic of *Märchen*" was one of her earliest recollections and therefore most deeply a part of her.

Again Wanda put her hand into the wonder box and this time drew out *The Funny Thing* and the following year, *Snippy and Snappy,* two more rejections but now, like *Millions of Cats,* classics which will go on living as long as there are children to hear them, and children to count in one of the drawings in *The Funny Thing* the seven nut cakes, the five seed puddings, the two cabbage salads, and the fifteen little cheeses. . . . (p. 311)

[Gag's revisions and years of retelling her tales to children is a method which] sounds to me like Beatrix Potter and the care and the listening and the rewriting that went into her brief but mighty classics. Certainly when we come to the *Tales from Grimm* and learn that four years of the most concentrated labor went into the preparation of these and other tales, we realize a little more what it means to be a truly dedicated human being. If Wanda had not loved the *Märchen* in childhood so deeply nor listened with such intensity to their telling, her work might have been easier—and of less value. (p. 312)

Wanda found that she didn't want always to translate freely. Sometimes, she says, a quite literal translation brought out the story as fresh and lively as it was in the original and this seemed especially true of stories in dialect. But others which had been smooth and vivid in German emerged lifeless and clumsy, so that a free translation was a necessity in order to deliver the pungency and vividness Wanda remembered. **"Hansel and Gretel,"** she found, could be presented almost as in the original, and yet was it the folktelling that gives us this magical mingling of consonants and vowels in "She fluffed up the feather bed and puffed up the pillows, she turned back the lily-white linen, and then she said: 'There, my little rabbits—a downy nest for each of you. Tumble in and slumber sweetly'"? For words in translating must be chosen from any number of possibilities, and the exact English equivalents to the German would not necessarily have delivered that soothing combination of *l*'s and *w*'s. We cannot be certain whom we have to thank for "So he sneaked out of the barn and, taking the path between his four paws, he made off for the town of Bremen" in **"The Musicians of Bremen."** But as for "They were dressed in satin and silk. Their bustles were puffed, their bodices stuffed, their skirts were ruffled and tufted with bows; their sleeves were muffled with furbelows. They wore bells that tinkled and glittering rings; and rubies and pearls and little birds' wings!" in **"Cinderella,"** that is pure Wanda.

In her illustrating, as she had in her translating, Wanda went back to early childhood to find truth and verification, and to get a powerful sense of place. She invoked the thick woods near Tante Klaus's for the dark forests in **"Hansel and Gretel,"** she hunted out her father's portfolios with their scenes of peasant interiors, and she explored her own memories of country weddings and her New Ulm background. (p. 313)

Wanda Gág freely and lovingly and unself-consciously created for children, at the same time she worked for her own joy and fulfillment as an artist through both words and drawings. Because she had the greatest possible respect for her audience, it followed that her standards of workmanship, the demands she made upon herself, were as high and as rigorous for children as for adults: the books she created for the young came from the same deep well of creative impulse—and were *required* to come from it—as the drawings she sent to exhibitions. The well was the same for both. (p. 314)

> *Eleanor Cameron, "Wanda Gág: Myself and Many Me's," in her* The Green and Burning Tree: On the Writing and Enjoyment of Children's Books *(© 1962,*

1964, 1966, 1969 by Eleanor Cameron; reprinted by permission of Little, Brown and Company in association with The Atlantic Monthly Press), Atlantic-Little, Brown, 1969, pp. 295-316.

For several decades the drawings, prints, and books of Wanda Gág of New Ulm, Minnesota, have charmed children and adults on both sides of the Atlantic. . . . Her picture books captured the verve of animal and human life as few illustrated volumes have done before or since. Such Gág works as *Millions of Cats, Snippy and Snappy, The Funny Thing,* and *Snow White and the Seven Dwarfs* offered some of the normal fare of children's literature: a love of nature, celebration of youth, wit and whimsy, and cuddly creatures. The infectious cadence of the first-named and most famous has also left parents and children chanting "hundreds of cats, thousands of cats, and millions and billions and trillions of cats" at the most unexpected moments. . . .

But this climb to success was an arduous one, a struggle that left a mark on her personality and art heretofore not widely appreciated. Underlying the charming tales of furry cats and wicked witches was an earnest regard for the underdog and a reverence for the working class. The artist's personal experience with economic hard times, her education in realist literature, and her brush with left-wing intellectuals in Minnesota and New York imparted a consciousness that at least indirectly affected her art. Her drawings, prints, and children's books of the 1920-40 era reveal a strong undercurrent of social concern, a rejection of easy sentiment, and even a disenchantment with American values and institutions. (p. 239)

When Wanda took her manuscript of *Millions of Cats* to publishers . . . , little did she suspect the significance of this moment to herself or American art. *Millions of Cats* became the prototype for the picture book, defined as one in which a single artist conceives, writes, illustrates, and supervises the printing of the whole book project. Her success in the children's book field should not have come as a surprise, as her upbringing and later training left her peculiarly prepared for the new genre. (p. 249)

The appeal to children of Wanda's work is not its easy sentiment but its honesty and rejection of the maudlin. She swam against the flood of sweet "pictorial baby talk" that dominated children's literature in that era. Her intelligence, philosophy, and rigid standards of art made it impossible for her to dilute the European folk tales or to crank out soppy picture stories. In her dealings with children Wanda never condescended. She had taught school and had played a major role in raising her sisters and brother, experiences which persuaded her that children were more alert to the outside world than most people thought. She believed children were blessed with forthrightness and innate good sense and need not be shielded from reality.

Out of Wanda's bedrock belief in the high potential of human behavior and in the artist's intellectual integrity came picture stories that strongly suggested aspects of the tense, modern era: stories featuring the same struggle, hardship, human frailty, violence, and even death that she had known in her own lifetime. In *Millions of Cats,* an old man's apparent beneficence (he cannot choose one cat over another to bring to his lonely wife) leads ultimately to mass carnage when the cats begin to fight to decide which one will be permitted to live with the poor farm couple. In another story, *Cinderella,* Wanda emphasized the irrevocable ill will between the heroine and her jealous stepsisters even after the prince proved Cinderella the rightful owner of the glass slipper. (p. 250)

(In most accounts, they all go off together to the castle.) Wanda did not feel bound to any rule of virtuous finish that locked in Walt Disney artists. Instead, her books consistently exhibit the same brand of realism that is found in her prints of urban and small-town America. Although most of her stories were fairy tales, she viewed them as a palliative against, not an escape from, the grim, impersonal, industrial living of the twentieth century. She wrote of mythical places where good sense, communication between people, and a sense of humor still were prized. Yet even here she would not soft-pedal human folly, and frequently the fairy tales were partly allegories of modern problems.

Inevitably, Wanda's social consciousness emerged in her children's illustrations. (p. 251)

The cat battle in *Millions of Cats* may reflect her revulsion against the destruction caused by World War I. Peasants abound in nearly all her stories, and Wanda's regard for the peasant class was almost legendary. Her seven dwarfs are frugal, hardworking, sensible men, not Disney's famous likable, comic fools who anxiously stumbled around the forest cottage awaiting Snow White's next kiss. Wanda spoke of peasants in the sense of all honest workers trying to maintain their integrity amidst the pressures of the industrial Western world. The picture book proved to be a good way for her to serve humanity and to vindicate herself from earlier accusations of "elitism" and being out of touch with ordinary human beings.

She also revealed in her children's books the strength and dignity of women. Like Wanda herself, females in her books asserts their opinions and make decisions. They suffer the same sins of pride, vanity, and greed as men. With few exceptions, their faults are those of commission, not omission: Rarely do they emerge as fragile housewives baking cookies while their he-man husbands till the fields and decide on the urgent family matters. The wife in *Millions of Cats* suggests that her husband find a cat, tells him that they can only afford to keep one after he returns with "trillions" of cats, and then takes charge of feeding the lone survivor of the ensuing cat fight. A more direct sally into feminist issues can be seen in her version of the folk legend, *Gone Is Gone; or, The Story of the Man Who Wanted to Do Housework.* (p. 252)

A commitment to lofty art standards also mitigated against false sentimentalism in Wanda's picture books. She had undertaken the rigors of academic classwork and made a careful study of the old masters and modern artists such as [Paul] Gauguin, [Vincent] Van Gogh, and [Paul] Cezanne. Her prints, drawings, and paintings drew ideas from the classics, modern realists, and abstract artists, and she did not alter her carefully developed style when she began producing for a younger audience. . . . [Her] illustrations revealed many of the same features of her earlier drawings and prints: stylized human figures, slight spatial distortions, asymmetrical compositions, and, as Carl Zigrosser put it, the "interplay of complex repetitive rhythms." The animal and human figures of *Millions of Cats, The Funny Thing, Gone Is Gone,* and her three books based on fairy tales of the brothers Grimm are more representational than some of the hybrid creatures and surreal settings of more recent picture books that draw heavily on post-World War II abstract art movements. (p. 253)

For all her appreciation of Cezanne and modern European art, Wanda never risked obscuring her stories through an adventuresome abstract vocabulary. Making pictures and stories comprehensible to a wide audience was ultimately her best response to those who questioned her "democratic" sentiments. Her images were recognizable but hardly photographic. They were halfway steps between academic realism and the European *avant-garde,* like so much of American art of this era. (pp. 253-54)

Wanda simply would not discard the fruits of her hard-earned education—humanist and technical—to appeal to a young audience. She epitomized Lynd Ward's description of the realist credo: "I will make the best pictures of which I am capable, whether for children or grown-ups."

In all of her art forms, Wanda refused to use push-button sentimentality. Unconventional parents, liberal and radical friends, personal contests with poverty and provincialism, a steady diet of realist literature, and a close study of art history all made her a questioning art-humanist, alert to human problems and eager to deal with them in her prints, paintings, and children's books. She was fortunate to have had such a rich past. (p. 254)

> *Richard W. Cox, "Wanda Gág: The Bite of the Picture Book," in* Minnesota History *(copyright, 1977, by the Minnesota Historical Society; used by permission), Vol. 44, No. 7, Fall, 1975, pp. 239-54.*

MILLIONS OF CATS (1928)

Millions of cats and no two alike! Whether one likes cats in the flesh, or whether one doesn't, Wanda Gág's drawings of them are irresistible.

Not since J. G. Francis's "Cheerful Cats" came to enliven the pages of "St. Nicholas" has there been a cat book in any way comparable to this one. It bears all the earmarks of becoming a perennial favorite among children and takes a place of its own, both for the originality and strength of its pictures and the living folk-tale quality of its text. A child will almost feel that he has made this book, printed in a hand lettering clearer than type. In form it is, indeed, an incentive for any child who makes pictures to set about making a book of his own.

Here is neither sophistication nor writing down, nor what seems to me infinitely more demoralizing to taste, *drawing down* to children. Everything lives in this book—cats, humans, trees, the little house "which had flowers all around it, except where the door was," the grass on the hills, the pond from which each cat took a sip and drained it dry, the delightful procession of cats following the very old man over the hills, and the frightened kitten who becomes "the most beautiful cat in the world." The atmosphere of domesticity which pervades the whole book is not the least of its charms. The very old man is still in sight of his home, even when climbing over numberless sunny hills and along cool valleys to the hill "which was quite covered with cats."

Wanda Gág sees everything as a child sees and she draws with a strength and beauty far removed from the commercialized art which is flooding the market with flashy picture books in crude colors. We have needed just such a regenerating American influence in this particular field, which, in my experience, is the most important of all in the formation of children's taste in reading and in art. . . .

A picture book for a child! As the few great books for children have been written in the leisure hours of great men and women, so all memorable picture books must spring out of the natural desires of artists who have something special to say to children.

Wanda Gág has something special to say, something to share, in this first picture book of hers which is so sure of a place among early American children's books of the future. Back of all the sharply differentiated amusing cats and their fight for a place in the home of the very old man and the very old woman lies a profound sense of beauty at the heart of all life.

Those who are familiar with the prints, etchings and water colors of this gifted young artist whose work has been recognized by the leading museums and collectors of the country, will not be surprised to know that Wanda Gág's first picture book has more in it than children who chuckle over the pictures are at all likely to realize. There is more, too, than the delightful individualization of cats so dear to cat lovers. . . . [These] drawings stir deeper emotions. One marvels at the vigorous technique and the fertility and variety of an imagination which could give birth to such an old world picture story book in present-day New York. That Wanda Gág will not do another in the least like it is assured by her rejection of every opportunity to standardize any given triumph in her art. . . .

Wise Wanda Gág! I hope she may be "amused" enough by something to do another picture book for children, but it is good to know that she cannot be persuaded to do anything against her own conviction. Her publishers have made a very fortunate choice in giving first place to this distinctive book in their first list of children's books, since it is a book of universal interest to children living anywhere in the world.

> *Anne Carroll Moore, "A Distinguished Picture Book," in* New York Herald Tribune Books *(© I.H.T. Corporation; reprinted by permission), September 9, 1928, p. 9.*

Each page of Wanda Gág's **"Millions of Cats"** should be considered as a whole, a whole made up of interwoven story and decoration. The text runs like a streamlet around the very old man and the very old woman and their house that had flowers, and through the hills where the old man walked hunting for a cat, and in and among the millions of cats which he finally found. . . .

If these cats lap ponds and browse on pastures they are true cats in the pride which is their undoing. Only the scraggly kitten survives to grow nice and plump in a series of studies posed with a large bowl of milk. Her end is the end of all good kittens—to play with a ball of yarn on a round rag rug in the radiant light of a lamp, the center of admiring attention. The pictures are quaint and bold, the cats thoroughly feline, and the kittens in their settings of luminous flowers enchanting.

> *Elizabeth Coatsworth, "Reviews: 'Millions of Cats'," in* The Saturday Review of Literature *(copyright © 1928 by Saturday Review; all rights reserved; reprinted by permission), Vol. 5, No. 9, September 22, 1928, p. 149.*

[*Millions of Cats* is a tale that will last as long as Jakob and Wilhelm Grimm or Hans Christian Andersen. It] is as important as the librarians say it is. Not only does it bring to book-making one of the most talented and original of American lithographers, an artist who has a following both here and abroad, but it is a marriage of picture and tale that is perfectly balanced. And the story pattern, so cunningly devised with such hearty and moral simplicity, is told in a prose as skilful as jingle. . . . Easily the best novel since Cinderella, in that genre. (p. 548)

> *Ernestine Evans, "This Year's Crop," in* The Nation *(copyright 1928 The Nation magazine, The Nation*

From Millions of Cats, *written and illustrated by Wanda Gág.*

Associates, Inc.), Vol. 127, No. 3307, November 21, 1928, pp. 547-48.*

In reviewing the life of the author-artist of this first true "picture book" by an American artist it seems the most natural thing in the world that *Millions of Cats* should have come into being from the genius of Wanda Gág. It has the sureness of the tale told for generations. It could only be the conception of an artist steeped in traditional lore. At a time when originality of artistic expression was only beginning to be encouraged, Wanda Gág dared to be herself, and the immediate success of her first book proved that children were ready for her fresh expression, which was at the same time perfectly in tune with the storytelling tradition. The pictures of *Millions of Cats* tell the story with vitality and atmosphere; yet the story can stand alone. (p. 634)

> *Ruth Hill Viguers, "The Artist as Storyteller: Picture Books," in* A Critical History of Children's Literature *by Cornelia Meigs, Anne Thaxter Eaton, Elizabeth Nesbitt, and Ruth Hill Viguers, edited by Cornelia Meigs (reprinted with permission of Macmillan Publishing Co., Inc.; copyright © 1953, 1969 by Macmillan Publishing Co., Inc.), revised edition, Macmillan, 1969, p. 633-53.**

An example of ultra-simplicity of plot and the extensive use of rhythmic patterns and refrains is the story *Millions of Cats*. . . . It resembles the brief folk anecdote in which the body of the tale is filled out with repetitive verses and parallel incidents. The construction is so compact that within half a dozen sentences we learn everything we will ever know about the characters, their location, their problem, and their plan to solve it. A "very old woman" says she wishes she had a cat and her husband, a "very old man," says he'll find her one. The rest is all rhythm and pattern centering around the selection of the pet. As the cats follow the man home they stop twice: each has one drop of water (leaving the pond dry) and one blade of grass (leaving the hillside bare). The refrain provides a unifying, chant-like effect. . . . (pp. 84-5)

A ferocious battle among the cats culminates in the impossible, nonsensical, and wondrous fact that they "eat each other up," that is, all except one kitten. This is a proper climax because it's strong enough to enable the listener to feel deeply about the resolution. The child has a sense of relief and satisfaction because the one modest kitten has found a good home. There can be no literal awareness of cats "eating each other up" because such a happening is clearly impossible; it's as fantastic as the rest of the story. (p. 85)

> *Donnarae MacCann and Olga Richard, "Literary Elements," in their* The Child's First Books: A Critical Study of Pictures and Texts *(© 1973 by Donnarae MacCann and Olga Richard; reprinted by permission of The H. W. Wilson Company), Wilson, 1973, pp. 79-94.*

THE FUNNY THING (1929)

[*The Funny Thing*] is the work of an artist of distinction. Two years ago Wanda Gág was known to art lovers as an artist whose work was already placed in the Metropolitan Museum. Last year she published *Millions of Cats* and straightway belonged to children everywhere. *The Funny Thing* has the same quaint charm.

> *Helen Ferris, "Books to Delight Our Youngest: 'The Funny Thing'," in* The Bookman, *New York (copyright, 1929, by George H. Doran Company), Vol. LXX, No. 3, November, 1929, p. 307.*

Wanda Gág has followed in the steps of her own last year's success "Millions of Cats" with "The Funny Thing." This is a pleasant, simply written little tale. . . . Once more we have a humor and a curious, grotesque charm that are highly individual. There is excellent technique here. Miss Gág knows how to draw and while to us personally the designing of some of the double-page pictures seemed over conscious and mannered at times, still there is certainly no one else who can touch her in her own particular line.

> *Rachel Field, "A Sheaf of Picture Books," in* The Saturday Review of Literature *(copyright © 1929 by Saturday Review; all rights reserved; reprinted by permission), Vol. VI, No. 17, November 16, 1929, p. 403.**

"The Funny Thing" bears strong witness to the great talents of Wanda Gág, creator of "Millions of Cats." If the history of the art of the picture book is ever written the name of this artist will undoubtedly be graven there in large letters, for she, writing her story as well as drawing it, has discovered the richest potentialities of each factor, and to the process of integration has brought a wealth of originality. No other books have quite that feeling of the artistic whole. And though one regrets that this story is, inevitably perhaps, lacking in the quality of proximity that made "Millions of Cats" a classic, yet there is here a charm that is more real after the fifth reading than after the first. And that fact is significant.

> *Lynd Ward, "Some Picture Books of the Year," in* New York Herald Tribune Books *(© I.H.T. Corporation; reprinted by permission), November 17, 1929, p. 9.**

SNIPPY AND SNAPPY (1931)

If the new book, "Snippy and Snappy" wants labeling, it can best be tagged by saying that there is strong probability it will find a place for itself on the shelf alongside the cat book, regardless of the fact that it deals with a couple of field mice. There is a great deal of movement in the book; the story moves up hill and down, pulling both text and pictures with it, and you go from one page to the next confident (here is an acid test of picture book technique) that new things for both the eye and the mind are ahead.

I am, as a rule, not overfriendly toward the practice of putting clothes on small animals such as mice. But with Snippy and Snappy the tailoring is not overdone, and there are so many other things to take in that the matter becomes of secondary importance. There is a delightfully bright end paper to start you off, a well designed title page, and then the succession of drawings of a great variety of things: hay fields, flowers, toadstools, front doors, kitchen cupboards: all objects of everyday existence. It is Miss Gág's peculiar triumph, that she sees familiar objects as distinct phenomena and can so set them down in black and white that they take on in our eyes that same individuality. Several of the drawings are particularly distinguished for this quality: the mop leaning against the wall, the floor lamp writhing up to its enormous blossom. The page whereon Snippy and Snappy cross the threshold of the house may well become to many a mind the visual expression of adventure.

> *Lynd Ward, "Two Field Mice," in* New York Herald Tribune Books *(© I.H.T. Corporation; reprinted by permission), September 27, 1931, p. 11.*

"Snippy and Snappy," though less universal in its appeal than "Millions of Cats," the first book by this clever and original artist, is nevertheless a very charming and satisfactory picture book. The pictures are amusing and full of delightful and carefully thought-out details and give the effect of a great deal of motion and action. Even inanimate objects, such as the mop which the two little field mice discover when they visit and explore a house for the first time and call a "plant with a wooden stem and its roots outside of the ground," or the lamp which they think is also a plant, "with beautiful curly roots outside the ground and leaves and a flower," have so much personality and individuality that they seem about to take part in the action of the story. Miss Gág's drawings are like the charms in the old fairy tales and make the reader the right size to share the adventures of "Snippy and Snappy" and see a house and its contents as a mouse might see it. There is a feeling of drama in the story that pleases children, and it reads aloud well, for the author's very simple prose has distinction and style.

> *Anne T. Eaton, "New Children's Books: 'Snippy and Snappy'," in* The New York Times Book Review *(© 1931 by The New York Times Company; reprinted by permission), November 1, 1931, p. 24.*

Very little children will like . . . the mouse tale by Wanda Gág, "Snippy and Snappy," so very much in the mood of her popular "Millions of Cats". . . . To my way of thinking the pictures in this third book by Miss Gág are better than any she has done for children. She has not made as many of the queer oyster-shell shaped full-page effects as in the earlier ones, and she has continued her fascinating portrayal of familiar household furnishings. These, in their detail and fantastic size as compared with the two small mice who are the chief actors, give it a charm and piquant quality sure to attract children, both the imaginative and matter-of-fact sort. The story, too, is simply and gaily written, for fun and not for information, although it has an excellent moral about meddling. (p. 296)

> *Rachel Field, "Picture Books Ahoy," in* The Saturday Review of Literature *(copyright © 1931 by Saturday Review; all rights reserved; reprinted by permission), Vol. VIII, No. 17, November 14, 1931, pp. 296-97.**

The two little mice are given personality in Wanda Gág's pictures principally by very expressive gestures and attitudes which attractively suggest the movements of small children. The humour of incongruity is the most important ingredient in this charming picture-book. (p. 327)

> *Margery Fisher, "Who's Who in Children's Books: 'Snippy and Snappy'," in her* Who's Who in Children's Books: A Treasury of the Familiar Characters of Childhood *(copyright © 1975 by Margery Fisher;*

reprinted by permission), Holt, Rinehart and Winston, Weidenfeld & Nicolson, 1975, pp. 326-27.

THE ABC BUNNY (1933)

In this entrancing volume the alphabet is only incidental; what the drawings do is to create a real and utterly engaging bunny. Children respond to him immediately, as in fact do readers of all ages. His adventures from the time when you discover him, under B, snug in bed, through C for crash, D for dash, E for "elsewhere in a flash," and so on; the animals he meets, "K for kitten catnip crazy," "L for lizard—look how lazy," all make up a perfect example of an absorbing tale for small children. In the course of it Bunny is lovable, frightened, daring, sleepy and frolicsome and he is equally irresistible in every mood. This is no rabbit brought to children to play with; on the contrary, it is the child who follows Bunny as he dashes from one experience to the next, always with a background of the open country.

The book has the freshness of invention, and the drawings the beauty, humor and originality characteristic of this artist's work. . . . **"The ABC Bunny"** is a distinguished piece of bookmaking as well as a book that children will promptly take to their hearts.

Anne T. Eaton, "This Year's Books for Children," in The New York Times Book Review *(© 1933 by The New York Times Company; reprinted by permission), November 12, 1933, p. 21.**

First of all the books of the year I would place . . . **"ABC Bunny"** and for a very special reason. Wanda Gág has a feeling for the rightness of words that no other maker of picture books can approach. Children love to follow the bunny's adventure through charming pictures and clever rhyming couplets full of pleasant words. . . .

Alice Dalgliesh, "Picture Books: 'The ABC Bunny'," in The Saturday Review of Literature *(copyright © 1933 by* Saturday Review; *all rights reserved; reprinted by permission), Vol. X, No. 18, November 18, 1933, p. 279.*

It is easily understood why this book made a happy addition to children's literature and stimulated an interest in ABC books. The letters of the alphabet lead Bunny into a series of fascinating experiences. The expressions on his face and on the faces of the little creatures he meets complement the catchy rhymes with their lilting rhythm. (p. 188)

Bernard J. Lonsdale and Helen K. Mackintosh, "A Is for Apple," in their Children Experience Literature *(copyright © 1973 Random House, Inc.; reprinted by permission of Random House, Inc.), Random House, 1973, pp. 187-89.**

Wanda Gág avoids the problem of having to force terminology by setting the antics of her *ABC Bunny* within the scope of youthful vocabulary. Her plot is reminiscent of "Chicken Little." Bunny is "snug a-bed" when he is suddenly awakened by the "Crash!" of a falling apple. . . . And he is off on a route that includes some exciting adventures with appropriate supporting characters, and that eventually circles back to Bunny Town, where the action began. The ending of the story particularly claims reader involvement. The dashing bunny and all his relations "exit" into burrows, and in the finest tradition of the old oral art of the storyteller, the author briefly concludes

with "That's enough for us today. Y for You, take one last look. Z for Zero—close the book!''

Stylistically, *ABC Bunny* is structured as a folktale and as such is particularly well suited to the story needs of the preschool child. (p. 175)

Mary Agnes Taylor, "From Apple to Abstraction in Alphabet Books," in Children's literature in education *(© 1978, Agathon Press, Inc.; reprinted by permission of the publisher), Vol. 9, No. 4 (Winter), 1978, pp. 173-81.**

GONE IS GONE; OR, THE STORY OF A MAN WHO WANTED TO DO HOUSEWORK (1935)

Many of us cherish for years a misty memory of some favorite story of our childhood. Often we never find the tale again, or, if we do, it lacks the remembered charm. Wanda Gág, however, has magic at her command. . . . [Unable to find a satisfactory copy of her favorite tale,] Miss Gág straightway went to work to reconstruct the story as she remembered it, giving to it the full-flavored conversational style and sly peasant humor with which it had been told to her as a little girl.

The result is an irresistible volume in which both text and pictures provide genuine and dramatic fun. Boys and girls from 5 to 9 who dearly love to chuckle over a story will take it to their hearts at once. It is excellent for reading aloud and will also appeal to those beginning to read for themselves. The black and white drawings . . . make us eager for the illustrated edition of Grimm which, it is rumored, Miss Gág is preparing.

From The ABC Bunny, *written and illustrated by Wanda Gág.*

Anne T. Eaton, ''New Books for Boys and Girls,'' in The New York Times Book Review *(© 1935 by The New York Times Company; reprinted by permission), October 6, 1935, p. 10.**

Wanda Gág, like many children, loved the old story of the man who said he could do more work a day than his wife could do in three, but when she grew up she could never find a version in all the books like the tale as her grandmother had told it to her in Bohemia. The plot might be the same, but where were the savory details, where the ''sly peasant humor''? So, coming at last to realize that her grandmother's version was her peculiar treasure, she determined to share it with American children, and now, supplied with plenty of fat little pictures in the same spirit, it makes one of the smallest and funniest story books of the season.

Laura Benet, ''Reviews of Children's Books: 'Gone Is Gone: or, The Story of a Man Who Wanted to Do Housework','' in New York Herald Tribune Books *(© I.H.T. Corporation; reprinted by permission), November 17, 1935, p. 11.*

TALES FROM GRIMM   (1936)

Richly and truly educational . . . is Wanda Gág's **Tales from Grimm**. . . . Several of the best tales she discovered were scarcely known in English. **'Six Servants,'** for which she has made inimitable pictures of the **'Fat One and the Thin One,'** is a good example of the less known group. The illustrations, from the beautiful frontispiece in color, 'Rapunzel, Rapunzel, let down your hair,' to the last black and white drawing for **'The Musicians of Bremen,'** are in the true tradition of the folk tale, freshly rendered with the keenness of perception, the intellectual integrity, and the complete mastery of technique which distinguish the work of Wanda Gág.

While the book is very definitely designed for younger children (who will read it with utmost ease and pleasure), the older reader will relish the new vitality given to tales as familiar as **'Hansel and Gretel'** by Miss Gág's pictures and choice of words. She is a natural storyteller.

Anne Carroll Moore, ''The Atlantic Bookshelf: 'Tales from Grimm','' in The Atlantic Monthly *(copyright © 1936, by The Atlantic Monthly Company, Boston, Mass.; reprinted with permission), Vol. 157, No. 3, September, 1936.*

Here is one of those rare books that makes a reviewer experienced in children's reading matter rub his eyes and ask himself if he is dreaming; if anything has really come to pass so simply and exactly right. We needed a thoroughly good selection for the use of children of the tales of the Brothers Grimm, using the ones that carry most in the way of shrewd peasant sense and the woodland beauty of the Teutonic fairy tale.

Wanda Gág has made that selection—tales that are or should be familiar to every household, most of them already so and one or two that I find, somewhat to my surprise, have the charm of novelty to American children. These sixteen priceless tales she has translated afresh, or, rather, lifted them out of one language into another so deftly that wherever there was a special tang, at least a taste of it remains. She has kept and given the sense of spoken language: reading is like listening to a story-teller. And then——then she has put all this into pictures that simply can't be matched for the purpose.

May Lamberton Becker, ''Old Fairy-Stories in Their New Dresses,'' in New York Herald Tribune Books *(© I.H.T. Corporation; reprinted by permission), November 15, 1936, p. 9.*

The Grimm stories come from the soil, their home was in the forest and the peasants' huts; as Wanda Gág says in her introduction, they are folktales rather than fairy stories, and in them the fairy world, though properly weird and strange, has a convincing three-dimensional character. Because she feels this quality in the tales, because their magic is a part of her earliest recollections, and because she has re-read them many times, and worked over them with the boy and girl of today in mind, Miss Gág has made a thoroughly satisfying book, and one that children will at once feel belongs to them. In her translations and in her drawings Miss Gág has caught the essence of the folktale, its drama, its wonder, its humor, its joy, and with a fine freshness and zest she is bringing these qualities to boys and girls.

The book is beautifully and appropriately made; its large print and uncrowded page combined with the many illustrations in black and white, and the beautiful frontispiece in color of Rapunzel in the tower, will make an instant appeal to young readers, and will prove a genuine incentive to children who do not read easily. This is a book that should not only be in public libraries and school libraries, but in the home library of every boy and girl from 6 to 10. Adult readers, too, will enjoy the new life that this rare artist has brought to a classic of childhood. Story-tellers will find the book invaluable.

Anne T. Eaton, ''The Changing Art of Writing for Children,'' in The New York Times Book Review *(© 1936 by The New York Times Company; reprinted by permission), November 15, 1936, p. 12.**

GROWING PAINS: DIARIES AND DRAWINGS FOR THE YEARS 1908-1917   (1940)

The keeping of a diary is not an uncommon practice among the young, but this journal cannot be classed with the feverish indulgences and moping introspections of the ordinary girl. It was pursued with remarkable pertinacity and recorded with an objective truthfulness that sets it apart from the innumerable examples of verbal exhibitionism put forth by artists in their nonage. It is quite possible that a measure of its naturalness and restraint may be attributed to the author's upbringing in a community where the artist was not regarded with undue suspicion. . . .

When Wanda Gág, in her twentieth year, enrolled in the art schools of the Twin Cities, she was a self-taught professional, somewhat conventional in her technical habits, but by no means conventional in her conception of the dignity of her chosen career. In the latter part of her diary she tells the story of her gropings, errors and occasional triumphs; her social life with friends and cavaliers, and her undeviating efforts to make her own way in the world. These chapters are intimate and much too long. But as they stand they are entirely free from the usual maunderings of those who foster the genius cult in art—there is never a trace of morbidity and the psychotic nonsense of the swooning intellectual.

This diary is not a conscious literary exercise; it is the unaffected account of the struggles of a girl who was determined to make herself an artist, and who succeeded nobly. Throughout the book the author's extraordinary purity of mind shines out;

she had talent and what is rarer than talent and finer than facility—character. She faced life, never whined, truckled, or hoped for miracles, and with enormous self-discipline, developed her capacities to the fullest extent.

There are no absolute rules for the training of artists, and I would be the last to recommend hardships as the panacea for creative ills. But Wanda Gág's diary brings into sharp relief one indispensable factor to the growth and healthy development of the expressive impulse. The young artist must be conditioned by the rigors of practical life if he is to produce anything worthy of the attention of men and women who are interested in human values and not in the whimsicalities of protected weaklings.

> Thomas Craven, "The Diary of a Working Artist," in New York Herald Tribune Books (© I.H.T. Corporation; reprinted by permission), September 29, 1940, p. 2.

That [Wanda Gág] will continue to contribute to children's books I believe more firmly than ever after reading **Growing Pains** and tracing the development of her art to the point of its mastery of form and design without loss of the intensity and vividness with which she sees and feels when a "drawing fit" is upon her. "When I draw I simply feel. I do not think of what kind of lines I am making." (pp. 338-39)

It required great courage for one so sensitive as Wanda Gág to publish diaries reaching from her fifteenth to her twenty-fourth year. I found the record so moving and so important at this time of storm and stress and great confusion regarding youth all over the world that it seems to me another proof of her intelligence and keen awareness of what youth has to give if left free to meet life on its own terms. She has known extreme poverty and great sorrow, but she has also known the love of children, the influence of poetry, music, dancing, the joys of reading and of friendship, the stimulation of endless discussions. Her "dreams" and "drawing moods" make rare reading. Over and above everything else she knows the truth of the old Irish proverb: "Beauty like sorrow dwelleth everywhere." (p. 339)

> Anne Carroll Moore, "The Three Owls' Notebook," in The Horn Book Magazine (copyrighted, 1940, by The Horn Book, Inc., Boston), Vol. XVI, No. 5, October, 1940, pp. 338-40.*

"Growing Pains" . . . makes it easy to understand [Wanda Gág's] achievement. . . .

These diaries are remarkable for many reasons, for their lively style, for their "documentary" value, for their droll appraisals. They are chiefly memorable, however, as a joyful testament of faith.

> Frances Smyth, "Testament of Faith," in The Saturday Review of Literature (copyright © 1940 by Saturday Review; all rights reserved; reprinted by permission), Vol. XXII, No. 24, October 5, 1940, p. 12.

[This is a singularly] candid and evocative book. . . .

"Growing Pains" has an immediate interest which goes well beyond the remembered facts of autobiography. It is a girl's diary, written between the ages of 15 and 24, as childishness passes slowly into maturity. The girl, to be sure, has become a celebrated artist. . . . And there is eventful action (even though set down with unconscious restraint) in her active struggle against the cramping ills of poverty. She is a personality,

and one can see that personality growing up through quite specific circumstance. But there is a larger value than that in this diary: here is the universality of normal sturdy youth.

There are the literary and artistic raptures of Wanda's years and period. . . . We are to watch the objects of her enthusiasm change, see her personal revulsion to "cleverness," already we look on as she considers the nature of sentimentality with amusing detachment and surprising poise. But it's a concrete record, by and large, which the diary of these early years sets forth with spontaneous reaction and natural vocabulary. It is alive and young and gallant and American. And for all the writer's need for self-expression, it is closer to [Betty Evelyn Davies's] "Six Girls" and [Louisa May Alcott's] "Little Women" than to Marie Bashkirtseff—which is one of the reasons that we find it so good, as we chuckle, admire and sympathize.

The book tells a real story, and it does it with freshness and a flavor that only long quotation could reproduce.

> Katherine Woods, "The Diary of An Artist's Growth," in The New York Times Book Review (© 1940 by The New York Times Company; reprinted by permission), October 20, 1940, p. 9.

NOTHING AT ALL (1941)

The appearance of anything by the creator of **"Millions of Cats"** is an event. This time she appeals to children for the first time in colors, bright, clear and set on with the tidiness that delights a small child. Otherwise she keeps, for the shape of the book, the hand-lettering of its story and the easy blend of the every day and the impossible in its plot, the same plan as in her already classic debut. The pretty little volume will please at sight children who loved **"Snippy and Snappy,"** for it has an appearance to which they are accustomed plus the touch of color for which they have been asking.

The story is of three little dogs, orphan but happy, living each in a house with a special roof. Pointy lives in the house with a point, Curly in the one with scallops, and under the roundish roof lives a dog whom no one could see because he was invisible.

This naturally creates problems for an illustrator. At first, all Miss Gág can do for him is a round white spot, trusting—not in vain—that children will "love you even if we cannot see you," as the other two puppies do. But when these two are adopted and Nothing-at-All trails along after, he begins to look something like a comet in the grass; the only way to see him is by the track he leaves. He takes advice from a bird, whirls rapidly and begins to shake down into the general shape of a puppy. Then he gets spots, then rolling eyes and, at last, a flashing red tongue. His friends cry, "Oh, little Something-After-All, it *is* so nice to see you!" There is just enough of the abstract about the situation—one can scarcely call it a drama—to put it among books for children a little beyond their years. But as many children belong to just this age group the little piece will have a large audience, even without the universal, almost hypnotic, appeal of Miss Gág's famous cat story.

> May Lamberton Becker, "Books for Young People: 'Nothing at All'," in New York Herald Tribune Books (© I.H.T. Corporation; reprinted by permission), September 21, 1941, p. 8.

It does make me happy whenever I find in a children's book that which leads me to feel it is the real thing. Wanda Gág has not "done it again" in *Nothing At All* . . . , for Wanda Gág never repeats herself in idea, text, or drawing. It is a pity to break the spell of surprise in this utterly charming picture book by hinting that Nothing-at-all is such an invisible, resourceful dog as might emerge from the pages of the Brothers Grimm into the light of our day. With the aid of a jackdaw, a magic chant, his two brothers and two adorable children, he gradually emerges from a shape. In a series of lithographic drawings in colors, Wanda Gág has invested the unseen with a reality that goes straight to the heart of child or grown-up. Here are humor, beauty, strength of draughtsmanship and a fresh childlike conception of life most reassuring in a world even more upset for animals than for human beings. (p. 381)

> *Anne Carroll Moore, "The Three Owls' Notebook,"*
> *in* The Horn Book Magazine *(copyrighted, 1941, by*
> *The Horn Book, Inc., Boston), Vol. XVII, No. 5,*
> *September-October, 1941, pp. 380-82.*

Once upon a time, Wanda Gág tells us, beginning her tale in time-honored fashion, there were three little orphan dogs. . . .

And in her inimitable drawings Miss Gág proceeds to show us the two occupied kennels and the one all full of nothingness. When the two little visible dogs were adopted and taken gently away by a little boy and a girl, little Nothing At All did not stay behind, and as he trotted after the others we see a white ball of Nothingness and the track it made. . . . Wanda Gág, who is something of a magician herself, shows us little Nothing At All becoming more and more of a shape, until he was a really truly see-able dog, and a most lovable round-eared puppy at that.

The lithographic drawings in soft tones of red, green and rust, have a gentle humor and an irresistible charm. Everything that Wanda Gág does is fresh and new. As appealing as **"Millions of Cats,"** and perhaps even more lovable, **"Nothing At All"** has an individuality of its own. It will take a permanent place among the books cherished by children and their elders.

> *Anne T. Eaton, "Invisible Dog," in* The New York
> Times Book Review *(© 1941 by The New York Times*
> *Company; reprinted by permission), November 2,*
> *1941, p. 38.*

I had hoped, though it didn't seem possible, that Wanda Gág's new book might be as good as her masterpiece, *Millions of Cats.* Well, it isn't. But who cares? If she never gives us worse we will not complain. "Nothing-at-all was as nice a dog as anyone could wish for, but no one could see him—he was invisible." And from that very intriguing beginning Wanda Gág has created a story with a happy and visible ending. The story shows a lively and original imagination. To illustrate it she has drawn many bewitching pictures in colour. Her literary and artistic skill is of a high order, but the latter has not the scope in these smallish pictures which the larger pages of *Millions of Cats* allowed. I cannot feel that the book is up to the high standard reached by most of this author's earlier work.

> *"New Books: 'Nothing at All'," in* The Junior Book-
> shelf, *Vol. 6, No. 2, July, 1942, p. 95.*

THREE GAY TALES FROM GRIMM (1943)

Wanda Gág takes the child with her straight into the folk-tale world, where a key is sure to unlock the little door among the rocks that leads to a magical secret underground and where every fir tree, every little peasant house and garden seem to suggest that wonders are close at hand.

In this little volume which will take its place beside Miss Gág's delightful version of **"Snow White and the Seven Dwarfs,"** her larger collection of **"Tales from Grimm"** and the tiny volume containing **"Gone Is Gone,"** she has retold three of the lesser-known tales: **"The Clever Wife," "The Three Feathers"** (sometimes known as **"The Frog Bride"**) and **"Goose Hans." "The Three Feathers,"** with its delightful pictures of the helpful Toad, in her dim underground cavern, surrounded by her attendants, the wrinkly crinkly little green toads, who so cleverly aided Simple Sepp to carry out his appointed tasks and win a princess, is the gayest and most charming of the three tales. But Kotti, the wife who so consistently did the wrong thing to the confusion of her patient Friedel, and whose final triumph was due not to good sense but good luck, will provide a chance for the laugh which children so enjoy.

> *Anne T. Eaton, "New Books for Younger Readers:*
> *'Three Gay Tales from Grimm'," in* The New York
> Times Book Review *(© 1943 by The New York Times*
> *Company; reprinted by permission), October 24, 1943,*
> *p. 21.*

Wanda Gág presents three comparatively unknown folktales, worded as only Wanda Gág can word them, and illustrated as only she can illustrate them. . . . The drawing of the three thieves sitting under the tree counting Friedal's gold while Kotti pours the vinegar on them from her safe perch on the bough is the kind of picture that children study for a long, long time. It will be fun to hear them chuckle over it. The second story is called **"The Three Feathers."** . . . Here Wanda Gág's wording is at its best. This story will be an unending joy to storytellers. The third story is about a very stupid fellow called Goose Hans. The children are going to find it difficult to believe that *anyone* could be as stupid as Hans is. They will applaud Gretel for running home to her mother instead of marrying him! Why should a girl marry a man who is so stupid that he smears himself all over with honey and feathers and sits on the goose's nest to hatch out the eggs? Boys and girls, we feel sure, are going to have lots of fun with these three gay tales.

> *M.G.D., "Folk and Fanciful Tales: 'Three Gay Tales*
> *from Grimm'," in* The Saturday Review of Literature
> *(copyright © 1943 by* Saturday Review; *all rights*
> *reserved; reprinted by permission), Vol. XXVI, No.*
> *46, November 13, 1943, p. 27.*

Wanda Gág's *Three Gay Tales from Grimm* looks as pleasant as her previous books. She has a faithful audience which would probably be disappointed to see her deviate from her approved and accustomed style. But I think it might not be a bad idea for her to try a new technique that would create renewed interest in her fine work. I am thinking of the large lithos she did for her *ABC Bunny* some years ago and a very refreshing difference it was. (pp. 20-1)

> *Fritz Eichenberg, "New Picture Books: 'Three Gay*
> *Tales from Grimm'," in* The Horn Book Magazine
> *(copyrighted, 1944, by The Horn Book, Inc., Bos-*
> *ton), Vol. XX, No. 1, January-February, 1944, pp.*
> *20-1.*

Wanda Gág is undoubtedly the best translator we have because she has been so completely saturated in the spirit of the Household Tales. Yet, do I detect a falling off, a rather more sophisticated attitude in this new collection of stories? Miss Gág, born and grown up in America must by now be far removed from the Bohemia of her parents. Her latest volume is given an apt title; the stories included are gay and amusing. . . . Miss Gág's pictures have a simplicity that suits these tales. Perhaps they are a little stylized and show too much evidence of the artist's sense of design, but they are nevertheless delightful and amusing and will, without doubt, be thoroughly enjoyed by all the young readers who have the good fortune to have this book.

> *"The New Books: 'Three Gay Tales from Grimm',"*
> *in* The Junior Bookshelf, *Vol. 10, No. 3, October,*
> *1946, p. 130.*

MORE TALES FROM GRIMM   (1947)

I read the illustrated galleys of **More Tales from Grimm** on the way over from Boston to New York and never did the journey seem so short. There is no letting down of the high spirit in the rendering of the stories, and if there are fewer pictures than the artist intended, we may be deeply grateful that so many had been completed. (p. 347)

> *Anne Carroll Moore, "The Three Owl's Notebook,"*
> *in* The Horn Book Magazine *(copyrighted, 1947, by*
> *The Horn Book, Inc., Boston), Vol. XXIII, No. 5,*
> *September-October, 1947, pp. 346-47.*

All of us who have realized, through our own delight or through sharing them with children, the great value of Wanda Gág's

wording and illustration of the German folktales have a feeling of gratitude, of very real happiness that this book has "come through." . . . Certainly the humor and imagination of these drawings, the fascinating detail of the backgrounds will waken the same pleasure in the children as did her first volume of the fairy tales of the Brothers Grimm. (p. 40)

> *"Folklore—Fantasy: 'More Tales from Grimm'," in*
> The Saturday Review of Literature *(copyright © 1947*
> *by Saturday Review; all rights reserved; reprinted*
> *by permission), Vol. XXX, No. 46, November 15,*
> *1947, pp. 40, 42.*

This last book of Wanda Gág was written and illustrated under the shadow of a fatal illness, but no hint of that can be found in it anywhere. The thirty-two stories are retold with all the gaiety and cunning skill which have made her earlier translations and her original stories so much beloved. They have a fluid quality, a spontaneity and an easy touch of the colloquial which give one the illusion of hearing rather than reading them. A few of the pictures were not entirely completed, but if we miss in these the rich blacks, the three-dimensional contours of the finished drawings, it is all the more interesting to have a glimpse of the artist at work. Like the majority of the illustrations they are full of her humor and imagination, and they reveal the marvelous sense of design which distinguished her work.

> *Ellen Lewis Buell, "Fantasy: 'More Tales from*
> *Grimm'," in* The New York Times Book Review *(©*
> *1947 by The New York Times Company; reprinted*
> *by permission), November 16, 1947, p. 5.*

Eloise Greenfield

1929-

Black American author of fiction, nonfiction, picture books, and poetry for children. Greenfield's works share the theme of the importance of childhood as the time to establish the inner strength necessary to face life with success. This confidence is built through learning from the accomplishments of past generations, from the examples of positive historical role models, and from the love and support of family and friends.

Greenfield's biographies attempt to provide young readers with experiences they can relate to and examples to apply to their own lives. They evolved from her work with the D.C. Black Writers Workshop in Washington and from her recognition of the short supply of good biographies on black historical figures. With *Rosa Parks,* Greenfield offers readers a black heroine—much-needed, according to several critics—and recreates both the political and social atmosphere of the sixties and the impact of Parks's pursuit of her rights. Her biography of Mary McLeod Bethune is praised for its effective portrayal of Bethune's inner strength and for its unidealized, natural characterization. *Childtimes: A Three Generation Memoir* is perhaps Greenfield's most important book. This autobiography, written by Greenfield and her mother with dictations from her grandmother, shows that harsh conditions and lack of material possessions need not destroy family bonds. She uses the experiences of her own family to represent the obstacles facing all black people and to demonstrate how they can be surmounted.

Greenfield's fiction deals with such childhood trials as death, divorce, the intrusion of a new sibling, and the fear of being alone. Greenfield's characters also find strength through the support of family members. She has earned praise for authentically portraying the affection and tenacity that exists within the black American family. Her family stories include not only the traditional nucleus of mother, father, sister, and brother, but also have major roles for aunts, uncles, grandmothers, and cousins.

Honey, I Love, Greenfield's first book of poetry, is appreciated for its warm family relationships, its positive images, and its Afro-American emphasis, but occasionally the collection is criticized for monotonous rhythm and lack of poetic quality. There is also some dissatisfaction with *She Come Bringing Me That Little Baby Girl:* Greenfield's solution to Kevin's problem is accused of being sexist. She is usually praised, however, for her realistic characters and dialogue and for presenting optimistic themes to her young readers. Her works strengthen confidence and build hope by using authentic, positive images of ancestry and family—important influences on the child's world. Greenfield received the first Carter G. Woodson Award in 1974 for *Rosa Parks,* the Irma Simonton Black Award in 1974 for *She Come Bringing Me That Little Baby Girl,* the Jane Addams Children's Book Award in 1976 for *Paul Robeson,* the Coretta Scott King Award in 1978 for *Africa Dream,* and a citation for her body of work from the Council on Interracial Books for Children in 1975. (See also *Contemporary Authors New Revision Series,* Vol. 1 and *Something about the Author,* Vol. 19.)

AUTHOR'S COMMENTARY

Writing is my work. It is work that is in harmony with me; it sustains me. I want, through my work, to help sustain children.

My attempts and those of other writers to offer sustenance will necessarily be largely ineffectual. Not only do we as human beings have limitations—so also does the written word. It cannot be eaten or worn; it cannot cure disease; it cannot dissipate pollution, defang a racist, cause a spoonful of heroin to disintegrate. But, at the right time, in the right circumstances, falling on the right mind, a word may take effect.

Through the written word I want to give children a love for the arts that will provoke creative thought and activity. . . . A strong love for the arts can enhance and direct their creativity as well as provide satisfying moments throughout their lives.

I want to encourage children to develop positive attitudes toward themselves and their abilities, to love themselves. When they are infants, other people have the complete responsibility for their health and safety; but when they are older, they must say, ''I am the only human being who is always with me, and I must care enough, must love myself enough, to make the decisions that are best for me.'' As for abilities—self-confidence is half the battle. Children must be able to face their mistakes and weaknesses without losing sight of their strengths.

I want to present to children alternative methods for coping with the negative aspects of their lives and to inspire them to seek new ways of solving problems. One of these alternative methods—so beautifully expressed in the words of Lucille Clifton, "oh children think about the good times"—I used in *Sister*. . . . Sister, who is Doretha, discovers that she can use her good times as stepping stones, as bridges, to get over the hard times—the death of her father, the alienation of her older sister, her struggles with school work. My hope is that children in trouble will not view themselves as blades of wheat caught in countervailing winds but will seek solutions, even partial or temporary solutions, to their problems.

I want to give children an appreciation for the contributions of their elders, contributions that may not be news but that make daily survival possible. . . . Children who are unaware of the practical guidance, moral support, and wisdom that older people have given and are willing to give are deprived of valuable assistance in growing up.

I want to give children a true knowledge of Black heritage, including both the African and the American experiences. The distortions of Black history have been manifold and ceaseless. A true history must be the concern of every Black writer. It is necessary for Black children to have a true knowledge of their past and present, in order that they may develop an informed sense of direction for their future.

I want to write stories that will allow children to fall in love with genuine Black heroes and heroines who have proved themselves to be outstanding in ability and in dedication to the cause of Black freedom. Rosa Parks, Paul Robeson, Harriet Tubman, Nat Turner, Sojourner Truth, Marcus Garvey, Malcolm X, Dr. Martin Luther King, Nina Simone, and so many others deserve our love and our respect. And this love and respect must be given for the right reasons. Jackie Robinson was a great athlete long before the major leagues decided they needed him. The fact that he was selected for entry into the major leagues does not enhance his worth nor does it diminish the worth of all the great ones who were never allowed to enter.

I want to reflect back to children and to reinforce the positive aspects of their lives. The media, especially television, for the most part do not reflect the strength of the Black family. The mirror that they hold up for children is a carnival mirror, a funhouse mirror, reflecting misshapen images, exaggerated or devaluated as the needs of situation comedy demand. Love is a staple in most Black families. (pp. 624-26)

Accompanying all of my other wants for children is the desire to share the feeling that I have for words. A few weeks ago, while reading Keorapetse Kgositsile's book, *The Present Is a Dangerous Place to Live* (Third World), I came across the words, "Home is where the music is"—plain words, quiet words, understated. But the excitement they created was too much for me to contain. I had to repeat them softly. I wanted to stand up and shout them, but I was afraid the neighbors would think that I had suddenly gone mad. And they would have been right—I had gone mad, word-mad. Because, if you love home and you love music and you love words, the miracle is that the poet chose *those* words and put them together in *that* order, and it is something to shout about. I felt like the Southern Black preachers who, in reciting from the Scriptures, would suddenly be surprised by an old, familiar phrase and would repeat it over and over to savor and to celebrate this miracle of words.

I want to be one of those who can choose and order words that children will want to celebrate. I want to make them shout and

laugh and blink back tears and care about themselves. They are our future. They are beautiful. They are for loving. (p. 626)

Eloise Greenfield, "Something to Shout About," in The Horn Book Magazine *(copyright © 1975 by the Horn Book, Inc., Boston), Vol. LI, No. 6, December, 1975, pp. 624-26.*

BUBBLES   (1972; reissued as *Good News*, 1977)

Bubbles can help children deal with the times when adults are unable to give them the attention they want. It can also help youngsters understand that families adopt different lifestyles for survival. These are important issues to talk about with young children. The book is out of print. . . . We urge our readers to send letters to publishers of their choice requesting that the book be reissued.

"Toward a Multicultural Collection: 'Bubbles'," in Interracial Books for Children Bulletin *(reprinted by permission of* Interracial Books for Children Bulletin, *1841 Broadway, New York, N.Y. 10023), Vol. 6, Nos. 5 & 6, 1975, p. 9.*

James Edward is excited because he has learned to read some words, and he runs home from school to tell Mama. But she only says, "That's nice, James Edward," and, instead of listening to him read, asks him to amuse baby Deedee so she can fix dinner before she goes to work. Coming out of his own funk when Deedee starts to feel neglected, James Edward tells *her* his news—and "even though she didn't know what it meant" she laughs with him. The deflating "That's nice" from a busy mother will win James Edward sympathetic allies, and the black family and working mother will score with librarians on the lookout for that extra recognition. There's not much to it, however, beyond the cathartic model. . . . Still, as Greenfield avoids manipulation and false solutions, it's a creditable example of its limited genre.

"Picture Books: 'Good News'," in Kirkus Reviews *(copyright © 1977 The Kirkus Service, Inc.), Vol. XLV, No. 11, June 1, 1977, p. 573.*

Mama doesn't come off very well in this story. . . . The writing style is not as deft as Greenfield's later work, but she conveys nicely a sense of James Edward's elation . . . and draws a tender picture of the affection between the two children.

Zena Sutherland, "New Titles for Children and Young People: 'Good News'," in Bulletin of the Center for Children's Books *(reprinted by permission of The University of Chicago Press; © 1977 by The University of Chicago), Vol. 31, No. 2, October, 1977, p. 32.*

Greenfield does convey the boy's quiet joy of accomplishment, but there is little more plot than that and this lacks the appeal of *Olaf Reads* by [Joan M.] Lexau (Dial, 1961) and [Miriam] Cohen's *When Will I Read?* (Greenwillow, 1977).

"Pre-school and Primary Grades: 'Good News'," in School Library Journal *(reprinted from the December, 1977 issue of* School Library Journal, *published by R. R. Bowker Co./A Xerox Corporation; copyright © 1977), Vol. 24, No. 4, December, 1977, p. 44.*

ROSA PARKS (1973)

Greenfield begins with an incident in which Rosa as a child in Montgomery, Alabama, is pushed by a white boy and pushes back; throughout she highlights all the small insults and observed injuries that help account for her subject's historic decision, one tired evening on the bus, that she had had enough. Also relevant and duly reported are Rosa's pre-bus strike work with the NAACP and the Montgomery Voters' League and the precedent set by a 15 year-old Montgomery girl who refused to give up her bus seat to a white man, and was carried off handcuffed by three policemen, some time before Mrs. Parks' act of defiance. The same eye for telling detail distinguishes Greenfield's account of the progress and eventual triumph of the bus boycott inspired by Mrs. Parks and organized by Dr. King and other ministers. This is sure to replace [Louise] Meriwether's pedestrian *Don't Ride the Bus on Monday*. . . .

> *"Younger Non-Fiction: 'Rosa Parks',"* in Kirkus Reviews *(copyright © 1973 The Kirkus Service, Inc.), Vol. XLI, No. 21, November 1, 1973, p. 1206.*

Effective balance between dialogue and narrative relates facts about Rosa Parks' life and about segregated southern society. The engaging text . . . builds quickly to the climax—the Montgomery, Alabama bus boycott precipitated by the arrest and jailing of Rosa Parks who refused to give up her bus seat to a white rider. This is a valuable addition for elementary school and public libraries needing supplementary material on the Civil Rights Movement.

> *Betty Lanier Jenkins, "Preschool & Primary Grades: 'Rosa Parks',"* in School Library Journal, *an appendix to* Library Journal *(reprinted from the April, 1974 issue of* School Library Journal, *published by R. R. Bowker Co./A Xerox Corporation; copyright © 1974), Vol. 20, No. 8, April, 1974, p. 50.*

Like Louise Meriwether's *Don't Ride the Bus on Monday*, this covers Rosa Parks' childhood, her historic stand that precipitated the Montgomery bus strike, her increasing participation in the civil rights struggle, and the Supreme Court decision that ended the Jim Crow rule in transportation. Here, however, the writing has more vitality, and the author's use of other incidents, earlier in Rosa Parks' life, that had evoked her resentment, makes the stand this quiet, self-contained woman took more convincing.

> *Zena Sutherland, "New Titles for Children and Young People: 'Rosa Parks',"* in Bulletin of the Center for Children's Books *(reprinted by permission of The University of Chicago Press; © 1974 by The University of Chicago), Vol. 27, No. 10, June, 1974, p. 157.*

Ms. Greenfield's book beautifully captures the sense of urgency which prevailed at the time and gives the young reader a good feeling for the early movement days of the Montgomery bus boycott. I might also mention that Ms. Greenfield's recent *Sister* is even more striking.

> *Judy Richardson, "Black Children's Books: An Overview,"* in The Journal of Negro Education, *Vol. XLIII, No. 3 (Summer, 1974), pp. 380-400.**

SISTER (1974)

Doretha, the young black heroine of **"Sister,"** loses her father. In fitful words like stroboscopic flashes Eloise Greenfield describes his death. . . .

The death of Doretha's father is transformed and transcended, so that our reaction is not pain at a sad scene we are witnessing but something more like wonder and joy, the reaction to a work of art. I don't mean, of course, that we are not affected by the sadness too. We believe it and are affected by it all the more readily because it has been transmitted so intensely. . . .

"Sister" is full of [the kind of transformation to be found in Vera and Bill Cleaver's "Where the Lilies Bloom," and] many other good things as well, including the author's tender way of projecting character through speech (*"You in a good mood. Say it."*) Eloise Greenfield is a writer of substance.

> *Jane Langton, "Five Lives,"* in The New York Times Book Review *(© 1974 by The New York Times Company; reprinted by permission), May 5, 1974, p. 16.**

The impressionistic jottings in Doretha's diary bring back a flood of memories—all part of the lesson of learning to laugh through one's pain. . . . Greenfield has a good ear for the spontaneous banter of teenagers, and she portrays Doretha's rejection by a cruel teacher, her mother's worries about Alberta and backbreaking labor in a laundry, and a whole spectrum of family sorrows without ever trying to shock or solicit pity. Doretha's past is a montage of fleeting dreams, hurts and feelings, but one can tell from the sureness of her own reactions that she will be one of the survivors who can laugh from strength.

> *"Younger Fiction: 'Sister',"* in Kirkus Reviews *(copyright © 1974 The Kirkus Service, Inc.), Vol. XLII, No. 10, May 15, 1974, p. 535.*

Despite the fragmentation of the literary format, the story reads smoothly, and the variety of the episodes compensates for the absence of a strong story line. The book is strong, nevertheless, strong in perception, in its sensitivity, in its realism. (p. 9)

> *Zena Sutherland, "New Titles for Children and Young People: 'Sister',"* in Bulletin of the Center for Children's Books *(reprinted by permission of The University of Chicago Press; © 1974 by The University of Chicago), Vol. 28, No. 1, September, 1974, pp. 8-9.*

A thoroughly real child shines through the unpretentious story. . . . To the author's credit, she does not adopt the easy, obvious device of letting the diary speak for the child in the first person; it is the sensitive touch of the adult writer that gives the story an artless simplicity. (pp. 136-37)

> *Ethel L. Heins, "Stories for the Middle Readers: 'Sister',"* in The Horn Book Magazine *(copyright © 1974 by the Horn Book, Inc., Boston), Vol. L, No. 5, October, 1974, pp. 136-37.*

SHE COME BRINGING ME THAT LITTLE BABY GIRL (1974)

"I asked Mama to bring me a little brother from the hospital, but she come bringing me that little baby girl wrapped all up in a pink blanket." Sensitively in touch with his natural idiom and troubled feelings, Greenfield lets us in on one left out older sibling's complaints. . . . And if the little boy's revised assessment of the baby ("I looked at her again and she wasn't all that ugly anymore'') and his willingness to share his parents' affection after Mama tells him she'll need his help caring for the newcomer seem unrealistically sudden, we've already been down far enough with him to accept a change.

> *"Picture Books: 'She Come Bringing Me That Little Baby Girl',"* in Kirkus Reviews *(copyright © 1974 The Kirkus Service, Inc.), Vol. XLII, No. 18, September 15, 1974, p. 1004.*

"She Come Bringing Me That Little Baby Girl" is excellent while describing the common situation of a first child's reaction to a new baby and, in this instance, depicting the virulent sexism of a young boy. The book fails, however, in its resolution of the problem. Kevin's mother tells him that she needs him to help care for the little girl, and, even more, she herself used to be a baby girl and her own brother had taken care of her. Conveniently mother's big brother, Uncle Roy, happens to be there and adds, "I wouldn't let nobody bother my little sister." Kevin's jealousy turns to instant love with an ease only possible in a book.

Resolving Kevin's problem in this way is sexist, because the boy is put into the role of strong protector and his sister into that of weak female. Moreover children's emotions are as intense, if not more so, than those of adults, and this book fails to recognize that fact. What we have here is an adult's idea of a child, instead of a child's emotional reality.

> *Julius Lester, "Children's Books, Fall 1974: 'She Come Bringing Me That Little Baby Girl',"* in The New York Times Book Review *(© 1974 by The New York Times Company; reprinted by permission), November 3, 1974, p. 48.*

The birth of a sibling can be a traumatic experience for an only child, and adults must be sensitive and intelligent in their handling of this delicate situation. In *She Come Bringing Me That Little Baby Girl,* Kevin, an only child, faces a new baby with little preparation. It is obvious that he is loved by his mother and father as well as by other relatives, but love is exactly what is questioned by children at a time like this: They are afraid their place will be taken by the new child.

In the course of the story, Kevin has to cope with several misconceptions about babies. He feels that if the baby had been a boy he would have been different. His hands would have been larger, and, therefore, better suited to ball playing. He is afraid to hold his new sister because she might break. Kevin is disappointed by the baby's wrinkled skin and loud cries. The sexism that we unfortunately see emerging as Kevin gropes for a way to accept his sister is fostered by a simplistic attempt to deal with Kevin's real problem of accepting a sibling.

Kevin is left to contend with these problems alone but is put at ease by his mother's assurances that she was a baby girl once and that his uncle, her big brother, had helped to take care of her. She then solicits Kevin's help in caring for his sister. This marks a turning point in the story, leading to a happy ending. It's all a little too simple, although the story is warm and shows a strong Black family grouping.

Parents or teachers can use this book to help children adjust to a new brother or sister, but only if they use it as a starting point for discussion and go on to deal more directly (and in an anti-sexist fashion!) with the concerns a child has.

> *Mary Ellen Shepard, "The Bookshelf: 'She Come Bringing Me That Little Baby Girl',"* in Interracial Books for Children Bulletin *(reprinted by permission of* Interracial Books for Children Bulletin, *1841 Broadway, New York, N.Y. 10023), Vol. 6, No. 1, 1975, p. 4.*

There have been many books like this, in which a child's jealousy is overcome and he or she accepts a sibling, but there's always room for another when it's well done, and this is: the story catches that wistful pathos of the child who is feeling displaced. Although the conversion is suspiciously easy, it's not unbelievable. . . .

> *Zena Sutherland, "New Titles for Children and Young People: 'She Come Bringing Me That Little Baby Girl',"* in Bulletin of the Center for Children's Books *(reprinted by permission of The University of Chicago Press; © 1975 by The University of Chicago), Vol. 28, No. 7, March, 1975, p. 113.*

PAUL ROBESON (1975)

It is fortunate to have this significant book about the great Black artist and leader, Paul Robeson, for young readers. It documents his militant international struggle to end the oppression of Black and poor people.

The author notes the support and inspiration afforded the young Robeson by his family . . . which created a foundation for his achievement as a scholar . . . , athlete, concert singer and actor. That support also contributed to the strength of conviction and purpose he was to manifest later in his activities as a political figure.

The book describes Robeson's use of his extraordinary singing talent to inform audiences around the world about the rich heritage of Black people, his outspokenness as a critic of oppression, and the persecution that befell him when he became a political activist. . . .

This book is an excellent introduction to a man of universal stature whose record has been suppressed for too long.

> *Marjorie Johnson, "Bookshelf: 'Paul Robeson',"* in Interracial Books for Children Bulletin *(reprinted by permission of* Interracial Books for Children Bulletin, *1841 Broadway, New York, N.Y. 10023), Vol. 6, Nos. 3 & 4, 1975, p. 9.*

[In *Paul Robeson* Greenfield] smoothly compresses both the highpoints of Robeson's careers as athlete, singer and actor and the course of his developing political commitment and repressive reactions against it. Best of all, Greenfield is obviously familiar with Robeson's music and conveys something of the timbre, style and emotional impact of his performances. (pp. 570-71)

> *"Younger Non-Fiction: 'Paul Robeson',"* in Kirkus Reviews *(copyright © 1975 The Kirkus Service, Inc.), Vol. XLIII, No. 10, May 15, 1975, pp. 570-71.*

Greenfield gives good insights into the personality of this world renowned Black entertainer. . . . The author has obvious respect for Robeson but remains objective, neither condemning nor glorifying his communist sympathies in the 1940's.

> *Joyce White Mills, "Preschool & Primary Grades: 'Paul Robeson',"* in School Library Journal *(reprinted from the September, 1975 issue of* School Library Journal, *published by R. R. Bowker Co./A Xerox Corporation; copyright © 1975), Vol. 22, No. 1, September, 1975, p. 82.*

An adequate biography of the great singer emphasizes his role as a political activist. The writing has occasional moments of awkwardness, but is smooth on the whole, although not as well written as the author's *Rosa Parks.*

> *Zena Sutherland, "New Titles for Children and Young People: 'Paul Robeson'," in* Bulletin of the Center for Children's Books *(reprinted by permission of The University of Chicago Press; © 1976 by The University of Chicago), Vol. 29, No. 5, January, 1976, p. 77.*

ME AND NEESIE   (1975)

A familiar situation is depicted in this picture book—the relationship between an only child and her imaginary friend. Janell's alter ego, Neesie, is a happy-go-lucky free spirit who defies all parental authority in an amusing and delightful way. . . .

When Janell's first day at school leads to the formation of new and real friendships, she returns home to find that Neesie has mysteriously disappeared—the need for her existence having faded away. (Parents who read this book to their children should be prepared to explain Neesie's disappearance and Janell's final adjustment to her absence.)

This story about a Black family has a very warm texture. Janell's mother and father are portrayed as being sensitive and sympathetic regarding their daughter's growing pains. . . . There are so few good stories written about young Black children that this book is especially welcome for its portrayal of a warm family relationship.

> *Joyce Toney, "The Bookshelf: 'Me and Neesie'," in* Interracial Books for Children Bulletin *(reprinted by permission of* Interracial Books for Children Bulletin, *1841 Broadway, New York, N.Y. 10023), Vol. 6, Nos. 5 & 6, 1975, p. 15.*

Janell describes her mother's exasperation with her insistence on Neesie, an imaginary friend and—presumably—her alter ego. . . . [The] story has a familiar situation and its own vitality, but it is weakened by the abruptness of the change at the end of the story. (pp. 96-7)

> *Zena Sutherland, "New Titles for Children and Young People: 'Me and Neesie'," in* Bulletin of the Center for Children's Books *(reprinted by permission of The University of Chicago Press; © 1976 by The University of Chicago), Vol. 29, No. 6, February, 1976, pp. 96-7.*

An easy, natural style, with occasional conversational bits of Black English ("if you not talking to me, you talking to yourself"), distinguishes this brief story of a little girl and her imaginary friend. . . . The simple text . . . [brings] Neesie to life as strongly as Janell—too clearly perhaps for a nonexistent character.

> *Virginia Haviland, "Stories For Younger Readers: 'Me and Neesie'," in* The Horn Book Magazine *(copyright © 1976 by the Horn Book, Inc., Boston), Vol. LII, No. 1, February, 1976, p. 44.*

FIRST PINK LIGHT   (1976)

Tyree's mother is depicted as understanding, patient and sensitive to Tyree's needs and individuality. Especially impressive

is the way she elicits obedience without resorting to parental tyranny. The text implies that she is a student, and she is shown doing *homework* rather than housework.

The father's going to care for Tyree's sick grandmother is another example of concern and sharing of responsibilities in this Black family.

First Pink Light exudes love. . . . An excellent book for children of any age—this adult enjoyed it!

> *Lynn Edwards, "Bookshelf: 'First Pink Light'," in* Interracial Books for Children Bulletin *(reprinted by permission of* Interracial Books for Children Bulletin, *1841 Broadway, New York, N.Y. 10023), Vol. 7, No. 7, 1976, p. 16.*

[Despite] a very simple story, this is a book that just manages to avoid sentimentality. The emotions are real, not exaggerated. But a lingering doubt was left in this reviewer's mind as to whether this is not more of a book about children, rather than for them.

> *David Anable, "Meet Some Sensible, Silly Pals," in* The Christian Science Monitor *(reprinted by permission from* The Christian Science Monitor; *© 1976 The Christian Science Publishing Society; all rights reserved), November 3, 1976, pp. 22-3.**

MARY McLEOD BETHUNE   (1977)

Mary McLeod Bethune, who wanted to be a missionary to Africa but wound up educating black Americans, lacks the obvious dramatic appeal of ***Rosa Parks*** . . . , and, as projected here, she is a dull study compared to June Jordan's *Fannie Lou Hamer* (1972). . . . However, Greenfield does take readers a brisk step ahead of [Ruby L.] Radford's 1973 MMB— as she traces Mary's progress from the fields of her family's South Carolina farm to the first black school in the area, then on scholarship to Scotia Seminary and Moody Bible Institute, at last to Daytona Beach, Florida, to found her own school for black children. . . . Serviceable.

> *"Younger Non-Fiction: 'Mary McLeod Bethune'," in* Kirkus Reviews *(copyright © 1977 The Kirkus Service, Inc.), Vol. XLV, No. 6, March 15, 1977, p. 287.*

Bethune and Greenfield are a winning pair. Children of all colors should enjoy hearing or reading about Ms. Bethune, and will learn some important truths about Black history in the process. The author makes skillful use of simple language to communicate complex ideas, interweaving background information about the post-Civil War and Jim Crow eras with a description of Bethune's determination to learn how to read and of her commitment to teach other Blacks. . . .

[This is a] beautifully told story.

> *Linda Humes, "Bookshelf: 'Mary McLeod Bethune'," in* Interracial Books for Children Bulletin *(reprinted by permission of* Interracial Books for Children Bulletin, *1841 Broadway, New York, N.Y. 10023), Vol. 8, Nos. 4 & 5, 1977, p. 32.*

Eloise Greenfield's ***Mary McLeod Bethune*** is a fine addition to the Crowell collection of biographies about black Americans. A day or so before this book appeared on my desk, my youngest son, aged 9, was interviewing me for a homework assignment. To his question, "Who were your childhood heroes?" my first and most immediate response was "Dr. Mary McLeod Bethune." Since he had never heard of her (along with thousands of other black youngsters), I am happy now to pass my copy along to him and happier still that she has been written about in a style that will be both accessible and delightful to all of his age-mates in the country.

It is precisely the fact that Mary McLeod Bethune functioned as a stunning, living role model for the members of my generation that makes it imperative that she be remembered by the generations to come. Eloise Greenfield has written charmingly and sensitively about Dr. Bethune's life work and dedication to the education of black youths. She has shown in full force the web of love and the caring styles of those around her who impelled Mary McLeod Bethune to do all the things she did. She has shown the strength, durability and tenacity of the first generation out of slavery. She has also shown us Mary McLeod Bethune's own role models, the hordes of strong, black folks who built schools out of nothing and sustained them with their love. All of this has been accomplished by Eloise Greenfield in a few simple, well chosen episodes by which she gives to children in her own words, "words to love, to grow on."

> C. Maxine Byrd, "Book Reviews: 'Mary McLeod Bethune'," in The Black Scholar (copyright 1978 by The Black Scholar), Vol. 9, No. 7, April, 1978, p. 57.

Have any children asked you about new books on courageous black women? Or have you gone to a library hoping to locate some excellently written biographies on outstanding black women? Perhaps then, the biography **Mary McLeod Bethune** by Eloise Greenfield may be just the answer.

Eloise Greenfield in her biography **Mary McLeod Bethune** provides the young reader with an informative and beautiful story of one of the great heroines in American history. Ms. Greenfield also does a superb job of excitingly presenting many of the major highlights of Ms. Bethune's life from childhood through adulthood. . . .

[The] author skillfully describes the hopes, dreams, and accomplishments which Mary encountered in her life. In addition, the biography illustrates how Mary's determination as a child in spite of the numerous obstacles she had to endure, led to her success later in life. . . .

The reader is made to fully empathize with the endless struggles that Ms. Bethune underwent to make her dream of becoming a school teacher and to start a school for black children a reality. One cannot help but gain additional strength and pride while reading and learning of this aspect of her career.

Throughout the book there are several positive and strong messages that the author conveys to children. One of the positive messages that the biography attempts to teach is that a person does not have to be a "superstar" to aid others or to make worthwhile contributions to humanity. Instead, it demonstrates through the life of Ms. Bethune, that self love, love for others, hard work, and determination can help one achieve their goals. The biography further illustrates that individuals have to make the very best of whatever situation they find themselves in.

Another interesting feature of **Mary McLeod Bethune** lies in the fact that it consistently emphasizes that Black people must take advantage of every opportunity and share their skills and talents (whatever they may be) with each other. . . .

This biography also deals effectively with discussing what many would define as a quandary in Ms. Bethune's life concerning her great desire to work as a Christian missionary in Africa. . . .

Mary McLeod Bethune is a powerfully written biography which tells a beautiful black story. And as Ms. Bethune once spoke, "I leave you Faith, I leave you hope, I leave you love"—so does this book.

> Beryl Graham, "Reviews: 'Mary McLeod Bethune'," in The Negro History Bulletin (reprinted by permission of The Association for the Study of Afro-American Life and History, Inc.), Vol. 41, No. 5, September-October, 1978, p. 894.

AFRICA DREAM (1977)

It is a pure delight to recommend this lovely book of poignant text. . . . It is fictional, a fantasy, but the writing and the pictures project the beauty and culture of the African continent.

The title is literally descriptive of the content. A black child visits Africa in a dream where she is welcomed joyfully by her long-ago grandparents, other relatives like cousins and uncles, and old-new friends. It is a magic dream trip with which youngsters (and oldsters) can identify, and enjoy. . . .

[It is] a fantastic book.

> Thelma D. Perry, "Reviews: 'Africa Dream'," in The Negro History Bulletin (reprinted by permission of The Association for the Study of Afro-American Life and History, Inc.), Vol. 41, No. 1, January-February, 1978, p. 801.

[A poetic but simple text describes] a child's dream (or is it a daydream?) of going back across the sea, back in time, to the Africa of long ago. There are strange words in old books, but she can understand them; there are strange faces but they welcome her. A grandfather with her father's face reaches out to embrace her, a grandmother of long ago—with her mother's face—cradles her in loving arms. And she becomes a baby and sleeps in that safe clasp. This is almost a prose poem, but the concepts it presents may be difficult for some children to grasp; the bridging of time and space, the fragmentary nature of a dream.

> Zena Sutherland, "New Titles for Children and Young People: 'Africa Dream'," in Bulletin of the Center for Children's Books (reprinted by permission of The University of Chicago Press; © 1978 by The University of Chicago), Vol. 31, No. 6, February, 1978, p. 93.

[Africa Dream] has a strange power that is only half realized; the threads of the first-person narrative are subtly tangled (at one point, the teller becomes a baby rocked in the arms of her "long-ago grandma" who has her Mama's face) and may confuse the youngest audiences.

> Marjorie Lewis, "Book Reviews: 'Africa Dream'," in School Library Journal (reprinted from the March, 1978 issue of School Library Journal, published by R. R. Bowker Co./A Xerox Corporation; copyright © 1978), Vol. 24, No. 7, March, 1978, pp. 118-19.

HONEY, I LOVE AND OTHER LOVE POEMS (1978)

Honey, I Love is an appropriate title for this first collection of poems by Eloise Greenfield. These 16 poems explore facets of warm, loving relationships with family, friends and schoolmates as experienced by a young Black girl. Central to the theme of the book is the idea that the child loves and loves herself and is very confident in expressing that love.

These poems are a fine example of Ms. Greenfield's talent for using rhythm, imagery and cadence in a manner which gives a definite Afro-American emphasis to universal experiences.

Teachers who have been searching for materials of high caliber to use with Black children will find this volume especially valuable. There are positive messages also for young children of all races. . . .

This book is definitely a must for classroom and school libraries.

> *Beryle Banfield, "Bookshelf: 'Honey, I Love and Other Love Poems'," in* Interracial Books for Children Bulletin *(reprinted by permission of* Interracial Books for Children Bulletin, *1841 Broadway, New York, N.Y. 10023), Vol. 9, No. 2, 1978, p. 19.*

There are 17 short selections in all, varied in subject (love, fun, things, riding on a train), colloquial and undemanding, but never forceful. The funkiest, **"Way Down in the Music,"** sounds more like Tin Pan Alley . . . than the cited Jackson Five, and overall the weak, unimaginative meter is a let-down: **"Rope Rhyme,"** with the bounciest title, sounds more like a jog . . . ; the inspirational intent of **"Harriet Tubman"** doesn't jibe with its light verse rhythms; and the title poem has some nice sounds and observations ("My cousin comes to visit and you know he's from the South / Cause every word he says just kind of slides out of his mouth") but goes on too long with the same monotonous beat. Nevertheless, easy to slide through. . . . (pp. 308-09)

> *"Younger Non-Fiction: 'Honey, I Love and Other Love Poems'," in* Kirkus Reviews *(copyright © 1978 The Kirkus Service, Inc.), Vol. XLVI, No. 6, March 15, 1978, pp. 308-09.*

Greenfield herself can be heard through the voice of a young Black girl in this book of love poems. She speaks in an easy way, of everyday things, sometimes rhyming, sometimes not. Most of the poems don't attempt complex perceptions. Greenfield's child is younger and less intense than the women Nikki Giovanni's adolescents grow up to be; and she is older and less political than Lucille Clifton's Everett Anderson. . . . The strongest images come in portraits of other people, like her older brother Reggie who has forsaken his family for basketball and Aunt Roberta who sits "All wrapped up in quiet / and old sweaters."

> *Sharon Elswit, "The Book Review: 'Honey, I Love and Other Love Poems'," in* School Library Journal *(reprinted from the May, 1978 issue of* School Library Journal, *published by R. R. Bowker Co./A Xerox Corporation; copyright © 1978), Vol. 24, No. 9, May, 1978, p. 55.*

The poems have moments of vision, some felicitous phrases, and a consistency in showing a child's viewpoint, but they often have a less than poetic quality and seem merely fragmentary attitudes or reactions of rather prosaic calibre.

> *Zena Sutherland, "New Titles for Children and Young People: 'Honey, I Love and Other Love Poems'," in* Bulletin of the Center for Children's Books *(reprinted by permission of The University of Chicago Press; © 1978 by The University of Chicago), Vol. 31, No. 11, July-August, 1978, p. 177.*

TALK ABOUT A FAMILY (1978)

It looks like Genny's family will be complete again when her older brother Larry comes home from the army, and she arranges a surprise party in a neighbor's yard to celebrate the return. The party is a success, but the family is already breaking up; next morning the parents announce that Daddy will be moving out. For a while Genny almost blames Larry for not being able to patch up their parents' marriage, but then she reminds herself that families come in all shapes and that the shapes are always changing. Greenfield's portrayal of Genny's feelings, her family's interactions, and her conversations with an old neighbor is sensitive enough to make this one of the more honest and effective entries in its limited, problem/consolation genre.

> *"Younger Fiction: 'Talk about a Family'," in* Kirkus Reviews *(copyright © 1978 The Kirkus Service, Inc.), Vol. XLVI, No. 8, April 15, 1978, p. 436.*

[*Talk about a Family*] portrays a middle-income Black family facing change. Without denying the pain and hurt that divorce causes, it shows the warmth of family ties, the bond of friendships, and a strong sense of neighborhood. Moralizing is kept to a minimum, and the characters are remarkably well developed, especially considering the confines of 64 pages. (p. 68)

> *Christine McDonnell, "The Book Review: 'Talk about a Family'," in* School Library Journal *(reprinted from the May, 1978 issue of* School Library Journal, *published by R. R. Bowker Co./A Xerox Corporation; copyright © 1978), Vol. 24, No. 9, May, 1978, pp. 67-8.*

CHILDTIMES: A THREE-GENERATION MEMOIR (with Lessie Jones Little, 1979)

That history is the composite experiences of many individuals is ably demonstrated through the reminiscences of three Black women—grandmother, mother, and daughter—recalling significant aspects of their respective childhoods. A brief introduction precedes the individual accounts, setting each in perspective against the climate of the times during which the narrator was born. A distinct voice emerges from each of the three segments, reflecting the personality of the teller and the style of discourse appropriate to her own era. The effect is poignant and moving, at once poetic and childlike, for the diverse images reflect the kinds of experiences which impress children during the formative years. And the selection of memories and expressions vividly re-creates those impressions as patterns linking one childhood with the next: household chores, school life and socials, encounters with prejudice, love of family, and pride of heritage. "There's a lot of crying in this book, and there's dying, too, but there's also new life and laughter. It's all part of living." Few books have conveyed that message more memorably or more artistically.

> *Mary M. Burns, "Early Winter Booklist: 'Childtimes: A Three-Generation Memoir'," in* The Horn Book Magazine *(copyright © 1979 by The Horn Book,*

Inc., Boston), Vol. LV, No. 6, December, 1979, p. 676.

Three first-person narratives make up this very warm, straight-from-the-heart-family history. . . . The book has a pretty broad scope: life in rural North Carolina and in the inner city of Washington, D.C. from the middle 1800s to the present. It gives an excellent overview of this period and shows how life styles changed and the way in which historical events and friends actually affected the everyday lives of black people. . . . But mostly the book is about what it was like to be a little girl and then a young woman for Pattie, Lessie and then Eloise—what kind of food each ate, chores and games, changing styles in clothing, family weddings and births, first memories and daydreams, parties and boyfriends. The intimate details of loving and growing up and the honesty with which they are told, in an easy-to-read colloquial style, will involve all readers, both white and black, and broaden their understanding of this country's recent past.

Marilyn R. Singer, "Grades 3-6: 'Childtimes: A Three-Generation Memoir'," in School Library Journal *(reprinted from the December, 1979 issue of* School Library Journal, *published by R. R. Bowker Co./A Xerox Corporation; copyright © 1979), Vol. 26, No. 4, December, 1979, p. 85.*

Author Greenfield and her mother have assembled the first of these three first-person recollections from the autobiographical writings and oral accounts of Patti Frances Ridley Jones, born in North Carolina in 1884. . . . In the same direct, down-to-earth manner, Mrs. Jones' daughter Lessie Jones Little, born in 1906, then recalls her youth—chores, parties, silly rhymes, and the Parmele, North Carolina, train station where "fellas and their girls" would come "all the way from other towns" just to spend a Sunday afternoon. Her daughter Eloise Greenfield's memories are more self-consciously related, her examples of racism more pointed and expository, her treasuring of her family and blackness more explicit, and her recollections less concrete and more deliberately evocative—appropriately so, perhaps, as a summing-up of the sequence. For each of the three memoirs there's a very brief introduction placing the childhood in a general context: post-slavery exploitation of Southern blacks for the first, new technology and emerging black movements for the second, and the Depression for the last—but mostly the emphasis is on the immediate, personal, family-centered experience. A genuine, fondly inscribed record. . . .

"Younger Non-Fiction: 'Childtimes: A Three-Generation Family Memoir'," in Kirkus Reviews *(copyright © 1980 The Kirkus Service, Inc.), Vol. XLVIII, No. 1, January 1, 1980, p. 7.*

In African life, one of the ways you can show respect and admiration for those who do great deeds is to bow down. . . . [Truly] you will want to "bow down low" to these three women, linked to each other through that many generations, for having worked to bring us *Childtimes.* Pattie Frances Ridley Jones who delivered Lessie Blanche Jones Little who delivered Eloise Glynn Little Greenfield delivered to us—old and young alike—a history of their family. I hesitate to say that for fear of evoking collective groans resulting from our skirmishes with history poorly taught from distorted, inaccurate books written by racist historians, but that reaction is off-set by our expectation of good, solid, *serious,* soulful books from Eloise Greenfield. . . .

The book is built on the major recognition that children can and must learn to handle truth and history at an early age. The format of the book reenforces that awareness in ways that will say to children, "Now this is what a good history book is about." . . . Each introduction conveys a sense of the era by describing briefly some of the significant events of the period. Bravo to the authors for highlighting the Niagara Movement and its demands for the education of Black children. Bravo for their accurate assessment of the great migration of Blacks to the North. . . . Bravo for the Landscape that makes clear that Black people resisted slavery and participated in securing their own freedom, which was then taken away. (p. 14)

As you turn the pages, the authors flip the bolts of their lives over and over, spreading out the fabric of their experiences for young folk to look at, examine closely, to stand back from and contemplate.

Men and women talk together through the re-telling of three generations of the Jones-Little-Greenfield family, important in each other's eyes and rearing children to understand and learn to struggle with love, tragedy, difference of opinion, spirituality, separation, loss, oppression, joy, humor and the importance of their African and African-American heritage. A chapter on **"Hot Rolls"** is a worthy subject for history! Say "hot rolls" to Black folk and see if, after swooning, they don't have a brief history to tell. There is a chapter on **"Separation."** How courageous and correct to include that women have left home (not the family!) while the men and children carried on. A chapter entitled **"Getting Baptized"** makes you *know* that we have to write more for children about our important African relationship to water. You will cry in sympathy and empathy in the chapter **"Doing the Laundry."** This present generation will write their history bout floodin the Laundro-mat with ankle-high detergent suds, but ain't nothin like a broken clothesline and muddy clothes! And my dear, the chapter on Black Music is so-o-o moving. . . . As our young ones say, Dee-e-p! Then, there is heartache handled well: "They dragging the river again." Greenfield tells about the "boy for whom the fireplugs were not enough" and by so doing children learn about the uncounted victims of racism through the reality of segregated swimming pools.

Childtimes is a carefully considered and thoughtful book, moving deliberately, constructed with loving care. The authors respect their child-readers (or listeners) and honor them with candor and honesty, tragedy and tears, providing chuckles and smiles as well. *Childtimes* is like the gingerbread my mother used to make. The smell of it filled you up inside, the ginger and other spices penetrating the place behind your eyes like few things did. And when you finished eating and savoring it, you were full, but wanted more. Parents, teachers, family members, get this book into classrooms, homes, churches. Read it yourselves, read it to young children; older children will read it by themselves. Then bow down, low! And to the writers, continue to "Speak the Truth to the people" about the importance of childtimes. (pp. 14-15)

Geraldine L. Wilson, "Bookshelf: 'Childtimes: A Three-Generation Memoir'," in Interracial Books for Children Bulletin *(reprinted by permission of* Interracial Books for Children Bulletin, *1841 Broadway, New York, N.Y. 10023), Vol. 11, No. 5, 1980, pp. 14-15.*

DARLENE (1980)

Unlike [Elizabeth] Fanshawe's *Rachel,* Darlene's wheelchair is not part of the story. In fact, the preschoolers who listened to this sympathized so completely with Darlene's impatience for her mother's return that they ignored her wheelchair altogether.

> Elizabeth Monette, "Picture Books: 'Darlene'," in Children's Book Review Service *(copyright © 1981 Children's Book Review Service Inc.), Vol. 9, No. 5, January, 1981, p. 31.*

[*Darlene* contains one] small turnabout incident s-t-r-e-t-c-h-e-d out—and slightly enhanced, perhaps, by the heroine's being (wordlessly) confined to a wheelchair. "Darlene wanted to go home," the text begins; and we see her looking mopey. "Uncle Eddie said, 'Your mama's coming to get you at two o'clock.'" Thereafter, as cousin Joanne devises one after another way to keep Darlene entertained, she keeps asking the time—but from her perceptible brightening we strongly suspect that, by the time her mama does arrive, she'll have changed her mind. And not only that but, when Uncle Eddie says, "Darlene, you don't know *what* you want," she pertly replies: "Yes, I do. I want to change my mind when I want to." As a demonstration that handicapped kids (Darlene, it should be mentioned, is black too) are no different from anyone else, fair enough; but otherwise not much of anything. . . . (pp. 137-38)

> "Picture Book: 'Darlene'," in Kirkus Reviews *(copyright © 1981 The Kirkus Service, Inc.), Vol. XLIX, No. 3, February 1, 1981, pp. 137-38.*

Darlene is beautiful. . . .

Being disabled is not a phenomenon solely restricted to white people, but for far too long, writers have failed to recognize and ameliorate this situation. Eloise Greenfield has admirably succeeded in beginning to fill the need for books for young readers whose main characters are both Third World and disabled. . . . *Darlene* clearly deserves a big round of applause for a job well done.

> Emily Strauss Watson, "Bookshelf: 'Darlene'," in Interracial Books for Children Bulletin *(reprinted by permission of* Interracial Books for Children Bulletin, *1841 Broadway, New York, N.Y. 10023), Vol. 12, No. 2, 1981, p. 22.*

DAYDREAMERS (1981)

This is not a poem as such but rather a picture essay. . . . The text captures the inner feelings of children, but it is written for adults. It may be difficult to justify the purchase of this luxury item, but this is a book that deserves a place in both the home and school/public libraries.

> Leila Davenport Pettyjohn, "Picture Books: 'Daydreamers'," in Children's Book Review Service *(copyright © 1981 Children's Book Review Service Inc.), Vol. 9, No. 11, June, 1981, p. 92.*

The text is poetry, minimal, unforced. "Daydreamers . . . holding their bodies still for a time / letting the world turn around them / while their dreams hopscotch, doubledutch, dance. . . ." Greenfield keeps the reader focused on the thoughts of the children in their moments of quiet while they question silently, reach back in memory and see things more clearly now, in this growing time "toward womanhood / toward manhood."

> "Children's Books: 'Daydreamers'," in Publishers Weekly *(reprinted from the June 12, 1981 issue of* Publishers Weekly, *published by R. R. Bowker Company, a Xerox company; copyright © 1981 by Xerox Corporation), Vol. 219, No. 4, June 12, 1981, p. 54.*

Greenfield celebrates daydreamers, whose reverie-filled pauses become a creative connection through which they grow and learn. Though the text is spare—a poem, in fact, that's spread thinly through the pages—the sentiments are richly expressed, with artful images and canny turns of phrase. . . . A slim but meaningful piece.

> Denise M. Wilms, "Children's Books: 'Daydreamers'," in Booklist *(reprinted by permission of the American Library Association; copyright © 1981 by the American Library Association), Vol. 78, No. 2, August 15, 1981, p. 105.*

The conventional relationship of author and illustrator is reversed in a book whose dust jacket states what is obvious to the perceptive eye: that the poetic text was inspired by [Tom Feelings's] drawings. . . . Expressive, soul-searching portraits of Black young people—ranging from early innocent childhood to adolescence on the brink of maturity—are uncannily echoed by the pellucid, sensitive words. . . . [Accompanying] lines of the extended poem provide a kind of spiritual illumination.

> Ethel L. Heins, "Poetry: 'Daydreamers'," in The Horn Book Magazine *(copyright © 1981 by The Horn Book, Inc., Boston), Vol. LVII, No. 5, October, 1981, p. 547.*

Marguerite Henry

1902-

American author of fiction and nonfiction for children. Henry is perhaps the most acclaimed writer of horse stories for children. She uses exciting plots, realistic characters, and historical accuracy to create her tales, which center mainly on horses but portray a variety of animal subjects. She spends months researching her books prior to their composition, and utilizes thousands of letters, personal interviews, and trips to her story's locale. Henry does not humanize her animals, but depicts their individual personalities and qualities of loyalty, courage, and perseverance as true to their species. Her children and adults are considered as fully developed as her animal characters. Critics note Henry's ability to identify with the feelings of both animals and humans, thus bringing a range of emotion to the imagination of her readers. Succinct word pictures drawn in language often called powerful and beautiful and a simple, warm style characterize the writing of this popular author.

First published at the age of 11, Henry began her adult career as a technical writer. She wrote *Auno and Tauno*, her first work for children, after hearing the childhood reminiscences of two Finnish friends, and the satisfaction she received from writing it convinced her to become a full-time children's author. *Justin Morgan Had a Horse*, the first of her many stories featuring horses, characteristically combines historical fact with imagination. *Misty of Chincoteague* introduces readers to one of Henry's most popular characters and the family that adopts her. Together with her filly, Stormy, whose story is told in *Stormy, Misty's Foal*, Misty made personal appearances nationwide and delighted thousands of children. *King of the Wind* gained Henry national prominence and won the Newbery Award for 1948. Reviewers praise her skillful character development of both the Arabian stallion Sham and his loyal friend Agba, and they note the effectiveness of her writing in eliciting sadness, joy, and excitement. Henry has also written biographies of both famous and less familiar figures in addition to well-received informational books including *Album of Horses, Birds at Home*, and *Wagging Tails: An Album of Dogs* which characterize various breeds and species and give pertinent facts and anecdotes about them.

Critics credit Henry with being the first author to provide a body of horse stories for the younger reader. While not all of her writing is seen as excellent, she is praised for her storytelling ability, use of historical perspective, attention to detail, and use of authentic speech patterns such as slang and broken English. Though often sentimental, her stories are not considered overly moralistic, and she is felt to invest them with realism and common sense. May Hill Arbuthnot called Henry "the poet laureate of horses," and consistent readership for almost forty years has proven the validity of this statement. Henry's awards include the Newbery Honor Book Award and the Friends of Literature Award in 1946 for *Justin Morgan Had a Horse;* the Newbery Honor Book Award in 1947 and the Lewis Carroll Shelf Award in 1961 for *Misty of Chincoteague;* the Newbery Award in 1948 for *King of the Wind;* the William Allen White Children's Book Award in 1956 for *Brighty of the Grand Canyon;* and the Children's Reading Round Table Award in 1961 and the Kerlan Award in 1975 for the body of

Tony Francis Photography

her work. Several of Henry's books have been adapted for film. (See also *Contemporary Authors*, Vols. 17-20, rev. ed., and *Something about the Author*, Vol. 11.)

AUTHOR'S COMMENTARY

King of the Wind was a long time growing. At first it was nothing but a letterhead. A letterhead and a wish.

Cupped in a fertile valley at the foot of the Blue Ridge Mountains lies a vast breeding farm for thoroughbreds. Several years ago the owner, Walter Chrysler, wanted the head of the Godolphin Arabian engraved on his stationery; for it was the blood of this famous horse that had flowed down the centuries to give speed and stamina to the stallions and broodmares in Mr. Chrysler's stable. So proud was he of this heritage that he engaged the artist, Wesley Dennis, to draw a faithful likeness of the head. The artist sent his assistant to the library to find in old books an accurate portrayal. As the Godolphin Arabian was foaled in 1724 there were, of course, no photographs of him but only artists' likenesses. It was not the drawings of the little horse with the extraordinary crest that intrigued the assistant, however; it was the fact that all through his life no one had foreseen any greatness in him! Overworked and underfed, he drew a wood cart in the streets of Paris. Yet in spite of his degrading experiences and menial tasks, no one could quench the fire in his veins. He lived to become one of the greatest foundation sires of the thoroughbred line.

The assistant wished to write the Godolphin story, and for years Wesley waited to do the illustrations, while the excitement grew within him. "If only I could tell you about another horse of history!" he would say while we were putting the book of Justin Morgan together. And I would reply with a quick imploring, "Don't! I can't trust myself to know about it if someone else is at work on the idea." But the hints were like nettles.

The story of Little Bub was completed; and before the sound of his hoofbeats had dimmed, I was lost in the wilds of Pennsylvania with a Quaker lad named Benjamin West. Then pony Misty was foaled and her story, too, was finished. At last Wesley's assistant decided that it was unlikely she would ever find time to write the Godolphin story; so Wesley was free to talk about it.

With great excitement I began to probe and pry into the life of this famous stallion who had rubbed shoulders with sultans and kings, with cooks and carters. Here were no burned-out cinders of history. Here were live coals showering their sparks over Morocco, France, England.

Sultan Mulai Ismael of Morocco, the stableboy Agba, the blackhearted wood carter, Quaker Coke of London, the Keeper of the Red Lion, the Earl of Godolphin—here were real characters. And Roxana, Hobgoblin, Regulus, Cade, Lath were real horses. Little by little and quite of their own volition they began to collaborate with me, to take me into their confidence.

I began to see the Earl of Godolphin not just as an aristocrat who owned a stable of pleasure horses. His passion was horses, blooded horses. He longed to improve the English strain. I felt the fear in him, the secret fear that just when he was on the eve of creating a new breed of horses his money was running out faster than sands in an hourglass.

And Jethro Coke made it plain that it was from pity he bought the little horse from between the shafts of the wood cart, not because he saw any greatness in him.

For *King of the Wind* querying letters went out by the basketful, to librarians and historians, to horsemen and Quakers. From Mary Alice Lamb, birthright Quaker and authority on early Quaker history, I learned my English "thee's" and "thou's" as against the American. She taught me, too, what I should have known, that the plural forms of "thee" and "thy" are "you" and "your." She agreed that "you" did sound un-Quakerish, but that was the way of it.

From Joachim Wach, Professor of Comparative Religion, I learned that Mohammedans believe in heaven, that in their Koran are many references to the "garden" and the happiness of those dwelling there. And so when Agba and Sham and Grimalkin were on the highroad to Gog Magog, I found myself saying, "If the road to the hills of Gog Magog had been the road to the garden of heaven, the three silent creatures could not have been happier." I'd write a whole horse van of letters for little nuggets like this.

In planning a book I like to think it out in scenes and I am always astounded that they cannot hang in mid-air. I'm in such a state of eagerness to get on to the next big scene that I forget there must be bridges between them. Children need them for security. Often little catwalks will do.

These bridges have always been my big problem. On the manuscript describing the scene in *Justin Morgan* where Joel Goss enlisted in the War of 1812, Helen Ferris of the Junior Literary Guild noted: "Danger! Bridge out! Don't you think disposing of the War of 1812 in a sentence and a half is a little abrupt?"

Her warning led me on one of my most exciting quests. I attacked the war from the viewpoint of doctors and veterinarians. The next thing I knew I was in the heat of the battle of Lundy's Lane, thrusting muskets in sleeves to make litters for the wounded men, then going to the horses, pouring alum in their wounds, quieting their screaming. And so what was once a gossamer thread became strong enough for hobnailed boots.

As time went on, some of the characters not only collaborated; they began to do a little bossing. Certain things were inevitable, and they made me see this. For example, I thought I was arguing with myself that Agba could not be a mute. Children might be repelled. But all the time Agba's dark burning eyes, his thin hands, his shoulders were talking to me more articulately than any words. It was he who made the decision.

To put myself into the long ago and far away I peppered my study walls with photostats. There were Arabian boys in their hooded mantles; sultans swaying along on their horses with wondrous fringed parasols held over them; wood carters snaking bullwhips over little cobs drawing big-wheeled carts; foppish French nobles admiring their curls in a beauty salon where wigs were pegged on the wall like scalps. And there were English scenes of thatched-roof cottages, of kitchens with hares and partridges dangling from the rafters like furry swords of Damocles, of Newmarket at the height of a royal race meeting.

There were pictures of actual characters such as the Earl of Godolphin, magnificent in his cascade of white ruffles; Sultan Mulai Ismael the Fat, sitting on his dais; the boy king, Louis XV, riding his stout horse; George II of England, strutting big to make up for his littleness; Queen Caroline, tall as a pikestaff, followed by her stepping-stone daughters in their little wired hoods.

Suddenly I was no longer hemmed in by study walls. I had leaped across the years. I was Agba flying through the streets of Meknes. I was Sham struggling to keep my footing on icy cobblestones. I was the Godolphin Arabian being crowned with royal plumes from the Queen's own headdress.

It was the present that grew dim and the long ago that became real! Even at noon when I set aside my work and went to the barn to water Misty and Friday, I was still in the past. It was not Misty's blond eyelashes that brushed along my hand as I held her water bucket, but those of Sham, the fleet one.

Present-day people helped play the little game with me. There was Samuel W. Riddle, owner of Man o' War. It was his beloved Big Red that helped to fasten draw-chains on the past. If I could make children understand that this hero of theirs was a direct descendant of the Godolphin Arabian, history would no longer sleep with closed, waxen eyelids; it would quicken to life.

Old press notices said that Man o' War was retired because of a bowed tendon, and checking on this statement brought me my cherished friendship with Mr. Riddle. I sent my opening chapter on Man o' War to him and he replied as follows:

Dear Mrs. Henry:

I liked your Morgan story, but I was shocked at what you wrote about Man o' War. He retired to the stud without a mark on him, never broke down or had a bowed tendon. Whoever told you this is a word of four letters beginning with L. I retired him as a three-year-old because his handicapper told me he would give him more weight than ever a horse carried as a four-year-old.

I will be 87 years old next July and I have tried to tell the truth all my life. Now I am too old to change. If you want to know anything more about Man o' War, come and see me.

> Very sincerely,
> S. D. Riddle
> (pp. 327-31)

I did go to Florida and there wrote and re-wrote the chapter. On the day I took it to Mr. Riddle, I found him sitting with his back to the sun and the sea. His eyes were the blueness of the sea and his hair the whiteness of the breakers. When I finished reading to him about his immortal Man o' War, I looked up to find a tear spilling down his cheek. Then I cried too, and we were friends. The rest of the day we spent at his stable at Hialeah, where I met more descendants of the Godolphin Arabian than a body can dream of.

Always there seems to be a gentle man with blue eyes and whitened hair who lends encouragement and faith to my stories. For *Misty* there was the inimitable Grandpa Beebe with his salty philosophy. It was he who dealt such wisdom as "Facts are fine, fer as they go, but they're like water bugs skittering atop the water. Legends, now—they go deep down and bring up the heart of a story."

With *Justin Morgan* it was David Dana Hewitt. He was 98 years old but young enough to ride my questions with a loose rein. In his fine, steady handwriting he made me see Vermont. Not the Vermont that greets you from paved highways, but the Vermont that lies deep in the soul of its people.

One would think I might have learned about transitions from this experience. But no. In *King of the Wind* I hopscotched from continent to continent with thoughtless abandon. Signor Achmet with his stallions and horseboys aboard ship at Tangier. The horses are sleek, their haunches gleam satin in the sun. In the next scene in Versailles they are bags of bones. This is where I need help and it comes in the form of a pertinent question by Dr. Mary Alice Jones, my editor, "What happened to make them thin?"

Then, quite gallantly, the blackguard of a captain prompts me in a stage whisper. With a sly wink and a twirl of his moustaches, he admits to pocketing the money for oats and feeding the horses on nothing but straw. (pp. 331-32)

"Putting a book to bed"—that is, preparing it for the press—is as much fun to me as the writing of it. It provides the excitement of playing in an orchestra, with none of the dull hours of practising. (p. 332)

The visual properties of a book, the tactile qualities—picture layout, size and kind of type, the cloth for the cover, the stamping—are as deeply important to me as the context. Working with all departments is akin in my mind to playing in a great orchestra. The tumult and triumph and cymbals and swells of sound are all there. So too is the sense of belonging, not as a solo player, but as part of the whole! The ecstasy of belonging! It must be the same feeling that horses have when they switch tails for each other in flytime!

At home I still have this sense of belonging because of the children who come to help on my new book. My tiny study is a child's paradise. The walls are covered with pictures. . . . Horses walking, horses trotting, horses galloping, horses blown, horses in repose, colts frisking, foals suckling.

The child who crosses my threshold gazes in wild delight. It is his dream room come true. It is mine, too. Perhaps his childhood room is not unlike the one I remember with walls painted fresh and clean and not to be desecrated with a motley collection of disarming animals with liquid, questing eyes.

I think when a child steps into this little world of mine he subconsciously rips off the pictures I have posted and puts up his own. For an instant this room becomes his. Then often he will look around and say with grave earnestness, "Will you write a book for me? Not for any other boy. Just for me?"

I'm a long time answering. How can I tell him that is what I am trying to do? How can I say, "Johnny, I'm trying! I'm trying to write a book that you can crawl into as snugly as you do into your own bed, a book about which you can say, 'This is mine. It fits around me. I fit into it. It fits under and over and around me. It warms me. It is mine, mine, *mine!*'"

Haltingly, I do say, "Johnny, books aren't just one-sided. It takes an understanding reader to discover his own book. The writer is no more than the farmer with his bag of seeds. The reader is a field, new plowed in spring. The farmer scatters his seeds, but all the plants that grow from them do not come up alike. Some are small and spindling and some are big and strong. That's the way it is with books. Sometimes a book gives you a small moment of happiness; and sometimes when you close the cover, the book grows big within you, like a boll of cotton bursting its seams. Some day, Johnny, I hope you'll say to me, 'This book you wrote for *me*.'"

It is children like Johnny who make me loath to give up a manuscript. In fact, if it weren't for deadlines I'd still be working on *King of the Wind*. The doing is always so much more fun than the getting through. The only really dismal days in my life are those when I turn in a manuscript. I am suddenly bereft. It is as if the sun had slid into the horizon and a cold curtain of rain had slapped across my face. A whole lifetime of emptiness seems to stretch out before me.

And then, oh happy relief! In a little while the manuscript is back home, with blessed little question marks along the margins. Then once again I'm happy. I've got work to do! The editor's in her chair; all's right with the world. (pp. 332-34)

> *Marguerite Henry, "Acceptance Paper," in* Newbery Medal Books: 1922-1955, *edited by Bertha Mahoney Miller and Elinor Whitney Field (copyright © 1955 by The Horn Book, Inc., Boston), Horn Book, 1955, pp. 327-34.*

GENERAL COMMENTARY

Is it because Marguerite Henry is a throughbred, is it because she has that extra quality called "heart" that she is able to make us laugh a little and cry a little, and satisfy us wholeheartedly when she tells a story? (p. 387)

Today many of us believe her to be the best author of children's horse stories in this era, perhaps of all time.

Whence comes her insight into the minds and hearts of people and animals? Can it be from the warmth of her own family living, her happy childhood? Whence comes this sensitivity to the fundamental needs of all creatures, human and four-footed, for love, for independence, for security, for achievement, for companionship, for solving problems, for growing up? Can the phenomenal amount of research which she has done for each book account for the depth of understanding she evidences in her writing? What are the qualities, the characteristics, the aspirations of this creator or interpreter of Little Bub, of Reddy, Misty, Rosalind, and Grimalkin and Little or Nothing? But the animal characters are not the only heroes. Grandma and Grandpa Beebe, Joel and Agba, Gibson and Benjamin White, and scores of other humans share the "Queen's Plate" as youths, four-footed and two, stretch toward maturity. For each animal one or more human friends, for each youth the wisdom and guidance of age. While all of the writing is not equally powerful, it is within the stories themselves that one must look for "the thread that runs so true," the thread that reveals Marguerite Henry in the truest light. (pp. 387-88)

Many readers agree that [the author/illustrator team of Marguerite Henry and Wesley Dennis] has produced some of the most beautiful and worthwhile books ever published for children. Although written for children, people of all ages thrill to the beauty of language, . . . homely philosophy; authentic information spiced with imagination and phantasy; the portrayal of characters, four-footed and two, rich in human values; and the awareness of the fundamental needs of all God's creatures. (pp. 388-89)

[*Justin Morgan Had a Horse*] is the kind of book that makes you proud and sometimes brings a lump to your throat. . . . But this was only the forerunner of better books to come in which all of the original values were enriched and deepened.

Following *Justin Morgan* came *Robert Fulton, Boy Craftsman.* This is believed by many to be best of the series of "The Childhood of Famous Americans." In *Robert Fulton*, the same rich human values are present. It isn't fiction, yet it reads like a novel. In it a real boy comes alive. Days of the past flash with color and hum with activity.

The writing in this story does not have the quality of later books nor of *Justin Morgan.* The sentences are short and choppy, the vocabulary limited, but to serve the purpose for which it was written, this probably had to be. It is the story of a boy whose mother understood the needs of her children for love and understanding, for security despite economic limitations, who encouraged children to discover and experiment and meet life situations, one who loved wholeheartedly and one who was loved. It is a satisfying book and helps to make history live for young insecure readers. . . .

[*The Little Fellow*] lacks the gripping poignancy of books written for older children. This story for young children, however, spells out for them two very real and personal problems, present in the four-footed animal society as well as in the two-footed human one, the task of growing up and that of adjusting to the other and younger children. . . .

In 1945 and 1946 the second eight geography books were published. . . . These, like the former [titles about Latin American and neighboring countries], are good, informational books. . . .

Benjamin West and His Cat, Grimalkin was published in 1947. This suspenseful tale of a boy who grew up to be an artist and his cat, Grimalkin, is one of the most unusual and best of the biographies for children. (p. 390)

Always Reddy is a calm little tale of a man and his dog, perhaps inspired by Mr. Henry's love of his pet dog. It is a good story,

but it does not tug at the heart strings as do some of the others. . . . While the plot is a substantial one, some of the incidents and settings seems less natural and lifelike than those in most of the books. It doesn't seem to be that it's dogs rather than horses, for Benjamin West has those "horse story qualities." In some unexplainable way, something seems to be lacking. Perhaps it's just the reader missing the rich drama, the suspense, or the laughter of children.

For those of us who first met Marguerite Henry in *Misty of Chincoteague,* probably none of her books will ever take its place in our hearts. . . . [For] us there will never be another Misty. For Misty is just Misty, and our introduction to a magical land of fact, phantasy, and legend woven into stories that entwine around our heart strings like ivy clinging to the wall. . . .

It is one of the finest horse stories ever written. Chincoteague is a way of life. The salt air of the Atlantic is in it. The fine sense of values, the feeling of drama, the deft characterization all blend together to give us Misty. [*King of the Wind* and *Sea Star, Orphan of Chincoteague* followed Misty.] (p. 391)

And then there was *Little or Nothing from Nottingham.* One wonders whether a book of this nature isn't a necessity for both the author and the reader after the highly charged emotional experience of stories like *King of the Wind* or *Sea Star. Little or Nothing* is a gentle book, a laughing book, a circus book. . . . It's a joyous book that delights circus fans young and old, as well as thousands of children to whom a dog is a second self and the circus is the epitome of romance and glory. In the opinion of this writer, this is the best of Henry's books for *younger* readers, but it seems to have no age limit. (pp. 392-93)

[*Born to Trot*] is fun to read, but in addition, it is packed with information about, enthusiasm for, and the excitement of harness racing. . . .

There is majesty, splendor, grandeur in *Album of Horses.* . . . As one pores over the fascinating legends and facts of all breeds of horses, one can hardly fail to realize the painstaking research that has gone into the book. Ponies, mules, Arabians parade through the pages. It's as exciting as a novel, as dramatic as a play, and as informative as an encyclopedia, but it's more than that. In it one senses the glories of the past, the hopes for the future. To those who have not known the horse world, it swings wide the gates, and to those already initiated there is romance and glamor and color and "heart." . . .

Brighty of the Grand Canyon [is] wild, free, lovable. A story of adventure, mystery, beauty, and human-animal companionship. A bond stronger than ropes, chains, or distance that existed between a man and a burro.

Brighty gave up freedom voluntarily, but no one, *no one* could take it away from him except temporarily. His need of humans when he was ill, when he was hurt, when he was hungry, or when he was lonely brought him back again and again to human dangers, but always he was a bright free spirit. With Jack Irons, the mountain lion, the jacks, the blizzard on the other side of the river, he lost to win again. Always Uncle Jim brought to him sympathy and healing brews, always Brighty brought to Uncle Jim loyalty, love, and faith and a willingness to serve. But because Brighty gave of his free will to Uncle Jim, he was ever free to go. . . . (p. 393)

Extensive, painstaking, thorough research has gone into each book. . . .

Here are no preachy, moralistic goody-goody characters. Here are creatures good, bad, and indifferent parading through the pages of the books. Here are pictures painted with words, people characterized by their behavior. Here is an honest forthright author who has never failed or fooled her readers. . . . Every detail must be accurate, every statement true.

But, furthermore, she seems to have the ability [as Alberita R. Semrad says,] "to be inside the skin of the story's protagonist." It is this ability, we suspect, that explains the secret of her success in presenting characters as they really are. Solutions to problems are not the pat "happy ever after" endings, but a realistic meeting of conflict carried through to a logical conclusion. King of the Wind never raced, but his colts did; Misty was sold, but Sea Star came to fill the gap; Gibson White did not ride Rosalind in the Hambletonian, although he was later to ride her foals; Reddy did not hunt again, but he found another responsibility. All creatures must grow up to face life as it is and always there is the wisdom of age to gentle, to help, and to push a little. There's no saccharine sweet moral to her stories, but a salty common sense, laced with humor, a few tears, and a "heart." . . .

[Mrs. Henry] has complete faith in animals and in children and it is returned full measure. And because children and animals *know*, we believe Mrs. Henry is a *"thoroughbred"* with that something extra called "heart." (p. 394)

> *Miriam E. Wilt, "In Marguerite Henry—The Thread That Runs So True," in* Elementary English *(copyright © 1954 by the National Council of Teachers of English; reprinted by permission of the publisher and the author), Vol. XXXI, No. 7, November, 1954, pp. 387-95.*

Everyone who knows children's literature knows the power and the popularity of books written by Marguerite Henry. (p. 7)

Individuals of all ages who read Marguerite Henry's horse stories know these stories introduce the reader to horses and to much more. Persons and places are a vivid and integral part of each story. The reader may begin to read because the book looks like a horse story. When he finishes reading, he has visited new places and he has met interesting, real people. (p. 8)

A perfect blending of text and illustration is characteristic of Marguerite Henry's work.

The Beebe family is convincingly human in *Misty of Chincoteague* . . . Maureen and Paul are a real brother and sister who know how it feels to want a pony. Grandpa Beebe's warm and friendly wisdom and wit are transmitted to the reader. In *Stormy,* . . . the story of Misty's foal, the tidal wave and winds are terrifyingly real. The ponies of Chincoteague are no "once upon a time" story for thousands of boys and girls. Misty and the Beebe family are special friends of the readers.

The Old Timer, Uncle Jim, and Homer are persons the reader meets in *Brighty of the Grand Canyon*. . . . The burro, Brighty, is an independent but loyal animal, never seeming to forget his good friend and master, the Old Timer, after the Old Timer disappears. Descriptions of the Grand Canyon country are evidence that the author visited the location and can convey the natural setting in words which help the reader see the places where Brighty traveled. Feelings of suspense, sadness, loyalty, and bravery are genuine, not contrived. Dialect in the conversation helps the reader hear the characters talk.

In each of the Henry horse stories before *Mustang,* one animal is the center of the reader's attention. In *Mustang, Wild Spirit of the West,* . . . Marguerite Henry has written about horses but she has not designated any one horse as the focus of the story. The story of the mustangs is a plea for saving one of the last symbols of the west. (pp. 8-9)

Each of Marguerite Henry's books . . . introduces the reader to persons who helped to make the animal story a real human drama. The age at which a reader will enjoy the book most will depend on the experiences in living which the reader can bring to the story. Repeated reading of Henry books is a frequent occurrence. . . . (p. 9)

Paul Hazard, as part of his answer to the question, "What are good books?" wrote ". . . books that awaken in them not maudlin sentimentality, but sensibility; that enable them to share in great human emotions; that give them respect for universal life—that of animals, of plants; teach them not to despise everything that is mysterious in creation and in man." And so Marguerite Henry's books are described. (p. 10)

> *Norine Odland, "Marguerite Henry: Mistress of Mole Meadows," in* Elementary English *(copyright © 1968 by the National Council of Teachers of English; reprinted by permission of the publisher and the author), Vol. 45, No. 1, January, 1967, pp. 7-11.*

Without "humanizing" animals, Mrs. Henry creates horses that are consistent with their species yet have qualities of courage, loyalty, and endurance. Plot does not take precedence over characterization. Each person is real, consistent, and fully developed. There is no lengthy descriptive prose, for a few words create a picture. One horse is described: "The Phantom ain't a hoss. She ain't even a lady. She's just a piece of wind and sky." There is realism in Marguerite Henry's writing; the pains of birth are described in *Black Gold,* yet the reader's senses are not shocked. (p. 515)

> *Charlotte S. Huck and Doris Young Kuhn, "Books for Special Interests," in their* Children's Literature in the Elementary School, *2nd ed. (copyright © 1961, 1968 by Holt, Rinehart and Winston, Inc.; reprinted by permission of Holt, Rinehart and Winston, Publishers, CBS College Publishing), second edition, Holt, Rinehart and Winston, 1968, pp. 507-42.*

As far as children are concerned, Marguerite Henry is the poet laureate of horses. (p. 137)

The quality of Marguerite Henry's books lies not only in her compelling storytelling power, but in her ability to make her creatures live and act true to their own species with all the helplessness and suffering of animals in the hands of cruel or ignorant men. Another great quality of these books is that they are peopled by admirable human characters who command as much interest as the animal heroes. These books stir deep compassion in young readers and the desire to nurture and protect. (p. 138)

> *May Hill Arbuthnot, "Animal Stories: 'King of the Wind'," in her* Children's Reading in the Home *(copyright © 1969 by Scott, Foresman and Company; reprinted by permission), Scott, Foresman, 1969, pp. 137-38.*

Marguerite Henry is probably the most successful writer of horse stories we have ever had. Her success rests on a sound basis. Every book represents careful research, the stories are well told, the animal heroes are true to their species, and the people in her books are as memorable as the animals. . . .

What gives [the] books by Marguerite Henry their unique quality? First of all, she can make the true pattern of animal life so vivid that readers identify themselves with the animals. Yet the animals are never humanized. With complete integrity to their species, these creatures exhibit traits that children admire in human beings—fortitude, loyalty, and a blithe zest for life. (p. 407)

> *May Hill Arbuthnot and Zena Sutherland, "Animal Stories: 'King of the Wind'," in their* Children and Books *(copyright © 1947, 1957, 1964, 1972, by Scott, Foresman and Company; reprinted by permission), fourth edition, Scott, Foresman, 1972, p. 407.*

AUNO AND TAUNO; A STORY OF FINLAND   (1940)

[This is a] pleasant book for four-year-olds, and through . . . the text a little American can come close to the daily life of a pair of Finnish twins. But the most important feature of the book, so far as the little listener is concerned, is that . . . its easy words tell a real story. . . .

> *May Lamberton Becker, "Books for Young People: 'Auno and Tauno, A Story of Finland'," in* New York Herald Tribune Books *(© I.H.T. Corporation; reprinted by permission), June 30, 1940, p. 7.*

BIRDS AT HOME   (1942; revised edition, 1972)

The discussion of 21 common birds emphasizes their nesting habits, care of the young, and how they help man by eating insect pests. This edition includes . . . an introduction by the author. In Chapter 11, two references to Southern Negroes hanging gourds for Purple Martin homes near their cabins have been changed to more general statements, and, in the chapter on Starlings, their range is changed from ". . . found west of the Rocky Mountains" to ". . . found over the entire country." Otherwise, the text is substantially the same.

> *Linda Lawson Clark, "The Book Review: 'Birds at Home'," in* School Library Journal, *an appendix to* Library Journal *(reprinted from the January, 1973 issue of* School Library Journal, *published by R. R. Bowker Co./A Xerox Corporation; copyright © 1973), January, 1973, p. 680.*

The author explains in an enlightening introduction that she was "a boxed-in city mouse" until she moved to the country and became fascinated with the birdlife around her. Almost immediately she conceived the idea of writing a book about birds and couldn't be dissuaded by an ornithological advisor who told her it would take a lifetime of study to produce such a book. Within two years she produced **Birds at Home,** little essays . . . written in a lively, enthusiastic style. . . . From an ornithological standpoint the accounts leave much to be desired. Anthropomorphisms abound, and there are many questionable observations; however, the book is recommended for those small children whose parents do not raise an eyebrow at having a bird "like to," "love to," or "prefer to" do this or that.

> *"Life Sciences: 'Birds at Home'," in* Science Books *(copyright © 1973 by the American Association for*

the Advancement of Science), Vol. IX, No. 1, May, 1973, p. 170.

JUSTIN MORGAN HAD A HORSE   (1945; revised edition, 1954)

In a book that is rich in human values—the sort of book that makes you proud and sometimes brings a lump to your throat—Marguerite Henry has told the story of the common little work horse which fathered a line of famous American horses.

> *"Sire of Fine U.S. Steeds," in* Book Week—Chicago-Sun Times *(© Field Enterprises, Inc.; reprinted with permission), November 11, 1945, p. 19.*

The descendants of Justin Morgan's namesake are known in America wherever men know horses. They have helped make American history in war and are equally valuable in peacetime. Around the true history of that sire of the first distinctively American breed of horses is built this appealing story of the Vermont school teacher who took an unwanted, short-legged little colt in part payment of a bad debt, and of Joel Goss, the boy who loved the colt at first sight, gentled and trained him. . . . Seven to 12-year-olds will warm to this story and so will a good many older readers.

> *Ellen Lewis Buell, "For Younger Readers: 'Justin Morgan Had a Horse'," in* The New York Times Book Review *(© 1945 by The New York Times Company; reprinted by permission), November 25, 1945, p. 12.*

ROBERT FULTON, BOY CRAFTSMAN   (1945)

Fulton, a mechanical genius apprenticed to a kindly and appreciative gunsmith who allowed the boy freedom to develop his natural tendencies, fulfilled the expectations of his neighbors. The early sections, dealing with Fulton up to his 17th year, are good, while the latter half is rather loose and haphazard and fails to hold the interest of the young reader. As inventor of dozens of useful articles, painter of importance in his own time, protege of Benjamin Franklin, loyal son and brother, and, ultimately inventor of the steamboat, Fulton's life is packed with interesting and ingenious material. There is excellent detail on manufacturing processes, materials, schools and family life. . . . Third and fourth graders may be able to read it themselves for the type is clear and good and the paragraphs and chapters short.

> *"Fact Books for the 9-12's: 'Robert Fulton: Boy Craftsman'," in* Virginia Kirkus' Bookshop Service, *Vol. 12, No. 14, August 1, 1945, p. 340.*

Simple text and large print make this another biography that third and fourth graders can read. Robert Fulton is a real boy who comes alive in the first part of the book.

> *Elizabeth Johnson, "New Books Appraised: 'Robert Fulton: Boy Craftsman'," in* Library Journal *(reprinted from* Library Journal, *November 1, 1945; published by R. R. Bowker Co. (a Xerox company); copyright © 1945 by Xerox Corporation), Vol. 70, No. 19, November 1, 1945, p. 1027.*

In adding the story of Robert Fulton to the Childhood of Famous Americans series, Marguerite Henry had to match her skill against that of a number of illustrious predecessors who have contributed to the list. It is delightful to find that she has made good to the extent of writing one of the best of the series.

The young Bob Fulton comes to life so believably in these pages that no youngster who reads the book is likely to forget him. . . .

His story is one to inspire other young Americans.

> *"Robert Fulton Began Career in School Days," in Book Week—Chicago-Sun Times (© Field Enterprises, Inc.; reprinted with permission), November 11, 1945, p. 17.*

BENJAMIN WEST AND HIS CAT GRIMALKIN (1947)

Even Americans proud of the distinctions of our pioneers seldom know but one thing more about Benjamin West than that he was a painter who flourished early in our history. We may have forgotten, if we ever knew, that he became president of the Royal Academy of England and court painter to King George III, but if we know his name we know that when he was very young, and couldn't get camel's hair brushes to paint with, he made brushes out of hair from his pet cat's tail. On this familiar anecdote Miss Henry weaves a pleasant pattern of early days among the Friends in Pennsylvania, of an eager little boy rescuing a kitten and forming with this intelligent creature such friendship as intelligent children at once recognize. She shows a little chap with kind parents and favorable surroundings—except that Benjamin wanted to make pictures, and to the devout Quakers pictures were ornaments and ornaments were needless. . . .

There is personal triumph in his series of discoveries: learning from the Indians to dig colors from the earth, trying with duck feathers, timothy grass and wooden paddles to lay the colors on smoothly, hearing about proper brushes, and suddenly realizing what fur might do in their place.

The romantic element in the real story makes natural the part the cat plays in all this. Grimalkin can "do anything but talk" and on occasion—as when somebody sits in his favorite chair—say something out loud and to the point.

> *May Lamberton Becker, "Books for Young People: 'Benjamin West and His Cat Grimalkin'," in New York Herald Tribune Weekly Book Review (© I.H.T. Corporation; reprinted by permission), June 22, 1947, p. 8.*

We do not know if Benjamin West's cat was really named Grimalkin. We are told, however, that his first brushes were made from the family cat's fur; that friendly Indians showed him how to make his colors from American earth; that his first picture, a portrait of his baby niece, was drawn when he was 7. From these and sundry other picturesque legends Marguerite Henry has fashioned an endearing story of the very beginnings of the painter's remarkable career. We wish that all artists could be introduced in such a sympathetic, human fashion to young readers.

> *Ellen Lewis Buell, "For Younger Readers: 'Benjamin West and His Cat Grimalkin'," in The New York Times Book Review (© 1947 by The New York Times Company; reprinted by permission), June 22, 1947, p. 27.*

The happy way in which Benjamin West's biography is combined with a real cat story gives this book an unusually friendly appeal. The cat whose tail furnished the Quaker lad with his first paint brushes has hitherto been merely a cat. Now, with Marguerite Henry's love of animals, Grimalkin is endowed

with personality and a share in developing a great talent. This is a delightful picture of American Quaker life before the Revolution and of the man who became court painter in England. (pp. 262-63)

> *Alice M. Jordan, "New Books: 'Benjamin West and His Cat Grimalkin'," in The Horn Book Magazine (copyrighted, 1947, copyright renewed © 1974, by The Horn Book, Inc., Boston), Vol. XXIII, No. 4, July-August, 1947, pp. 262-63.*

ALWAYS REDDY (1947)

Reddy [was] the best red setter, the best bird dog, up and down the river. Also she was the most devoted: one of the charms of this story is that it so communicates the love of man and dog for one another, and shows its every-day but always lovely ways. . . .

[After Reddy's owner Mr. Hoops discovers that his mother-in-law, who is allergic to dogs, was coming to live with them] he made a desperate resolve. Reddy and [her son] Snippet would live in the City Hall.

How he walked in and found the office staff delighted, how he set up housekeeping for the dogs, how they won—and lost temporarily—that support of the mayor, by their too-perfect conduct when this amateur sportsman took them out hunting; and in what a burst of bravery old Reddy saved the housing situation and covered herself with glory, makes a cheerful story of bird dog training, performance and lovable character.

> *May Lamberton Becker, "Books for Young People: 'Always Reddy'," in New York Herald Tribune Weekly Book Review (© I.H.T. Corporation; reprinted by permission), December 28, 1947, p. 6.*

MISTY OF CHINCOTEAGUE (1947)

The islands of Chincoteague and Assateague, just off the coast of Virginia, are the setting for an exceptionally appealing book. . . . The capture, near loss, and gentling of Phantom and Misty, the excitement of the annual pony roundup, the little-known and colorful background, and good characterization make a story that is vividly real. . . .

Children may regret the final disposition of the mole but adults will admire the dexterity with which the author "gets out of that one."

> *"Children's Books: Henry, Marguerite, 'Misty of Chincoteague'," in The Booklist (reprinted by permission of the American Library Association; copyright © 1947 by the American Library Association), Vol. 44, No. 6, November 15, 1947, p. 117.*

"Misty of Chincoteague" makes the most of an unusual setting off the coast of Virginia. . . . The simple story is told with a fine sense of values, a feeling for drama, deft characterization.

> *Francis Smith, "The Animal Kingdom: 'Misty of Chincoteague'," in The New York Times Book Review (© 1947 by The New York Times Company; reprinted by permission), November 16, 1947, p. 41.*

[This is an] exciting horse story. . . . The salty atmosphere of the Atlantic pervades this story, which discloses much about the peculiar life on Chincoteague and introduces some fine appealing characters. It is . . . absorbing reading. . . .

Alice M. Jordan, "Stories for Younger Children: 'Misty of Chincoteague'," in The Horn Book Magazine (copyrighted, 1948, copyright renewed © 1975, by The Horn Book, Inc., Boston), Vol. XXIV, No. 1, January-February, 1948, p. 38.

KING OF THE WIND (1948)

[The author of *Misty of Chincoteague* has] again produced a book to delight all horse lovers. . . . Sham, Agba and the cat, Grimalkin, are so well drawn in word . . . that they will long be remembered by all who read this fine book.

Jennie D. Lindquist, "New Books for Christmas: 'King of the Wind'," in The Horn Book Magazine (copyrighted, 1948, by The Horn Book, Inc., Boston), Vol. XXIV, No. 6, November, 1948, p. 463.

This is the story of a very King of the Wind—Sham, the great Godolphin Arabian, ancestor of Man o' War and many another brave-hearted racer. Of course there is a boy in the story of Sham—Agba, a young horseboy in the stables of the Sultan.

Agba was at Sham's side when the horse was sent as a gift to the French King. Mute, unable to put his love for the horse into words, the boy could show his loyalty only by staying with him through poverty and later troubles in England. Not even the Earl of Godolphin recognized at once the quality of the little horse which looked so slight beside the sturdy English breed.

In **"King of the Wind"** Marguerite Henry stirs the reader's imagination, holds his interest, makes him laugh a little and cry a little—satisfies him. [There is a] moving quality [in the] writing . . . , and the book . . . [tells] a story which boys and girls will read again and again.

P.A.W., "Castaways: 'King of the Wind'," in New York Herald Tribune Weekly Book Review (© I.H.T. Corporation; reprinted by permission), November 14, 1948, p. 18.

The Godolphin Arabian is the most romantic horse to appear in literature for youth for some time. . . .

Boys and girls from 8 to 14 won't care a hoot about the impressive list of "books consulted," but will accept every thrilling word of the story . . . as gospel truth.

Gladys Crofoot Castor, "Folk-Tales, Elephants, Mysterious Islands," in The New York Times Book Review (© 1948 by The New York Times Company; reprinted by permission), November 14, 1948, p. 3.*

Story is reminiscent of the author's *Justin Morgan Had a Horse,* with a different setting, of course. Vivid portrayals of Morocco, France, and England during the 1700's are presented while the story unfolds. . . . [This] is one of the most distinguished books of the year. (pp. 1825-26)

Janie M. Smith, "Children's Books: 'King of the Wind'," in Library Journal (reprinted from Library Journal, December 15, 1948; published by R. R. Bowker Co. (a Xerox company); copyright © 1948 by Xerox Corporation), Vol. 73, No. 22, December 15, 1948, pp. 1825-26.

SEA STAR, ORPHAN OF CHINCOTEAGUE (1949)

All the many thousands of children who loved **"Misty of Chincoteague"** will be thrilled to have a sequel. Here they will learn another true story of that wild pony island, of the Beebes and Pony Ranch, and of the round-up Mrs. Henry has made famous.

Paul and Maureen sadly let Misty go off with the movie men; she has to help finish the movie, also to meet children when the movie is shown. A kind fate sends a tiny orphan colt to take Misty's place in their hearts. How the children found him and began to bring him up make a moving tale. Grandma Beebe with her good sense, good cooking, and wonderful picnic Bible lesson, is more lovable than ever: so is Grandpa, with his horse sense and deep understanding of the children's feelings.

A second book about Chincoteague has not the impact of the first, but this one is both a good sequel and a good document, ending with a map of the island and a footnote about the truth of the story from the author. She does not, however, tell the children what the publisher's news note tells, that Misty now really is with her at her home near Chicago.

Mrs. Henry's books about horses were the first to fall in that age-range of the younger readers, where they have made a real contribution and won her the Newbery Medal. None are perhaps very fine writing but they all have all the elements that bring them close to children's hearts, above all their reality.

Louise S. Bechtel, "Books for Young People: Adventures with Animals, 'Sea Star'," in New York Herald Tribune Book Review (© I.H.T. Corporation; reprinted by permission), November 13, 1949, p. 16.

BORN TO TROT (1950)

Perhaps Miss Henry's book should be classed as biography this time. For, more than any other of her mostly true horse stories, this one is based on facts, on the life of a champion trotting mare, the boy who owned her and the boy's father who trained her. Her achievement will be very satisfying to all who love that great American institution, harness racing. To youngsters who may not have seen such races, it will be both a fine horse story and a revealing introduction.

We meet young Gib White, whose one aim in life was to be a real reinsman on the "Grand Circuit." Now, for the first time, he is allowed to go along with his father, to work along with him and all the other big trainers. He proved a hero when his first chance came. But fate sent him to a hospital, where the doctor thought he'd never get well, until his father gave him the colt he names Rosalind. From there on, the book is the story of this filly who became world champion trotting mare. In with her story, goes Gib's reading of an old book, the life of a great Hambletonian of one hundred years ago. Such a device might be awkward, but it adds trotting-horse history cleverly to the main tale. And it brings the boy in the hospital deeper into his beloved world of horses. . . .

It's a grand horse story, far above the usual run of such books, appealing to ages ten to fourteen.

Louise S. Bechtel, "Books about Boys and Their Horses," in New York Herald Tribune Book Review (© I.H.T. Corporation; reprinted by permission), November 12, 1950, p. 16.*

Against an exciting background of horses and harness racing, the author writes of real people and real events in her latest and best book. Actually there are two stories: the one about Rosalind, world champion trotting mare and her young owner, Gibson White, son of "Hambletonian Ben," trainer and driver; the other concerns William Rysdyk and his horse, Hambletonian, greatest of all progenitors of the trotting horse. So deftly have the two tales been interwoven that they vie with each other in appeal and drama. The comradeship between the boy and his father is of special note. (pp. 120-21)

> *"Children's Books" 'Born to Trot',"* in The Booklist *(reprinted by permission of the American Library Association; copyright © 1950 by the American Library Association), Vol. 47, No. 6, November 15, 1950, pp. 120-21.*

[A Hambletonian trophy goes] to Marguerite Henry. . . . The true story of Rosalind, world champion trotting mare, is made vivid and moving, and her royal ancestry is attractively presented through a story within a story device. Informative, exciting; everyone from 10-90 will love it.

> *Elaine E. Beatty, "New Books Appraised: 'Born to Trot'," in* Library Journal *(reprinted from* Library Journal, *December 1, 1950; published by R. R. Bowker Co. (a Xerox company); copyright © 1950 by Xerox Corporation), Vol. 75, No. 21, December 1, 1950, p. 2084.*

ALBUM OF HORSES (1951; as *Portfolio of Horses*, 1952; as *Portfolio of Horse Paintings*, 1964)

Boys and girls from ten up are so fond of this author . . . that they will greet an informational book by [her] with joy. There are many with similar contents this year, but this is definitely the best for boys and girls. [It has a] lively, intelligent text. . . .

The twenty-four kinds of horses include the shire horse and the Lipizzans from Vienna. The list ends with three kinds of ponies, the burro or donkey, and the mule. The last excellent chapters tell some very worthwhile things about keeping your horse or pony happy. It's an elegant book, one of the best gift-books of the year. This horse-lover longs for time to read it all over again at leisure.

> *Louise S. Bechtel, "Broncs and Ponies, West and East: 'Album of Horses'," in* New York Herald Tribune Book Review *(© I.H.T. Corporation; reprinted by permission), November 11, 1951, p. 6.*

More than just another collection of horse stories. **"Album of Horses"** presents facts, legends and authentic bits of genealogy concerning all the major breeds of horses in this country. The reader is shown not only how the different types of horses look and move and how they vary from one another but also their uses now and in the days before motors. Miss Henry makes clear the connection between historical need and present-day blood lines. In several cases the facts about a given breed are amplified by a true and exciting story of one specific horse who typifies his forbears virtues.

"Album of Horses" will do more than please enthusiasts, it is likely to create many new ones.

> *Lavinia R. Davis, "Horses, Horses & Horses," in* The New York Times Book Review *(© 1951 by The New York Times Company; reprinted by permission), November 11, 1951, p. 34.*

BRIGHTY OF THE GRAND CANYON (1953)

Sure fire—with Bright Angel destined to join Misty among candidates for the animal Hall of Fame. For Bright Angel, too, has a factual past, on which Marguerite Henry has built an enchanting story. Brighty was a little grey burro, a wild creature with a more than human faculty for picking friends and making enemies—and getting into and out of scrapes. There's adventure and mystery here, set against the superb backdrop of the Grand Canyon, where Brighty made the trail that others follow. . . . Some may quarrel with his human reasoning, but Marguerite Henry has made him very convincing, very appealing.

> *"'Brighty of the Grand Canyon'," in* Virginia Kirkus' Bookshop Service, *Vol. XXI, No. 20, October 15, 1953, p. 710.*

Good frontier adventure keeps **"Brighty of the Grand Canyon"** rolling too fast to miss a word.

This latest of Marguerite Henry's fine books differs somewhat from the others, but only those who are unfamiliar with the West would say it is too packed with drama to be true. And the author's understanding warmth for all of God's creatures still shines through her superb ability as a story teller making this a vivid tale for seven to fourteen-year-olds.

> *Alberita R. Semrad, "Adventuring with a Burro," in* The Christian Science Monitor *(reprinted by permission from* The Christian Science Monitor; *© 1953, copyright renewed © 1981, The Christian Science Publishing Society; all rights reserved), November 12, 1953, p. 10.*

Brighty is the most winning of all Mrs. Henry's four-footed heroes. He is a comic, like all burros, but lonely too. His search for companionship, his loyalty to those who are kind to him, and his gay flights back to freedom make a thrilling story of animal and human adventure. (p. 407)

> *May Hill Arbuthnot and Zena Sutherland, "Animal Stories," in their* Children and Books *(copyright © 1947, 1957, 1964, 1972 by Scott, Foresman and Company; reprinted by permission), fourth edition, Scott, Foresman, 1972, pp. 392-419.**

WAGGING TAILS: AN ALBUM OF DOGS (1955; as *Album of Dogs*, 1970)

[This is a] companion volume to Marguerite Henry's **"Album of Horses."** Miss Henry . . . has used a light and lively style in her descriptions and anecdotes about 25 pure-bred dogs, and also the mongrel. The facts are here, and they are presented in such a way as to delight young dog lovers.

> *"Children's Forecasts: 'Album of Dogs'," in* Publishers Weekly *(reprinted from the December 28, 1970 issue of* Publishers Weekly, *published by R. R. Bowker Company, a Xerox company; copyright © 1970 by Xerox Corporation), Vol. 198, No. 25, December 28, 1970, p. 61.*

In her typically simple, warm, sympathetic style, the author describes . . . varied breeds in terms of their appearance and history and relates anecdotes that reveal the general personality traits of each. Properly called an album, this book is by no means an encyclopedia of dogs. Nor is it a manual for dog training and care. It is a very personal weaving of words, and pictures, making obvious the author's . . . affection and admiration for man's four-legged friends. Youngsters seeking detailed information about dog breeds should consult such titles as [Francene and Louis] Sabin's *Dogs of America* (Putnam, 1967) or an encyclopedia. Those just browsing will find that this book offers enjoyable light reading.

> Lea R. Pastorello, "The Book Review: 'Album of Dogs'," in School Library Journal, *an appendix to* Library Journal *(reprinted from the January, 1971 issue of* School Library Journal, *published by R. R. Bowker Co./A Xerox Corporation; copyright © 1971), Vol. 17, No. 5, January, 1971, p. 52.*

CINNABAR, THE ONE O'CLOCK FOX   (1956)

Children always enjoy a good chase and Cinnabar, the one o'clock fox, leads the hunters a merry one all through this book. Every exciting twist and turn and doubling back is described in the text. . . . The chase itself would have made an excellent animal story, with the pert Cinnabar laughing at the dogs and horsemen after each clever escape. Marguerite Henry, however, has chosen also to add fantasy and imagines the life of Cinnabar and his vixen Vicky and four cubs . . . as though they were any jolly human family with plenty of witty conversation, a well-furnished den with cooking utensils, and even a copy of "Julius Caesar." Children will probably enjoy all this though it does not satisfy this, perhaps obtuse, adult.

> "Through Magic Casements," *in* New York Herald Tribune Book Review *(© I.H.T. Corporation; reprinted by permission), November 18, 1956, p. 6.**

Although stories endowing animals with human habits and homes usually suffer in comparison to Beatrix Potter's tales, this one must be rated unique in pace and excitement. Both the prose and pictures make an intelligent and successful appeal to the reader's five senses.

> Lavinia R. Davis, "Losing the Hounds," *in* The New York Times Book Review *(© 1956 by The New York Times Company; reprinted by permission), November 18, 1956, p. 46.*

BLACK GOLD   (1957)

Those children who like sad stories . . . those who like true stories . . . those who love horse stories . . . will all find satisfaction in Marguerite Henry's life story of Black Gold, that real stallion who won the fiftieth anniversary of the Run for the Roses at Kentucky Derby. . . . A winner this.

> "Eight to Eleven—Fiction: 'Black Gold'," *in* Virginis Kirkus' Service, *Vol. XXV, No. 20, October 15, 1957, p. 772.*

Marguerite Henry shuttles neatly from person to person, scene to scene, to spin a narrative of triumph mixed with tragedy— but it is the tragedy that accents the triumph. Miss Henry is frequently, unabashedly sentimental, but I have never known a horse-fan to object to that, especially when she can create such a sharp sense of immediacy as she does here.

> Ellen Lewis Buell, "Three Legs and a Heart," *in* The New York Times Book Review *(© 1957 by The New York Times Company; reprinted by permission), December 22, 1957, p. 16.*

MULEY-EARS, NOBODY'S DOG   (1959)

Muley-Ears was a big dog who got his name from his huge, pricked-up ears. He lived on the beautiful island of Jamaica, belonging to nobody but the families who spent their vacations in the house he had made his home. Everyone loved Muley-Ears and shared their fun and food with him, while he returned their affection by showing them his favorite haunts. Then one day along came a disagreeable man, who refused all his overtures. How the two finally became friends winds up a simple little tale, pleasant enough but far below [Henry's] usual high standard. . . .

> Polly Goodwin, "A Mixture of Fancy, Fact for Ages 7-11," *in* Chicago Tribune, Part 4 *(© 1959 Chicago Tribune), May 10, 1959, p. 4.**

[Henry's] latest book . . . is a slight, sentimental affair. . . . As a portrait of an amiable, individualistic dog, this is all well and good. However, when Muley-Ears reforms one surly, ungenerous man the story trails away in simon-pure Victorian sweetness.

> Ellen Lewis Buell, "On the Beach," *in* The New York Times Book Review *(© 1959 by The New York Times Company; reprinted by permission), May 17, 1959, p. 30.*

For a younger audience than most of this author's books, this has a simple plot and a good lesson and leaves one with the feeling of having been on the beach in the story.

> Sonja Wennerblad, "Junior Books Appraised: 'Muley-ears, Nobody's Dog'," *in* Junior Libraries, *an appendix to* Library Journal *(reprinted from the September, 1959 issue of* Junior Libraries, *published by R. R. Bowker Co./A Xerox Corporation; copyright © 1959), Vol. 6, No. 1, September, 1959, p. 75.*

GAUDENZIA, PRIDE OF THE PALIO   (1960; as *The Wildest Horse Race in the World*, 1976)

As always, Miss Henry has told a good story for boys and girls who admire horses, and she has made her readers feel the boy's devotion to animals. She has not, however, entirely succeeded in giving us much genuine Italian atmosphere, and her Italian characters speak an irritating kind of broken English.

> "PW Forecasts: 'Gaudenzia, Pride of the Palio'," *in* Publishers Weekly *(reprinted from the October 3, 1960 issue of* Publishers Weekly, *published by R. R. Bowker Company; copyright © 1960 by R. R. Bowker Company), Vol. 178, No. 14, October 3, 1960, p. 60.*

It is small wonder that Marguerite Henry, whose horse stories are loved by children everywhere, should have chosen the Palio, famed horse race run twice annually around the town square of Siena, Italy, for the setting of her latest book. A more spectacular event would be hard to find.

Gaudenzia is a real horse and Giorgio Terni, who rode and trained and loved her, is a real boy. They first met when Giorgio, son of a poor farmer, with a burning desire to ride in the Palio, was horse trainer for Signor Ramalli in Siena, and Guadenzia was a bony carthorse with a nervous tic but with a noble Arabian head which strangely moved the boy. How unlikely it seemed then that one day these two would race together and win, only to be forced to compete with one another in the race to follow.

Emotions run strong in this gripping tale: hope alternates with despair, defeat with victory, grief with joy. And along with the poignant boy-horse relationship, the pageantry—and savagery—of the centuries-old race . . . lend color and excitement to one of the author's finest books.

> Polly Goodwin, "Stories of Horses—Each One a Winner," in Chicago Tribune, part 4 (© 1960 Chicago Tribune), November 6, 1960, p. 22.*

Here is the pageantry and color of the Palio, its history and complicated inner workings, a swiftly moving plot which reaches a terrific climax, and characterization which is deft and convincing. . . . [This is a truly] distinguished book. (p. 72)

> Marian Herr, "Junior Books Appraised: 'Gaudenzia: Pride of the Palio'," in Junior Libraries, an appendix to Library Journal (reprinted from the January, 1961 issue of Junior Libraries, published by R. R. Bowker Co./A Xerox Corporation; copyright © 1961), Vol. 7, No. 5, January, 1961, pp. 71-2.

In a skilfully constructed story based on fact, Marguerite Henry once again writes magnificently of a horse and the boy who loved it, this time evoking the pageantry of the dangerous Palio races in Siena. As the plot moves toward its breathtaking climax, it extends itself to include a good many characters, ranging from an Umbrella Man to Monsignor Tardini of the Vatican, with the result that the reader has a very live sense of Italy and its people at the end. A slightly broken English is employed to simulate the Italian spoken by the children and peasants, but the device has been used artistically and effectively. [Excitement and warmth of feeling] pervade this book. (p. 45)

> Irma Simonton Black, "A Child's World of Ideas," in Saturday Review (copyright © 1961 by Saturday Review; all rights reserved; reprinted by permission), Vol. XLIV, No. 8, February 25, 1961, pp. 44-5.*

ALL ABOUT HORSES   (1962; revised edition, 1967)

An excellent piece of merchandise which, when one thinks of the thousands and thousands of young horse lovers there are, promises to be one of the most popular titles in this very successful series. . . . All the facts that most children can take in about the horse and its habits have been clearly presented by Miss Henry. It can't miss.

> "PW Forecasts: 'All About Horses'," in Publishers Weekly (reprinted from the September 24, 1962 issue of Publishers Weekly, published by R. R. Bowker Company; copyright © 1962 by R. R. Bowker Company), Vol. 182, No. 13, September 24, 1962, p. 65.

STORMY, MISTY'S FOAL   (1963)

There is no doubt which book will be the children's favorite this fall. . . . How Misty and her foal were saved, and how the children of this country and Misty . . . helped the islands to buy back some of the ponies they had sold, and so replenish their herds, make a thrilling tale for children. Adults may see a touch of the publicity of our times, but let us not be captious.

> Alice Dalgliesh, "Middle Group: 'Stormy, Misty's Foal'," in Saturday Review (copyright © 1963 by Saturday Review; all rights reserved; reprinted by permission), Vol. XLVI, No. 45, November 9, 1963, p. 61.

An eagerly awaited book . . . will be grabbed up avidly by that vast army of girls who love horse stories. The startling and tragic circumstances described—the birth of Misty's foal, Stormy, just after a hurricane had decimated the wild herds and destroyed almost everything on Chincoteague and Assateague its "outrider" island—are such that young readers will not be disappointed.

Children's imaginations fill in where authors falter, but certainly the narrative is in need of tightening. The book is written almost entirely in dialogue, much of which should have been pruned, and reads like a combination of publicity releases for the island's chamber of commerce, script for the forthcoming movie about Misty and her colt, and a realistic and sympathetic report on every thought and action of the members of the family who own Misty during this crisis.

Many of the factual details are interesting—the mare waiting out the storm in the kitchen with the cat and her newborn kittens, the helicopter rescue of the family, the sad homecoming with a nearly ruined house and stable and more dead ponies than could be counted, and the "personal appearance" of Misty and her foal as publicity for a movie produced to earn money for the rehabilitation of the island's pony herds. This book will have considerable appeal with its well-publicized subject . . . , although it is not as good as we could hope for from Marguerite Henry.

> Margaret Sherwood Libby, "The Long March Home," in Book Week—The Washington Post (© 1964, Washington Post Co.), January 26, 1964, p. 14.

Stormy, Misty's Foal is frankly a tear-jerker. . . . Misty of Chincoteague is, we are told, a nation-wide American darling, and the story of flood on the island is told from the point of view of the precious foal, whose rescue is marked by thanksgiving all over the country. . . . Horse-doters will wallow in the story: horse-lovers may prefer [Anna Sewell's] Black Beauty and could learn from comparing the two books the difference between sentiment and sentimentality. [Stormy's] saga made me feel rather sick. . . . (p. 655)

> Margery Fisher, "The Friendly Creatures," in her Growing Point, Vol. 4, No. 8, March, 1966, pp. 654-55.*

WHITE STALLION OF LIPIZZA   (1964)

Absolutely sure-fire for Marguerite Henry's fans . . . , this book will be loved by all horse-crazy children. . . .

While I am not horse crazy . . . I found the story interesting, though I confess to being a little sorry for the stallions that have to undergo such rigorous training.

> Alice Dalgliesh, "'White Stallion of Lipizza'," in Saturday Review (copyright © 1964 by Saturday Review; all rights reserved; reprinted by permission), Vol. XLVII, No. 50, December 12, 1964, p. 49.

To Vienna, to the Spanish Court Riding School with its famous equestrian ballet dancers, the Lipizzan stallions, a well-loved author . . . has turned for a new story. Young Hans Haupt was only a baker's son, but every morning as he waited for a glimpse of the magnificent animals crossing the street from their stables to the riding school, he was determined to know more about them and to understand the mystery of their mighty leaping and graceful prancing. And when Hans is finally admitted to the school to begin rigorous years of apprenticeship in the ancient art of classical riding, the passionate devotion to his new career is focused upon one horse in particular, his aging "four-legged professor," the celebrated Borina. The author's writing is often awkward and effusive; illogically the speech of her characters is sprinkled with literal translations from the German; and her incidents occasionally border on the melodramatic. But her careful research, fascinating material, and enthusiastic storytelling commend her to horse lovers of all ages. (pp. 53-4)

> Ethel L. Heins, "Late Winter Booklist: 'White Stallion of Lipizza'," in The Horn Book Magazine (copyright © 1965, by The Horn Book, Inc., Boston), February, 1965, pp. 53-4.

There is perhaps more about boy than horse in **White Stallion of Lipizza**, with the action centering on Hans' hopes and gradual achievements, rather than on the performance of the horses. The book lacks depth of character development and ethical values present in **Gaudenzia**. Nevertheless, satisfying as a dream-come-true story with much background on the riding school and on the horsemanship required there.

> Mary Munro, "Junior Books Appraised: 'White Stallion of Lipizza'," in School Library Journal, an appendix to Library Journal (reprinted from the February, 1965 issue of School Library Journal, published by R. R. Bowker Co./A Xerox Corporation; copyright © 1965), Vol. 11, No. 6, February, 1965, p. 47.

[**White Stallion of Lipizza**] seems over-extended . . . , with many incidents that do not contribute to the story line; the writing style is pedestrian, the authenticity of detail about the horses giving the book its chief value.

> Zena Sutherland, "New Titles for Children and Young People: 'White Stallion of Lipizza'," in Bulletin of the Center for Children's Books (reprinted by permission of The University of Chicago Press; copyright 1965 by the University of Chicago), Vol. 19, No. 1, September, 1965, p. 10.

MUSTANG; WILD SPIRIT OF THE WEST   (1966)

"If God has a kind of plan for all of us, I like to think he coupled me with horses right from the start." It's an unfortunate beginning for Wild Horse Annie and for this highly fictionalized, hoof-in-mouth story of the Nevada woman who fought to save the mustangs from the Last Roundup. . . . When she saw "the very critter that helped build America" being rounded up and ground up for horsemeat, Annie went on the warpath. The result was a barrage of letters to Congress and an invitation to testify in Washington. "I just can't go . . . I'm just plain scairt!" But she mustered her courage and her facts, and told the whole story of the mustang's role in history to the Committee. The result was a standing ovation. "What was I to say . . .?" With thoughts of Lincoln and Patrick Henry and John Paul Jones, she concluded "'We—we the people have won.' That was the Plan." God works his will in mysterious ways.

> "Fiction: 'Mustang: Wild Spirit of the West'," in Virginia Kirkus' Service (copyright © 1966 Virginia Kirkus' Service, Inc.), Vol. XXXIV, No. 21, November 1, 1966, p. 1140.

Take a sure-fire author like Marguerite Henry; add a sure-fire title like "Mustang"—with a subtitle like "Wild Spirit of the West" for good measure, and what have you got? You've got a sure-fire block-buster, that's what you've got. The author has added to her stable of hits the biography of "Wild Horse" Annie Johnston, a determined character who carried her fight to save the mustangs all the way from her home state, Nevada, to Washington and Congress. And a fast-paced biography it is. *I* found the dialog in it a little too folksy for my taste, but shucks, I'm just an old city slicker—*and* a critter that has enough horse sense to know nothing in the world is going to keep this entry from being—if not the winner of the Christmas Best-Seller Race, one of the titles way out in front of the field.

> "Children's Books: 'Wild Spirit of the West'," in Publishers Weekly (reprinted from the November 21, 1966 issue of Publishers Weekly, published by R. R. Bowker Company; copyright © 1966 by R. R. Bowker Company), Vol. 190, No. 21, November 21, 1966, p. 76.

The fact that the story is written in first person gives it both conviction and urgency. . . . Although the last pages of Annie's story strike a lyric note, the book is the best this author has written for many years, engrossing as a story of the preservation of wild animals and truly moving as a story of a dauntless woman.

> Zena Sutherland, "New Titles for Children and Young People: 'Mustang, Wild Spirit of the West'," in Bulletin of the Center for Children's Books (reprinted by permission of The University of Chicago Press; copyright 1967 by the University of Chicago), Vol. 20, No. 5, January, 1967, p. 74.

DEAR READERS AND RIDERS   (1969)

Marguerite Henry, the biggest name in horse stories for children, has answered questions sent to her from readers all over the world. They are questions about her books—why they were written, whether the characters are real—and general questions on horses and riding. The book is written in a light yet informative style, and is sure to be a hit with young horse lovers.

> "Some Horse Stories: 'Dear Readers and Riders'," in Publishers Weekly (reprinted from the December 29, 1969 issue of Publishers Weekly, published by R. R. Bowker Company, a Xerox company; copyright © 1969 by Xerox Corporation), Vol. 196, No. 25, December 29, 1969, p. 68.

This delightfully informal book features letters from Miss Henry's readers. . . . A chapter is devoted to each of the author's stories . . . , with an explanation as to what motivated her to write it and the background against which the story was written. Questions sent in by readers concerning that particular book are then presented and answered. . . . Upon finishing the book, readers will feel that they have met the author personally and listened to adventures of far and near; they will quite likely be inspired to read any of the books that they may have overlooked, or perhaps to reread some old favorites with new insight.

Lea Rae Pastorello, "The Book Review: 'Dear Readers and Riders'," in School Library Journal, *an appendix to* Library Journal *(reprinted from the May, 1970 issue of* School Library Journal, *published by R. R. Bowker Co./A Xerox Corporation; copyright © 1970), Vol. 16, No. 9, May, 1970, p. 73.*

SAN DOMINGO: THE MEDICINE HAT STALLION　(1972)

Peter knows that some event in his father's past has made him cold and critical, but he doesn't find the solution that establishes better relationships until he has left home and become a courier for the Pony Express. The bandit he kills is the man who had wronged and embittered his father. This element of coincidence is the one weak note in a book that should otherwise satisfy readers who enjoy action stories of the western frontier. Set in the Nebraska Territory in the mid-nineteenth century, the book stresses the boy's love for his pony, San Domingo, who is traded away by his father, and whom he finds again when he rides for the Pony Express. The story has good setting and structure, adequate style, and more perceptive characterization than is usual in Marguerite Henry's writing. Appended is a list of source materials. (pp. 91-2)

Zena Sutherland, "New Titles for Children and Young People: 'San Domingo; The Medicine Hat Stallion'," in Bulletin of the Center for Children's Books *(reprinted by permission of The University of Chicago Press; © 1973 by The University of Chicago), Vol. 26, No. 6, February, 1973, pp. 91-2.*

Saturated with horse lore, this story will keep Marguerite Henry's reputation secure with young animal fanciers. . . . The resolution of the father-son relationship and of the mystery surrounding Jethro Lundy's past and his attitudes toward his family provides a satisfying ending. . . . [The] characters convey the spirit of the period of westward expansion.

Rose S. Bender, "The Book Review: 'San Domingo; The Medicine Hat Stallion'," in School Library Journal, *an appendix to* Library Journal *reprinted from the May, 1973 issue of* School Library Journal, *published by R. R. Bowker Co./A Xerox Corporation; copyright © 1973), Vol. 19, No. 9, May, 1973, p. 72.*

One is ever grateful when a horse story does not fall into the basic categories of cosy canters through the Home Counties or noble beast of the wild gentled by only one human juvenile hand. . . .

As much an historical novel as an animal story, this book is a sympathetic study of a boy growing to manhood in a difficult and turbulent background. . . .

Despite the skill and obvious talent of [the] author . . . this book loses impact because of its format. It is larger than usual for books intended for the age group to which it should appeal, and the general style is more suited to children younger than those who will be able to appreciate the story. This gives it a 'dated' appearance which makes it most likely the object of a gift rather than a child's own choice.

"For Children from Ten to Fourteen: 'San Domingo'," in The Junior Bookshelf, *Vol. 39, No. 4, August, 1975, p. 266.*

THE ILLUSTRATED MARGUERITE HENRY　(1980)

The author of **"Misty of Chincoteague"** and other beloved horse stories shares memories of what journalist Charles Hillinger calls in his introduction to her new book, "the interplay of artist and author." Henry gives generous credit to Wesley Dennis (he illustrated the Misty trilogy and 15 more of her books), to Robert Lougheed, Lynd Ward and Rich Rudish. The author's warm style animates stories that are entertaining in themselves but also revelations about how collaboration—sometimes at long distance—results in a book with pictures and text in harmony. Photos of the artists illustrate the vignettes and their expressions of their regard for Henry. There are also pictures from the famous stories, paintings in glowing colors and equally distinctive black-and-white drawings, in a volume that animal lovers, certainly the author's fans, will want.

"The Illustrated Marguerite Henry," in Publishers Weekly *(reprinted from the December 5, 1980 issue of* Publishers Weekly, *published by R. R. Bowker Company, a Xerox company; copyright © 1980 by Xerox Corporation), Vol. 218, No. 23, December 5, 1980, p. 53.*

In this personal, anecdotal account, Marguerite Henry introduces her readers to the artists who have collaborated with her on her books. The sketches, paintings, letters, and notes scattered throughout take on added interest when filtered through Henry's reminiscences. These are open, warm, and often humorous ("If what Wesley wanted couldn't be found in his magazines he'd resort to illusion. His specialty was the use of roiling dust to hide the detail of a rider's garb or saddle in, say, the year 1793"). The art of Wesley Dennis, who illustrated much of her writing, expectedly takes the most space; for him and subsequent painters, Henry describes how each book idea came to be and how the artist went about developing the story's visual elements. The whole encounter is a treat for Henry's readers; art students, too, will profit from this sage insider's look at those who helped give form to her work. (pp. 963-64)

Denise M. Wilms, "Children's Books: 'The Illustrated Marguerite Henry'," in Booklist *(reprinted by permission of the American Library Association; copyright © 1981 by the American Library Association), Vol. 77, No. 13, March 1, 1981, pp. 963-64.*

Erich Kästner

1899-1974

German author of fiction for children, novelist, poet, satirist, journalist, critic, and editor for adults. Kästner is perhaps the most well-known German writer of books for children. He attempted to prepare young readers for life by alerting them to moral and social problems through his literature. His books often contain sections of authorial comment or italicized paragraphs of instruction delivered in a casual way, and his ability to combine dialogue, action, and humor with his moral views is considered noteworthy for not disturbing the narrative flow or offending readers with didacticism. Using exciting plots, realistic characters, and an informal writing style, Kästner's presentation of the child's world is seen as accurate. He creates both positive and negative experiences for his protagonists, and treats topics considered daring for his day with sincerity and understanding. His heroes and heroines draw on their inner strength to overcome odds, coming closer to maturity in the process.

Using many of his own experiences as background, Kästner consistently impressed on his readers the importance of remembering and utilizing their early moral training. He believed that the quality of one's family life largely determines future happiness and productivity. The only child of a devoted and aggressive mother, Kästner was raised in an atmosphere touched by poverty but enriched with love and learning. His desire to become a teacher was dampened by his disenchantment with the German educational system, which discouraged individuality. Kästner remained in Germany throughout the Nazi reign, despite the fact that his books were banned and burned. Twice arrested by the Gestapo, he felt it was his personal duty to stay and fight moral corruption. Though the majority of Kästner's literary output was for adults, he considered children his most important audience and sought to teach them the importance of freedom so that their generation might banish the threat of dictatorship.

Kästner's first children's book, *Emil and the Detectives*, is perhaps his most enduring work. Considered the inspiration for the gang-story genre, *Emil* deals with injustice, group loyalty, adherence to a strict moral code, and powerful family commitment—themes which recur in many of Kästner's later works. Many of his boy characters, including Anton of *Annaluise and Anton* and most especially Emil, closely parallel Kästner's own life and close relationship with his mother. *Lisa and Lottie*, thought to be the first children's book with divorce as its subject, is concerned with the reunification of identical twins, separated since birth, who switch roles in an attempt to reconcile their parents. The fact that the girls cannot exchange places without emotional problems points to Kästner's belief that how we are raised greatly affects our basic nature. Here, as in *Emil, The Animals' Conference, The Little Man and the Big Thief,* and other books, Kästner uses humor, action, and fantasy to cushion a harsh topic without being sentimental.

Though Kästner's later books are sometimes seen as lacking the quality of his earlier titles, critics are generally positive in reviewing his works for young readers. These stories are regarded as universally appealing despite their exclusive con-

©Lutfi Özkök

cern with German children, and Kästner's place in the forefront of children's literature seems assured. During his lifetime he was richly applauded by the literary world. Kästner's awards include the Literature Prize of Munich in 1956; the Büchner Prize in 1957; the Hans Christian Andersen Award in 1960; the Lewis Carroll Shelf Award in 1961 for *When I Was a Boy;* and the Mildred L. Batchelder Award in 1968 for *The Little Man. Emil and the Detectives* has been adapted worldwide for stage and film, and *Lisa and Lottie* has been filmed in several languages. (See also *Something about the Author,* Vol. 14.)

GENERAL COMMENTARY

[Kästner has said] that children cannot be trained too early for their role as members of the state and of society. The stake which each individual has in the group and the group in each individual, a readiness to help, a spirit of enterprise, the war against injustice, such things as these form the themes of his stories for children. By their means he seeks both consciously and unconsciously to awaken a socio-political sense of responsibility. His books would not be his without their humour and their vivid plots, but they would never have penetrated into so many countries if they did not have this serious core which Kästner, like [Charles] Dickens, discovered from his own youthful experiences. (p. 179)

*Bettina Hürlimann, ''Politics in Children's Books,''
in her* Three Centuries of Children's Books in Europe, *translated and edited by Brian W. Alderson
(English translation © Oxford University Press 1967;
reprinted by permission), Oxford University Press,
Oxford, 1967, pp. 173-94.**

There are many and diverse reasons why a work of children's literature emerges from the rest and becomes a 'classic'. Some of these reasons are negative, such as a refusal on the part of the author to write down to his audience or to undervalue the emotional depth and intellectual maturity of quite young children; other reasons are positive, like an ability to hold the rapt attention of the young reader from beginning to end and to allow the child's imagination the fullest possible rein within the broad context of the narrative. All these skills and many more are possessed in abundance by Kästner. But the central quality which has created the truly great classics, such as the Alice adventures [by Lewis Carroll] or Mark Twain's novels for children, and which Kästner certainly displays in full measure, is a willingness to affirm without reservation or condescension the validity of the world of the child.

Childhood, argues Kästner, is not to be regarded as a clumsy, disobedient, pimpled and incommodious prelude to the fulfilment of adulthood; it is, rather, a valid and complete experience within itself, with its own being and its own laws, and it must be lived through in all its richness, for it alone is the foundation for the rest of life. The quality of the adult depends upon the quality of his childhood. In no way is childhood a lesser kind of experience, to be regarded patronisingly by the adult. It is, on the contrary, a time when the nerve ends are at their most sensitive, when life has its most direct and immediate impact. . . . What marks the child off is a curious blend of independence within a private world to which the adult has no access and, on the other hand, a powerful need for affection and dependence. The latter must be neither mocked nor left unsatisfied, for this would have inevitable and dire consequences both on the imaginative life of the child and on his later attitudes and responses. The greater the affection given, the more the child will be able to explore to the full the world of his childhood and thus grow and develop into a moral, independent and effective adult member of society.

Kästner takes a moral approach to the function of his works for children as for adults; but he is certainly no defender of the establishment, affirming the status quo at all costs and stifling doubts and questionings about the world. His eyes, moreover, are firmly fixed upon the present: perhaps the child comes trailing clouds of glory, but Kästner is preoccupied, not with the vague aeons before birth, but with the real experiences and opportunities of childhood itself.

As the child develops and grows older, he or she begins to channel and direct the emotions and to acquire a sense of right and wrong; and Kästner regards it as his prime function to help to guide this developmental pattern along fruitful and positive lines. He argues forcibly that since the present adult is the sum total of his past experiences, particularly those of that period vaguely designated as 'childhood', it is to the child that the greatest creative effort must be directed, not in order to provide him with the appropriate set of blinkers to wear in adult life; on the contrary, the aim is to expose him to the richest and most diverse range of experience and to optimise his awareness of the social and moral problems of the day, and particularly, of the fact that many of these problems are painful, unpleasant and some, in the last analysis, insoluble. (pp. 69-71)

[Kästner] is convinced that the child should neither be lured into a false world of adventure (this is not to deny the importance of fantasy and the imagination), nor should it be dragged prematurely into a semblance of adulthood; it must first be allowed to develop to the full as a child within the boundaries prescribed by childhood. The focal point of the child's world and interest . . . lies in the home, and in human relationships, particularly those between brothers and sisters, parents and children.

There is no attempt on Kästner's part to idealise the family situation, to pretend that all parents are ideal, all families unbroken, all suffering a mere passing dark cloud with the inevitable silver lining. Nor is he afraid to place the emotions in a central position in his works, as he does, for example, in *Das fliegende Klassenzimmer* [*The Flying Classroom*], set in the boarding school situation which in countless other hands has been used as just another springboard for adventure situations with parents conveniently out of the way except as an occasional source of tuck boxes.

Kästner is anxious to maintain a personal relationship between himself and his young reader, and to this end he does not rest content with the uniformity of a narrative mode where the fictional narrator sees all but is never seen himself. He habitually prefaces his novels for children with introductory observations which have as their object the establishment of an easygoing personal friendship with his readers and also a swift exposition for the ensuing narrative. And from time to time he intervenes in the course of the narrative, sometimes to point out the moral or social implications of a situation. . . . Or again, he may highlight some aspect of the plot, as in *Das doppelte Lottchen* [*Twice Lotte,* published in the United States as *Lisa and Lottie*], where he is particularly anxious that his reader should not be bewildered by the complexities of the action. . . . In *Das fliegende Klassenzimmer,* Kästner goes a stage further by introducing a framework in which he depicts himself near the Zugspitze at the height of summer, trying to write a Christmas story under the inspiration of the eternal snows. He uses this device, not only as a lead-in to the story proper, but in order to highlight from the outset the key moral of this and all his work for children: 'Never forget your childhood. Do you promise? Word of honour?' . . . (pp. 73-4)

Kästner does not gloss over the problems facing Jonathan [when he realizes his father has sent him to Hamburg to get rid of him] nor over the fact that his plight is not one that can be overcome by the wave of a magic wand, but only through the individual himself drawing on his inner strength, thus allowing him to come to terms with his situation and to profit from the experience. Nothing in life is purely negative or destructive, unless the individual involved loses the will or the courage to face up to it.

The atmosphere of the school and the world of the small boy are swiftly and expertly captured with a few deft touches: it is a world which is physically circumscribed, largely confined as it is to school and home environments, but boundless from the point of view of the imagination. (p. 75)

Kästner does not indulge in profound characterisation—neither in his fiction for children nor for adults—because he is concerned with general relationships rather than psychological states within individuals, but it does not follow that because this is so his figures are either static or two-dimensional. Simplified they may be, but they do grow and respond to their environment, and, equally importantly, they are confronted not only with situations involving action and excitement, but also with moral and emotional situations and conflicts.

The boys' independent spirit is characterised by Jonathan's play, 'The Flying Classroom', which the class are rehearsing for performance just before the end of the Christmas term. The play concerns a school of the future, and the plot, although hyperbolic and clearly the product of an amateurish boy's hand . . . reflects a need on the part of the children to experience the teaching situation as a real thing, not as an arid expanse of chalk and talk: it concerns a class taking an aeroplane and flying round the world in order to experience lessons in geography at first hand. (p. 76)

A rehearsal of 'The Flying Classroom' is interrupted by a member of the class who rushes in to inform the young actors that one of the day-boys, the son of the German teacher, who was taking home the class dictation books for his father, has been waylaid by a gang from the Secondary School and kidnapped. The two groups confront each other on a piece of waste ground and a battle of the champions ensues, a confrontation with all the drama and symbolism—but little of the dignity—of the conflict on the off-shore island in the medieval epic *Tristan* between Tristan and Morold.

In defiance of the terms of the combat, the losing side—the Secondary School boys—refuse to hand over their prisoner; he is ultimately rescued, although not before the dictation books have been burned.

This episode underlines Kästner's desire to reflect as honestly as possible the world of the child, in two ways specifically: first, the cruelty that children are capable of, particularly in the vicious cuffs on the ear dealt out to the unfortunate prisoner at regular intervals by his captors; and secondly, the moral conflict in the defeated champion, the leader of the Secondary School gang, who is torn between loyalty to his group and obedience to the moral code which states that all promises should be honoured. In fact, he finally decides to relinquish leadership of the gang, but Kästner in no way minimises the difficulty of his choice and the personal struggle it demands.

Although Kästner is concerned to project the situation of the boys and the school in the most credible possible terms, he is guilty of causing one compound fracture of the long arm of coincidence by causing the Non-Smoker and Justus to turn out to be long-lost school friends, but he does this so disarmingly that the reader accepts the improbable as if it were the inevitable. Their reunion serves to underline once more the central moral of the work. . . . The message is clear: childhood is the foundation for adult life; and only if that foundation is secure will adulthood be in the cause of a better world.

The plot of *Das fliegende Klassenzimmer* is thin, and deliberately so. Kästner does not ignore the child's interest in 'what happens next', but he does not let this dominate the narrative. He is aware, too, that the child is interested in personalities, in situations and settings, and much of the novel is taken up with the exploration of the world of the boarding school and the boys within it. Kästner does not pretend that the individual can carve out his own unaided destiny in defiance of the world about him; much of life is concerned with coming to terms with other individuals and recognising the nature of society at large.

Kästner by no means idealises society. The Non-Smoker may be gently rebuked by implication for opting out of the obligation to contribute to the sum total of social endeavour and to try to turn society into a more positive and humane direction, but Kästner still permits him this plea for time to think, to withdraw . . . from the superficial bustle of the everyday and consider the deeper issues of social existence. . . . Of course money is unimportant to those who are living above subsistence level; but even here Kästner does not oversimplify the issue. One of the boys in the school is unable to go home for Christmas, because his parents cannot afford the return fare—the father is out of work and the family have no financial reserves; Justus finds the boy alone, weeping, discovers the reasons for his distress, and makes him a present of more than enough money to spend Christmas with his family. Kästner is not afraid to make the closing scene of his novel the unexpected homecoming of the boy Martin. The emotion is intense, but unsentimentalised; he permits the full emotional weight of the situation of the unexpectedly reunited family to come across to his young reader. (pp. 77-9)

The more general significance of commitment and involvement comes across in Justus's reaction to Martin's predicament. (p. 79)

Kästner does not treat the boarding school atmosphere in negative terms: there is none of the nonsense of romps in the dorm—in fact, very little emphasis is placed on this aspect of school life—which one suspects belong more in the cherished memories of the present adult than in the preoccupations of the actual pupils. He stresses instead the relationships with teachers and other pupils, and the work situation in class. And in the background all the time there is to be observed Kästner's concern for educational excellence, not only, by implication, in the boys' imaginative dramatic undertaking, but also in direct statements such as 'We need teachers who must themselves develop if they are to cause us to develop.' . . . The staff hold the key to the educational life of the school and the development of the pupil. As Kästner says elsewhere, 'Young people need ideals just as they need milk, bread, and air.' . . . And in pursuit of this objective, Kästner widens the horizons of the children's novel by introducing themes that many would consider taboo, notably in *Das doppelte Lottchen*. (p. 80)

The work opens in a lakeside summer camp for young girls where Luise Palfry, one of the holidaymakers, is astonished to see emerging from the bus bringing a batch of new arrivals a girl, Lotte, who is her mirror image. It soon transpires that they are indeed twin sisters: their parents had divorced, and each had taken one of the twins, who were then brought up, ignorant until this moment of the fact that each had a twin sister. It does not matter that the initial coincidence is somewhat far-fetched—as with reunited old friends in *Das fliegende Klassenzimmer*, Kästner carries the situation off with such flair that no one would venture to challenge his veracity—since the situation is exploited with such entertaining mastery. The two girls resolve to change places. . . . (pp. 80-1)

Kästner underlines the power and abilities of these young children to control their own destinies: the two set out quite deliberately on their daunting plan to bring their parents together again, utterly convinced that divorce is an unnatural state, and equally convinced of their ability to effect a change.

The situation being developed is one highly charged with emotional potential; and Kästner demonstrates his extreme skill in handling and controlling the intensity of emotion at any given point in the novel. . . . There is none of [the] aura of 'little girl all alone' in *Das doppelte Lottchen;* and Kästner avoids sentimentality and tear-jerking emotion by the simple expedient of pacing the development of the action and the degree of emphasis on emotion with great skill. Until the very last moment, the emotional potential of the situation is suppressed and other aspects stressed. Only at the end is emotion allowed full play. When Luise, playing the role of Lottchen, is supposed to cook for her mother, although—unlike her twin—she is incapable of cooking, the humorous side of the situation is exploited to the limit. Luise may be exhausted and despairing at her inability to follow the careful instructions her sister has laid down, but the tone of the narrative is sparkling and witty rather than tragic and grief-stricken, as it might well have been. . . . [Lotte's] mother works for an illustrated paper; and whilst Luise, playing out the part of Lotte, slaves unproductively over a hot stove, Lotte herself tries to act out her twin sister's rôle as the daughter of a rich and famous conductor and composer.

Kästner exploits this situation in order to underline his conviction of the supreme importance of art in the development and maturation of the young. For children, there is no such thing as Romantic Irony, a gap between art and life, as the young girl in *Pünktchen und Anton* [*Annaluise and Anton*], slipping readily between fantasy and real life, amply demonstrates. Whatever they read, see, and hear is real, whether it be a novel, a drama, or in the case of Lotte, a performance of [Engelbert] Humperdinck's opera *Hansel and Gretel* conducted by her father.

The woman sitting near Lotte in a box is the recipient of her father's smiles as he acknowledges the applause; and, in Lotte's eyes, she takes on the destructive, but superficially alluring, qualities of the witch. The opera itself deals in a very adult fashion with the problems of marriage, poverty, and children, and the severely difficult moral dilemmas facing the destitute parent.

Luise experiences culinary difficulties, and Lottchen has her own problems in trying to fit into a strange environment; thus is demonstrated Kästner's concern for character: these are not two cardboard figures able to change places with consummate ease. Kästner underlines his thesis that nurture is more significant by far than nature by showing that it is impossible for the two girls to change places without severe problems of adjustment, despite their physical similarity and their considerable personal resources and determination. Each retains her own personality, which is the product of her home environment and those about her. . . . (pp. 81-3)

If Kästner shows any bias, it is on the side of the mother. This is not out of anti-male chauvinism, but because circumstances have left her the poorer of the two. The father's wealth is demonstrated to be of no positive value in the building up of a home environment, whereas financial deprivation, as has been seen earlier, almost turns into a positive advantage in the maintenance of a balanced and flourishing family situation. Constantly Kästner underlines the fact that money is a divisive factor: extreme poverty can, of course, destroy a home, but so too can an excess of wealth. In the case of the latter, it offers a seemingly easy way out of emotional involvement. Emotional relationships demand a strong and constantly renewed commitment by those involved; and Kästner recognises within individuals a latent tendency to shy away from such commitment in any situation where it can readily be pushed to one side. It is all too easy to feel cushioned by money from the basic need of human beings for deep and lasting bonds with others. Such a situation has emerged in the case of the twins' father, now separated from his wife, who concentrates almost exclusively on music. So great is his absorption in his work that his only

remaining strong attachment is to his daughter, although even that relationship is becoming ever more tenuous; and his lack of practice, so to speak, in emotional relationships enable him to become ensnared by Fräulein Irene Gerlach, the 'other woman'.

Kästner boldly places this theme at the forefront of the novel, and portrays the open struggle between Lotte and Irene Gerlach for the father's love. . . . Like all of Kästner's child heroes and heroines, Lotte reveals considerable courage beyond her years, and she confronts Irene [and forbids her to marry her father]. . . . (pp. 83-4)

So the twins succeed in their endeavour to reunite their estranged parents. It is significant that Kästner avoids the pitfall into which so many writers for children fall: namely, the facile apportioning of bouquets and punishment to those who have proven themselves morally worthy or reprehensible in the course of the action. The father of the family may have been 'guilty' of looking at another woman, but the emphasis is on forgiveness, on the preservation of the family unit. Irene Gerlach is seen as an aberration, no more: the family is the true norm, and the twins keep the secret of their father's susceptibility to the charms of Irene. The rightness of the family unit, and the prime necessity for bringing the family together again under one roof are what really matters, not a superficial allotting of punishment and reward.

As in the adult novels, the themes of travel and adventure are of central significance. . . . [In] *Das doppelte Lottchen* they play a central rôle. . . . [What travel] actually does is to highlight the central importance of the home environment and the necessity for the existence of the home as the vital focal point of all human life. . . . [The] two twins, even though physically identical, still retain their separate personalities and this causes those about them to react in a puzzled and disorientated manner when one or the other of them apparently acts out of character. . . . Individual and environment are intertwined in a complex interlocking network of relationships, not static, like the clockwork of the best of all possible rationalist worlds, but dynamic, ever-growing, demanding constant interaction among individuals for its survival and growth. And the transplantation of the twins causes considerable repercussions among family, teachers and friends who find them responding in a marginally or even substantially different manner from what they have come to expect over the years. It is an exercise in exchange of personalities which gives rise to a great deal of amusement and entertainment, but one which nevertheless has a [serious] purpose behind it. . . . (pp. 85-6)

Adventure and travel are also central themes in the most celebrated of all Kästner's works, *Emil und die Detektive* [*Emil and the Detectives*]. . . . (p. 86)

In *Emil und die Detektive,* many of the familiar Kästner themes can be found: the gang of children with their strong sense of group loyalty and strict moral code; the presence of a master-criminal in the shape of Grundeis . . . ; and the powerful commitment to the family and to family life. And, as in the other novels, the central figure is taken out of his own environment and, by dint of his courage, determination and independent spirit, carries through to its end his objective—in this case, unmasking the criminal and securing the return of the money. (p. 87)

The moral emerges naturally from the narrative: the thief is caught and revealed in all his pathetic frailty as the guilty man, and Emil is rewarded for his efforts. At the end of the narrative, there is a deliberate avoidance of heavy-handed morality. *Das doppelte Lottchen* and *Das fliegende Klassenzimmer* close on a note of emotion, whilst *Emil und die Detektive* concludes humorously, with a mock-moral to the effect that money should always be sent in the form of a postal order. Technically, the ending of the work has its weaknesses in that it is unduly drawn out: the thief is caught in Chapter 14, but the proceedings are not closed for another four full chapters.

There is one feature of *Emil und die Detektive* which merits particular attention, namely the dream sequence during the train journey. It is a device which Kästner employs elsewhere in his work, but here it appears in its most developed and extended form. (pp. 87-8)

In *Das doppelte Lottchen*, Lotte has a dream during her first night in her sister's bed in the home of her father. The two twins find themselves as Hansel and Gretel, with Irene Gerlach acting as the witch. Their father then appears, sawing them in half, so that each parent has two half-twins. (p. 89)

Emil's dream concerns the painful feelings of guilt about his chalking of the statue of the Grand Duke; it obsesses him to the point that it dominates his mind, and can only be fully worked out in the context of a dream. It serves to underline the child's respect for and fear of authority as a nameless and insuperable absolute, and too the way in which a relatively small incident can grow to assume gigantic proportions if it is not resolved at an early stage. Kästner deliberately depicts Emil as a basically 'good boy' with a bad conscience: he has no sympathy with the artificial view of the small boy as moral anarchist perpetrated by writers such as Richmal Crompton, the inventor of William. Kästner recognises in the child the paradox of the will to observe the moral code, and the conflicting sudden impulse which causes that code to be broken in the heat of the moment, and subsequently regretted bitterly and at length. Only in a dream situation could such emotions be explored openly and directly, in a vivid and pictorial fashion. . . .

Lotte's fear is that the enterprise she and her twin sister has undertaken will founder; that they will not succeed in reuniting their parents, but on the contrary help to make the rift between them final and absolute. (p. 90)

[From] the technical point of view, [the dream sequences] are important devices for Kästner who, as a writer, is more than reluctant to describe emotional states in a static fashion. He operates through dialogue and action . . . ; and only the dream situation permits the acting out of those emotions which are beneath the surface or which are too painful to explore openly.

The dreams also form part of the important field of fantasy, which Kästner regards as particularly vital in his novels for children. (pp. 90-1)

The main level of Kästner's novels for children is as close as it is possible to get to 'real life', but he does introduce much material which can only be described as fantastical, although he does so with such skill that the reader accepts the situation without demur. . . . (p. 91)

[In his novels for children], fantasy is employed as an extension of reality, but is no less acceptable since it forms part of every child's experience, and for a child it is every bit as 'real' as reality. . . . One novel, *Pünktchen und Anton*, has as its central figure a young girl who seemingly is a permanent inhabitant of a fantasy world. . . . The antics of Pünktchen—herself, as her nickname suggests, a diminuitive figure—are no more in-credible than the Little Man of *Der kleine Mann* [*The Little Man*] and *Der kleine Mann und die kleine Miss* [*The Little Man and the Little Miss*] who is so small that he sleeps in a matchbox.

But even in the midst of all the fantasy, real issues are never far from the surface. The sequel to *Emil und die Detektive*, *Emil und die drei Zwillinge* [*Emil and the Three Twins*], opens on an even more delicate and sensitive issue than that which forms the basis of *Das doppelte Lottchen*. Jeschke, the sergeant whom Emil imagined was pursuing him because of the chalk marks on the Grand Duke's statue, wants to marry Emil's mother. . . . Emil is asked for his approval; and the central part of the novel—which is largely irrelevant to this decision—acts as a contrasting childish adventure to the adult choice Emil has to make.

Along with the other members of the gang from *Emil und die Detektive,* he is invited to stay by the Baltic. . . . [The] really important moment comes when Emil and his grandmother discuss the home situation alone. . . . His journey to the Baltic [is] like so many journeys in Kästner's works: a voyage of self-discovery, part of the process of growth and maturation. (pp. 91-3)

> R. W. Last, "Works for Children," in his Erich Kastner (© 1974 Oswald Wolff (Publishers) Limited), Oswald Wolff, 1974, pp. 69-96.

EMIL AND THE DETECTIVES   (1930; German edition, 1928)

[Emil brings] the reminder that boys are boys the world over. Country bred or city boys matter not, if only the boy himself is the real thing, and Emil Tischbein is very much the real thing. Moreover, Emil has a most perfect mother and grandmother, a charming cousin, Pony Hutchen . . . , and innumerable friends in Berlin who are as real as he is. . . . Gustav, the boy with a good kind heart and an automobile horn is sure to be a prime favorite. . . . [When] he finds what trouble Emil . . . is in, he calls out his whole gang to help chase and catch "the man in the stiff hat," who has robbed the sleeping Emil in the railway train. Robbed him of the 140 marks he is bringing to his grandmother, but not of that gift of imagination which sets him dreaming a wonderful dream, nor yet of his practical resourcefulness as a detective when put to the test in the streets of Berlin. . . .

This is [Erich Kästner's] first book for children and we trust it will not be his last. There are indications here of great promise as well as a record of solid accomplishment on behalf of the small boys of the world. He has not changed in essential characteristic, in the strong fibre of his natural affections, his distaste for best suits, his inherent sense of obligation whatever his outward bearing. . . . There is more boy psychology to be learned from such books as [this], than from any number of elaborate tabulations of texts with expert comment. . . .

It should enlarge the world of many an American teacher of the fourth grade and beyond to know that the small boys of Berlin are so near of kin to the small boys of Buffalo and Chicago. . . . [On] close comparison with the original I believe [translator May] Massee has been forced to use Americanisms for lack of German equivalents. This will doubtless endear the book to young American readers and need have no permanent effect on their vocabularies. Far more potent will be the effect of the lively companionship of the likeable and resourceful Emil, who is neither too wise nor too good for boys of eight to ten to take on as a friend in another country. To see Berlin one day with Emil is an experience for any one young or old to anticipate.

Anne Carroll Moore, "Password, Emil!" in New York Herald Tribune Books (© I.H.T. Corporation; reprinted by permission), September 14, 1930, p. 8.

If there is any aversion more justifiably well-rooted than that to books in which the child heroes or heroines reform their elders, brighten their lives, or in some other way show themselves the superiors of grown-ups in intelligence and resource and what not, it is yet to be discovered. The situation is contrary to good sense and good manners. So, when we confess that we were quite bowled over by this story from the German whose plot is nothing less than the capture of a thief by a small boy and his friends, readers will understand that a wall of prejudice had to be surmounted. Evidently it's all in how it is done. . . .

The undeniable charm of the story is attributable to two things— the situation and the characters. There is something very beguiling, absurdly moving, in the picture of this bold thief surrounded by a swarm of youngsters who by mere force of numbers nullify their weakness as adversaries. As for the characters— not for a long time have we met in a book children so real, real as salt and bread; simple, natural, so absolutely true that you find yourself nodding mentally and saying "Yes. Just so do children think and talk and act."

There isn't a sentimental touch in the book and yet you are in no doubt as to the warmth of the affection existing between Emil and his mother, or, so far as that goes, the devotion of the whole family connection. A charming home life is implicit throughout. Not every writer of children's books could give you without offending conversations between a small boy and his mother in which the word "fresh" is the only one that describes the boy's remarks. Erich Kästner . . . has done it. The delightful verbal give and take among members of a family who are sure of each other, and imbued with a mutual respect which is not dependent on lip-service, has seldom been better done than in this simple story. . . .

Temptation to quote must be resisted, and, too, the dialogue for full effect needs its own setting. But let no one who really cares for children and finds a peculiar appeal in that which goes on beneath their apparently unsubtle surfaces, let no one who believes in and loves the idea of the family as an institution, miss this book.

Marcia Dalphin, "The Children's Bookshop: 'Emil and the Detectives'," in The Saturday Review of Literature (copyright © 1930 by Saturday Review; all rights reserved; reprinted by permission), Vol. VII, No. 11, October 4, 1930, p. 191.

"Emil and the Detectives" is up-to-date—a story for children whose minds have been formed by the cinema. . . . This story of a gang of Berlin kids is entertaining enough, but I wonder why it has been translated—there must be many more entertaining books for children written in German today. (p. 23)

Padraic Colum, "Animals, Fairies and Children" (reprinted by permission of the Estate of Padraic Colum), in The New Republic, Vol. 65, No. 833, November 19, 1930, pp. 22-4.*

["**Emil and the Detectives**"] plays in post-war Berlin, but we find no reference to the war, and the poverty of the hero's mother might be due to any cause. Only once do we feel that the boys are touched by the reparation atmosphere, that is when they talk jokingly about taking up foreign credits, being much in need of money. Otherwise the story shows the life of the children untouched by the effects of war and revolution. . . .

[How the boys recover Emil's money] in a spectacular chase through the metropolis makes excellent reading for children and adults. (p. 176)

Ruth J. Hofrichter, "Erich Kästner as a Representative of 'Neue Sachlichkeit'," in The German Quarterly, Vol. V, No. 4, November, 1932, pp. 173-77.

The ancestor of the gang-story is probably Erich Kästner's *Emil and the Detectives*. . . . Kästner had the advantage of an unselfconscious approach to class-distinction. At a time when, in England, adventure stories were still largely middle-class, Kästner could write as a matter of course of a very mixed Berlin street-gang, in which one member has a father working as night-watchman in an hotel and another belongs to a professional family; while Emil, whose journey to the city to stay with his grandmother sparks off the whole comical business, lives with a widowed mother who takes in washing. The adventure rises naturally out of this very background. Emil goes to Berlin by train, with an envelope in his pocket containing his money. For safety, he pins the notes to his jacket, and it is the pin-marks which finally convict smooth Mr. Grundeis, who has stolen the notes while Emil is asleep in the carriage. Nothing was ever more convincing than that Emil should awake just in time to see his chatty companion hurriedly leaving a station, and should be able to keep him in sight until the happy accident of his meeting with the gang of street boys. Nothing was ever more utterly lifelike than the swift, efficient deploying of the gang—one to stand by for telephone reports, one to lurk in the hotel where Grundeis has taken refuge, others to shadow him until the triumphant moment when they all close in on him at the bank with the cry, 'Stop him. That is stolen money.' Kästner has not once had to go beyond probability, and yet here are all the requirements of the adventure-story—tension, speed, surprise.

The course of such stories in England might have been happier if more writers had taken note of Kästner's technique; his brilliant selection of detail, his crisp, utterly unpadded narrative, broken up with racy dialogue; his strict attention to character. For if his crook, shady and meagre, is horrifyingly real, his boys are too, each one set in his proper environment. We know who they were, what they were like, where they lived and how they lived. (pp. 251-52)

Margery Fisher, "Innocents in the Underworld," in her Intent Upon Reading: A Critical Appraisal of Modern Fiction for Children (copyright © 1961 by Margery Fisher), Hodder & Stoughton Children's Books (formerly Brockhampton Press), 1961, pp. 251-69.

[Books] with a plot enhanced by a mystery, atmosphere, and good characterization, and remain true to natural childhood are rare. During the forties and fifties a trend could be noticed toward a type of mystery story in which groups of children track down criminals, with far from childlike purpose and technique, finally outwitting not only the criminal but the police. This was an unfortunate deterioration of the plot and treatment in Erich Kastner's *Emil and the Detectives*. . . . Emil's single purpose—very true to boy nature—was not primarily to capture a thief but to get back his stolen money, and the boys of Berlin entered the chase to right a wrong done to one of their kind.

Leadership, teamwork, determination, not violence, got Emil's money back and caught a thief. The emphasis in later stories of this kind was less childlike. (p. 580)

> *Ruth Hill Viguers, "Experiences to Share: Modern Realistic Stories, Family Stories, Social Trends," in* A Critical History of Children's Literature *by Cornelia Meigs, Anne Thaxter Eaton, Elizabeth Nesbitt, and Ruth Hill Viguers, edited by Cornelia Meigs (reprinted with permission of Macmillan Publishing Co., Inc.; copyright © 1953, 1969 by Macmillan Publishing Co., Inc.), revised edition, Macmillan, 1969, pp. 567-600.**

ANNALUISE AND ANTON   (1933; German edition, 1931)

The story of **"Annaluise and Anton"** . . . is a most engaging affair. It will probably make a good many little girls wish they had a wicked governess who took them out at night to beg in the streets and afterwards regaled them with fruit salad in a restaurant. . . . The children's chatter and their adventures are very lively and natural, and even the moral lectures printed in italics . . . are sensible and amusing and likely to promote lively argument. Annaluise, although she readily told fibs, has so much spirit and heart that she will be an addition to any home. Her history is quite one of the leading books of the season. . . .

> *"Schoolroom Mixture," in* The Times Literary Supplement *(© Times Newspapers Ltd. (London) 1932; reproduced from* The Times Literary Supplement *by permission), No. 1608, November 24, 1932, p. 902.**

In **"Emil and the Detectives"** this same author gave us an adventure story for children that had, together with an engaging spontaneity and humor, a genuinely human and childlike quality. . . . To Emil's many friends **"Annaluise and Anton"** will be a disappointment. In the author's attempt to follow the same pattern, the spontaneity and proportion of the first book have disappeared, and although the incident of the governess who takes a little girl to sell matches and to beg on the streets at night, when the father and mother believe the child to be safe in bed, may have its origin in fact, the story of Erich Kästner has made of it fails to ring true.

Annaluise herself, the precocious little girl, has occasional moments of reality. But Anton never comes to life, and the descriptions of his affection for his mother and his assiduous care of her when she is ill seem a deliberate attempt to recapture what was in **"Emil"** an entirely natural and convincing background of fine home relationships.

The rich, quarrelsome household of Herr Pogge and his wife, Annaluise's parents, the sentimentalized poverty and affection of Anton and his mother; the governess, Fraulein Andacht; her young man, who tries, with her help, to burglarize Annaluise's home; fat Berta, the cook, who hits the robber over the head with an Indian club and dances with the policemen who come to her aid; the father and mother in evening dress who discover their daughter begging on the street—all lend themselves more readily to melodrama and cheap comedy than to a book for children.

> *Anne T. Eaton, "Books for Children: 'Annaluise and Anton'," in* The New York Times Book Review *(© 1933 by The New York Times Company; reprinted by permission), August 27, 1933, p. 15.*

Kästner is indeed a writer whose style—piquant, unexpected, yet straightforward as a telegram—catches the eye of an intelligent grown-up opening the book at random, keeps him reading and quite likely sends the book home in his pocket to be given second hand to a child.

In this case the child will get, as he did in the brisk adventures of Emil, a happily rowd story. This time it is about a girl, but there is a boy in it so like Emil that, though in the story they never meet, in the epilogue they are compared and on the cover introduced. The unpredictable Annaluise has the precise blend of bad conduct and good intentions that endears a young heroine to young readers. . . .

[Annaluise] is furiously interested in the adventure of being alive. When she talks, it is with the punch of the fearless. You never know what on earth she will do next.

[While masquerading as a beggar-girl] she meets Anton, who really has to sell bootlaces to feed a sick mother. This is the definite purport of the book: to show children whose lives are easy, in the most vivid and memorable way, that there are children whose lives are hard. "If people who are well off don't keep trying to help those who are badly off," says Herr Kästner, "I don't know what will become of us all."

This he says, and so much more, not in the story but at the end of each chapter, where a running commentary on the tale appears in italics. If not the chief feature of the book—a sparkling and sensational plot is that—it is distinctive. Contrary to adult belief, children are not at all averse to moralizing in books, provided it is without disguise, intensely personal and done with snap. If it can be skipped, all the better, and these italicized sections may be easily dropped out, though I think they will not be. They are too amusing.

> *"Books for Young People: 'Annaluise and Anton',"*
> *in* New York Herald Tribune Books *(© I.H.T. Corporation; reprinted by permission), September 3, 1933, p. 5.*

THE 35th OF MAY; OR, CONRAD'S RIDE TO THE SOUTH SEAS (1934; German edition, 1931)

[*The 35th of May*] is different in kind and quality from its predecessors, but there is no denying its attraction for the adventure-minded child who likes to stretch his imagination full length.

> *"Old Enchantment: 'The 35th of May'," in* The Times Literary Supplement *(© Times Newspapers Ltd. (London) 1933; reproduced from* The Times Literary Supplement *by permission), No. 1660, November 23, 1933, p. 829.*

To those who remember **"Emil and the Detectives"** as the prime children's book of some four or five years ago, . . . **"The 35th of May"** was bound to excite curiosity. . . . **"The 35th of May"** was written either just before or just after the triumph of National Socialism. It is not fair to take it too seriously, and be too disappointed over it. It is cerebral fantasy, a pot boiler maybe, an innocent smoke screen, before a troubled breast that may later tell us what this year in Germany has really been like.

Conrad goes to his uncle the chemist on Thursday afternoons and always has an absurd time with the eccentric chemist who pours raspberry vinegar over salmon mayonnaise. (Is this just dull nonsense, or satire on the vast over-ornamentation of foods and drinks in the magazines?) On this particular afternoon, when Conrad has the chore of writing an essay on the South Sea Isles, because he is good at arithmetic and has no imagination (now is this slant just invention or is it something else ever so sly on the progressive schools of the fatherland?). Well, anyway, Conrad and his Uncle Ringel walk out and they come on a swaybacked circus horse, ace roller skater of all horses, and really in trouble, because even the circus horse union's secretary now rides in a motor car, and they give the beast sugar; and Negro Caballo (that's the horse) returns the call, which is hardly ever done by any horse in any apartment house. . . .

The story is nice enough and crazy enough, as the three go through the wardrobe, over the land of Cockayne and Topsy Turvey to the Southern Seas, to serve as escape literature, and maybe stimulating yarn, but one has to work too hard to tether it to sense to make one relish it in repetition. I would not recommend it for reading or for purchase except that I am sure that Kastner will do a great story about or for young people under the Swastika, and the friends of Emil . . . had best stand by. This is not to say that **"The 35th of May"** (strange beguiling title) does not pleasure me at all. There is the forest of bluebells ten times higher than Conrad and his uncle, and the sweet wind blowing through it. There is ELECTROPOLIS! THE AUTOMATIC CITY DANGER! HIGH TENSION! where the cattle-converting machines had ceased to run because the cattle were all converted; then the machines reversed, and all the sausages were changed back, and the oxen, cows and calves ran bellowing madly down the street and into the city. . . .

Shades of Lewis Carroll and Upton Sinclair, how can a body tell what the future holds on the first and thirty-fifth of May, when German authors go so fast in so many directions, and advertise their works, and most sincerely, as juveniles?

> *Ernestine Evans, "Books for Young People: 'The 35th of May'," in* New York Herald Tribune Books *(© I.H.T. Corporation; reprinted by permission), December 30, 1934, p. 5.*

LISA AND LOTTIE (1951; German edition, 1949; British edition as *Lottie and Lisa*)

[How Lottie and Lisa set about repairing their parents's broken marriage] makes a joyous, hilarious and pathetic story, told with that deceptively casual manner which is Mr. Kästner's own.

The author deals effectively, in parenthesis, with the objectors who regard divorce as a subject unfit for a children's book, but indeed the story itself is its own defence. Here is the glow of living colours. The twin heroines are recognisable and lovable children, and their story has humour and suspense. Even the least character is a defined personality. . . . I think that few children will resist the appeal of this book, and that readers will gain from it the joy of a delightful story and an understanding of some of the perplexities of this bewildering world.

An English writer might well have turned the pathos into sentimental mawkishness. How Mr. Kästner does it I know not—it is the secret of his art—but his deft, sympathetic and nonchalant manner makes us accept without embarrassment the affectionate and intimate tone of the narrative, into which he does not hesitate to draw the reader. I have perhaps said enough to indicate how deeply I have enjoyed this book, which tackles so gallantly a difficult subject and which introduces so cou-

rageous and endearing a pair of characters. I hope it will enjoy the same success as *Emil,* for in its own way it is as memorable and enduring an achievement. (pp. 131-32)

> *"The New Books for Children under 10: 'Lottie and Lisa'," in* The Junior Bookshelf, *Vol. 14, No. 4, October, 1950, pp. 131-32.*

Artificial as [the] situation sounds, the author of **"Emil and the Detectives"** has made a very good thing out of it. It is impossible, but one doesn't care. It is complicated, funny, frankly sentimental—and where is the little girl who doesn't like sentiment? Mr. Kastner's good-humored, old-fashioned asides are also quite wise.

> *Ellen Lewis Buell, "Turnabout," in* The New York Times Book Review *(© 1951 by The New York Times Company; reprinted by permission), August 12, 1951, p. 18.*

The outstanding children's book author of post-war Germany probably is Erich Kästner. . . . His remarkable style, so alive, humorous, and true to children, here again is very well translated. . . .

The plot is amusing in essence—playing on their similarity, these twins of nine years bring their divorced parents together. But we do not recommend the book for average nine-year-old American girls. Even if they happen to be the children of a divorce, such a story would not be good for them. In its frank, European way it shows a temperamental orchestra-conductor father being pursued by a sleek seductress in Vienna and a nine-year-old being clever enough to break up the affair. The feelings of the little girls are so well done that we do recommend the book to any parents considering divorce.

> *Louise S. Bechtel, "Books for Boys and Girls: 'Lisa and Lottie'," in* New York Herald Tribune Book Review *(© I.H.T. Corporation; reprinted by permission), August 19, 1951, p. 10.*

There is a lively charm about Kästner's books that is hard to define, but lovers of his *Emil and the Detectives* will realize what kind of treat they have in store in this book. . . . Imagine how you'd feel if you were a little girl of nine at a summer camp and suddenly another little girl appeared who looked exactly like you! And who turned out to be the twin you never had known existed! . . . The original way in which they [reunite their family] makes an entertaining tale with a most satisfactory ending. If what the little girls accomplish is not quite credible, their feelings about the need for both parents are entirely so. (pp. 328-29)

> *Jennie D. Lindquist and Siri M. Andrews, "Early Fall Booklist: 'Lisa and Lottie'," in* The Horn Book Magazine *(copyrighted, 1951, by The Horn Book, Inc., Boston), Vol. XXVII, No. 5, September-October, 1951, pp. 328-29.*

When I read *Lisa and Lottie* . . . I couldn't understand why no one had thought of this novel twist for a twins book before. . . . I can easily understand why the book has already been translated into six languages. It has originality of idea and piquancy of style. Gay, but without even a dash of anything saccharine, it made me feel very happy—something Pollyanna never did.

> *"For Girls under Twelve: 'Lisa and Lottie'," in* The Atlantic Monthly *(copyright © 1951, renewed 1979, by The Atlantic Monthly Company, Boston, Mass.;*

reprinted with permission), Vol. 188, No. 6, December, 1951, p. 104.

Until quite recently the broken home was taken as a subject in only one children's book, **Das doppelte Löttchen** (**Lotte and Lisa**) by Eric Kästner. Here we are given a child's-eye view of the relationship between parents and the tragedy of their divorce, but Kästner resorts to fantasy and humour in order to make this subject acceptable. He gives his serious problem an improbable, whimsical tale, which he then organizes like a ballet, making use of doubles, substitute-children and all the devices of comedy; the parallel is further stressed by the fact that the story unfolds in the world of the theatre. This is perhaps the best novel by the author of **Emil and the Detectives;** it has the great merit of dealing with a serious subject and the further advantage of doing so without being ponderous; furthermore artists are depicted here in a realistic way—a rare achievement in children's literature where they usually appear as *deus ex machina* or a Father Christmas, crudely portrayed and with a total lack of conviction.

Eric Kästner probably chose the surest way of representing family conflicts objectively by adopting a humorous tone for his novel; his parents are repressive and stupidly authoritarian, their manners are often humiliating, their quarrels frequent and unpredictable, yet far from inciting to rebellion like [Jules] Vallès or turning the situation into a tragedy like Jules Renard, he simply makes it funny. (pp. 112-13)

> *Isabelle Jan, "The Home," in her* On Children's Literature, *edited by Catherine Storr (originally published in French by Les Editions ouvrieres; copyright © 1969; translation copyright © Allen Lane, 1973), Schocken, 1974, pp. 90-121.**

THE ANIMALS' CONFERENCE (1949)

Gay, rollicking fun, hilarious bits, and clever twists run through the story . . . from the first to last. And still the book is packed with a heap of good common sense. Some say the story is for ages 10 to 14. Better say from 9 to 99. You will be chuckling over it long weeks after the book has been passed on to a friend.

> *Ruth C. Barlow, "When the Animals Get Together," in* The Christian Science Monitor *(reprinted by permission from* The Christian Science Monitor; *(© 1953, copyright renewed © 1981, The Christian Science Publishing Society; all rights reserved), May 14, 1953, p. 14.*

For centuries, the Germans have been expert at making fun of men by caricaturing them as animals. Now comes a hilarious [story], . . . a satire on our failure to achieve world peace. Here animals are animals, and men are men. The wealth of amusing detail will amuse children from about nine or ten up; the story is one for all ages.

As it opens, we read "news headlines all over the world," about peace conferences that have failed, and we hear the comments on them in various animal homes. Finally, Oscar the elephant could stand it no longer. He got on long distance to all corners of the earth and summoned an Animal Conference, to be held at Animal Skyscraper.

Now we see animals of all sorts choosing their delegates, the delegates making ready, the marvelous ways they all traveled. The imagination here . . . is wonderful. As they gather, it develops that there are present five children of all races, favorites of various creatures. The conference motto is "A better world for the children."

Meantime, men are having still another big conference at Capetown. To it the Animal Conference sends ultimatums which have no effect, so they use force. . . . Then, at last, the men sign the simple rules for peace, and the conferences are over forever. No more frontier barriers, no more wars, and what changes in education!

To us, it was all irresistible. It is a dozen Babar books crowded into one, with a story on an older age level. The treaty is so simple, so much what we, of childish hearts pray for, that it does make us feel rather silly. Must we ask the animals to take over? We think children all over the world will laugh at it and love it.

> *Louise S. Bechtel, "Books for Boys and Girls: 'The Animals' Conference',"* in New York Herald Tribune Book Review, *June 7, 1953, p. 10.*

[Erich Kästner tells **"The Animals' Conference"**] with brilliant use of detail, with warmth and wit. . . . This is a genial fantasy, sensible and loving—and with enough satire to entertain adults. Highly recommended.

> *Marjorie Fischer, "New Books for the Younger Readers: The Animals' Conference'," in* The New York Times Book Review *(© 1953 by The New York Times Company; reprinted by permission), July 12, 1953, p. 18.*

[**The Animals' Conference** is] funny, witty, and gaily packed with much-needed wisdom. . . .

Mr. Kästner [has] managed to put across a high-power sermon without preaching once.

Children are not the only ones who are going to have a beautiful time with this book, which makes sense. Personally we are all for the animals taking over! Meanwhile let us hope representatives of peoples the world over read this book and learn something from its memorable contribution to the peace of our planet.

> *Ernestine Evans, "Summer Solace: 'The Animals' Conference'," in* The Saturday Review, *New York (copyright © 1953 by Saturday Review, all rights reserved; reprinted by permission), Vol. XXXVI, No. 34, August 22, 1953, p. 38.*

The Animals' Conference . . . is a lighter hearted satire [than George Orwell's *Animal Farm*], but its propaganda is just as acid. The dreadful human race, the animals decide, is responsible for spoiling the entire planet and making life impossible for animals and the innocent—in this case, every nation's children.

How often, and how uncomfortable, one has thought just the same thing. But this is animal vengeance with no violence. Erich Kästner tells the story of how the animals—mostly living peacefully in the depths of Africa—suddenly wake up to the state of the world and decide to do something about it. They do not intend to usurp the human position, but copy the human design for getting things done—the conference, committee or parliament. The basic joke is, of course, not that they succeed (they have to) but that in order to succeed, they beat Man at his own game. The moral is serious, the means amusing. . . . (p. 68)

The animals' victory is achieved, of course, not by force but by united effort and cunning: the tactical destruction by the rats and the moths of what they consider to be the *real* enemy— the things that make the humans pompous—paper and clothes, especially documents and uniforms. They are abolishing, in clothes and written communications, two of the chief differences between men and animals; but as a sanction it is very effective. . . .

The liberating gaiety of this fable is an antidote to the pessimism of *Animal Farm* and the book deserves a wider public. (p. 69)

> Margaret Blount, "Four Satires," in her Animal
> Land: The Creatures of Children's Fiction (reprinted
> by permission of Georges Borchardt Inc.; copyright
> © 1974 by Margaret Ingle-Finch) William Morrow
> & Company, Inc., 1975, pp. 62-9.*

WHEN I WAS A BOY (1961; German edition, 1956(?); British edition as *When I Was a Little Boy*)

If anything could disarm a reviewer, looking at the title with a morose surmise, it is Herr Kästner's piercing sentence: 'Not everything that children experience is suitable for other children to read about'. Not everything is suitable for adults, either. Whoever recalls his childhood primarily for a reader's pleasure? Why, people even *pay* for others to listen to the compulsive theme—the sad self-love, the affectionate disgust— week after week of it. Professional listener! It is a role that Samuel Butler might have devised, or even, if you follow the thought more closely, [Jonathan] Swift. But Herr Kästner seems to have forestalled these thoughts. His trick is to reverse the usual stance; where others might adopt the refractory or confessional manner, he chooses to write with the selective assurance of an adult addressing a child. Other autobiographers might study the effect.

Most children know that they are not interesting in themselves: therefore the endless acting and daydreams. But they are fine observers of the rich inscrutable life in which they have their minor part. A book about childhood should supply this view of the larger scene and here the ground is Dresden before the First World War, the busy daily lives of tradesmen, craftsmen and shopkeepers (who were mostly the author's relatives) and of teachers (who were not). (p. 661)

Outside the house were the streets where he fetched the shopping; the river, in which his mother occasionally tried to throw herself; the splendid house of portly Uncle Franz, where they sometimes visited—an occasion of high comedy. But it is not the distant Kaiser or the homely King of Saxony round the corner that reminds us now and then where we are, but some odd pervasive details—the black puddings and chitterlings, perhaps, and still more the obsessional gymnastics (which Erich started at six). It says much for Herr Kästner's craft that he gives interest even to mysteries such as these. (p. 662)

> Naomi Lewis, "Erich or Little by Little," in New
> Statesman (© 1959 The Statesman & Nation Pub-
> lishing Co. Ltd.), Vol. 57, No. 1469, May 9, 1959,
> pp. 661-62.

It is hard to think offhand of any other autobiographies aimed so specifically at children and it seems altogether appropriate that such an experiment should have been made by the author of that pioneer, *Emil and the Detectives*. The pleasant truth of the matter, as Herr Kästner well knows, is that these rambling

memories of his boyhood in Dresden will give great satisfaction to adults, too. He has obliquities of manner that permit him to work, when he wishes, on two levels. *When I Was a Little Boy* is in many respects a hymn of praise to his extraordinary mother, a woman of fantastic energy, enterprise and will, a sketch of whom already exists in *Emil*. But he is never mawkish: the scene in which he describes his agonies every Christmas Eve as he stood between the rivalries of his parents, the elaborate toys made for him by his mild father and the mound of gifts from his mother, is cleverly done; there is shade as well as light. He gives amusing details of his family tree, but not too many; there is a fierce portrait of his rich bullying Uncle Franz, surrounded by terrorised women, and a sad account of a rock-climbing expedition with a chilly schoolmaster struggling to be amiable. Only here and there are there traces of the Vein Avuncular: '"No!" cries memory, shaking her curly locks,' etc.

> John Coleman, "No Harm Done," in The Spectator
> (©1959 by The Spectator; reprinted by permission
> of The Spectator), No. 6833, June 12, 1959, p. 844.

[Exactly the same didactic instinct as made Kästner] a satirical poet led him, and still leads him, to write for children. He writes for children because he is interested in producing civilized grown-ups, and one of the results is that he always treats children in an astonishingly grown-up way.

This was perhaps the secret of *Emil* . . . which creates no false atmosphere of cosiness and makes no bones about the financial hardships of a working-class home in 1928; and it is even more evident in the post-war books. *Lotte and Lisa* deals with the very delicate subject of children of divorced parents, and does so with great understanding. [*The Animals' Conference*] is an optimistic counterpart to *Animal Farm*. . . . The new autobiography describes, with absolute directness, the obligations laid on a child by a self-sacrificing mother like Frau Kästner, and the pangs of unhappiness that strike it when relations in the home are not right. It is full of incidental pleasures, comic, nostalgic or picturesque. . . . But what distinguishes it from any ordinary told-to-the-children story is its continual willingness to draw hard-thought conclusions: its awareness that moral problems can seem as difficult to a man of sixty as to a little girl of six.

This last book shows how deep-rooted are many of Herr Kästner's special characteristics. He came from a poor home, which allowed him to appreciate some of the problems of the working class without attributing false virtues to it. He was a model pupil and a model son for much the same reasons as Emil, because he owed it to his parents; and this gives him a certain moral stability which angry writers sometimes lack. He was on the whole so happy and healthy that he now sees childhood as providing a standard by which every adult ought to be able to check himself. At the same time he is a deliberately clear and simple writer not so much because he is writing for simple readers as because he has got something which he wants to put in an unmistakable way. (p. 362)

> "The Story of a Moralist," in The Times Literary
> Supplement (© Times Newspapers Ltd. (London)
> 1959; reproduced from The Times Literary Supple-
> ment by permission), No. 2990, June 19, 1959, pp.
> 361-63.

In reading [*When I Was a Boy*] one realizes how much of Mr. Kästner's own childhood is in his stories for children. The beginning is rather self-conscious but most of the book seems to have been written out of sheer pleasure of reminiscence. Some children will doubtless enjoy this for it has much warmth and gentle humor, but its appeal seems largely for people primarily interested in all that childhood memories can reveal, in the delightful vignettes of young Erich's relatives (and a varied and colorful lot they were), and in the glimpses of German life and the city of Dresden before the First World War. Those who like such books as Ernest H. Shepard's *Drawn from Memory* (Lippincott) will undoubtedly find pleasure in this story of the people and events which formed the personality—thoughtful, humorous, understanding—of this writer.

> *Ruth Hill Viguers, "Of Interest to Adults: 'When I Was a Boy',"* in The Horn Book Magazine *(copyright, 1961, by the Horn Book, Inc., Boston), Vol. 37, No. 5, October, 1961, p. 451.*

The noted author of **"Emil and the Detectives"** . . . is showing in this book that he has lost nothing of his literary inspiration and his subtle humor. . . . He is a writer of rare charm and deep sincerity. In his unpretentious memoirs he gives a perfect picture of his youth. . . . He sets a memorial of unending love to his mother who struggled very hard to assure her only son of the opportunity to develop his talents. . . . Warmly recommended. . . .

> *Felix E. Hirsch, " 'When I Was a Boy',"* in Library Journal *(reprinted from* Library Journal, *November 15, 1961; published by R. R. Bowker Co. (a Xerox company); copyright © 1961 by Xerox Corporation), Vol. 86, November 15, 1961, p. 3945.*

THE LITTLE MAN   (1966; German edition, 1963)

["The Little Man" is] Erich Kästner's beautiful novel of a circus performer who is only two inches tall. . . .

The problems of Maxie's size, his longing to be a normal boy, his attachment to his tutor—all are rendered to make the story more than the sum of its parts. It is significant to me that the author suffered persecution under Hitler in the 1930's, for there is an indomitable quality to **"The Little Man"** that is deeply moving.

> *Barbara Wersba, "Ages 9 to 12: 'The Little Man',"* in The New York Times Book Review *(© 1966 by The New York Times Company; reprinted by permission), November 6, 1966, p. 40.*

The circus background is amusingly drawn, but the hero's master, Professor Hocus von Pocus, hardly comes to life. It would be wrong to take the book too seriously, and Herr Kästner has the disadvantage of having made his name with a masterpiece.

> *"The Sense of Nonsense,"* in The Times Literary Supplement *(© Times Newspapers Ltd. (London) 1966; reproduced from* The Times Literary Supplement *by permission), No. 3378, November 24, 1966, p. 1077.**

It would be nice to report that the author of the classic *Emil and the Detectives* has done it again; but this book about the life and adventures of a two-inch magician's assistant who sleeps in a matchbox is merely a moderately entertaining, modernized Life of Tom Thumb. The over-elaborate plot and the language larded with exclamation points, obscure references, and elaborate puns, seem apt to discourage most readers under ten. Moreover, some episodes, like the hero's dream of being

eight feet tall, and his unsuccessful search for a wife his size, are positively depressing. (p. 29)

> *Alison Lurie, "Intellect and Non-Violence" in* The New York Review of Books *(reprinted by permission of the author), Vol. 7, No. 10, December 15, 1966, pp. 27-9.**

Children will surely enjoy this amusing and always lively story, and will quickly see themselves in Maxie's position and predicaments. Erich Kästner has a gay, easy approach to his characters and his readers, an approach which is well captured in this translation; the dialogue is particularly good. (p. 240)

> *Richard Doubleday, "Book Reviews: 'The Little Man',"* in The School Librarian and School Library Review, *Vol. 15, No. 2, July, 1967, p. 240.*

THE LITTLE MAN AND THE BIG THIEF   (1969; German edition, 1967; British edition as *The Little Man and the Little Miss*)

"What about the kids who haven't read the first book about the Little Man?" Jakob Hertig asks Mr. Kästner at the beginning of **The Little Man and the Little Miss.** "I know what! You must begin the second volume by first telling us the contents of the first one." This is ingeniously done. . . . Having put the reader in the picture, the second volume continues where the first left off. Unfortunately this reminder of the earlier story only underlines, as sequels often do, the true paucity of the second. In the new story Maxie is involved with making a film of his previous adventures, while the police chase the kidnappers. Sadly, the latter half of the book loses tempo badly.

It is padded out with inconclusive episodes which, while having a certain gaiety (a visit to the Sausage God in Breganzona, for example), give an insipid colouring to the whole. The Little Miss of the title conveniently arrives to share a minuscule home with Maxie so that Hokus von Pokus, his conjurer guardian, is free to marry his own girl. The book is a pale shadow of **The Little Man** whose exciting kidnapping, reminiscent of the best of **Emil,** is replaced by sentiment.

> *"Continental Characters,"* in The Times Literary Supplement *(© Times Newspapers Ltd. (London) 1969; reproduced from* The Times Literary Supplement *by permission), No. 3529, October 16, 1969, p. 1200.*

Erich Kästner's individual brand of humour is well in evidence here, but alas, the extravagance of a plot gets wildly out of hand, and the book launches into a prolonged happy ending before half the ends are properly tied up. The Lilliputian joke on its own, carried over into blissful domesticity, may not satisfy readers who would like to know what happened to the comic and inventive villains of the piece; however, there is a good deal of incidental amusement to be found here. (pp. 107-08)

> *Anthea Bell, "Book Reviews: 'The Little Man and the Little Miss',"* in The School Librarian, *Vol. 18, No. 1, March, 1970, pp. 107-08.*

[The Little Man and the Big Thief is the] tallest of tales of the shortest of boys. . . . All [the chapters] are immensely indulgent, indulgeable, playful and punful as translated superbly into American. For the sentient child or unjaded adult—a fountain of youthful fantasia to please every Peter Pan.

"Younger Fiction: 'The Little Man and the Big Thief'," in Kirkus Reviews *(copyright © 1970 The Kirkus Service, Inc.), Vol. XXXVIII, No. 6, March 15, 1970, p. 322.*

There's lots of excitement, plenty of speed and a satisfactory plot of wheels-within-wheels [in **"The Little Man and The Big Thief"**]. . . .

The spirit of the Continental circus, the techniques of today's film and television, and the old, old sense of magic in story-telling, are all together in this novel and the combination sounds perfectly natural. . . .

The book is about performers—but it's also about behavior and manners, the way people of any age and any size treat one another. Its touch is light and its world one of gaiety, but the story never says there's no sadness in experience. . . .

There is nothing sugary, no talking-down from Mr. Kastner toward his two-inch-high hero nor toward his young reader. Rather, he tells the story as though he's sharing in a common pleasure with them both, with an occasional remark addressed straight to the reader, "Have you ever tried to pack a conjurer's magic tails into a suitcase? No? Well, it takes at least an hour and a half." He tells the story, too, with its proper vocabulary; words like "confounded effrontery" are not left out.

And although nothing has been underlined, it's there for the young reader to observe for himself: in a human being, no matter if he is only two inches high, feelings may lie too deep for words, and actions may reach up to giant size in courage and high spirits.

Eudora Welty, *"Four Reviews by Eudora Welty: 'The Little Man and the Big Thief',"* in The New York Times Book Review *(© 1970 by The New York Times Company; reprinted by permission), May 24, 1970, p. 4.*

We have another book by the author of **Emil and the Detectives**. It is, however, a fantasy of a different nature—and a distinguished one. . . . The book introduces some fine and crazy characters—the film director 'six and a half feet in his socks'; the strange and wonderful sausage king of Breganzona (the author's German heritage obviously influencing his choice of food); and also revives for our delectation several of the notable characters of the earlier book.

Fantasy writing for children of nine to twelve is beset by pitfalls—the danger of becoming patronizing, of taking flight into the realms of adult fantasy where children are unwilling to follow, the complications of keeping the fantasy consistent to the climax of the book. All these Mr. Kästner avoids in a masterly manner. . . . [There is] mannered wit in every paragraph. Altogether an attractive addition to the fiction shelf.

"Fiction: 'Little Man and the Little Miss'," in Children's Book News *(copyright © 1970 by Baker Book Services Ltd.), Vol. 1, No. 3, May-June, 1970, p. 131.*

Readers who enjoyed **The Little Man** will appreciate the sequel, which ties up loose ends and enlarges and clarifies the reader's understanding of certain characters and events. However, because much of the action takes place off stage—in the earlier book or in South America—this book is somewhat less exciting and less hilarious than its predecessor. (p. 389)

Diane Farrell, *"Stories for the Middle Readers,"* in The Horn Book Magazine *(copyright © 1970 by The Horn Book, Inc., Boston), Vol. 46, No. 4, August, 1970, pp. 384-92.*

Yuri Korinetz

1923-

(Also transliterated as Iurii Iosifovich Korinets, Yuri Korinets, and Juri Korinetz) Russian novelist for children, poet, radio playwright, and translator for adults. Korinetz's works are thematically concerned with the importance of the past as an influence on the present. Set in both contemporary and historical Russia, his three translated novels for children allow readers to become familiar with Russian attitudes through storytelling, fantasy, and the reactions of his characters to everyday events and unexpected conflicts. Korinetz's books stress the importance of relationships between generations. Strong role models impress the boy narrators with their experience and values; the narratives, often written as reminiscences, show how they accept and use this knowledge in their own approaches to life.

Korinetz's observations of human nature are recognized as accurate and truthful; his characterization of Uncle Petya in *There, Far Beyond the River* is called especially memorable. Occasionally the structure and the uniquely Russian aspects of Korinetz's works are thought to be unclear and he has also been criticized for authorial interjections within some of the narratives. However, Korinetz's contribution to international children's literature is valued for his eloquence and sensitivity toward children and for the positive background his books provide on Soviet life and thought. *There, Far Beyond the River* was awarded the first prize in the U.S.S.R. Children's Book Competition dedicated to Lenin's Centenary in 1968, and his works were selected among the best of the year for inclusion in the UNESCO International Youth Library from 1972 through 1974. (See also *Contemporary Authors*, Vols. 61-64, and *Something about the Author*, Vol. 9.)

THERE, FAR BEYOND THE RIVER   (1973; Russian edition, 1967)

Confidence in the future lies at the heart of *There, Far Beyond the River*. A little boy in Soviet Russia learns about the past, and about his place in the present, by contact with his uncle. . . . The idiom of the story is strange to English readers, but one quickly adjusts to its unfamiliar cadences and to a certain pedantry of manner. The story moves slowly—an unavoidable characteristic of oblique narrative—and it is probable that not all young readers will persist for long enough, but in time the strength and wisdom of the narrative become irresistible. The second two-thirds of the book are magnificent in their quiet, sustained eloquence.

Here for once a good children's book is essentially a book for children. The boy narrator has no grafted adult characteristics; he is all boy, although a very serious, very Russian boy. Uncle, the gigantic old revolutionary Porfiri, and the other adult characters are all seen through the boy's eyes and so legitimately seem rather larger than life. In its integrity, its action and its philosophy this is a very good book indeed. For English children it will offer an additional bonus, for it opens a door upon a strange, fascinating, profoundly alien world.

"Fighting to Survive," in The Times Literary Supplement *(© Times Newspapers Ltd. (London) 1973; reproduced from* The Times Literary Supplement *by permission), No. 3734, September 28, 1973, p. 1113.*

[*There, far beyond the river*] is an enchanting book about the friendship between the boy narrator Misha and his much-admired uncle, a magnificent and tremendously vital figure. . . . (p. 125)

It all sounds very simple, but the book is beautifully written, having a vivid feel of place and time with its graphic descriptions of brooding northern landscapes of forests and rivers, or evocations of the pleasures of brewing punch over a sweet-smelling juniper fire in a pine forest lit by the midnight sun hanging in the branches low on the horizon. Beyond this it is also the story of a boy coming to terms with new experiences and acquiring a sense of values. . . . *There, far beyond the river* illustrates the essential continuity of a Russian literary tradition which runs from [Ivan] Turgenev's *Sportsman's Sketches* through the pastoral works of [Ivan] Bunin to the recent short stories of Yuri Kazakov, with his characters who like those of Yuri Korinetz are questioners and brooders with a longing for some intense, high experience, who fail to fit into the snug niche of modern industrial society but respond instead to the mystery and wonder of nature. (pp. 125-26)

Konstantin Bazarov, "Young Readers: 'There, Far Beyond the River'" (© copyright Konstantin Bazarov 1973; reprinted with permission), in Books and Bookmen, *Vol. 19, No. 1, October, 1973, pp. 125-26.*

This Russian book has walked off with several prizes, and rightly. The short chapters and episodic treatment help to convey a dreamy quality enhanced by the boy's only half-comprehending hero-worship. Into this, the details of the boy's life, going to the ballet or camping with his uncle and eating fresh salmon, are vividly inserted. And all the time the political history conveyed by the uncle's Revolutionary past gives the story a special poignancy.

> *John Fuller, "Nine to Thirteen: 'There, Far Beyond the River'" (© British Broadcasting Corp. 1973; reprinted by permission of John Fuller), in* The Listener, *Vol. 90, No. 2328, November, 1973, p. 642.*

[*There, far beyond the river*] is a strange mixture: basically the story of a boy's relationship with a beloved uncle and their adventures fishing and camping around Moscow and on the Kola peninsula in northern Russia, it embraces so much more. It is a hymn of praise to the outdoor life, the beauty of wilderness, the joy of self-reliance, the warmth of friendship. It is a study of a remarkable man pursuing an ideal through several decades of Russian politics. It is the story of a boy's growth in knowledge and awareness of human values. It is streaked and flecked with the magic of fantasy, the certain 'something' so valued by the uncle because it adds to the quality of life.

And yet the young reader will be led from chapter to chapter by the pace of the action, the vividness of the description, the constant humour, the affirmation of life. Highly recommended. (pp. 354-55)

> *C.E.J. Smith, "Eleven to Fifteen: 'There, Far Beyond the River'," in* The School Librarian, *Vol. 21, No. 4, December, 1973, pp. 354-55.*

No generation gap exists between Misha and his ebullient, adventure-loving Uncle Petya whose abilities as hunter, fisherman, storyteller, and revolutionary are both infinitely fascinating and apparently limitless. . . . Although Misha is the narrator, Uncle Petya—indulgent, wise, and humorous—dominates the story and commands the reader's attention. He is larger than life whether he is describing his audacity in outwitting the Czarist police or is reprimanding Misha for his chauvinism. . . . As intimate as a conversation, as precise as poetry, as pungent as a folktale, the narrative depends for its compelling vitality on superb evocation of character and setting rather than on situation. . . . Misha's story is a celebration of living and an exploration of life's meaning.

> *Mary M. Burns, "Folk Tales and Legends: 'There, Far Beyond the River'," in* The Horn Book Magazine *(copyright © 1974 by The Horn Book, Inc., Boston), Vol. L, No. 2, April, 1974, pp. 148-49.*

["**There, Far Beyond the River**"] has a stiffness that detracts from Yuri Korinetz's bouncy story. . . . But there is still great fascination in the novel's incident and atmosphere. . . .

[It] is a true portrait of the mixture of exuberance and resignation that is Russia—which, for the sake of the future, is one of the things we should all want our children to understand.

> *Susan Cooper, "Strains of Mark Twain," in* The Christian Science Monitor *(reprinted by permission from* The Christian Science Monitor; *© 1974 The Christian Science Publishing Society; all rights reserved), May 1, 1974, p. F5.**

IN THE MIDDLE OF THE WORLD   (British edition, 1976)

Character . . . gives authenticity to a picture of Moscow in the 1930's, in *In the middle of the world*. . . . Jura looks back to the time when as a small boy he lived with his parents in a tenement block. . . .

History for Jura is epitomised by the statue of Vorovsky, hero of the Revolution, which stands in the courtyard and becomes in a way the boy's confidant. Reporting what he saw but did not altogether understand, the boy also conveys a sense of the past as he describes sly Lyapkin and his spiteful little boy; to Jura, Lyapkin is sinister because he wants to have the dog Dick destroyed after his master Whiskers has killed himself, but the reader realises that the informer and blackmailer was also responsible for the death of a man once a Tsarist soldier and later a loyal fighter for the Bolshevik cause. The undercurrents in the book are all the more telling because of the open, almost naïve manner of the narrative. (p. 3159)

> *Margery Fisher, "Ways to the Past," in her* Growing Point, *Vol. 16, No. 3, September, 1977, pp. 3158-61.*

The adults are a rich Dickensian collection, and human nature is as it always is: the gossip, the good and the silly, the dislike of high-ranking bureaucrats, the things that puzzle small children about their elders' behaviour. Fortunately, little Jura needs to ask the very questions about everyday life in Russia and the early years after the Revolution that foreign readers need answers to, so that a fascinatingly full picture builds up of the system, the divided loyalties and sense of purpose, the lawless gangs of orphans roaming the streets, and the customs and landmarks of Moscow. The Russians remain a religious people: the author firmly rejects church teaching, but finds the need to preach political and moral lessons as fervently as any Maria Edgeworth! But this is not merely hirtorical party propaganda. Jura is an unusual child: he has struck up a friendship with the stone statue of the patriot Vorovsky in the middle of the palace courtyard and shares with it his secrets, sorrows and joys. We find ourselves right inside the mind of this very sensitive child, not only through the writer's wonderfully imaginative observation, . . . but also a delightfully Pooh-like style of thought and conversation for Jura. A most unusual and moving book. (pp. 289-90)

> *"For Children under Ten: 'In the Middle of the World'," in* The Junior Bookshelf, *Vol. 41, No. 5, October, 1977, pp. 289-90.*

Readers of [Konstantin] Paustovsky and [Kornei] Chukovsky will recognize the characteristic manner of those reminiscences; the lyrical chat that recalls the laundry steaming on the primus stoves in the communal kitchen, the delirium of measles, the fitting of the boy's first suit, the capture of crayfish in summer. . . .

Andrea Bell's translation is pleasantly readable, but it comes not from the original but from the German, and, passing through this double filter, subtleties elude us. Ideas in a Soviet context are difficult to place. What are we to make of the religious thought that creation was "well-planned by someone", or of the political menace in a child's boast: "My father can put your father in prison"? Ideology apart, it is all very friendly and very foreign.

> *Marion Glastonbury, "Running in Families," in* The Times Educational Supplement *(© Times Newspapers Ltd. (London) 1977; reproduced from* The Times

Educational Supplement *by permission), No. 3264, December 30, 1977, p. 13.**

THE RIVER AND THE FOREST　　(British edition, 1978)

[*The River and the Forest*] comes to us through the double filter of a Russian-German and German-English translation—a lot of trouble but well worth it. Volodya, an 11-year-old Siberian, sets out alone on a five-day journey in autumn from his native village to his grandfather's hunting lodge. Sustained by dreams and memories, fresh grayling and cranberries, he struggles through storms and a forest fire, until, half-dead with hunger and exhaustion, he meets hope of rescue in a chance encounter with the drunken Prokop and his motorboat. But Prokop, vengeful son of a dispossessed kulak, has already caused the death of Volodya's parents on the mountain, and now leaves Volodya to his fate, which he survives only by hallucinating help from the community of ants.

I take this to be a gentle ideological hint, though the exact meaning of Korinetz's occasional political remarks escapes me. However, I'm sure he's right about the mating of elks and the antics of bear cubs. The intense life of a wild landscape is made present to the reader until cities "trapped in stone" seem unfamiliar, and the reminder of centralized government comes as a shock: "Anyone living in Moscow would fetch the moon down from the sky for a piece of salmon like that."

　　　Marion Glastonbury, "Foreign Parts," in The Times Educational Supplement *(© Times Newspapers Ltd. (London) 1978; reproduced from* The Times Educational Supplement *by permission), No. 3281, May 19, 1978, p. 32.**

Frontispiece maps of fictional journeys can be a nuisance to the reader, who wants to get on with the story and feels obliged to check routes and landmarks that seem irrelevant compared with the mental picture he is building up. But the map of Volodya's path through the Siberian *taiga* does help us to understand many points—why at one stage the lad had to leave the guide-lines of the Ilych River which flowed by his own village, why he is confusingly said to be travelling south when one feels he must be going north, how indeed a lad could be lost when year after year he had travelled with his grandfather from the winter home in the village to old Matemyan's hunting hut in the forest. A preliminary glance at the map, a look back now and then, a closer study at the end, and the whole escapade becomes at once clearer and more admirable. (p. 3346)

The journey is described in a precise but leisurely fashion. The author projects his account through the boy's mind as much as by direct narrative and he writes so pictorially that we have a strong illusion of pushing forward with his young hero, as he makes camp by the river or salts fish for carrying. We come to know the small, isolated community he belongs to, with its odd mixture of the 'seventies, with helicopters and political controls, and the age-old subsistence life of forestry, trapping and hunting. As Volodya makes his way along the river bank or through the forest his thoughts go back to moments in the past—to the still unexplained death of his parents in the snow-bound *taiga*, to the dubious dealings of vicious Prokov with the geologists and his malice towards the boy and his grandfather, to Prokov's daughter Alevtina, the boy's playmate and his intended companion for the future.

There is another way, too in which Volodya's thoughts and fancies broaden the scope of the book. At the outset of his

journey he falls asleep in a meadow and dreams that he is talking to the Great Ant and accepting her advice; later, when he is in real trouble, the same Queen bullies him into stumbling on when he is on the verge of collapse. . . . The fantasising is one aspect of the attitude to nature which has been instilled in the boy by his grandfather; it seems entirely natural that the people in this corner of Siberia should personify the forces of nature, since they live so close to them.

The observant, contented relations of the boy with his environment is stated simply and for the most part without authorial comment. . . . There is never any sentiment in the boy's reaction to animal life. Shortly after [Volodya sees two ravens on the riverbank] the ravens steal the rest of the salmon which he has cached by the river; he tries to get it back, is attacked by the birds and has to take to the water to protect himself. The instinctive antagonism of the birds contrasts forcibly with the moment when Prokov, passing along the river in his boat on one of his poaching forays, ignores the obviously lost and suffering boy, tossing to him the evil observation that he might as well die like his parents. Because the story is based on a sturdy acceptance of probability, Prokov does not come to a bad end as a result of his present and past misdeeds. To the boy, as to the author, he seems as natural a piece of evil, and almost as motiveless, as the snow that ultimately killed Volodya's parents or the fire and storm that nearly killed him. The acceptance of life with its rewards and its hazards provides the theme of this finely structured narrative. (pp. 3346-47)

　　　Margery Fisher, "Special Review: 'The River and the Forest'," in her Growing Point, *Vol. 17, No. 2, July, 1978, pp. 3346-47.*

Something of the clarity of sequences seems to have been lost in Anthea Bell's translation, or else one is distracted by Volodya's own digressions on his long walk to his grandfather's cabin. . . . Dreams, memories of earlier childhood and many thoughts are recorded as his journey progresses and these demand tight concentration from the reader. Still it is a kindly country tale of a Siberia which appears less hostile to survival than tradition has led most of us to believe. Nature can still be treacherous but the river and the woodland suggest freedom and a variety of life in sharp contrast to the snowy wastes, forbidding forests and penal settlements which are more usually the stuff of westernised fiction. Something of a tonic after the dour pictures of [Leo] Tolstoy and [Fëdor] Dostoiewsky.

　　　"For Children from Ten to Fourteen: 'The River and the Forest'," in The Junior Bookshelf, *Vol. 42, No. 5, October, 1978, p. 269.*

The strength of the work lies in its natural observation, the depiction of a boy completely in tune with his surroundings, and the subtle use of the solitary journey as a means of recollection and contemplation of other experience. At the end we know Volodya very well. Some children might find the dividing lines between actuality, recollection and dream difficult to detect at times. They may also find not to their taste the presence of an obtrusive author ready to point a conclusion or form an attitude. The authorial stance is one now abandoned by most western authors for children. Nevertheless, this is a sensitive work, well worth introducing to discriminating children.

　　　Dennis Hamley, "Fiction: 'The River and the Forest'," in The School Librarian, *Vol. 26, No. 4, December, 1978, p. 357.*

Karla Kuskin

1932-

(Also writes under the pseudonym Nicholas J. Charles) American author/illustrator and illustrator of poetry and fiction for children, and critic and scriptwriter for adults. Although many of Kuskin's works are picture books, she is most highly acclaimed for her poetry. She is especially well-known for her appeal to the child's sense of humor and for the pleasure her verse gives when read aloud.

Kuskin's first picture book, *Roar and More*, was the result of a graphic arts course project at Yale University in which she constructed an entire book, including text, illustrations, cover, and binding. The book was immediately successful upon publication and is considered unique for its typography, which varies the sizes and shapes of the letters to reflect the sounds of different animals, a technique she also used for *All Sizes of Noises*. Kuskin's picture books written in verse receive positive reviews for their rhythmic, imaginative text and ability to relate to children. *A Boy Had a Mother Who Bought Him a Hat* is also praised for its handsomely detailed illustrations and for its timeless appeal. Critics see most of her illustrations as whimsical, gay, and neatly drawn.

Kuskin has said that her writings developed from her imagination and memories of her youth. As a poet, Kuskin attempts to capture the pleasing sounds and rhythms of language she enjoyed as a child. In *Near the Window Tree* and *Dogs and Dragons, Trees and Dreams: A Collection of Poems* she includes the background incidents and inspirations behind each poem. While some reviewers feel that the added notes are not useful and detract from the literary value of the poems, most state that this method is good for helping children to understand and appreciate poetry. Critics praise Kuskin's precise view of the child's world, the musical quality of her texts, and her ability to make poetry accessible to children. The success of her works suggests her accuracy in determining how to bring children and language closer together through the enjoyment of the sound and sight of words. She has received the American Institute of Graphic Arts Award for Best Children's Books in 1955-57 for *Roar and More* and in 1958-60 for *Square as a House*, the American Institute of Graphic Arts Award for Best Fifty Books in 1958 for *In the Middle of the Trees*, the Children's Book Showcase selection in 1972 for *A Boy Had a Mother Who Bought Him a Hat*, the New York Academy of Sciences Children's Science Book Award for Younger Children in 1979 for *A Space Story*, and the National Council of Teachers of English Award for Excellence in Poetry for Children in recognition of her aggregate work in 1979. (See also *Contemporary Authors*, Vol. 1-4 and *Something about the Author*, Vol. 2.)

AUTHOR'S COMMENTARY

I want to talk through my verses to anyone: mice, fireplugs, assorted trees and children, anyone who will listen. And I want to talk in any voice: an old lady's, a child's, my cat's—in any voice that I choose to use. The children who hear my verses or read them to themselves will, hopefully, recognize a familiar feeling or thought. Or possibly an unfamiliar feeling or thought will intrigue them. If that spark is lit, then my verse may

Photograph by Piper Productions; courtesy of Harper & Row, Publishers, Inc. and Harriet Wasserman Literary Agency

encourage its individual audience to add his own thought or maybe even a poem of his own, to try his own voice in some new way.

Like most people who write, I want to be heard and understood. A very direct way of finding out if someone out there is listening and if he understands is to read him what you have written. (pp. 38-9)

The only way I know of getting the words out of my head and into the light is to try to meet them as you would a stranger and catch them unaware to learn how they *really* sound. Is the sense still there? Has an image collapsed? How does the silent reading differ from reading aloud? Does it work both ways? I've written a lot of verses that sounded splendid in a corner of my mind, but once they were echoing across the objective air, they lost their luster. They resemble those jewel-like stones you bring home from the beach on Sunday only to wonder on Tuesday why you brought home all those *stones*.

I am a firm believer in reading aloud because, I suppose, I loved it so much as a child. Both roles were wonderful—reader and listener. Truthfully I think that I liked reading best. It combines the advantage of listening to that fascinating sound—your own voice—with the feeling that whatever you were reading was a gift you were bringing to your audience. Because it was your discovery, you had part ownership. That's a marvelous feeling to have about T. S. Eliot's *Old Possum's Book of Practical Cats* or speeches from *A Midsummer Night's Dream.*

In the last dozen years I have often read my verses in quite a few different areas and to a variety of age groups, ranging from the pupils in private schools of New York City to children in inner-city schools of Washington, D.C. It's easy to read poetry to children who know and love poetry. It's very difficult to read to children who don't know what poetry is and care less.

Last spring I went to Washington, D.C., for a government agency called CAREL. That is the Central Atlantic Regional Educational Laboratory. Like most government agencies, its title is a veritable poem in itself. It was a terrible time to be in Washington or anywhere else. I made the trip on the morning Robert Kennedy died. The area I went to had suffered the worst effects of the rioting and destruction that erupted after the assassination of Martin Luther King a month before.

One of the schools I visited still had a good many windows broken. Its metal doors with their tiny chicken-wired windows were constructed to keep people out, not invite them in. Yet the children I read to were young and seemed completely unaffected by the current and terrible events. And for many of the older children, I suspect, the world had been hard enough, long enough so that they were not as surprised and shocked by the chaos as some of our more comfortable and better-protected citizens. Include me among the latter.

I first read to children of eight and nine years and realized quickly that they weren't with me. The poem I read was **"The Witches Ride."** . . . (pp. 39-40)

A verse like that one—one that I would generally read to children of this age—just wasn't right. At the moment I didn't have time to figure out why. Instead, I had to do some quick experimenting to try to find a place where we could meet each other. I tried some shorter, funnier verses like [**"When I Went Out to See the Sun"**]. (p. 41)

If a child laughs at what you say, he's listening; and he may keep listening even when you get a little more serious. I read my very shortest poem from a book called *Alexander Soames: His Poems.* The title is **"Bugs."**

> I am very fond of bugs.
> I kiss them
> And I give them hugs.

The response should be poetic: *bugs . . . ugh(s?).* I got the response. I also began to draw, fast and messy, but I wanted to hold attention. The words and the way they were put together may have been unfamiliar, but I hoped that the sketches would make the words plainer.

I read the first book I had written, *Roar and More,* and drew some of the animals. We were finally on common ground. There were a great many requests for animals and for "a picture of me . . . draw Ellie" and best of all "Let me draw," until we were all drawing together. *Roar and More* was effective here because the verses are short, simple and demand a response. (pp. 41-2)

Another book I have used is *Square as a House,* which is also in verse and which asks for a response quite directly. (p. 43)

Which Horse Is William? does the same thing in prose. I told this story more than I read it. As with everything I read, I skipped freely and changed things if I thought they might seem too strange in their original form. This is the way I read the more flowery sections of [Kenneth Grahame's] *Wind in the Willows* to my son. Essentially, I am a great believer in using an unfamiliar word or phrase when it is called for, but when all the territory is unfamiliar, the going can get so discouraging that instead of gaining a questioner, you lose a listener.

The younger children I read to in these schools were very alive, anxious to hear, to talk and to possess. They all wanted the drawings I was doing and were also fascinated with the idea of making or having a book of their own. (pp. 43-4)

I read very much the same kinds of poems to the older children that I had read to those who were younger. The older ones weren't as eager—perhaps the word is "free"—to talk, listen, take, give. I felt that a lot of them had been bored too long and had gotten used to not listening. They came around, but I had to work harder.

One of the things small children respond to first is rhythm as in clapping games and songs. Poems are tuneless songs. Beginning with short verses, using books that have built-in points for response, drawing pictures to hang ideas on or asking listeners to draw their own reactions while you are reading or when you have finished are all friendly ways of introducing poetry to a young child. With the phrase "young child," I am including all of those children who do not have a speaking— even a *nodding*—acquaintance with poetry.

The building materials of a poem are sound and the swing of it: words in their infinite color, length, shape, rhythm and, at times, rhyme. When they are used freely and impressionistically, a listener can enjoy the sound—just abstractly at first. Later he will listen to what is being said. "The Congo" by Vachel Lindsay is a drum solo. W. S. Gilbert's "When You're Lying Awake" from *Iolanthe* is a waterfall of words and silliness. "Jabberwocky" by Lewis Carroll is another handsome example of what the sound and roll of words can do. If we continue along this winsome road, we approach James Joyce country, where the terrain gets rougher.

However it is done—as formally as in a narrative poem like [Robert Browning's] "The Pied Piper of Hamlin" or [Alfred Noyes's] "The Highwayman," as subtly as in haiku or with the simplicity of some short descriptive Emily Dickinson poetry—a poem is written to carry feeling and thought. Usually the two are combined into a mood. Reading both prose and poetry (even reading the back of the Sugar Smacks Box) expands our private world and lets us in on moods and lives that we are not familiar with. Through reading we can become someone else anywhere else.

When I said before that I want to use different voices when I write, I was referring to this kind of exploration of other lives. If I can go into new thoughts and places in my imagination, perhaps whoever is listening will follow. I do not wish to make this sound more complicated than it is. Quite simply, I do not spend all my days writing from the point of view of the New York-born mother of two I am. (pp. 44-5)

How do I know if what I have written says what I want the way I want it to? By the reaction or lack of it. When a class of 30 children in Towson, Maryland, recited a poem of mine to me, I had two feelings. One, I wanted to become quietly invisible; and two, I knew my words had reached them from the way they muttered and roared them back at me. You know you have a good reaction when there is laughter, if you are trying to be funny and when there is an absorbed silence, if you are not. On occasions when my eight-year-old son suddenly quotes a few lines from something I have written or I overhear him reading a book of mine to his four-year-old sister, I momentarily feel that I have bridged that famous gap and said something both to them and me.

I want to add one thought here. Despite my pleasure when I am able to write something that communicates, I am, finally, not writing for my audience first, but for myself. In other words: if I don't think something is funny, I won't feel better about it if my son or a lot of other people's sons laugh at it. When it comes down to the crunch, as they say in *Time,* it is my feelings I finally have to trust.

But I was talking about children's reactions to reading. One of the very best of these happens when a child listens for awhile and then is inspired to take up his own pencil and write. Then you know that he has enjoyed what he's heard or read so much that he wants to create some of the same. It may also mean that he wasn't entirely satisfied and thinks he can do better. Sometimes he's right. (pp. 46-7)

Reading and writing encourage each other. Once you want to write, you read more. In each way, that private world of knowledge and feeling is expanded. (p. 48)

> *Karla Kuskin, "'Talk to Mice and Fireplugs . . .',"* *in* Somebody Turned on a Tap in These Kids: Poetry and Young People Today, *edited by Nancy Larrick (copyright ©1971 by Nancy Larrick Crosby; reprinted by permission of Delacorte Press/Seymour Lawrence), Delacorte Press, 1971, pp. 38-48 [the excerpt of Karla Kuskin's poetry used here was originally published in her* Alexander Soames: His Poems *(copyright © 1962 by Karla Kuskin; reprinted by permission of the author), Harper & Row, Publishers, Inc., 1962].*

ROAR AND MORE   (1956)

Certainly all you will need to do with this clever book is to invite a very small child to come and sit beside you. As soon as you read:

> If a lion comes to visit
> Don't open your door
> Just firmly ask "What is it?"
> And listen to him roar.

quickly turn the page and watch his delight as that ROAR you read fills the page with black, black letters. This is sure-fire, for fun, for art, for originality, a miracle to have come from a dissertation. . . . A grown-up can enjoy the clever use of typography to show sounds, the odd and interestingly stylized pictures, and the light gay verses, but the four and five year olds will just plain love it. A hearty welcome to Karla Kuskin.

> *"Fun and Beauty for the Youngest: 'Roar and More',"* *in* New York Herald Tribune Book Review, *Part II (© I.H.T. Corporation; reprinted by permission), November 18, 1956, p. 5.*

Kuskin's first venture into the field of children's books is something of a typographer's delight. Eleven animals are presented here in illustration—each accompanied by a rhyming verse. . . .

"Roar and More" as a spirited romp through a part of animal-land is satisfyingly unconventional. The drawings are simple and bold, nicely counter-pointed by the near-nonsense verses. But the most fun will come from the reader who can sound out the animal noises without inhibition.

> *George A. Woods, "From Snarls to Purrs," in* The New York Times Book Review, *Part II (© 1956 by The New York Times Company; reprinted by permission), November 18, 1956, p. 49.*

In [William Wondriska's] *The Sound of Things* and **Roar and More,** it is the turn of letter combinations, patterns, configurations, whether or not words, to signify sounds. . . . **Roar and More** is more—the meaning of the title apart—for each sound-picture is introduced by a rhyme and a portrait that together key us to the coming sound. . . .

Roar and More is the one that succeeded with children and, presumably, parents—because it is more than sounds, because the sounds can more easily be uttered, because it's for the presenting, the sharing, the reacting. It moves, things happen. (p. 359)

> *Barbara Bader, "New Looks" in* American Picture Books from Noah's Ark to the Beast Within *(reprinted with permission of Macmillan Publishing Co., Inc.; © 1976 by Barbara Bader), Macmillan, 1976, pp. 332-63.*

[**Roar and More** is an example of a book whose structure and patterns lead young children slowly through the steps of a joke. It's] learn-to-laugh and laugh-as-you learn, as the author skillfully wrings humor from the zoological fact that giraffes are mute. The book asks, "What does the lion say? the horse? the cow? the pig?" The roar, the neigh, the moo, the oink are reported as expected. Then the book asks, deadpan, what the giraffe says? Each question has been followed by the phonetic approximation in English of the animal's response. Therefore the "nothing" response in the case of the giraffe is experienced as funny. The build-up is part of the process. (p. 39)

> *Joan W. Blos, "Getting It: The First Notch on the Funny Bone," in* School Library Journal *(reprinted from the May, 1979 issue of* School Library Journal, *published by R. R. Bowker Co./A Xerox Corporation; copyright © 1979), Vol. 25, No. 9, May, 1979, pp. 38-9.**

JAMES AND THE RAIN   (1957)

Mrs. Kuskin's second book is one of the best read-aloud stories for very young children to appear in a long, long time. The story of James and his walk in the rain with his animal friends is very entertaining. Even two year olds can understand it. The pictures are graceful and gay and precisely drawn so that it can be recognized by little children. Best of all, the verse has a fine easy rhythm that makes it a joy to read aloud. If Mrs. Kuskin had refrained from using the word "like" when she should have used "as" her book would be quite perfect.

> *"Juvenile Forecasts: 'James and the Rain'," in* Publishers Weekly *(reprinted from the July 22, 1957 issue of* Publishers Weekly, *published by R. R. Bowker Company; copyright © 1957 by R. R. Bowker Company), Vol. 172, No. 4, July 22, 1957, p. 67.*

Books which place their emphasis on something besides a narrative line could be cited by the hundreds. But it is perhaps enough to mention one more example, [*James and the Rain*]. . . . All the excitement and giddy pleasure that rainy days produce in young children can be found here, and the jingling text makes it difficult for anyone to escape the fever.

> *Donnarae MacCann and Olga Richard, "Specialized Texts," in their* The Child's First Books: A Critical Study of Pictures and Texts *(copyright © 1973 by Donnarae MacCann and Olga Richard; reprinted by permission of The H. W. Wilson Company), Wilson, 1973, pp. 107-13.**

IN THE MIDDLE OF THE TREES   (1958)

Kittens, balloons, snowmen and dragons, Spring and children are the subjects of [Kuskin's] small chants. Though the poems themselves are not of the stature of Rachel Field or of [Robert Louis Stevenson], the rhymes are definite and recognizable and some of the imagery is inventive and amusing. This is a good conditioner toward sound similarities and as such a good building block toward phonics.

> *"Picture Story Books: 'In the Middle of the Trees'," in* Virginia Kirkus' Service, *Vol. XXVI, No. 4, February 15, 1958, p. 133.*

These poems are full of imagination and humor—and also of poetry—which is a rather rare combination. They also contrive to be individual, and practically every one has some line that is a mouth-curving surprise, so that you race eagerly on to see what is around the next corner. Sure to be entrancing to children from four to eight—and no doubt equally entrancing to the grownup who is privileged to read it aloud.

> *Silence Buck Bellows, "Books: 'In the Middle of the Trees'," in* The Christian Science Monitor *(reprinted by permission from* The Christian Science Monitor; © 1958 The Christian Science Publishing Society; *all rights reserved), May 15, 1958, p. 13.*

Amusing verses that sing and prance and dance, and equally amusing pen and ink sketches (touched with vivid emerald green), half formal, half absurd, make up Karla Kuskin's latest picture book. Usually the child is speaking about the happiness of waking up early, about the seasons, about the fun of pretending when you are full of delight. The rhymes and rhythms used are the simple ones young children respond to readily. We are sure they will love the verse that begins: 'There's a tree by the meadow, by the sand, by the sea, on a hillock, near a valley, that belongs to me," with the haunting beat of "Over in the Meadow," and what fun to chant and then disentangle the meaning of **"Around and Around."** . . .

> *Margaret Sherwood Libby, "For Boys and Girls: 'In the Middle of the Trees'," in* New York Herald Tribune Book Review *(© I.H.T. Corporation; reprinted by permission), June 15, 1958, p. 11.*

THE ANIMALS AND THE ARK   (1958)

All the animals are brought together as Noah's Ark sails again in Karla Kuskin's fourth book. . . . The treatment is whimsical—text in a bouncy, breezy verse and drawings that range from a hold full of squalling, scratching beasts to the Ark floating right off the page. It's mostly a pleasurable voyage except at trip's end where the Ark, like the reader, is left high and dry. (p. 53)

> *George A. Woods, "For the Very Young It's Always the Picture Book That Tells the Story: 'The Animals and the Ark'," in* The New York Times Book Review, *Part II (© 1958 by The New York Times Company, reprinted by permission), November 2, 1958, pp. 52-3.*

The familiar Noah's Ark story becomes here a fresh listening experience in spontaneous verse that heightens the drama of the tale. The pictures, in amusing line with two-color wash, at the same time create an atmosphere of gaiety and humor. The rhymes are natural and the words flow in a happy Pied-Piperish sequence. . . . Interesting layout, with gray pages or portions of pages to indicate the raining world and white areas for the interior of the ark.

> *Virginia Haviland, "Christmas Booklist : 'The Animals and the Ark'," in* The Horn Book Magazine *(copyright, 1958, by the Horn Book, Inc., Boston), Vol. XXXIV, No. 6, December, 1958, p. 467.*

JUST LIKE EVERYONE ELSE   (1959)

A rather silly story about a child who is quite ordinary except that (we learn on the last page) he can fly. Or, perhaps, he only thinks he can fly. Small children are likely to greet this phenomenon with "Why, mommy?" or "How?" or just "Oh." Though the text isn't up to Miss Kuskin's standard, her pictures are as attractive as ever.

> *"Fiction Forecast: 'Just Like Everyone Else'," in* Publishers Weekly *(reprinted from the February 9, 1959 issue of* Publishers Weekly, *published by R. R. Bowker Company; copyright © 1959 by R. R. Bowker Company), Vol. 175, No. 6, February 9, 1959, p. 112.*

Although the idea [of Jonathan James being able to fly off to school] is absurd and the story lacking in incident this little book with its repetitive text, unpretentious drawings, and surprise ending will tickle many small children.

> *"Children's Books: 'Just Like Everyone Else'," in* The Booklist and Subscription Books Bulletin *(reprinted by permission of the American Library Association; copyright © 1959 by the American Library Association), Vol. 55, No. 18, May 15, 1959, p. 514.*

After her breezy jingles to tell the story of Noah, Karla Kuskin now tries a very brief prose tale decorated with her characteristic droll line drawings of scarlet. We follow Jonathan James who is "just like everybody else." . . . But just turn to the last page and watch your four-year-old as he sees how Jonathan James goes to school, not in any way like everybody else. We think he will laugh at the mild surprise. A slight but jolly little square book.

> *Margaret Sherwood Libby, "For Boys and Girls: 'Just Like Everyone Else'," in* New York Herald Tribune Book Review *(© I.H.T. Corporation; reprinted by permission), August 23, 1959, p. 9.*

WHICH HORSE IS WILLIAM? (1959)

The emotional power of recognition between those who love one another is portrayed with tender humor in this story of little William and his mother. Question: "Can you tell me from everyone else in the world?" "Certainly," mother replies as she places a pie in the oven. At this point William embarks on a little detective game in which the reader will participate, assuming the forms of various animals, challenging his mother to distinguish him from the others. In each case some detail gives him away—the only mouse with mittens, the only songbird who stands on his head, the only skunk with an ascot. Fun from cover to cover picking out the features which distinguish William in the gay illustrations. A delightful and pertinent fantasy. . . .

> *"Books for Young People: 'Which Horse is William?'" in* Virginia Kirkus' Service, *Vol. XXVII, No. 12, June 15, 1959, p. 399.*

There is much to intrigue and satisfy small children in this original picture book: the imaginative play between William and his mother, her delightful responses to his questions, the boldly drawn pictures which invite reader participation, and the sense of security derived from the knowledge that mothers always know their own children.

> *"Children's Books: 'Which Horse Is William?'" in* The Booklist and Subscription Books Bulletin *(reprinted by permission of the American Library Association; copyright ©1959 by the American Library Association), Vol. 56, No. 5, November 1, 1959, p. 161.*

When William tests his mother's knowledge of him by a series of fantasied transformations into familiar animals, she identifies him with happy ease. It is unfortunate that neither text nor pictures make the extent of the fantasy sufficiently clear. The book may be truly funny for five- and six-year-olds but there is the possibility that it will confuse the youngest listeners.

> *"Literal and Make Believe: 'Which Horse Is William?'" in* Saturday Review *(copyright © 1959 by Saturday Review; all rights reserved; reprinted by permission), Vol. XLII, No. 45, November 7, 1959, p. 62.*

SQUARE AS A HOUSE (1960)

An amusing little picture book with attractive stylized pictures and a text that makes a kind of game of teaching children a bit about various shapes and colors. Children over 5 or 6, however, will find it very elementary.

> *"Fiction Forecast: 'Square As a House'," in* Publishers Weekly *(reprinted from the March 7, 1960 issue of* Publishers Weekly, *published by R. R. Bowker Company; copyright © 1960 by R. R. Bowker Company), Vol. 177, No. 10, March 7, 1960, p. 65.*

Here's a better than ever book by that wonderful, rhythmical writer for the 4 to 8 set. . . . Even those younger will be captivated by the magic of imagining: "What would you choose if you were free, to be anything . . . that you wanted to be?" Children will take delight in considering each choice, dramatizing the possibilities—fat, thin, long, tall—square, soft, loud, small—and chiming in on the refrain: "Who would you, which would you, what would you be?" Both eye and ear catching,

this book rates with the author-artist's **"Roar and More"** as high among contenders for the top rank in current children's classics.

> *Ruth Moss Buck, "Who Would You Be?" in* Chicago Sunday Tribune, Magazine of Books *(© 1960 Chicago Tribune), May 8, 1960, p. 2.*

This alliterative performance, almost nonsensical, is too abstract to impress many readers or listeners. The illustrations, compared to this author-illustrator's previous work, seem routine.

> *George A. Woods, "The World Through Multi-Colored Magnifying Glasses: 'Square As a House'," in* The New York Times Book Review *(© 1960 by The New York Times Company; reprinted by permission), May 8, 1960, pp. 30-1.*

Admirers of last season's **"Which Horse Is William?"** are likely to like Mrs. Kuskin's new book, too. The idea may not be quite such fresh fun, but the pictorial presentation has a combination of boldness and delicacy—tiny lines, thick black strokes, little dabs of color, big fence-paint blocks—that may sharpen the responsiveness of the 4-8's to design even as they wonder about other things.

> *Rod Nordell, "The Artist Helps Tell What Things Are For: 'Square As a House'," in* The Christian Science Monitor *(reprinted by permission from* The Christian Science Monitor; *© 1960 The Christian Science Publishing Society; all rights reserved), May 12, 1960, p. 4B.*

THE BEAR WHO SAW THE SPRING (1961)

The illustrations in this simple picture book are, perhaps, the best that Mrs. Kuskin has ever done. . . . There are pages covered with beautiful patterns of leafy trees or bordered with charming bright colored birds and butterflies. The rhymed text, however, which is made up largely of conversation between a dog and a bear about the wonders of nature, is overlong and decidedly monotonous. The average four-year-old will probably not sit still with nothing to look at but patterns, however lovely, or half a dozen tiny spot drawings, while some 48 lines of rather awkward verse is read aloud to him.

> *"Juvenile Forecast: 'The Bear Who Saw the Spring'," in* Publishers Weekly *(reprinted from the May 1, 1961 issue of* Publishers Weekly, *published by R. R. Bowker Company; copyright © 1961 by R. R. Bowker Company), Vol. 179, No. 18, May 1, 1961, p. 55.*

The wonders of nature through winter, summer, spring and fall are taught to a young dog named Lou, and thus to the reader, by a bear who has been around. . . . Mrs. Kuskin's verses are pleasing, her illustrations are prettily decorous but the whole is a rather large lesson to take in during one or two sittings as Bear educates Lou. . . .

> *George A. Woods, "Sometimes the Picture's Half the Story: 'The Bear Who Saw the Spring'," in* The New York Times Book Review *(© 1961 by The New York Times Company; reprinted by permission), May 14, 1961, pp. 4, 35.**

Both pictures and rhyming text in this lovely big picture book share a simplicity, tenderness, and gentle humor that will captivate small children and make reading aloud a pleasure for adults.

> *Polly Goodwin, "The Junior Bookshelf: 'The Bear Who Saw the Spring'," in* Chicago Sunday Tribune, Magazine of Books *(© 1961 Chicago Tribune), August 13, 1961, p. 7.*

Although rather long for beginning reading or for reading aloud, this picture-book introduction to the four seasons has considerable appeal. . . . The colors in the illustrations change with the seasons, adding to the effectiveness of the book. Because of the length and a few instances of unnatural natural history, this is not as satisfactory a book as [that by Doris V.] Foster, *A pocketful of seasons*, but will appeal to Kuskin fans. (pp. 375-76)

> *"Easy and Picture Books: 'The Bear Who Saw the Spring'" (originally published under a different title in* The Booklist, *Vol. 57, No. 22, July 15, 1961), in* Books for Children: 1960-1965 *(copyright © 1960, 1961, 1962, 1963, 1964, 1965 by the American Library Association), American Library Association, 1966, pp. 375-76.*

ALEXANDER SOAMES: HIS POEMS   (1962)

Of course you're allowed to pronounce it *pomes,* How else would you rhyme it with *Soames*? And rhyme is important in this book, for Alexander Soames is a boy who can't talk without rhyming. But just let him rhyme, and he becomes voluble on any subject his patient and companionable mother may introduce. Cleverly wacky and gay, Soames' pomes will delight not only the 4-8's, but any grownup privileged to do the reading aloud.

> *Silence Buck Bellows, "Pomes and Poems: 'Alexander Soames'," in* The Christian Science Monitor *(reprinted by permission from* The Christian Science Monitor; *© 1962 The Christian Science Publishing Society; all rights reserved), November 15, 1962, p. B3.**

These attempts at nonsense verse only succeed in being smart-alecky. . . . Rhyming is poor, e.g., the word "poems" is made to rhyme with "Soames" throughout. Not recommended.

> *"Junior Books Appraised: 'Alexander Soames: His Poems'," in* School Library Journal, *an appendix to* Library Journal *(reprinted from the January, 1963 issue of* School Library Journal, *published by R. R. Bowker Co./A Xerox Corporation; copyright © 1963), Vol. 9, No. 5, January, 1963, p. 88.*

I am naturally predisposed to like a poet so unpretentious as to rhyme "Poems" with "Soames." Karla Kuskin's fantasy about a small boy who speaks only in rhymes is as amusing as its title's promise. These verses are good nonsense, light-hearted, swiftly paced. And who wouldn't abide by Alexander's "Rules," which include "Do not jump on ancient uncles. / Do not yell at average mice. / Do not wear a broom to breakfast. / Do not ask a snake's advice."

> *Ellen Lewis Buell, "For Younger Readers: 'Alexander Soames'," in* The New York Times Book Review *(© 1963 by The New York Times Company; reprinted by permission), May 5, 1963, p. 22.*

ALL SIZES OF NOISES   (1962)

If sounds of the city and the park, of climbing down stairs and munching toast can be translated visually, Karla Kuskin can do it. Her morning alarm is heard in big black letters, sending little John scurrying into the bathroom where the gurgles and gargles of washing are accomplished in quick order. Then on to breakfast and the blast, clank, grind of the city street. . . . Rhymes and "noises" sing out pleasantly for any youngster worth his salt in imagination.

> *"Books for Younger Readers: 'All Sizes of Noises'," in* Virginia Kirkus' Service, *Vol. XXX, No. 5, March 1, 1962, p. 233.*

Karla Kuskin has a way with words and a technique with type that make each page of this story a pleasant surprise. It is a gay rhyming account of the day of a boy and a dog. . . . Fans who rated her first published book "A" for originality and rhyme will welcome more in **"Roar and More"** manner.

> *Ruth Moss Buck, "Delightful Stories Made More So by Pictures: 'All Sizes of Noises'," in* Chicago Sunday Tribune: Magazine of Books *(© 1962 Chicago Tribune), May 13, 1962, p. 6.*

The device of oddly placed and outsize letters to convey sounds used so successfully in . . . **"Roar and More,"** is again employed in a new book dealing with the sounds of a child's day. The alternate pages are in startling contrast: first, precisely-drawn little scenes in various bright colors showing John asleep, John washing, John eating; then a page on which the sounds of the preceding scene are shown in huge and oddly placed lettering. Explanations are in rhyme. . . . Not as much fun as the first book but usable with young children to stimulate interest in noticing different sounds around them.

> *Margaret Sherwood Libby, "Boys and Girls: 'All Sizes of Noises'," in* Books—New York Herald Tribune *(© I.H.T. Corporation; reprinted by permission), July 29, 1962, p. 10.*

Love of language and special joy in poetry shine through the twenty-odd books Kuskin has written and illustrated. . . .

It is entirely clear from Kuskin's books that she knows what is worth saving and what is important to children. Her pictures and her verse and poetry are brimming over with the experiences of children growing up in a big city. (p. 935)

Her pictures and page decorations add a note of fun or an extension of the printed words. [*All Sizes of Noises*] shows this harmony between words and pictures vividly. In one picture, John sleeps in his bed, and his dog sleeps on a rug beside the bed; the verse on the opposite page tells how quiet the house is. The next double-spread contains fourteen letters, six inches tall and printed in bold black ink: BRRrrrmnnnggg. The visual suggestion of noise needs no explanation. Effect on boy and dog, Arf, is instantaneous both in verse and pictures. The following two pages present a strong blue background with white bubbles containing letters of different sizes for *gargle, slosh, scrub,* and *rub.* And as John dresses, Arf brings him his socks. Any child would love such assistance. (pp. 938-39)

> *Alvena Treut Burrows, "Profile: Karla Kuskin" (copyright © 1979 by the National Council of Teachers of English; reprinted by permission of the publisher and the author), in* Language Arts, *Vol. 56, No. 8, November-December, 1979, pp. 934-40.*

GRRRRRRRind   CLANK   DINDINDINDINDIN

"Hot enough for you?"   "Don't push"   "sure is"   bleepbleepbleepbleepbleepbleep   CLICKCLACKCLICKCLACK

HONNNNNNK   THUDthudTHUDthud   "WATCH OUT!"   Screeeeeeeeeeeeeeeeeeeechb u m p

                      "Ooops Sorry"   "Hello"   grrrrrRRRRRMMMMMM

"Hurryuphurryhurryup"

BLAST   BOOOOP   tootootoot BOOM toot   HONKHONK   carooooom

                SCREECH   toot CRASH

brrrrmmmmmmMMMMMM   grrrrrrrind   THUDthudTHUDthud
                                          RRRRRRRRRrrrrrr

"What a nice HAT BOOOOPboopboop   "I forgot my gloves"

CLONK   arf   "steptotherearofthebus"   bangbingbangbing   SLAM

From All Sizes of Noises, *written and illustrated by Karla Kuskin.*

ABCDEFGHIJKLMNOPQRSTUVWXYZ (1963)

[A variation of the ABC theme] is offered by Karla Kuskin in a little square book with stylized drawings, quaintly Victorian in flavor and reproduced in full color. Each letter in the time-honored fashion stands for an object beginning with that letter, then a rhyming couplet tells what that object likes: "A is for Ants. Ants like plants" (the picture shows ants swarming over plants that appear to be assorted zinnia and daisylike forms). The letters themselves, boldly drawn and each in a different style, are interesting as designs but a little confusing for the child, who also may be puzzled by the unusual words "pipers like vipers," "sages like pages," "Utes like buttes." However, an interested and appreciative adult can explain away the difficulties, and especially alert youngsters will enjoy the verbal oddities.

> *Margaret Sherwood Libby, "For Boys and Girls: 'ABCDEFGHIJKLMNOPQRSTUVWXYZ'," in* Book Week—New York Herald Tribune *(© 1963, The Washington Post), September 15, 1963, p. 24.*

["**ABCDEFGHIJKLMNOPQRSTUVWXYZ**"] presents the notion that words have friends: each letter stands for a word, and the word is accompanied by something it likes. "A is for ants / Ants like plants." So far so good. But some of the words get pretty esoteric when you consider the average age of a child learning his alphabet. Even grownups may need a dictionary to explain "U is for Utes / Utes like buttes." Visually, however, this tiny volume is a delight, with subtle color and exquisite drawings. Each letter is presented in a different style of calligraphy, which again makes a lovely sight, but might cause difficulties to a youngster just learning to distinguish one letter from another.

> *Alberta Eiseman, "Selections from the Picture Book Shelf: 'ABCDEFGHIJKLMNOPQRSTUVWXYZ'," in* The New York Times Book Review *(© 1963 by The New York Times Company; reprinted by permission), November 10, 1963, p. 51.*

An attractive variation on the usual single-object ABC book. Each letter here not only stands for something but has a further qualification because that something *likes* something else. . . . It has captivated one ex-kindergartner who has had school fun with rhyming words, although a few of the identifications were meaningless to him (e.g., "Utes like buttes"). A precise three- or four-color drawing illustrates each facing letter and couplet. The letters themselves will interest the careful examiner, for each is in a different style.

> *Virginia Haviland, "Christmas Booklist: 'ABCDEFGHIJKLMNOPQRSTUVWXYZ'," in* The Horn Book Magazine *(copyright © 1963, by the Horn Book, Inc., Boston), Vol. XXXIX, No. 6, December, 1963, p. 590.*

THE ROSE ON MY CAKE (1964)

A group of verses full of childlike humor and many with surprise endings. Although there is no unifying theme, all the verses describe a child's everyday experiences, both real and imaginary. This is not the author's best work, for at times the rhymes are uneven in quality and somewhat forced. This is also true of the delicate line drawings, for in spots the technique changes and their effectiveness is lost. This picture book is worthwhile, however, as an additional purchase for the apt humor so well exemplified in "**I Woke Up This Morning.**"

> *Harriet B. Quimby, "Junior Books Appraised: 'The Rose on My Cake'," in* Library Journal *(reprinted from* Library Journal, *July, 1964; published by R. R. Bowker Co. (a Xerox company); copyright © 1964 by Xerox Corporation), Vol. 89, No. 13, July, 1964, p. 2872.*

The author-artist again demonstrates her undeniable gift for turning the unspoken thoughts of childhood into affable, light-hearted poems and pictures. Her verses are of many moods, and there is plenty of wisdom along with the fun. Straight from a child's mind are lines like these: "I woke up this morning / At quarter past seven. / I kicked up the covers / And stuck out my toe. / And ever since then / (That's a quarter past seven) / They haven't said anything / Other than 'no.'" But there is also the tempered irony of "**William's Toys,**" the tender resignation of **"I Have a Lion,"** the tonal painting of **"The Witches' Ride"** and the daft nonsense of **"Hughbert and the Glue."** "The trouble with parties is / All of them end"'; unfortunately, so does this quite delightful book. But it will bear repeated reading.

> Ethel L. Heins, "Poetry: 'The Rose on My Cake'," in The Horn Book Magazine (copyright © 1964, by The Horn Book, Inc., Boston), Vol. XL, No. 4, August, 1964, p. 389.

[*The Rose on My Cake* is a] book of poems, illustrated with attractive drawings some of which are lightly humorous, all of which are lively. The poems are deft, some amusing, some ingenuous, some more profound than the others—yet not too sophisticated. A very pleasant book to read aloud. (pp. 56-7)

> Zena Sutherland, "New Titles for Children and Young People: 'The Rose on My Cake'," in Bulletin of the Center for Children's Books (reprinted by permission of The University of Chicago Press; copyright 1964 by the University of Chicago), Vol. 18, No. 4, December, 1964, pp. 56-7.

SAND AND SNOW (1965)

It's an immediate Northern juvenile quandry that gets a lot of discussion among small children—which is preferable? Summer or winter? The rhyme is clever and has great dignity as the stanza alternate between the satisfactions that Annabella Peach finds in masses of soft summer beach sand while her friend, Joseph J. Tempestossed, welcomes the extra clothing and the challenges that go with ice and snow. The illustrations are done in very clean lines, their near severity softened by their miniature size and the use of primary colors. The delicacy of sand and snow is suggested in the dotted marginal decorations. Small, handsome, quiet reading.

> "Books to Read Aloud: 'Sand and Snow'," in Virginia Kirkus' Service (copyright © 1965 Virginia Kirkus' Service, Inc.), Vol. XXXIII, No. 13, October 1, 1965, p. 1038.

Each new book by Karla Kuskin is a delight to the eye and the ear. Her poetry *must* be read aloud to be appreciated, and it bears repetition well. Unlike some of her previous works, such as **Alexander Soames: His Poems,** and *The Rose on My Cake,* this new book is really one long poem rather than a series of short ones. . . . Mrs. Kuskin's rhymes are fresh and her rhyme schemes are original. She contrasts such prosaic activities as getting dressed for winter with lovely descriptions of animals in a snowfall. The verses are light and will speak directly to a child's heart. The gay illustrations are bordered by a delicate frame of snowflakes or beach designs, and the warm oranges used for the sunny beach sections contrast with the blues of the winter pages. The world she shows is the world of childhood, for she has the gift of looking at things as children do. Though this seems like a slight book of verse at first glance, a re-reading preferably aloud, and a careful examination of the pictures, preferably with a child, reveal the charm of the complete book.

> Phyllis Cohen, "Sand and Snow," in Young Readers Review (copyright © 1966 Young Readers Review), Vol. II, No. 7, March, 1966, p. 15.

Sand and Snow is a good-humored little essay in phenomenology opposing the seasons by their characteristic substances, associating summer with passive femininity and winter with a more energetic imagery of boyhood. Mrs. Kuskin makes, for all the anodyne cuteness of her literal drawings, one or two literary observations that somewhat redeem her inability as an artist to suggest a difference in *feeling* between "grains of stone" and "numberless crystals" (sand and snow). . . .

Alas, to use her word, the verses are shaky and willing to sacrifice a rhythmic achievement to one of rhyme (which I am not at all certain very young children hear). Still, the ritual of dressing for the cold is given something of that twist by which we recognize a real experience. . . . And there is a mythological marriage of the elements at the end, when "two friends will race the windy beach / And watch snow / Snow on sand," which indicates that Mrs. Kuskin understands the need for an agent-scene ratio. Her difficulty is that she cannot, or in any case does not, dramatize it.

> Richard Howard, "What Comes Naturally," in Book Week—New York Herald Tribune (© 1966, The Washington Post), March 27, 1966, p. 14.*

JANE ANNE JUNE SPOON AND HER VERY ADVENTUROUS SEARCH FOR THE MOON (1966)

A read-'em-to-sleep bit of nonsense that soothes with the crooning sound of June, Spoon, Moon, to regular cadence and scratches the back of listener superiority with its mad assortment of adults and articulate animals gathered up by Jane Anne when she went looking for the moon in a series of unlikely places. Quiet fun and nicely, neatly cartooned in color.

> "Books to Read Aloud: 'Jane Anne June Spoon and Her Very Adventurous Search for the Moon'," in Virginia Kirkus' Service (copyright © 1966 Virginia Kirkus' Service, Inc.), Vol. XXXIV, No. 2, January 15, 1966, p. 55.

WATSON, THE SMARTEST DOG IN THE U.S.A. (1968)

Watson, the dog who reads, presents a terrible problem. How can I stop laughing at him long enough to write about him? It's awful! I just looked again at the first picture of him and of Huey Middle, the boy he lives with; I just reread the first page and I'm laughing so hard I can't hold the pen! I've *got* to stop! Copy's due by five o'clock! I know, I'll think about serious things. I can see the Time-Life building out the window. I'll think about Henry Luce. Maybe *Life* will run an editorial story on Watson titled "Watson—An Incentive to Reading." Watson *does* come to a *Life*-worthy conclusion. "Barkingly stated Watson, 'There's nothing like a good book.'" But the way he *looks* when he says it! Oh, I'm laughing again! I *can't* write about him. Sorry. You'll just have to work out the whole thing by yourself.

> "Children's Books: 'Watson, the Smartest Dog in the U.S.A.'," in Publishers Weekly (reprinted from the April 8, 1968 issue of Publishers Weekly, published by R. R. Bowker Company, a Xerox company; copyright © 1968 by Xerox Corporation), Vol. 193, No. 15, April 8, 1968, p. 51.

A pet whose pastime is reading, Watson lives each part; he gets so wrapped up in the story of a mean witch who imprisons a royal cowboy (the princess' favorite) that he bursts into tears and can't be consoled. "It's best to finish whatever you begin," advises the father of the family: that story within a story comes out all right and Watson comes out dancing. Patterns are deployed ingeniously in the illustrations and ingenuity is the chief attribute altogether—pawky amusement for the smart set.

> *"Picture Books: 'Watson, the Smartest Dog in the U.S.A.','"* in Kirkus Service *(copyright © 1968 The Kirkus Service, Inc.), Vol. XXXVI, No. 9, May 1, 1968, p. 508.*

A read-aloud story with nonsensical appeal and lively (but often distracting) illustrations. . . . Reading to his boy, Watson is carried away repeatedly by imagining himself each character in turn—a procedure that palls slightly with repetition.

> *Zena Sutherland, "New Titles for Children and Young People: 'Watson, the Smartest Dog in the U.S.A.','"* in Bulletin of the Center for Children's Books *(reprinted by permission of The University of Chicago Press; copyright 1968 by The University of Chicago), Vol. 22, No. 2, October, 1968, p. 30.*

Some young listeners may find the transitions between the main story and Watson's assumption of the many roles of the story-within-the-story confusingly abrupt, but all can enjoy the multicolored illustrations which delightfully reflect the humor of the text.

> *Dorothy Gunzenhauser, "The Book Review: 'Watson, the Smartest Dog in the U.S.A.','"* in School Library Journal, *an appendix to* Library Journal *(reprinted from the October, 1968 issue of* School Library Journal, *published by R. R. Bowker Co./A Xerox Corporation; copyright © 1968), Vol. 15, No. 2, October, 1968, p. 142.*

IN THE FLAKY FROSTY MORNING (1969)

The brief span of a snowman from mittened start ("They rolled cold snow together / and they built my bottom part") to "dwindle, / droop (and) snowman soup." You could call this evanescent too, especially since the pictures lack Mrs. Kuskin's usual snap.

From Watson, the Smartest Dog in the U.S.A., *written and illustrated by Karla Kuskin.*

> *"Picture Books: 'In the Flaky Frosty Morning','"* in Kirkus Reviews *(copyright © 1969 The Kirkus Service, Inc.), Vol. XXXVII, No. 3, February 1, 1969, p. 95.*

An agreeable narrative poem, told in first person by a snowman, that will help fill the demand for snow-season stories. . . . [This] book features pictures on each page that are large enough for group viewing. The rhymes, though unevenly successful, are for the most part satisfying, and the black, blue, and purple-pink pictures are uncluttered and crisp, paralleling the freshness of a winter day. Third graders can read this independently; preschoolers through second-graders will listen and look with pleasure, and will probably incorporate the last image, "snowman soup," into their winter play vocabulary.

> *Evelyn Stewart, "The Book Review: 'In the Flaky Frosty Morning','"* in School Library Journal, *an appendix to* Library Journal *(reprinted from the April, 1969 issue of* School Library Journal, *published by R. R. Bowker Co./A Xerox Corporation; copyright © 1969), Vol. 15, No. 8, April, 1969, p. 102.*

ANY ME I WANT TO BE: POEMS (1972)

Occasionally Karla Kuskin comes up with a phrase or a few that make you think it would have been worth her while to try harder—like "I rest / In my domed home / In the middle of a small sea. / Me." in the middle of a bland little chirp about a hatching bird. But despite the novel frames of reference (each poem is the first person statement of some everyday object or creature) most of the undisturbing sentiments expressed are as commonplace as their subjects. . . . However Kuskin's facile rhymes are always smooth ("One thing that you can say about roaring. / It is not boring. / And if rushing around the jungle being king / Is your kind of thing . . ."), and sometimes amusing ("Being a strawberry isn't all pleasing. / This morning they put me in ice cream. / I'm freezing"), and her pictures are comfortable and unassuming.

> *"Younger Non-Fiction: 'Any Me I Want to Be','"* in Kirkus Reviews *(copyright © 1972 The Kirkus Service, Inc.), Vol. XL, No. 18, September 15, 1972, p. 1103.*

The best ideas are often the simplest, and one of the simple—though by no means unprofound—ideas behind Karla Kuskin's sprightly new book of poems . . . is that children find it intriguing to imagine being someone or something else. . . .

The thirty author-illustrated poems in *Any Me I Want to Be* do not describe; instead, the poet has tried—and, with refreshing, edged but gentle humor and not an ounce of condescension, succeeded—"to get inside each subject and briefly be it." . . .

The subjects—and moods and pacing, too—range from a mirror to the moon. Along the way one becomes a dog (who, between arfs, growls, and barks, wonders how people can possibly manage on only two legs), a ruefully impatient clock, a highly individualistic leaf, a bird who makes up in song what he lacks in appearance, a sled who harbors death wishes against flowers, a happy baby ant, tired shoes, a dragon basking in the knowledge that children in fact do love him, a whale who masks his cautionary pragmatism with the rhetoric of Edward G. Robinson in *Little Caesar* ("I'm swimming around the sea, see / And the sea belongs to me, see"), a forlorn single mitten, a strawberry unhappily destined for ice cream, a grateful doll, a very stately tree, and an adventurous bicycle who is eager to zoom with its sneakered rider through fall leaves and be "off to anywhere": "Together we can see at least a million blocks." There is more than a touch of A. A. Milne here, and a bit of Edward Lear, and a bit of Ogden Nash. But mostly it is Karla Kuskin, who, as any of you might like to be, is fun, funny, and therefore wise.

> *"Books for Children: 'Any Me I Want to Be: Poems',"* in Saturday Review *(copyright © 1972 by* Saturday Review; *all rights reserved; reprinted by permission), Vol. LV, No. 42, October 14, 1972, p. 82.*

These riddles are of high quality: the language is simple yet musical ("I am a snake. / I snake alone / Through rushes and bushes / Past moss and stone."), evocative ("Come picture this lovely and frightening scene; / You're in the river just floating. / You're green.), or wistful ("What there is of me to see / Is short with feathers. / My eyes blink small."). The mild humor of the text is reinforced by the delicately detailed line and watercolor drawings, among which the tree, the lion in the forest and the crocodile lying in wait beneath a curtain of tropical lianas stand out. Children will delight in this book and pick it up again and again.

> *Daisy Kouzel, "The Book Review: 'Any Me I Want to Be: Poems',"* in School Library Journal, *an appendix to* Library Journal *(reprinted from the January, 1973 issue of* School Library Journal, *published by R. R. Bowker Co./A Xerox Corporation; copyright © 1973), Vol. 19, No. 1, January, 1973, p. 62.*

WHAT DID YOU BRING ME? (1973)

A platitudinous little morality tale in which Edwina Mouse who loves Things too much is switched by a witch with her mother, who then—as Edwina—puts on such a demonstration of temper and greed and willfulness that Edwina, in her mother's shoes, is moved to utter the magic words: "If only I could be myself again I would never ask for one thing more." So she is and she doesn't, and Kuskin's naively neat little pictures don't disguise the prescriptive banality.

> *"Picture Books: 'What Did You Bring Me?'"* in Kirkus Reviews *(copyright © 1973 The Kirkus Service, Inc.), Vol. XLI, No. 20, October 15, 1973, p. 1154.*

An amusing play on the problem of greed. . . . The story skims along at a light, brisk pace, and the freshness of the writing and pictures gives personality and appeal to what could easily have become just another mousy lesson.

> *Marilyn R. Singer, "The Book Review: 'What Did You Bring Me?'"* in School Library Journal, *an appendix to* Library Journal *(reprinted from the November, 1973 issue of* School Library Journal, *published by R. R. Bowker Co./A Xerox Corporation; copyright © 1973), Vol. 20, No. 3, November, 1973, p. 40.*

A BOY HAD A MOTHER WHO BOUGHT HIM A HAT (1975)

A cumulative nonsense story in verse, enhanced by a clean, modern format, has the timeless appeal of a traditional folk rhyme. The little boy's hat was such an instant success "[t]hat whatever he did / Or whatever he said / He wore his new hat /

From Any Me I Want to Be, *written and illustrated by Karla Kuskin.*

Which was woolly and red. / He stood in a wood / In his hat / On his head." His mother then bought him, one after the other, a mouse, new shoes, rubber boots, a pair of skis, a Halloween mask, a cello, and finally, an elephant, which was "not just a small one—a heavy, gray, tall one." Since the boy cannot bear to part, even momentarily, with any of his possessions, the sequence of events becomes increasingly ludicrous. The simple verses bowl along at an energetic pace—accompanied by handsomely composed pictures in tones of black, gray, and blue, punctuated with bright red. Literal-minded children may be dubious about the illustrations of the skis and of the Halloween mask, which do not, of course, show them to be yellow, as the text plainly states.

> *Ethel L. Heins, "Poetry: 'A Boy Who Had a Mother Who Bought Him a Hat',"* in The Horn Book Magazine *(copyright © 1976, by the Horn Book, Inc., Boston), Vol. LII, No. 6, December, 1976, p. 635.*

[What] is especially interesting about this book as a piece of bookmaking is the way the illustrations match the text: they are drawn as if they were in verse and are filled with visual equivalents of rhyme and rhythm.

The drawings are in color, but yellow and green are absent, giving the pages a cool, clean wintry look. And they are made cheerful and bright by the use of small touches of red, mostly for the eponymous hat.

> *Alvin Eisenman, " 'A Boy Had a Mother Who Bought Him a Hat','' in* Children's Book Showcase 1977, *Barbara Bader, Betty Binns, Alvin Eisenman, eds. (© 1977 The Children's Book Council, Inc.), Children's Book Council, 1977, p. 20.*

"Red as a rose and it kept off the snows" is the accompanying line to the title of this variation on "The House That Jack Built". . . . The familiar dactyls of the nursery rhyme original keep the story bouncing along, complete with repetitions that underline childhood's pride of possession. . . .

As always, there is much to praise in Kuskin's art—the delicate, thoughtful little details, the varied pacing, the skillful use of color, the fine attention to design. But for all the refinements of the art, the central idea—the absurd accumulation of goods by one small individual—somehow goes by the way side; there's no sense of the preposterous, of build-up, or of anticipation. The idea of wearing jeans, boots, skis and a mask just isn't that funny. What emerges is a fragile joke tastefully told and executed with expertise, but one that doesn't quite come off.

> *Ann Sperber, "For Young Readers: 'A Boy Had a Mother Who Bought Him a Hat','' in* The New York Times Book Review *(©1977 by The New York Times Company; reprinted by permission), February 27, 1977, p. 12.*

NEAR THE WINDOW TREE: POEMS AND NOTES   (1975)

Kuskin explains at the start that when she reads her poems in schools children often ask her where she gets her ideas, and this is an attempt to show how the inspiration for poetry is anywhere you are. Here then is a series of short, superficially autobiographical paragraphs describing the author's chair near her window, her tree, her cats, her summer at camp, her children's habits, toys and coats, etc.—with each paragraph followed by a verse to show how the experience has been turned into poetry. The examples, both playful . . . and pensive . . . could certainly succeed in convincing children that poetry is accessible and that it can be related to everyday life—provided that you are willing to call this poetry. But if you bring the two together by taking the poetry out of the lines rather than putting it into everyday life, the point hardly seems worth making.

> *"Younger Non-Fiction: 'Near the Window Tree','' in* Kirkus Review *(copyright © 1975 The Kirkus Service, Inc.), Vol. XLIII, No. 8, April 15, 1975, p. 462.*

If you write poetry yourself, don't miss **"Near the Window Tree."** . . . To each of her poems [Karla Kuskin] adds a note telling how the poem began. Nothing pedantic, only encouragement for young readers to try their own. The poems are clear, simple and musical enough to stick in your head after the first reading.

> *Nancy Willard, " 'Near the Window Tree','' in* The New York Times Book Review *(© 1975 by The New*

So then she went out and she bought him a mouse.
Sniffing and squeaking and seeking and peeking.

He loved it so much
That whatever he did
Or whatever he said
When dressed in his hat
Which was woolly and red

He included his mouse
And he built it a small,
Very comfortable house
Which he painted sky blue.
He went to a party.
The mouse went there too.

From A Boy Had a Mother Who Bought Him a Hat, *written and illustrated by Karla Kuskin.*

York Times Company; reprinted by permission), May 4, 1975, p. 24.

Kuskin states in the beginning of her introduction: "Encourage children to read [and then] write poetry . . . [thus] they will be encouraged to reach into themselves and articulate feelings and dreams." . . .

Kuskin follows the introduction with alternating pages of text explaining the birth of the poem she is presenting. The texts of both prose and poetry are exemplified by her own pen and ink drawings in black and white. . . . Kuskin's book can lead a child to envisioning any kind of poem. If a librarian believes with teachers that a love of literature (including poetry) must begin with the very small child then this book should be selected by school media people as well as librarians in children's rooms of public libraries with the idea that it needs introducing to most children with follow-up of children's activities (skillfully handled) being imperative. Knowledgeable parents could, also, buy this book for their own children. (p. 29)

Alice Smith, "Children's Reference Books: 'Near the Window Tree'," in Reference Services Review *(© 1975 by The Pierian Press, Inc.), Vol. 3, Nos. 3 & 4, July-December, 1975, pp. 29-31.*

These poems have all the variety, disarming imagery, and seeming simplicity of the poet's *A Rose on My Cake* . . . and more. Kuskin has a child's eye view of the world plus an enchanting ability to interpret everyday things in fresh and truly poetic terms meaningful to young children. . . . The book also features notes preceding each group of poems—memories and glimpses of how the poems came to be written—which encourage children to write down their own thoughts and make the poet accessible as a confiding friend and not a remote grownup with unattainable talents. This is a must for all children interested in poetry—and that includes all children. (pp. 64-5)

Lynn Bradley, "The Book Review: 'Near the Window Tree'," in School Library Journal *(reprinted from the November, 1975 issue of* School Library Journal, *published by R. R. Bowker Co./A Xerox Corporation; copyright © 1975), Vol. 22, No. 3, November, 1975, pp. 64-5.*

A SPACE STORY   (1978)

Both elements suffer in this attempt to combine a quiet, secure nighttime mood piece with a simple description of the solar system. The sudden shift from peaceful night to the fiery sun breaks the mood, and the information on the solar system is so scant and oversimplified that the outdated number of Jupiter's moons given is painfully obtrusive. . . . Readers would do better to go to [Astrid] Lindgren's *The Tomten* (Coward, 1961) for a night mood book and, for a picture of the solar system, to [Franklyn Mansfield] Branley's *A Book of Planets for You* (Crowell, rev. ed. 1966), which is not current but still contains a higher percentage of accepted figures than Kuskin.

Margaret L. Chatham, "The Book Review: 'A Space Story'," in School Library Journal *(reprinted from the December, 1978 issue of* School Library Journal, *published by R. R. Bowker Co./A Xerox Corporation; copyright © 1978), Vol. 25, No. 4, December, 1978, p. 45.*

Karla Kuskin's *A Space Story* . . . mixes the wandering spirit of science fiction with the unalterable facts of astronomy. Gazing at a night full of stars, Sam asks his mother what kind of people could possibly live out there. Galaxies away, another boy gazes out a different sky and wonders what kind of people could possibly live out there. Meantime, the planets silently whirl and the stars blaze and die. . . . Karla Kuskin's poetic narrative has the concentration of an odyssey compressed to the size of a parable.

Stefan Kanfer, "A Rainbow of Colorful Reading: 'A Space Story'," in Time *(copyright 1978 Time Inc.; all rights reserved; reprinted by permission from* Time*), Vol. 112, No. 23, December 4, 1978, p. 101.*

The book answers very clearly some fundamental questions concerning our solar system. The sun and each planet are described in terms understandable to a child aged 6-8, and the differences between our Earth and the other worlds are always emphasized. . . . [The] writing style [is] rhythmic as well as informational.

Ethna Sheehan, "Truth Wrapt in Tales: 'A Space Story'," in America *(© America Press, 1978; all rights reserved), Vol. 139, No. 19, December 9, 1978, p. 440.*

Kuskin has written a space story to introduce young readers to the sun and planets. . . . [The] book's content is an enigma. . . . There are several problems with this book. There is no distinction made between the factual information and the speculation about life elsewhere, leaving young readers with the impression that life does exist elsewhere exactly like life on earth. Some of the information about the sun and planets is beyond the comprehension of this age level, and there is no distinction made between stars, planets and moons. It seems the author has oversimplified information to a degree that makes it either obscure or meaningless.

Esther Fagan, "Children's Books: 'A Space Story'," in American Association for Advancement of Science, *Vol. XV, No. 3, December, 1979, p. 164.*

HERBERT HATED BEING SMALL   (1979)

Herbert isn't so small. It's just that everyone else in Loomington is much taller. And Philomel isn't so tall. It's just that everyone else in Littleville is much shorter. Prompted by the misery of their respective situations, each packs candy and a favorite bear and heads for "the world out there." Herb, climbing up the hill, meets Phil climbing down. What a relief to discover they're both the same size! . . . Kuskin's rhyming text is always playful and for the most part nimble, but it occasionally stumbles over its own intricacy, e.g., "Now that was certainly a sight / well calculated to ignite excitement / and invite delight." Her illustrations are bright and clean lined, in a plain, appealing style.

Yvette Tetrault, "The Book Review: 'Herbert Hated Being Small'," in School Library Journal *(reprinted from the October, 1979 issue of* School Library Journal, *published by R. R. Bowker Co./A Xerox Corporation; copyright © 1979), Vol. 26, No. 2, October, 1979, p. 142.*

The illustrations, washed over in shades of red and green, are clear and uncluttered but ordinary. It's a pleasant, sprightly story that makes a nice point.

Marilyn Kaye, *"Children's Books: 'Herbert Hated Being Small','" in* Booklist *(reprinted by permission of the American Library Association; copyright © 1979 by the American Library Association), Vol. 76, No. 3, October 1, 1979, p. 279.*

When a child wonders about size—Am I big for my age? Or too small? Will I always be short? Or too tall?—there can be no more elegant and reassuring self-help book than [*Herbert Hated Being Small.*] . . . Everything is relative, observes this cascade of wise rhymes. Einstein would have been pleased. (pp. 99-100)

Stefan Kanfer, *"Books: A Child's Portion of Good Reading," in* Time *(copyright 1979 Time Inc.; all rights reserved; reprinted by permission from* Time*), Vol. 114, No. 23, December 3, 1979, pp. 99-100.*

DOGS AND DRAGONS, TREES AND DREAMS: A COLLECTION OF POEMS (1980)

Kuskin arranges some of her previously published verses to illustrate the simple lesson in poetics with which they are interspersed. But the verses could make their points as well without these direct instructions to listen to the sounds of the words, compare them to colors in a painting, or whatever. In fact the second entry, **"Take a Word Like Cat,"** is a poem about writing a poem, and perhaps, in itself, the most successful example in the volume. All too often, though, holding them up as examples only shows up the verses' essential vapidity. The occasional touch of mild humor might amuse, but one can only express dismay at the prospect of classrooms full of children being taught to emulate such pale shades of poetry.

"Younger Fiction: 'Dogs and Dragons, Trees and Dreams: A Collection of Poems'," in Kirkus Reviews *(copyright © 1981 The Kirkus Service, Inc.), Vol. XLIX, No. 3, February 1, 1981, p. 143.*

Kuskin's stated purpose in *Dogs & Dragons,* beyond delighting children with her own charmingly illustrated verses, is to encourage young readers to write poetry. "No imagination is freer than a child's, no eye is sharper," she writes in her introduction. As for ear, the one with me since childhood—tuned to the cadence of speech or rhythm of song, to assonance, consonance, rhyme—is satisfied by Kuskin's poems. Her appealing ideas, her quirky observations of nature and her original juxtapositions of the ordinary and the bizarre strike chords of memory—mostly happy, occasionally melancholy—echoing for me now as a chant or a chime.

Variety, wit and unfailing sensitivity mark the words and drawings through which Kuskin addresses children. Her subjects are trumpets, turnips, witches, glue, parties, gray days, snakes and yarn. She instructs not by assignment but by suggestion and example. Above about half the poems is an elementary observation or two on her own writing of them. . . .

A vivid poem about a black night with a white moon is prefaced by the observation that words are like colors put together with care to make a painting. A poem that surprised the poet and "wrote itself" begins "Write about a radish. / Too many people write about the moon." We are reminded that rhythm alone may be strong enough to hold a poem together, as in [her] poignant, unrhymed evocation of the wind. . . .

Kuskin may not be the best poet who passes her craft on to children (in case you play "Botticelli," his initials are also KK—Kenneth Koch), but *Dogs & Dragons, Trees & Dreams* works nicely. (p. 10)

Rose Styron, *"A Pocketful of Rhyme: 'Dogs and Dragons, Trees and Dreams'," in* Book World— The Washington Post *(© 1981, The Washington Post), March 8, 1981, pp. 10-11.**

Newly illustrated by the author with brisk, usually small, line drawings, this collection of her poems, previously published and culled by Kuskin, is designed, she points out in an introduction, to introduce children to poetry. Therefore, throughout the book—but not for every poem—there are italicized comments or suggestions. . . . The comments don't add much, although adults who need help in encouraging children's enjoyment of poetry may find some of the comments useful; the poems are deft and pleasant, but since all are readily available, this seems a regrouping useful primarily if there are specific collection needs.

Zena Sutherland, *"New Titles for Children and Young People: 'Dogs and Dragons, Trees and Dreams: A Collection of Poems'," in* Bulletin of the Center for Children's Books *(reprinted by permission of The University of Chicago Press; © 1981 by The University of Chicago), Vol. 34, No. 9, May, 1981, p. 174.*

NIGHT AGAIN (1981)

Kuskin sets a quiet, contented bedtime mood in a few small words that bring out the comfortable regularity of the routine and the links between nighttime inside and outside the little boy's bedroom. The link is first made in connection with the stuffed bears on his bed: "Here we go / into our lairs. / You have yours / they have theirs / in the woods / where the night rains begin." Later, after the boy is tucked in and left alone, "Lights from cars / wash the wall. . . ." The images are a little rundown, a little soft, but it's all low-keyed and pleasantly calming.

"Picture Books: 'Night Again'," in Kirkus Reviews *(copyright ©1981 The Kirkus Service, Inc.), Vol. XLIX, No. 8, April 15, 1981, p. 500.*

[*Night Again*] shows every sign of scrupulous attention: the diminutive size of the book, the uniform circular shape of the pictures, the soft blues and yellows, the carefully elliptical chanting text ("Here we go / bed again . . .), carefully paced and laid out opposite the illustrations of a little boy's nighttime routine—these all could have made a distinguished children's book. But unfortunately neither the words nor the pictures have the charm or evocative power they aspire to. The pictures have a sameness of scale and tone, and the words seem more anxious to keep in step than to communicate any genuine thoughts and feelings; they certainly don't achieve a cumulative poetic effect. The whole project seems fatally haunted by the ghost of Margaret Wise Brown's magnificent and now classic nighttime story "Goodnight Moon." **"Night Again"** is a disappointment, despite its evident intelligence, taste and good intentions. (p. 71)

Harold C.K. Rice, *"The Subject Is Night," in* The New York Times Book Review *(© 1981 by The New York Times Company; reprinted by permission), April 26, 1981, pp. 51, 71.**

From ascent of the stairs at bedtime to cozy sleep, tucked in with toy and a confident "Wake me soon!", vignetted images employ line drawings in three colors against darkish blue pages. . . . The text, a poem, has more in common with [Margaret Wise] Brown's *A Child's Goodnight Book* (Addison-Wesley, 1943) than with *Goodnight Moon* (Harper, 1947). Almost atavistically, it recalls the goodnight books of the 1940s and 50s; an interesting revival.

Joan W. Blos, "Book Reviews: 'Night Again'," in School Library Journal *(reprinted from the May, 1981 issue of* School Library Journal, *published by R. R. Bowker Co./A Xerox Corporation; copyright © 1981),* Vol. 27, No. 9, May, 1981, p. 57.

Jean Little

1932-

(Real name Flora Jean Little) Canadian author of fiction and poetry for children. In each of her books, Little attempts to deal with childhood problems optimistically. Her subjects include physical handicaps, mental retardation, compulsive lying, and coping with death. She writes realistically and forcefully without overt sentimentality, drawing upon her own experience: she is a teacher of motor-impaired children and has only partial sight. Although many of Little's protagonists have physical disabilities, her themes focus on the strengths and weaknesses of the inner personality, not the outward obstacles. Little does not end her books with miracle cures, although at times she has been charged with solving problems too neatly. One of her main objectives in writing is to guide children toward self-discovery. One of the central preoccupations in her books is the interpersonal relationships of her protagonists with both peers and adults. In each story there are tense family situations with which the troubled child must also contend.

Most of Little's characters confront problems caused by the psychological frailties and imperfections in their friends, their families, and in themselves. They also inevitably encounter learning experiences and insight into personal strength of character. She wrote her first book, *Mine for Keeps*, when she realized the lack of handicapped protagonists in children's fiction. This book is praised for its sensitivity, realistic conclusion, and for allowing the physical disability to recede into the background of the story. In *From Anna* and its sequel *Listen for the Singing*, Little presents the hindrances caused by partial and total blindness, but she also focuses on the political atmosphere of Canada and the normal struggles of childhood. A complaint that recurs in many critiques of Little's books is that forced moralizing often makes her situations seem contrived and strained. This aspect has brought disapproval from reviewers who classify her works as bibliotherapy rather than literature. It is generally agreed, however, that Little is adept at establishing characters quickly and effectively, and that her dialogue is convincing and natural. She receives praise for the emotional tone of her books, her sensitivity, and her insight into the personalities of the characters. Little won the 1961 Canadian Children's Book Award for *Mine for Keeps*, and the Vicky Metcalf Award in 1974 for a body of work inspirational to Canadian children. (See also *Contemporary Authors*, Vols. 21-24, rev. ed., and *Something about the Author*, Vol. 2.)

GENERAL COMMENTARY

City life and modern family life in particular form a basis for the books by Jean Little. Since they were written for therapeutic purposes, they have little in common with the traditional stories of child and family life that extol the innocence, fun, and gaiety of childhood. Miss Little's children do not live in Kenneth Grahame's 'golden age' but face serious problems of adjustment. In *Mine for Keeps* . . . a child crippled by cerebral palsy learns to adjust to normal family and school life; in *Home from Far* . . . the accidental death of the eldest son in the family and the resulting disturbance to his twin sister lead the parents to offer a home to two foster children. These books have no

Courtesy of Jean Little

stories as such but concentrate on a problem to the extent that they might well fall within the realm of bibliotherapy—'guidance in the solution of personal problems through directed reading'. If this is indeed their purpose they are in a sense beyond the range of literary criticism. If, on the other hand, they are intended as 'heartwarming' stories that give children an insight into the problems of others, they can be justly criticized for contrived situations, quick and easy solutions, and the intimation that problems of magnitude can be solved completely. (pp. 186-87)

> *Sheila Egoff, "And All the Rest: Stories," in her* The Republic of Childhood: A Critical Guide to Canadian Children's Literature in English *(© Oxford University Press, Canadian Branch, 1975; reprinted by permission), Oxford University Press, Canadian Branch, 1975, pp. 161-206.**

Nowadays, children learning to cope with physical or mental handicaps are central to the themes of many children's books. Many of Jean's books have been in the vanguard of this relatively recent movement, dealing forthrightly but sensitively with such problems as cerebral palsy (*Mine for Keeps*), mental retardation (*Take Wing*), and partial sightedness and blindness (*From Anna* and its sequel, *Listen for the Singing*), in a way that makes such differences "natural and comprehensible" to

146

the young reader. . . . In other novels she explores the lives of children facing psychological handicaps or problems—lying (*One to Grow On*), being a shy and withdrawn only child (*Look Through My Window*), or just social and ethnic difference (*Kate*). Jean Little's characters may have the same handicaps at the end of a book as they do at the beginning, but there is this difference: they have grappled with and conquered the real disabilities—fear, for example (*Stand in the Wind*), or resentment (*Spring Begins in March*), or self-centeredness (*Home from Far*), or self-pity and resignation (*Listen for the Singing*). For ultimately, that is the real thrust of Jean Little's novels—recognizing and mastering the enemy within rather than tilting at the one without. (p. 89)

The measure of worth of a child's book, Jean Little believes, is in fact its capacity to enable its reader to grow. For this reason, because the child's first and most important social context is his or her family, Jean writes essentially what is called "the family novel." That is, the action of the Little novels is played out in the milieu of the family, both natural and adopted, where Jean's main focus is the child's interpersonal relationships. Here she explores, in turn: the complexities of sibling relationships . . . ; the trials and joys of the extended family . . . ; and the conflicts between child and adult that are part and parcel of every growing up. After family, friendship is the other dimension of social relationships that all the Little novels probe in depth—friendship between children and adults as well as between children, making friends, breaking friends, losing friends, finding friends. (pp. 89-90)

What she strives for in her own writing is not realism so much as truth; not a cataloguing of the exterior world of circumstances and events but, rather, a sensitive, perceptive portrayal of the inner realms of experience, feeling, and thought—for example, a family's grief over a death, and their courage in overcoming it (*Home from Far*); a child's discovery of and coming to terms with her roots (*Kate*); the agonies and ecstasies of friendship (*Take Wing*). In this way, her books have a power to extend and enrich experience; to touch and, by touching, to enlarge the capacity for feeling. From all this comes the quality of vision that Jean Little's books bring to the reading child. (p. 90)

> *Meguido Zola, "Profile: Jean Little" (copyright © 1981 by the National Council of Teachers of English; reprinted by permission of the publisher and the author), in* Language Arts, *Vol. 58, No. 1, January, 1981, pp. 86-92.*

MINE FOR KEEPS   (1962)

[*Mine for Keeps* is an] unusual story, deeply moving but with no sentimentality. Sally, who has been living for five years at a school for handicapped children, comes home to face the problems of family life and attendance at the local school. . . . One of the most valuable aspects of the book is in the depiction of Sally's family: they are real people, who try to help, but who make mistakes and lose their tempers. All of the handling of the difficulties of a child who has cerebral palsy is matter-of-fact; the handicap recedes into a background fact that simply gives validity to a lively and satisfying story. (pp. 11-12)

> *Zena Sutherland, "New Titles for Children and Young People: 'Mine for Keeps'," in* Bulletin of the Center for Children's Books *(reprinted by permission of The University of Chicago Press; copyright 1962 by the University of Chicago), Vol. XVI, No. 1, September, 1962, pp. 11-12.*

In the nineteenth century many children's books had their invalids and long scenes in a sick-room. Too often there the story ended in tears, though sometimes there was a joyous recovery. . . . But very seldom had a heroine to live with an illness for life as does Sally Copeland in *Mine for Keeps*. . . . The story is told without sentimentality and has a style of simplicity and distinction. There are many details of daily life which add to the reader's knowledge of children's lives in Canada, and Sally, her family, and her friends are all well rounded characters. (pp. 170-71)

> *"For Children from Ten to Fourteen: 'Mine for Keeps'," in* The Junior Bookshelf, *Vol. 28, No. 3, July, 1964, pp. 170-71.*

HOME FROM FAR   (1965)

[*Home from Far* is a] good family story with unusual facets, since the Macgregors are not only adjusting to the death of one of the children but also to the advent of two foster-children. . . . Sensitive and percipient, the author has written a beautifully balanced story: there is, for example, the candid picture of the difference in the adaptability of the two foster children.

> *Zena Sutherland, "New Titles for Children and Young People: 'Home from Far'," in* Bulletin of the Center for Children's Books *(reprinted by permission of The University of Chicago Press; copyright 1965 by the University of Chicago), Vol. XVIII, No. 10, June, 1965, p. 152.*

The author's gift for characterization and her skill at making people live save this from impossible melodrama. It would have been excellent if only some of the problems had been left unsolved. Life is not so easily tied in neat packets.

> *Anne Izard, "Junior Books Appraised: 'Home from Far'," in* Library Journal *(reprinted from* Library Journal, *June 15, 1965; published by R. R. Bowker Co. (a Xerox company); copyright © 1965 by Xerox Corporation), Vol. 90, No. 12, June 15, 1965, p. 2886.*

Each child is a real individual, the dialogue is natural and amusing, and the values are wholesome. Mrs. Macgregor's lecture to Jenny and Mike after they had played a cruel trick on a younger brother reveals the kind of relationships which the parents attempt to build within the family. . . . This is a family in which parents do not abdicate when faced with problems, but who apply firmness with affection to guide their children toward self-understanding and sound values.

> *Elizabeth D. Hodges, "Damsels in Distress," in* Book Week—New York Herald Tribune *(© 1965, The Washington Post), July 25, 1965, p. 16.**

Dramatic and moving are the reactions and adjustments of children and parents. And family adventures that start out hopefully often end in near tragedy. So individual and real are the characters that everything happening to them is of vital importance to the reader; seldom is every member of a storybook family so completely realized. Absorbing from beginning to end, the book is deeply satisfying.

> *Ruth Hill Viguers, "Stories for the Middle Years: 'Home from Far'," in* The Horn Book Magazine *(copyright © 1965, by The Horn Book, Inc., Boston), Vol. XLI, No. 4, August, 1965, p. 387.*

[Jean Little] evidently writes out of her own knowledge of how to cope with tragic loss. [*Home from Far*] comes to the verge of being bibliotherapy, but because of its catharsis goes far deeper and is of the tragic sense of life, probing artistically the ever-recurrent question of how to cope with loss.

For Jenny, the tragic heroine of *Home from Far,* peace comes when she learns to look outward rather than inward and to understand that others beside Michael need her love. In this reciprocity, she finds a necessary balance that brings her home from far—home to the living, instead of far away with one who can no longer be a part of her life except in memory. But the beauty of the story lies in the idea that memory need not be erased, but rather furbished and cherished. (p. 134)

> Carolyn T. Kingston, ''The Tragic Moment: Loss,'' *in her* The Tragic Mode in Children's Literature *(© 1974 by Teachers College, Columbia University; reprinted by permission of the publisher), New York: Teachers College Press, 1974, pp. 124-167.*

SPRING BEGINS IN MARCH (1966)

The problems of the older generation in an active, crowded household and of a physically handicapped sister are handled with good-natured honesty [in *Spring Begins in March*]. And the unity of a family behind one of its members needing extra love shines through the petulant thinking of the child who struggles and finally finds herself.

> Barbara S. McCauley, ''Coping and Muddling,'' in The Christian Science Monitor *(reprinted by permission from* The Christian Science Monitor; © 1966 The Christian Science Publishing Society; all rights reserved), November 3, 1966, p. B8.

The characters are completely alive, as Miss Little's book people invariably are, and though Meg can often be so tiresome that she tries even the reader's patience, she can also be very engaging. And those who remember the torments of being eleven, as well as those in the midst of experiencing them, will sympathize with her.

> Ruth Hill Viguers, ''Stories for the Middle Years: 'Spring Begins in March','' in The Horn Book Magazine *(copyright © 1966, by The Horn Book, Inc., Boston), Vol. XLII, No. 6, December, 1966, p. 717.*

Meg, the little sister in *Mine For Keeps,* reappears as the heroine of this book. She has grown older and has her own problem of under-achievement in school. Vigor, humor, and compassion characterize this book, which, like others by the author, has a message but is, primarily, a good story which children will read eagerly. Many little girls will identify with Meg as she daydreams about herself in wildly successful situations.

> Gertrude B. Herman, ''Junior Books Appraised: 'Spring Begins in March','' in School Library Journal, *an appendix to* Library Journal *(reprinted from the December, 1966 issue of* School Library Journal, *published by R. R. Bowker Co./ A Xerox Corporation; copyright © 1966), Vol. 13, No. 4, December, 1966, p. 56.*

[*Spring Begins in March*] is all a little too tidy. The characters are wooden and unreal, and all have a lesson to teach, including the dog! Parts of the narrative read like a social worker's casebook. Even a Victorian child wouldn't have found this palatable!

Miss Little has an easy, readable style entirely lacking in self-consciousness. She obviously loves dogs and is at her best when writing about them. It is unfortunate that she seems to ascribe only therapeutic reasons for their presence in her books. (pp. 35-6)

> Callie Israel, ''Reviews: 'Spring Begins in March','' in In Review: Canadian Books for Children, *Winter, 1967, pp. 35-6.*

WHEN THE PIE WAS OPENED (1968)

Although they may enjoy the rhythmic, singing quality of Jean Little's poetry, children will find her subject matter almost totally dull and alien. Writing primarily in the ballad form (replete with forced rhymes), she moves from pseudo-philosophical discussions of romantic love to a visit from her sister to her father's death and sentimentally on and on. The sections dealing with dogs and family life at first glance seem more relevant, but the former is as sticky as a dog's kiss, the latter as obvious as a sermon. Although a poem will occasionally flash a well-conceived image, most of the lines are totally unimaginative, and dominated by a feeble, moralistic attempt at universality. Here's a pie that's far better left unopened.

> ''Older Non-Fiction: 'When the Pie Was Opened','' in Kirkus Service *(copyright © 1968 Virginia Kirkus' Service, Inc.), Vol. XXXVI, No. 3, February 1, 1968, p. 127.*

[*When the Pie Was Opened*] should be appealing to young readers because the compiler deemed it best to speak these particular messages through verse. Some of her favorite lyrics will be favorites also among her readers, for they are an expression of her many feelings and delights, shared by many who have felt the same but felt inadequate and incapable of expressing themselves thus. (pp. 466-67)

> ''Young People's Books: 'When the Pie Was Opened','' in Best Sellers *(copyright 1968, by the University of Scranton), Vol. 27, No. 23, March 1, 1968, pp. 466-67.*

I thoroughly enjoyed these poems and feel that Miss Little has achieved her best success so far in them.

She captures many different moods in this collection, from the twelve-year-old trying on dresses to the senile old woman, running the gamut from happiness to sadness. The author nicely varies her style to create these impressions. She uses many different rhyme schemes and actually paints pictures by her choice of words. . . .

The poems contain quite a variety of choice for the reader; however, I do feel that they would not appeal to boys at all, but only to girls who can identify with the themes.

> Pat Exell, ''Reviews: 'When the Pie Was Opened','' in In Review: Canadian Books for Children, *Vol. 2, No. 4, Autumn, 1968, p. 13.*

TAKE WING (1968)

Laurel had always had a special love for her brother James, had always tried to hide her fear that he was not quite normal, and had always protected him. . . . Not until a series of small crises, during mother's absence, did shy Laurel dare to talk to her father about a medical examination, and only after it proved that James was mentally retarded but educable did Laurel acknowledge that she had coddled her brother. There are several other themes to give the story balance: Laurel's shyness causes her trouble in making friends and also in accepting, with composure, a role in a school play. The ending is satisfying, with some problems solved but no occurrence of miracles; the book's only contrived aspect is that the girl with whom Laurel has been hoping to become friends also has a retarded sibling, an older sister.

> Zena Sutherland, "New Titles for Children and Young People: 'Take Wing'," in Bulletin of the Center for Children's Books (reprinted by permission of The University of Chicago Press; copyright 1968 by The University of Chicago), Vol. 22, No. 2, October, 1968, p. 31.

[With Take Wing the] author has written an absorbing story that is a thoroughly realistic treatment of a too common situation in which parents ignore reality to the detriment of the whole family. Recommended reading for parents and teachers as well as for young people. (p. 565)

> Diane Farrell, "Stories for Older Boys and Girls: 'Take Wing'," in The Horn Book Magazine (copyright © 1968 by The Horn Book, Inc., Boston), Vol. XLIV, No. 5, October, 1968, pp. 564-65.

Jean Little's earlier stories revealed exceptional understanding of children with handicaps and their relations with family and friends. In [Take Wing] the author takes up with insight and compassion the problem of a mentally retarded boy. . . .

This is a meaningful and engrossing story. All the characters are believable and win one's whole concern. At story's close it is good to know that hope is held out for James and that Laurel finds friendship through "the courage to take wing."

> Polly Goodwin, "Children's Book World: 'Take Wing'," in Book World—Chicago Tribune (© 1968 Postrib Corp.; reprinted by permission of Chicago Tribune and The Washington Post), October 20, 1968, p. 14.

[Take Wing is a] well-written, realistic novel with strong characterizations. . . . Laurel's attempts at forming friendships fail until the end of the book, when she discovers that Barbara, the girl she has been trying to become close to, has a retarded sister. A similar bond becomes a basis for friendship—an unfortunate contrivance which is, however, redeemed by generally good plot and character development.

> Trevelyn Jones, "Grades 3-6: 'Take Wing'," in School Library Journal, an appendix to Library Journal (reprinted from the January, 1969 issue of School Library Journal, published by R. R. Bowker Co./A Xerox Corporation; copyright © 1969), Vol. 15, No. 5, January, 1969, p. 74.

ONE TO GROW ON (1969)

Janie Chisholm had developed a habit of lying, or call it prevarication, and this worried her parents and brought ridicule from her brothers and sisters. . . . The author has written many good books for young people and this can be listed high among them as easy to read and conveying (painlessly) an important message.

> "Young People's Books: 'One to Grow On'," in Best Sellers (copyright 1969, by the University of Scranton), Vol. 29, No. 3, May 1, 1969, p. 57.

Jean Little's **"One to Grow On"** is the story of an imaginative and sensitive girl who exaggerates—or makes wild claims—through intensity of feeling and imagination. We soon learn not to believe her, but we must believe in her: she and her family and friends are highly credible. . . . [This is a] gentle, compassionate story. . . .

> Neil Millar, "From 8-12—A Wide Country," in The Christian Science Monitor (reprinted by permission from The Christian Science Monitor; © 1969 The Christian Science Publishing Society; all rights reserved), May 1, 1969, p. B4.*

"I think most of the lies you tell are like 'dress-up clothes.' You try them on to make a different impression," godmother Tilly tells Janie Chisholm. But lying is just a symptom of how a child can be a part of and yet apart from her family, here handled with acumen and verve. . . . [With] Tilly's oblique prods, Janie's increased confidence (via a shift in the Chisholm family gears), and some Little talent it works out. Affecting and sensible.

> "Younger Fiction: 'One to Grow On'," in Kirkus Reviews (copyright © 1969 The Kirkus Service, Inc.), Vol. XXXVII, No. 9, May 1, 1969, p. 504.

This author's latest excursion into bibliotherapy for the jellybean set deals with the problem of lying. . . . Fortunately, Janie's all-understanding godmother arrives on the scene in time to convert trauma to modest triumph. (The Chisholms incidentally are vaguely connected with the Copelands of several earlier books, which must make them and their confrères the most problem-oriented characters in current juvenile fiction.)

This is still not literature. There is no real plot, and the style is forced, while thin or stereotyped characters are manipulated paper-doll fashion in over-explicit illustration of the psychology. And as liars, neither Janie nor Lisa approaches the creativity or the élan of [Vera and Bill Cleaver's] Ellen Grae. (pp. 15-16)

> Shirley Ellison, "Reviews: 'One to Grow On'," in In Review: Canadian Books for Children, Vol. 3, No. 3, Summer, 1969, pp. 15-16.

LOOK THROUGH MY WINDOW (1970)

Miss Little's novel has all the acceptable trappings of what, I must confess, I had sincerely hoped was a dying syndrome of American juvenile fiction: insecure parents struggling with a temporarily enlarged family, sensitive girls trying to discover themselves, and a problem. Of course there must be an all too obvious problem. In this case, it's a half Jewish girl with an identity crisis, and an excuse to deal with that unpleasantness of polite Canamericans: prejudice. And how to solve the identity crisis? Why, invite the girl to spend a perfectly lovely Christmas with her new found friend's family of course. And how to deal with prejudice for nice kids—you know, a WASP'S first conscious encounter with a Jewish . . . oops, pardon me, half Jewish girl? (Don't want to make the thing too traumatic first go.) Well, Jews invented God, didn't you know? And add a few children's bloopers, just to grow on, amid the adults' ever so careful explanation of others' sensibilities.

If I sound less than convinced and the book sounds less than convincing you are absolutely right. The whole scene is just too too polite and predictable. Never so much as a nasty thought, word or character. Everyone copes with great good sense all around and is tearfully fulfilled. Oddball eccentrics are brought into the fold by winsome good will. And every child grows up learning to be himself.

Miss Little just can't seem to stop flogging her former role of the tactful, reassuring schoolmarm. No pain, no anguish, no problem without a neat solution, no laughter. And no fun. To be fair she can occasionally get inside the thoughts of kids and show how foolish and hurtful to themselves their conclusions can be. And of course, her kids often understand and cope more effectively than impatient, obtuse, and unobservant adults. But that's in an earlier novel, *Take Wing*.

Sorry Miss Little. I prefer my problems straight or slapstick. And I hope children will too. You only prove that our children's lives are too bland. Truth and reality are ugly. But they are better teachers for those who are ready to face up to them. (pp. 24-5)

> *Ralph J. Wintrob, "Reviews: 'Look through My Window'," in In Review: Canadian Books for Children, Vol. 4, No. 4, Autumn, 1970, pp. 24-5.*

Details of friendship, family relationships, and household domesticities enliven the author's everyday stories, creating scenes and situations immediately satisfying to little girl readers. . . . The inclusion of the poetry by each girl adds much to their characterization.

> *Virginia Haviland, "Stories for the Middle Readers: 'Look through My Window'," in The Horn Book Magazine (copyright © 1970 by The Horn Book, Inc., Boston), Vol. XLVI, No. 6, December, 1970, p. 621.*

Jean Little's *Look Through My Window* is a quiet, unassuming, and realistic portrayal of three friends, Emily Blair, Kate, and Lindsay, whose lives are enriched by writing and reading poetry. Little makes it clear that for these girls making a poem is not just a "fun thing to do," but a means of revealing aspects of their character otherwise hidden or undisclosed, and a way of expressing deeply felt emotions. (p. 81)

[The] quality of the poetry is not very good, but Little does manage to give each girl an individual voice.

The novel takes seriously the girls' discussions of their dreams of becoming professional writers. . . . [In] general, the girls are tolerant of each other's differences and respectful of the need to write.

Although *Look Through My Window* has not received much attention, it is a valuable novel because it realistically portrays its main characters writing and responding to verse. Interestingly, two of the girls' favorite books are *Harriet the Spy* and *Up a Road Slowly*. Little may have intended her novel to be linked with both [Louise] Fitzhugh's and [Irene] Hunt's as part of the small group of novels which depict children's dreams of becoming writers and their initial attempts at this craft. (p. 82)

> *Francis Molson, "Portrait of the Young Writer in Children's Fiction," in The Lion and the Unicorn (copyright © 1977 The Lion and the Unicorn), Vol. 1, No. 2, Fall, 1977, pp. 77-90.**

KATE (1971)

Emily's best friend from *Look Through My Window* . . . tells her own story a year or two later in a sequel that has all the quiet insights of its predecessor, the same resonating allusions to favorite books . . . , and more of Kate's engaging unrhymed poetry. . . . Kate's affection for little Susan Rosenthal is a bit overdone, but otherwise her vexing, mercurial feelings are sensitively and unsentimentally projected. As in the previous book, Miss Little plants Kate's probing introspection and her concerns about religion and identity in the vitalizing context of breezy conversation, firmly realized locations (her parents' crammed book store, the gloomy living room of her querulously tyrannical grandfather), and the minute realities of babysitting, walking to and from school, and working on bothersome class projects. Girls of any faith or nation . . . will have no trouble looking through Kate's window. (pp. 1070-71)

> *"Younger Fiction: 'Kate'," in Kirkus Reviews (copyright © 1971 The Kirkus Service, Inc.), Vol. XXXIX, No. 19, October 1, 1971, pp. 1070-71.*

["**Kate**"] is a moving, thematically contemporary book, about a 13-year-old's search for identity. . . . Girls with more on their minds than future housekeeping and maternity will find "**Kate**" more to their taste than many other books intended for them.

> *Nancy Garden, "Romance and Realism," in The Christian Science Monitor (reprinted by permission from The Christian Science Monitor; © 1971 The Christian Science Publishing Society; all rights reserved), November 11, 1971, p. B5.**

The story is balanced by a continuation of the friendship with Emily, and by Kate's delighted appreciation of a younger child she finds endearing. Stimulating and smoothly written, the book has fine characterization and relationships and a realistic development of a modest but significant plot. (p. 60)

> *Zena Sutherland, "New Titles for Children and Young People: 'Kate'," in Bulletin of the Center for Children's Books (reprinted by permission of The University of Chicago Press; © 1971 by The University of Chicago), Vol. 25, No. 4, December, 1971, pp. 59-60.*

The concentration with which Kate considers her situation seems occasionally forced, and the school and friendship relationships are portrayed more successfully than the socio-ethnic ones. However, the child characters have a strong reality, and their responses to each other make a lively story.

> *Virginia Haviland, "Stories for the Middle Readers: 'Kate'," in The Horn Book Magazine (copyright © 1972 by The Horn Book, Inc., Boston), Vol. XLVIII, No. 1, February, 1972, p. 49.*

[With *Kate*,] Jean Little has written a fascinating multifaceted girl's novel revealing the many dimensions of an adolescent girl's character. Younger adolescent readers who enjoyed *Look Through My Window* will welcome another story with the same heroines. . . . In *Kate* the title character meets several situations head on. Kate's personal integrity is threatened, her pride is challenged, her knowledge of adult integrity is skewed, her knowledge of adult faith is broadened. The novel is really a long flashback in which Kate explains how she and Emily split and eventually become friends again. Emily seems the more assured of the two; perhaps her comfortable Gentile background is responsible. . . . *Kate* is a beautiful tribute to the power of love.

John W. Conner, "Book Marks: 'Kate'," in English Journal (copyright © 1972 by the National Council of Teachers of English; reprinted by permission of the publisher and the author), Vol. 61, No. 3, March, 1972, pp. 434-35.

FROM ANNA (1972)

The gemutlichkeit in the Christmas day finale is as thick as Anna's glasses and Anna has none of the vitalizing dimension of *Kate* . . . or Emily in *Look Through My Window* . . . , but there are readers who will see themselves in her persecution and perversity.

"Younger Fiction: 'From Anna'," in Kirkus Reviews (copyright © 1972 The Kirkus Service, Inc.), Vol. XL, No. 18, September 15, 1972, p. 1098.

In 1934 Anna's father . . . decides to flee with his family from the injustices in Germany and makes a new start in Canada. . . . [Anna] is found to have severely limited vision—the cause of her awkwardness and inability to read. That her severe handicap had not been discovered in the city-school she had attended in Germany seems implausible. Yet, the appealing narrative unfolds the development of a child whose admirable imagination and creativity are no longer hidden by shyness. The political background, though minimized, forms a significant, enriching element. The story successfully deals with Anna's handicap and her family's adjustment to a new homeland. (pp. 467-68)

Virginia Haviland, "Stories for the Middle Readers: 'From Anna'," in The Horn Book Magazine (copyright © 1972 by The Horn Book, Inc., Boston), Vol. XLVIII, No. 5, October, 1972, pp. 467-68.

Seeing what the Nazis were doing to his Jewish friends, and convinced that things would get worse in Germany made Papa decide that the family must emigrate to Canada. The other children faced the change with varying degrees of equanimity; for Anna it meant disaster. Always the awkward ugly duckling of the brood, unable to learn reading, she dreaded both the new language and the prospect of another set of scornful teachers. Although it seems not quite believable that it occurs to nobody that the child needs glasses, and the change from duckling to swan has moments of sentimentality, this does show convincingly what a sympathetic teacher, a special class, and new friends who are understanding can do to help a child gain self-confidence. . . . The writing style and the characterization are excellent, and the double themes of loving freedom and understanding the handicapped are values sustained throughout the story. (pp. 78-9)

Zena Sutherland, "New Titles for Children and Young People: 'From Anna'," in Bulletin of the Center for Children's Books (reprinted by permission of The University of Chicago Press; © 1973 by The University of Chicago), Vol. 26, No. 5, January, 1973, pp. 78-9.

STAND IN THE WIND (1975)

[Predictably,] Martha helps timid, babyish Kit, her own age, to stand up both to the wind (until now she's been terrified by all sorts of storms) and to her domineering mother and older sister. The days, some rainy, drag on, and though all the incidents are described with an eye for revealing personalities and relationships, nothing is brought out during a detailed gin rummy game, for example, that we didn't already know. Somehow the story seems too trivial for its length, which could have been cut if Little trusted her readers to catch on without all the repetition and spelling out. Disappointingly slight and unsubtle, then, after the charm and insight of *Kate* . . . and *Look Through My Window*. . . .

"Younger Fiction: 'Stand in the Wind'," in Kirkus Reviews (copyright © 1975 The Kirkus Service, Inc.), Vol. XLIII, No. 22, November 15, 1975, p. 1287.

[In *Stand in the Wind*, the] give and take required by four different personalities, as well as Martha's disappointment at missing camp, provide the plot's interest and its easy, natural movement from one incident to the next. The four thoroughly knowable girls emerge naturally through their actions, each with her own strengths and weaknesses. . . . Although the girls, especially Martha, seem too wise for their years—Martha instinctively how to combat Kit's shyness—the conclusion is consistent with the rest of the book, an appropriate mixture of success and failure. As a whole, this is a worthy addition to Little's other popular fiction. . . .

Carolyn Johnson, "Book Review: 'Stand in the Wind'," in School Library Journal (reprinted from the January, 1976 issue of School Library Journal, published by R. R. Bowker Co./A Xerox Corporation; copyright © 1976), Vol. 22, No. 5, January, 1976, p. 35.

Some of Jean Little's books are better than others, and this one falls in between. At times her writing is rather strained and self-conscious leaving the reader with the uncomfortable feeling that she is trying hard to get across some other message. On the whole though, this is a rather satisfying story; it has a pleasant quality. Although character transformation seems too sudden, the main characters have real personality, a nice atmosphere is sustained, and the incident of a few summer days is entertaining. . . . Conversation is natural, and the outcome believable. The title is symbolic as well as literal, and although the characters have developed, the answers are not too pat or contrived.

The author depicts child characters better than adult, and the parents have a very sketchy appearance. (pp. 57-8)

Not great literature, but still a good read for "middle-aged" girls who like family stories. (p. 58)

Bonnie Clark, "Reviews: 'Stand in the Wind'," in In Review: Canadian Books for Children, Vol. 10, No. 3, Summer, 1976, pp. 57-8.

I remember reading somewhere that whereas American children's fiction nowadays tends to deal with "real life" things such as parental divorce, alienation, drugs and the like, in Canadian children's fiction kids still go to summer cottages and ride ponies. This made it sound as though our fiction for children was aeons out of date and naive to the point of silliness. . . . I do not believe it is necessary to present children totally with the gloom-and-doom view of life, nor do I think it would be an accurate reflection of most children's lives in this country to do so. The summer cottage experience is still a pretty common one to Canadian children, and I'm delighted that Jean Little, in [*Stand in the Wind*], deals with a subject which will, I am convinced, touch chords in the hearts of many of today's children. (p. 123)

One can always be certain, with Jean Little's characters, of true feelings and characteristics. There are no good guys and bad guys; all are ambiguous mixtures. Martha is capable of maliciously hurting Ellen's feelings, and of failing to realize that Rosemary, the snobbish one, is not as secure as she seems. Ellen is capable of treating Martha like a little kid, or of embarrassing her in front of the newcomers. There are also some very perceptive nuances of feeling, as when Martha, having previously and patiently tamed some seagulls, allows Kit to feed them and then feels a sharp and also half-ashamed sense of loss, wanting the birds to be hers alone. The sense and love of place are very strong here, and the descriptions of the shore and the land, although necessarily brief, are tellingly done.

The story is concerned with the ways in which all four begin to adjust to one another's flaws and to discover points of common interest and respect. Stated thus briefly, it may sound as though this were a moral tale. In a sense, all serious writers, whether for children or adults, are moralists at one level, in that they examine both the strengths and weaknesses of individual human relationships and the responsibilities involved in these. This is only a drawback in fiction when it becomes didactic, and Jean Little's writing is not didactic. It has, rather, a sense of faith in the possibilities of human relationships, and that is another thing entirely. These four girls learn something about one another and about themselves through a series of mishaps, through laughter, and through unexpected moments of joy, such as that experienced by Kit in feeding the gulls.

The only overt moralizing which bothered me to some extent occurs when the American-Canadian theme is introduced, and when it turns out that both have some stereotyped concepts of the other's national characteristics. On the other hand, we *do* have stereotyped concepts of each other's national characteristics, and perhaps it is as well that these should be brought into the light and dealt with. The resolution of this situation here, however, seems slightly strained, when they proceed to teach one another their respective national anthems.

The main theme, however, remains that of individual personal relationships. Rosemary keeps putting down Kit, and Martha attempts to bolster up Kit's confidence. Kit turns out to be a whiz at learning card games, but when the four play together, she is so intimidated by Rosemary that she loses when she could have won. This small scene is chilling, and is meant to be. Rosemary does not even realize the effect she is having on her young sister. Thus do members of families unwittingly hurt one another.

The key scene in the book is the one in which Martha, who is fearless in an outdoors which is familiar to her, drags the reluctant and terrified Kit out into a high wind. Kit finds that she can overcome her fear of storms, can indeed "stand in the wind". I like this central image, both theme and title. It works very well indeed, and is never overplayed or unnecessarily explained.

Through a series of humourous scenes which will, I think, appeal to kids very much, the four girls come to a better understanding of one another. Even the intrepid Martha, so fiercely independent, learns that she must follow the faith she tried to give to Kit, to stand in the wind. She still longs for a "real" camp, and tries to make the cottage life into one, with predictable failure. She is disappointed and depressed, ready to give up. But the others, and notably Kit, finally give her, as

a true surprise gift, a day and night of "real camp", when they sleep out under the stars. Martha is younger than her sister Ellen, and in some ways, in terms of experiencing life's sadness, she is the youngest of all four girls, but she is at the same time, within herself, actually the strongest. She learns—and this is never explained, only implied, but sensitive children will understand—that it is a good and lucky thing to be strong, but the strong must be able to accept love and help, too.

In the end, the lives of the four are not radically altered. They go back to their own situations; the week is over; the parents reappear. But they go back with some newly found insights which they don't analyse or even totally understand, some sense of growth of the spirit. (pp. 124-25)

It will probably be put forward as a "girls' book", but I hope that boys will read it as well, not just for what they may learn from it, but because it's a funny and sad and interesting story for all. (p. 125)

> *Margaret Laurence, "Jean Little's Latest," in* Canadian Children's Literature: A Journal of Criticism and Review *(Box 335, Guelph, Ontario, Canada N1H6K5), Nos. 5 & 6, 1976, pp. 123-25.*

LISTEN FOR THE SINGING (1977)

The stubborn heroine of *From Anna . . .* , having adjusted to her German family's relocation in Canada, now faces the trauma of entering high school. However, her personal fears about her partial blindness and about coping with new friendships become overshadowed by the rumblings of W.W.II. Anna's family feels the sting of anti-German sentiment, but the war still seems remote until her much feared eldest brother, Rudi, enlists. In a contrived ending, Rudi is accidently blinded, and Anna, who has accepted her own impaired vision, must encourage him to face up to his handicap. Characterizations remain strong and, although this story is not as involving as its predecessor, readers of the earlier book will want to know what happens to Anna and her family as they face each new trial with characteristic courage.

> *Julia B. Fuerst, "Book Reviews: 'Listen for the Singing'," in* School Library Journal *(reprinted from the September, 1977 issue of* School Library Journal, *published by R. R. Bowker Co./A Xerox Corporation; copyright © 1977), Vol. 24, No. 1, September, 1977, p. 132.*

The characterization is as discerning here as in the first book, and the author is just as adept at picturing the wartime atmosphere in Canada as she is in describing the warmth and mutual supportiveness of the family circle. Good pace, good style.

> *Zena Sutherland, "New Titles for Children and Young People: 'Listen for the Singing'," in* Bulletin of the Center for Children's Books *(reprinted by permission of The University of Chicago Press; © 1977 by The University of Chicago), Vol. 31, No. 3, November, 1977, p. 50.*

Stories of an adolescent's troublesome freshman year are common enough, but this one is exceptional not only for its subtle handling of the domestic tensions created by the war between the refugee family's new country and its old one, but also for the way this circumstance is used to link together an array of remarkably well-realized characters. . . .

Milton Meltzer, "Victims and Survivors," in The New York Times Book Review (© 1977 by The New York Times Company; reprinted by permission), November 13, 1977, p. 39.**

I wish I could be more than luke-warm about this book, because it has merits that never go amiss—sympathy, for instance, for the frailties of well-meaning people, and insight, born of personal experience, into the special traumas of the physically handicapped. Like her creator, Jean Little, Anna of *Listen for the Singing* suffers from severe visual impairment, and as a result the usual stresses of adolescence take on major dimensions for her. . . . This is a story of courage, then, in one of its more unspectacular guises: the courage of a young person who anticipates almost certain humiliation and nonetheless wins through to a number of small victories.

Had Jean Little kept to this single theme, at this relatively limited (but not ignoble) plane, there might be less provocation for the reviewer to resort to faint praise. Two complications are introduced into Anna's story, however, and in neither case does the author succeed in justifying the presence of these intrusions by convincing presentation. One of the complications is Anna's unsettled relationship with her older brother Rudi; the other is the troubled atmosphere created for Anna and her family by the outbreak of war. . . . The problems encountered by German families in Canada, and particularly by young men like [Rudi], were real and painful ones in historical terms, and no one would question that they deserve sympathetic exploration through fiction. But Anna herself is too young (fifteen, we are told, although at many points she seems younger) to understand Rudi's dilemma herself, and so her brother's torments remain peripheral and somewhat obscure. For his part, Rudi, torn between his hatred of the Hitler regime and the prospect of a promising career at university, treats his awkward little sister with an insensitivity which, for all the author's efforts at providing adequate motivation, still strikes the reader as contrived.

Yet it is out of these two additional plot elements—the brother-sister relationship, and the upheaval of Canada in war-time—that the major dramatic events in the book arise. Anna's German background is made the occasion for introducing a quite-implausible villain, a teacher who begins by persecuting Anna on the grounds of her alien name, and ends by revealing his fellowship-in-suffering: he too is acutely shortsighted, physically as well as (we must inescapably conclude) morally. Even making allowances for the terror of a high-school freshman at encountering "the meanest man alive" as her home-room teacher, the characterization of Mr. Lloyd is too shallow to pass muster. (pp. 81-2)

Rudi goes to Halifax to train for the Navy, and while there is involved in an accident—unexplained in the novel, and thereby all the more gratuitous—which leaves him totally blind. *Voilà la réconciliation:* Anna can now help her brilliant but embittered older brother adjust to the very handicap, in its most extreme form, which has so far shaped her own young life. Tidy, of course, but all the more unconvincing on that very account. Furthermore, by playing for sentiment in this fashion, Little succeeds only in undermining her central theme and character.

The writing style, too, is somewhat pedestrian, and suffers on occasion from Little's evident desire to get her research right. There are touches that work very well—the horse-drawn delivery wagons in Anna's city, the platoon of soldiers marching by in time to [a] jaunty chant. . . . Authentic recreation of times past is so demanding an art that perhaps one should not cavil at only partial success. Yet the fact remains that Little never quite manages to establish that crucial note of authenticity. (pp. 82-3)

Susan Jackel, "Brief Reviews: 'Listen for the Singing'," in The World of Children's Books (© 1978 Jon C. Stott), Vol. III, No. 1, Spring, 1978, pp. 81-3.

Jean Little's *Listen for the Singing* . . . is one of the author's finest books. . . .

While internationally translated and known for her ten earlier novels, Jean Little has never received the fullest recognition in her native land although her books are particularly meaningful to Canadians not only for their authentic local settings but for their persuasive social reality. . . .

Fortunately *Listen for the Singing* does not follow the usual sequel syndrome. Continuation books are often paler versions of the originals. In this warm and provocative book Jean Little does not allow herself to be caught in a repetitive time warp. While *Singing* will be welcomed by all of Anna's earlier fans the story takes place several years later and we see the Solden family from a different perspective with the roles of the characters newly defined.

The story begins in Canada in 1939 on that September day Britain declared war on Germany. It immediately presents us with a double concept: not only is Anna confronted with her personal problems as she prepares to enter her first public high school, but it is also a time of family despair as the Soldens face the complexities of being German immigrants in a land that is at war. . . .

What distinguishes Little's novel is her ability to weld together a story which deals with the impact of world-shaking events and the equally disturbing intricacies of her heroine's daily world.

The tale unfolds swiftly as Anna prepares to face her first day in Grade Nine of Davenport Collegiate. (p. 94)

Anna meets the sympathetic Maggie de Vries and the outspoken Paula Kitsch. Not only do they defend her against Mr. Lloyd [their prejudiced teacher], but they also offer their services to her as guide both in and out of school and eventually include her as a member of their "gang".

Miss Little has great perception and a fine ear for youthful speech in showing the development of the girls' relationship. "And their grins met like hands clasping" she writes of Anna and one of her new friends. As usual her characterizations are plausible whether she is depicting the fourth member of the gang, the unthinking Suzy, who is always saying the wrong thing about Anna's disability, or the daily life of the three sisters and two brothers of the family.

The narrative pace is fast enough to delight even the most impatient young reader as the author reveals the series of nightmares the heroine must overcome. . . .

Jean Little's is a unique voice in juvenile fiction. Her own personal vision handicap enables her to deal with this subject honestly and forcefully without the sentimentality which mars the works of lesser talents when they write of comparable situations.

One of the most intriguing themes of the entire book is the relationship that gradually evolves between Anna and her oldest brother, Rudi, whom she has avoided, remembering his rudeness to her in the years before her ailment was finally diagnosed. She discovers that Rudi is capable of affection when he not only undertakes responsibility for assisting her with her dreaded algebra but also attempts to help her as she reluctantly explains her fears about attending the school dance. (p. 95)

[The scene where Rudi] serves as her dance instructor . . . offers new insights into family relationships.

In this taut novel the author shows the irony of the family being discriminated against because of their background while on the other hand they are stunned by the fate of their friends and family still in Germany. (pp. 95-6)

Little offers a realistic picture of wartime Canada and the effects of Rudi's decision [to enlist in the Canadian navy] on the members of the household, particularly the mother, Klara.

I refuse to destroy the impact of the story by being specific about the tragedy that befalls Rudi—it is the only element in the novel that I found almost too ironic.

The major theme and Anna's resulting credo come from an Armistice Day speech by the school principal who insists: "Faith is when you hear the bird singing before the egg is hatched."

And indeed Anna is revealed as the strongest, most forceful member of the family when she attempts to save Rudi in a scene fraught with suspense.

Listen for the Singing is an important book. In these days of transitory literature, when so many novels in the juvenile field seem to be written only for their momentary shock value as sensational subjects (e.g. child abuse or homosexuality) it is refreshing to read a book which deals not only with personal dilemmas but with history itself. . . .

It is a family story for those who do not dwell in never-never land and one which all children will relate to not only for its great entertainment value also because it convincingly portrays an authentic world without being "preachy".

Above all, it is an invaluable book because it deals with a period in Canadian history which has been largely neglected by contemporary children. It will help make World War Two real to a generation largely unfamiliar with this era, their opinions diluted by the reruns of fatuous TV sit-coms. *Listen for the Singing* has a universal poignance and is a powerful book for children today and in the decades to come. (p. 96)

Myra Paperny, "History Confronted," in Canadian Children's Literature: A Journal of Criticism and Review *(Box 335, Guelph, Ontario, Canada N1H6K5), No. 12, 1978, pp. 94-6.*

Walter Dean Myers

1937-

Black American author of picture books, fiction for children and young adults, and nonfiction for children and adults. Although Myers has written in a variety of genres, his humorous works for preteens about growing up in a racially diverse, urban environment are perhaps his most popular. The protagonists of *Fast Sam, Cool Clyde, and Stuff, Mojo and the Russians,* and *The Young Landlords* are gang members, but Myers presents them in a favorable light rather than as negative examples of ghetto life. The characters receive positive support from their groups as they face the mysteries, joys, and harsh realities of living. Critics recognize Myers's understanding of his characters and praise his natural dialogue and the accuracy of his portraits.

In contrast with the realistic backgrounds in Myers's works, his storylines are often outrageous farces; *Mojo,* for instance, intertwines the antics of Russian consuls, a group of Harlem children, and a relocated southern sorceress. Some reviewers criticize Myers's premises as unbelievable, but most applaud his imagination and sense of humor. With *It Ain't All for Nothin'* Myers departs from his lighthearted approach to present a frank portrayal of a son's relationship with his father and the difficult decisions he must make to reach maturity. This work is considered especially noteworthy for its eloquence, compassion, and honesty. Myers has also published versions of folk and fairy tales, a picture book with a subtle philosophical message, a nonfiction book on social welfare, a science fiction novel for younger children, and works in other genres. It is generally agreed that he is at his best when he writes about city children and communities, where his light touch and sensitivity are most apparent. Myers received the Interracial Council for Children's Books Award in 1968 and the Woodward School Annual Book Award in 1976 for *Fast Sam.* (See also *Contemporary Authors,* Vols. 33-36, rev. ed.)

Photograph by E. Algonaldo Thomas; courtesy of The Viking Press, Inc. and Harriet Wasserman Literary Agency

WHERE DOES THE DAY GO? (1969)

Following Steven's question to his Daddy, an exchange of views among the (polyglot) children he's taken to the park and then a terse explanation—not much grist for a picture book . . . but, in the conjectures of the youngsters, some refreshing outreach: Karen imagines the day breaking up into little pieces that become . . . ''The stars!'' while Kiku remembers it sinking into the sea; but ''then it would keep the fishes awake,'' counters Karen. . . . A supportive little book (with a wise black Daddy) though somewhat static.

"Picture Books: 'Where Does the Day Go?'" in Kirkus Reviews *(copyright © 1969 The Kirkus Service, Inc.), Vol. XXXVII, No. 23, December 1, 1969, p. 1252.*

Integration, involvement, and togetherness are all deftly handled when Michael observes that ''day and night are like two people''—refreshingly different and both important. A good book for story hour because it is sure to stimulate feedback from inquiring minds who might have other ideas on where the day goes.

Mary Eble, ''The Book Review: 'Where Does the Day Go?''' in School Library Journal, *an appendix to* Library Journal *(reprinted from the April 15, 1970 issue of* School Library Journal, *published by R. R. Bowker Co./A Xerox Corporation; copyright © 1970), Vol. 16, No. 8, April 15, 1970, p. 111.*

Although there is little action in Walter Myers' *Where Does the Day Go?* it has other strong values in addition to its exploration of the mystery of night and day. The discussion among a group of children shows some of the misconceptions that can arise. The book explains natural phenomena accurately, and it presents an exemplary father who takes an evening walk with his children and their friends, commenting on the fact that people are as different as night and day, and how wonderful that is. (p. 99)

Zena Sutherland, Dianne L. Monson, and May Hill Arbuthnot, ''Books for the Very Young,'' in their Children and Books *(copyright © 1947, 1957, 1964, 1972, 1977, 1981 by Scott, Foresman and Company; reprinted by permission), sixth edition, Scott, Foresman, 1981, pp. 78-123.*

as they depend on their computer for everything). Passable in a remedial reading situation for its fast pace and photos of young people in futuristic garb, this **Brainstorm**'s lack of cohesiveness makes it a dubious choice. . . .

Patricia Manning, "Book Reviews: 'Brainstorm'," in School Library Journal (reprinted from the November, 1977 issue of School Library Journal, published by R. R. Bowker Co./A Xerox Corporation; copyright © 1977), Vol. 24, No. 3, November, 1977, p. 60.

The great attraction to reluctant older readers of this short pithy science-fiction story will be in its presentation. Excellent black and white photographs alternate with pages of text and do much to convey the atmosphere of life in the future and yet preserve the feeling that these are still humans as we know them. Humans who can have fear (though they can control it), humans who can and do feel great affection for their companions, and yet humans who do have an instinct for survival above all else. This gripping, easy to read, fast-moving story is ideal for older boys who feel that books are no longer for them.

"For Children from Ten to Fourteen: 'Brainstorm'," in The Junior Bookshelf, Vol. 43, No. 1, February, 1979, p. 58.

IT AIN'T ALL FOR NOTHIN' (1978)

[*It Ain't All for Nothin'* is an] exceptionally vivid story of a difficult summer in the life of twelve-year-old Tippy, a Black boy in Harlem. His mother died when he was born, and the boy had lived with his grandmother Carrie ever since. When she went to a nursing home, he moved in with his father Lonnie. But the boy had no place in Lonnie's life except as a means of obtaining welfare money, and Lonnie alternately neglected and abused him. Tippy's loneliness and fear led to a growing sense of isolation which he attempted to drown in soda-flavored whiskey. When Lonnie and his cohorts robbed a store and one of the group was dying from a gunshot wound, Tippy called the police and turned his father in. . . . The levity of **Fast Sam, Cool Clyde, and Stuff** and of **Mojo and the Russians** doesn't appear in the account of these desperate circumstances. The author's use of language is remarkably varied considering the strictures of a first-person novel: extravagant run-on sentences when Tippy was drunk, flat realism when he described his contact with welfare workers and hospital personnel, and heartbreaking eloquence when he expressed his feelings toward his father. The people surrounding Tippy are characterized clearly, without sentimentality but with compassion. The reader comes to understand the defeat suffered by Lonnie and his friends and to recognize how perilously close Tippy came to losing himself. (pp. 518-19)

Charlotte W. Draper, "Fall Booklist: 'It Ain't All for Nothin'," in The Horn Book Magazine (copyright © 1978 by The Horn Book, Inc., Boston), Vol. LV, No. 5, October, 1978, pp. 518-19.

Tales of woe concerning ghetto living often degenerate into tirades against the system or checklists of injustices. This, happily, is not the case in Walter Myers' novel. . . . Through the characters, from street-wise, adaptable Motown to slow, dreamy, exploited Denise, readers see a vivid slice of New York City life. Tippy's wrestling with the decline of his grandmother, his ambivalent feelings toward his father, alcohol, and the overwhelming magnitude of the city make this a first-rate

read, in the class of Alice Childress' *A Hero Ain't Nothin' But a Sandwich* (Coward, 1973).

Steven Matthews, "Junior High Up: 'It Ain't All for Nothin'," in School Library Journal (reprinted from the October, 1978 issue of School Library Journal, published by R. R. Bowker Co./A Xerox Corporation; copyright © 1978), Vol. 25, No. 2, October, 1978, p. 158.

As both [Robbie] Branscum and [Berniece] Rabe come out with grit-and-hardship dramas of 1930s orphans, Myers gives us a contemporary Harlem kid whose problems seem more real and more serious even though he has a father and, thanks to welfare, knows he will eat. . . . Kindly Mr. Roland's convenient presence in the wings constitutes perhaps an easy out for Tippy and for Myers, but it doesn't undermine Myers' demonstration that however the cards are stacked, the choice is there to be made. And instead of the broad-stroke characterization of the orphan books, Myers gives us people—you'll even come to feel for the hopelessly no-good Lonny before he ends up in jail. Sound base, authentic surface—like Tippy, a winner.

"Older Fiction: 'It Ain't All for Nothin'," in Kirkus Reviews (copyright © 1978 The Kirkus Service, Inc.), Vol. XLVI, No. 20, October 15, 1978, p. 1143.

Tippy tells, in completely convincing fashion, the story of a crisis in his life. . . . Myers doesn't soften the scene; while with Lonnie, Tippy drinks, he gets beatings, he lies when he goes to the hospital to visit Grandma. Yet he remains a sympathetic character, and in this first really serious book by Myers, that is one of the strengths: none of the characters is superficially drawn as all good or all bad. Not a happy book, but a trenchant and touching one. . . . (pp. 84-5)

Zena Sutherland, "New Titles for Children and Young People: 'It Ain't All for Nothin'," in Bulletin of the Center for Children's Books (reprinted by permission of The University of Chicago Press; © 1979 by The University of Chicago), Vol. 32, No. 5, January, 1979, pp. 84-5.

This book deals frankly with the stark realities of ghetto life. It pretties up nothing; not the language, not the circumstances, not the despair. It sucks the reader into a whirlpool of emotions. When the health of Tippy's grandmother deteriorates and she experiences the humiliation of dealing with welfare bureaucrats, we feel her defeat. When Tippy's world crumbles as his grandmother—who raised him from infancy—is removed to a nursing home, we experience his fear; we share his conflict and confusion as he wonders how his grandmother's benevolent God can allow such dreadful things to happen. When Tippy is forced to move in with his father, his misgivings are ours. And when he is viciously beaten by his father and forced to violate the principles instilled in him by his grandmother, we touch his pain—the hurt in his body and the hurt in his heart.

The torment which this child experiences is virtually unrelenting and on several instances I put the book down simply to gain respite from it. But that only underscored the fact that Tippy and the people who populate his world cannot escape so easily.

This is a devastating book which needed to be written; not only does it delineate the sufferings of this youngster, it also details the caring and support offered to him by members of his community.

The main problem I have with *It Ain't All for Nothin'* is its failure to fully explore the political realities behind the situations in which the characters find themselves. They did not construct the system which grinds them under its heel. They do not benefit from their deprivation, even if they contribute to it. But *someone* does benefit and it is inadequate to assume that the reader is aware of the political ramifications; they need to be stated openly and clearly. We are dealing with society's surplus people and they deserve to have their position squarely examined.

I was also uncomfortable with Tippy's solution to the conflict he faces after his father is involved in a robbery—he turns his father over to the police. I felt it could have been resolved in a way which did not so strongly suggest that feeding into the existing system was the right and proper way to handle things. (And how many kids are really going to "drop a dime" on their father?) . . . My son feels that Tippy's story is uplifting and encouraging. I, however, am only aware of the knot in my stomach.

Ashley Jane Pennington, "Bookshelf: 'It Ain't All for Nothin' '," in Interracial Books for Children Bulletin *(reprinted by permission of* Interracial Books for Children Bulletin, *1841 Broadway, New York, N.Y. 10023), Vol. 10, No. 4, 1979, p. 18.*

THE YOUNG LANDLORDS (1979)

The account of the summer experiences of a group of Black teenagers in New York is similar in spirit to the author's earlier books *Fast Sam, Cool Clyde, and Stuff*. . . . Paul Williams narrates the many adventures—ranging from the hilarious to the dangerous—that he and his friends encountered when they unwittingly became the owners of a run-down slum building. At first the group was excited by the idea of being landlords, but it was soon apparent that the responsibilities far outweighed the privileges. . . . In the course of the summer, Paul learned that compassion and business did not always mix; he and his friends were forced to devise ingenious—but not always successful—methods of raising money for the building. In the meantime, they took some risky chances while trying to prove the innocence of a friend who had been accused of robbery. Paul eventually concluded that "answers were a lot easier to come by when you stood across the street from the problem"; all in all he came to a better understanding of the human condition. The story is presented with a masterful blend of humor and realism; dialogue is lively and authentic, and the many characters are drawn with compassion. The author has once again demonstrated his keen sensitivity to the joys and frustrations of adolescence as well as his thorough knowledge of the New York City street scene.

Kate M. Flanagan, "Fall Booklist: 'The Young Landlords'," in The Horn Book Magazine *(copyright © 1979 by The Horn Book, Inc., Boston), Vol. LV, No. 5, October, 1979, p. 535.*

While Myers inserts a few chapters that do nothing to further the story, they are just as funny as the rest of the book; like *Mojo*, the story has lots of action, good characterization and dialogue, and a casual but warm relationship among the members of the gang. The book gives an attractive picture of a black urban neighborhood, and while it has its yeasty share of zany characters, it is given depth by the tenderness of the shy romance between Paul and Kitty, and by the deepening un-

derstanding between Paul and the stern father from whom he had at first felt alienated.

Zena Sutherland, "New Titles for Children and Young People: 'The Young Landlords'," in Bulletin of the Center for Children's Books *(reprinted by permission of The University of Chicago Press; © 1979 by The University of Chicago), Vol. 33, No. 3, November, 1979, p. 52.*

There is humor in this latest Myers entry, but the story line is unrealistic. The idea of a Harlem slum landlord selling one of his buildings for one dollar to a group of teenagers after they visit his office to complain about its state of disrepair is rather farfetched. On top of that, they make a success of it and end up managing a second building. Cute, but I question whether today's pre-teens and teenagers are going to want to read an inner-city black fantasy.

James S. Haskins, "'The Young Landlords'," in Children's Book Review Service *(copyright © 1980 Children's Book Review Service Inc.), Vol. 8, No. 5, January, 1980, p. 48.*

"The Young Landlords" isn't a novel; it's a neighborhood block party! Never were more zany characters gathered around so small—and condemned—an apartment house. . . .

The plot—kids running a slum building, The Joint, and catching a stereo thief—stretches the imagination at more than one point.

It works as a convenient vehicle, however, for introducing . . . great characters. . . .

There are ideas, too, about the conflict between tenants and slumlords. About the hot-goods industry, police lethargy, newspapers' predilection for story over facts. Important ideas, particularly for the reader who doesn't live next to The Joint.

Mr. Myers's story starts slowly; tightening would have helped. But there are funny lines and scenes, the dialogue is real, and as the narrator says, "Mostly the whole experience was an up kind of thing."

Patricia Lee Gaugh, "Children's Books: 'The Young Landlords'," in The New York Times Book Review *(© 1980 by The New York Times Company; reprinted by permission), January 6, 1980, p. 20.*

Walter Dean Myers has taken an implausible story line and created an entertaining novel complete with humor, pathos and sensitivity. It is a well-written book which I enjoyed in spite of certain drawbacks. . . .

Unlikely as the story is, I enjoyed it. I especially liked the respect with which Myers treats his young heroes. He carefully explores their feelings and perspectives. A case in point is his portrayal of the relationship between Paul and his father. Paul frequently feels overwhelmed and oppressed by Mr. Williams, who he thinks sets him up to be ridiculed. Paul responds by withdrawing, but later in the book he sees things from his father's side. He doesn't like his father's attitudes any better, but he at least begins to understand their origin.

I applaud the author's attempts to present a balanced picture, to suggest that there are at least two sides to most situations—not only with Paul and his father but in tenant-landlord relationships, male-female relationships, people-to-people situations.

As much as I enjoyed *The Young Landlords,* I would have appreciated it even more if there had been some acknowledgment that the dilemma of a deteriorating neighborhood is directly related to a political system which fosters the emotional and physical decay of certain segments of this society. The solution goes well beyond taking over one building on one block in one city. In addition, I get the sense that the author intended to be nonstereotypic by presenting both sexes as creative, courageous, caring and energetic. However, it quickly becomes apparent that the boys will save the day. A disappointment.

In spite of these objections, I feel that this book can be one vehicle through which these issues can be introduced and explored. Some lively class discussions could be generated after reading *The Young Landlords.* I heartily recommend that it be used in this way.

Ashley Jane Pennington, "'The Young Landlords'," in Interracial Books for Children Bulletin *(reprinted by permission of* Interracial Books for Children Bulletin, *1841 Broadway, New York, N.Y. 10023), Vol. 12, No. 1, 1981, p. 15.*

THE GOLDEN SERPENT (1980)

Walter Dean Myers' *The Golden Serpent* . . . [is] a folkish tale of a king and a wise man. Naturally the discontented ruler will learn something from the guru (the setting is the Indian subcontinent), and maybe little readers will as well. What's the lesson? Myers coyly leaves that up to his audience, a trick that seems less like authentication and more like a cop-out. It may be that kids are not ready for the wisdom of the East, or at least such a bogus rendering.

Michele Slung, "The Artful Menagerie," in Book World—The Washington Post *(© 1980, The Washington Post), November 9, 1980, p. 14.*

A well-known writer of realistic and humorous fiction has written a story in the style of a folk tale or even of an apologue. Most of the sentences are short and simple in structure, and the terse narrative runs along until its somewhat baffling conclusion, which teases the interpretive skill of the reader.

Paul Heins, "Picture Books: 'The Golden Serpent'," in The Horn Book Magazine *(copyright © 1980 by The Horn Book, Inc., Boston), Vol. LVI, No. 6, December, 1980, p. 636.*

If it's appropriate for a story about a kvetch "to have a Yiddish flavor" (see [Carol Chapman's *The Tale of Meshka the Kvetch*]), it may be appropriate for a story of ineffable wisdom to be set in India; the problem is that it has *no* flavor. It starts out in fact . . . as still another tale of a wise-man-on-a-mountain and his young helper, related in banal primer prose. . . . [The] king gets wind of Pundabi's gifts, calls him to the palace, and asks him to solve a mystery—what mystery "is for you to discover!" . . . Pundabi observantly walks around and discovers, he says, "the mystery of the Golden Serpent." The king of course didn't know he had one; and, searching, can't find it—the people are too crippled to steal anything, too poor to conceal anything. The king, disconcerted, pays Pundabi his promised golden coins to get rid of him, and Pundabi gives them to the poor folk just met. A "wise and generous solution," as Ali says; but what of Pundabi's promise to the king that, when he opens his eyes, he'll find the Golden Serpent. "No," he won't, Pundabi agrees; "Some people never do. But that is another mystery." However kids construe this, it has only Pundabi's wise stratagem to commend it: the telling has no lift. . . .

"Picture Books: 'The Golden Serpent'," in Kirkus Reviews *(copyright © 1980 The Kirkus Service, Inc.), Vol. XLVIII, No. 23, December 1, 1980, p. 1515.*

This is one of those unique stories that will be most appreciated by older children, even though it has a picture-book format. Though the publisher recommends ages six to nine, I would use it with junior-high age. . . . The unusual, mystical story should provoke discussion and critical thinking. A lovely book.

Beverly Woods, "Picture Books: 'The Golden Serpent'," in Children's Book Review Service *(copyright © 1981 Children's Book Review Service Inc.), Vol. 9, No. 5, January, 1981, p. 32.*

D(aniel) Manus Pinkwater

1941-

(Also writes as Manus Pinkwater) American author/illustrator of fiction and nonfiction for children. Pinkwater's books for children provide a wealth of fantasy and imagination. His characters are ordinary people from ordinary places (often boys from Rochester, New York or Hoboken, New Jersey), thrust into incredible situations in unlikely places with odd creatures, both human and otherwise. His illustrations incorporate the details of his descriptions with the outlandishness of a child's imagination and are considered simple yet effective.

Critics agree that Pinkwater's nonsensical names and phrases and his absurd plots and pictures delight both children and adults. However, some reviewers complain that his overwhelming reliance on the ridiculous diminishes the appeal of some later works. At his most effective, Pinkwater is said to present the ludicrous as commonplace, often entwining the bizarre with important lessons and ending his tales with a familiar moral most children understand. Pinkwater's longest work, *Alan Mendelsohn, the Boy from Mars*, is a novel written in the same exaggerated comic vein as his shorter books. In a break from the whacky and whimsical, Pinkwater and his wife have written a common-sense guide to raising dogs, emphasizing pet ownership in an urban environment. Says Pinkwater, "My books are a portrayal of real life. In life things fall out in a random fashion. Preposterous things happen all the time. . . . I've seen things that make a 200-pound chicken [*The Hoboken Chicken Emergency*] seem like nothing." (See also *Contemporary Authors*, Vols. 29-32, and *Something about the Author*, Vol. 8.)

GENERAL COMMENTARY

[Mr. Pinkwater has an] uncluttered, generous style—slightly reminiscent of [Tomi] Ungerer, with a touch of [Leo] Lionni. . .

"**Alan Mendelsohn**" is his most ambitious book to date, a 252-page novel that is, in spots, reminiscent of E. Nesbit, and everywhere vintage Pinkwater. Though its hero, Leonard, has a different name, he is the continuation of the heroes in the earlier novels, all various shades of Mr. Pinkwater himself: curious, oddball, moral, pre-teen lovers, not-too-hassled by authority figures, who stumble onto some incredible power and, along with it, a fantastic adventure, usually otherworldly. The exception is "**The Last Guru**," a satire, which brings the otherworldly down to earth.

Mr. Pinkwater's formula for fantasy is simple: he doesn't strain anybody's credibility. The power or key to it, in each of his novels resides in some impotent adult, such as an over-the-hill, obvious con artist—Samuel Klugarsh is the latest one—whose fraud is so blatant that it can be topped only by the surprise of his actually having the power without even knowing it. Even the fantasy in "**The Hoboken Chicken Emergency**," superimposed on the tired plot of banished pet turned mean without understanding, here concerning the love of Arthur Bobowicz for a 266-pound chicken, succeeds with the easy touch of Mr. Pinkwater.

Though he will never win any awards strictly for his prose, neither will he collect any booby prizes for it. The writing

itself is adequate, no more, no less. But for imaginative plot and decorative detail, Mr. Pinkwater's scores go off the charts.

Ann S. Haskell, "The Fantastic Mr. Pinkwater," in The New York Times Book Review (© 1979 by The New York Times Company; reprinted by permission), April 29, 1979, pp. 32, 43.

THE TERRIBLE ROAR   (1970)

A little lion, his mother and his sleeping father are "waiting in the tall grass for something good to eat." Just as they're about to pounce on an unsuspecting zebra, the little lion feels a sneeze-like tickle. "But instead of a sneeze it came out a roar, a terrible roar." The zebra disappears and with each subsequent terrible roar something else disappears, until the little lion is left all alone. But one final roar sends him to the place where everything else has gone—and only the terrible roar is left behind. Though the text is simple and rhythmically repetitive, the story is skimpy, so the book is made by the exceedingly bright, flat-planed, simple and humorous color pictures which pre-schoolers will love.

Ann D. Schweibish, "The Book Review: 'The Terrible Roar'," in School Library Journal, an appendix to Library Journal (reprinted from the March, 1971 issue of School Library Journal, *published by R. R. Bowker Co./A Xerox Corporation; copyright © 1971), Vol. 17, No. 7, March, 1971, p. 123.*

BEAR'S PICTURE   (1972)

A bear can paint a portrait of his dreams, regardless of what two "fine, proper gentlemen" say in **"Bear's Picture."** . . . His painting progresses, page by page, volubly unappreciated by two bird-like critics—and, when finished, "the bear looked at his picture and was happy."

This book begins with a fine idea: elements in the line background can be sought out and compared with the bear's interpretations in the full-color easel painting. However, what could have been an exciting visual game is soon forsaken for a weak and wordy description of the picture's literal meaning, and the book's message becomes as muddied as the intended poster colors. No matter, the bear isn't much of an artist anyway. If his purpose is to encourage the young reader to arrange colors on paper, maybe he will.

Ellen Raskin, *"Bears and Forebears," in* The New York Times Book Review *(© 1972 by The New York Times Company; reprinted by permission), December 24, 1972, p. 8.*

WIZARD CRYSTAL   (1973)

Wizard Crystal is at least the happiest frog story to come along since Eliner L. Horwitz's *Strange Story of a Frog Who Became a Prince*. The magic crystal, which has the power to bring happiness, lies at the bottom of a pond where resident frogs sing contentedly GUNK GAGUNK of the warm sun, bright stars, safe home, and happy place. Then a wizard who "had been unhappy every day for 307 years and was tired of it" finds the crystal with a magic compass and takes it to his home. All night the frogs surround the wizard's house, singing of their home and dreaming of their crystal, until at last "the wizard changed." The fun here is as much in the freewheeling doodles as in the plot—but that ends well when "Morning came. When the wizard woke up he was not unhappy any more. He was not a wizard any more either. He was a frog." Sparkling.

"Picture Books: 'Wizard Crystal'," in Kirkus Reviews *(copyright © 1973 The Kirkus Service, Inc.), Vol. XLI, No. 3, February 1, 1973, p. 110.*

For sheer fun, smashing pictures, and a socko ending, this book is hard to beat. (Grownups will appreciate it as well as, maybe better than, children.)

"Children's Books: 'Wizard Crystal'," in Publishers Weekly *(reprinted from the February 26, 1973 issue of* Publishers Weekly, *published by R. R. Bowker Company, a Xerox company; copyright © 1973 by Xerox Corporation), Vol. 203, No. 9, February 26, 1973, p. 123.*

In this bog, ah, book, there's a wizard unhappy for 307 years; some happy frogs caring for a magic crystal at the bottom of their pond. Wizard takes crystal. Now unhappy frogs follow now happy wizard, surround house and sing "gunk, gunk, gagunk" which, in frog talk means "think hard . . . what to do." Crystal works its magic, and frogs end singing same song, different words apparently "gunk, gunk, gagunk" now mean-ing "this pond . . . warm sun." And the whole thing sinks slowly into the illogical swamp.

George A. Woods, *"'Wizard Crystal'," in* The New York Times Book Review *(© 1973 by The New York Times Company; reprinted by permission), April 1, 1973, p. 10.*

FAT ELLIOT AND THE GORILLA   (1974)

[*Fat Elliot and the Gorilla* is] essentially an overextended attempt to make offbeat fun out of a get thin message, and we tend to agree with Elliot's doctor who tells him early on "You ought to go on a diet. Of course, nobody ever sticks to one." However this and other bluntly honest acknowledgments of what a fat kid is really up against are funny in their unexpectedness and disarming enough to make his program worth a try.

"Younger Fiction: 'Fat Elliot and the Gorilla'," in Kirkus Reviews *(copyright © 1974 The Kirkus Service, Inc.), Vol. XLII, No. 4, February 15, 1974, p. 186.*

Elliot is another friendless fatty who predictably loses a few pounds and wins some self-confidence. . . .

Pinkwater's hybrid fantasy cum diet manual results in a mixed and muddled bag of sound suggestions (he counsels lots of exercise and good eating habits) and crank cure-alls (Elliot's method of extracting his sweet-tooth won't offer much comfort to overweight kids). Moreover, thinner Elliot's sudden rise in popularity unnecessarily reinforces the notion that fat equals freak. Despite many wry touches in the text (notably the scales's snide remarks) and cartoons (an especially funny drawing shows Elliot's family shoveling in their dinner) Elliot's loss is not the reader's gain.

Jane Abramson, *"Preschool and Primary Grades: 'Fat Elliot and the Gorilla'," in* School Library Journal, *an appendix to* Library Journal *(reprinted from the April, 1974 issue of* School Library Journal, *published by R. R. Bowker Co./A Xerox Corporation; copyright © 1974), Vol. 20, No. 8, April, 1974, p. 52.*

MAGIC CAMERA   (1974)

Magic Camera is just the sort of discovery every kid would want Dad to bring up from the cellar to make that boring day in bed with the flu pass quickly, and its fascination rests as much in its "cranks and knobs and buttons and switches" and in the "real" things it sees in a different way (the lamp chain in which each link reflects the whole room) as in the camera's special midnight magic. When Charles learns that everything the camera snaps disappears inside and can later be released through the back of the camera, he keeps his discovery private, and his experimentation—shown in black and white doodly drawings—leaves most of the view through the lens to the imagination while showing the camera's own gadgetry in detail. All in all, Charles just thought "it was a very nice camera"—and so it is.

"Picture Books: 'The Magic Camera'," in Kirkus Reviews *(copyright © 1974 The Kirkus Service, Inc.), Vol. XLII, No. 2, January 15, 1974, p. 53.*

Sick in bed, Charles reads about photography in his encyclopedia and decides that cameras are magic. He is hardly surprised, therefore, when the dusty antique camera his father finds for him in the basement turns out to have lots of special tricks. . . . In black-and-white illustrations Charles seems to be sloppily drawn on the pillow, but a fanciful and warmly naive quality leaves no doubt that the magic of childhood has remained to grace this author-artist's work.

> *"Children's Books: 'Magic Camera'," in* The Booklist *(reprinted by permission of the American Library Association; copyright © 1974 by the American Library Association), Vol. 70, No. 15, April 1, 1974, p. 878.*

WINGMAN (1975)

[Pinkwater's] pictures—combining the look of black and white comic book pages and sketches from Donald's Big Chief pencil tablet—show us all along just how things appear to Donald. His story is told with such absolute conviction that it's easy to believe it's "mostly true." You might also say that this is a wonderfully internalized report on the growth of a creative vision . . . or, more simply, that Donald is an artist for sure.

> *"Younger Fiction: 'Wingman'," in* Kirkus Reviews *(copyright © 1975 The Kirkus Service, Inc.), Vol. XLIII, No. 7, April 1, 1975, p. 375.*

You don't have to be a comic book freak to be sympathetic to Donald Chen's escapist fantasies as he hides with armfuls of Capt. Marvels and Flash Gordons in the superstructure of the George Washington Bridge. Humiliated by an insensitive teacher, Donald has decided to play truant rather than go back to P.S. 132, where he was the only Chinese child in the class and probably the poorest one as well.

Day after day in this precarious perch he immerses himself in adventure comics until suddenly Wingman appears!

Unfortunately, this Chinese Superman does not quite come off as the splendid character he could have been, and the part of the story dealing with Wingman's flights cruises on leaden wings. The problem, perhaps, is the difficulty of injecting a fantastic element into a real and touching situation. The reader never sees him as a striking figure, separate from an unhappy child's imaginings. Instead our interest goes to Donald, whom it is easy to believe in and identify with. We also care about the kindly teacher who takes over Donald's class at midyear. It is her recognition of Donald's talents as an artist that brings us to the happy resolution we are hoping for.

The story is told in the same matter-of-fact, unadorned style the author uses in his pen drawings. Intended, presumably, to evoke a comic-book format, the illustrations are kept from the danger of occasionally seeming amateurish by the snappy optical shading effects reminiscent of Roy Lichtenstein's work.

> *Jane Geniesse, "'Wingman'," in* The New York Times Book Review *(© 1975 by The New York Times Company; reprinted by permission), May 4, 1975, p. 40.*

Wingman [is] a gentle Chinese version of Superman, who takes [Donald] on a trip to ancient China. After a truant officer sends him back to school, an understanding teacher helps Donald to become an accepted member of the class and to channel his imagination into art. A decidedly different, easy to read story

From Wingman, *written and illustrated by Manus Pinkwater.*

which effectively deals with how fantasy provides a protective covering from hurts and prejudices. (pp. 109-10)

> *Cynthia T. Seybolt, "'Wingman'," in* School Library Journal *(reprinted from the September, 1975 issue of* School Library Journal, *published by R. R. Bowker Co./A Xerox Corporation; copyright © 1975), Vol. 22, No. 1, September, 1975, pp. 109-10.*

BLUE MOOSE (1975)

[Another star performance] has resulted in a witty and touching fantasy. Mr. Breton . . . is a "very good cook" and he runs a thriving restaurant on the edge of a big woods. People flock to Mr. Breton's place, but they are a taciturn lot. They eat—tons of clam chowder, beef stew and homemade bread. None of them, however, ever says the food is delicious or passes the time of day with the sad, lonely chef. But all that changes when the hero of this tale arrives. He is a blue moose and he joins forces with the restaurant keeper, changing his life forever. The plot, besides providing exceptional wish-fulfillment fare, is charged with suspense and adventure based on close calls and misunderstandings, all satisfactorily resolved in an understated finale.

> *"Fiction: 'Blue Moose'," in* Publishers Weekly *(reprinted from the June 9, 1975 issue of* Publishers Weekly, *published by R. R. Bowker Company, a Xerox company; copyright © 1975 by Xerox Corporation), Vol. 207, No. 23, June 9, 1975, p. 63.*

Pinkwater of course puts all the joy and buzz between the words, which seem to be plunked onto the page with the same matter-of-fact aplomb that the moose exhibits clumping into the dining room—where we see him, placid and unselfconscious, waiting on a table of woodsmen. But then this author's "yup" is worth more than another's whole thesaurus.

> *"Younger Fiction: 'Blue Moose',"* in Kirkus Reviews *(copyright © 1975 The Kirkus Service, Inc.), Vol. XLIII, No. 12, June 15, 1975, p. 661.*

Serio-comic narration is perfectly complemented by black-and-white line drawings of a very professional moose—mittens drying on his antlers, serving bowls lined up properly between the antler tips, etc. A quietly pleasing and most rewarding book. (p. 89)

> *Marjorie Lewis, "Preschool and Primary Grades: 'Blue Moose',"* in School Library Journal *(reprinted from the September, 1975 issue of* School Library Journal, *published by R. R. Bowker Co./A Xerox Corporation; copyright © 1975), Vol. 22, No. 1, September, 1975, pp. 88-9.*

An ingratiating piece of nonsense, adequately illustrated in black and white, is successful primarily because of the bland blend of nonsensical situation and straightforward writing. . . . The idea is affably silly, the writing style pseudo-simple (really, rather sophisticated).

> *Zena Sutherland, "New Titles for Children and Young People: 'Blue Moose',"* in Bulletin of the Center for Children's Books *(reprinted by permission of The University of Chicago Press; © 1976 by The University of Chicago), Vol. 29, No. 5, January, 1976, p. 84.*

[Manus Pinkwater] evokes perfectly the half-and-half world of an animal who manages to have human characteristics without becoming unconvincingly anthropomorphic. The numerous drawings are stylish, eloquent and funny.

> *Lesley Lancaster, "Wild Streaks of Humour: 'Blue Moose',"* in The Times Educational Supplement *(© Times Newspapers Ltd. (London) 1978; reproduced from* The Times Educational Supplement *by permission), No. 3275, April 7, 1978, p. 20.*

THREE BIG HOGS (1975)

In a funky turnabout on all those little escapades that end with a reassuring welcome home, three crybaby hogs—the smallest weighs 150 pounds—find themselves thrust out into the cruel world and decide it isn't so bad after all . . . but not until they've wallowed in self-pity, broken into an empty house, made a mess Goldilocks would be ashamed of, and fled the town in tears after catching sight of a butcher shop. Then, lost in the forest, the trio run smack into a looming, beady-eyed brute (and we don't blame them for addressing him as "sir") who shuts up their whining with an explosive "Phooey!" . . . [Our] friends take the hint and if their transformation into "regular forest hogs" hairy, toothy and tough doesn't do much for their looks, we're convinced it was the right decision. The three hogs "liked it very much" and you will too.

> *"Picture Books: 'Three Big Hogs',"* in Kirkus Reviews *(copyright © 1975 The Kirkus Service, Inc.), Vol. XLIII, No. 21, November 1, 1975, p. 1225.*

From Blue Moose, *written and illustrated by Manus Pinkwater.*

LIZARD MUSIC (1976)

Lizard Music is that rarity, a children's fantasy that is truly contemporary in sensibility as well as setting. It's funny, properly paranoid, shot through with bad puns and sweet absurdities, and all about a baffled kid intent on tracking reality (as slippery as lizards) in a media-spooked milieu. Television figures here as prominently as it does in most kids' lives—or as comics did in *Wingman* (1975). It's on late night TV that Victor, eleven, first sees the movie about pods invading the earth and replacing their human doubles . . . and then sees what he is sure are pod people on a talk show. Differently scary, it's on unlisted late TV that he first sees the lizard band whose music he likes "more than anything I'd ever heard." After that "all of a sudden I was running into lizards every five minutes". . . weirdest of all, alive in the hand of the strange, bony-fingered old black "chicken man" he meets on [a] bus with a performing chicken named Claudia. All of a sudden the chicken man, too starts turning up everywhere, on and off TV, under a variety of aliases; he seems to have some answers—not only about lizards . . . but also about pods . . . ; and, though he's not at all straight about telling what he knows, he finally takes Victor to an invisible floating island, inhabited by hospitable, harmonious lizards, where Claudia hatches the egg that lizard legend says will grow to lead them in conquering the pods. Which is certainly a more significant feat, and far less pretentiously brought forth, than are any of those traditionalist victories of light over darkness that are still being (over) sold as high fantasy.

> *"Younger Fiction: 'Lizard Music'," in* Kirkus Reviews *(copyright © 1976 The Kirkus Service, Inc.), Vol. XLIV, No. 15, August 1, 1976, p. 846.*

Not for everyone's ears, . . . *Music* is a decidedly different fantasy—sometimes fuzzy, occasionally forced, nearly always funny—that will grab the same audience that loves Ellen Raskin's arcane flights of fancy.

> *Melinda Schroeder, "Preschool and Primary Grades: 'Lizard Music'," in* School Library Journal *(reprinted from the October, 1976 issue of* School Library Journal, *published by R. R. Bowker Co./A Xerox Corporation; copyright © 1976), Vol. 23, No. 2, September, 1976, p. 110.*

Pinkwater's productions have all been notably imaginative and appealing. His latest looks like a shoo-in for awards and for popularity among readers, young and old. . . . The story is believable and enhanced by Victor's astute comments on the Tube and other subjects.

> *"Fiction: 'Lizard Music'," in* Publishers Weekly *(reprinted from the October 18, 1976 issue of* Publishers Weekly, *published by R. R. Bowker Company, a Xerox company; copyright © 1976 by Xerox Corporation), Vol. 210, No. 16, October 18, 1976, p. 64.*

[*Lizard Music*] is a wonderful science-fiction style fantasy firmly rooted in the familiar. Who would have thought television, that well-known threat to our children's imagination, could be the center of inspired fantasy?

> *Brigitte Weeks, "Young Bookshelf: 'Lizard Music'," in* Book World—The Washington Post *(© 1977, The Washington Post), February 13, 1977, p. G10.*

[This author] has a clear recollection of childhood and its effect on the imagination. . . . Youngsters from 8 to 12 will enjoy this story of a young boy on his own for 2 weeks who tracks down the origin of the lizard musicians he sees on television late at night. Youngsters will also be intrigued by the black-and-white drawings that illustrate the text. (p. 217)

This humorous story of a boy's fantastic adventure has a theme that augments its value as an exciting story. Its abstract concerns with simplicity of life-style, genuineness of human beings, and awareness of the environment are woven into the fabric of the story by a masterful plotter. It speaks directly to children who will absorb and appreciate the deep underlying message. (pp. 219-20)

> *Diana L. Spirt, "Appreciating Books: 'Lizard Music'," in her* Introducing More Books: A Guide for the Middle Grades *(© 1978 by Diana L. Spirt; reprinted by permission of the author), R. R. Bowker Company, 1978, pp. 217-20.*

AROUND FRED'S BED (1976)

What Fred sees around his bed, first in a bad dream but still when he wakes up are monsters . . . , ugly to be sure but just too goofy-looking to be the stuff of nightmares. (Even their teeth and claw nails are rounded off.) Fred himself is not seen at all: he covers his face with a blanket or pillows when he's hiding and with his hands when he unsuccessfully orders the

From Lizard Music, *written and illustrated by D. Manus Pinkwater.*

monsters from the room, and he shows his back when he walks out . . . and when he tells his parents about the visitation. The reason for this inept coquetry is apparent after Daddy says, "There are no monsters here. Get into bed with us." Fred does, and then you do see him, and get the joke—that he and his fat but vaguely saurian parents are monsters too. Indeed they might well strike you as more revolting than the ones that frightened Fred, but the fact that they look like a different sort of monster altogether tends to undercut the point. In any case, the truncated story [doesn't] rate any space in your nightmare closet.

> *"Picture Books: 'Around Fred's Bed'," in* Kirkus Reviews *(copyright © 1976 The Kirkus Service, Inc.), Vol. XLIV, No. 23, December 1, 1976, p. 1262.*

A nice, if not wholly new, concept (a monster afraid of monsters). . . . Frightened by monsters in his room who refuse to leave, Fred trots off to his parents' bedroom. "There are no monsters here," says Daddy, "Get into bed with us." Parental comforting is certainly in order, but the inference (if not the implication) may be that it's safe in Mommy's and Daddy's room, but not in one's own. Otherwise the story is succinctly told.

> *Zena Sutherland, "New Titles for Children and Young People: 'Around Fred's Bed'," in* Bulletin of the

Center for Children's Books *(reprinted by permission of The University of Chicago Press; © 1977 by The University of Chicago), Vol. 30, No. 9, May, 1977, p. 149.*

A toddler's twilight zone. Fred sees nightmare monsters, runs to his parents for security, and the reader discovers Fred and parents are monsters too, though friendly ones. Introduces a common childhood fear, but doesn't do much to assuage it.

"Picture Book Notes: 'Around Fred's Bed'," in Curriculum Review *(© 1977 Curriculum Advisory Service; reprinted by permission of the Curriculum Advisory Service, Chicago, Illinois), Vol. 16, No. 2, May, 1977, p. 128.*

THE BIG ORANGE SPLOT   (1976)

Nonconformity becomes the rule on Mr. Plumbean's street, but only after he shakes up his neighbors (squares, all of them, down to the lines of their jaws) by becoming the exception on a "meat street" where every house is the same. The turnaround begins when a seagull ("no one knows why") drops a splot of orange paint on Mr. Plumbean's roof. The neighbors urge him to repaint. . . . But Mr. Plumbean has made his house look like his dreams, and as, one by one, the neighbors visit to talk sense, they end up changing their own houses to match their dreams—as pictured in splashy color, there's a ship, a balloon, a medieval castle, etc. And no one cares that strangers think they've all got "bees in their bonnets, bats in their belfrys, and knots in their noodles"—phrases that grownups might not appreciate but small listeners are likely to go round repeating. And like the residents of Plumbean's street, Pinkwater makes something groovy out of an ordinary beginning.

"Picture Books: 'The Big Orange Splot'," in Kirkus Reviews *(copyright © 1977 The Kirkus Service, Inc.), Vol. XLV, No. 5, March 1, 1977, p. 219.*

Who better than a Pinkwater to write about a Plumbean?

When you can make a hero out of a ***Big Orange Splot,*** you've got it made. And the Splot made over Mr. Plumbean's life—and his street. . . .

The illustrations are just right for drawing a Splot, and that is intended as a compliment.

Gene Langley, "Picture Books: 'The Big Orange Splot'," in The Christian Science Monitor *(reprinted by permission from The Christian Science Monitor; © 1977 The Christian Science Publishing Society; all rights reserved), May 4, 1977, p. B4.*

The rhythmic text, incorporating a series of cumulative details, is well-suited for reading aloud; the architectural modifications, ranging from a ship to a pseudo-Greek temple, are a marvelous blend of absurdity (from an adult's point of view) and logic (from a child's point of view). The vibrant, full-color illustrations are executed in a deceptively ingenuous style reminiscent of children's art. A rib-tickling tribute to individuality, presented with a sure sense of the comic spirit.

Mary M. Burns, "Late Summer Booklist: 'The Big Orange Splot'," in The Horn Book Magazine *(copyright © 1977 by the Horn Book, Inc., Boston), Vol. LIII, No. 4, August, 1977, p. 432.*

In the morning the other people on the street came out of their houses. Their houses were all the same. But Mr. Plumbean's house was like a rainbow. It was like a jungle. It was like an explosion.

From The Big Orange Splot, *written and illustrated by Daniel Manus Pinkwater.*

THE BLUE THING   (1977)

A sort of free-floating, alternative origin tale, about an unnamed thing that turns up out of nowhere. . . . Eventually, perhaps when you see the spot of blue "as big as a mountain and getting bigger," you'll catch on; if not, the last picture, all blue above the wavey line that signifies mountains, will confirm that what the small blue thing has grown into is the sky. Slight, but Pinkwater's spacey, craftily simple drawings make that seem a virtue.

"Picture Books: 'The Blue Thing'," in Kirkus Reviews *(copyright © 1977 The Kirkus Service, Inc.), Vol. XLV, No. 14, July 15, 1977, p. 725.*

Judging by his creations so far, Pinkwater's middle name could as well be Versatility as Manus. In novels and in ingenious picture books, he has attracted critical praise and an eager audience, children who will find his new book well worth their time. To classically simple ink drawings with lots of white he adds "the blue thing." At first, it's a dot, so small, "Nobody knew it was there." It's a sort of seed thing, he says, unnoticed by a frog, a fox and others. But it grows. It becomes as big as the frog, the fox and a cow, and they see it then. It becomes as big as a tree. No one can miss it. Pinkwater says it's still there: "You can go and see it for yourself." It's the sky. Everyone can figure out hidden meanings here, of course, but no one will question the book's basic attraction—grand entertainment.

"Picture Books: 'The Blue Thing'," in Publishers Weekly *(reprinted from the July 18, 1977 issue of* Publishers Weekly, *published by R. R. Bowker Company, a Xerox company; copyright © 1977 by Xerox Corporation), Vol. 212, No. 3, July 18, 1977, p. 137.*

A simple whimsy about the origin of the blue sky. Educators always have conscientious scruples about attractive tales based on misleading ideas, but children have an instinctive ability to differentiate between fact and fantasy, especially with a little help. Not Pinkwater's most original work, either in story or illustration, but intriguing enough to keep the attention of pre-school listeners—no small accomplishment.

> *Brigitte Weeks, ''Young Bookshelf: 'The Blue Thing','' in Book World—The Washington Post (copyright © 1977 The Washington Post), September 11, 1977, p. E6.*

THE HOBOKEN CHICKEN EMERGENCY   (1977)

Though the word from New Jersey is that they're not laughing at Hoboken any more, kids should at least get some chuckles out of 266-pound Henrietta—the only chicken left in town. . . . A disarming resolution all round, and if Henrietta is a feather-weight compared to Claudia in last year's *Lizard Music,* she's no turkey.

> *''Younger Fiction: 'The Hoboken Chicken Emergency','' in Kirkus Reviews (copyright © 1977 The Kirkus Service, Inc.), Vol. XLV, No. 4, February 15, 1977, p. 166.*

The last line of **"Lizard Music,"** Mr. Pinkwater's previous book, reads: "I'm looking around for a really intelligent chicken." His search, evidently, led to [**"The Hoboken Chicken Emergency"**].

Arthur Bobowicz, sent to the market for a Thanksgiving turkey, comes home with a live, six-foot tall, 266-pound chicken—and his parents are only mildly upset. If you can believe that, then maybe you're ready for the rest of the story.

Henrietta, this "superchicken," runs afoul of Arthur's father and is returned from whence she came. She then flies the coop and scares the good citizens of Hoboken. The rest of the story is a chicken chase. . . . The overloaded slapstick falls flat, and neither Arthur nor Henrietta has enough going for him to make a reader care whether they are reunited or not: Mr. Pink-water didn't find his intelligent chicken.

However, if you know a young reader who has always wanted a six-foot tall, 266-pound chicken for a pet, he or she may like this book. As for me, when I finished reading I had the feeling that I'd just sat through a Saturday morning television cartoon. (pp. 44-5)

> *Sue Alexander, ''For Young Readers: 'The Hoboken Chicken Emergency','' in The New York Times Book Review (© 1977 by The New York Times Company; reprinted by permission), March 27, 1977, pp. 44-5.*

If you throw enough ingredients into a pot you get an unusual stew, and the *Hoboken Chicken Emergency* is no exception. Of course, the 266-pound chicken . . . doesn't get stewed. . . .

[Justice] wins through, though slightly henpecked, and all live happily ever after. And with this chicken story inside him the reader will, too.

> *Guernsey LePelley, ''Sir Rosemary to the Rescue,'' in The Christian Science Monitor (reprinted by permission from The Christian Science Monitor; © 1977 The Christian Science Publishing Society; all rights reserved), May 4, 1977, p. B8.**

A big step up in reading level and length, but . . . using humor to draw the reader out of himself, is Daniel Manus Pinkwater's *The Hoboken Chicken Emergency*. . . . This highly idiosyn-cratic author-illustrator puts the town of Hoboken under

siege. . . . The looney adventures of Arthur and Henrietta the chicken cater precisely to the transition from fairy-tale to space wars, and the drawings are as zany as the text. (p. 28)

> *Brigitte Weeks, ''Brigitte Weeks on Children's Books,'' in The New Republic (reprinted by permission of The New Republic; © 1977 The New Republic, Inc.), Vol. 177, No. 23, December 3, 1977, pp. 26, 28-9.**

SUPERPUPPY: HOW TO CHOOSE, RAISE, AND TRAIN THE BEST POSSIBLE DOG FOR YOU   (with Jill Pinkwater, 1977)

A super puppy book, refreshingly flexible and undogmatic, offering sensible guidance and alternative procedures on ev-erything from selecting a dog to fit your family, home, and habits (but "forget all these rules" if nothing happens between you and the dog so selected) to identifying and dealing with various diseases and parasites. Relaxed as they are about in-dividual differences in dogs, owners, and "experts," the Pink-waters are firm about pet shops (they give several good reasons why you should never buy a dog in one), rigorous about pet and vet selection, careful to structure their obedience-training procedures, and openly contemptuous of people who buy ad-vertised canine junk food, acquire pets without the necessary commitment of time and love, or allow their pets to saddle the world with unwanted animals. Drawing on their own experi-ence as professional obedience trainers and owners of two Alaskan malamutes with distinctive personalities, and empha-sizing throughout that they don't know it all, that their book is not "complete," and that there might be better ways for you than the ones they suggest, the Pinkwaters quietly and personably set forth a thorough, thoughtful, and sympathetic Dr. Spock of puppy care.

> *''Young Adult Non-Fiction: 'Superpuppy: How to Choose, Raise and Train the Best Possible Dog for You','' in Kirkus Reviews (copyright © 1977 The Kirkus Service, Inc.), Vol. XLV, No. 14, July 15, 1977, p. 731.*

The Pinkwaters have created a book so much fun to read, so informative and altogether so valuable that it should almost be reading required of anyone thinking about owning a pet. Ab-sorbing the contents could certainly cut down on the number of dogs abandoned by people who change their minds about having a canine in the house. The authors begin by suggesting that you examine your reasons for owning a dog. The rest of the book details all the problems and rewards of caring for a dog and, in short, does everything promised in the title. The most attractive feature of this guide is that it is grounded in common sense and in unmistakable affection for man's and woman's best friend.

> *''Nonfiction: 'Superpuppy, How to Choose, Raise, and Train the Best Possible Dog for You','' in Pub-lishers Weekly (reprinted from the August 1, 1977 issue of Publishers Weekly, published by R. R. Bowker Company, a Xerox company; copyright © 1977 by Xerox Corporation), Vol. 212, No. 5, August 1, 1977, p. 115.*

This is yet another "how to raise and train a dog" book, written at a slightly lower level than some and with perhaps less em-phasis on purebred dogs. Like all participants in the dog "fancy" (those who spend most of their time training, showing, groom-ing, talking and thinking about purebred dogs), the Pinkwaters have their canine prejudices (which they *do* acknowledge in an amusing way), which might irritate dog owners who don't agree with them. The book is definitely written about the urban pet; anyone who believes dogs should live and work outdoors will find scant sympathy here. The Pinkwaters do a good job discussing choosing a puppy—from a breeder of purebreds, from a neighbor, from the dog pound or even taking in an adult stray. They suggest possible dangers in each case and recommend ways to minimize them; this flexibility distinguishes the Pinkwaters from some other dog experts, who assume the only worthwhile dogs are of known parentage. The amount of exercise needed by large dogs, especially those in urban environments, is oddly understated in the introductory sections; much later, almost in passing, the authors mention that their huskies are walked four times a day. Very few people with full time jobs or school work could contemplate such an obligation. If the prospective urban dog owner reads all of this book carefully, he or she should be well informed about whether dog ownership is wise and how to care for and train the dog chosen. Such information is also available in a host of other books, some of which may be a bit more daunting to a city dweller who wants a mutt.

> *D. Covalt Dunning, "Animal Husbandry," in* Science Books & Films *(copyright © 1978 by the American Association for the Advancement of Science), Vol. XIV, No. 2, September, 1978, p. 115.*

FAT MEN FROM SPACE   (1977)

[*Fat Men From Space* is] told from the viewpoint of William, whose dentist gives him one of those rare but actually occurring fillings that turn out to function as radio receivers. At first William has fun putting on his teacher . . . and his mother. . . . Then, to boost reception, he hooks up his tooth to a chain-link fence and finds himself zapped into contact with voracious fat men from space, arriving in their spaceburgers to strip the earth of its junk food. Because they know he's overheard their plans, the spacemen snatch William up in their ship, and from there he witnesses the invasion: millions of fat men in plaid sports jackets falling through the sky to gobble up frozen pizza . . . Twinkies . . . breaded clams . . . the President's private store of Milky Ways. . . . At last a giant potato pancake launched in space near the invaders' home planet diverts the fat men, leaving earthlings awash in Big Mac wrappers and allowing William to free-fall home in a plaid spacejacket provided for the journey. That's all—just another wiggy, preposterous fabrication from D. M. Pinkwater, himself a fat man from space with an ear for our planet's absurdities.

> *"Younger Fiction: 'Fat Men from Space'," in* Kirkus Reviews *(copyright © 1977 The Kirkus Service, Inc.), Vol. XLV, No. 17, September, 1977, p. 934.*

The only thing each work by Pinkwater has in common is excellence. As usual [*Fat Men from Space*] is different from what has gone before, a wildly comic fantasy with a solid moral.

> *"Picture Books: 'Fat Men from Space'," in* Publishers Weekly *(reprinted from the September, 1977 issue of* Publishers Weekly, *published by R. R. Bowker Company, a Xerox company; copyright © 1977 by Xerox Corporation), Vol. 212, No. 11, September 12, 1977, p. 133.*

I am ashamed to admit that I laughed out loud several times while reading this gripping narrative. But do not be deceived.

The enemy is everywhere. Already they have caused the real Daniel Manus Pinkwater's photograph to be removed from the book jacket and have replaced it with one of . . . a fat man in a plaid sports jacket with a crew cut, a tasteless tie and horn-rimmed glasses.

> *Georgess McHargue, "Children's Books: 'Fat Men from Space'," in* The New York Times Book Review *(© 1977 by The New York Times Company; reprinted by permission), October 16, 1977, p. 47.*

THE LAST GURU   (1978)

Harold, at 12, wins a small fortune at the racetrack . . . and a large fortune by investing the money in stocks. So large that he, his parents, and his uncle must figure out how to live a normal life once the public learns that Harold is the fifth richest person in the world. With the aid of "friends" (Armand Virmin, the investment man, and Hamish MacTavish, the millionaire Croco-Cola man) Harold and his parents end up in India where monks of the order of the Silly Hat discover in Harold the reincarnated soul of their founder and whisk him off to Tibet for a two-year training course. Harold returns to Rochester, New York both wealthy and enlightened enough to solve what the author obviously feels is a real problem—too many people meditating without finding happiness, too many gurus who are in the business for the money, and too few people who can laugh. Pinkwater's sense of humor is as quirky as ever, though he's grinding the axe pretty hard in this one. Harold is a delightfully no-nonsense type who can handle being the reincarnation of a great soul with complete insouciance; but much of the fun here is based on a working knowledge of the meditation scene, and the names of the characters (Reverend Goon, for instance) *do* seem to connect rather obviously with certain well-known religious leaders. (pp. 66-7)

> *Sara Miller, "Grades 3-6: 'The Last Guru'," in* School Library Journal *(reprinted from the November, 1978 issue of* School Library Journal, *published by R. R. Bowker Co./A Xerox Corporation; copyright © 1978), Vol. 75, No. 3, November, 1978, pp. 66-7.*

This starts out even better than *Lizard Music,* with twelve-year-old Harold Blatz putting his three-years' savings on his first racetrack bet, investing the 90-to-one winnings in the stagnant Hamish MacTavish Zenburger chain, and ending up the fifth richest person in the world. . . . From wacky satire, the vibrations change to a virtual hum as the Blatzes settle happily in an Indian village—where, as a gift to townspeople who can't think of anything they need, Harold orders a prefabricated bowling alley from England. The bowling alley becomes a shrine after Harold goes off to the Tibetan monastery of the 1000-year-old Silly Hat sect—whose founder, the monks believe with some reason, has been reincarnated in Harold. When Harold returns to Rochester, New York, two years later, there's a hilarious scene at the airport as guru after guru is disgorged from the midnight plane from Bombay and whisked off by crowds of devoted followers. Harold, it seems, has returned to an America in the midst of an Eastern-inspired (or, more specifically, Hodie MacBodhi-inspired) spiritual rebirth—and from here on Pinkwater begins to come down too hard. Compared, for example, with his throwaway list of painters' names in *Lizard Music,* there's something a little heavy, and more than a little testy, in his repeated reference to Buttered Rum Crass, the Hairy Cricket Brotherhood, Alan Plotz, and the rest—and, in Harold's climactic, didactic speech puncturing the whole guru craze, the direct attack somehow violates the message. Nevertheless, the message is not tacked on; the whole crazy adventure has been building to it all along, and the road is paved with Pinkwater's delightful, straight-faced observations of everyday absurdities and outlandish manifestations. (pp. 1189-90)

> *"Younger Fiction: 'The Last Guru'," in Kirkus Reviews (copyright © 1978 The Kirkus Service, Inc.), Vol. XLVI, No. 21, November 1, 1978, pp. 1189-90.*

ALAN MENDELSOHN, THE BOY FROM MARS   (1979)

Like *Lizard Music,* this Hogboro adventure begins realistically and little by little has readers assenting to such . . . phenomena. . . . The story begins when Leonard Neeble "a short, portly, wrinkled kid with glasses," moves unhappily to a new neighborhood but soon makes friends with Alan Mendelsohn, another weird new kid at Bat Masterson Junior High School. Soon Leonard and Alan have attained State Twenty-six with used-book-dealer Samuel Klugarsh's crackpot, cabalistic Mind Control System, and thus can mentally command mindless people to do silly things and bricks to rise into the air. These tricks soon grow boring, however, and then Venusian Clarence Yojimbo, whom they meet in the Chili Parlor, explains that "the point of State Twenty-six is not to make yourself into a radio transmitter—but to make yourself into a radio receiver." After that intriguing suggestion, the boy's subsequent adventure in the existential plane of Waka-Waka might be a bit of a let-down philosophically, but Leonard's ultimate happy-ending adjustment back at Bat Masterson is his own show, and unlike any other. Throughout Pinkwater gets away with long explanatory conversations because the conversations are so ridiculous and the explanations so wild—dizzying in their ever-expanding revelation, pure Pinkwater in their spacey view of our existential plane.

> *"Older Fiction: 'Alan Mendelsohn, the Boy from Mars'," in Kirkus Reviews (copyright © 1979 The Kirkus Service, Inc.), Vol. XLVII, No. 12, June 15, 1979, p. 690.*

In this exaggerated, tongue-in-cheek story of time-slips and thought control, Pinkwater lampoons con men and dupes, psychic powers, quack medicos, natural food faddists and assorted weird characters with great humor if, occasionally, at great length. Leonard and Alan repeatedly fall for confidence tricks and repeatedly profit from them, as when they buy a Mind Control Omega Meter and find that, for them, it works. If nothing succeeds like excess, the author has achieved a triumph of improbable folderol.

> *Zena Sutherland, "New Titles for Children and Young People: 'Alan Mendelsohn, The Boy from Mars'," in Bulletin of the Center for Children's Books (reprinted by permission of The University of Chicago Press; © 1979 by The University of Chicago), Vol. 33, No. 3, November, 1979, p. 54.*

Pinkwater writes hilarious, outrageous, delightful novels about intelligent lizards, pig-shaped submarines, gurus in silly hats and other fantastic and wonderful things. Pinkwater's books don't always succeed—*The Last Guru* and *Yobgorgle* fall apart about half-way through—but when they do, the result is exhilarating.

Alan Mendelsohn is Pinkwater's best book since *Lizard Music*. The plot concerns the adventures of Leonard Neeble and Alan Mendelsohn, fellow students at Bat Masterson Junior High School. Things are pretty dull around Hogsboro until Leonard and Alan discover the Bermuda Triangle Chili Parlor, meet Samuel Klugarsh, and start learning the Klugarsh Mind Control System. . . . And I almost forgot Clarence Yojimbo. You see, he's a member of the Laughing Alligator Motorcycle Club, a folk singer, and an extra-terrestrial, and . . . well, maybe you'd better just read the book. It's terrific! And then give it to your favorite young adult to enjoy.

> *Fran Lantz, "Fiction: 'Alan Mendelsohn, the Boy from Mars'," in Kliatt Young Adult Paperback Book Guide (copyright © by Kliatt Paperback Book Guide), Vol. XV, No. 6, September, 1981, p. 14.*

PICKLE CREATURE   (1979)

Pinkwater, an incorrigibly zany children's book writer, has done it again. This time his young hero, a boy named Conrad who's visiting his grandmother, finds a sweet-tempered pickle-thing (a cross between "a dinosaur, and a big dog, and a crocodile") when sent on a late-night run to the corner grocery. It accompanies Conrad back to his grandma's and settles down to sleep. And that's all . . . but even when this author creates an uncluttered story he manages to infuse it with a feeling of delightful lunacies left unsaid. Brightly colored, comically lumpy pictures.

> *Michele Slung, "Young Bookshelf: 'Pickle Creature'," in Book World—The Washington Post (© 1979, The Washington Post), March 11, 1979, p. F5.*

Heavy outlines and solid blocks of brash color are used in the simple, ingenuously drawn pictures that accompany a slight fantasy. . . . There's some humor in the fact that the clerk at the grocery store and Conrad's grandmother both calmly accept the pickle creature . . . but the story has a static tone and the ending is limp. (pp. 15-16)

> *Zena Sutherland, "New Titles for Children and Young People: 'Pickle Creature'," in Bulletin of the Center for Children's Books (reprinted by permission of The University of Chicago Press; © 1979 by The University of Chicago), Vol. 33, No. 1, September, 1979, pp. 15-16.*

RETURN OF THE MOOSE   (1979)

Second go arounds rarely rival the first, and the *Return* . . . of Pinkwater's *Blue Moose* . . . is no exception. Still maître d' at Mr. Breton's gourmet eatery, he's no longer the moose who melted the reserve of the chef's north country customers. Now endowed with an artistic temperament and monumental ego, he's a moose on the make, penning his memoirs . . . , wrangling with publishers, going Hollywood. Pinkwater may have been going for self-parody (the hero's nom de plume is D. Moosus Moosewater), but satirizing authors is an adult joke, and a familiar one at that. The mellow camaraderie of the earlier book was as warming as Breton's best-in-the-world chowder. The sequel has its moments, but the further Moose strays from the restaurant the more he leaves a bad taste in the mouth.

> *Pamela D. Pollack, "Preschool and Primary Grades: 'Return of the Moose'," in School Library Journal (reprinted from the April, 1979 issue of School Li-*

brary Journal, *published by R. R. Bowker Co./A Xerox Corporation; copyright © 1979), Vol. 25, No. 8, April, 1979, p. 47.*

[*Blue Moose*] is probably Pinkwater's most lovable creation, and for a while here Mr. Breton and his helper the moose are running their North Woods restaurant as harmoniously as ever. But then the clicking of the typewriter in the moose's room replaces the companionable hum in the kitchen: Blue Moose, it seems, is writing his own "True Story." . . . Surprisingly (to Mr. Breton), the moose does sell his book, but he is so incensed when his publishers Klotz, Yold & Co. turn it into a hot love story that he storms off to New York and eats all 6,000 copies—plus two electric typewriters. It's a fitting response and there are other such touches, but somehow this hackneyed satire of the publishing world (and later of the successful-author circuit) seems imposed on our old friend the moose. And though it's nice to see Mr. Breton's supporting partner strike out on his own, the result is far less resonant than the first *Blue Moose*.

> *"Younger Fiction: 'Return of the Moose'," in* Kirkus Reviews *(copyright © 1979 The Kirkus Service, Inc.), Vol. XLVII, No. 8, April 15, 1979, p. 452.*

A sequel to *Blue Moose,* but standing solidly on its own, this is a hilarious tall tale, the exaggerations given a nice foil by the dead-pan sobriety of the telling. . . . Pinkwater has a yeasty style and he knows just how far to carry nonsense without letting it degenerate into senselessness. This is a good choice for reading aloud to younger children.

> *Zena Sutherland, "New Titles for Children and Young People: 'Return of the Moose'," in* Bulletin of the Center for Children's Books *(reprinted by permission of The University of Chicago Press; © 1979 by The University of Chicago), Vol. 33, No. 2, October, 1979, p. 36.*

YOBGORGLE: MYSTERY MONSTER OF LAKE ONTARIO   (1979)

Pure fun from Pinkwater, all about what happens to Eugene Winkleman when his parents win a trip to Europe and he spends two weeks in a Rochester motel with 280-pound fast-food-junkie Uncle Mel. Early on, Eugene meets Professor Ambrose McFwain of the Piscean Discovery Institute—the "weirdo in a rowboat" Eugene and Uncle Mel have just seen in a low-grade documentary movie—and before long McFwain entices Uncle Mel with a fat man's safari suit to let Eugene come along as assistant on his upcoming Lake Ontario monster hunt. Also on board is Colonel Ken Krenwinkle. . . . Yobgorgle turns out to be an enormous pink pig—no, it's a pink, pig-shaped submarine—and the final encounter, in the depths of Lake Ontario, is with the submarine's mad captain who in turn turns out to be the Flying Dutchman—and who holds the monster hunters captive until, in a final life-or-death ride, they free him from his curse. There's lots more preposterous craziness, tossed in and built up. . . . Much of it is just plain silly, but all of it bears the stamp of Pinkwater's unstoppable, inspired imagination.

> *"Younger Fiction: 'Yobgorgle: Mystery Monster of Lake Ontario'," in* Kirkus Reviews *(copyright © 1979 The Kirkus Service, Inc.), Vol. XLVII, No. 18, September 15, 1979, p. 1068.*

Pinkwater has a deft facility for placing his improbable plots in real settings, and *Yobgorgle, Mystery Monster of Lake On-*

tario is comfortably ensconced in conservative Rochester, New York. . . . When Pinkwater is good, he is very, very good, and even when he's not so good there are still a few laughs in each chapter. This, despite a change of scene and a wildly dissimilar plot, reads like a spin-off from his far more successful *Alan Mendelsohn, the Boy from Mars.* . . .

> *Patricia Manning, "Grades 3 to 6: 'Yobgorgle: Mystery Monster of Lake Ontario'," in* School Library Journal *(reprinted from the November, 1979 issue of* School Library Journal, *published by R. R. Bowker Co./A Xerox Corporation; copyright © 1979), Vol. 26, No. 3, November, 1979, p. 80.*

[*Yobgorgle: Mystery Monster of Lake Ontario*] is crammed with outrageous bits and bizarre characters (à la Roald Dahl) but Pinkwater lacks the satiric bite of Dahl. His imaginative flamboyance seems forced, superficial, and gratuitous. The overabundance of weirdness strains and ultimately drains suspense and credibility from the story. It is good for a chuckle or two, but, like the Yobgorgle, it is without substance. (p. 69)

> *John Cech, "Older Readers: 'Yobgorgle: Mystery Monster of Lake Ontario'," in* Children's Book Review Service *(copyright © 1980 Children's Book Review Service Inc.), Vol. 8, No. 7, Winter, 1980, pp. 68-9.*

THE WUGGIE NORPLE STORY   (1980)

["**The Wuggie Norple Story**"] is surely one of the most inane and boring [texts] I or my kids have encountered in many months. It consists of repetitious, stupid-name jokes (Lunchbox Louie is the father, Bigfoot the Chipmunk is the mother, King Waffle is the kid) strung out along a story of a cat called Wuggie Norple who gets bigger and bigger every day.

> *Harold C.K. Rice, "Picture Books: 'The Wuggie Norple Story'," in* The New York Times Book Review *(© 1980 by The New York Times Company; reprinted by permission), April 27, 1980, p. 49.*

Laugh along with some of the zaniest characters that have ever been gathered together in one book. . . . Classes to whom this book has been introduced insist that it is a "must" for library purchase. (pp. 93-4)

> *Margaret M. Nichols, "Picture Books: 'The Wuggie Norple Story'," in* Children's Book Review Service *(copyright © 1980 Children's Book Review Service Inc.), Vol. 8, No. 10, May, 1980, pp. 93-4.*

Contrary to the author's evident assumption, giving characters jawbreakingly ever-so-funny names does *not* constitute the creation of a humorous story. . . . Even those who quite enjoy this sort of thing will suffer from circuit overload before the multisyllabic crew take themselves off to Nosewort Pond for the grand finale picnic.

> *Joan McGrath, "Preschool and Primary Grades: 'The Wuggie Norple Story'," in* School Library Journal *(reprinted from the May, 1980 issue of* School Library Journal, *published by R. R. Bowker Co./A Xerox Corporation; copyright © 1980), Vol. 26, No. 9, May, 1980, p. 62.*

THE MAGIC MOSCOW (1980)

A slight but humorous tale of Steve, an ice-cream shop owner in Hoboken, New Jersey, who idolizes Sergeant Schwartz of the Yukon on television. His dream comes true when he buys a malamute who is the grandson of Schwartz's famous TV dog. . . . Black-and-white illustrations of all the characters add to the fun. Pinkwater fans will love it.

> Linda Worden, ''Younger Readers: 'The Magic Moscow','' in Children's Book Review Service (copyright © 1980 Children's Book Review Service Inc.), Vol. 9, No. 2, October, 1980, p. 15.

Take a good-natured but gullible collector of comic books, antique sneakers, and just about anything; a shyster malamute dealer; a scrawny malamute puppy; a former radio actor known for his role as a Canadian mountie; a self-described world-famous dog expert; a friendly milkman; the milkman's delivery horse Cheryl; and 121 dogs assembled for the Hoboken Sled Dog Club's annual show. Give them all unlikely names (Sergeant Schwartz of the Yukon) and put them all together . . . in the Magic Moscow (formerly Magic Moocow), a soft ice cream stand in Hoboken, New Jersey. The result is as irresistibly unbalanced as proprietor Steve's health-food specialty, a concoction called Moron's Delight made up of a banana, a carrot, three kinds of syrup, whole roasted peanuts, a slice of Swiss cheese, a radish, yogurt, wheat germ, and a kosher pickle. The story more-or-less centers on Steve and his new puppy Edward, whom the dealer claims to be descended from the faithful companion of Steve's old hero Sergeant Schwartz. As Steve's young part-time helper Norman Bleistift tells it, the dog-show that brings Steve's hero to Hoboken ends a fiasco; Edward wins by default but then disappears; and everyone gallops off in the milk wagon to rescue him from Slade, Blackie, and Nick, the trio of dog rustlers who exist only in the mind of the former Sergeant Schwartz. Related with Pinkwater's usual straight-faced drollery, a funny story.

> ''Younger Fiction: 'The Magic Moscow','' in Kirkus Reviews (copyright © 1980 The Kirkus Service, Inc.), Vol. XLVIII, No. 20, October 15, 1980, p. 1357.

[The Magic Moscow presents] the dizziest ending yet devised by bumptious Pinkwater. Don't try to understand; just enjoy, particularly the artist's sharp ink drawings highlighting the burlesque.

> ''Children's Books: 'The Magic Moscow','' in Publishers Weekly (reprinted from the October 17, 1980 issue of Publishers Weekly, published by R. R. Bowker Company, a Xerox company; copyright © 1980 by Xerox Corporation), Vol. 218, No. 16, October 17, 1980, p. 66.

THE WORMS OF KUKUMLINA (1981)

The zany Mr. Pinkwater takes the reader on an African safari to track down the intelligent, giant earthworms of Kukumlima, a place known only to a very few. The explorers find the earthworms and also the long-lost prospector, Gordon Whillikers. (''G. Whillikers, I presume.'') The characters include Seumas Finneganstein, wealthy inventor of the little metal snaps on salamis, his grandson Ronald Donald Almondotter, and his best friend Sir Charles Pelicanstein. The characters they meet along the way are just as nutty. The usual Pinkwater elements—fast foods, comic books and pinball machines—are present. The running joke of the book is that Los Angeles doesn't exist: it's just an example of poor mapmaking. The whole thing is a delightful romp that children will adore.

> Nelda Mohr, ''Younger Readers: 'The Worms of Kukumlima','' in Children's Book Review Service (copyright © 1981 Children's Book Review Service Inc.), Vol. 9, No. 8, March, 1981, p. 65.

If readers can suspend not only disbelief but also common sense and logic, as many fantasy fans can, this should prove to be one of Pinkwater's most popular books. Its narrator, Ronald Donald Almondotter, is privileged to go along on an African safari with his grandfather (Seumas Finneganstein) and Grandpa's old friend Sir Charles Pelicanstein to find the elusive worm, enormous and intelligent, that is reputed to live in wildest Kukumlima, wherever that is. It's a nonsensical romp from start to finish, with ridiculous adventures, exaggerated characters, and—somehow—a plot that actually develops and has a dénouement.

> Zena Sutherland, ''New Titles for Children and Young People: 'The Worms of Kukumlima','' in Bulletin of the Center for Children's Books (reprinted by permission of The University of Chicago Press; © 1981 by The University of Chicago), Vol. 35, No. 2, October, 1981, p. 35.

TOOTH-GNASHER SUPERFLASH (1981)

Funny-man Pinkwater takes us on another ride, this time in the versatile Tooth-Gnasher Superflash with Mr. and Mrs. Popsnorkle and the five little Popsnorkles. But if the silly names recall The Wuggie Norple Story, we're not done in by them here. The Tooth-Gnasher does perform. Specifically, after Mr. Popsnorkle takes the wheel of the Superflash from car salesman Mr. Sandy, the car turns into a dinosaur, an elephant and then a giant turtle. When Mr. Sandy says uneasily, ''This is not the way the Tooth-Gnasher Superflash is supposed to behave,'' Mr. Popsnorkle answers that the only other thing he'd like the car to do is turn into a huge chicken and fly. And so it does, obligingly. . . . Mrs. Popsnorkle, playing the role she would in a mindless car commercial, can only comment repeatedly on the car's lovely color. Kids will have no trouble recognizing the whole outing as part spoof, part whimsy, and more fun than most knobs and buttons provide.

> ''Picture Books: 'Tooth-Gnasher Superflash','' in Kirkus Reviews (copyright © 1981 The Kirkus Service, Inc.), Vol. XLIX, No. 6, March 15, 1981, p. 353.

Pinkwater's spoof of jazzy cars is illustrated in boldly colored, scribbly cartoons. The book proves again that no one can accuse the author of subtlety or sense—which is all to the good so far as his devotees are concerned.

> ''Fiction: 'Tooth-Gnasher Superflash','' in Publishers Weekly (reprinted from the April 3, 1981 issue of Publishers Weekly, published by R. R. Bowker Company, a Xerox company; copyright © 1981 by Xerox Corporation), Vol. 219, No. 14, April 3, 1981, p. 74.

Laurence Pringle

1935-

(Also writes as Sean Edmund) American author of nonfiction for children, and photographer. Pringle, a wildlife biologist and past editor of *Nature and Science* magazine, has developed his knowledge of science into books on biology and environments which handle a wide range of topics (dinosaurs, death, ecosystems) in an informative and interesting manner. Several of his works are specifically concerned with the effects of man-made hazards—chemical pollution, over-population, food shortages—and possible solutions to such ecological perils. He also discusses alternative energy sources, including the pros and cons of nuclear power.

Although some critics charge that Pringle is too simplistic in his descriptions and terminology, most reviewers observe that while his approach may occasionally be general it is not condescending. It is generally felt that Pringle transforms complex scientific material into a group of appealing and plainspoken books which may interest young readers enough to lead them to more advanced and detailed studies. Three of Pringle's titles were chosen A.L.A. Notable Books: *Listen to the Crows* in 1976, *Death Is Natural* in 1977, and *Wild Foods* in 1978. (See also *Contemporary Authors*, Vols. 29-32, and *Something about the Author*, Vol. 4.)

AUTHOR'S COMMENTARY

The nineteenth-century philosopher Søren Kierkegaard told of a man who saw a sign in a shop window: "Philosophy Done Here." He rushed into the shop to buy some, only to be told that the sign itself was for sale.

The subject here is science books, and Kierkegaard's story can easily be adapted to the late twentieth century: change the words to "Science Done Here" and put them on a T-shirt. This essay explores what it means to "do science," why an understanding of science is especially important now, and how children's books can help. (p. 108)

Doing science means being curious, asking questions. It means having a healthy skepticism toward authority and announced truths. It is both a way of looking at the world and a way of thinking. It values both fantasy and reality, and provides a framework for telling the difference. . . .

To do science is to acknowledge that the world is a complex place but that the complexity can be explored and understood, and that there is order and unity in its diversity. At its core, science is a hopeful activity. Psychiatrist Karen Horney believed that young children are naturally joyful, unafraid, warm, and spontaneous. To this I think we can add curious and hopeful. Since science at its best stands for hope, curiosity, truthfulness, and the joy of discovery, you might suppose that children would clamor for more science in their lives. This is not the case. (p. 110)

Science teaching is scarce in elementary and middle schools, and many science programs reinforce the notion that doing science means memorizing facts, jargon, and numbers that seem irrelevant to everyday life. Scientists themselves have contributed to illusions about how they work and what the

results mean. As a result, the public feels that science is much too complex for ordinary folks, and that it is a source of final, absolute answers rather than a continual search for truth.

This massive misunderstanding of science is taking its toll. Although there is no lack of scientists, women and ethnic minorities are poorly represented. Ill-prepared to tell facts from fantasies and wishful thinking, people support a thriving UFO industry, astrology industry, and other pseudoscience enterprises with millions of dollars annually. By itself, this may be harmless, but irrationality spills over into other areas. Science illiteracy has other, greater costs.

We live in an age when decisions involving science and technology can have enormous effects on everyone. Scientific knowledge—or a lack of it—plays a vital part in food-growing, health, and energy matters, for example. Decisions about such matters affect the quality of our lives, and perhaps the lives of many generations to come. (pp. 110-11)

Books reflect our culture, so it is not surprising to find some children's books that could only thrive amidst science illiteracy. In a recent children's book about astrology, for example, nearly all of the text was neutral or mildly positive in tone. Readers were even given detailed instructions for preparing a horoscope. Only in the last few pages was the validity of astrology questioned seriously. Finally, in the last line, it was dismissed as nonsensical magic. This attempt to have it both ways—to appeal to ignorance, then belatedly appeal to reason—was disrespectful to readers of any age, and especially so to children. (pp. 111-12)

Commercial exploitation of ignorance is never pretty, but books like [this], fortunately, are only a small fraction of those published. Furthermore, the overall quality of children's science books has improved in the past decade or two. The "gee whiz" approach to scientific and technological developments is vanishing. People are more conscious of interconnections. They have learned to expect side effects—which someone called "wormholes in the fruits of technology"—so that few books now read like press releases from industry or government. There are also fewer books about animals as isolates; the interdependence of living things and their environment is acknowledged and celebrated.

There have also been some encouraging changes in other media. For decades, commercial television has abounded with pseudoscience of the worst sort. The few programs dealing with real science tended to emphasize colorful, charming subjects. (p. 112)

The public television series "Cosmos," first shown in 1980, may have helped viewers begin to distinguish between some truths and some illusions about themselves and the universe. (p. 113)

Aiming at eight- to twelve-year-olds, Children's Television Workshop produced "3-2-1 Contact" with a goal of showing "science as rational, but also intuitive, neat, but also messy, and characterized not only by patience and rigor, but by wit and playfulness as well."

These goals have been met by the finest children's science books down through the years. Whether the subject is the moon or a mouse, you can find a core of integrity in these books. Both subject and reader are treated with respect.

Scientists are portrayed as humans. They sometimes make mistakes, and compete or squabble among themselves. Their curiosity leads them to ask questions much like the ones other people ask. What they learn may or may not stand the test of time or the scrutiny of other minds. It will certainly lead to more questions.

There is, of course, some jargon in most of these books. An irreducible minimum of terms is vital in order to tell a story or explain an idea. Authors who are obsessed with naming things, who feel that a sort of crossword-puzzle knowledge is wisdom, usually aim for maximum jargon. But a minimum of terms and their definitions helps clear the reader's path from idea to idea, and it is the ideas that really matter.

As a writer, I felt the burden of scientific terms and their definitions most acutely in my book *Death Is Natural*. The main ideas of the first chapter were that death is inevitable and necessary, and that minerals and other matter making up living things are continually recycled on earth. The chapter's "character"—a rabbit—died on the first page, but there was still a story to tell. What happens to a dead animal? Where does it *go*?

Just as readers may feel an urgency to find out, I wanted to get on with the story. Before long, however, there was that irreducible minimum of terms (element, atom, molecule) to explain. I felt impatient with those paragraphs, and suppose

that readers do too. That I chose *not* to use a dozen other terms having to do with decay is some consolation.

At a recent conference on children's books, an editor declared that accuracy is the single most important characteristic of science books. Well, sure, accuracy ranks right up there with apple pie, but I wonder, "accuracy of what?" Minor details, major ideas, values, attitudes? Which would you rather read: a book marred by some factual errors that is also sprightly, inspiring, and memorable, or one that is perfect in every factual detail but dull as a hoe? We should not have to make such a choice, since most publishers routinely pay experts to check manuscripts of nonfiction books. (Of course, experts can be careless, make or miss mistakes, and also may disagree among themselves.) The perfect book has yet to be published, but the best science books are accurate in details and especially in concepts. Respect for the truth, to the extent it is known, is part of the appealing integrity of doing science. (pp. 113-14)

The doing of science depends on such special human qualities as curiosity, passion, creativity, and veracity. Partly because of these characteristics, science has been called the greatest hope of the human race. Children's books have a vital role to play. They can make science and the universe more accessible to young people. They can stand for and appeal to the finest characteristics and highest aspirations of the human species. (p. 115)

Laurence Pringle, "Science Done Here," in Celebrating Children's Books: Essays on Children's Literature in Honor of Zena Sutherland, *edited by Betsy Hearne and Marilyn Kaye (copyright © 1981 by The Zena Sutherland Lectureship Fund; reprinted by permission of Lothrop, Lee & Shephard Books, A Division of William Morrow & Co.), Lothrop, Lee, & Shepard Books, 1981, pp. 108-15.*

GENERAL COMMENTARY

Laurence Pringle combines in his books the ability to explain logical relationships and the succinct marshalling of facts that clarify such relationships, especially when they are intricate. In one of his earlier books, *Follow A Fisher* . . . , Pringle demonstrates his understanding of writing for younger children as he describes in crisp, straightforward style the habits and habitat of a member of the weasel family. His concern for conservation of species and for preservation of ecological balance as smoothly incorporated into the simply written, continuous text.

Nuclear Power: From Physics to Politics . . . , is for older readers, an objective approach to the complex dilemma of the nuclear power plant. Although he states that he is "not neutral," Pringle is in fact quite objective in discussing the safety hazards, the violations, the problems of nuclear waste, and the role of the Atomic Energy Commission. The text is as lucid in descriptions of processes as it is in evaluation of moral and ethical questions involved in the provision of energy through nuclear power. (pp. 456-57)

The breadth of Pringle's interests is indicated by the fact that, although he trained as a wildlife biologist, his books often consider the total environment, sociological factors, and legal or ethical implications of biological problems. (p. 457)

May Hill Arbuthnot, Dianne L. Monson, and Zena Sutherland, "Informational Books: 'Follow a Fisher'," in their Children and Books *(copyright © 1947, 1957, 1964, 1972, 1977, 1981 by Scott, Fores-*

man and Company; reprinted by permission), sixth edition, Scott, Foresman, 1981, pp. 456-57.

DINOSAURS AND THEIR WORLD   (1968)

You'd expect another book about dinosaurs to be a new breed, in some way different from or superior to its precursors, but this is neither distinctively angled nor especially effective. A brief survey of the origin, varieties and disappearance of dinosaurs, it combines a determinedly instructive, often interlocutory text, young in style and tone, with black-and-white illustrations (photographs, drawings, diagrams) that are adequate for identification but won't awe anyone. Moreover, the "monster" image is lost without a corresponding gain in scholarship: explanations (of the evolution from amphibians to reptiles, of the characteristics of different groups of dinosaurs) are fragmentary and often superficial. It's the last book most youngsters would choose from a wide assortment and there's no reason why they should.

> *"Younger Non-Fiction: 'Dinosaurs and Their World',"* in Kirkus Service *(copyright © 1968 Virginia Kirkus' Service, Inc.), Vol. XXXVI, No. 5, March 1, 1968, p. 267.*

[One] of the best [of new dinosaur books] is this graphic presentation. The animals and their remains are displayed in drawings and photographs, and the text successfully combines both archaeological and biological introductions to their world. After a dramatic account of the first discoveries of the prehistoric evidence, there is an easy-to-follow, simply worded, and well outlined discussion in a series of short chapters. Of particular interest is the description of how fossil clues are used by paleontologists to reconstruct the appearance and trace the life cycles of dinosaurs. A good addition to any elementary collection. . . .

> *Rose Henninge, "The SLJ Book Review: 'Dinosaurs and Their World',"* in Library Journal *(reprinted from* Library Journal, *June 15, 1968; published by R. R. Bowker Co. (a Xerox company); copyright © 1968 by Xerox Corporation), Vol. 93, No. 12, June 15, 1968, p. 2542.*

There are in print a great many dinosaur books for children, but this is one of the best because it is a well-researched and carefully written narrative. . . . Irrespective of how many dinosaur books elementary school and public libraries own, they need this one.

> *"Archeology: 'Dinosaurs and Their World',"* in Science Books *(copyright © 1968 by the American Association for the Advancement of Science), Vol. 4, No. 2, September, 1968, p. 114.*

[**Dinosaurs And Their World**] is an elementary treatment of selected dinosaurs, their evolutionary antecedents, and the problems and processes of paleontological investigation. In several instances the author has attempted to achieve simplicity by deleting significant detail and substituting such frustratingly imprecise phrases as "a kind of" or "something like." The book is further weakened . . . by occasionally imprecise technical terminology (e.g. sandstone rock); and by the inconsistent inclusion of phonetic pronunciation aids that are occasionally ambiguous (e.g. "am-FIB-e-ns"). (pp. 27-8)

> *Ronald J. Kley, " 'Dinosaurs and Their World',"* in Appraisal: Science Books for Young People *(copy-*

About 180 million years ago, a dinosaur walked across some mud, leaving three-toed tracks. The mud later hardened into rock. Over a thousand dinosaur tracks have been found near this spot, in Rocky Hill, Connecticut. *From* Dinosaurs and Their World, *written and illustrated by Laurence Pringle.*

> *right ©1970 by the Children's Science Book Review Committee), Vol. 3, No. 1, Winter, 1970, pp. 27-8.*

THE ONLY EARTH WE HAVE   (1969)

In summary form, what every conservationist would like every child to absorb—the dangers to *the only earth we have* from air pollution, water pollution, undisposed and indisposable waste, from pesticides that are really biocides (life killers) and from the disruption of plant-animal communities. An introductory chapter emphasizes the importance of living *with* nature, the closing chapter tells quite specifically "what you can do"; the balance consists of an introduction to each of the threats listed. Mr. Pringle . . . knows whereof he speaks but he sometimes speaks rather broadly, especially in regard to the deleterious effects of irrigation: there is no explanation of the assumption that irrigation water is salty water, no recognition that engineers have methods of countering silting. But, as the examples indicate, he is alert to the more insidious, less apparent by-products of progress. The arguments would have been bolstered and the book made more instrumental by inclusion of a bibliography—or, preferably, of a separate bibliography for each topic containing some of those articles in *Science* and *Scientific American* to which the author refers loosely. Considering its brevity also—it's really akin to a position paper—such implementation would not have been inappropriate. But as a succinct statement of the position, precisely exemplified and illustrated, this is as good a way to get young or older people to react as any we have.

> *"Older Non-Fiction: 'The Only Earth We Have',"* in Kirkus Reviews *(copyright © 1969 The Kirkus Service, Inc.), Vol. XXXII, No. 17, September 15, 1969, p. 1017.*

"Man's survival depends on understanding and living with nature." [In **The Only Earth We Have,** the] author develops this theme in a few brief chapters covering air pollution, water pollution, unwise use of pesticides, the problem of a throwaway society and our diminishing wildlife. . . . The incidences of killer smogs in New York and London are grimly described, along with a quote on Los Angeles: "Where you can wake up in the morning and hear the birds cough." . . . This introduction to our tremendous environmental problems, written by an interested naturalist, will be attractive to young readers because of its brevity, clear writing and handsome format.

> *Jean Coleman, "The Book Review: 'The Only Earth We Have',"* in School Library Journal, *an appendix to* Library Journal *(reprinted from the October, 1970 issue of* School Library Journal, *published by R. R. Bowker Co./A Xerox Corporation; copyright © 1970), Vol. 17, No. 2, October, 1970, p. 132.*

ONE EARTH, MANY PEOPLE: THE CHALLENGE OF HUMAN POPULATION GROWTH   (1971)

A balanced discussion of human population growth that conveys a sense of urgency and emphasizes the need to change, in Kenneth Boulding's words, from a "cowboy" orientation toward nature to a "spaceman" economy. Pringle points out both the advantages and disadvantages of zero population growth, and discusses the accomplishments and limitations of the "green revolution," which he maintains must fail in the long run to keep pace with an ever-growing population. (Nor is harvesting the ocean a panacea, though its yield can be increased and more efficiently utilized.) Biologists, ecologists and demographers of varying persuasions are widely quoted in an informative survey of the effects of crowding on animal populations; the depletion of soil, minerals, water and energy sources . . . ; and the disproportionate drain effected by rich Americans on the world's resources. . . . Pringle is no alarmist but the conditions he discusses are alarming. His book—less optimistic than John Scott's *Hunger* (1969), less importunate than [Paul R.] Ehrlich's *Population Bomb*—should be required reading for the generation that stands to inherit the earth and its problems.

> *"Older Non-Fiction: 'One Earth, Many People',"* in Kirkus Reviews *(copyright © 1971 The Kirkus Service, Inc.), Vol. XXXIX, No. 8, April 15, 1971, p. 448.*

Although Pringle believes that overpopulation is an urgent problem, he has tried to present different viewpoints on the issue in this brief, introductory book. . . . Curiously, the author only specifically mentions induced abortion and vasectomies as means of birth control, though other methods are certainly more widely used today. The text is straightforward, interesting, and clearly written; the numerous photographs are superfluous but will make the book more attractive to reluctant readers.

> *Ann P. Michalik, "SLJ Book Reviews: 'One Earth, Many People!'"* in School Library Journal, *an appendix to* Library Journal *(reprinted from the July, 1971 issue of* School Library Journal, *published by R. R. Bowker Co./A Xerox Corporation; copyright © 1971), Vol. 96, No. 13, July, 1971, p. 2366.*

Discussion of the world's population problem is becoming common as the current rash of books indicates. Rarely does a book present so completely in so little space the basic components of population dynamics. . . . The author has combined an interesting and direct writing style with a good mix of generalizations supported by pertinent and interesting statistical facts. Obviously, he has a firm grasp of a wide range of materials in this field. Above all the author has presented both the optimistic and pessimistic sides of the population problem without any polemics while he manages to hold the reader's attention. The book is enhanced by a careful use of photos which drive home the verbal message. Necessary technical terms are not avoided but are presented in an explanatory way without using dry definitions.

> *"Ecology: 'One Earth, Many People: The Challenge of Human Population Growth',"* in Science Books *(copyright © 1971 by the American Association for the Advancement of Science), Vol. VII, No. 2, September, 1971, p. 144.*

IN A BEAVER VALLEY: HOW BEAVERS CHANGE THE LAND (1970)

[This] book offers an explanation of the beaver's significant role in the ecological scheme of nature. It shows how the building of a dam and the resultant formation of a pond bring about changes in the surrounding plant and animal life. . . . The clear text, accompanied by fine black-and-white photographs, will encourage an appreciation for and sense of wonder at nature's plan in young readers, who will enjoy the book even more if they share it with an adult.

> *Eleanor Glaser, "The Book Review: 'In a Beaver Valley',"* in School Library Journal, *an appendix to* Library Journal *(reprinted from the April, 1971 issue of* School Library Journal, *published by R. R. Bowker Co./A Xerox Corporation; copyright © 1971), Vol. 17, No. 8, April, 1971, p. 100.*

The approach in [**In a Beaver Valley: How Beavers Change the Land**] is unique in that a realistic picture of changing ecology is painted. This would be a relevant experience for children today who are growing up in a society that has little understanding of ecology. Although change in society is generally accepted, environmental change is not. Many feel that ecosystems should stay constant; this book suggests in a simple way that there is a continually shifting inter-relationship in the natural world.

> *Ann E. Matthews, "'In a Beaver Valley',"* in Appraisal: Science Books for Young People *(copyright © 1971 by the Children's Science Book Review Committee), Vol. 4, No. 3, Fall, 1971, p. 21.*

ECOLOGY: SCIENCE OF SURVIVAL   (1971)

Important though it is, the environmental issue is in danger of the bandwagon effect, and one must ask whether new contributions to its literature are justified. I think [**Ecology: Science of Survival**] survives that stern test, for here is a plain and clear treatment, simple without condescension . . . , which presents the problem in a manner well adapted to the needs of the younger teenager. The American origin of the book, though it means a preponderance of American examples, is less of a disadvantage than it can sometimes be, because of the global perspectives. The broad issues of life on earth, energy flow, cycling of materials and the population problem are introduced through down-to-earth particular examples. There is something cool and critical about the presentation, too, which is a further recommendation. (pp. 78, 81)

> *H. M. Thomas, "Book Reviews: 'Ecology: Science of Survival'," in* The School Librarian, *Vol. 21, No. 1, March, 1971, pp. 78, 81.*

A prime source of basic information on "the study of relationships between living things and their environments." Nothing is done on earth that does not affect something or someone else. . . . Ecosystems, biomes, energy flow, cycles of life (carbon, nitrogen and phosphorous), man-made biogeochemical cycles, constant change, and animal and human patterns of population are clearly described and explained. The writing is lucid and factual but will require the full attention of readers for complete understanding. . . . There are many good books about pollution and its effects on the environment, but they all deal with parts of the subject whereas this provides an overview of the entire "web of life" of which "man is just one thread"; it should serve as excellent background reading for . . . other books on ecology. . . .

> *Mary I. Purucker, "The Book Review: 'Ecology: Science of Survival'," in* School Library Journal, *an appendix to* Library Journal *(reprinted from the March, 1972 issue of* School Library Journal, *published by R. R. Bowker Co./A Xerox Corporation; copyright © 1972), Vol. 18, No. 7, March, 1972, p. 128.*

An introductory survey that is partly a running glossary, italicizing and defining such relevant terms as *niche, estuary, detritus,* and *biotic potential.* Outlined are the ways of life in an *ecosystem,* patterns of life in the various *biomes* and other spheres, the flow of energy in nature from the sun through *food chains,* the *biogeochemical cycles* of life, and the patterns of plant, animal and human populations. Cautionary examples of man's disturbance of the environment are woven throughout, so that the dangers of rash predation, DDT, mercury, and strontium 90 pollution, and accelerated *eutrophication* are understood in the context of life's tenuous web. . . . [Pringle's] text-bookish treatment can be a useful addition in meeting the proliferating school assignments on the subject and (with its vocabulary emphasis) as an introduction to further reading.

> *"Younger Non-Fiction: 'Ecology: Science of Survival'," in* Kirkus Reviews *(copyright © 1971 The Kirkus Service, Inc.), Vol. XXXIX, No. 13, July 1, 1980, p. 680.*

COCKROACHES: HERE, THERE, AND EVERYWHERE (1971)

The ubiquitous cockroach, tolerantly depicted here, there, and all over dinner plates, bathroom pipes, and floor boards, is followed in simple words and diagrams through egg pack, nymph stage, molting, and pesky adulthood, with due attention to his ancient lineage, efficient anatomy, indiscriminate appetite, and development of strains resistant to poisons. To know him might not be to love him, but to read about him here is to get to know this tenacious survivor.

> *"Younger Non-Fiction: 'Cockroaches: Here, There, and Everywhere'," in* Kirkus Reviews *(copyright © 1971 The Kirkus Service, Inc.), Vol. XXXIX, No. 18, September 15, 1971, p. 1018.*

One would hope that a book for children entitled "Cockroaches" would be written with accurate content combined with a lot of child appeal. Pringle's *Cockroaches* meets that standard. It can be read rewardingly by the eight-and-nine-year-old, and the ten-and-eleven-year-old would be easily tempted to duplicate the "real scientist" experiments referred to towards the end of this well-written, appealing little book.

> *Jerome Wagner, "'Cockroaches: Here, There, and Everywhere'," in* Appraisal: Science Books for Young People *(copyright © 1972 by the Children's Science Book Review Committee), Vol. 5, No. 3, Fall, 1972, p. 29.*

THIS IS A RIVER: EXPLORING AN ECOSYSTEM (1972)

[This] is a brief, straightforward description of how rivers form and change, what kinds of life exist in swift and quiet waters, and how man uses (and abuses) rivers. It's strictly utilitarian and Pringle's course here closely parallels Delia Goetz's in *Rivers* (1969), but his pertinent examples, diagrams (of the water cycle and of a stream food web), and photographs can justify the addition.

> *"Younger Non-Fiction: 'This Is a River'," in* Kirkus Reviews *(copyright © 1972 The Kirkus Service, Inc.), Vol. XL, No. 4, February 15, 1972, p. 198.*

Effective environment education must begin early. Pringle's book does a good job of presenting the river ecosystem to younger readers without either overwhelming them with details or boring them with a condescending style. . . . Descriptions of clean and polluted rivers are given, and there are enough hints to lead the interested child into making some first hand observations. The latter in turn should lead him to more detailed books.

> *"Biology: 'This Is a River: Exploring an Ecosystem'," in* Science Books *(copyright © 1972 by the American Association for the Advancement of Science), Vol. VIII, No. 2, September, 1972, p. 140.*

Pond study and oceanography are common subjects for ecological writings, but the topic of flowing water is often neglected. There is a dearth of children's books on this subject, which makes this a welcome edition. The author emphasizes life in and around rivers and streams. It is regrettable that so many books on aquatic habitats slight physical characteristics and favor biological ones. The habitat is placed in a modern perspective by relating it to the necessity of a water cycle, importance to technology, and problems of pollution.

> *John R. Pancella, "'This Is a River: Exploring An Ecosystem'," in* Appraisal: Science Books for Young People *(copyright © 1973 by the Children's Science Book Review Committee), Vol. 6, No. 2, Spring, 1973, p. 27.*

FROM POND TO PRAIRIE: THE CHANGING WORLD OF A POND AND ITS LIFE (1972)

How a pond slowly changes into a prairie: the pond's formation by man or glacier, the initial appearance of bacteria and plank-

These drawings show how a lake goes through a series of changes over thousands of years, finally becoming dry land.

From Ecology: Science of Survival, *written and illustrated by Laurence Pringle.*

ton, the muck build-up which supports other forms of life, the "edge creeping in" for hundreds or thousands of years until the pond becomes a marsh with ducks and muskrats in residence, then the filling in of the marsh until the burrowing animals of the prairie take over. It's another undramatic chronicle of natural change; the subject these days is far from novel but Pringle still handles it with more style and authority than most.

> *"Younger Non-Fiction: 'From Pond to Prairie',"* in Kirkus Reviews *(copyright © 1972 The Kirkus Service, Inc.), Vol. XL, No. 7, April 1, 1972, p. 407.*

[*From Pond to Prairie: The Changing World of a Pond and Its Life*] is a good little book which children should enjoy. The text is informative and readable. . . . It is nice to see that the publisher assumed a sufficient degree of literacy on the part of the reader to include an index. Even though the book is short, its overall educational usefulness is enhanced by this inclusion.

> *"Fresh-Water Biology: 'From Pond to Prairie: The Changing World of a Pond and Its Life',"* in Science Books *(copyright © 1972 by the American Association for the Advancement of Science), Vol. VIII, No. 2, September, 1972, p. 142.*

The basic concept that every pond is in the process of evolution is lost in this confusing presentation. . . . Although the idea of tracing the history of a pond from its formation until it becomes a prairie is valuable and the text is simply written and scientifically sound, the jumbled information could not be assimilated by the middle-grade children for whom this book is geared.

> *Suzanne Bitterman, "The Book Review: 'From Pond to Prairie: The Changing World of a Pond and Its Life',"* in School Library Journal, *an appendix to* Library Journal *(reprinted from the March, 1973 issue of* School Library Journal, *published by R. R. Bowker Co./A Xerox Corporation; copyright © 1973), Vol. 19, No. 7, March, 1973, p. 111.*

PESTS AND PEOPLE: THE SEARCH FOR SENSIBLE PEST CONTROL (1972)

Stating unequivocally that "old weapons are best," Pringle disposes of DDT and other biocides in an opening chapter, then concentrates on documenting the successes of biological controls—predators, parasites, and ("still in the study and testing stage") pathogens. . . . Pringle adds to his credibility by pointing out the exaggeration inherent in fashionable (and commercial) claims for the "good effects" of mantises and ladybugs; at the same time he faults the biocide industry for promoting (and the federal government for permitting) expensive and damaging pest control programs. (The finding that "about 80 percent of farmers get their pest control information from biocide salesmen" indicates what conservationists are up against.) . . . *Pests and People* is eminently sensible.

> *"Older Non-Fiction: 'Pests and People: The Search for Sensible Pest Control',"* in Kirkus Reviews *(copyright © 1972 The Kirkus Service, Inc.), Vol. XL, No. 21, November 1, 1972, p. 1254.*

[The] treatment of the pest problem and future pest management programs is thoughtful and provocative. The material is new to children and will be of interest to those concerned with solving environmental problems.

> *A. C. Haman, "'Pests and People: The Search for Sensible Pest Control',"* in School Library Journal, *an appendix to* Library Journal *(reprinted from the April, 1973 issue of* School Library Journal, *published by R. R. Bowker Co./A Xerox Corporation; copyright © 1973), Vol. 19, No. 8, April, 1973, p. 78.*

TWIST, WIGGLE, AND SQUIRM: A BOOK ABOUT EARTHWORMS (1973)

It has all been covered in other easy books on earthworms—their rings of muscle (and no bones), their ability to regenerate, their peculiar androgyny, the benefits to plants from their castings and their burrowing—but Pringle has an eye for telling detail and a way of making the essentials clear and immediate for youngest readers. . . .

complex subject and explains some of the methods that ecol-ogists use to trace the flow of food energy in nature.

> *Diane Holzheimer, "'Chains, Webs, and Pyra-mids: The Flow of Energy in Nature'," in* Appraisal: Science Books for Young People *(copyright © 1976 by the Children's Science Book Review Committee), Vol. 9, No. 2, Spring, 1976, p. 33.*

CITY AND SUBURB: EXPLORING AN ECOSYSTEM   (1975)

The city/suburb is a complex ecosystem often ignored in en-vironmental studies. Pringle explores this ecosystem with straightforward text and clear black-and-white photographs, describing plants and animals that might be found and showing the effect of the urban environment on them. Although not sufficiently detailed for research, this book, with its open for-mat and appealing photographs, is a good introduction to and overview of the subject.

> *Carole Ridolfino, "The Book Review: 'City and Sub-urb: Exploring an Ecosystem'," in* School Library Journal *(reprinted from the February, 1976 issue of* School Library Journal, *published by R. R. Bowker Co./A Xerox Corporation; copyright © 1976), Vol. 22, No. 6, February, 1976, p. 48.*

Beginning with the description of an ecosystem as "a place in nature with all of its living and nonliving parts," the author presents an effective argument for studying the complex city-suburb environment as well as forests, ponds, and estu-aries. . . . Written in a simple, straightforward style, the text is an excellent, concise introduction to the varied forms of life—people, plants, animals—found within the noisy, crowded metropolitan areas which have replaced woods, plains, and prairies. Although a relatively new kind of ecosystem, the city with its suburb is the most complex of such systems now extant, a structure which affects and is affected not only by its im-mediate surroundings but also by areas far away. A concise, explicit overview of urban ecology.

> *Mary M. Burns, "Cities: 'City and Suburb: Explor-ing an Ecosystem'," in* The Horn Book Magazine *(copyright © 1976 by the Horn Book, Inc., Boston), Vol. LII, No. 2, April, 1976, p. 167.*

Key concepts discussed include ecosystem, change in time, food chains, climatic change, air pollution, animal habitat, adaptive behavior, invader or foreign species, population growth and distribution and diversity. Of these, "ecosystem" is the only concept explicitly defined in the text. The author empha-sizes that, despite man's drastic alteration of nature in the city-suburb environment, many of the same nonhuman interaction patterns—as well as methods for studying these patterns—remain the same. . . . A unique and probably valid aspect of Pringle's approach is the treatment of city and suburb envi-ronments as essentially the same. Specific criticisms: the pic-tures are interesting, but they are either soft focus or fuzzy; and the explicit discussion of ecosystem is not as clear as in other introductory books.

> *Laura B. Williamson, "Ecology: 'City and Suburb: Exploring An Ecosystem'," in* Science Books & Films *(copyright © 1976 by the American Association for the Advancement of Science), Vol. XII, No. 2, Sep-tember, 1976, p. 103.*

THE MINNOW FAMILY—CHUBS, DACE, MINNOWS, AND SHINERS   (1976)

The minnow family, called the *Cyprinidea*, is the largest of all fish families. The reader of this book will learn the physical characteristics of these small freshwater fish and how specific ones such as the longnose dace, golden shiner, and cutlips minnow are unique. A clear informative text details the hab-itats, adaptations, mating and nest building behavior of these most interesting creatures. . . . A glossary of minnow names, suggestions for further reading, and an extensive index com-plete this definitive reference. (pp. 35-6)

> *Diane Holzheimer, "'The Minnow Family'," in* Ap-praisal: Science Books for Young People *(copyright © 1976 by the Children's Science Book Review Com-mittee), Vol. 9, No. 3, Fall, 1976, pp. 35-6.*

[With *The Minnow Family* the author has] done an exceptional job for young readers. It is not a field identification guide but it will be very useful for the novice ichthyologist and aquar-ologist. It includes many species and their descriptions, hab-itats, habits and life cycles. Interesting research is included on nest building, behavior, and sensing underwater sound and chemicals for survival. An excellent, readable, and scholarly reference.

> *John R. Pancella, "'The Minnow Family'," in* Ap-praisal: Science Books for Young People *(copyright © 1976 by the Children's Science Book Review Com-mittee), Vol. 9, No. 3, Fall, 1976, p. 36.*

Pringle attempts to tell all there is to know about North Amer-ica's 200 different species of freshwater minnows; that he does not succeed in a more noteworthy manner is not surprising. He first describes the physical characteristics of minnows and then their various habitats. Regrettably, however, the reader has to plow through a welter of common names, sizes and other essentially dull information about the many different types of minnows before reaching the stimulating material: how dif-ferent species of minnows are adapted to various factors in their environments, unique behavior patterns revealed by ex-periment, and mating and nesting behavior. Pringle concludes with a somewhat less than satisfying account of the role of minnows in the grand scheme of living things. . . . This book does contain a considerable amount of basic information, and thus deserves space on the library shelf as a source book. (pp. 212-13)

> *A. H. Drummon, Jr., "Children's Books: 'The Min-now Family'," in* Science Books & Films *(copyright © 1977 by the American Association for the Ad-vancement of Science), Vol. XII, No. 4, March, 1977, pp. 212-13.*

LISTEN TO THE CROWS   (1976)

Trust Laurence Pringle to avoid the lockstep animal biography formulas. His appreciation of the common but redoubtable crow avoids generalities and focuses on the amazing versatility of the bird's voice box through the work of Dwight Cham-berlain, who recorded and classified twenty-three separate calls, and the studies of Nicholas Thompson which proved that crows can actually count—up to six—and use their ability to identify themselves to other members of the flock.

> *"Younger Non-Fiction: 'Listen to the Crows'," in* Kirkus Reviews *(copyright © 1976 The Kirkus Ser-*

vice, Inc.), Vol. XLIV, No. 19, October 1, 1976, p. 1099.

[**Listen to the Crows**] is a] very brief explanation of why and how crows caw. Scientific studies of calls that may mean identification, warning, or assembly are clearly summarized, but Pringle does not quote directly or even cite the three studies he's drawn from. Though interesting and well written, this offers such a tiny glimpse of the subject that it's hard to justify the price.

Susan Sprague, "The Book Review: 'Listen to the Crows'," in School Library Journal *(reprinted from the January, 1977 issue of* School Library Journal, *published by R. R. Bowker Co./A Xerox Corporation; copyright © 1977), Vol. 23, No. 5, January, 1977, p. 96.*

Crows emerge in this book as much more than mischievous imps or menaces to gardens: They are among the most intelligent of birds. . . . In a clear, interesting manner, Pringle reports on studies of crows' calls, adding his own observations and comments to those of other scientists. . . . The book is well written, and holds the reader's attention, but the various facets of crow communication would be better emphasized if occasional subheadings were used. No references for further reading are given, but an adequate index is included.

Marie M. Jenkins, "Children's Books: 'Listen to the Crows'," in Science Books & Films *(copyright © 1977 by the American Association for the Advancement of Science), Vol. XIII, No. 3, December, 1977, p. 167.*

OUR HUNGRY EARTH: THE WORLD FOOD CRISIS   (1976)

The most serious and important children's science book to appear recently is *Our Hungry Earth.* The text is gripping, and the information about current events may be new to many readers. . . . Not only the subject matter but the manner of presentation is outstanding. . . . [The] bibliography is graded and annotated; and a helpful glossary is included.

Sarah Gagne', "World Hunger," in The Horn Book Magazine *(copyright © 1977 by the Horn Book, Inc., Boston), Vol. LIII, No. 1, February, 1977, p. 79.*

The author discusses food supplies, population growth and natural resources as components of the world food crises. The author's malthusiam message is population must ultimately be brought into line with environmental resources, especially food resources. . . . A well written, rational analysis of the complexities of food crises, how they came to be and why humankind can no longer ignore the problem. A book with which adolescents will be very much impressed. (p. 43)

John J. Padalino, " 'Our Hungry Earth: 'The World Food Crises'," in Appraisal: Science Books for Young People *(copyright © 1977 by the Children's Science Book Review Committee), Vol. 10, No. 2, Spring, 1977, pp. 42-3.*

Our Hungry Earth is a provocative survey of problems facing humankind as world population increases. The account is not overly pessimistic; rather the nature of the problem, the progress made thus far and the areas of needed continued progress are treated equally, objectively and dispassionately. . . . Examples abound in an easy-to-follow fashion, and numbers and technical discussions are minimal. . . . **Our Hungry Earth** will

be interesting to thoughtful junior and senior high school students.

William Cape, "Ecology and Community: 'Our Hungry Earth: The World Food Crisis'," in Science Books & Films *(copyright © 1977 by the American Association for the Advancement of Science), Vol. XIII, No. 1, May, 1977, p. 7.*

DEATH IS NATURAL   (1977)

Pringle characteristically treats his natural history subjects in an ecological context, and this is an attempt to do the same with death. . . . Pringle mentions different beliefs in an afterlife, but essentially in an aside, then returns to the idea of death as a natural and "necessary part of the continual recycling of the earth's elements." Later chapters deal with population cycles and the need for thinning; the "weeding out" process of natural selection; adaptation and the extinction of species; and the interdependence of all life. With pauses to explain the concepts of genes, elements, evolution, etc., this lacks Pringle's usual direct, on-target clarity; certainly it's no competition for [Herbert S.] Zim and [Sonia] Bleeker's thorough-going primer on *Life and Death* (1970). But Pringle's aim is for a different, more holistic sort of understanding, and perhaps for some it will all come together. (pp. 288-89)

"Younger Non-Fiction: 'Death Is Natural'," in Kirkus Reviews *(copyright © 1977 The Kirkus Service, Inc.), Vol. XLV, No. 6, March 15, 1977, pp. 288-89.*

Elementary students should find this book fascinating reading about one of the natural occurrences of life (i.e., death). . . . Pringle stresses how the death of living things makes life possible for succeeding generations, and he gives a good introduction to further classroom discussions of how the balance of nature eventually changes. This book would be a useful addition to elementary school and classroom libraries.

Renarick Hodgdon, "Biology: 'Death Is Natural'," in Science Books & Films *(copyright © 1978 by the American Association for the Advancement of Science), Vol. XIII, No. 4, March, 1978, p. 221.*

A remarkable book for children, as well as some adults! Pringle shows clearly how death in the plant and animal world is indeed a necessary part of life. His style is so simple and clear that the idea of death is introduced to the child in a most acceptable manner. . . . The last chapter is superb—but no better than the rest of the book. Excellent photographs, mostly by the author, add much. (pp. 39-40)

R. Gregory Belcher, " 'Death Is Natural'," in Appraisal: Science Books for Young People *(copyright © 1978 by the Children's Science Book Review Committee), Vol. 11, No. 1, Winter, 1978, pp. 39-40.*

THE HIDDEN WORLD: LIFE UNDER A ROCK   (1977)

Pringle offers a species-by-species catalog of the creatures—sowbugs, spiders, wood roaches, etc.—commonly found in the cool, damp "microclimate" under a rock, board, or indeed "any object that covers the ground." A second section on the crayfish, leeches, mayfly nymphs, and a few others you might find under rocks in streams is less cohesive—probably because, as Pringle remarks, "almost any small, aquatic fresh-water animal can be found under a rock at some time." Overall there

From Death Is Natural, *written and illustrated by Laurence Pringle.*

is no larger view of the "procession of life" . . . which Pringle himself has chronicled in other contexts. But with a clear, closeup photo for each species and ample hints for finding and identifying it, this could be an inviting and supportive first field guide.

> *"Younger Non-Fiction: 'The Hidden World: Life under a Rock',"* in Kirkus Reviews *(copyright © 1977 The Kirkus Service, Inc.), Vol. XLV, No. 8, April 15, 1977, p. 432.*

[The book] should interest even the children who usually say "ugh." The author describes not only commonly found land animals that hide, but water animals such as crayfish, leeches, hellgrammites, and caddis flies. If, after reading the book, a child doesn't lift a stone or a log on his next walk, I doubt he ever will. Except for a lapse in referring to a yellow jacket as a bee instead of a wasp, the book is distinctive.

> *Sarah Gagné, "Exploring the Outdoors: 'The Hidden World: Life under a Rock',"* in The Horn Book Magazine *(copyright © 1977 by the Horn Book, Inc., Boston), Vol. LIII, No. 5, October, 1977, p. 559.*

Pringle first describes the physical characteristics of under-rock environments, explaining why they are desirable places in which to live. He cleverly—and almost incidentally—include what methods and equipment to use in exploring. In lively style, the author continues with highlights about several groups of animals (sowbugs, millipedes and centipedes, slugs, spiders, beetles), encouraging exploration. Just when it seems that he must have exhausted his source, he turns to rocks in water: There the excitement begins again. Each kind of animal discussed is shown in a good drawing or in a natural environment photo-

graph. There are well-placed photographs of children exploring under rocks. The index and the suggestions for additional readings are excellent. My only criticisms are the inadequate definition of the term ecosystem . . . , the absence of any girls in the photographs of the children and the failure to emphasize the need to turn the rocks back to their original positions after exploring. This book will serve as an excellent stimulus for the young naturalist. (pp. 221-22)

> *Norman A. Engstrom, "Ecology: 'The Hidden World: Life under a Rock',"* in Science Books & Films *(copyright © 1978 by the American Association for the Advancement of Science), Vol. XIII, No. 4, March, 1978, pp. 221-22.*

THE CONTROVERSIAL COYOTE: PREDATION, POLITICS, AND ECOLOGY (1977)

Which side can you believe? Perhaps neither, suggests Pringle in this unusually objective attempt to separate fact from the prejudices of either conservationists or sheep ranchers. Citing wildlife biologists' ongoing studies as the most reliable source of information, and filling readers in on the economics of sheep raising and the behavior and population patterns of coyotes, Pringle comes to no all-encompassing conclusion but does report on several seemingly well established items: Coyotes do kill sheep and can threaten the livelihood of some ranchers; contrary to predator behavior in the wild, coyotes are not "culling" the herd by taking the most unhealthy sheep; many of the sheep killed by coyotes are not eaten; control efforts have not had much effect on coyote populations in the West and, because of their tremendous ability to bounce back, "body counts" have little meaning. Coming from a longtime environmentalist like Pringle, such findings must give pause.

> *"Young Adult Non-Fiction: 'The Controversial Coyote',"* in Kirkus Reviews *(copyright © 1977 The Kirkus Service, Inc.), Vol. XLV, No. 10, May 15, 1977, p. 546.*

This text is a very well-written report of coyote-sheep interrelationships, an emotionally-charged issue in the American West today. Pringle, a wildlife biologist, presents the facts in a clear, straightforward manner, never sacrificing accuracy. In relating how Americans have viewed coyotes and other predators over the years, he gives an excellent summary of the development of wildlife management. . . . Containing the results of recent coyote studies, the text is up to date. A generous number of black-and-white photographs document the report and add a touch of wild beauty. The text is sure to become a classic in the study of predator-prey relationships.

> *Martha T. Kane, "'The Controversial Coyote',"* in Appraisal: Science Books for Young People *(copyright © 1978 by the Children's Science Book Review Committee), Vol. 11, No. 2, Spring, 1978, p. 29.*

Pringle's efforts to be fair and unemotional are refreshing. Although aimed at a young audience, this book would be valuable reading for members of the general public who are prepared to objectively reconsider the coyote controversy.

> *B. Dennis Sustare, "Book Reviews: 'The Controversial Coyote: Predation, Politics, and Ecology',"* in Science Books & Films *(copyright © 1978 by the American Association for the Advancement of Science), Vol. XIV, No. 1, May, 1978, p. 26.*

ANIMALS AND THEIR NICHES: HOW SPECIES SHARE RESOURCES (1977)

By defining key words clearly and arranging the increasingly complex relationships carefully, Pringle has produced a fine introduction to food use in animals habitats. Without oversimplifying or needlessly repeating information, he provides several examples of competition and co-existence and identifies the scientists whose research is represented in each chapter. . . . [This] is most satisfying for those first looking at natural connections.

> *"Younger Non-Fiction: 'Animals and Their Niches: How Species Share Resources',"* in Kirkus Reviews *(copyright © 1977 The Kirkus Service, Inc.), Vol. XLV, No. 19, October 1, 1977, p. 1052.*

Pringle discusses the knowledge scientists have gained about "resource partitioning," the sharing of food and space within an ecological community by related species, through descriptions of individual research projects. . . . Despite the use of "parameciums" rather than "paramecia," the text is lucid and accurate; Pringle shows, more clearly than if he had made a statement on the subject, how painstaking and objective the scientific method is and how a body of knowledge grows through a diversity of research findings.

> *Zena Sutherland, "New Titles for Children and Young People: 'Animals and Their Niches: How Species Share Resources',"* in Bulletin of the Center for Children's Books *(reprinted by permission of The University of Chicago Press; © 1978 by The University of Chicago), Vol. 31, No. 7, March, 1978, p. 117.*

This little book is superb. It deals with an important aspect of ecology—how species share resources. The writing is clear and concise, and the good glossary supplements definitions appearing in the text. Many classic research studies are described clearly, identifying the scientists and conveying not only what scientists know, but how scientists go about finding out such data as how five species of warblers can live in the same kinds of trees. The reader gets a strong message that finding out about the natural world is a human endeavor involving asking questions, observing organisms in their natural environment and performing laboratory experiments. At the same time, the reader is alerted to unanswered questions. Anyone wishing to understand the fundamental ideas of how animals live together and what scientists do—without being overwhelmed by scientific jargon—will find this book suitable.

> *Dale E. Ingmanson, "Children's Books: 'Animals and Their Niches: How Species Share Resources',"* in Science Books & Films *(copyright ©1978 by the American Association for the Advancement of Science), Vol. XIV, No. 2, September, 1978, p. 114.*

THE GENTLE DESERT: EXPLORING AN ECOSYSTEM (1977)

"This book introduces desert ecosystems," says Pringle with characteristic straightforwardness, and his lucid essay examines the great variety of plant and animal life and their essential interrelatedness. The aim, of course, is to correct the notion that deserts are harsh, empty wastelands. In keeping with that, he questions the common attitude that the desert is "a place to be used and changed." The damaging effects of those uses—stripmining, illegal motorcycling that tears up the turf, and growing populations that draw on limited water supplies and continually lower the water table—underscore Pringle's belief

that the desert should be appreciated on its own terms. With the author's careful, well-chosen black-and-white photographs.

> *Denise M. Wilms, "Children's Books: 'The Gentle Desert: Exploring an Ecosystem',"* in Booklist *(reprinted by permission of the American Library Association; copyright © 1977 by the American Library Association), Vol. 74, No. 7, December 1, 1977, p. 615.*

A disappointing treatment of American desert ecosystems. . . . In the last three pages, Pringle, like many conservationists before him, deplores the impact of people and technology on the fragile, desert ecosystem. He mentions only the broadest and most obvious features of desert life, and the text sorely lacks first-hand observations.

> *George Gleason, "The Book Review: 'The Gentle Desert: Exploring an Ecosystem',"* in School Library Journal *(reprinted from the January, 1978 issue of School Library Journal, published by R. R. Bowker Co./A Xerox Corporation; copyright © 1978), Vol. 24, No. 5, January, 1978, p. 96.*

Two cheers for this desert book—one for the handsome photographs, format and production—the second for the wealth of information. The author has touched base on most of the important facts about the desert, which will make this book useful for school units on the subject. I especially like the view of the desert as a large ecosystem within which are many smaller ones. Now for the cheer-less part: the book badly needs chapter headings or some other device to make it easier for the reader to take command of the many separate ideas and facts presented. And I wasn't comfortable with the *tone* of the book. Everything was given the same weight of emphasis, whether it was a plant experiment, a flash flood or the ravaging of the Mohave by motorcyclists. The result is a text notably lacking in excitement, with as much "color" as a sand dune. The desert, one of the most unique and dramatic environments on earth, deserves better. (pp. 29-30)

> *Barbara Brenner, "'The Gentle Desert: Exploring an Ecosystem',"* in Appraisal: Science Books for Young People *(copyright © 1978 by the Children's Science Book Review Committee), Vol. 11, No. 2, Spring, 1978, pp. 29-30.*

WILD FOODS: A BEGINNER'S GUIDE TO IDENTIFYING, HARVESTING, AND COOKING SAFE AND TASTY PLANTS FROM THE OUTDOORS (1978)

[Pringle] calls this a beginner's guide to identifying, harvesting, and cooking safe and tasty plants and he claims "with some preparation and study, almost anyone can become a confident forager."

If this book were to be used only by children, for whom it is written, it should more specifically describe and illustrate similar appearing but harmful plants, but if adults are along to supervise the collecting and cooking, [Paul] Breeden's botanical illustrations are a sufficient aid to safe picking. . . .

And you won't have to wander in the wilderness to earn your fare. Pringle says the greatest variety of edible plants are more likely found close to home.

Indeed, after a brisk day's outing one may agree with Pringle that "unreasonable fear of poisonous plants robs people of pleasure."

Janet Domowitz, "Books That Break the Age Barrier: 'Wild Foods: A Beginner's Guide to Identifying, Harvesting, and Cooking Safe and Tasty Plants from the Outdoors'," in The Christian Science Monitor *(reprinted by permission from* The Christian Science Monitor; © *The Christian Science Publishing Society; all rights reserved), October 23, 1978, p. B4.*

You may not believe it, but some of the best things in life are still free. At least Laurence Pringle feels they are in **"Wild Foods"**. . . . Wisely included are warnings about what to stay away from, and both Mr. Pringle's photographs and the illustrations by Paul Breeden are excellent aids to identification.

Susan de Jong, "Ambrosia and Watercress," in The New York Times Book Review *(© 1978 by The New York Times Company; reprinted by permission), December 10, 1978, p. 78.*

By dint of intense search I have been able to find only three minor points with which I can find fault! (1) The difference between simple and compound leaves should have been stressed rather than taken for granted. (2) Some may accept the relative worth of maples other than *acer saccharum* for producing high quality syrup in large quantities but no syrup connoisseur would. (3) "Maple seeds grow in pairs, each with a wing" should read ". . . each seed with a wing." This is indeed nit-picking! The whole book is delightful, and what lover of wild strawberries would not be delighted with the recipe for "Instant Jam" on page 72: ". . . be sure to make Instant Jam (while picking) . . . by popping some . . . in your mouth." I don't see how I can wait for spring!

R. Gregory Belcher, " 'Wild Foods'," in Appraisal: Science Books for Young People *(copyright © 1979 by the Children's Science Book Review Committee), Vol. 12, No. 2, Spring, 1979, p. 51.*

DINOSAURS AND PEOPLE: FOSSILS, FACTS, AND FANTASIES (1978)

This sketchy report of some important 19th- and 20th-Century fossil discoveries fails to give much information about either dinosaurs or the scientific and human efforts involved. The author concludes with the proposition that "a revolution in ideas about dinosaurs is underway" but the text doesn't convey the sense of excitement or momentum implied by "revolution." The black-and-white photographs and drawings are only adequate in subject matter and composition and lack interest compared to those in Pringle's *Dinosaurs and Their World*. . . . Maps showing discovery sites are lacking, and the frequently used term "sauropod" is not fully explained. Some contemporary changes in theory about dinosaur physiology and behavior not widely covered in other books make this an acceptable source of additional information.

Margaret Bush, "The Book Review: 'Laurence, Dinosaurs and People: Fossils, Facts, and Fantasies'," in School Library Journal, *(reprinted from the April, 1979 issue of* School Library Journal, *published by R. R. Bowker Co./A Xerox Corporation; copyright © 1979), Vol. 25, No. 8, April, 1979, p. 61.*

Dinosaurs and People focuses on those individuals who were the pioneers in paleontology—their backgrounds, motivations, the hardships they often endured, their single-minded devotion to their investigations as well as their occasional political greed,

and the excitements of their pursuits. Pringle takes the reader from the great North American dinosaur "rush" of the late 1800's to East Africa and finally to the Gobi Desert, sites of the most significant fossil finds. He discusses paleontological techniques, the discoveries of lesser-known dinosaurs, and the questioning of old ideas. His explanations of the evidence for the theory of endothermic, or warm-blooded, dinosaurs are crystal clear. . . . [The] book is a gem. (pp. 46-7)

Arlene Bernstein, " 'Dinosaurs and People'," in Appraisal: Science Books for Young People *(copyright © 1979 by the Children's Science Book Review Committee), Vol. 12, No. 3, Fall, 1979, pp. 46-7.*

One of the better aspects of Laurence Pringle's volume lies in the fact that he obviously does not consider young readers a bunch of little muttonheads. He takes the trouble to explain things well without totally exhausting both material and reader. He goes into theories, both old and new, and identifies areas of conjecture. He asks the question whether the 100-million-year-old dinosaur community can be reconstructed with accuracy. And he suggests reasons and theories that may have validity and may indeed reflect what the past was like. The volume is up-to-date, including the recent discussions about whether some dinosaurs were warm-blooded.

Wayne Hanley, " 'Dinosaurs and People'," in Appraisal: Science Books for Young People *(copyright © 1979 by the Children's Science Book Review Committee), Vol. 12, No. 3, Fall, 1979, p. 47.*

NATURAL FIRE: ITS ECOLOGY IN FORESTS (1979)

Pringle begins with a hyped-up, melodramatic description of a destructive raging fire—but, being Pringle, he then reveals that such scenes exist only in people's minds. Not all forest fires are "bad," he explains; they have been a natural force in the environment for many thousands of years, and many trees and plants—and some animals who live off them—are "fire species," better off when natural blazes are allowed. Fire is "like decay speeded up," says Pringle, in that plants that grow after fires are richer in nutrients. . . . So goes the latest word in fire ecology, handed down with Pringle's usual concision, clarity, and good sense.

"Younger Non-Fiction: 'Natural Fire: Its Ecology in Forests'," in Kirkus Reviews *(copyright © 1979 The Kirkus Service, Inc.), Vol. XLVII, No. 21, November 1, 1979, p. 1265.*

The book will create a certain amount of fuss; some of the self-styled environmentalists who don't know a microtome from a chromosome will be shocked by it. The author points out that fire is a normal part of the environment and has been since plants first grew on land dry enough for a fire to spread. He also points out that we may well have been mistaken in the past when we went to great trouble and expense to prevent forest, brush, and prairie fires and to put them out when they had started. He makes a very good case, and the book deserves to be read carefully and thoughtfully.

Harry C. Stubbs, "Ecology: 'Natural Fire: Its Ecology in Forests'," in The Horn Book Magazine *(copyright © 1979 by The Horn Book, Inc., Boston), Vol. LV, No. 6, December, 1979, p. 688.*

Quite rightly, Pringle . . . points out that ecologists and foresters have in recent years altered the view that forest fires are totally evil and must be controlled at all costs. . . . Some readers could be confused by Pringle's categorizing as forest fires the vicious brushfires of southern California. . . . A good book for forest-culture communities, but most young, urban readers lack the background to understand much of it.

> *George Gleason, "The Book Review: 'Natural Fire: Its Ecology in Forests'," in* School Library Journal *(reprinted from the February, 1980 issue of* School Library Journal, *published by R. R. Bowker Co./A Xerox Corporation; copyright © 1980), Vol. 26, No. 6, February, 1980, p. 71.*

Although such a brief book can only scratch the surface of such a complicated subject, Pringle's work is a provocative introduction to the influences—both benign and malignant—of fire on the flora and fauna of forests. . . . Pringle does add his influence against the over zealous "Smokey-the-bear" followers who would oppose all fire. No doubt some of the less informed will argue against the use of this book in schools. They will be wrong.

> *R. Gregory Belcher, "'Natural Fire: Its Ecology in Forests'," in* Appraisal: Science Books for Young People *(copyright ©1981 by the Children's Science Book Review Committee), Vol. 14, No. 1, Winter, 1981, p. 52.*

NUCLEAR POWER: FROM PHYSICS TO POLITICS   (1979)

As Three Mile Island has demonstrated, the nuclear safety issue is too important to be left to the experts. It is also next to impossible for a non-expert, of twelve or forty, to assess the situation at a technical level. That being the case, Pringle doesn't try to snow readers with complicated technical background which wouldn't equip them to judge for themselves anyway. Instead, he attempts to guide them through the controversy over pushing on with nuclear power. . . . Three Mile Island aroused a public that was already withdrawing support despite "thirty years of industry and government propaganda." To this thirty-year campaign, Pringle offers a valuable corrective.

> *"Older Non-Fiction: 'Nuclear Power'," in* Kirkus Reviews *(copyright © 1979 The Kirkus Service, Inc.), Vol. XLVII, No. 19, October 1, 1979, p. 1151.*

When exaggerated claims on both sides make reasonable analysis of the arguments difficult it is a help to have science writers like Pringle with us. He is clear-headed, crisp, and always informative in this brief overview of the nuclear power controversy. . . . Secondary students who are not strong in science might have difficulty with some of the text—especially when it gets around to breeder reactors—but Pringle seems to have a sixth sense when it comes to knowing when enough information is enough. . . . [There] are too many imposing titles used and there are not as many articles on alternative energy sources as promised. (pp. 127-28)

> *Robert Unsworth, "The Book Review: 'Nuclear Power: From Physics to Politics'," in* School Library Journal *(reprinted from the April, 1980 issue of* School Library Journal, *published by R. R. Bowker Co./A Xerox Corporation; copyright © 1980), Vol. 26, No. 8, April, 1980, pp. 127-28.*

The nuclear power controversy derives from a complexity of technical, economic, and political issues which have polarized the Western World. Pringle here in presenting the story makes the case against nuclear power skillfully in unemotional language. He admits a strong antinuclear bias and has not neglected any fact or event which supports his position. In the attempt at fairness and balance, he tries to give the pronuclear arguments. However, this is clearly not the book to get both sides of the controversy. The scientific and technical content of the book is well done and clearly reveals why the issue has become so controversial. If one feels that a children's science book may or should intermix science with politics, then this book ranks high.

> *David G. Hoag, "'Nuclear Power: From Physics to Politics'," in* Appraisal: Science Books for Young People *(copyright © 1980 by the Children's Science Book Review Committee), Vol. 13, No. 3, Fall, 1980, p. 54.*

LIVES AT STAKE: THE SCIENCE AND POLITICS OF ENVIRONMENTAL HEALTH   (1980)

With characteristic attention to clarity and detail, Pringle offers a solid, consciousness-raising introduction to the current state of the environment, concentrating on health hazards to which human beings in American society are exposed. Coming down hard on "consumer freedom of choice arguments" espoused by industry spokespeople, he calls for stricter controls and health standards together with increased grass-roots participation in decision making to protect the general public from unnecessary and dangerous pollutants, additives, and chemicals in water, air, and food and the worker from undue occupational hazards.

> *Stephanie Zvirin, "Books for Young Adults: 'Lives at Stake: The Science and Politics of Environmental Health'," in* Booklist *(reprinted by permission of the American Library Association; copyright © 1980 by the American Library Association), Vol. 47, No. 3, October 1, 1980, p. 204.*

In another thoughtful and thought-provoking book in his "Science for Survival" series, Pringle examines the known and suspected dangers in food, products, pollutants, job-related health hazards, and drugs that are a detrimental part of the total human environment. . . . A well-written and well-organized text concludes with a list of some national groups working in the public interest. . . .

> *Zena Sutherland, "New Titles for Children and Young People: 'Lives at Stake: The Science and Politics of Environmental Health'," in* Bulletin of the Center for Children's Books *(reprinted by permission of The University of Chicago Press; © 1981 by The University of Chicago), Vol. 34, No. 7, March, 1981, p. 138.*

Are children tired of hearing the words *environment, energy,* and *pollution*? The book is welcome for making the subjects fresh and urgent, with examples and references from the experience of the last ten years. . . . Some people would say that the book is biased, that examples are selective, that the author gives more weight to the consequences to society than to the cost of testing and safety. But he is not trying to say how compromises should be made; he is simply presenting information that, for a thoughtful reader, argues for a cautious approach and for constant testing to insure safety. In short, the unknown may be hazardous, and his PCB example bears him out. It is this information that children need in order to urge wise decisions upon future government leaders.

Sarah Gagné, "Environment: 'Lives at Stake'," in
The Horn Book Magazine *(copyright © 1981 by The
Horn Book, Inc., Boston), Vol. 57, No. 3, June,
1981, p. 330.*

WHAT SHALL WE DO WITH THE LAND?   (1981)

Readers will see that though land types vary from farm acreage
to forest to plain to coastal frontage, each with its special set
of circumstances, the same intertwined conflicts arise: should
the land be exploited for short-term gain or should it be carefully managed as an investment in the future? Should the personal property rights of local residents be subservient to the
right of the state or federal government to regulate how the
land is used? The author's environmentalist bent is quietly
apparent throughout and never without foundation; indeed, the
lucid presentation is eminently thought-provoking—a first-rate
starting point for background on a topic that will be increasingly
in the news.

*Denise M. Wilms, "Children's Books: 'What Shall
We Do with the Land? Land Choices for America',"
in* Booklist *(reprinted by permission of the American
Library Association; copyright © 1981 by the American Library Association), Vol. 78, No. 3, October
1, 1981, p. 239.*

This latest of Pringle's straight-talking, clear-thinking over-
views informs young readers on the hard land-use choices facing Americans and how they are being met. Digging as always
behind official rhetoric and weakened laws, he points to examples of private interests' influence on local, state, and federal
decisions—and to other examples of government units taking
steps in the right direction, that of preserving and managing
land for the greatest long-term public benefit. Thus, public
taxing and zoning policy can help save farmland and coastland
from developers. . . . The National Forest Service, we see,
does a better job of saving federal forests from commercial
exploitation than does the Bureau of Land Management. The
Administration-supported Sagebrush Rebellion, Pringle makes
clear, consists mostly of "an attempted takeover of federal
lands" by "wealthy ranchers, mining companies, developers,
energy companies, and other powerful private interests—and
politicians friendly to their cause." Opinion polls show that
most people in the West (and elsewhere) want federal control,
though "an opposite impression can be gained from hearings"
packed by these private interests. Whatever the issue, Pringle
can be counted on to draw the lines, identify the parties, make
the connections among interest, action, and effect—and demonstrate an approach that young readers can profitably apply
to other issues.

*"Older Non-Fiction: 'What Shall We Do with the
Land?'" in* Kirkus Reviews *(copyright © 1981 The
Kirkus Service, Inc.), Vol. XLIX, No. 21, November
1, 1981, p. 1350.*

What Shall We Do With the Land really asks the question, what
should we do with the land that is left. Pringle documents case
after case in which land use and misuse have ruined farmland,
rangeland, forests and coastal areas. . . . The prospects, however, are not entirely gloomy, according to Pringle. There has
been significant legislative activity on federal and state levels.
Pringle cites innovative range management practices that can
restore pasturelands; he credits Hawaii for having instituted
strict land zoning laws. The questions regarding land use are
important and, where there is a continuing dialogue concerning
the rights of society as a whole versus individual rights, this
thoughtful, well-written book should be a must.

*Julia Rholes, "The Book Review: 'What Shall We
Do with the Land: Choices for America'," in* School
Library Journal *(reprinted from the December, 1981
issue of* School Library Journal, *published by R. R.
Bowker Co./A Xerox Corporation; copyright © 1981),
Vol. 28, No. 4, December, 1981, p. 72.*

M(iroslav) Sasek

1916-1980

Czechoslovakian author/illustrator of nonfiction for children. Sasek's *This Is . . .* series provides a unique service for children by introducing them to great countries, cities, and landmarks in an entertaining and understandable way. Sasek approached his books as if he were visiting a place for the first time, as he often was. He began each visit by going to see the places and things he heard or read about, and explored the rest without the aid of a guidebook. His impressions in word and picture form the basis of the books, and he added historical asides when he thought they were warranted. Sasek wrote his facts simply, but with enough nuance and satire to entertain sophisticated readers; his colorful illustrations are accurate and architecturally precise, but are drawn with humor and detail to intrigue young readers. Throughout the series Sasek retains a childlike sense of wonder in his verbal and visual descriptions.

Sasek was educated as an artist in Czechoslovakia, but left in 1948 when the Communist Party came into power; he settled in Munich, but chose to remain stateless. Sasek started writing for children while on vacation in Paris. He noticed that parents in families of tourists tended to stay absorbed in their surroundings. Feeling these young people deserved to know about the things they would or could be seeing, Sasek created *This Is Paris* in 1959; he eventually published nearly twenty books in the series.

Most critics agree that Sasek presents his subjects to children successfully; some American reviewers say that his European outlook provides a lively, objective view of the American cities and subjects he covers. It is also noted that some of the language of Sasek's books is beyond the level of his intended audience, and that his later works lack the freshness of the earlier titles. However, the longevity of his series suggests that Sasek's respect for children's needs and his care in making his subjects exciting for them has secured his readership. Sasek was awarded the *New York Times* Choice of Best Illustrated Children's Book of the Year in 1959 for *This Is London* and in 1960 for *This Is New York*, which also received the Boy's Club of America Junior Books Award in 1961. *This Is the United Nations* was listed on the International Board on Books for Young People (IBBY) Honor List in 1979. (See also *Contemporary Authors*, Vols. 73-76; obituary, Vol. 101; and *Something about the Author*, Vol. 16; obituary, Vol. 23.)

GENERAL COMMENTARY

My only reservation about the now familiar series . . . on the great cities of the world . . . is that the people are all done in the same cartoon style and the human face doesn't change significantly from city to city. The artist's real interests are architecture and social details, and he has tried, successfully, I think, to catch the idiosyncrasies of each city. . . . (pp. 226-27)

> Emily Maxwell, "The Smallest Giant in the World, and the Tallest Midget," in The New Yorker *(© 1961 by The New Yorker Magazine, Inc.), Vol. XXXVII, No. 20, November 18, 1961, pp. 222-48.*

THIS IS PARIS (1959)

Marchons! lovers of Paris, *Marchons!* Straight to this big flat picture book with dozens of fine well-placed pictures of beloved Parisian landmarks. . . . Gaily modern are the half-caricatured people and the design, but the beautiful watercolors of buildings have an almost architectural accuracy. We love it. We hope many a teacher will use this book to awaken interest in *la civilization française* in boys, girls and their elders. (p. 30)

> "'First Books' and a 'Young Traveler' Offer Views of Far Lands," in New York Herald Tribune Book Review *(© I.H.T. Corporation; reprinted by permission), May 10, 1959, p. 30.*

[*This is Paris* is a] handsome and evocative picture book . . . , presenting a potpourri of Parisian landmarks and life. . . . Humor and sophistication mark the simple text, which is nonetheless direct and childlike in appeal. Even the child who has but a vague notion of what and where Paris is should have fun poring over the details of the distinctive illustrations and marvelling over the surprising glimpses of another way of life.

> Gertrude B. Herman, "Junior Books Appraised: 'This Is Paris'," in Library Journal *(reprinted from* Library Journal, July, 1959; published by R. R. Bowker Co.

(a Xerox company); copyright © 1959 by Xerox Corporation), Vol. 84, No. 13, July, 1959, p. 2224.

This Is Paris is a delightful, amusing travel guide for children. . . . [Sasek] has used the techniques of [Claude] Monet and [Georges] Seurat to express the reflections of the "City of Light" as tiny dots of color shimmer below the Eiffel Tower. The people's faces are reminiscent of [Amedeo] Modigliani, for example, the lady carrying the long bread stick. Famous landmarks, such as Notre Dame, Pont de Neuf, and the Louvre, as well as everyday bus stops, book stalls, and letter boxes are pictured with enough space for comfort. Wisely, he included the Monkey's Paradise at the zoo, French poodles, and a cemetery for dogs. Adults who have been in Paris may enjoy this book even more than children. (p. 183)

Charlotte S. Huck and Doris A. Young, "Children Seek Information about People and Places," in their Children's Literature in the Elementary School *(copyright © 1961 by Holt, Rinehart and Winston; reprinted by permission of Holt, Rinehart and Winston, Publishers, CBS College Publishing), Holt, Rinehart and Winston, 1961, pp. 153-92.**

THIS IS LONDON (1959)

This is a guided pictorial through London, its parks, its squares, its places, its river, a glimpse of its proper bankers and starched Nannies. This is the smell of violets, the bracing warmth of four o'clock tea, the chaos of Piccadilly and the lure of the Tower. This is London, a city of history and civilization, . . . a city of nostalgia for all those whose native language is English. M. Sasek, with his daring sense of design and his unusual use of color, conjures up the spirit of London town in a book so vivid and inviting that readers of all ages will take refreshment in this invitation to a delightful journey.

"Books for Young People: 'This Is London'," in Virginia Kirkus' Service, *Vol. XXVII, No. 20, October 1, 1959, p. 789.*

M. Sasek of Czechoslovakia gives us a painter's view of London, and it is, if anything, even handsomer and wittier than his earlier book. . . . In his text Mr. Sasek manages to be both succinct and genial, imparting a rather surprising amount of information, and the whole effect is fine.

Ellen Lewis Buell, "To See and to Admire," in The New York Times Book Review *(© 1959 by The New York Times Company; reprinted by permission), October 18, 1959, p. 46.*

There are not many words in Miroslav Sasek's ***This is London,*** but those few are most memorable. . . .

The colour is magnificent and uninhibited, the draughtsmanship brilliant but unobtrusive (one gradually realizes that these

So here we are.

There are five million people living here in the capital of France, one big river — the Seine — dozens of monuments, dozens of churches, dozens of museums — and thousands of cats.

From This Is Paris, *written and illustrated by M. Sasek.*

bold, stylized drawings are minutely accurate as well as true in general impression). The humour is characteristic and pervasive but always subordinate. The jokes are all pointed. Miroslav Sasek has drawn the visitor's London from foggy arrival to rainy departure. His book is a series of impressions, unrelated, one would think, but they add up to a remarkably complete picture of the modern city. The words and pictures are closely integrated; each has its terse style and humour.

> *"Our Capital Gains," in* The Times Literary Supplement *(© Times Newspapers Ltd. (London) 1959; reproduced from* The Times Literary Supplement *by permission), No. 3014, December 4, 1959, p. xx.*

A gay, witty, affectionate portrait of London, which matches last spring's **This Is Paris** in brilliance and imagination of color drawings and in generous page make-up. It will be a happy reminder for some children; a guide for those who may be going to visit London; and for all a charming interpretation, introducing famous landmarks and the personality and atmosphere of the great city. . . .

> *Virginia Haviland, "Early Spring Booklist: 'This Is London'," in* The Horn Book Magazine *(copyright, 1960, by the Horn Book, Inc., Boston), Vol. 36, No. 2, April, 1960, p. 142.*

THIS IS ROME (1960)

The young traveler, armchair or active, could have no better guide than M. Sasek. . . . In **This Is Rome** . . . he continues to delight and instruct with his wonderful, lively, word-and-picture views of the Eternal City. Forums and fountains, catacombs and carabinieri, statues and students, trams and temples—Mr. Sasek has recorded them all in a volume that is only second best to being there. (p. 30)

> *George A. Woods, "The World through Multi-Colored Magnifying Glasses," in* The New York Times Book Review, *Part II (© 1960 by The New York Times Company; reprinted by permission), May 8, 1960, pp. 30-1.**

The third of M. Sasek's picture-books about capital cities . . . is a little more formal than the others—there is the smallest breath of the guide book about it—but it has the sharp, simple sophistication which is this distinguished artist's characteristic manner. In spite of mannerisms, his is a refreshing, gay approach, and he gives children a picture of a great living city, a great museum certainly but also a home for ordinary people. . . . He has a feeling too for the absurdities as well as the splendours of the city.

Mr. Sasek's method is to show Rome as the visitor sees her, not tidily in an itinerary which takes the famous sites and buildings in their proper sequence but in a happy muddle of statues, museums, restaurants, churches, motor-cars, ruins. The drawing is most beautiful—and beautifully reproduced—with a particularly sensitive feeling for building; it is, however, essentially artful art. The book may seem to appeal to very small children, but it is designed for the sophisticated reader who will enjoy the incongruous contrasts and who will not be puzzled by the abrupt—and unexplained—turns of the text. The book is full of unanswered questions. Why does the Villa Medici belong to France? What are "Carabinieri", police or military? What was [English poet John] Keats doing in Rome? Older boys and girls will know the answers, or where to find

them; younger children attracted to the book by its gay colour and many pictures will be merely baffled.

Sophisticated readers will enjoy not only the brilliant draughtsmanship and the warm comedy but also the fine economy with which Mr. Sasek uses words. He employs no tricks but colours the plainest statement with his own wry humour.

> *"Roman Candles," in* The Times Literary Supplement *(© Times Newspapers Ltd. (London) 1960; reproduced from* The Times Literary Supplement *by permission), No. 3038, May 20, 1960, p. xxi.*

[In **This is Rome** Sasek] takes the reader on a delightful and instructive tour of Rome, recording in captioned colored drawings his impressions of sights seen along the way. The scenes are both interesting and significant, the pictures are stunning, and the brief comments enlightening.

> *"Children's Books: 'This Is Rome'," in* The Booklist and Subscription Books Bulletin *(reprinted by permission of the American Library Association; copyright © 1960 by the American Library Association), Vol. 56, No. 20, June 15, 1960, p. 634.*

THIS IS NEW YORK (1960)

Inevitably, M. Sasek, that witty, keen-eyed painter of cities came to New York and now . . . he presents the pageant of that "largest city in the Western Hemisphere *** full of the Biggest Things." Mr. Sasek pays due homage to all the bigness but, characteristically, he balances them with little shops (a hot dog cart) and little streets. . . . This book is for everybody, New Yorkers, native and adopted, exiles, outlanders, and anyone who appreciates fine pictures.

> *Ellen Lewis Buell, "All Around the Town," in* The New York Times Book Review *(© 1960 by The New York Times Company; reprinted by permission), October 23, 1960, p. 48.*

In his latest colorful big picture book Sasek shows he can do as superbly by an American city as he has done by the European capitals of Paris, London, and Rome. . . .

[All] the exciting sights of New York are pictured and captioned with wit and charm for the delectation of children and adults. We wager this book will be even more popular than its predecessors.

> *Polly Goodwin, "Artful Portrait of New York City," in* Chicago Tribune, *Part 4 (© 1960 Chicago Tribune), November 6, 1960, p. 38.*

To the *gendarmes* of Paris, the bobbies and guardsmen of London and the *carabinieri* of Rome M. Sasek has added the firemen of New York and a policeman or two. . . . His amusing representational pictures . . . are stiffer and more formal, but it is still a delight to see ourselves as he sees us. It was the firemen and the tall buildings, which he had to twist his neck to see, that struck him first, then the other big things, a few small ones like Greenwich Village's Macdougal Alley, and the fact that you can shop in any language. . . . His first view of New York is more conventional than his views of other cities. . . . Perhaps M. Sasek will make a longer visit, prowl some more and add intimacies of the city to match the little boy he shows so charmingly in this book feeding peanuts to "New York's huge fluffy squirrels."

The biggest store in the world

— and one of the smallest.

From This Is New York, *written and illustrated by M. Sasek.*

"America's Past and Present Seen Anew," in New York Herald Tribune Book Review *(© I.H.T. Corporation; reprinted by permission), November 13, 1960, p. 18.**

If there is a trace of vulgarity in the fourth of Mr. Sasek's picture-guides to capital cities, this may perhaps be attributed to his subject. *This is New York* is informal, gay and authentic. In a series of swift glimpses he gives an impression of a great city as it appears to a sharp eyed, intelligent and irreverent visitor. In this, as in the earlier books, the text is a discreet, unemphatic accompaniment of the pictures.

Parents of very small children who are attracted by the large page and the bold colourful drawing should be warned that this is a subtle book, essentially sophisticated in its humour and its social comment. It is likely to appeal most strongly to intelligent readers in their teens who have a feeling for design and a developed sense of humour.

"Big City," in The Times Literary Supplement *(© Times Newspapers Ltd. (London) 1960; reproduced from* The Times Literary Supplement *by permission), No. 3065, November 25, 1960, p. xii.*

No author has made cities more enticing than Miroslav Sasek. Despite the crime and grime, New York is beautiful in *This Is*

New York . . . , with gay, colorful pictures and a lively, humorous text describing the grandeur of a bridge span, the bustle of the garment district, the biggest traffic jams in the world. (p. 474)

Zena Sutherland, Dianne L. Monson, and May Hill Arbuthnot, "Information Books," in their Children and Books *(copyright © 1947, 1957, 1964, 1972, 1977, 1981 by Scott, Foresman and Company; reprinted by permission), sixth edition, Scott, Foresman, 1981, pp. 442-501.**

THIS IS EDINBURGH   (1961)

M. Sasek has been going about the world drawing the great cities, drawing in each case, quite candidly, the things that the tourist might see or be shown. . . . Edinburgh is a good subject, for it is a peculiarly civic city ('civic' is their favourite word), milling with monuments; its history is much commemorated and has a way of swallowing up the present situation; it certainly does so in the many books about the place, all of which somehow or other have a stoutly antiquarian air. Sasek's drawings run to caricature, but their observation of Edinburgh is accurate and acute, though it's an Edinburgh shorn unaccountably of its New Town. The wind and weather, the stone (both sorts of Edinburgh rock are included) of turret and tenement, are commemorated in a sheaf of wry and amiable pictures which have all the right greys and angularities. The sketch of Jenners Store, flanked by one of Princes Street's abundant commissionaires, is a piece of architectural satire not unworthy of the *doyens*, [Saul] Steinberg and [Osbert] Lancaster. He is not afraid to follow out his jokes and fantasies: the tartan tripes of the bagpipes are hung about his pages to great effect. . . .

Karl Miller, "M. Sasek," in New Statesman *(© 1961 The Statesman & Nation Publishing Co. Ltd.), Vol. LXI, No. 1573, May 5, 1961, p. 724.*

Those who know and love the cities for which M. Sasek has made his huge picture-book guides, with the brief, amusing and perceptive captions, enjoy them enormously and those who hope to visit them some day cannot help but find them alluring. In rapid succession he has given us his impressions of Paris, London, Rome, and New York. In each his keen perceptive eye caught not only the precise look of buildings, squares, monuments and people of all kinds, but the mood of various parts of these cities. Now he gives us Edinburgh. . . . He does not mention "Auld Reekie" at all. In fact his visit must have been a sunny one for he sees color everywhere in the gray capital of the north, in the flower clock on Princes Street, in the tartans (not pictured in quite the true colors in the text), in the brighter streets and gayly painted mews, and in school uniforms. His views of buildings are wonderful, architecturally precise yet softened to make interesting compositions and everyone surely will delight in his fine watercolors of the castle from Princes Street. We were surprised not to see the exquisitely harmonious Charlotte Square and some other of our favorite spots, but there is a limit to the number of these fine pictures, and we would not drop any of them. . . .

"Attractive and Interesting New Series," in Lively Arts and Book Review *(© I.H.T. Corporation; reprinted by permission), May 14, 1961, p. 30.**

It would be inaccurate to say that M. Sasek is in a groove. He has, rather, devised a most satisfactory formula and applies it with great skill, understanding and integrity. Thus, although all his studies of great cities are, at a superficial glance, alike, each is true both to the *genius loci* and to the artist's personal vision. If this seems too sober an approach to what are admittedly very funny books, it should be noted that M. Sasek's fun always has serious edge to it.

He has found much to love in Auld Reekie, particularly the incongruities, social and architectural. There is some very lovely drawing, particularly of the Edinburgh skyline, a sharply humorous enjoyment of folly, and an occasional neatness of phrase. Yet **This is Edinburgh,** for all its excellences, does not quite add up to a portrait of a city; rather a number of quick sketches in preparation for a portrait.

> *"City Portraits," in* The Times Literary Supplement *(© Times Newspapers Ltd. (London) 1961; reproduced from* The Times Literary Supplement *by permission), No. 3090, May 19, 1961, p. xviii.*

Miroslav Sasek has an eye that captures the underlying pattern of scenes, a sense of humor that adds originality, a publisher who preserves the just-painted freshness of his remarkably wide color range. He shows some history, what a sgian dubh is, and brings such an atmosphere that it is easy to hear the squeal of bagpipes and the soft burr of Scots voices.

> *P. M., "Widening Horizons for Children: 'This Is Edinburgh'," in* The Christian Science Monitor *(reprinted by permission from* The Christian Science Monitor; *© 1961 The Christian Science Publishing Society; all rights reserved), June 8, 1961, p. 11.*

THIS IS MUNICH   (1961)

By comparison [with **This is Edinburgh,** the text of **This is Munich**] is plodding, unsure whether to be informative or gay. There is some doubt, too, about who will read these books—not the earnest ten-year-old who wants to know. The younger child might be puzzled by the guide-book aspect and by the touches of sophistication: the father and son in lederhosen, for example, who stand unflinching in a hothouse of tropical plants, or the buxom girl in Bavarian costume who turns up in the Munich artists' quarter with the caption, 'this is an art student.'

> *Karl Miller, "M. Sasek," in* New Statesman *(© 1961 The Statesman & Nation Publishing Co. Ltd.), Vol. LXI, No. 1573, May 5, 1961, p. 724.*

[**This Is Munich** is an addition] to an alluring series which, one must confess, probably holds more appeal for the adults familiar with the various cities than for the children for whom they are intended. The drawings are bold, imaginative, creatively humorous—when occasion demands, and informative—but they have a somewhat mature sophistication, and their chief appeal lies in a recognition value rather than stimulating interest.

> *"Eight to Eleven—Non-Fiction: 'This Is Munich'," in* Virginia Kirkus' Service, *Vol. XXIX, No. 10, May 15, 1961, p. 428.*

[Sasek's] architectural drawing in **This is Munich** is exuberant; so is his enjoyment of human oddities. This is an affectionate, critical, highly intelligent impression of a great and complex city.

> *"City Portraits," in* The Times Literary Supplement *(© Times Newspapers Ltd. (London) 1961; repro-*

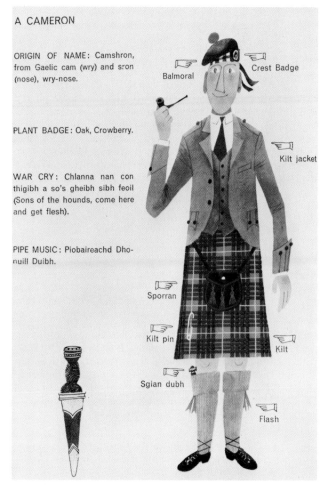

From This Is Edinburgh, *written and illustrated by M. Sasek.*

duced from The Times Literary Supplement *by permission), No. 3090, May 19, 1961, p. xviii.*

The large, striking picture books by M. Sasek have been most popular with adults. Children can share them, but the text certainly does little to introduce a city to a child who has not seen it. . . . ["**This Is Munich**" is] a bit over-crowded by churches and beer halls. Have you ever watched the faces of children as the famous clock strikes an evening hour and the Munich Child comes slowly out, carrying his lantern? Now the city fathers apparently prefer to picture him with a beer stein in one hand, a radish in the other. M. Sasek might watch children a little more closely on his future trips to cities, because he could give them so much.

> *Alice Dalgliesh, "Books for Young Children: 'This Is Edinburgh' and 'This Is Munich'," in* Saturday Review *(copyright ©1961 by* Saturday Review; *all rights reserved; reprinted by permission), Vol. XLIV, No. 29, July 22, 1961, p. 37.*

Author-Illustrator Sasek unwraps cities like Christmas presents. He does not have to simulate a child's natural wonder at what exists; he shares it. From the seven tons of bells in Munich's New Town Hall to the address of the oldest house (No. 5 Burgstrasse), he makes his facts sound like discoveries and his Munich sausages appetizing enough to nibble.

"Books: 'This Is Edinburgh' and 'This Is Munich'," in Time *(copyright 1961 Time Inc.; all rights reserved; reprinted by permission from* Time*), Vol. LXXVIII, No. 5, August 4, 1961, p. 73.*

THIS IS VENICE (1961)

"This Is Venice" is one of a series of big, handsome picture books by Miroslav Sasek, a sophisticated, skillful artist, whose illustrations are so good, so full of humor and color, that they must be looked at again and again. Every page is "suitable for framing," but even the most enthusiastic child would never want to take apart this near perfect piece of work. What a lovely Venice for any young reader to know and treasure.

Maureen Daly, "Scouring the World with Typewriter and Camera," in Chicago Tribune *Part 4 (© 1961 Chicago Tribune), November 12, 1961, p. 38.*

The pattern of M. Sasek's books is now firmly established. It would be difficult for him to introduce innovations, and these would not be welcomed by his admirers, who delight in the fixed conventions of his unconventional portraits. It is the more remarkable that each book is pure Sasek and at the same time each catches the characteristic atmosphere of his subject. . . .

This is Venice has many of the artist's gentle digs at tourists and at the vendors who feed on them. It shows, too, that M. Sasek is primarily an architectural draughtsman. His drawings of churches, palaces and odd corners are brilliant simplifications which never depart from the essential truths of building. That he draws buildings not in noble isolation but surrounded by the mess and muddle of a living city—washing on the line, telly-aerials on the roof—endears him more deeply to the reader.

"Writ on Water," in The Times Literary Supplement *(© Times Newspapers Ltd. (London) 1961; reproduced from* The Times Literary Supplement *by permission), No. 3118, December 1, 1961, p. xvii.*

The romantic background of Venice, both historical and present-day, naturally makes this newest addition to the artist's picture-book series on cities an especially fascinating volume. His paintings have their usual brilliance and flavor and, accompanied by humorous text, ensure a wide range of interest again.

Virginia Haviland, "Late Winter Booklist: 'This Is Venice'," in The Horn Book Magazine *(copyright, 1962, by The Horn Book, Inc., Boston), Vol. 38, No. 1, February, 1962, p. 63.*

THIS IS ISRAEL (1962)

Contrasting the old with the new an artist records his impressions of present-day Israel in eye-catching paintings and brief captions. [*This is Israel*] is strictly a tourist's view of the country; it seems however a little less effective than the earlier books which described cities rather than countries.

"History, Geography, Travel, Social Life and Customs: 'This Is Israel'," (originally published in The Booklist*, Vol. 59, No. 14, March 15, 1962), in* Books for Children: 1960-1965 *(copyright © 1962 by the American Library Association), American Library Association, 1966, p. 193.*

That diligent metropolis-hopper, Miroslav Sasek, . . . now

travels lightly through the Promised Land. Tourists are always a bit surprised to find that all those places the Bible talks about are really there, and Mr. Sasek shares some of this wide-eyed wonder. . . . As usual, he puts it all down with a witty, exuberant brush. But, charming as it is, the book doesn't quite live up to the others. For one thing, its layout is crowded and confusing. For another, color in some of the pictures seems strangely insipid. And Mr. Sasek's usually bright text has been interspersed with Biblical quotations, a device that has been overworked in books about Israel and that here seems somewhat pretentious and unnecessary.

Grace H. Glueck, "Among the New Books for the Younger Readers' Library: 'This Is Israel'," in The New York Times Book Review *(© 1962 by The New York Times Company; reprinted by permission), December 9, 1962, p. 36.*

To his series on famous cities of the world this Czech artist adds a book about a larger area, which, however, because of its unusual character, fits appropriately into the sequence. Covering the ancient and the modern in the same startling juxtaposition as that which the visitor finds, both text and pictures—his delightful full-color impressions—convey a vivid sense of scene and life, with occasional flashes of the humor that distinguishes this lively set of books. (pp. 182-83)

Virginia Haviland, "Early Spring Booklist: 'This Is Israel'," in The Horn Book Magazine *(copyright ©1963, by The Horn Book, Inc., Boston), Vol. XXXIX, No. 2, April, 1963, pp. 182-83.*

THIS IS SAN FRANCISCO (1962)

This is San Francisco is the eighth of Mr. Sasek's impressions of the world's great cities and there seems no reason why he should not continue so long as a city remains to prompt his sharp observation, shrewd social comment and pervading humour. The San Francisco album is in the now-familiar manner, and Mr. Sasek is particularly happy with the singular blend of brashness and beauty in the West Coast capital. If there is at least as much relish of absurdity, there is more than common tenderness and affection in this portrait. Like [Rudyard] Kipling, Mr. Sasek has found San Francisco hard to leave, and so will his readers.

"Sasek in S.F.," in The Times Literary Supplement *(© Times Newspapers Ltd. (London) 1962; reproduced from* The Times Literary Supplement *by permission), No. 3144, June 1, 1962, p. 397.*

San Francisco [is] the subject of Sasek's latest fascinating picture book. Cable cars and cars parked precariously on steep streets, bridges and freeways, Chinatown and Fishermen's wharf, lovely vistas and parks and not so lovely prisons, all the things that make up one of the most beautiful and distinctive cities in the world enchant the eye and stir the imagination as depicted by the artist with characteristic humor and zest.

Polly Goodwin, "The Junior Bookshelf: 'This Is San Francisco'," in Chicago Tribune *Part 4 (© 1962 Chicago Tribune), June 17, 1962, p. 7.*

Like most visitors to San Francisco, M. Sasek has fallen in love with that unusual city and has given it his best. His writing here is less guidebook-like and somewhat more informal than

California Street

Ladies are not permitted to hang on the outside.

From This Is San Francisco, *written and illustrated by M. Sasek.*

it has been. But at times one longs for just a few more words for those children who will view San Francisco only in the pages of the book. . . .

The book opens with a sweeping view of the city as seen from Berkeley, with the Golden Gate Bridge in the distance. Farther on there is a spectacular picture of the bridge, and for good measure the artist also swings the whole orange-red span across two pages. He handles the city's incredibly steep streets particularly well, as he does the cable cars and Chinatown. . . . It will be difficult for readers to resist rushing out to see San Francisco again—or for the first time.

> Alice Dalgliesh, *"Musical Chairs and Paperbacks: 'This Is San Francisco',"* in Saturday Review *(copyright © 1962 by* Saturday Review; *all rights reserved; reprinted by permission), Vol. XLV, No. 28, July 21, 1962, p. 35.*

THIS IS CAPE KENNEDY   (1964)

[*This Is Cape Kennedy*] is dramatic, though one misses the spectacular panoramas of large cities provided by his previous books. In the nature of the Cape, the most attention-getting pages are those showing the giant rockets, the radar-tracking devices, and the montage of world headlines when our astronaut made America's first orbit. The book also exposes the commercialism surrounding the Cape.

> Alice Dalgliesh, *"The Wonderful Silence: 'This Is Cape Kennedy',"* in Saturday Review *(copyright © 1965 by* Saturday Review; *all rights reserved; reprinted by permission), Vol. XLVIII, No. 4, January 23, 1965, p. 51.*

"We can trace it!" shouted the kindergartener as soon as he saw the marvelous rockets in *This Is Cape Kennedy*. . . . Contemporary in feeling, with an enticing combination of realism and whimsy, they are among the children's delights an adult can share. Cape Kennedy seems a hardly beatable subject for boys. . . .

> R.N., *"Children's Books: 'This Is Cape Kennedy',"* in The Christian Science Monitor *(reprinted by permission from* The Christian Science Monitor; *© 1965 The Christian Science Publishing Society; all rights reserved), August 26, 1965, p. 5.*

Sasek's pictorial presentation of the "Space Capital of the World" shows in colorful captioned paintings missiles and equipment at Cape Kennedy and tourist attractions at nearby Cocoa Beach. This is not among the best of the artist's guidebooks but it does contain quite a bit of information in its illustrations and captions and may well have the most appeal for children. (pp. 18-19)

> *"Social Sciences: 'This Is Cape Kennedy',"* in Books for Children: 1960-1965 *(copyright © 1960, 1961, 1962, 1963, 1964, 1965 by the American Library Association),* American Library Association, 1966, pp. 18-19.

THIS IS IRELAND   (1965)

[A] combination of topographical nonsense and visual fantasy is not uncommon in books about Ireland. We can be grateful that M. Sasek's book is not only decorative but unusually accurate. . . .

There are a few minor blemishes, but they do not detract from our pleasure in illustrations such as of Bernard Shaw's birthplace with a television aerial attached to the chimney, or in a vista of one of the most secret places in Ireland, rarely visited by strangers—Clonmacnoise, where "the warriors of Erin in their famous generations, slumber." . . .

A good many of Sasek's pictures give the impression of having been drawn from photographs, which adds greatly to their pleasing familiarity.

> Denis Johnston, *"Books for Young Readers: 'This Is Ireland',"* in The New York Times Book Review *(© 1965 by The New York Times Company; reprinted by permission), March 14, 1965, p. 30.*

Shamrocks, shillelaghs and sheep, bathed in an all-pervading green and accompanied by harps, jaunting carts and a leprechaun or two, enliven this gay, bright and pleasantly conventional book. The architectural drawings of castles, cathedrals, squares and public buildings are done with photographic care, and the many watercolor scenes of fields, bays and mountains attempt in poster fashion to show the lushness of the lowlands and the omnipresent veil of mist.

But the book lacks the originality and the fine humor and zestfulness M. Sasek brought to his first portfolios of cities. . . . Once in a while the mood of this enchanting country is caught, though the greens are reproduced a bit harshly in an attempt to have them look as truly emerald as they appear in reality.

> Margaret Sherwood Libby, "Happy in My Green Heaven: 'This Is Ireland'," in Book Week—The Sunday Herald Tribune (© 1965, The Washington Post), March 21, 1965, p. 17.

[This Is Ireland] comprises, as do the previous Sasek books, an often-amusing and quite informative text that consists chiefly of brief captions (a phrase, a sentence, or at most a few paragraphs) for utterly charming pictures. The book has a little less cohesion than do the books about individual cities, but it does convey atmosphere and give information. Because it attempts to describe an entire country, the book has noticeable omissions, but it is delightful for browsing.

> Zena Sutherland, "New Titles for Children and Young People: 'This Is Ireland'," in Bulletin of the Center for Children's Books (reprinted by permission of The University of Chicago Press; copyright 1965 by the University of Chicago), Vol. XVIII, No. 8, April, 1965, p. 123.

THIS IS HONG KONG (1965)

Primarily, This is Hong Kong belongs to Mr. Sasek's series of picture-books for the young, but there is good reason for their not monopolizing it. The artist sometimes works in cartoonist style, sometimes as though fancying a toy-box, and again in broad terms of direct landscape and seascape. The hints are often practical: below a fine panorama of heavy spring weather over skyscrapers, junks, tankers, and mountainous islands, one reads "you get this priceless view, plus the ferry ride across the harbour, for three half-pence (British), or just under two cents (U.S.)". If we do not know what a cheongsam is, two local beauties wearing this one-piece garment with high collar are illustrated. . . .

It is a sensibly arranged as well as a gorgeous volume, and at last we are gathering in a few more of the regular sights and singularities of Hongkong, until a large view of the city and the heights above, preparing for the night, practically concludes an agreeable, if limited, itinerary.

> "Sasek Goes East," in The Times Literary Supplement (© Times Newspapers Ltd. (London) 1965; reproduced from The Times Literary Supplement by permission), No. 3303, June 17, 1965, p. 501.

[For] children who don't have a rich Aunt Ethel to actually take them [to Hong Kong], this book is an excellent substitute. They won't capture the tang and scent of Hong Kong this way. But the book's bold and vivid illustrations give an accurate sense of the color and vigor and excitement of one of the world's most fascinating cities. There is a simple text as well. It avoids trivia. It doesn't insult a child's intelligence. It includes much of the information a good handbook would provide. But somehow, it's much more interesting.

> J. H., "A Travel Bargain," in The Christian Science Monitor (reprinted by permission from The Christian Science Monitor; © 1965 The Christian Science Publishing Society; all rights reserved), November 4, 1965, p. B5.

THIS IS GREECE (1966)

["This Is Greece"] is a humorous and inviting picture book that tours the landmarks with the younger reader. Though the layout is sometimes confusing, the poster pictures of ancient and modern Greece have a pleasing sense of vista, and the reader leaves the book with a definite idea of the country and its significance.

> Roger Jellinck, "Greek Glory, Roman Power: 'This Is Greece'," in The New York Times Book Review, Part II (© 1966 by The New York Times Company; reprinted by permission), May 8, 1966, p. 31.

A new Sasek book is always a treat, and [This Is Greece] presenting a land "rich in history, in light, in marble; the birthplace of western civilization," is as flavorful, colorful, and witty as his other picture book tours of lands and cities. . . . It's a rewarding journey, which anyone who has been to Greece, or who plans or longs to go there, will want to share.

> Polly Goodwin, "The Junior Bookshelf," in Chicago Tribune (© 1966 Chicago Tribune), May 15, 1966, p. 11.

[With This Is Greece] Mr. Sasek introduces a civilization as well as a place. Although this would be especially enjoyed by those with some background in Greek history and mythology, the entertaining pictures and brief text would also stimulate interest in the subject. A pleasing combination of fact and fun, this will be useful in elementary social studies classes.

> Marilynn McBeth, "Junior Books Appraised: 'This Is Greece'," in Library Journal an appendix to Library Journal (reprinted from the September, 1966 issue of School Library Journal, published by R. R. Bowker Co./A Xerox Corporation; copyright © 1966), Vol. 13, No. 1, September, 1966, p. 190.

THIS IS TEXAS (1967)

In "This Is Texas" . . . the artist gives us his realistic impressions of such diversities as grain elevators in the Panhandle, prairie dogs in Lubbock, El Capitan, the Alamo by night, the King Ranch and such modern attractions as the Houston Astrodome, amusement parks, Dallas's Neiman-Marcus Specialty Store—and the Kennedy assassination site. Everything in this Texas guidebook looks and sounds sensational.

> George A. Woods, "Picture Books: 'This Is Texas'," in The New York Times Book Review (© 1967 by The New York Times Company; reprinted by permission), May 7, 1967, pp. 52-3.

Texas is an ideal subject for Mr. Sasek's gifted gaiety; the Lone Star State's "mostestness" is gently pilloried and the wide variety of scenery and ways of life are shown to great effect, though the degree of certainty shown about the source of the shot that killed President Kennedy will not commend itself to recent critics.

> "Junior Information Books: 'This Is Texas'," in The Times Literary Supplement (© Times Newspapers Ltd. (London) 1967; reproduced from The Times Literary Supplement by permission), No. 3404, May 25, 1967, p. 465.

The text [of This Is Texas] consists of captions of varying length; the writing style has an easy, occasionally flippant, conversational tone. Perhaps because the book covers an area so large and so diverse, it seems to have less cohesion than its predecessors and gives almost an effect of being fragmented.

> *Zena Sutherland, "New Titles for Children and Young People: 'This Is Texas'," in* Bulletin of the Center for Children's Books *(reprinted by permission of The University of Chicago Press; copyright 1967 by the University of Chicago), Vol. 21, No. 2, October, 1967, p. 32.*

THIS IS THE UNITED NATIONS (1968)

Like a tour of UN headquarters which it simulates, this is informative and entertaining and exhausting. (One of the troubles is that—probably in deference to a world market—it asks the reader to examine the works of art contributed by each country.) In contrast to Sasek's earlier cityscapes, this is generally sober and straightforward, explaining the history, purposes and functions of the UN, identifying its chief components and associated organs; kids who begin to nod will perk up again in the press room, the post office and the gift shop. Adult fans of the series may miss the accustomed levity but teachers and parents can trade on the eye-appeal—including a spread of the maps of the 122 member nations—for a thorough briefing.

> *"Younger Non-Fiction: 'This Is the United Nations'," in* Kirkus Service *(copyright © 1968 The Kirkus Service, Inc.), Vol. XXXVI, No. 10, May 15, 1968, p. 553.*

Anything that can sustain enthusiasm in the work of the United Nations at this time when general interest has tended to decline is well worthwhile. Mr. Sasek's book is undoubtedly intended to do just this, but he has given so much prominence to the external structure and organization that young readers may well miss the purpose behind it all. His vivid illustrations accompanied by terse text are arresting and exciting, but so much is lacking that would give a child some idea of the high aims and practical achievements of the U.N. Mr. Sasek has had great success with the series to which this book belongs but the U.N. is the planned expression of an ideal rather than the gradual development of history and it calls for different treatment.

> *"Older Non-Fiction: 'This Is the United Nations'," in* The Times Literary Supplement *(© Times Newspapers Ltd. (London) 1968; reproduced from The Times Literary Supplement by permission), No. 3458, June 6, 1968, p. 596.*

In M. Sasek's familiar style, the spindly legged adults and puffy cheeked young children poke their pointy noses into U.N. meeting rooms on a breezy tour of the international headquarters on the East River. As always, M. Sasek is smoothly passing along the odd bits and pieces of data children seem to enjoy. . . . But there is plenty of basic historical information in the slim volume. The style is whimsical but not so whimsical that the read-aloud experience is a bore.

Inevitably U.N. fans will grumble that M. Sasek seems too engrossed with the tourist-type attractions and neglects the sound and serious matters: too much about girl guides, stamp-collecting and souvenirs, but not enough about the unique status of the U.N.'s staff as international civil servants, or the U.N.'s Peace Force accomplishments in the Middle East and Cyprus and the Congo.

But this is such an attractive introduction to the U.N. it seems a pity to carp. It's gay. It's informative. A book to be read once and again, handed down in the family, borrowed—and returned.

> *Kathleen Teltsch, "Good Neighbors," in* The New York Times Book Review *(© 1968 by The New York Times Company; reprinted by permission), June 23, 1968, p. 22.*

The book gives a straightforward account eminently suitable for the older junior range and upwards. The reader is told *how* the organization works, not *if* it works, and this is surely what such an introductory book should do for youngsters.

Amongst many other things, the young reader will be interested to see the coloured flags of the 122 member nations, the U.N. post office with its special stamp issues, the arrangements for simultaneous translations, facilities for the press and the pieces of art presented by different nations. Work of the several councils should promote discussion among older pupils.

> *E. Bowker, "Book Reviews: 'This Is the United Nations'," in* The School Librarian and School Library Review, *Vol. 16, No. 3, December, 1968, p. 372.*

THIS IS WASHINGTON, D.C. (1969)

Sasek roaming the streets was a wayward charmer; Sasek as the standard guide to the city is considerably stiffer. Here, crisply drawn, are the sites of Washington for the average tourist and a few special sights for children (especially in and around the Smithsonian). The descriptive captions are adequate except in a few instances when the choice of words is misleading (e.g. it is implied that the Library of Congress is solely *for* Congress, that the Washington Monument is made of bricks rather than blocks of stone).

> *"Picture Books: 'This Is Washington, D.C.'," in* Kirkus Reviews *(copyright © 1969 The Kirkus Service, Inc.), Vol. XXXVII, No. 11, June 1, 1969, p. 595.*

Perhaps Mr. Sasek is getting tired of globe-trotting after ten years, or perhaps there is a bubble of sanctity about the United States capital that he feels it would be sacrilege to prick. Whatever the cause, **This is Washington, D.C.** sags rather, compared with some of the early volumes in the same series.

For one thing, there is very much more text, and it is of a different kind. Whereas in the early books he succeeded in distilling the essence of the place in brief, telling sentences, here he crams in long paragraphs of factual information, not all of it accurate. . . .

It is sad to say that the illustrations are less witty too. Whereas the volume on, for example, London, is full of pictures of natives and visitors which evoke both a smile and the feeling that they are absolutely true, there is a much higher proportion of buildings and inanimate objects in the Washington book. Such people as are portrayed are comic in a conventional way and show little of the wit and discernment that characterized the first volumes in the series. Even the buildings seem more pompous. Indeed, one no longer has the impression that the artist has browsed around the city of his choice, getting to know the people and the feel of the place, but rather that he has tossed off his book with the aid of a guide and a collection of coloured photographs. Perhaps it is time he had a rest.

"Sasek in America," in The Times Literary Supplement *(© Times Newspapers Ltd. (London) 1969; reproduced from* The Times Literary Supplement *by permission), No. 3513, June 26, 1969, p. 701.*

A book about Washington's history must be well-rooted in the city's past, and M. Sasek shows a wide understanding of all the aspects—social, economic and political—which make up this complex seat of government. He highlights institutions and landmarks such as the Smithsonian museum, the Federal buildings, the White House and the Library of Congress, but equally interesting information is given about the Bureau of Engraving and Printing and the headquarters of the F.B.I. where a marksmanship demonstration is held by G-men at the end of every tour. This is a short but concise guide, full of humour and aided by bold, bright illustrations. It is highly recommended to anyone planning a trip to America's capital city.

A. B., "Geography & Travel: 'This Is Washington'," in Children's Book News *(copyright © 1969 by Baker Book Services Ltd.), Vol. 4, No. 4, July-August, 1969, p. 219.*

The sense of awe and reverence young Americans bring to the national capital need not be artificially nourished but neither should it be prematurely deadened. Instead of surmounting the bureaucratic barricades to reveal more pictorially interesting goings-on in Washington, Mr. Sasek settles too often for postcard representations. Under textbook verbiage and mini-deluges of irrelevant statistics he smothers the "gay sense of fun" promised on the jacket.

More's the pity, for the Czech artist-author does sometimes turn his keen eye discerningly. For example: in illustrating the Voice of America's operations, he shows an intriguing Master Control Panel and a child pushing a button to tune in an announcer in Tamil. Here he delights visually as well as stretches the imagination beyond building walls.

All the familiar tourist attractions are covered, some more successfully than others; but Mr. Sasek short-changes young readers by not suggesting less obvious spots, such as the Islamic Center with its exotic Mosque where shoes are shed at the door before entering, the Naval Observatory where time is "born" and the Museum of African Arts where ancient tribal masks mingle with contemporary works.

Barbara Dubivsky, "'This Is Washington, D.C.'," in The New York Times Book Review *(© 1969 by The New York Times Company; reprinted by permission), August 24, 1969, p. 20.*

Like other Sasek books, this is distinguished by the impressive exactness of the architectural details in pictures of sites and buildings, and by the rakish drawing of people; it includes general information about the city and minor details of exhibits, as well as the text about the paintings of points of major interest that constitute the bulk of the book. The whole is an attractive and fairly comprehensive guide to the city; it lacks only the flavor and the feeling of a metropolitan personality that gave the earlier Sasek books about great cities such verve.

Zena Sutherland, "New Titles for Children and Young People: 'This Is Washington, D.C.'," in Bulletin of the Center for Children's Books *(reprinted by permission of The University of Chicago Press; © 1969 by The University of Chicago), Vol. 23, No. 2, October, 1969, p. 30.*

THIS IS AUSTRALIA (1970)

Sasek's globe-trotting series is designed, we are informed, "for children of every age, including adults". Like the audience he aims at, he is in turn exasperating and endearing. He is exasperating when he is arch and jokey (particularly at Port Arthur): endearing when he catches a brilliant national likeness, like his pair of grinning reliable life-savers or his shy, big-hearted girl adorned with rainbow lorikeet. Sasek's Australia is a jolly place, where the sky is always blue and the people always beaming. Large towns are packed like mosaic around the shore; the predominantly suburban quality of Australian life is well-illustrated by a drawing of a family picnicking in a gum-fringed car-park, above the dead-pan caption "Every scenic place in Canberra has a picnic area with gas barbecue pits for weekenders". In the bottom corner of the back endpaper, the artist himself bounds away on a kangaroo's back, with a portfolio of sketches under his arm; but if his impressions have been superficial, they are nevertheless lively and affectionate.

"Myth and Reality: 'This Is Australia'," in The Times Literary Supplement *(© Times Newspapers Ltd. (London) 1970; reproduced from* The Times Literary Supplement *by permission), No. 3583, October 30, 1970, p. 1256.*

The sleek buildings, sprawling cities and wide open spaces of Australia have about them little of the picturesque or raffish and so, little to offer Mr. Sasek though he must perforce put them on repeated display; convicts, now, are something else—though just what (i.e. why 'the first British settlers came in chains') we never learn notwithstanding the several references to them. In fact, they're a stock joke: Port Arthur "provided accommodations for some 30,000 new arrivals. . . . No, it was not a hostelry. It was a penitentiary." Also, with picture, "This was a lifer's uniform. . . . But Port Arthur's design for living was something else again"—with an almost unreadable reproduction of a chart showing the number of lashes administered annually for various offenses. So it goes on, wanly whimsical and worth mentioning only because a child, not knowing what to make of it, may make more than he should. Sasek does get around and where there's sufficient visual variety—as in Alice Springs and environs—the book makes fairly interesting looking; otherwise a good deal of it looks alike and though this may be Australia, it is only a superficial aspect of it.

"Younger Non-Fiction: 'This Is Australia'," in Kirkus Reviews *(copyright © 1971 The Kirkus Service, Inc.), Vol. XXXIX, No. 6, March 15, 1971, p. 292.*

"This Is Australia" . . . will not disappoint readers accustomed to [Sasek's] bright, whimsical postcard tours. . . .

More about things than people, really, but leaving one with an impression of friendliness and vigor nonetheless. And it's such a painless way to learn a bit about a lot of things Australian, even if Sasek artfully sticks to all the pretty things.

Robert Berkvist, "Wombats in the Outback: 'This Is Australia'," in The New York Times Book Review *(© 1971 by The New York Times Company; reprinted by permission), May 2, 1971, p. 12.*

THIS IS HISTORIC BRITAIN (1974)

[**This Is Historic Britain** is an] excellent introductory guide. . . . Although the monuments of British tourism—such as the Tower of London, Shakespeare's Birthplace, and Stonehenge—are not scanted, there is a rich display of English cathedrals (Chester, Durham, Exeter, Gloucester, and Hereford—among others), and careful attention is given to Welsh and Scottish castles. Oxford and Cambridge Universities are each well-represented, and references are made to places associated with American history: Plymouth with the Pilgrims; Stratford-upon-Avon with John Harvard's mother; and Boston, England, with Boston, Massachusetts. Despite the regrettably erroneous statement that Shakespeare's last home—New Place—is still preserved, the genial text conveys a richly authentic feeling for the history of Britain as it is enshrined in its buildings and relics. (pp. 700, 702)

> *Paul Heins, "History and Biography: 'This Is Historic Britain'," in* The Horn Book Magazine *(copyright © 1974 by the Horn Book, Inc., Boston), Vol. L, No. 6, December, 1974, pp. 700, 702.*

Sasek's text is, as always, packed with facts that would be interesting to a sightseer, and the book can serve as an adjunct to a historical unit of the curriculum, but the primary appeal is visual: carefully detailed and accurate paintings in restrained color of the period architecture found in castles, cathedrals, and historic buildings throughout England, Scotland, and Wales. (pp. 98-9)

> *Zena Sutherland, "New Titles for Children and Young People: 'This Is Historic Britain'," in* Bulletin of the Center for Children's Books *(reprinted by permission of The University of Chicago Press; © 1975 by The University of Chicago), Vol. 28, No. 6, February, 1975, pp. 98-9.*

Once again Mr. Sasek lives up to his high standards both in illustration and text. I can see [*This is Historic Britain*] being a very popular addition to the series both with librarians and with adults as a gift for young readers who are discovering Britain for themselves for the first time. However not only children enjoy these books, many older readers get immense pleasure out of the series.

> *"The New Books for Librarians: 'This Is Historic Britain'," in* The Junior Bookshelf, *Vol. 40, No. 4, August, 1976, p. 211.*

Alfred Slote

1926-

American author of fiction and nonfiction for children and adults. Slote draws upon his experiences as a former baseball player and Little League coach for most of his stories. Hockey, tennis, and baseball games are the settings for basic life issues: relationships between father and son, life and death, and good and evil; Slote's characters learn to deal with personalities and situations both on and off the field. Besides his sports stories, Slote has written two science books, *The Moon in Fact and Fancy* and *Air in Fact and Fancy*, in which he combines myth and folklore with scientific facts, and three science fiction stories, *My Robot Buddy*, its sequel, *C.O.L.A.R.*, and *My Trip to Alpha I*. Like his sports stories, Slote's science fiction works are concerned with relationships, but between humans and robots. They also encompass more universal issues such as slavery and freedom. Slote has also written a group of short stories, *The Devil Rides with Me and Other Fantastic Stories*, which combine science fiction and fantasy.

Slote's science and science fiction works have not met with the same critical approval as his sports stories, although in general they have been well received. The consensus is that his sports stories are most successful because Slote has an agreeable, informal style and an ear for natural dialogue, and can incorporate descriptions of a game's action with believable story lines. By molding the popular genres of sports stories and science fiction around weightier issues, it is felt that Slote teaches as well as entertains. Slote received the Friends of American Writers Award in 1971 for *Jake*. (See also *Something about the Author*, Vol. 8.)

THE MOON IN FACT AND FANCY (1967)

In an agreeable, informal style the author recounts several legends about the moon, following each with a scientific explanation of the phenomenon that figures in the story. The paired chapters cover such subjects as the origin of the moon, its phases and features, eclipses, effect on the tides, and a journey to the moon. The legends, chosen from widely divergent sources, are well told; the science material is informative and simply expressed. . . . This is a title which may appeal to the reader who usually avoids science books. . . .

> Janet French, *"The Book Review: 'The Moon in Fact and Fancy',"* in Library Journal *(reprinted from* Library Journal, *July, 1967; published by R. R. Bowker Co. (a Xerox company); copyright © 1967 by Xerox Corporation), Vol. 92, No. 13, July, 1967, p. 2657.*

This is the kind of book that must have seemed like a good idea at the start. **"The Moon in Fact and Fancy"**—why not? A little fact, a little fancy . . . presto! But not quite, because the ready-made mixture refuses to jell. Here are some little-known folk legends about the moon, how it got there, why it waxes and wanes, what its markings are, but they are not especially well told, or retold. Here, too, are some scientific facts and informed speculation about the moon, how it got there, etc., but again the presentation is prosaic. There is nothing seriously wrong with either the idea or the presentation, nothing, that is, that a good storyteller couldn't remedy. A

well-maintained effort, no doubt, but as lifeless as the poor old moon itself.

> Robert Berkvist, *"For the Young Reader: 'The Moon in Fact and Fancy',"* in The New York Times Book Review *(© 1967 by The New York Times Company; reprinted by permission), July 9, 1967, p. 34.*

The Moon in Fact and Fancy . . . is interesting from a thematic point of view. . . . While I cannot vouch for the authenticity and accuracy of the legends gathered from all over the world, I can say that his astronomy is reasonably accurate. Of course, in a small book the treatment must be superficial, allowing little chance for major misstatement. If a youngster of ten or twelve seems ready to graduate from fairy stories, this book may be an excellent means of making the transition. (pp. 29, 66)

> K. L. Franklin, *"Astronomy,"* in Natural History *(copyright © the American Museum of Natural History, 1967; reprinted with permission from* Natural History*), Vol. LXXVI, No. 9, November, 1967, pp. 29, 66.**

AIR IN FACT AND FANCY (1968)

The suggestion of mental parallels is the main advantage of this presentation, which juxtaposes short mythic stories with modern scientific views of the same phenomena: the creation, the source of winds, the causes of rain, lightning and thunder. In most cases the ''primitive'' version reflects sharp observations even if the causal relationships (e.g. between water currents and the winds) have been revised. One can see a resemblance between Newton's invention of a ''force of gravity'' and the construct of Rangi, the earth god. Assuming that readers recognize a difference between natural and scientific observation, this should not mislead but should intimate the fecundity of each approach. Imaginative but without support from the textbook prose.

> *''Older Non-Fiction: 'Air in Fact and Fancy','' in* Kirkus Service *(copyright © 1968 The Kirkus Service, Inc.), Vol. XXXVI, No. 11, June 1, 1968, p. 611.*

This charming collection of folk tales and facts continues the original concept first developed by the author in his book *The Moon in Fact and Fancy*. . . . Underlying the structure of the expository treatment is the author's belief that ''science and story can share the same pages and receive equal welcome in the heart,'' and this again he has demonstrated successfully. . . . There is . . . a rich lode of legend and myth to explain the atmosphere and its happenings. In almost all cultures, early man had developed his own folk tales. Mr. Slote's problem obviously was to select from among riches. While one may disagree with some of these selections, they do present a broad and diverse cultural sweep; e.g., Greek mythology (what holds up the sky); Norway (what makes a rainbow); India (why we have thunder); South Pacific (what causes rain). More importantly, they serve well to sustain the reader's interest and entice him into the clear and concise technical explanations that follow. Only in the final chapters of the book which deal with air pollution, is there no companion folk tale. Modern man can apparently ascribe to no one but himself this new wholesome development in the story of our atmosphere.

> *''Meteorology: 'Air in Fact and Fancy','' in* Science Books *(copyright © 1969 by the American Association for the Advancement of Science), Vol. 5, No. 1, May, 1969, p. 38.*

STRANGER ON THE BALL CLUB (1970)

Tim had just moved to Arborville and the last thing he needed was to get off on the wrong foot with the other boys in fifth grade. His mother had died, his father was withdrawn, and his older sister just plain bossy. So when he found a baseball glove and carefully inked over the name ''Tad Myers'' it was a blow to find that Tad was in his room—and a very nice guy. Hostile and insecure, Tim had already irked most of the Little League Team when it was discovered that he had taken and clumsily, later, returned Tad's glove. . . . The outcome is believable and satisfactory, the story more cohesive than most baseball fiction for the young reader. There really is a plot, not a series of game descriptions strung together, and what baseball there is, is very good.

> *Zena Sutherland, ''New Titles for Children and Young People: 'Stranger on the Ball Club','' in* Bulletin of the Center for Children's Books *(reprinted by permission of The University of Chicago Press; © 1970 by The University of Chicago), Vol. 24, No. 4, December, 1970, p. 67.*

Most of the second half of Alfred Slote's *Stranger on the Ball Club* . . . is devoted to a detailed description of a single Little League practice game. Though the description is really too long, it does relate directly to the plot and serves as a bridge to the conclusion. . . . Characters are developed exclusively through standard dialogue; however, the book does have some merit as it conveys the unifying potential inherent in well-managed athletics for children.

> *''Sports Books: 'Stranger on the Ball Club','' in* School Library Journal, *an appendix to* Library Journal *(reprinted from the December, 1970 issue of* School Library Journal, *published by R. R. Bowker Co. / A Xerox Corporation; copyright © 1970), Vol. 17, No. 4, December, 1970, p. 76.*

Alfred Slote's *Stranger on the Ball Club* . . . is concerned with ethical values and has good sports writing and deeper characterization than is found in most books at [the nine to eleven-year-old reading] level.

> *May Hill Arbuthnot and Zena Sutherland, ''Sports Stories,'' in their* Children and Books *(copyright © 1947, 1957, 1964, 1972 by Scott, Foresman and Company; reprinted by permission), fourth edition, Scott, Foresman, 1972, pp. 471-72.**

JAKE (1971)

''My name is Jake Wrather, which doesn't mean much to you, and it doesn't mean much to me either. I never knew my father who gave me my last name, and my mother left two years ago to visit down south and never came back. I room with my Uncle Lenny and he doesn't care about anything except music. We get along fine because I don't care about anything except baseball. . . .'' Jake is no fake—in fact he puts a sturdy brand of spunk where his mouth is—and Alfred Slote is no *Stranger on the Ball Club*. . . . And Jake and Lenny make a super team (Lenny used to play semi-pro himself), but the spotlight is on the Print-Alls who are in first place in the Arborville eleven-year-old league and in trouble. Catcher John Fulton's mother is their nominal coach, only Jake's the one who actually holds the nine together (being, he says, not the best but the toughest among them); all's well till the opposing McLeod Builders raise an unsportsmanlike stink and the league president rules that nominal isn't good enough. The search for a male coach leads to the resolution of a bigger problem and the human relations are healthy all around; Slote engineers some pretty fancy choreography on the diamond too, and that Jake is a somebody. (pp. 740-41)

> *''Younger Fiction: 'Jake','' in* Kirkus Reviews *(copyright © 1971 The Kirkus Service, Inc.), Vol. XXXIX, No. 14, July 15, 1971, pp. 740-41.*

[Jake's] tough-minded outlook, his pluck and persistence win readers by page two. No crap for this kid. And no clichés from author Slote, who includes genuinely exciting baseball play action and makes his orphan-ball-player a nonpareil even when in the batter's box.

> *''Superbooks: 'Jake','' in* School Library Journal, *an appendix to* Library Journal *(reprinted from the December, 1971 issue of* School Library Journal, *published by R. R. Bowker Co. / A Xerox Corpo-*

ration; copyright © 1971), Vol. 18, No. 4, December, 1971, p. 75.

Jake is tough, takes what he needs and fights for what he wants. . . . A minimum of social comment, a good number of believable, well-drawn characters and a maximum of tense baseball actions add up to a superior sports book for boys *and* girls.

> Amy Kellman, "Books for Children: 'Jake'," in Teacher (copyright © 1973 by Macmillan Professional Magazines, Inc.; used by permission of The Instructor Publications, Inc.), Vol. 90, No. 9, May-June, 1973, p. 73.

MY FATHER, THE COACH (1972)

For once, a father's attempt to work out his own problems through the Little League meets with success all round. Though he's a terrible coach, Ezell Corkins' dad eventually wins the respect of team captain Obey Parker when he faces down "the man"—who happens to be the Vice President of the bank where Mr. Corkins is a parking lot attendant as well as coach of the rival team. Meanwhile the Sumpter Street team shows its speed on the basepaths and gets in some good between game raps. Ezell's reassessment of his unprepossessing father looks like the **Biggest Victory** of this baseball season.

> "Younger Fiction: 'My Father, the Coach'," in Kirkus Reviews (copyright © 1972 The Kirkus Service, Inc.), Vol. XL, No. 17, September 1, 1972, p. 1082.

Many's the baseball book in which the rookie team beats the league champions, but few of them have as substantial a plot as does this. . . . The characters and dialogue are convincing, the baseball sequences succinct and dramatic, and the ending a victory both for the team and for the little man whose courage is rewarded.

> Zena Sutherland, "New Titles for Children and Young People: 'My Father, the Coach'," in Bulletin of the Center for Children's Books (reprinted by permission of The University of Chicago Press; © 1972 by The University of Chicago), Vol. 26, No. 3, November, 1972, p. 49.

Not since Bessie Setzer managed the . . . B'nai Bagels [in E. L. Konigsburg's *About the B'nai Bagels*] has sports fiction seen the like of Willie Corkins in Alfred Slote's **My Father, the Coach**. . . . The characters are well drawn, and the book effectively deals with small town factions and the pressures exerted by leading citizens on those not considered social equals. It also touches on the ways adults maneuver kids, especially in sports. Willie Corkins should be nominated "Coach of the Year."

> "The Book Review: 'My Father, the Coach'," in School Library Journal, an appendix to Library Journal (reprinted from the December, 1972 issue of School Library Journal, published by R. R. Bowker Co./A Xerox Corporation; copyright © 1972), Vol. 19, No. 4, December, 1972, p. 76.

HANG TOUGH, PAUL MATHER (1973)

Slote, an expert at quick, casual sporting patter, handles a sticky subject with finesse, though with no particular insight beyond the stiff-upper-lip proposition that the same toughness that makes a boy a good pitcher will enable him to face a painful illness and the prospect of death. Paul Mather, a leukemia stricken twelve-year-old who equates life with pitching, manages to fulfill his dream of helping his team to victory in the final game of the season, even though he does his bit from a wheelchair on the sidelines instead of working on the mound. If it's hard to avoid the word heart-warming, Paul's story is never maudlin, and, while this isn't aimed at every little leaguer, there's definitely an audience for this kind of inspirational treatment. (pp. 116-17)

> "Younger Fiction: "Hang Tough, Paul Mather'," in Kirkus Reviews (copyright ©1973 The Kirkus Service, Inc.), Vol. XLI, No. 3, February 1, 1973, pp. 116-17.

Alfred Slote's **Hang Tough, Paul Mather** . . . deals realistically with human dignity and courage. Paul Mather loves to pitch but is handicapped by an incurable blood disease. Under plausible circumstances, Paul sneaks off to play for the locals. He ends up in the hospital but his outlook is optimistic. Steering free of sentimentality, Slote offers a good, sensitive story here in which baseball action is kept in perspective throughout.

> "Sports Books: 'Hang Tough, Paul Mather'," in School Library Journal, an appendix to Library Journal (reprinted from the May, 1973 issue of School Library Journal, published by R. R. Bowker Co./A Xerox Corporation; copyright © 1973), Vol. 19, No. 9, May, 1973, p. 93.

When Paul begins his story, he is in the hospital and talking to his doctor. Very deftly the author makes it clear that Paul's prime interest in life is baseball. . . . Paul's retrospective account is without sentimentality or self-pity, but the tragic fact is that he has leukemia and knows it. He has, against orders, seized a chance to play baseball and it has exhausted him. . . . Both the doctor-patient relationship and the bond between Paul and his younger brother are beautifully developed, and the story of Paul's candor and courage is convincing, sad but never morbid, in a book that has depth and integrity.

> Zena Sutherland, "New Titles for Children and Young People: 'Hang Tough, Paul Mather'," in Bulletin of the Center for Children's Books (reprinted by permission of The University of Chicago Press; © 1973 by The University of Chicago), Vol. 26, No. 10, June, 1973, p. 162.

TONY AND ME (1974)

Tony Spain, the new boy on the team is a super athlete and in fact, except for Bill, he's the only real ball player on the sad sack Miller's Laundry team. . . . He also is a nice guy who cooks great hot dogs and wants to be Bill's friend—his first, really, since moving to Michigan from California. Then when Tony involves Bill in the theft of a baseball, Bill's naivete leads to their getting caught, and Bill, whose Dad happens to be a store manager with strong feelings about shoplifting, is sandwiched between two conflicting loyalties. For a while it looks as though we may slide home to an easy resolution, but Tony's elderly out-of-touch Dad packs him off to relatives in Kentucky and Bill is left alone to mold himself into the leadership role Tony had come by naturally—a dramatic but not unsubstantiated transition. Slote himself may not be exactly an all-star, but his values—particularly those father/son relationships—are consistently strong and his line-ups packed with genuinely likable players. And here, as usual, he stays one pitch ahead of the formula hitters.

"Younger Fiction: 'Tony and Me'," in Kirkus Reviews *(copyright © 1974 The Kirkus Service, Inc.), Vol. XLII, No. 16, August 15, 1974, p. 878.*

[Inferior to his **Hang Tough, Paul Mather,** Alfred Slote's **Tony and Me**] has a transparent plot. Bill Taylor comes under the influence of Tony Spain, a brilliant athlete but a petty thief. The problem—Bill unwittingly gets involved in shoplifting—is predictably straightened out with Bill maturing a bit. Still, Slote's characterization is good, dialogue is realistic and intelligent, and sports action is kept to palatable proportions.

"Sports Books: 'Hang Tough, Paul Mather'," in School Library Journal, *an appendix to* Library Journal *(reprinted from the December, 1974 issue of School Library Journal, published by R. R. Bowker Co./A Xerox Corporation; copyright © 1974), Vol. 21, No. 4, December, 1974, p. 52.*

As always in Slote's stories there's some good baseball, and—as always—there's a good deal more. This is a convincing and candid presentation of the conflict a child can feel when faced with a choice between loyalty to a friend and adherence to the ethical standards instilled in the home; it has strong characterization and perceptive depiction of parent-child relationships. (pp. 84-5)

Zena Sutherland, *"New Titles for Children and Young People: 'Tony and Me',"* in Bulletin of the Center for Children's Books *(reprinted by permission of The University of Chicago Press; © 1975 by The University of Chicago), Vol. 28, No. 5, January, 1975, pp. 84-5.*

MATT GARGAN'S BOY (1975)

The author's prose is swift, full-bodied and surprisingly tender as he tells of the tribulations of Danny Gargan. Danny's father has long been a famous catcher with the Chicago White Sox, a career which has broken up his marriage. Danny's mother couldn't stand the life of a ballplayer, so she and the boy live in a small town where she works at the library and Danny is a star pitcher on his baseball team. The boy's main object in life is to keep his mom from remarrying. . . . This is the situation on which Mr. Slote has built a thoroughly satisfying story.

"Children's Books, Fiction: 'Matt Gargan's Boy'," in Publishers Weekly *(reprinted from the February 24, 1975 issue of* Publishers Weekly, *published by R. R. Bowker Company, a Xerox company; copyright © 1975 by Xerox Corporation), Vol. 207, No. 8, February 24, 1975, p. 116.*

Danny Gargan has all the problems you'd expect a big leaguer's son to have, and it's easy to imagine that he'd be even less sympathetic in person than he is in print. . . . Danny and Matt are one cautious step beyond the sunnier father-son teams Slote has given us in the past . . . nothing flashy but showing a sound grasp of the fundamentals.

"Younger Fiction: 'Matt Gargan's Boy'," in Kirkus Reviews *(copyright © 1975 by The Kirkus Service, Inc.), Vol. XLIII, No. 6, March 15, 1975, p. 309.*

All of Slote's baseball stories have clear, colorful game sequences and believable characters with real, soluble problems. As in earlier books, the two are nicely meshed in a book that is sturdily structured and smoothly written. . . . The ending is low-keyed, logical, and satisfying—a sports story with real substance. (pp. 167-68)

Zena Sutherland, *"New Titles for Children and Young People: 'Matt Gargan's Boy',"* in Bulletin of the Center for Children's Books *(reprinted by permission of The University of Chicago Press; © 1975 by The University of Chicago), Vol. 28, No. 9, May, 1975, pp. 167-68.*

[Alfred Slote] disappoints readers here, though he gets things to work out for the characters. Dan Gargan's mother divorced his major leaguer father because she didn't want to be a "baseball widow," but **Matt Gargan's Boy** . . . turns out to be an even bigger jock. Mom resists Dan's efforts to get her to remarry Dad and even wins his blessings on her budding romance with Herb Warren, father of Susie, the first girl to try out for the local baseball team. Infielder Susie makes the team, of course, after a "male chauvinist pig at the age of eleven," willingly puts aside his animosity. Dad makes out too, planning to marry divorcee Ruth (Babe?), daughter of a former jock and a baseball lover. Despite the neat solutions, it all adds up to a replay of the "acorn doesn't fall far" theme.

"Sports Books: 'Matt Gargan's Boy'," in School Library Journal *(reprinted from the May, 1975 issue of* School Library Journal, *published by R. R. Bowker Co./A Xerox Corporation; copyright © 1975), Vol. 21, No. 9, May, 1975, p. 72.*

MY ROBOT BUDDY (1975)

The notion that "well programmed robots . . . have lives of their own" might make [Isaac] Asimov wince. But even though Jack's Dad worries about the implications of buying his son a robot best friend, this is basically a domestic comedy wherein not-quite-human, very expensive Danny wins acceptance despite the strain he places on the family budget. The clincher comes when a gang of kidnappers can't tell the real boy from the robot and Danny must rescue Jack from being robotnapped. But the fun lies mostly in Slote's easygoing depiction of parents discomfited by the arrival of a perfect son who needs neither disciplining nor Mom's home cooking. Engagingly programmed to prove that kids know best.

"Younger Fiction: 'My Robot Buddy'," in Kirkus Reviews *(copyright © 1975 The Kirkus Service, Inc.), Vol. XLIII, No. 18, September 15, 1975, p. 999.*

An okay story about Jack Jameson who wants and gets a robot playmate made according to his specifications (even down to his belly button radio) for his birthday. The . . . **Robot Buddy** eventually saves this real boy from a robotnapper in a case of mistaken identities. Although the first person narrative has humor and action, it's all highly improbable (science fiction is supposed to have at least a toe in reality), and the slight characterization and superficial plotting put this into the category of Danny Dunn, Mad Scientists Club, and other popular formula fiction.

Cherie LaGess Zarookian, *"Pre-school and Primary Grades: 'My Robot Buddy',"* in School Library Journal *(reprinted from the October, 1975 issue of* School Library Journal, *published by R. R. Bowker Co./A*

Xerox Corporation; copyright © 1975), Vol. 22, No. 2, October, 1975, p. 92.

[*My Robot Buddy* is a] slickly written book that raises some provocative questions for young readers, only to dodge away from them in the end. Because Jack Jameson's family lives way out in the country and he has no one to play with, he convinces his parents to buy him a robot buddy for his tenth birthday. He even gets to pick the robot's face and personality and basic programming. The robot, named Danny One, is every child's imaginary playmate come to life. Of course, there are a couple of hitches. Danny can't taste anything, so he and Jack can't talk about favorite foods. And he can't play sports with Jack because he's programmed to be stronger and better co-ordinated than any "real" boy. As Jack and Danny get to know each other, they seem to be on the verge of asking what exactly a "real" boy is. What makes Jack a person and Danny a machine? Is there some important difference between them— or not? Unfortunately, the author wastes too much time on a routine sub-plot about robotnappers to follow up his own lead.

Gerald Jonas, "For Young Readers: 'My Robot Buddy'," in The New York Times Book Review *(© 1976 by The New York Times Company; reprinted by permission), January 25, 1976, p. 10.*

A first-person story told by a boy of future times is convincing in its establishment of setting. . . . The story has good plot development; its weakness is that the plot is a variant on an old formula: by an act of courage, an unwanted pet—or group member—or, as here, a robot—becomes accepted. (pp. 102-03)

Zena Sutherland, "New Titles for Children and Young People: 'My Robot Buddy'," in Bulletin of the Center for Children's Books *(reprinted by permission of The University of Chicago Press; © 1976 by The University of Chicago), Vol. 29, No. 6, February, 1976, pp. 102-03.*

THE HOTSHOT   (1977)

The first title in a series designed for slow or reluctant older readers should win the intended audience as well as readers in the middle grades. Slote has simplified his usual writing style adroitly, with crisp dialogue and short sentences. . . . The plot is not unusual: a team player learns that it's better to work with the hockey team than try to score alone. However, the first person writing gives the story a sense of immediacy, so that the plot is convincing, and the book has the appeals of action sequences in the hockey games and of a wish granted, for hotshot Paddy wins a place on the all-city team and a chance to play in the state tournament.

Zena Sutherland, "New Titles for Children and Young People: 'The Hotshot'," in Bulletin of the Center for Children's Books *(reprinted by permission of The University of Chicago Press; © 1977 by The University of Chicago), Vol. 30, No. 11, July-August, 1977, p. 180.*

["**The Hotshot,**" a book in the new Triumph series, promises fiction that will appeal to high schoolers reading at a fourth-grade level.] It is a straightforward account of a young hockey player's efforts to make the all-city team. Writing in the first person, Mr. Slote never falls into the common trap of adults using children's voices; he is neither too cute nor precocious.

Karla Kuskin, "Children's Books: 'The Hotshot'," in The New York Times Book Review *(© 1977 by The New York Times Company; reprinted by permission), October 9, 1977, p. 28.*

MY TRIP TO ALPHA I   (1978)

To visit his rich Aunt Katherine on planet Alpha I, 11-year-old Jack takes the newest, fastest means: "VOYA-CODE." (A substitute body is made at Jack's destination and his "mind" is sent by computer data.) The technology works perfectly, but Jack finds a suspicious situation when he arrives. The youngest member of his family, he is called upon to witness the deed whereby his aunt gives all her holdings to her overseers, and Aunt Katherine is acting very strangely. . . . There's precious little science fiction for this age level that is neither outdated nor hopelessly hokey, so it's a rare treat to find a second book as fresh and readable as Slote's *My Robot Buddy*. . . .

Margaret L. Chatham, "Grades 3-6: 'My Trip to Alpha I'," in School Library Journal *(reprinted from the October, 1978 issue of* School Library Journal, *published by R. R. Bowker Co./A Xerox Corporation; copyright © 1978), Vol. 25, No. 2, October, 1978, p. 150.*

This takes place in a future when "they" can make computer programs of people and thus send you off to a distant planet, where you'll go about in a duplicate dummy while your real body is kept in Sleep-Storage waiting your return. So that's how Jack travels to Alpha I to help Aunt Katherine pack for a move to Earth. . . . Slote doesn't bother with technological intricacies or with philosophy—"There's obviously a lot of tightening up to be done with this VOYA-CODE business" is Dad's comment upon hearing of Jack's adventure—but, like *My Robot Buddy*, the story moves along about as swiftly and effortlessly as a VOYA-CODE trip.

"Younger Fiction: 'My Trip to Alpha I'," in Kirkus Reviews *(copyright © 1978 The Kirkus Service, Inc.), Vol. XLVI, No. 22, November 15, 1978, p. 1249.*

A science fantasy and a mystery are neatly packaged in a crisp and ingeniously plotted story. . . . There's pace and suspense in Jack's plot to outwit the Arbos, logic within the fantasy, and good structure and style in the telling. (pp. 88-9)

Zena Sutherland, "New Titles for Children and Young People: 'My Trip to Alpha I'," in Bulletin of the Center for Children's Books *(reprinted by permission of The University of Chicago Press; © 1979 by The University of Chicago), Vol. 32, No. 5, January, 1979, pp. 88-9.*

LOVE AND TENNIS   (1979)

In a slick, first-person story that's no more subtle than its title, 15-year-old tennis whiz Buddy Berger faces two big decisions—one about tennis and the other, yes, about love. Ruled with a steely grip by his mother, "queen of the Arborville [Michigan] tennis scene," since his parents' divorce, Buddy is at the peak of his development; he's just beaten a nationally ranked player in a local tournament, and may have to play against his own father in the finals a week away. . . . Long before the week is up, it's apparent that although Buddy has the talent for professional tennis, he lacks the proper attitude, the will to win. . . . Buddy's dad wins the finals, and Buddy says he's through with tennis. As for love, he's still thinking. But he's such a cool, self-confident character for a 15-year-old, that there's not much to worry about.

> *"Older Fiction: 'Love and Tennis',"* in Kirkus Reviews *(copyright © 1980 The Kirkus Service, Inc.), Vol. XLVIII, No. 3, February 1, 1980, p. 136.*

This is probably the best of the few tennis stories that have been written; no formula plot here, but a realistic and perceptive account of the pressures of the game and the conflicts they can cause. The characters are rounded, and there are logical connections between what they're like, what they do, and how they react to each other.

> *Zena Sutherland, "New Titles for Children and Young People: 'Love and Tennis',"* in Bulletin of the Center for Children's Books *(reprinted by permission of The University of Chicago Press; © 1980 by The University of Chicago), Vol. 33, No. 7, March, 1980, p. 142.*

Slote attempts more in this book than do most writers of sports fiction for young people but he sidesteps the important issues he raises. Buddy Berger, a promising 15-year-old tennis player, is coerced by his domineering mother into attending a tennis school run by a monomaniacal martinet. Buddy's father, whom Buddy is scheduled to play against for the club championship, disapproves of his ex-wife's methods but feels powerless to intervene. The initial tension is deftly drawn, the emotion legitimate. Buddy's experience at the tennis camp is a chilling parable of a world in which all relationships, indeed all conventional moral principles, are sacrificed for the sake of the few who display extraordinary talent. Unfortunately, the truncated resolution falls completely flat, as if the author had quit in the middle and just tacked on an ending. Buddy's mother undergoes an unconvincing personality change off-stage, cheating readers of his long-awaited confrontation with her. And Buddy himself dissolves into a world-weary angst that falls just short of ludicrous.

> *Richard Luzer, "Junior High Up: 'Love and Tennis',"* in School Library Journal *(reprinted from the January, 1980 issue of* School Library Journal, *published by R. R. Bowker Co./A Xerox Corporation; copyright © 1980), Vol. 26, No. 5, January, 1981, p. 81.*

THE DEVIL RIDES WITH ME AND OTHER FANTASTIC STORIES (1980)

Six short stories from the borderland between science fiction and fantasy. The title refers to Joe, a young skier who learns firsthand how two local ski heroes went from accidents on Devil Mountain to Olympic gold medals to early deaths—with the luck of the Devil. Joe refuses the Devil's contract, but is the streak of luck he begins to enjoy really his own? Other stories tell of a girl's wormy revenge for her brother's repeatedly broken promises to take her fishing if she'll supply the worms; **"Willie Saxophone,"** a modern musician who brings the children back to upset the quiet town of Hamelin after he's defrauded by the town fathers; and **"The Picture Painter"** whose pictures come true. Less satisfying are the stories of an exchange of a drop of blood between a college freshman who's tired of being treated like a child and a fast aging frog, with absurd and rather pointless results; and the robot who kills **"The Last Dinosaur"** of Omega III to prevent the evolution of oppressive man on that planet, as if one dinosaur were a breeding population. Light entertainment in a popular genre.

> *Margaret L. Chatham, "Grades 3-6: 'The Devil Rides with Me and Other Fantastic Stories',"* in School Library Journal *(reprinted from the April, 1980 issue of* School Library Journal, *published by R. R. Bowker Co./A Xerox Corporation; copyright © 1980), Vol. 26, No. 8, April, 1980, p. 116.*

The Devil Rides with Me and Other Fantastic Stories is an exciting hi-lo book by Alfred Slote. In most of the stories, he takes familiar legends and gives them new twists, from the standard devil's offer for your soul to the pied piper. There's freshness, originality, and wickedness worth looking into.

> *"Critically Speaking: 'The Devil Rides with Me and Other Fantastic Stories',"* in The Reading Teacher *(copyright 1981 by the International Reading Association, Inc.; reprinted with permission of the International Reading Association), Vol. 34, No. 6, March, 1981, p. 736.*

C.O.L.A.R.: A TALE OF OUTER SPACE (1981)

Alfred Slote's specialty is making space travel seem as ordinary as piling in the family wagon for a jaunt to McDonald's. Which isn't bad, if you can pull it off. Mr. Slote does in **"C.O.L.A.R"**. . . . The Jameson family, familiar from the earlier book [**"My Robot Buddy"**], is stranded on an unknown planet when their spaceship runs out of fuel. Mr. and Mrs. Jameson must rely on their son, Jack, and his robot twin, Danny, to save the ship and all of their lives after a "rock" tries to kill them. When Danny disappears outside the ship, Jack goes out after him. Boy and robot find themselves prisoners of the strange C.O.L.A.R. society.

"C.O.L.A.R." is simply and lightly written with humorous touches; its themes are freedom versus slavery and Jack and Danny's loyalty to each other. (p. 62)

> *Virginia Hamilton, "Fanciful Words,"* in The New York Times Book Review *(© 1981 by The New York Times Company; reprinted by permission), April 26, 1981, pp. 60, 62.**

The Jameson family . . . is stranded on an asteroid where C.O.L.A.R., the Colony of Lost Atkins Robots, is hiding. The runaway robots want to keep their whereabouts unknown and urge the Jameson robot to join them. Danny the robot and Jack, the Jamesons' son, are virtually identical, which enables them to escape from C.O.L.A.R. and eventually reconcile the other robots with their inventor, Dr. Atkins. The idea of making robots as much like human beings as possible has lost its respectability in science fiction and has been replaced with specialized robots like those in recent movies. Slote's idea that robots could pass for people and would feel a longing to do so seems a cruel revival of slavery. The condescending, simplistic solution that owning thinking, feeling beings is okay as long as you're not mean to them is offensive. The background of the story shows little regard for readers' knowledge of science. The asteroid's earth-type atmosphere is never explained; people on the spaceship cannot detect that atmosphere; and the robots, able to radio each other with their "belly-buttons," cannot detect that Jack is not a robot. R2D2 has more to offer grade-school science-fiction fans.

> *Carolyn Caywood, "Book Reviews: 'C.O.L.A.R.: A Tale of Outer Space',"* in School Library Journal

(reprinted from the May, 1981, issue of School Library Journal, *published by R. R. Bowker Co./ A Xerox Corporation; copyright © 1981), Vol. 27, No. 9, May, 1981, p. 69.*

Slote's notion of robots with human emotions and feelings was a dubious one in the first place, but he gets in over his head here when he plays around with their rights: if we can accept their "humanity," we obviously can't accept their being "owned" at all. Light as this is, it only goes to demonstrate that Asimov's rules can't be frivolously abandoned.

"Younger Fiction: 'C.O.L.A.R.: A Tale of Outer Space'," in Kirkus Reviews *(copyright © 1981 The Kirkus Service, Inc.), Vol. XLIX, No. 11, June 1, 1981, p. 680.*

[**C.O.L.A.R.: A Tale of Outer Space**] is better constructed than [**My Robot Buddy**], with more suspense and drama, and in addressing the prejudices of the robot community it speaks to the bias within the human society.

Zena Sutherland, "New Titles for Children and Young People: 'C.O.L.A.R.: A Tale of Outer Space'," in Bulletin of the Center for Children's Books *(reprinted by permission of The University of Chicago Press; © 1981 by The University of Chicago), Vol. 35, No. 1, September, 1981, p. 17.*

Donald J. Sobol

1924-

American author of fiction and nonfiction for children. Sobol is best known for his popular *Encyclopedia Brown* series about Leroy Brown, the brilliant ten-year-old son of a police chief who deciphers clues and solves various mysteries by using his "little grey cells." Sobol has also written novels set in medieval times and the Civil War period as well as biographies of men involved in the American Revolution and has detailed thirteen of the world's most significant disasters. Critics observe that Sobol develops plot and situations more than characters in his novels and stories: the *Encyclopedia Brown* series, for instance, revolves around the same characters to leave young readers free to concentrate on the mystery-solving aspect of the books.

Sobol's works are regarded as especially useful to slow readers, particularly the *Encyclopedia Brown* stories, in which readers are invited to discover clues and solve mysteries along with Encyclopedia. Although some critics fault Sobol's occasional use of archaic language, his historical novels and surveys are noted for their clarity and readability. Sobol believes that the primary purpose of an author of juvenile works is to entertain children and the concensus among his readers is that he more than fulfills that obligation. In 1972 he received the Pacific Northwest Library Association Young Reader's Choice Award for *Encyclopedia Brown Keeps the Peace; Encyclopedia Brown Takes the Case* was awarded the 1976 Aiken County (Georgia) Children's Book Award. Sobol also won the Garden State Children's Book Award in 1977 for *Encyclopedia Brown Lends a Hand.* (See also *Contemporary Authors New Revision Series,* Vol. 1, and *Something about the Author,* Vol. 1.)

AUTHOR'S COMMENTARY

Stories originate in two ways. They start from a writer's own experience, or they start from his imagination. Most of my stories depend upon my imagination. (p. 18)

When I first began to write, I read a piece of advice that I considered sound. It was "Write about what you know." Alas, I'd had scant experience from which to spin stories that would not put my readers to snoring. But I took the advice so seriously that, having no exciting experiences, I wrenched entirely from my imagination the stories I wrote. Very few were published.

Happily, a year or so later I ran across another piece of advice, "Know what you write about." "Write about what you know"— "Know what you write about." There is a difference, and the difference is vital.

"Write about what you know" had limited me to my own experiences and so forced me to rely solely upon my imagination. "Know what you write about" set me free. Now if I had an idea for a story set in a foreign country, for instance, I could write about that country without ever having been there. I went to the library and dug up all the information I could find about the country. I got to know what I was writing about—from authors who had lived there. (pp. 18-19)

Encyclopedia Brown is an example of combining imagination with research. I am often asked if Encyclopedia is a real boy, or if I were like him when I was ten. The answer is no, he is

Lee Hunt

not real. He is not the ten-year-old Don Sobol. He is, however, the boy I wanted to be when I was his age, though I suspect I was more like Bugs Meany.

Encyclopedia represents many boys. Some I have read about, some I have met in real life, the rest of him is invented. Other characters in the Encyclopedia Brown books are often suggested by my own children. . . .

The majority of my ideas come from what I see, and most of these arise out of what I read. (p. 19)

A mystery idea must be simple—the simpler the better. If the detective in a story solves a crime because he knows something that has been withheld from the reader, or something that is outside the reader's general store of information, the writer has not played fair, and the reader will feel cheated. So I keep my clues easy, though not always easy to spot. But reader and detective must be given an equal chance at finding the clues. I don't want a reader to come to the last sentence and exclaim in anger, "How was I supposed to know that!" I want to outwit my reader the way Encyclopedia Brown outwits Bugs Meany, and have the reader groan with Bugs, "Man, oh man! Was I fooled!"

The ideas that I write down are usually no longer than a sentence each. The best ideas are little known facts about common subjects, or common subjects seen in a new way. Let me give you a few examples. After a long drive, the hood of a car will become hot from the heat of the motor. Ice will deaden the taste buds. A person who loses consciousness while standing will fall forward. Blueberries stain the teeth.

Simple? Yes, and within the general store of knowledge of young and old. You may have recognized the examples. All are ideas that became Encyclopedia Brown stories.

Outwitting you, the reader, is hard, but harder still is making you laugh. I try above all else to entertain. Yes, it is nice to have a message too. And I have one. It is that all men are brothers, and that a religion or a race cannot be blamed for the misbehavior of one of its members. . . .

I hope to be making children laugh for decades to come. (p. 20)

> *Donald J. Sobol, "Encyclopedia Brown: Young Reader's Choice," in* PNLA Quarterly, *Vol. 37, No. 2, Winter, 1973, pp. 18-20.*

THE DOUBLE QUEST   (1957)

A full fashioned historical novel, based on the little known fact of the invasion of England by Flemish troops in 1161, has all the color and romance and some of the delightful improbabilities of the days of knight errantry. . . . How Martin's and Brynoble's quests coincide and lead to a single man (*not* Velbane) who is both murderer and collaborator with the Flemish, makes a rich story and with its elements of tragedy, more intricately patterned than most books of this sort for the teen ages.

> *"Eight to Eleven—Non-Fiction: 'The Double Quest',"* in Virginia Kirkus' Service, *Vol. XXIV, No. 24, December 15, 1956, pp. 903-04.*

["**The Double Quest**"] is primarily a mystery with medieval trappings and as such is quite a novelty among boys' adventure stories. It is well-plotted, ingenious and exciting. . . .

While the tourney is very well done indeed, the rest of the medieval setting is sketched lightly as in a hero tale. All the emphasis is on romance—there are two fair ladies who share much of the danger without lessening the interest of the story for the boys.

> *"Daring Boys in Exciting Adventures," in* New York Herald Tribune Book Review *(© I.H.T. Corporation; reprinted by permission), May 12, 1957, p. 22.**

Intrigue piles on intrigue [in *The Double Quest*]. Tense reading, with rich sub-plots built on solid background and a close view of knighthood. References to Launcelot, Gawein, Arthur, and Guinevere bring the story nearer to present interests.

> *Virginia Haviland, "Stories for the Older Boys and Girls: 'The Double Quest'," in* The Horn Book Magazine *(copyrighted, 1957, by The Horn Book, Inc., Boston), Vol. XXXIII, No. 3, June, 1957, p. 231.*

THE LOST DISPATCH: A STORY OF ANTIETAM   (1958)

Based on an actual incident of the Civil War in which a vital dispatch was lost, Donald Sobol, whose *Double Quest* established him as a teen-age writer of distinction, tells here the story of the last crucial days of the Civil War. Were it not for the fact that Sergeant Wade Baxter had a double on the Con-

federate side the final battle between General McClellan and General Lee might have ended in a Confederate Victory. Haunted, baffled, and nearly destroyed by the sharp shooting, three-fingered rebel who seems dedicated to killing not him, but every sentry who stands beside him, Wade sets out to identify his tormentor, and in his discovery plays a vital part in the preservation of the Union. An excellent story, taut with suspence and historical impact, comes to life here with unusual dignity and stature.

> *"Twelve to Fifteen—Fiction: 'The Lost Dispatch',"* in Virginia Kirkus' Service, *Vol. XXVI, No. 13, July 1, 1958, p. 464.*

Based on the finding of Special Orders No. 191 in a meadow outside Frederick, Maryland, on September 13, 1862, which had such a decisive part in the Union victory at Antietam, the plot of this excellent story of the Civil War provides an explanation of the mystery of how the orders were lost. Through the experiences of young Sergeant Baxter, teen-age readers will feel the impact of war, prison, and death, and receive a fresh understanding of the issues that were decided on the field of battle.

> *Elizabeth Burr, "'The Lost Dispatch'," in* Junior Libraries, *an appendix to* Library Journal *(reprinted from the December, 1958 issue of* Junior Libraries, *published by R. R. Bowker Co./A Xerox Corporation; copyright © 1958), Vol. 5, No. 4, December, 1958, p. 43.*

This exciting novel of the Civil War is a possible explanation of the unsolved mystery of the lost dispatch that was responsible for giving the victory at Antietam to General McClellan instead of to General Lee, and thus changing the course of the War. A well-written book which will be a welcome addition to the Civil War shelves in our libraries.

> *Margaret Mahon, "Books for Young People: 'The Lost Dispatch'," in* Saturday Review *(copyright © 1959 by* Saturday Review; *all rights reserved; reprinted by permission), Vol. XLII, No. 16, April 18, 1959, p. 55.*

THE FIRST BOOK OF MEDIEVAL MAN   (1959)

The Middle Ages, vastly rich artistically, elaborately complex socially, emerge here in compelling clarity. Terms which every school boy employs casually—tournaments, knights, moats, serfs,—as well as religious, philosophical, and social concepts are precisely investigated in terms within the grasp of the grade school reader. Not only does Donald Sobol afford a comprehensive view of the world from which the renaissance at once grew and rejected, but conveys much of the richness of feeling, so vital to the medieval world.

> *"Eleven to Thirteen—Non-Fiction: 'The First Book of Medieval Man'," in* Virginia Kirkus' Service, *Vol. XXVII, No. 17, September 1, 1959, p. 655.*

This brief book undertakes a relatively rare, difficult, and thoroughly worth-while task. To youngsters, indeed sometimes to others, the Middle Ages are one of the most difficult segments of history to comprehend. Yet it is an era of major importance, in historical continuity, religiously and culturally (especially in architecture).

Mr. Sobol has done a highly creditable job of surveying, in few words and pages, the broad, complex web of medieval life. Choosing England as his theatre, he reviews the elaborate social structure of the feudal system and something of the life on most of its levels. . . .

Obviously this is not studied in depth, yet a considerable amount of fact, with a sense of continuity, is achieved. The book is bound to teach much to its young reader.

> Edmund Fuller, "Olde England," in The New York Times Book Review (© 1960 by The New York Times Company; reprinted by permission), January 10, 1960, p. 28.

Clear, interesting text . . . describes and explains the pattern and details of life in England during the Middle Ages. A book to delight children who have already become acquainted with the period and to excite others to read about it. This could add a great deal of pleasure if it stood on the shelves of home libraries along with the Arthurian legends, [Howard] Pyle's *Men of Iron* (Scribner), and other stories of feudal days.

> Ruth Hill Viguers, "'The First Book of Medieval Man'," in The Horn Book Magazine (copyright, 1960, by the Horn Book, Inc., Boston), Vol. XXXVI, No. 1, February, 1960, p. 49.

ENCYCLOPEDIA BROWN, BOY DETECTIVE   (1963)

Here is a sure-shot book for almost any young person. It is amusing as well as being challenging to their wits. The cases Leroy . . . solves must also be solved through deduction by the reader—unless he cheats and looks up the answers which are given at the back. A fine book for birthday presents or for taking to camp.

> "PW Forecasts: 'Encyclopedia Brown, Boy Detective'," in Publishers Weekly (reprinted from the March 4, 1963, issue of Publishers Weekly, published by R. R. Bowker Company; copyright © 1963 by Xerox Corporation), Vol. 183, No. 9, March 4, 1963, p. 69.

Once you have accepted the premise that Encyclopedia is twice as bright as his father, the Chief of Police of Idaville, this is an excellent and original book. Leroy (nicknamed Encyclopedia) can solve a mystery while washing the dishes—or almost any time. The answers to the more complex situations may be found at the end of the book, but the reader should try to solve them himself before turning to those pages. Good fun.

> Alice Dalgleish, "The First Golden Years: 'Encyclopedia Brown, Boy Detective'," in Saturday Review (copyright © 1963 by Saturday Review; all rights reserved; reprinted by permission), Vol. XLVI, No. 42, October 19, 1963, p. 40.

Is there a detective in the house? Then let him match wits with Encyclopedia Brown, the 10-year-old detective as he helps his police chief father uncover a bank robber's identity, or solves for the grocer the mystery of an attempted burglary of his store. . . .

A word of warning: Encyclopedia's nickname is well earned, for he has a very sharp ear for detecting flaws in a culprit's story. His cases are all short, and all offer legitimate clues—which Encyclopedia never misses but which the reader may, if he doesn't keep his eyes open and his mind on the job. If any case should baffle, solutions are given at the back of the book. It will be much more satisfying to "solve it" Encyclo-

pedia's way, though, by intelligent deduction—and a lot more fun. Mr. Sobol's book is as bright and entertaining as its hero. (p. 49)

> Margaret Berkvist, "For Ages 6 to 9: A Variety of Stories and Tales," in The New York Times Book Review, Part II (© 1963 by The New York Times Company; reprinted by permission), November 10, 1963, pp. 49-50.*

LOCK, STOCK, AND BARREL   (1965)

These 50 powerfully written vignettes of men actively involved in the American Revolution, on the battlefield as well as behind the scenes, are a welcome addition to the material on this period. Most of these men's names appear in all the history books, but very little biographical material is available on them for young people: William Howe, Henry Knox, Frederick von Steuben, Casimir Pulaski, Francis de Grasse, and Frederick North, to mention a few. The author conveys the background of the period, the mental, cultural, emotional, and physical makeup of each individual and shows both his virtues and his faults through his actions during a crucial incident directly related to the war. Both the selective and general bibliographies will be valuable to the student and the casual reader. (pp. 197-98)

> Carolyn W. Field, "Junior Books Appraised: 'Lock, Stock, and Barrel'," in School Library Journal, an appendix to Library Journal (reprinted from the March, 1965 issue of School Library Journal, published by R. R. Bowker Co./A Xerox Corporation; copyright © 1965), Vol. 11, No. 6, March, 1965, pp. 197-98.

This biographical approach to history is quite satisfying. The author has shown discernment in selecting the most lively and sophisticated details and has unobtrusively slipped in the vital statistics among the facts and fancies. The material is immensely varied. . . . The book can be dipped into with pleasure (a fine bedside table book) or read from the last to the first or vice versa, consulted for ready reference or further study, and has an index and bibliographies.

> M. S. Cosgrave, "'Lock, Stock, and Barrel'," in Book Week—New York Herald Tribune (© 1965, The Washington Post), June 13, 1965, p. 22.

ENCYCLOPEDIA BROWN AND THE CASE OF THE SECRET PITCH   (1965)

This case history of [Leroy (Encyclopedia) Brown's] deductions follows **"Encyclopedia Brown, Boy Detective."** 10 situations are presented in which Encyclopedia comes up with a surprising solution. . . . Detection purists may . . . be left hanging, because in most of the cases Encyclopedia has postulated guilt on the basis of a lie. For instance, in the first case, Encyclopedia is shown a letter sent to Bugs Meany by famous baseball pitcher Spike Browning. The letter is dated June 31. We decided that Spike Browning was a moron. Encyclopedia concluded that Bugs Meany had forged the letter. Nevertheless, young puzzle lovers will enjoy testing their wits. . . . (pp. 679-80)

> "Eight to Eleven—Fiction: 'Encyclopedia Brown and the Case of the Secret Pitch'," in Virginia Kirkus' Service, Vol. XXXIII, No. 14, July 15, 1965, pp. 679-80.

[The] short mysteries in ["**Encyclopedia Brown and the Case of the Secret Pitch"**] are up to the ingenious best of Donald J. Sobol. Each of the cases—from the hungry hitchhiker who is nailed by his frozen Hershey to the violinist who lost his Stradivarius to gingerale ice cubes—is puzzling enough to send the cleverest youngster flipping to the back of the book for the written solutions.

> *Ellen Goodman, "Old Friends in New Adventures," in* The New York Times Book Review, *Part II (© 1965 by The New York Times Company; reprinted by permission), November 7, 1965, p. 46.**

ENCYCLOPEDIA BROWN FINDS THE CLUES   (1966)

As in previous books, Mr. Sobol puts the facts clearly and concisely and then lets his hero pronounce judgment. Readers are free to match wits with the detective by solving the mysteries without looking up the solutions at the end of the book. Like Encyclopedia Brown himself, the problems are straightforward—no tricks, no catch solutions.

> *Patience M. Daltry, "Children's Books in Roundup: 'Encyclopedia Brown Finds the Clues',"* in The Christian Science Monitor *(reprinted by permission from* The Christian Science Monitor; © 1966 The Christian Science Publishing Society; all rights reserved), September, 1966, p. 11.*

[*Encyclopedia Brown Finds The Clues*] follows the pattern of the two preceding stories and presents 10 more cases which give the reader an opportunity to match wits with the boy detective before consulting the solutions in the back of the book. As usual, the stories are clever and fairly stated, and are short and easy enough to tempt the reluctant reader. At the same time, they offer plenty of challenge even to the confirmed mystery addict.

> *"Junior Books Appraised: 'Encyclopedia Brown Finds the Clues',"* in School Library Journal, *an appendix to* Library Journal *(reprinted from the November, 1966 issue of* School Library Journal, *published by R. R. Bowker Co./A Xerox Corporation; copyright © 1966), Vol. 13, No. 3, November, 1966, p. 5771.*

SECRET AGENTS FOUR   (1967)

Four secret agents trip over each other's feet and consistently, carefully come up with the wrong conclusions in a hilarious battle for Miami between the U.S. government organization *Mongoose* and the gangster enemy *Cobra*. . . . The plot—to immobilize Miami with a memory drug that puts everybody back twenty-four hours and out of contact with everybody else. Fantastic? Yes, and wildly funny, and full of teenage ironic understatement from the first fiasco to the final triumph.

> *"Older Fiction: 'Secret Agents Four',"* in Kirkus Service *(copyright © 1967 Virginia Kirkus' Service, Inc.), Vol. XXV, No. 16, August 15, 1967, p. 969.*

ENCYCLOPEDIA BROWN GETS HIS MAN   (1967)

Who would believe that the real brains behind Idaville's wonderful police record was Chief Brown's quiet ten-year-old son? The answer, of course, is anyone who's read the earlier books. With his usual alertness, Encyclopedia spots the inconsistency in each culprit's alibi, and the game is to match his wits. Easy reading but not easy reasoning, and good to the last hint dropped.

> *"Younger Fiction: 'Encyclopedia Brown Gets His Man',"* in Kirkus Service *(copyright © 1967 Virginia Kirkus' Service, Inc.), Vol. XXXV, No. 19, October 1, 1967, p. 1209.*

Like the first-rate sleuth he is, E. Brown never loses a case or misses a clue—though the reader may miss plenty. But Mr. Sobol kindly provides solutions at the end of the book for those who wonder just how Encyclopedia knew which man to get each time. As in previous books, Mr. Sobol plays fair, the evidence is all there—it's just a matter of remembering what one is told.

> *Patience M. Daltry, "Detectives at Work: 'Encyclopedia Brown Gets His Man',"* in The Christian Science Monitor *(reprinted by permission from* The Christian Science Monitor; © 1967 The Christian Science Publishing Society; all rights reserved), October 5, 1967, p. 10.*

Encyclopedia Brown, precocious young sleuth, pursues his latest cases in the style of his earlier crime-hunts. As an assortment of junior clients come up with mysteries involving everything from missing marbles to a blueberry-pie eater with white teeth, Encyclopedia pounces on the one clue which points logically to a solution. . . . Constructed with nimble words and diverting dialogue ("I've been smoking too many dried coffee grounds"), this book manages to put crime detection on a plane of good fun. (p. 46)

> *Jane Mathorne, "Fiction for Ages 9 to 12: 'Encyclopedia Brown Gets His Man',"* in The New York Times Book Review, *Part II (© 1967 by The New York Times Company; reprinted by permission), November 5, 1967, pp. 44, 46.*

ENCYCLOPEDIA BROWN SOLVES THEM ALL   (1968)

[*Encyclopedia Brown Solves Them All*] maintains the level of preceding books of the series, offering funny situations, corny dialogue, clever detective cases and reasonable solutions. Like the others, it should have appeal for slow readers . . . and younger advanced readers.

> *Marguerite M. Murray, "The Book Review: 'Encyclopedia Brown Solves Them All',"* in School Library Journal, *an appendix to* Library Journal *(reprinted from the November, 1968 issue of* School Library Journal, *published by R. R. Bowker Co./A Xerox Corporation; copyright © 1968), Vol. 15, No. 3, November, 1968, p. 90.*

If any book can break the habit for comic-book addicts it is Donald J. Sobol's **"Encyclopedia Brown Solves Them All."** . . . Short stories, big print, humor, lots of action, make the transition from funnies to real books easy, even tempting. Besides, every reader has a fair chance to match wits with that unbeatable boy detective, Encyclopedia (so called for his range of knowledge), since all the clues are concealed somewhere in the story.

> *Pamela Marsh, "Junior Sherlock,"* in The Christian Science Monitor *(reprinted by permission from* The Christian Science Monitor; © 1968 The Christian Science Publishing Society; all rights reserved), November 7, 1968, p. B6.*

GRETA THE STRONG   (1970)

King Arthur devotees will welcome this new tale of a feminine knight-errant who rides fifty years after Arthur's death. . . .

Donald Sobol, long a student of medieval times, wraps this new tale in the glitter and magic of the old legend.

> Martha Bennett King, "Legend Unvarnished: 'Greta the Strong'," in Book World—Chicago Tribune (© 1970 Postrib Corp.; reprinted by permission of Chicago Tribune and The Washington Post), May 17, 1970, p. 26.

In days long agone "mine arms" might have passed muster but wherever is "whereover" to be found? Or the interjection "Grammercy" with two *m*'s? Or 'gramercy' anyhow after say the 16th century? (Mayhaps the copyeditor was confounded too.) Or "ween" ditto? Or "rightwise," rightly the 13th-16th century form of righteous, here unrecognizable. With simple retellings pretentiously and senselessly archaicized let us now be done: in this Arthurian spin-off there are a mere nine or ten words to a line and almost none of them plain, short sentences and almost none of them direct.

> "Younger Non-Fiction: 'Greta the Strong'," in Kirkus Reviews (copyright © 1970 The Kirkus Service, Inc.), Vol. XXXVIII, No. 11, June 1, 1970, p. 603.

ENCYCLOPEDIA BROWN SAVES THE DAY   (1970)

"Really, he was more like a whole library than an encyclopedia. You might say he was the only library in America that closed at night to take a bath." You might wonder what he does with all those quarters, too, since in this departure our hero is in everybody's business for himself—BROWN'S DETECTIVE AGENCY, 25¢ per day plus expenses. And it's sneaky, funny business as always: ten cases, ten questions, ten answers set out at the back of the book, guaranteed to stymie.

> "Younger Fiction: 'Encyclopedia Brown Saves the Day'," in Kirkus Reviews (copyright © 1970 The Kirkus Service, Inc.), Vol. XXXVIII, No. 20, October 15, 1970, p. 1150.

As in other books about the astute ten-year-old sleuth, Encyclopedia Brown, this is a series of short mysteries, each of them solved by the boy detective, each ending with a query as to how he knew the solution. . . . The writing style is lively and humorous, and there is a challenge for the reader, but the book is weakened by the fact that Encyclopedia will on occasion pursue an investigation when he already knows the answer: for example, in **"The Case of the Kidnapped Pigs,"** one of the two children who report their prize pigs kidnapped gives his telephone number as "ZA 4-7575." Since the telephone dial has no "Z," he is immediately suspect—yet Encyclopedia rides six miles to talk to the four boys that the real culprit has said he suspected.

> Zena Sutherland, "New Titles for Children and Young People: 'Encyclopedia Brown Saves the Day'," in Bulletin of the Center for Children's Books (reprinted by permission of The University of Chicago Press; © 1971 by The University of Chicago), Vol. 24, No. 8, April, 1971, p. 129.

ENCYCLOPEDIA BROWN SHOWS THE WAY   (1972)

The wise-cracking fifth grade sleuth who has already shown countless kids the way to reading success solves ten more crimes for his police chief father and the kids of Idaville. Again the solutions are far from obvious but once you've looked them up in the back of the book you realize that the clues were there for the finding. Feminists like Sally, Encyclopedia's assistant, can only hope to be vindicated in a later volume (here Sally impotently stamps her foot at the culprit and says "Ooooh . . . I wish I could prove you're guilty!" only to have Encyclopedia answer "I can" and save the day once more), but the boys are already lining up for this one.

> "Younger Fiction: 'Encyclopedia Brown Shows the Way'," in Kirkus Reviews (copyright © 1972 The Kirkus Service, Inc.), Vol. XL, No. 14, July 15, 1972, p. 804.

The city of Idaville still rests safe from burglars, con artists, and other lawbreakers—if the police chief can't catch 'em, his son Encyclopedia will. The ten new mysteries here contain clues requiring such knowledge as that thunder follows lightning, that blue light causes red to look black, etc. . . . In the first story a footprint near a burglarized garage is too small for the suspect, a teenager who had previously stolen a car and who was seen in the vicinity. Unfortunately, when Encyclopedia explains that the print shrunk while drying, this seemingly proves the teenager's guilt. While he is not convicted without other evidence, there is no indication that Encyclopedia's clever deduction proved only that the boy *could* have made the print. As usual, youngsters will enjoy the situations in which the fifth grader shows up adult ineptitude. Nevertheless, the disregard for the suspect's rights in the above-mentioned story seriously hinders what is supposed to be an exercise in clear thinking.

> Katherine Heylman, "The Book Review: 'Encyclopedia Brown Shows the Way: Ten All-New Mysteries'," in School Library Journal, an appendix to Library Journal (reprinted from the December, 1972 issue of School Library Journal, published by R. R. Bowker Co./A Xerox Corporation; copyright © 1972), Vol. 19, No. 4, December, 1972, p. 62.

ENCYCLOPEDIA BROWN TAKES THE CASE   (1973)

That ten-year-old detective is still amazing Idaville . . . , his rival Bugs Meany is shifty as ever . . . , and Encyclopedia's assistant Sally—well, Sally is now a full-fledged partner who takes a case of her own and solves it by both outwitting and outjabbing a male karate school grad. Which if anything should only expand the unreluctant readership of Sobol's ten-at-a-time exercises in rapid crime detection.

> "Younger Fiction: 'Encyclopedia Brown Takes the Case'," in Kirkus Reviews (copyright © 1973 The Kirkus Service, Inc.), Vol. XLI, No. 15, August 1, 1973, p. 813.

The author's successful formula—ten-year-old Encyclopedia Brown solves ten mysteries by always asking the question that enables him to break the case—is sure to make this latest title as popular as the preceding nine. . . . It's a gimmick, but kids—especially reluctant readers—will appreciate this addition to the popular series.

> Cherie Zarookian, "The Book Review: Encyclopedia Brown Takes the Case'," in School Library Journal,

an appendix to Library Journal *(reprinted from the December, 1973 issue of* School Library Journal, *published by R. R. Bowker Co./A Xerox Corporation; copyright © 1973), Vol. 20, No. 4, December, 1973, p. 51.*

The cases [in *Encyclopedia Brown Takes the Case*] range from burglary to a fixed dog-paddle race (for dogs), to a poisoned pet skunk, and the ten-year-old sleuth and his right-hand-girl attack each problem with alacrity. As usual, the reader is invited to solve the cases for himself before reading the conclusions, which are puzzling even for a long-time reader of mysteries. The plots are varied, plausible, and fun while providing some mental exercise along with the entertainment.

"Children's Books: 'Encyclopedia Brown Takes the Case'," in The Booklist *(reprinted by permission of the American Library Association; copyright © 1974 by the American Library Association), Vol. 70, No. 9, January 1, 1974, p. 491.*

ENCYCLOPEDIA BROWN LENDS A HAND   (1974)

Clean as a whistle Encyclopedia solves the mysteries of the worn out phrases, the skunk ape, the exploding toilet, the salami sandwich . . . you name it, he solves it. His sidekick, Sally—"the prettiest girl in the fifth grade"—can now out-punch Bugs Meany and, on occasion, out-deduce Encyclopedia, but his is still basically a boy's world. In fact Encyclopedia may well be the preeminent boy rap artist of our time, and as for the cases . . . the "'most hair-raising experience since I pulled off my turtleneck sweater,' he joked weakly." And proof that he's got a lot on the ball, we add roundly.

"Younger Fiction: 'Encyclopedia Brown Lends a Hand'," in Kirkus Reviews *(copyright © 1974 The Kirkus Service, Inc.), Vol. XLII, No. 16, August 15, 1974, p. 878.*

If children pick up the well-placed clues (the back page of a newspaper will always be an even number or that a girl can't play the cello in a tight skirt) they'll be able to see just how Encyclopedia and Sally solve such cases as "**. . . the Exploding Toilet**," "**. . . the Skunk Ape**," etc. . . . Typical Sobol fun, a bit silly at times, but bound to please fans.

Katherine Heylman, "Book Reviews: 'Encyclopedia Brown Lends a Hand'," in School Library Journal, *an appendix to* Library Journal *(reprinted from the October, 1974 issue of* School Library Journal, *published by R. R. Bowker Co./A Xerox Corporation; copyright © 1974), Vol. 21, No. 2, October, 1974, p. 114.*

ENCYCLOPEDIA BROWN AND THE CASE OF THE DEAD EAGLES   (1975)

Encyclopedia and his hard-hitting girl assistant Sally are at it again putting a stop to Wilfrid Wiggins' con game . . . ; doing their bit for ecology by tracking down an eagle poacher; and figuring out why Bugs Meany's offer to give lessons in hypnotizing lobsters is a fraud (does it take a genius to do this?). Some of the solutions are problematical, especially Sally's ability to spot a woman disguised as a man because she takes the seat facing the room at the pizza parlor as etiquette would dictate. It seems that Sobol is trying hard to liberate Sally from her sidekick role but isn't always sure how to go about it. Give

him credit for the effort, just as Encyclopedia's fans will give him credit for being consistently right.

"Younger Fiction: 'Encyclopedia Brown and the Case of the Dead Eagles'," in Kirkus Reviews *(copyright © 1975 The Kirkus Service, Inc.), Vol. XLIII, No. 15, August 1, 1975, p. 850.*

[The] 12th collection of detective cases solved by the boy wonder, follows the familiar pattern of presenting all the clues and giving readers a chance to solve the cases themselves before they turn to the back of the book for solutions. Encyclopedia's girl assistant Sally is given a larger role than usual; otherwise these are more of the same.

Sarah Law Kennerly, "Mystery and Suspense: 'Encyclopedia Brown and the Case of the Dead Eagles'," in School Library Journal *(reprinted from the December, 1975 issue of* School Library Journal, *published by R. R. Bowker Co./A Xerox Corporation; copyright © 1975), Vol. 22, No. 4, December, 1975, p. 67.*

The short cases [in *Encyclopedia Brown and the Case of the Dead Eagles*] are presented as open-ended riddles. These mysteries are solved with great aplomb by precocious Brown. The characters are undeveloped and lifeless. Brown's only redeeming quality seems to be that he outsmarts everyone in his bold, condescending manner. (p. 53)

Joan Weller, "Detective-Mysteries for Young People," in The World of Children's Books *(© 1978 Jon C. Stott), Vol. III, No. 2, Fall, 1978, pp. 51-5.**

TRUE SEA ADVENTURES   (1975)

You may have heard some of these sea yarns before: the saga of the original Crusoe; the man who was pulled alive out of the belly of a whale; the ghost ship *Octavius*. But of Sobol's 22 anecdotes, some are bound to be new (how about Project Habakkuk, the abortive British plan to launch an iceberg aircraft carrier which makes Gathorne-Hardy's *Operation Peeg* not so far-fetched after all?) and all are fast-paced entertainment (provided episodes of frostbite and lifeboat triage are your notion of diverting reading). We would prefer that retailers of this sort of "strange but true" material make some mention of sources. Not much ballast for library collections, but this should attract a full roster of readers.

"Younger Non-Fiction: 'True Sea Adventures'," in Kirkus Reviews *(copyright © 1975 The Kirkus Service, Inc.), Vol. XLIII, No. 21, November 1, 1975, p. 1237.*

Twenty-two tales of the sea, ranging from the story of a late nineteenth century Jonah to an account of the last patrol of the U.S. submarine *Tang* in 1944, are presented as brief and intriguing vignettes. Written in a reportorial style, highlighted with the connotative phraseology associated with journalistic eyewitness accounts, the stories . . . will appeal to younger adventure buffs as well as to adolescents seeking interesing yet short, easy-to-read selections. (pp. 179-80)

Mary M. Burns, "Also of Interest: 'True Sea Adventures'," in The Horn Book Magazine *(copyright © 1976 by the Horn Book, Inc., Boston), Vol. LII, No. 2, April, 1976, pp. 179-80.*

ENCYCLOPEDIA BROWN AND THE CASE OF THE MIDNIGHT VISITOR (1977)

Ten-year-old Encyclopedia Brown, Idaville's "secret weapon against crime," gets ever sharper as he gets—er—remains the same age. The junior genius and partner Sally solve three big-time crimes and a passel of neighborhood cases of varying degrees of farfetchedness, including that of the Painting Gerbils. Bugs Meany's usual frame-up job is foiled once again and Sally gets to punch out Cuthbert DeVan DeVoe, local catnapper. The puzzles occasionally require knowledge not provided by the text (e.g., ambulance patients are loaded *head* first) to keep detectives on their toes. However, with two fist-fights cheerfully resorted to, it looks like due process is taking a downswing.

> *"Younger Fiction: 'Encyclopedia Brown and the Case of the Midnight Visitor'," in* Kirkus Reviews *(copyright © 1977 The Kirkus Service, Inc.), Vol. XLV, No. 17, September 1, 1977, p. 934.*

In the usual format of this series, there are brief bafflers (each a separate mystery) and answers given at the back of the book. Sometimes the clues are ones the readers might have spotted; at other times, the answers seem contrived, as in **"The Case of the Red Sweater,"** where a boy who has claimed to be wearing a girl friend's sweater is spotted as the culprit because "Encyclopedia realized that Bugs was wearing his sweater inside out!" That is, the sweater was reversible. However, the brisk, brief presentation of the cases plus the infallible, if incredible, perspicacity of the ten-year-old detective will appeal to many readers.

> *Zena Sutherland, "New Titles for Children and Young People: 'Encyclopedia Brown and the Case of the Midnight Visitor'," in* Bulletin of the Center for Children's Books *(reprinted by permission of The University of Chicago Press; © 1978 by The University of Chicago), Vol. 31, No. 8, April, 1978, p. 135.*

DISASTER (1979)

Beginning with the bubonic plague, Sobol's book describes 13 disasters (a significant number?) chronologically. Some were natural, others caused by men and a few exacerbated by humans. Tartars in Asia Minor massacred Italian traders for infecting them with the plague which killed millions during the 14th century. Germans murdered Jews for the same stupid reason although they were also victims of the disease. Following these tragic accounts are reports on Port Royal, a Caribbean town that sank into the sea in 1612, the destructive eruption of Mount Pelee in 1792 (politicians needing votes barred the populace from leaving the city near election day and thus doomed 30,000 men, women and children), the mine cave-in in Illinois in 1901, and other disasters. Sobol says he chose these in the belief they would interest the young. Perhaps, but some of the graphic details here are too dreadful even for iron nerves.

> *"Nonfiction: 'Disaster'," in* Publishers Weekly *(reprinted from the January 22, 1979 issue of* Publishers Weekly, *published by R. R. Bowker Company, a Xerox company; copyright © 1979 by Xerox Corporation), Vol. 215, No. 4, January 22, 1979, p. 370.*

Sobol's prose is brisk and vivid, usually steering clear of the sensational. He provides a degree of analysis where appropriate: an upcoming election played a crucial role in keeping St.

Pierre's population in the city as Mt. Pelee blew; politics also kept East Pakistan from receiving necessary aid after the cyclone. Informative at a newsreel level for browsers or report researchers.

> *Denise M. Wilms, "Children's Books: 'Disaster'," in* Booklist *(reprinted by permission of the American Library Association; copyright © 1979 by the American Library Association), Vol. 75, No. 22, July 15, 1979, p. 1630.*

Sobol begins with a discussion of the Black Death of the Middle Ages which does not fit his definition of a disaster in the foreword as, "A nightmare come true . . . over in a matter of seconds or minutes." The author does treat some of the classic disasters. . . . Recent disasters such as the collision of two 747s, the winter of 1976-77 and the New York City Blackout of 1977 comprise almost half the book. Although the lack of illustrations is a disappointment, the book is useful because of its currency. The style is readable, but the lack of an index hampers the book's use for quick reference.

> *Edward W. Menke, "Junior High Up: 'Disaster'," in* School Library Journal *(reprinted from the January, 1981 issue of* School Library Journal, *published by R. R. Bowker Co./A Xerox Corporation; copyright © 1981), Vol. 27, No. 5, January, 1981, p. 73.*

ENCYCLOPEDIA BROWN'S RECORD BOOK OF WEIRD AND WONDERFUL FACTS (1979)

This is a collection of unrelated facts, anecdotes, etc. They are funny, or interesting, or. . . . Each page is headed by an appropriate, if ugly, cartoon, followed by the interesting fact in a short paragraph. A good browsing item, or for program use. The name ENCYCLOPEDIA BROWN is gratuitous, having nothing to do with the book, except to sell it.

> *Lenore Rosenthal, "Older Readers: 'Encyclopedia Brown's Record Book of Weird and Wonderful Facts'," in* Children's Book Review Service *(copyright © 1979 Children's Book Review Service Inc.), Vol. 8, No. 3, November, 1979, p. 30.*

A few years ago I made a grave error. As a thank-you-for-inviting-us gift I brought some friends a paperback copy of the "Guinness Book of World Records." The host buried his nose in the book. . . . He was lost for the duration. I never again made the mistake of bringing such a gift, but I recently found a clue to people's fascination with such books, especially the need to astound others with tidbits of amazing information. I read Donald J. Sobol's **"Encyclopedia Brown's Record Book of Weird and Wonderful Facts."** (p. 56)

[The] kind of stuff you have to share, to read aloud, is [all] from a chapter called **"Flabbergasting Facts."** In addition there are chapters on young sports record breakers (**"Gym Dandies"**), animal facts and fancy, curiosities of the human body and a very funny chapter called **"Aspirin Alley,"** dedicated to the nudnicks who tried but failed, like Joe Hayden, 17, who issued a challenge to play chess with 180 people at one time. Unfortunately, only 20 people showed up to accept the challenge. Eighteen defeated him, including a 7-year-old boy. Joe beat only his mother and a man who quit early to go shopping.

Basically I trust Encyclopedia Brown, boy detective, star of a number of books wherein young readers have to solve a series of mysteries. But I do question some of the data in this book.

For instance, Encyclopedia Brown says that the average American eats 2 doughnuts a day. Come on! That's 730 doughnuts a year. Most people I know (an average lot) won't eat that many in a lifetime. So if I'm to believe Encyclopedia Brown, I must assume somebody's eating a heck of a lot more than his share.

There's one weird and wonderful fact Encyclopedia Brown didn't include. His books, hardcover and paperback, including sales to book clubs and in 13 foreign countries, have sold over 10 million copies. Now let's see. If those books were laid end to end they'd reach from the North Pole to. . . . (pp. 56, 69)

> *Barbara Karlin, "Guinness Junior," in* The New York Times Book Review, *Part II (© 1979 by The New York Times Company, reprinted by permission), November 11, 1979, pp. 56, 69.*

ENCYCLOPEDIA BROWN CARRIES ON   (1980)

[*Encyclopedia Brown Carries On*] presents a series of brief cases that Encyclopedia quickly solves; at the back of the book is a series of one-page solutions. At times the clue is there for the reader to pick up, but at other times it is absent although not illogical. The writing style is breezy and repetitive; there's some challenge in the puzzle element, but the anecdotes otherwise are on the frothy side.

> *Zena Sutherland, "New Titles for Children and Young People: 'Encyclopedia Brown Carries On,'" in* Bulletin of the Center for Children's Books *(reprinted by permission of The University of Chicago Press; © 1980 by The University of Chicago), Vol. 33, No. 10, June, 1980, p. 202.*

Dry humor seems stronger than usual in this latest group of Encyclopedia cases, and crisp dialogue and action move the minimysteries along at their usual speedy pace. The biggest flaw is in several of the 10 stories that tax the reader beyond fair limits for deducing a solution. In **"The Case of the Marvelous Egg,"** for example, the reader has no way of knowing that the chute pack worn by a parachute jumper has no backup chute in it. The majority of the stories are solvable by clear thinking, however; so add this where Encyclopedia has a following.

> *Denise M. Wilms, "Children's Books: 'Encyclopedia Brown Carries On,'" in* Booklist *(reprinted by permission of the American Library Association; copyright © 1980 by the American Library Association), Vol. 76, No. 20, June 15, 1980, p. 1536.*

In one of the few episodes that's a story and not just a puzzle, Sally and Encyclopedia are framed by Bugs and cohort Edsel—and have to explain to a suspicious policeman how Edsel comes to be tied up in a garden hose, with demon pitcher Sally throwing grapes at his head. And while some of the solutions truly call for encyclopedic knowledge that few would have or necessarily want (a dollar is 6.14 inches long, but appears as 6⅛ inches on a ruler), others are the sort that one at least *thinks* one might puzzle out—like a left-hander's way of cutting his sideburns (shorter on the left side). That story, too, is a likely conceit, turning on an equal-opportunity club for left-handers. Some cases of sheer ingenuity, but no let-up in energy.

> *"Younger Fiction: 'Encyclopedia Brown Carries On'," in* Kirkus Reviews *(copyright © 1980 The Kirkus Service, Inc.), Vol. XLVIII, No. 13, July 1, 1980, p. 838.*

ANGIE'S FIRST CASE   (1981)

Is it plausible for a young female detective to catch the Wolfpack, a gang of teenage thieves? Perhaps not, but Sobol takes us skillfully through Angie's escapades. . . . Although the story takes some very preditable turns, there is enough action and suspense to keep the reader intent right on through the conclusion.

> *Fellis L. Jordan, "Older Readers: 'Angie's First Case'," in* Children's Book Review Service *(copyright © 1981 Children's Book Review Service Inc.), Vol. 10, No. 13, July, 1981, p. 119.*

A widow is beaten by an intruder in her home; a teenage boy steals trifles from a neighbor's garage; counterfeit 20s are floating around town; a teenage "wolfpack" is vandalizing homes; an auto body shop revamps stolen cars; a bloody shooting is staged on a fishing boat; and twelve-year-old Angie, who eventually noses out or stumbles upon the connections among all these events, is followed by a sinister man in tan. As school lets out for summer, Angie determines to catch the wolfpack for the glory of her older sister Kit. . . . There's nothing more to the story than the too-neatly interlocked plot—an acceptable limitation in Sobol's Encyclopedia Brown puzzle-stories, but more noticeable here, where one story (albeit three cases deep) is stretched out to fill the volume. However, for addicts of straight detection Sobol keeps the curve balls flying; and the calculated appeal to feminists will give Angie a push.

> *"Younger Fiction: 'Angie's First Case'," in* Kirkus Reviews *(copyright © 1981 The Kirkus Service, Inc.), Vol. XLIX, No. 13, July 1, 1981, p. 801.*

If [Angie's] ability to link seemingly small occurrences and to untangle the mysteries seems farfetched, the exciting pace, likable characters, and readability more than compensate. Sobol's lively female counterpart to Encyclopedia Brown will have equal appeal.

> *Barbara Elleman, "Children's Books: 'Angie's First Case'," in* Booklist *(reprinted by permission of the American Library Association; copyright © 1981 by the American Library Association), Vol. 78, No. 2, September 15, 1981, p. 111.*

Tobi Tobias

1938-

American author of picture books, fiction and nonfiction for children, and journalist. Tobias's study of the arts and her experience as a contributor to dance magazines provide her with background for biographies of successful musicians, dancers, and sculptors from minority cultures. She emphasizes the determination and perseverance the artists display in their struggles to achieve acceptance and distinction in their particular fields. Most of Tobias's other books are about facing situations traumatic to children. She treats the characters and their dilemmas sensitively in a simple style designed for easy comprehension. Her remaining works are regarded as pleasant stories for very young children.

While Tobias's biographies are generally well received, some of her books have not met with the same critical approval. Her resolutions to the predicaments of childhood dissatisfy some reviewers because of a lack of conviction in the way they are presented. *The Quitting Deal* is especially praised for dealing with the bad habits and problems of adults as well as children, though it again is a work that has been accused of offering no solution to these problems. Perhaps Tobias's greatest appeal to children is through her biographies, which introduce young readers to contemporary artists in an accessible and informative way. (See also *Contemporary Authors*, Vols. 29-32, and *Something about the Author*, Vol. 5.)

MARIA TALLCHIEF (1970)

At forty-one Maria Tallchief "'hung up her toe shoes' and went home'' and the answer to a question adults might pose tells children something they seldom hear; an auspicious career is not the less so for being terminated. Especially as it retains its luster here . . . in the recounted triumphs and its basis—natural talent plus utmost dedication. Interest inheres besides in the 'story' of Maria Tallchief: an Indian father who golfed on oil revenues; a Scotch-Irish mother ambitious for her daughter to become a concert pianist; and Betty Marie herself, with "no time for doing nothing," torn at twelve between the two things she loved doing most, playing the piano and dancing. With [choreographer George] Balanchine comes a glimpse of recent ballet history, and the break-up of their marriage rings truer than in most juveniles. At the last we see a glowing photograph of Maria Tallchief and the daughter who figured in her decision to give up dancing: there's a rightness about this that's reassuring in a world of many wrongs.

> *"Younger Non-Fiction: Maria Tallchief'," in* Kirkus Reviews *(copyright © 1970 The Kirkus Service, Inc.), Vol. XXXVIII, No. 16, August 15, 1970, p. 883.*

In what is the only book on Tallchief for this age level, Tobias offers a clear, simple, accurate—if sometimes flat—treatment of the American Indian girl who became a famous ballerina. . . . Slow readers with an interest in ballet might well be tempted by the book, which is very easy to read.

> *Susan Stanton, "The Book Review: 'Maria Tallchief'," in* School Library Journal, *an appendix to* Library Journal *(reprinted from the December, 1970 issue of* School Library Journal, *published by R. R.*

Bowker Co./A Xerox Corporation; copyright © 1970), Vol. 17, No. 4, December, 1970, p. 56.

Tobi Tobias has had a lifetime interest in the dance and she writes of Maria Tallchief, world renowned ballerina, with clarity and admiration. She conveys to young readers the dedication and hard work that go into making a person a superstar. Tobias handles tastefully Tallchief's divorce from choreographer George Balanchine and, without belaboring the point, informs readers that family life is very difficult to combine with a ballet career.

> *May Hill Arbuthnot, Dianne L. Monson, and Zena Sutherland, "Books for Younger Children: 'Maria Tallchief'," in their* Children and Books *(copyright © 1947, 1957, 1964, 1972, 1977, 1981 by Scott, Foresman and Company; reprinted by permission), sixth edition, Scott, Foresman, 1981, p. 414.*

MARIAN ANDERSON (1972)

[*Marian Anderson* is a] lifeless, platitudinous text. Beginning with the undemonstrated assertion that "The Anderson family did not have much money, but they cared about each other and had many happy times together," Tobias refers repeatedly to Marian's "beautiful voice" but never conveys any real appreciation of her music. And as we're told when she is a school girl singing in the church choir that though a contralto "she could reach up to the high soprano notes, too, and even down to the low music of the baritone," it's hard to be impressed much later, re her Metropolitan Opera performance in 1955, that "Marian's part was not easy. She had to reach very high and very low notes. . . ," Marian Anderson's landmark performances and her encounters with discrimination—including the 1939 DAR refusal to let her sing at Constitution Hall—are dutifully catalogued, but it's all devitalized by the tone of knee-jerk piety.

> *"Younger Non-Fiction: 'Maria Anderson'," in* Kirkus Reviews *(copyright © 1972 The Kirkus Service, Inc.), Vol. XL, No. 23, December 1, 1972, p. 1358.*

This biography of Marian Anderson will impress readers with her determination and pride. . . . Tobias has captured her subject's enthusiastic response to life and conveys it by means of a concise, clearly written narrative. However, Anderson's birth date is inaccurately listed, and the book is further flawed in that it ends with the 1956 farewell tours of Europe and America and completely neglects her 1958 appointment as a delegate to the United Nations and the presentation to her of the Presidential Medal of Freedom in 1963. . . . [This] book could be used as an introduction to her career for a younger audience than would read her autobiography, *My Lord What a Morning* (Watts, 1966) and [Shirlee P.] Newman's *Marian Anderson: Lady from Philadelphia* (Westminster, 1966).

> *Helen Wright, "Book Reviews: 'Marian Anderson'," in* School Library Journal, *an appendix to* Library Journal *(reprinted from the April, 1973 issue of* School Library Journal, *published by R. R. Bowker*

Co./A Xerox Corporation; copyright © 1973), Vol. 19, No. 8, April, 1973, p. 72.

[**Marian Anderson**] is simply written, dispassionate in tone, and balanced in treatment. The text describes the now-familiar (but never before so competently written for very young readers) story of the small girl in Philadelphia whose big, golden voice was so appreciated by the members of her church that they financed her first professional training.

> *Zena Sutherland, "New Titles for Children and Young People: 'Marian Anderson'," in* Bulletin of the Center for Children's Books *(reprinted by permission of The University of Chicago Press; © 1973 by The University of Chicago), Vol. 26, No. 10, June, 1973, p. 163.*

The biography reads like an adventure story and Ms. Tobias handles the story of the brilliantly talented black singer, her perseverence and pride and how she turned racial barriers into triumphs with rare insight and understanding.

> *Robert J. Pierce, "Marian Anderson," in* Dance Magazine *(copyright 1973 by Danad Publishing Company, Inc.), Vol. XLVII, No. 7, July, 1973, p. 81.*

ISAMU NOGUCHI: THE LIFE OF A SCULPTOR   (1974)

Regarding Noguchi's personal life Tobias emphasizes the loneliness of growing up without a father, being sent off across an ocean by his American mother living in Japan, hanging on here and there while belonging nowhere, and never having a family of his own despite a late, brief unhappy marriage. By implication, then, Noguchi's life is his work, and Tobias concentrates on his development as an artist—the early dissatisfaction with realistic sculpture, his apprenticeship with Brancusi whose work seemed a realization of Noguchi's own dreams, further traveling to which, we're told, he adapted his style by using sharp, shining metal in modern New York, soft clay in Japan where he felt close to nature, and strong marble from the mountains in Italy. Always, "he felt that locked inside this material were great adventures"—and though Tobias doesn't quite communicate either the excitement of "making them happen" or the uniqueness of Noguchi's unlocking, she does provide some orientation for viewing nonrepresentative sculpture as well as an unromanticized picture of an artist's commitment.

> *"Younger Non-Fiction: 'Isamu Noguchi'," in* Kirkus Reviews *(copyright © 1974 The Kirkus Service, Inc.), Vol. XLII, No. 19, October 1, 1974, p. 1065.*

Too much of Tobias' text is devoted to the facts of Noguchi's troubled life and not enough attention is given to the artist's career and to his methods of creation. However, this contemporary sculptor's genius for working in stone, metal, and clay and his desire to capture "in his shapes the power of the sun, the flow of rushing water, and the strong spirit of women and men," comes through in the striking black-and-white photographs. . . . Not an absorbing biography, but an interesting browsing book for middle graders.

> *Shirley M. Wilton, "Book Reviews: 'Isamu Noguchi: The Life of a Sculptor'," in* School Library Journal, *an appendix to* Library Journal *(reprinted from the November, 1974 issue of* School Library Journal, *published by R. R. Bowker Co./A Xerox Corporation;*

copyright © 1974), Vol. 21, No. 3, November, 1974, p. 59.

[**Isamu Noguchi: The Life of a Sculptor** is a] biography written in a grave, direct style. . . . While the book has a subdued tone, it is candid about the unhappy aspects of Noguchi's life and makes a very strong statement about the isolation and dedication of the artist. . . . An interesting and unusual biography, this should be of special concern to readers who are students of any art form. (pp. 99-100)

> *Zena Sutherland, "New Titles for Children and Young People: 'Isamu Noguchi: The Life of a Sculptor'," in* Bulletin of the Center for Children's Books *(reprinted by permission of The University of Chicago Press; © 1975 by The University of Chicago), Vol. 28, No. 6, February, 1975, pp. 99-100.*

[The biography of Isamu Noguchi] is thorough, albeit somewhat bland. In simple, clear language and images, the author has managed to integrate the personal life experiences, motivations and outside forces which contributed to Noguchi's development as a sculptor. He emerges as a real person—neither a god because of his fame nor a cardboard stereotype.

The author is also to be commended for attempting to deal straightforwardly with the sensitive questions of Noguchi's interracial/intercultural identity and his particular predicament during the World War II internment of Japanese Americans. Originally, because of his half-white status, Noguchi was not forced to go into a camp. He then chose to do so, hoping to make the camps better places to live. Ironically, when he asked to be released, the government refused for seven months on the ground of his being Japanese American. This rude awakening led Noguchi to admit that he still felt "like a prisoner in his own country." Yet, by equating the camps with "jails" and the effects of racism with the tribulations of a prison experience, the author reveals her unwillingness to unequivocally indict the government's unjust actions. Nor does she exonerate Japanese Americans from any charges of disloyalty. Her superficial, non-controversial treatment of these issues leaves the impression that she wanted to dispense with this unpleasant matter quickly and move on to the safer subject of Noguchi's artistic endeavors.

The effort is made to deglamorize the artist's life by not focusing on gallery openings, personal fame and wealth. Instead, Ms. Tobias stresses the hard work, risks, compromises and commitment required of all artists. She also emphasizes the artist's concept of popularizing sculpture—taking it out of the galleries and museums into the streets, parks and homes to give it a wider base rather than reserving it for the elite few. Most importantly, Noguchi is presented in a down-to-earth, humanistic manner. . . . This is a good introductory work for young readers who are interested in art and how it expresses an artist's personal values and lifestyle. However, mature supervision would be required to offset its often weak treatment of the Japanese American experience. (pp. 20-1)

> *Asian-American Task Force, "Book Reviews: 'Isamu Noguchi: The Life of a Sculptor'," in* Interracial Books for Children Bulletin *(reprinted by permission of Interracial Books for Children Bulletin, 1841 Broadway, New York, N.Y. 10023), Vol. 7, Nos. 2 & 3, 1976, pp. 20-1.*

THE QUITTING DEAL   (1975)

''The Quitting Deal'' concerns the way children and adults cope with problems together and admits the possibility that children can and often do help their parents.

The problem here is twofold: a mother needs to quit smoking and cannot; her daughter wants desperately to stop sucking her thumb. They make a pact to help each other, trying a variety of ''quitting deals'' which range from ''The Nasty Stuff Cure'' to ''The Penny Cure,'' a form of bribery.

Mrs. Tobias clearly shows us the insidious nature of habits: cutting out one often leads to taking on another. The mother, who once sucked her fingers, gave it up to start biting her nails. She left that, the text implies, to begin smoking.

Despite all its talk of quitting, however, **''The Quitting Deal''** ultimately fails: The characters are left with their nasty habits, and we feel let down. I wish they'd been able to ''stop being silly . . . and then quit'' as the mother had suggested instead of promising to ''just do it a little bit less,'' which we know is not going to really work. After all, quitting means stopping, not tapering off.

> *Marge Blaine, '' 'The Quitting Deal','' in* The New York Times Book Review *(© 1975 by The New York Times Company; reprinted by permission), May 4, 1975, p. 40.*

The combination of words and pictures here is inspired telling and showing. Jenny is the small-girl narrator who reveals the lengths to which she and her mother go to stop their bad habits. Jenny sucks her thumb; mom smokes incessantly. With father's encouragement, mother and child join forces in a grim try at self-improvement. . . . Without any kind of falsity or sentimentalizing Tobi Tobias explores real problems.

> *''PW Forecasts: 'The Quitting Deal,' in* Publishers Weekly *(reprinted from the June 2, 1975 issue of* Publishers Weekly, *published by R.R. Bowker Company, a Xerox company; copyright © 1975 by Xerox Corporation), Vol. 207, No. 22, June 2, 1975, p. 53.*

[*The Quitting Deal* is a] winning story about how much easier it is to make resolutions than to keep them. . . . Although Jenny's father sometimes gives the impression of being Judy's father as well, all the relationships reflect love and understanding as well as a sense of humor—especially that of mother and daughter who have an unusually egalitarian relationship. . . . [This is an easy-flowing] tale of human frailty and struggle.

> *Melinda Schroeder, ''Book Reviews: 'The Quitting Deal','' in* School Library Journal *(reprinted from the September, 1975 issue of* School Library Journal, *published by R.R. Bowker Co./A Xerox Corporation; copyright © 1975), Vol. 22, No. 1, September, 1975, p. 92.*

[The text of **The Quitting Deal**] is brisk, ingenious, and often funny. Perhaps because there is no didacticism and no all-problems-solved ending, the story—which is really just an expanded situation—is successful both as a gentle indictment of smoking and thumb-sucking, and as an understanding, rueful, and realistic acceptance of people's hangups.

> *Zena Sutherland, ''New Titles for Children and Young People: 'The Quitting Deal','' in* Bulletin of the Center for Children's Books *(reprinted by permission of The University of Chicago Press; © 1975 by The University of Chicago), Vol. 29, No. 2, October, 1975, p. 36.*

ARTHUR MITCHELL   (1975)

A vigorous narrative, and what else could it be considering the energy of Arthur Mitchell—who had no money for dancing lessons and got into the High School of Performing Arts on the basis of a soft-shoe routine, who studied modern dance and later classical ballet with Balanchine only to hear a woman in the audience exclaim ''look . . . they've got a nigger in the company'' on the night of his leading role debut. And then bringing young black dancers and black style into ballet through his Dance Theatre of Harlem. Briskly executed. . . .

> *''Younger Non-Fiction: 'Arthur Mitchell','' in* Kirkus Review *(copyright © 1975 The Kirkus Service, Inc.), Vol. 43, No. 11, June 1, 1975, p. 611.*

Tobias notes the hard work and strong discipline required of Mitchell, as well as the barriers of racial prejudice that frustrated his efforts. The smooth text generally avoids condescension, though occasional sentences render simplistic rather than simple description. However, the flaws are slight, and this portrait of the contemporary black dancer is most welcome.

> *''Children's Books: 'Arthur Mitchell','' in* The Booklist *(reprinted by permission of the American Library Association; copyright © 1975 by the American Library Association), Vol. 71, No. 21, July 1, 1975, p. 1130.*

Without oversimplifying some of the less pleasant facts (e.g., family problems, prejudice), Tobias has written an easy-to-read biography of the Black ballet dancer, choreographer, and founder of the Dance Theatre of Harlem. She clearly explains why it was extremely difficult for Mitchell to achieve success in the world of classical ballet and why he eventually abandoned his career to encourage and train other Blacks for classical dance. . . . [A] fine biography of a male dancer.

> *Helen Gregory, ''Book Reviews: 'Arthur Mitchell','' in* School Library Journal *(reprinted from the September, 1975 issue of* School Library Journal, *published by R. R. Bowker Co./A Xerox Corporation; copyright © 1975), Vol. 22, No. 1, September, 1975, p. 92.*

MOVING DAY   (1976)

The many changes and the bustle which a moving day brings—sorting, packing, boxes, vans, saying good-bye, one last look, new room, strange noises, new faces, saying hello—are all seen through the eyes of a small girl whose stuffed bear remains a constant, comforting companion throughout. The gentle, poetic text [is] direct and childlike in word and tone. . . . This is an intensely personal lap book that parents will find great pleasure in sharing with very young children as a reassuring prelude to the big day.

> *Mary Jane Anderson, ''Children's Books: 'Moving Day','' in* The Booklist *(reprinted by permission of the American Library Association; copyright © 1976 by the American Library Association), Vol. 72, No. 19, June 1, 1976, p. 1410.*

The bittersweet excitement of moving day is readily evoked in a totally childlike fashion through a poetic, easy-to-read text. . . .

The details of preparation—sorting, discarding, packing, and protecting a favorite toy—as well as the pangs of separation and the pleasures of finding new friends are precisely cataloged by the small female narrator. . . .

Mary M. Burns, "Late Summer Booklist: 'Moving Day'," in The Horn Book Magazine *(copyright © 1976 by the Horn Book, Inc., Boston), Vol. 52, No. 4, August, 1976, p. 389.*

[There is simple precision in the text of *Moving Day,*] which is a small girl's running commentary. . . . The experience of moving as well as the relegation of reactions to a toy have been described in other picture books for the very young; this is not highly original, but it's nicely done.

Zena Sutherland, "New Titles for Children and Young People: 'Moving Day'," in Bulletin of the Center for Children's Books *(reprinted by permission of The University of Chicago Press; © 1976 by The University of Chicago), Vol. 30, No. 1, September, 1976, p. 19.*

JANE, WISHING (1977)

Jane, plain Jane . . . wishes herself into a romantic realm where her name would be Amanda or Melissa, her eyes would be sea-green sea-blue, her skin would be see-through pale, she would be an only child, with a room of her own, etc., etc.— only to be put down . . . by the obtuse-to-obnoxious members of her notably unsympathetic family. So she decides—on the final page—"to be happy anyway." Jane's wishes are years ahead of most picturebook youngsters, even assuming that they're today's wishes to the extent that the cloddy family—smiling for the first time in the finale—is today's waking bad dream. What she has to be happy about is hard to perceive.

"Picture Books: 'Jane, Wishing'," in Kirkus Reviews *(copyright © 1977 The Kirkus Service, Inc.), Vol. XLV, No. 9, May 1, 1977, p. 485.*

The main difference between Jane, Tobias's likable heroine, and young girls in real life is that she's indiscreet enough to let her family in on her dreams of glory. Most readers will recognize (probably with an embarrassed wince) Jane's fantasies. She wished she had a waterfall of red hair and sea-green, sea-blue eyes instead of plain brown hair and brown eyes. She yearns for a rich room of her own, a beautiful singing voice and a *beau ideal.* Jane's parents, grandmother, brother and sister puncture the girl's dreams consistently in a story that's half humorous and half wistfully sad. (pp. 107-08)

"PW Forecasts: 'Jane, Wishing'," in Publishers Weekly *(reprinted from the June 13, 1977 issue of* Publishers Weekly, *published by R. R. Bowker Company, a Xerox company; copyright © 1977 by Xerox Corporation), Vol. 211, No. 24, June 13, 1977, pp. 107-08.*

Jane's daydreams are recounted in lyrical prose on pages imprinted with soft pinks, coppers and browns, showing distant trees, flowers, a silky black kitten and a prancing horse. Encounters with her family are on alternate pages with black-and-white drawings which depict the crowding and conflict in a modern three-generation family. The text is printed entirely in dialogue, near or over the picture of the speaker. The result is visual crowding of people and text, which suggests the sound and fury, the relentless voices of the TV scene. It is a sensitive

and artistic book, and maybe this is the technique to use with the children of Television Man as opposed to the children of Gutenberg Man.

Nancy Larrick, "Children's Books: 'Jane, Wishing'," in The New York Times Book Review *(© 1977 by The New York Times Company; reprinted by permission), July 24, 1977, p. 18.*

Harried Mom, hassled Dad, cute teen sister, jeaned and sneakered brother, sensible, nostalgic Grandma all answer [Jane's wishes] with plain talking, and their personalities and preoccupations emerge in dialogue through their reactions to Jane's longings. There is reassurance and love here amidst the familiar family bickering, and a pleasant togetherness that [the author has] . . . caught in a friendly way that rings true, with a comfortable balance between dreams and reality.

Marjorie Lewis, "The Book Review: 'Jane, Wishing'," in School Library Journal *(reprinted from the September, 1977 issue of* School Library Journal, *published by R. R. Bowker Co./A Xerox Corporation; copyright © 1977), Vol. 24, No. 1, September, 1977, p. 117.*

CHASING THE GOBLINS AWAY (1977)

Tobias has been thanked for several winning books for youngsters but this is below her standards. The story is far too long for the flimsy subject and not very convincing. Jimmy is a small boy, bedeviled by a dread of the dark. Night after night, he suffers nightmares as the most fearsome monsters advance upon his bed. One is his infant sister. One is a black, empty space you "could fall through, forever and ever." Others are slithery snakes, "the electric one" and many more. Jimmy's parents help him, at first, to get through the nights but finally insist that he conquer his fears himself, which he does. That will surprise some grownup readers who are bound to feel that the child needs professional attention.

"PW Forecasts: 'Chasing the Goblins Away'," in Publishers Weekly *(reprinted from the September 26, 1977 issue of* Publishers Weekly, *published by R. R. Bowker Company, a Xerox company; copyright © 1977 by Xerox Corporation), Vol. 212, No. 13, September 26, 1977, p. 137.*

Why don't we stop trying to fool children about the things that go bump in the night? They're there and that's it and there's nothing can be done about them. Oh you can try water, handholding, a game of cards, a stuffed dog or a light on. But a child has to meet them on his own terms, in his own good time. . . . You see, it's kind of hopeless, except for Jimmy, who gives them what for and 40 whacks in a gargantuan struggle one night.

Tobi Tobias describes the catalogue of demons and tells of the midnight tussle in smooth, literate prose. . . . But where does the vanquished foe go? Perchance to haunt someone else's dreams?

George A. Woods, "Children's Books: 'Chasing the Goblins Away'," in The New York Times Book Review *(© 1977 by The New York Times Company; reprinted by permission), October 23, 1977, p. 32.*

Another picture book in the bedtime blues genre, here a young boy conquers his fears by becoming the aggressor. . . . [The] message is pat, and it is debatable whether an older child need undergo an instant conversion to independence just because a new baby has arrived.

> *Corinne Camarata, "The Book Review: 'Chasing the Goblins Away'," in* School Library Journal *(reprinted from the February, 1978 issue of* School Library Journal, *published by R. R. Bowker Co./A Xerox Corporation; copyright © 1978), Vol. 24, No. 6, February, 1978, p. 51.*

PETEY (1978)

[*Petey* is] Tobias' first-person story of the death of a girl's pet gerbil. One day, on her usual after-school checkup, Emily finds Petey huddled and shivering in his cage. Daddy helps her fuss with him while discussing the implications, and by morning Petey is dead. Emily cries, and then she and her parents remember the good times with him and bury him in the yard; at the end she's "thinking over" the offer of two new gerbils. Tobias' telling is relatively natural and no doubt other gerbil owners will see nothing sappy in Emily's "think[ing] about how cute he was when he was a little baby." . . . But by now there are so many requiems for dead pets that Tobias offers nothing new.

> *"Picture Books: 'Petey'," in* Kirkus Reviews *(copyright © 1978 The Kirkus Service, Inc.), Vol. XLVI, No. 8, April 15, 1978, p. 434.*

The pensive mood created by Tobias is similar to that of Carol Carrick's *The Accident* (Seabury, 1976) with the family showing a like understanding of the youngster's loss. . . . [This] is one of the more thoughtful books about death for this age level. It is easy to empathize with Emily and the parents deal with her problem matter-of-factly without sugarcoating or sentimentalizing.

> *Carol Chatfield, "The Book Review: 'Petey'," in* School Library Journal *(reprinted from the May, 1978 issue of* School Library Journal, *published by R. R. Bowker Co./A Xerox Corporation; copyright © 1978), Vol. 24, No. 9, May, 1978, p. 60.*

[Following Petey's death, when friends offer Emily a pair of gerbils] from their unexpected litter, she wavers: "No one, no one could be like Petey." Mommy sagely counsels, "I never said it would be the same. It can be different, Em, and still be good," and Emily thoughtfully hedges: "I'm going to think it over and let her know." That simple finish . . . is just right for the very true-to-life story. Details of ownership are vivid as is Emily's emotion; any small pet owner will sorrowfully empathize. . . .

> *Denise M. Wilms, "Children's Books: 'Petey'," in* Booklist *(reprinted by permission of the American Library Association; copyright © 1978 by the American Library Association), Vol. 74, No. 17, May 1, 1978, p. 1439.*

[*Petey* is] nicely-told story about the death of a pet. . . . Not unusual in structure, the book still is one of the better stories about accepting death, especially for the reader to whom it is a new experience.

> *Zena Sutherland, "New Titles for Children and Young People: 'Petey'," in* Bulletin of the Center for Children's Books *(reprinted by permission of The University of Chicago Press; © 1978 by The University of Chicago), Vol. 31, No. 10, June, 1978, p. 168.*

AT THE BEACH (1978)

A low-key, unassuming text nevertheless captures the enjoyment two youngsters experience during their day at the beach. Small events strung together give the story body.

> *Denise M. Wilms, "Children's Books: 'At the Beach'," in* Booklist *(reprinted by permission of the American Library Association; copyright © 1978 by the American Library Association), Vol. 74, No. 21, July 1, 1978, p. 1682.*

A quiet mood is instantly set as a little girl is awakened early in the morning by the singing of birds outside her seaside bedroom. From this readers are lead, along with the girl and her family, through a pleasant sun-filled day *At the Beach*. No fast-paced thriller here, but a peaceful first-person description of building sand castles, walking on the beach, eating lunch, and napping in the hot sun. At day's end everyone saunters home and rounds out the occasion singing happy songs. . . . A gentler complement to [May] Garelick's *Down to the Beach* (Four Winds, Scholastic, 1973).

> *Hayden Atwood, "The Book Review: 'At the Beach'," in* School Library Journal *(reprinted from the September, 1978 issue of* School Library Journal, *published by R. R. Bowker Co./A Xerox Corporation; copyright © 1978), Vol. 25, No. 1, September, 1978, p. 126.*

[*At the Beach* is simply] told, but there is a paucity of action in the story and of vitality in the writing, although the book does convey a sense of the child's content in a peaceful, sunny day and the security of her family.

> *Zena Sutherland, "New Titles for Children and Young People: 'At the Beach'," in* Bulletin of the Center for Children's Books *(reprinted by permission of The University of Chicago Press; © 1978 by The University of Chicago), Vol. 32, No. 2, October, 1978, p. 37.*

HOW YOUR MOTHER AND FATHER MET, AND WHAT HAPPENED AFTER (1978)

Despite the suggestive title, this is *not* a how-you-were-made story. It is a boy-girl-meet-marry-and-live-happily-ever-after book. One wonders for what audience it is intended, as it is too difficult for beginning readers who would be confused to hear a story about strangers told in terms of "your mother and father," and too cutesy for older kids. Characters are stereotypes, from the Irish belle mother and the serious, wants-to-be-a-doctor Jewish father to his matzoh ball making aunt. The narrative is super-sentimental and clichéd. . . . (pp. 51-2)

> *Joan Scherer Brewer, "The Book Review: 'How Your Mother and Father Met, and What Happened After'," in* School Library Journal *(reprinted from the November, 1978 issue of* School Library Journal, *published by R. R. Bowker Co./A Xerox Corporation; copyright © 1978), Vol. 25, No. 3, November, 1978, pp. 51-2.*

Written as if told by an elderly friend of the family, [*How Your Mother and Father Met, and What Happened After*] is a rather sentimental but not mawkish story about the parents of Jimmy, to whom the book is addressed. Jeanie McLaren was nineteen when she met William Singer; he was older than she and dedicated to his medical career, but they fell in love. He went off to serve in the Korean War, and when he came back they were married. . . . Tobias handles the interreligious aspect with gentle candor and the pacific feelings of the young soldier (which increased when he, a man dedicated to saving lives, saw the carnage of the front lines) with directness and dignity. The book can help younger children to whom it may be read aloud understand concepts of family relationships and generations.

> *Zena Sutherland, "New Titles for Children and Young People: 'How Your Mother and Father Met, and What Happened After'," in* Bulletin of the Center for Children's Books *(reprinted by permission of The University of Chicago Press; © 1979 by The University of Chicago), Vol. 32, No. 5, January, 1979, p. 91.*

THE MAN WHO PLAYED ACCORDION MUSIC   (1979)

Anton Zoltany plays subversive tunes. No question about it. From his apartment, the music seeps next door and hires Mrs. McGeorge away from her tasks. The housewife dances outside, leaving her cat meowing for its breakfast. George McGeorge comes into the deserted kitchen, aghast at having to fend for himself before he leaves to work with his computers. Where is his wife? Where are his tidy, smart twins? Sam and Samantha waltz into view and out of doors, on their way to freedom: so does the cat, tempted by Zoltany's siren tones. Only poor Mr. McGeorge is left, wondering what has happened to his sane world. . . . [Tobias presents] an inspired piece of daffiness, with McGeorge's plaints expressed in computerlike type, and the music! It swirls and rushes and soars up and around the pages in writing as seductive as the squeeze box.

> *"PW Forecasts: 'The Man Who Played Accordian Music'," in* Publishers Weekly *(reprinted from the November 19, 1979 issue of* Publishers Weekly, *published by R. R. Bowker Company, a Xerox company; copyright © 1979 by Xerox Corporation), Vol. 216, No. 21, November 19, 1979, p. 79.*

Unfortunately, George McGeorge is too obvious a stereotype: the Uptight, White Anglo-Saxon Male Computer Expert. And somehow—despite the . . . well-chosen words that would be easy to listen to, full of repeated sounds and varied cadence—

the story is oddly disappointing. Maybe because it talks so of romance and adventure, but all that occurs offstage; meanwhile, readers are left sitting with unpleasant, unresolved George—and never get to hear the music, only the loud message.

> *Marilyn R. Singer, "The Book Review: 'The Man Who Played Accordian Music'," in* School Library Journal *(reprinted from the February, 1980 issue of* School Library Journal, *published by R. R. Bowker Co./A Xerox Corporation; copyright © 1980), Vol. 26, No. 6, February, 1980, p. 50.*

HOW WE GOT OUR FIRST CAT   (1980)

Juice up the repartee a little, and this laconic sketch about a family's adoption of an uninvited cat could be a TV sitcom episode. Mother, of course, doesn't want the cat. The kids, naturally, have answers to her every objection (Jamey will have allergy injections, Timothy will put chicken-wire around the bird's cage), plus an extra comeback for added laughs: if Jamey had allergy shots, "Then I'd never sneeze." Timothy: "What would you do when you had a cold." Jamey: "Give it to you." And Dad comes around just when Mom, too, is weakening. It's snappy, off-hand, up-to-date—but not really about the fate of a homeless cat but about who will win the family battle of wits.

> *"Picture Books: 'How We Got Our First Cat'," in* Kirkus Reviews *(copyright © 1980 The Kirkus Service, Inc.), Vol. XLVIII, No. 19, October 1, 1980, p. 297.*

Tobias tells her brief tale in a bemused, low-key style, making the story of the acceptance of a stray cat into a large family a warm one readers will smile over. . . . It is easy to see that Sylvestress is growing on the family, quietly and inevitably, in spite of the superficial aloofness of the parents.

> *Judith Goldberger, "Children's Books: 'How We Got Our First Cat'," in* Booklist *(reprinted by permission of the American Library Association; copyright © 1981 by the American Library Association), Vol. 77, No. 10, January 15, 1981, p. 703.*

Harvey Weiss

1922-

American author/illustrator of fiction and nonfiction for children. Weiss is best known for his books on how to make boats, models, games, gadgets, art pieces and other functional creations. These works are noted for their variety of simple and advanced examples, their clear instructions, and their ability to inspire young readers towards achieving professional results. Weiss has also written several well-received fictional works which are noted for their imagination and humor.

Weiss worked in advertising, printing, and sculpture before he married children's author Miriam Schlein, for whom he created his first illustrations. He combined his experiences as an illustrator with his knowledge of sculpture to create his first book, *Clay, Wood, and Wire*, which concentrates on the techniques and materials used in sculpting and creating collages. For several of his following works, Weiss combined realism and fantasy to create fiction that is generally praised for the comic tone of its texts and its expressive illustrations. His succeeding nonfiction books are all based on personal interests and skills which he relates to the interests of young readers.

Weiss receives praise for his blending of these activities with an appreciation for the excellence of the masters. He includes examples of their works, explanations of how they were produced, and their museum or gallery locations. Another feature of Weiss's work which critics appreciate is his emphasis on creativity through improvisation: he encourages his readers to improve and expand on the projects he presents. One reason for his thoroughness and enthusiasm for the reader's creativity may be that he chooses subjects which reflect his private involvements. *Sailing Small Boats*, for example, reveals his personal zeal, covering everything from the techniques of sailing, to boating safety, to actually building a life-size vessel. He says that he writes to please himself and enjoys illustrating and writing in areas which capture his interest; hence, many of his books concentrate on art and the artistic aspects of his topics. Weiss's nonfiction receives sporadic criticism for attempting to cover too much material and for not presenting enough information, but Weiss is usually admired for his exemplary style of handling his topics with creativity, clarity, and thoroughness and for inspiring his audience to build on the basis he presents and develop their own techniques. (See also *Contemporary Authors*, Vol. 5, rev. ed., and *Something about the Author*, Vol. 1)

GENERAL COMMENTARY

A major criterion for an activity book is that the instructions tell the reader exactly how to perform the activity. Harvey Weiss's arts and crafts books are clear in explaining procedures, and they encourage readers to use their own initiative.

Pencil, Pen, and Brush . . . has a sophisticated approach for a how-to-do-it book. Using the work of major artists, from Leonardo da Vinci to Maurice Sendak, as well as photographs for models, Weiss presents his instructions in easy steps, never talking down to his readers. Practical advice is given for each step, and readers are given suggestions for striking out on their

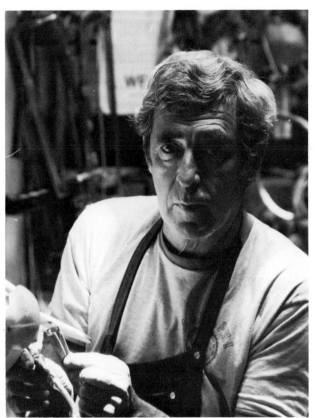

Courtesy of Harvey Weiss

own; the discussion ends on an encouraging note, with questions and suggestions. . . .

Weiss is always clear and explicit, moving from simple projects to more complicated ones; in *Model Cars and Trucks and How to Build Them* . . . , for example, the first model is a solid, one-piece racing car, and the last a large, intricate car that can be ridden. The same careful progression from the familiar and simple to the less familiar and intricate is evident in *How to Run a Railroad* . . . , a book on model trains.

Motors and Engines and How They Work . . . [is] an accurate and useful book for the child with a mechanical bent, and one that requires no previous knowledge.

Zena Sutherland, Dianne L. Monson, and May Hill Arbuthnot, ''Evaluating Informational Books: Harvey Weiss,'' in their Children & Books, part five, edited by Dorothy M. Broderick (copyright © 1947, 1957, 1964, 1972, 1977, 1981 by Scott Foresman and Company; reprinted by permission), sixth edition, Scott, Foresman, 1981, p. 463.

TWENTY-FOUR AND STANLEY (1956)

When twenty-five children try to rehabilitate a beached boat, the practiced reader of juvenile books automatically expects

219

them to work miracles. Not so with this story and therein lies the surprise and a considerable part of its appeal. . . . In both text and pictures Harvey Weiss catches all the urgency and the furious commotion among a gang of children engaged in a project of their own making.

As for the vociferous Stanley, he plays a rather anomalous role. He's too young to supply the beginning reader with a sense of self-identification yet, if not the hero, he is a focal character. Perhaps he'll remind the reader of that ever-present younger brother who tries so hard to stand up and be counted. In any case Stanley is so full of bounce that one is awfully glad when he succeeds.

> Ellen Lewis Buell, "The Boatmen," in The New York Times Book Review (© 1956 by The New York Times Company; reprinted by permission), June 10, 1956, p. 20.

CLAY, WOOD, AND WIRE; A HOW-TO-DO-IT BOOK OF SCULPTURE   (1956)

A book on sculpturing by an earnest and imaginative teacher of the art helps set a new standard in how-to-do-it books for youngsters by looking to the best in the field for its examples and closely allying it with the simple things one can make to begin with. Horses, lions, heads, figures and so forth—on to mobiles—these are the things in which Mr. Weiss instructs. Each section is laid out so as to give first something of the idea of sculpturing—its free form, the possibilities for interpreting one's surroundings. These are supplemented with examples of all kinds of art from the ancient Chinese to [Alexander] Calder and Henry Moore. Then comes doing it for oneself, and the process is simple and logical. With elementary materials—pipe cleaners for a horse and its movements, clay for a simple head, constructions done with odd bits around the house, wire and metal for mobiles—one can begin anywhere and basic instructions are clear and step-by-step. An excellent book to engender a feeling for art as a personal, interpretive matter and, with notes on the many pictures, an art book in itself.

> "Eight to Eleven: 'Clay, Wood, and Wire'," in Virginia Kirkus' Service, Vol. XXIV, No. 20, October 15, 1956, p. 789.

Written by a young sculptor, the artist-author stimulates the reader to do his own work in various simple materials by showing him more than fifty examples of some of the world's great sculpture. . . . Each series of examples is followed by step-by-step directions in making a simple object in the same general area. In some cases we feel that the instructions are a little too specific and may lead to verbatim imitation. There are clear directions (too clear at times) on making horses out of pipe cleaners, lions with plasticene, heads and figures out of clay, mobiles with cardboard and other materials, constructions out of cardboard and wood, masks from papier-mâché, cows out of plaster, carvings from wood, and so on. The book of 48 large pages is beautiful in design. It includes a bibliography and information about the museum examples used as illustrations. The approach is certainly unique. While it may seem to be a big jump from bronze examples to pipe cleaners and stone examples to plasticene, the author deserves a chance to see how well it works.

> D. Kenneth Winebrenner, "New Teaching Aids: 'Clay, Wood, and Wire'," in School Arts (reprinted with

permission of School of Arts), Vol. 56, No. 3, November, 1956, p. 45.

A GONDOLA FOR FUN   (1957)

Mr. Weiss's story about a gondolier's son who takes over his father's craft and rows a party of tourists right out to sea is overlong and rather monotonous. This is a pity, because the pictures of Venice have a wonderful exuberance that is all too rare in books for children.

> "PW Forecasts for Booksellers: 'A Gondola for Fun'," in Publishers Weekly (reprinted from the April 8, 1957 issue of Publishers Weekly, published by R. R. Bowker Company; copyright © 1957 by R. R. Bowker Company), Vol. 171, No. 14, April 8, 1957, p. 62.

Mario wanted very much to be allowed to row, but his father said, "Certainly not! A gondola is not for fun. A gondola is a serious thing. For us it is a business—not a thing of pleasure." But there came a day when Father fell overboard and Mario was suddenly forced to row. How he tried to prove himself a true gondolier as he continued the sightseeing trip makes a hilarious picture-storybook of the tall-tale variety most six- to ten-year-olds love.

> Jennie D. Lindquist, "Stories for the Younger Children: 'A Gondola for Fun'," in The Horn Book Magazine (copyrighted, 1957, by The Horn Book, Inc., Boston), Vol. XXXIII, No. 4, August, 1957, p. 298.

PAPER, INK, AND ROLLER; PRINT-MAKING FOR BEGINNERS (1958)

Art-interested young people from sixth graders to senior high students will find this a stimulating and informative book. The continuity from the simplest process to the more complex ones is excellent. Step-by-step directions are set forth in clear and interesting style and accompanied, appropriately, by illustrations made in the printing technique being described. Recommended for any library needing good books on subjects in the art field for junior and senior high school students.

> Elsa Berner and Frank L. Shupe, "Junior Libraries: 'Paper, Ink, and Roller; Print-making for Beginners'," in Library Journal (reprinted from Library Journal, December 15, 1957; published by R. R. Bowker Co. (a Xerox company); copyright © 1957 by Xerox Corporation), Vol. 83, No. 22, December 15, 1957, p. 44.

Harvey Weiss has chosen a more specific subject, **"Print-Making for Beginners,"** to follow his fine **"Clay, Wood, and Wire,"** but he, too, is urging his readers to enjoy, to experiment, while showing them how to achieve different effects. His book is divided into six parts explaining how to do press, transfer, potato, cardboard and linoleum prints and how to stencil, with a few comments on silk-screen printing, lithography and relief and intaglio work. Very simple step-by-step directions are given in each case with examples printed in black and red so the kind of results to be expected may be seen beforehand. These examples range from a bottle-cap impression and a crudely cut potato print to a Maurice Sendak rooster, linoleum prints from John and Clare Romano Ross' "Manhattan Island," and a [Henri] Matisse, a [James Abbott McNeill]

How To Make A Lion Out Of Plasticene

1. First get some plasticene. (You can get it in any art store.) Plasticene is a kind of clay that never dries up. It is strong and easy to manage, and you can use it over and over again.

2. To start your lion, you need a flat piece of wood for a base. A heavy piece of cardboard will do if you can't get wood. About 4 x 6 inches is a good size.

3. Make four balls of plasticene. These will be the legs. You'll find that the plasticene is hard and stiff if you use big lumps of it, but if you break off little pieces and squeeze them in your fingers a few times they will become soft and workable.

4. Make another, larger, longer ball and put it on top of the four legs. This will be the body. Make sure the legs are squeezed firmly into the body.

5. Then make another large oval ball for the head. Squeeze it on good and tight, or it may fall off later.

6. Here the fun begins. You have somewhat the shape of a lion. Now push and poke and squeeze and pinch. Add plasticene or take it away. Keep at it until your lion begins to look the way you want it to. Be bold. Get the graceful "sweep" of the back. Get the powerful, round chest and big, proud head. At first it may not look like a lion to anyone but you. But take your time about it, and keep trying until you begin to get what you want.

7. You are making a lion, and the thing about lions is that they roar. So let's make him roar. Just scoop out a big mouth. Put in his teeth. Now is he roaring? If you were making a hippopotamus instead of a lion, you would make him big and round and lumpy and heavy. If you were making a snake, you would make him thin and wriggly and squiggly. If you were making a wart hog, you would make him wrinkled and bumpy and warty and ugly. Every animal has some one special thing you will want to emphasize.

8. Last of all put in the smaller details, like eyes and ears and paws and tail. You can make the eyes just by poking a couple of holes in the head with the point of a pencil. A little ball of plasticene can make the nose. You can make the lion's mane with thin strips of plasticene stuck on, one on top of the other, all around the head.

9. When you think you're through with your lion, try holding him up against a strong light and look to see if he has a clean, definite outline or silhouette. Look at him from all sides. If he is bumpy and unsure, work on him some more.

If you feel that you would rather make your lion some other way—do it. Maybe you would rather have him sitting down, or yawning, or all curled up sleeping.

Or maybe you'd rather make an elephant, or an airplane, or a tugboat, or a kangaroo with a baby in its pouch, or a tiny mouse with big ears and a long tail.

If you like, you can make the lion out of clay instead of plasticene. But if you do, read the next chapter first, so you will know how to handle the clay.

From Clay, Wood, and Wire: A How-To-Do-It Book of Sculpture, *written and illustrated by Harvey Weiss.*

Whistler, an [Albrecht] Dürer. The special delight in this handsome book is the artistry of its design, the simplest prints arranged to make the pages beautiful so they are art lessons in themselves. It left us anxious to stop reviewing books and start print-making immediately.

> *"Art Is Fun," in* New York Herald Tribune *(© I.H.T. Corporation; reprinted by permission), November 2, 1958, p. 9.**

A welcome, basic how-to book, strikingly illustrated to make it not only helpful but interesting to look at page by page as it explains processes of hand printing. Very young children may print by the simple methods of press (one's finger is a press) or transfer (as of leaves and grasses), and even by raw potato or stencil. For the more deft are cardboard, linoleum, woodcut, and silk screen work. Lithography, engraving, and etching are only briefly, though understandably, introduced. Prints in richly varying tones of red, black, and gray illustrate each step and provide examples of striking effects to be achieved when patterns are moved or printed in different colors or on different kinds of paper. Comparisons of the results of different techniques may be clearly seen from the picture of a goat printed by each process. . . . A bibliography for older young people is appended.

> *Virginia Haviland, "Christmas Booklist: 'Paper, Ink, and Roller; Print-Making for Beginners'," in* The Horn Book Magazine *(copyright, 1958, by the Horn Book, Inc., Boston), Vol. XXXIV, No. 6, December, 1958, p. 476.*

PAUL'S HORSE, HERMAN (1958)

This story of a lackadaisical horse with a straw hat, illustrated with whimsical drawings by the author, sustains comic force throughout, and never departing from the realm of possibility, it moves brightly along the brink of hilarious nonsense.

> *"'Paul's Horse, Herman'," in* Virginia Kirkus' Service, *Vol. XXVI, No. 11, June 1, 1958, p. 380.*

A delightfully humorous, ridiculous story. . . . It is interesting to note that one of the boys, a Negro, is part of the group, and his relationship with the other children is natural and real. This is what we need in intercultural books.

> *"Junior Books Appraised: 'Paul's Horse, Herman'," in* Junior Libraries, *an appendix to* Library Journal *(reprinted from the September, 1958 issue of* Junior Libraries, *published by R. R. Bowker Co./A Xerox Corporation; copyright © 1958), Vol. 5, No. 1, September, 1958, p. 52.*

Few children can own a horse, but they go right on wishing that they could—and reading about luckier children who do.

From Paul's Horse, Herman, *written and illustrated by Harvey Weiss.*

Readers of Harvey Weiss' tale, **"Paul's Horse, Herman,"** will have some good laughs about Herman, a tired work horse who is not exactly the answer to a boy's dream—plus some ideas of their own on how to wake him up. . . . The situations are at times forced and not as convincing as in Mr. Weiss' **"Gondola for Fun,"** but Herman, who emerges as a worthy creature, will be remembered with affection.

> *Alice Low, "6-9: For Those Who Read and Those Who Are Read To," in* The New York Times Book Review *(© 1958 by The New York Times Company; reprinted by permission), November 2, 1958, p. 44.**

THE EXPEDITIONS OF WILLIS PARTRIDGE (1960)

An amusing picture book in which a small boy on his way to school imagines that he is a series of glamorous characters having all kinds of exciting adventures. It may be just a bit overdone, but children with lively imaginations will enjoy it. The pictures are brightly colored and so full of action that they almost seem about to leap from the pages.

> *"PW Forecasts: 'The Expeditions of Willis Partridge'," in* Publishers Weekly *(reprinted from the October 31, 1960 issue of* Publishers Weekly, *published by R. R. Bowker Company; copyright © 1960 by R. R. Bowker Company), Vol. 178, No. 18, October 31, 1960, p. 54.*

Although still quite young, Willis Partridge lives his own secret Walter Mitty-ish life and, being a boy of imagination, it is a dizzy one. . . . Harvey Weiss details all [his] exploits, switching back and forth from daily routine to the higher life, in a matter-of-fact style and in spirited pictures, and since there is no malice or ridicule, small boys ought to enjoy his good-humored kidding.

> *Ellen Lewis Buell, "The Hero," in* The New York Times Book Review *(© 1961 by The New York Times Company; reprinted by permission), February 5, 1961, p. 38.*

The "conspicuous gaps of consciousness—a sort of faraway look," often noticed in children by the observant Harvey Weiss, have inspired a [thoroughly] engaging book and daydreaming hero with whom small boys are sure to identify. . . .

His mother, the cop on the corner, and his teacher may be unaware of Willis' heroic secret life, but readers will love sharing it in story and bright colored, hilarious pictures.

> *Polly Goodwin, "The Junior Bookshelf: 'The Expeditions of Willis Partridge'," in* Chicago Tribune *(© 1961 Chicago Tribune), February 19, 1961, p. 10.*

It is fairly difficult to sort out from the pictures the real and the imaginary, heroic lives of Willis going on at the same time. The idea is not one that children are likely to enjoy. It is too near the bone. Every child imagines him or herself [as a] hero or heroine. To have a grown-up putting this private ploy into pictures, into a book, is surely too embarassing for any Mittyish child to accept.

The author-artist, Harvey Weiss, has made an easy miscalculation, like those who put real baby sayings and real funny ways of children into stories *for* children. The popular heroes of children's fiction will always be those who perform not as children really do but as children like to think of themselves as doing. (p. xiv)

> *"Big Flat Country: New Decorations Demand New Ideas," in* The Times Literary Supplement *(© Times Newspapers Ltd. (London) 1961; reproduced from* The Times Literary Supplement *by permission), No. 3118, December 1, 1961, pp. xiv-xv.**

PENCIL, PEN, AND BRUSH DRAWING FOR BEGINNERS (1961)

A very useful book for children who like to draw and want to improve their skills. Mr. Weiss is concerned chiefly with teaching young artists to observe their subjects. . . . The child who uses this book will emerge with a heightened awareness of the quality of the paintings and drawings that he sees.

> *"PW Forecasts: 'Pencil, Pen, and Brush'," in* Publishers Weekly *(reprinted from the May 8, 1961, issue of* Publishers Weekly, *published by R. R. Bowker Company; copyright © 1961 by R. R. Bowker Company), Vol. 179, No. 19, May 8, 1961, p. 45.*

[This is] the third of Harvey Weiss' introductory books on the techniques of art—the previous ones were the excellent **"Clay, Wood, and Wire"** and **"Paper, Ink, and Roller."** Here again the artist-author suggests how one might go about representing an object or an idea, gives some hints on procedure (composition, use of pencil, pen and ink, wash, tones or color) and then stimulates the young artist further by arranging fine examples of great artists' work to inspire him. The sections of the book deal rapidly (almost too rapidly, for there is material for many books here) with the drawing of animals, figures, heads, landscapes, scenes, and with experimentation in different methods and in abstract design. A few photographs are shown as models, and a variety of interesting examples of the work of Maurice Sendak and Joe Lasker, modern illustrators, as well as drawings of the great masters like [Jacopo Robusti] Tintoretto, [Leonardo] da Vinci, [Pablo] Picasso, [Albrecht] Dürer and others, some rather too small and crowded to be effective.

> *Margaret Sherwood Libby, "Great Variety in Honor Books," in* New York Herald Tribune *(© I.H.T. Corporation; reprinted by permission), May 14, 1961, p. 3.**

[Mr. Weiss] shows how other artists have found the quality [of the object drawn] that seemed special to them. So his book is an appreciation course as well as an entertaining drawing lesson with examples from [Edgar] Degas, [Paul] Klee, Leonardo [da Vinci], as well as from children's book illustrators. Clear advice on how to use a pencil, chalk, charcoal, color washes and ink will send the most casual doodlers eight years old and older running for their drawing paper. Mr. Weiss knows how to draw, how to explain, how to spread enthusiasm.

> *Pamela Marsh, "Widening Horizons for Children: 'Pencil, Pen, and Brush Drawing for Beginners',"* in The Christian Science Monitor *(reprinted by permission from* The Christian Science Monitor; *© 1961 The Christian Science Publishing Society; all rights reserved), June 22, 1961, p. 7.*

STICKS, SPOOLS, AND FEATHERS   (1962)

Among the many books planned to aid and inspire children and those who work with them in drawing, sculpture, graphics and other imaginative activities with their hands, our favorites are those by Harvey Weiss. **"Pencil, Pen, and Brush," "Paper, Ink, and Roller"** and **"Clay, Wood, and Wire"** eschew all facile talk about creativity and art and set the children free to be imaginative and original by guiding them in the choice of materials, giving precise and extremely helpful information on techniques and showing them a few models. The latest in the series shows how many miscellaneous objects can be used to make things of beauty. First, brief directions for nailing, using screws, and dowels, gluing, sandpapering and painting are given. Then with pictures, photographs and step-by-step instructions, beginners are shown exactly how to make a stick tower, a model locomotive, a totem pole, spool people, wooden animals, a tightrope walker, paper-made hats and even how to weave or make a simple electric motor that works and a naval cannon that shoots. Finally a brief discussion of collage ends a most helpful, stimulating book which insists that "there is no limit to the imagination."

> *Margaret Sherwood Libby, "Books for Boys and Girls: Sticks, Spools, and Feathers," in* New York Herald Tribune *(© I.H.T. Corporation; reprinted by permission), October 7, 1962, p. 14.*

Many handicraft books offer projects which can only be classed as "busy work"; Mr. Weiss, here as in his previous books on block printing and sculpture, suggests projects of lasting value. He emphasizes techniques and methods which can be applied in many ways and which encourage the use of the maker's own ideas and imagination. . . . Directions are clear, illustrations excellent.

> *Margaret Warren Brown, "Christmas Booklist: 'Sticks, Spools, and Feathers'," in* The Horn Book Magazine *(copyright ©1962, by The Horn Book, Inc., Boston), Vol. 38, No. 6, December, 1962, p. 615.*

CERAMICS: FROM CLAY TO KILN   (1964)

Ceramic techniques are presented so well that one wishes to begin at once on some clay pieces of his own. Basic processes, from clay preparation through work with tiles, slabs, coils, and figure-shaping to glazing and firing, are explained with clear, step-by-step text and drawings. Limitations and difficulties are indicated; a small bit on using a potter's wheel is included. Each section is introduced with fine photographs of simple, choice ceramic pieces that exemplify the particular technique to be described for making bowls, animals, heads, and so on. An artful combination of instruction and inspiration for beginners of ten years and up.

> *Priscilla L. Moulton, "Arts and Crafts: 'Ceramics: From Clay to Kiln'," in* The Horn Book Magazine *(copyright ©1965, by The Horn Book, Inc., Boston), Vol. XLI, No. 1, February, 1965, p. 64.*

A very good book for the beginner. The explanations and the illustrations are clear, the progression of difficulty well-paced. Mr. Weiss strikes a nice balance between detailed, step-by-step instruction and an encouragement of experimentation and creativity. He suggests simple equipment and modest designs, but suggests to the reader that the more complicated procedures should be understood; the reader is referred, for example, to textbooks on glazing, although the method for adding a simple glaze is given.

> *Zena Sutherland, "New Titles for Children and Young People: 'Ceramics: From Clay to Kiln'," in* Bulletin of the Center for Children's Books *(reprinted by permission of The University of Chicago Press; copyright 1965 by the University of Chicago), Vol. 19, No. 4, December, 1965, p. 71.*

PAINT, BRUSH, AND PALETTE   (1966)

In this brief book there is a great deal of information that will be useful to the beginning student and the beginning teacher as well. Painting is approached through experimentation with basic design problems and fundamental techniques. The uses of color and form are discussed in a clear, well-organized manner. The book is well illustrated with diagrams and excellent reproductions. It should have definite appeal at the secondary level.

> *Allan T. Marsh, "Junior Books Appraised: 'Paint, Brush, and Palette'," in* School Library Journal, *an appendix to* Library Journal *(reprinted from the October, 1966 issue of* School Library Journal, *published by R. R. Bowker Co./A Xerox Corporation; copyright © 1966), Vol. 13, No. 2, October, 1966, p. 5257.*

It's a clear call to the colors from the master of mixed media (***Sticks, Spools, and Feathers; Clay, Wood, and Wire***); it's a simple text on traditional methods of painting which does not require a progressive school or a progressive parent in the background. Mr. Weiss covers the subject of color (and covers the pages with full-color illustrations); he shows how shapes and forms influence color and are influenced by it; he instructs on the use of various painting materials. Step-by-step demonstrations, starting from a photograph, explore the multiple possibilities of a single subject. This is a do-it-yourself, see-it-yourself approach that starts with the rules and ends with the imagination. Integral illustrations that demonstrate concepts as well as methods give it an edge over many painting manuals.

"Eleven to Thirteen—Non-Fiction: 'Paint, Brush, and Palette'," in Virginia Kirkus' Service *(copyright © 1966 Virginia Kirkus' Service, Inc.), Vol. XXXIV, No. 21, November 1, 1966, p. 1144.*

["**Paint, Brush, and Palette**"] will delight any beginning artist. Harvey Weiss always turns a clean bright light on any kind of creative work he presents, from Pottery to Printmaking, a light that illuminates the obvious—and beyond. . . . It shines bright on "**Paint, Brush, and Palette**."

"Children's Books: 'Paint, Brush, and Palette'," in Publishers Weekly *(reprinted from the December 5, 1966 issue of* Publishers Weekly, *published by R. R. Bowker Company; copyright © 1966 by R. R. Bowker Company), Vol. 190, No. 23, December 5, 1966, p. 67.*

THE BIG CLEANUP   (1967)

[For] boys, Harvey Weiss depicts a familiar chore in "**The Big Cleanup**" . . . , and gives them the reasons for never throwing out a hoard of junk. Peter tries to weed out his, but being a Walter Mitty j.g., everything—from the rusty spark plug to the radio run over by a truck—stays, essential to his dreams. Almost as tedious as cleaning up your room, the story is saved by a glimmer of imaginativeness and the lighthearted abandon in the illustrations.

Margaret F. O'Connell, "Stories, Ages 6 to 9: 'The Big Cleanup'," in The New York Times Book Review *(© 1967 by The New York Times Company; reprinted by permission), May 7, 1967, p. 51.*

Once again Harvey Weiss reveals a sympathetic understanding of small boys' preoccupation with hoarding in a very funny book. From parents it will evoke wry chuckles, and children will identify happily with Peter's efforts to dispose of what his mother sternly called the mess in his room. . . . The author's merry illustrations reflect the humor and imagination of the text.

Polly Goodwin, "Children's Book World: 'The Big Cleanup'," in Book World—The Washington Post *(© 1967 Postrib Corp; reprinted by permission of* Chicago Tribune *and* The Washington Post), *October 29, 1967, p. 20.*

SAILING SMALL BOATS   (1967)

This book should fill the growing need to supply youngsters with a well-planned introduction to the sport of sailing. Beginning with a simple but clear explanation of historical back-

Notice in the illustration below how different the cube appears in different lights. And see how the ball can appear as either a simple flat circle or a solid heavy object, depending on where the light comes from.

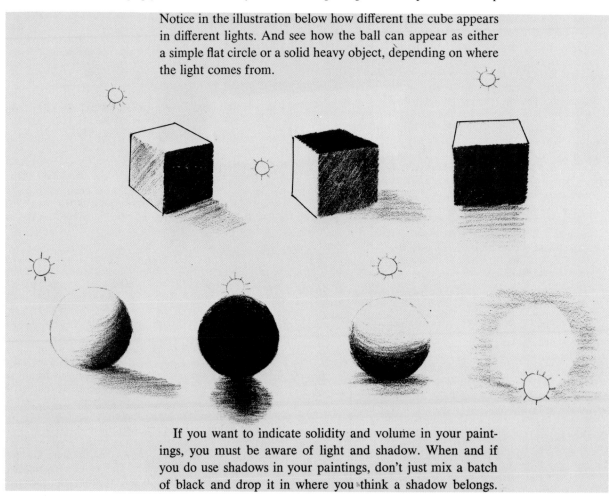

If you want to indicate solidity and volume in your paintings, you must be aware of light and shadow. When and if you do use shadows in your paintings, don't just mix a batch of black and drop it in where you think a shadow belongs.

From Paint, Brush, and Palette, *written and illustrated by Harvey Weiss.*

ground and the scientific principles underlying this form of transportation, the reader is drawn into a series of simple experiments which clarify the mysteries of flotation, stability, movement, control, and basic construction. Instructions are given for building a model sailboat which include nomenclature and the effects of rudder and set of sail. The next stage is the construction of a full-sized sailboard. Many well chosen diagrams and photographs amplify the clearly written step-by-step procedures outlined. When boat prices are considered, enthusiastic young readers might well undertake the building of their own boats. This beautifully printed and illustrated volume should prove to be a valuable passport to an exciting pastime.

> *Oscar Wright, "The Book Review: 'Sailing Small Boats'," in* School Library Journal, *an appendix to* Library Journal *(reprinted from the January, 1968 issue of* School Library Journal, *published by R. R. Bowker Co./A Xerox Corporation; copyright © 1968), Vol. 14, No. 5, January, 1968, p. 91.*

It's now April, time for fitting out your boat and polishing up your sailing skill. Harvey Weiss, an artist and seasoned sailor, here offers the novice an inviting and helpful handbook on the handling of small boats. Though it is difficult enough to teach a landlubber the mysteries of sailing when he's on board, it is much harder on shore to instruct him through the printed word. This, however, is what the author has accomplished in direct, unfrilled language and many clear diagrams. . . . There's also a brief sailor's vocabulary as well as complete instructions on how to build your own sailboat and, once you get it out on the water, sound advice on getting under sail.

> *Holger Lundbergh, "For Young Readers: 'Sailing Small Boats'," in* The New York Times Book Review *(© 1968 by The New York Times Company; reprinted by permission), April 7, 1968, pp. 26, 28.*

HOW TO BE A HERO   (1968)

An inventive game book that poses a series of fantastic, though sometimes possible, situations, along with several alternative solutions so readers may check their hero-potential against their ability to select the correct answers. Clever cartoon-like illustrations in watercolor heighten the absurdity of each incident, and a simply stated moral points out its relevancy to everyday conduct. Although similar in approach to Sesyle Joslin's *What Do You Say, Dear?* this title will appeal to older readers.

> *Barbara S. Miller, "The Book Review: 'How to Be a Hero'," in* School Library Journal, *an appendix to* Library Journal, *(reprinted from the September, 1968 issue of* School Library Journal, *published by R. R. Bowker Co./ A Xerox Corporation; copyright © 1968), Vol. 15, No. 1, September, 1968, p. 142.*

MOTORS AND ENGINES AND HOW THEY WORK   (1969)

By means of photographs and cleverly-executed drawings, the term "engine" is explained as "a machine that changes one form of energy into another form that can produce mechanical work." Each type of motor or engine is described briefly in terms of the mechanical principles involved: water wheels, windmills, sails, gravity machines (pile drivers and a grandfather's clock, for example), spring-wound engines, steam engines, steam turbines, electric motors, gasoline engines, diesel engines, jet and rocket engines, and solar engines. There are instructions for making simple working models of many of the engines. The simple introductory descriptions will make the student's later introduction, by other more detailed books, to physical mechanics more lucid. It is a fundamental book for science-minded youngsters.

> *"Mechanical Engineering: 'Motors and Engines and How They Work'," in* Science Books *(copyright © 1969 by the American Association for the Advancement of Science), Vol. 5, No. 1, May, 1969, p. 68.*

Mr. Weiss brings to this book about technology the same clarity of writing that has made his beginning art books . . . so popular. Informative, well-captioned drawings and diagrams, and clear photographs, complement Weiss's discussions. . . . The author charts the history of machinery and thus, in a minor way, of man's progress. From the first definition of an engine to the last speculation that man may yet harness tides or falling snow in his never-ending demands for power, Mr. Weiss describes each engine with authority, lucidity, humor—and fondness. Including do-it-yourself projects for readers, this is a fine follow-up to [Thomas] Aylesworth's *It Works Like This* (Doubleday, 1968) and a good lead into [John D.] Michel's *Small Motors You Can Make* (Van Nostrand, 1963).

> *Barbara Korn, "The Book Review: 'Motors and Engines'," in* School Library Journal, *an appendix to* Library Journal *(reprinted from the October, 1969 issue of* School Library Journal, *published by R. R. Bowker Co./A Xerox Corporation; copyright © 1969), Vol. 16, No. 2, October, 1969, p. 145.*

COLLAGE AND CONSTRUCTION   (1970)

Sensible advice on materials and techniques, firm adherence to esthetic precepts, and a broad spectrum of media make this a better-than-most book on art experience. While some of the suggestions are quite concrete, most advance ideas about concentrating on realism, or abstract form, or a theme, or simply on contrast of texture or shape. The writing is informal, serious, and encouraging, and the media discussed include box pictures, paper collage, wire sculpture, and string pictures.

> *Zena Sutherland, "Children's Books for Spring: 'Collage and Construction'," in* Saturday Review *(copyright © 1970 by* Saturday Review; *all rights reserved; reprinted by permission), Vol. 53, No. 19, May 9, 1970, p. 46.*

The seventh book in Weiss's [Beginning Artist's Library] series develops his **Sticks, Spools, and Feathers** . . . motif into a more specific art. Collages and constructions (solid, three-dimensional collages) are determined by the materials available and are limited only by the imagination and confidence of the creator. The explicit, persuasive text is clearly illustrated with black-and-white, or sepia photographs of amateur and professional productions. Young practitioners will be emboldened to create; teachers will find the book idea-filled; and hoarders of odd bits and pieces will find a raison d'etre.

> *Leone R. Hemenway, "The SLJ Book Review: 'Collage and Construction'," in* Library Journal *(reprinted from* Library Journal, *June 15, 1970; published by R. R. Bowker Co. (a Xerox company); copyright © 1970 by Xerox Corporation), Vol. 95, No. 12, June 15, 1970, p. 2310.*

THE GADGET BOOK   (1971)

Not just another step-by-step guide, this book of 24 gadgets to make from simple materials will definitely inspire readers to tinker. The emphasis is on having fun, with only incidental discussion of the scientific principles involved. Nevertheless, all necessary details are included—e.g., there is a particularly succinct explanation of working with electricity. Instructions are given for making a lighthouse, water clock, flashlight, muscle-coordination tester, cigar-box guitar, letter holder, etc. Weiss also encourages reader initiative by supplying suggestions for individual application of and variations on the projects. Illustrations are big, clear and well correlated with the text; print is large enough to make direction-following easy. This unusual, stimulating title, with its gadgets "both useful and useless," can complement such books as [Robert Emmett] Mueller's *Inventor's Notebook*. . . .

> *Shirley Smith, "The Book Review: 'The Gadget Book'," in* School Library Journal, *an appendix to* Library Journal *(reprinted from the November, 1971 issue of* School Library Journal, *published by R. R. Bowker Co./A Xerox Corporation; copyright © 1971), Vol. 18, No. 3, November, 1971, p. 119.*

Here is a delightful collection of fun projects for kids who like to tinker. The gadgets are described, well illustrated by line drawings, and are all based upon the application of one or more scientific principles. . . . The science is in this book if you look for it. But first and foremost, *The Gadget Book* is a technological reference for children in their own world. Grownups keep out! Average fourth graders can probably handle the text, although the illustrations are really the basis of the book. What is needed, however, is an ability on the part of the child to translate the two-dimensional diagrams into three-dimensional structures. Completion of any of the gadgets in this book will certainly provide practice in this skill.

> *Thomas A. Butler, "Children's Science Books Review: 'The Gadget Book'," in* Appraisal: Science Books for Young People *(copyright © 1972 by the Children's Science Book Review Committee), Vol. 5, No. 2, Spring, 1972, p. 39.*

The author, believing that "the fun of a gadget comes not only from using it, but from putting it together," presents basic instructions for various gadgets . . . but leaves many problems for the young inventor to solve. While allowing room for creative genius, the book carefully describes many intriguing projects.

> *"Early Spring Booklist: 'The Gadget Book'," in* The Horn Book Magazine *(copyright © 1972 by The Horn Book, Inc., Boston), Vol. 48, No. 2, April, 1972, p. 166.*

The Gadget Book offers starting help and background principles rather than detailed instructions for making twenty-four objects—games, flashlight, burglar alarm, guitar. The objects are likely to be enjoyable to make but of limited practical value. . . . All good fun for someone with a scientific bent.

> *"Starters Science: 'The Gadget Book'," in* The Times Literary Supplement *(© Times Newspaper Ltd. (London) 1974; reproduced from* The Times Literary Supplement *by permission), No. 3760, March 29, 1974, p. 336.*

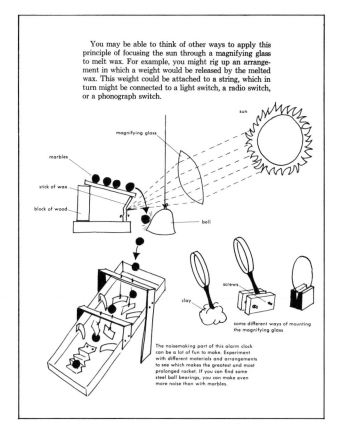

From The Gadget Book, *written and illustrated by Harvey Weiss.*

LENS AND SHUTTER; AN INTRODUCTION TO PHOTOGRAPHY (1971)

Lens and Shutter, whose author is a well-known sculptor who has written similar books for beginners in the arts from collage to pottery, surveys the technique and samples the art in an open, brief text accompanied by many splendid photographs: from the Matthew Brady cameramen to Walker Evans, from the Canyon de Chelly to a frog worriedly clinging to a pencil. Weiss seeks to tell what makes good pictures no less than how to mix Dektol. The result is a good overall treatment for any would-be beginner, complete with the worthwhile hint to buy your gear at a specialized camera shop, where you can make friends with people who can aid you. Schools, clubs and young readers who are on the brink of photography will find the book a real help. Its technical directions are clear and honest; they probably fall just short of providing enough detail to enable anyone to do it all without further advice. (p. 110)

> *Philip Morrison and Phylis Morrison, "Books about Science for the Young Reader: An Annual Christmas Survey," in* Scientific American *(copyright © 1971 by Scientific American, Inc.; all rights reserved), Vol. 225, No. 6, December, 1971, pp. 106-15.**

[An] excellent introduction to the craft and art of photography. Clarity of expression, logical and imaginative organization, and a wealth of illustration contribute to the effectiveness of this presentation. The beginning section on the camera, although fairly brief, is particularly lucid. Throughout the book, as processes and materials are described, enough essential background is supplied so that the beginner can understand not only what is taking place—but even more important to his development as a photographer—exactly why it is taking place. Creative techniques for photographic expression of many kinds of interests make up a substantial portion of the book. . . . A chapter on darkroom techniques concludes the attractive and stimulating book. (pp. 63-4).

> *Beryl Robinson, "Arts and Crafts: 'Lens and Shutter; An Introduction to Photography',"* in The Horn Book Magazine *(copyright © 1972 by The Horn Book, Inc., Boston), Vol. 48, No. 1, February, 1972, pp. 63-4.*

HOW TO MAKE YOUR OWN MOVIES; AN INTRODUCTION TO FILMMAKING (1973)

An introduction to the craft of movie-making that is comprehensive enough to give a novice an understanding of the ways and means of making a film. Written simply and clearly by an author who has a string of craft books to his credit, the book could easily be used by grade-school children.

> *Sidney D. Long, "Early Spring Booklist: 'How to Make Your Own Movies; An Introduction to Film-making',"* in The Horn Book Magazine *(copyright © 1974 by The Horn Book, Inc., Boston), Vol. L, No. 2, April, 1974, p. 166.*

SHIP MODELS AND HOW TO BUILD THEM (1973)

With characteristic clarity Weiss instructs beginners in the construction of a few basic models that are "not scientifically exact reproductions of any particular boat." There is a tugboat that can be modified to make a fireboat or fishing boat (modification is encouraged provided there is "some experimental testing in a bathtub"), a simple sailboat with the same type of hull, a Mississippi stern-wheeler propelled with rubber band, a working submarine, and a powerboat that calls for an electric motor (available at hobby shops for under a dollar). There is the usual prefatory rundown on materials and tools (if you don't have all of them, "remember what a beaver can do with just his teeth"), a chapter on hollowing out a hull, and in the end a few diagrams of particular vessels without detailed instructions, for those who are ready to proceed on their own. Trim, bilge-free and watertight.

> *"Younger Non-Fiction: 'Ship Models and How to Build Them',"* in Kirkus Reviews *(copyright © 1973 The Kirkus Service, Inc.), Vol. XLI, No. 17, September 1, 1973, p. 971.*

For beginning model builders who are interested in ships, this provides a good basic understanding of tools and materials and their correct use. . . . Instructions are combined with drawings and photographs to make this an easy course for would-be naval architects.

> *Ann D. Schweibish, "The Book Review: 'Ship Models and How to Build Them',"* in School Library Journal, *an appendix to* Library Journal *(reprinted from the January, 1974 issue of* School Library Journal, *published by R. R. Bowker Co./A Xerox Corporation; copyright © 1974), Vol. 20, No. 5, January, 1974, p. 54.*

A useful elementary book . . . on model-making which should give the beginner some useful hints to set him on the right track. . . . Instructions are given for making hollow hulls,

more advanced power-driven and sailing models and a submersible submarine. Plans are easy to follow.

I am not keen on the statement 'Never mind that your model of the *HMS Bounty* may have only two masts whereas the original had three.' I do not quarrel with the thought behind it: the aim is to produce a model which has character and works well. But if it is named it should be as accurate as possible—and children will be the first to agree.

> *Rowland Purton, "'Ship Models and How to Build Them',"* in The School Librarian, *Vol. 24, No. 3, September, 1976, p. 260.*

HOW TO MAKE YOUR OWN BOOKS (1974)

More concise and accessible than [Susan] Purdy's *Books for You to Make*, . . . this also represents a more general approach to creating a book, with instructions for selecting paper, cutting, folding, binding and glueing, adding covers and hand lettering followed by suggestions for types of books to make—diaries, albums, comic books, etc. Unintimidating and easy to follow.

> *"Younger Non-Fiction: 'How to Make Your Own Books',"* in Kirkus Reviews *(copyright © 1974 The Kirkus Service, Inc.), Vol. XLII, No. 13, July 1, 1974, p. 686.*

After a brief introduction gets readers of all ages involved. the author breaks his own book into two parts: Part One on **"How It's Done,"** covering kinds of paper, size, thickness, cutting and folding, stapling and sewing, gluing, making covers, writing and printing; and Part Two on **"Books You Can Make,"** which illustrates and provides instructions for just about everything you can think of, from travel journals to nonsense books, and some excellent examples of experimental formats. An unusual book, and unusually good. (pp. 24-5)

> *Ralph Fabri, "Art Books: 'How to Make Your Own Books',"* in American Artist *(copyright © 1974 by Billboard Publications, Inc.), Vol. 38, No. 389, December, 1974, pp. 24-5.*

A useful, practical, do-it-yourself book likely to arouse the enthusiasm of most lively-minded youngsters for making 'personal one-of-a-kind books'. The author's introduction explains his purpose and his method. . . . The ground covered by [the] second part is wide. . . . The copious illustrations are as clear and as sensible as the text—though most readers would find difficulty in trying to cut a large sheet of paper in precisely the way shown on page 10.

> *S. G. Colverson, "Eleven to Fifteen: 'How to Make Your Own Books',"* in The School Librarian, *Vol. 24, No. 4, December, 1976, p. 356.*

MODEL CARS AND TRUCKS AND HOW TO BUILD THEM (1974)

No expertise is needed to follow the clear and comprehensive step-by-step directions in an excellent book for the beginning hobbyist of any age. Weiss describes the tools and materials needed, giving advice on using them, and he stresses the fact that the reader need not adhere rigidly to details of projects shown in the book. Instructions are given for a variety of models: racing cars, trucks, tractors, derricks, and even a large model that can be ridden. There are separate chapters on special techniques, such as making wheels or finishing and painting. Photographs and diagrams are well-placed and informative. A very model of a model guide.

> Zena Sutherland, "New Titles for Children and Young People: 'Model Cars and Trucks and How to Build Them'," in Bulletin of the Center for Children's Books (reprinted by permission of The University of Chicago Press; © 1975 by The University of Chicago), Vol. 28, No. 8, April, 1975, p. 139.

It is both encouraging and delightful to read in the introduction that "the cars and trucks described in this book are really most enjoyable in their own right . . . not because they are a substitute for or imitation of the real thing." The information in the first two chapters of the clearly written and easy-to-follow text—"The Tools and Materials," and "Finishing and Painting"—is of value for all kinds of projects in carpentry and wood finishing; and the third chapter, "How to Make the Wheels," concentrates on the dual problem of making wheels for and attaching them to model cars. . . . [The] final two chapters—"A Motor-Driven Model" and "A Large Model to Ride On"—further expand the scope of the model-car builder. The clear text is full of practical suggestions and reminders and is reinforced by the simple plans and drawings. The format of the book is comfortable and convenient, and the photographs of the finished models are a pleasure to behold. (pp. 157-58)

> Paul Heins, "Early Spring Booklist: 'Model Cars and Trucks and How to Build Them'," in The Horn Book Magazine (copyright © 1975 by the Horn Book, Inc., Boston), Vol. LI, No. 2, April, 1975, pp. 157-58.

GAMES AND PUZZLES YOU CAN MAKE YOURSELF (1976)

Directions for making more than three dozen games and puzzles are included in an attractively designed, meticulously detailed volume, which will appeal to hobbyists as well as to those who have exhausted the imaginative possibilities of commercial products. Because the instructions, in many cases, suggest alternative methods of construction, materials are readily available as standard household supplies or as leftover scraps from other projects; however, the more skilled enthusiast will find the book an equally valuable source for making distinctive and personalized gifts. Some of the games—Ticktacktoe and its three dimensional variant, for example—are familiar; others, such as Nine-Men's Morris, may be less well known; still others, such as Similarity, could be readily adapted for classroom use. And for baby-sitters, parents, scout leaders, or recreation directors, the easy, inexpensive suggestions for setting up action games—including a miniature golf course—offer instant relief. A versatile and practical guide. (pp. 172-73)

> Mary M. Burns, "Arts and Crafts: 'Games and Puzzles You Can Make Yourself'," in The Horn Book Magazine (copyright © 1977 by the Horn Book, Inc., Boston), Vol. LIII, No. 2, April, 1977, pp. 172-73.

With this in his suitcase any uncle can face visiting his nephews and nieces with equanimity. With only the simplest of materials he can construct 9 games and 10 puzzles.

Actually making the games will prove as much fun as subsequently playing them. Highly recommended.

> "The New Books: 'Games and Puzzles You Can Make Yourself'," in The Junior Bookshelf, Vol. 42, No. 1, February, 1978, p. 32.

HOW TO RUN A RAILROAD: EVERYTHING YOU NEED TO KNOW ABOUT MODEL TRAINS (1977)

Libraries still running on [Raymond Francis] Yates and [Harry] Zarchy will clear the track for the new Harvey Weiss—a typically careful, thorough, imaginative introduction to model railroading. Terminology and "locomotive anatomy" precede, so you'll know what he's talking about, and then it's over to the kinds of trains—O gauge, HO (aitch-o), N—and their advantages (in plain words, N "is a little too delicate and fussy" for many people), with a strong plug for freight over passenger models (more realistic-looking in a small layout, and far more interesting to operate). The electrical apparatus is explained, and instructions are given for attaching connectors, for switching and coupling. Best of all, predictably, is the discussion of laying the track and constructing the setting. Weiss recognizes that "a lot of people like to use . . . kits" ("They can be sure of accurate scale and correct detail") but of course he's not one of them: for his railroad, the NP & H (running between North Piddleton and Happenstance), he's built barns, stations, bridges, trestles, water tanks . . . and landscaped the layout so that it looks "truly realistic—a scaled-down version of some small part of the earth's surface!" Operating the line is a story in itself, with a scenario describing an extended freight operation. Subsequently Weiss adds a second, inner oval, allowing for the operation of two trains at a time (a friend can come over with "his or her" train), and then converts the whole setup into a wildly unrealistic, amusement-park-like complex. With everything clearly and precisely illustrated, the clean-cut layout of all Weiss craft books, and sufficient challenge to make model trains more than "merely toys which you'll quickly tire of."

> "Younger Non-Fiction: 'How to Run a Railroad: Everything You Need to Know about Model Trains'," in Kirkus Reviews (copyright © 1977 The Kirkus Service, Inc.), Vol. XLV, No. 15, August 1, 1977, p. 787.

In his usual meticulous fashion, Weiss gives a full and logically arranged sequence of facts about buying, building, and operating a model railroad. The diagrams are adequately labelled and are nicely placed in relation to textual references, and the writing is clear, informal, and authoritative. The text describes the several gauges and the advantages and disadvantages of each; gives advice about power packs, transformers, coupling and track plans; it leaves to the kits (about which Weiss also gives some suggestions) the directions for putting cars and engines together, but every aspect of assembling and running the whole system and of making such ancillary equipment as tunnels or mountains is explained.

> Zena Sutherland, "New Titles for Children and Young People: 'How to Run a Railroad'," in Bulletin of the Center for Children's Books (reprinted by permission of The University of Chicago Press; © 1978 by The University of Chicago), Vol. 31, No. 5, January, 1978, p. 88.

WHAT HOLDS IT TOGETHER (1977)

The author of several superior crafts books takes a novel cross-section approach in this introduction to joiners and fasteners of all sorts. In 48 pages that pop with corky incidental drawings, Weiss chats informatively about hammering nails and matching adhesives to the job at hand, and he touches on the basics of screws, bolts, rivets, soldering, and forging as well. Just to give the concept its due, some knots, sewing stitches, magnets, and suction cups are also thrown in. Put them all together and you have a few how-to tips, a few curious facts, a bit of nuts-and-bolts knowledge—and, more important, another way to look at a lot of things.

> *"Young Non-Fiction: 'What Holds It Together',"* in Kirkus Reviews *(copyright © 1977 The Kirkus Service, Inc.), Vol. XLV, No. 19, October 1, 1977, p. 1053.*

[Mr. Weiss] has illustrated his book himself, and, while some of the pictures are a little questionable for the practical-minded (see page 23 where a worker, balancing on a steel girder, holds in his bare hand a block against which a second worker hammers with a riveting machine!) for the most part it is explicit and informative. There is not a vital need for a book like this, but as an additional purchase or for a special project it is interesting, fun, and can be a source of considerable practical knowledge about the various methods of construction. There are experiments at the end of several chapters which are just right to do either in a classroom or at home. . . .

> *Heddie Kent, "What Holds It Together,"* in Appraisal: Science Books for Young People *(copyright © 1978 by the Children's Science Book Review Committee), Vol. 11, No. 2, Spring, 1978, p. 49.*

There are only a dozen or so basic ways in which the things we use are fastened together. . . . This excellent book covers most of them, and does so in a sprightly, interesting fashion. Simple, clear drawings on every page illustrate each topic in an entertaining and often amusing way. The result is a high-interest format that should lead every youngster who starts this book to finish it. Most chapters have a simple experiment that deals with some aspect of the topic. No index is provided or needed. Many alert young readers will detect one error: sea-level atmospheric pressure is about 15 pounds per square inch, not 32.

> *Norman F. Smith, "What Holds It Together,"* in Appraisal: Science Books for Young People *(copyright © 1978 by the Children's Science Book Review Committee), Vol. 11, No. 2, Spring, 1978, p. 49.*

Weiss is not only a successful writer, he is also an excellent illustrator who combines both talents to produce a lucid description of a very general topic. . . . A very nice feature is the nine, well-planned, inexpensive experiments, each illustrating one of the major subjects. The chapter on magnets could have been a bit more complete, but it still contains interesting information. This book is a must not only for those specifically interested in construction, but also for those of us who always wanted to know "what are those used for" or "how and why does one do this." **What Holds It Together** is also recommended as reference reading for any industrial arts related course from fifth grade through adult education. Light, enjoyable, practical and refreshing . . . well worth reading, even for those in levels below fifth grade.

> *Jason R. Taylor, "Technology (Applied Sciences): 'What Holds It Together',"* in Science Books & Films *(copyright © 1978 by the American Association for the Advancement of Science), Vol. XIV, No. 3, December, 1978, p. 184.*

WORKING WITH CARDBOARD AND PAPER (1978)

Another of the author's creative craft books, produced in a familiar format and containing clear directions in text and diagrams. Designs for such objects as mobiles, airplanes, and castles call for easily and inexpensively obtained materials. Of particular interest is the inclusion of instructions for making paper.

> *Virginia Haviland, "Non-Fiction: 'Working with Cardboard and Paper',"* in The Horn Book Magazine *(copyright © 1978 by The Horn Book, Inc., Boston), Vol. LIV, No. 4, August, 1978, p. 415.*

A competent introduction to the creation of models, sculpture, designs, and geometrics from cardboard and paper. Through crisp explanations and well-placed sketches and photos, Weiss offers basic skills while leaving room for individual creativity. Beginning with information on tools, types of paper, and cutting/scoring techniques, Weiss continues with suggestions for projects that are moderately difficult but rewarding. Most of the projects require patience, dexterity, and some sense of spatial relationships. Measurements and shapes are suggested through the illustrations, rather than being laid out in traceable patterns. Similar in tone and format to [John] Lidstone's *Building With Cardboard* (Van Nostrand Reinhold, 1968), this is a well organized, informative, and attractive treatment. . . .

> *Lynn S. Hunter, "Book Reviews: 'Working with Cardboard and Paper',"* in School Library Journal *(reprinted from the September, 1978 issue of School Library Journal, published by R. R. Bowker Co./ A Xerox Corporation; copyright © 1978), Vol. 25, No. 1, September, 1978, p. 151.*

MODEL BUILDINGS AND HOW TO MAKE THEM (1979)

An excellent introduction to an intriguing hobby. The book offers techniques for constructing different types of model buildings, including a dollhouse, a town house, a castle, and a cathedral. Divided into two parts—wood and cardboard construction—the text notes the relative difficulty of using wood. Photographs, diagrams, and explicit directions for the selection and use of tools and materials are included. Terms are carefully explained and described within the context of a particular project. Because the text is brief, the table of contents serves as an adequate index. Thoughtfully presented and logically designed, the volume should be useful for hobbyists as well as for the more casual reader whose curiosity has been piqued by the current interest in model building as an art form and as a means of re-creating the past. (pp. 551-52)

> *Mary M. Burns, "Fall Booklist: 'Model Buildings and How to Make Them',"* in The Horn Book Magazine *(copyright © 1979 by The Horn Book, Inc., Boston), Vol. LV, No. 5, October, 1979, pp. 551-52.*

In his typical casual but informative style, Weiss teaches the basics of making model buildings. . . . Weiss not only tells what can be used, but also explains why some methods and materials are preferable to others. Weiss' directions for model buildings begin with a simple cardboard structure and progress through increasingly sophisticated variations. Instructions for wood structures progress similarly, leading up to the construction of a dollhouse. Throughout, Weiss encourages individual creativity, stressing ways in which his plans can be varied. There is some overlap between this and Weiss' **Working with**

Cardboard and Paper . . . , but the narrower focus of ***Model Buildings*** allows for greater depth and detail. (pp. 156-57)

Lynn S. Hunter, "Book Reviews: 'Model Buildings'," in School Library Journal *(reprinted from the October, 1979 issue of* School Library Journal, *published by R. R. Bowker Co./ A Xerox Corporation; copyright © 1979), Vol. 26, No. 2, October, 1979, pp. 156-57.*

HOW TO BE AN INVENTOR   (1981)

The old-time, putzing-around inventor may have lost glamour to the laboratory scientist, but Weiss' latest freely structured how-to book is attractive enough to spark a revival. Weiss talks about both practical inventors (those who create devices to solve particular problems) and those who do it just for fun. He classes himself in the latter group, and shows some of his ingenious if perfectly worthless inventions, which include a steam-powered beckoning hand. Also pictured are inventions of da Vinci, sculptures by [Jean] Tinguely that fit Weiss' concept of useless inventions, a lot of crackpot devices (some of which were taken seriously by their inventors), and a more predictable sampling from [Thomas] Edison, [James] Watt, and their ilk.

"Younger Non-Fiction: 'How to Be an Inventor'," in Kirkus Reviews *(copyright © 1981 The Kirkus Service, Inc.), Vol. LXIX, No. 4, February 15, 1981, p. 217.*

A joyful and humorous discussion of the process of invention. Ranging from the sophisticated conceptions of Leonardo da Vinci to the zany improbabilities of Rube Goldberg, the author considers useful and practical as well as nonsensical and aesthetic possibilities. He discusses how to get started, suggests the making of models and drawings, cautions about the use of electrical equipment, and supplies lists of materials and devices. The photographs and diagrams supplement each other and at times reflect the humor of the text. In addition to a chapter on patents, there is also a short but lively section devoted to some inventors and their inventions. With a brief bibliography. (pp. 206-07)

Paul Heins, "Early Spring Booklist: 'How to Be an Inventor'," in The Horn Book Magazine *(copyright © 1981 by The Horn Book, Inc., Boston), Vol. LVII, No. 2, April, 1981, pp. 206-07.*

Kit Williams

1948-

British picture book author/illustrator for children. Williams's fantasy *Masquerade* is among the most controversial and popular children's books of recent years. It combines elements of myth and folklore with riddles in both text and illustration to create clues which, when deciphered, lead the reader to a buried treasure. *Masquerade* tells the story of the moon's love for the sun. She sends him a jewel as a token of her affection through her messenger, Jack Hare, who loses it on his journey through earth, air, fire, and water. It was up to the reader to find the spot where Jack Hare dropped the jewel, an 18-karat gold pendant crafted by Williams in the shape of Jack Hare himself. According to Williams, the treasure could have been found just as easily by a bright child of ten as by an Oxford don; however, the jewel was recently unearthed by a British design engineer.

A self-taught artist, Williams created his first book as an answer to a challenge to write and illustrate something totally original for children. While growing up he was often frustrated when treasures offered in advertisements proved false, so he created *Masquerade* "for my lost childhood." History, nature, logic, and ingenious constructions, which figure prominently in Williams's paintings, are used as the basis for the book; Williams chose its title to underscore the elements of fun, mystery, and changeability he sought to convey.

Readers were immediately fascinated by the challenge and the prize offered by *Masquerade*. Men, women, and children from around the world attempted to dig up the treasure, which Williams acknowledged was buried on public land somewhere within the British Isles. Critical reception, however, is mixed. The book's success is occasionally credited to the gimmickry of the prize rather than to its artistry. The complexity of some of the riddles and the underlying malevolence in some of the pictures have raised questions about *Masquerade*'s suitability for children. But the cleverness of Williams's text, the fascination of his illustrations, and, especially, the uniqueness of his concept have also been recognized, and the book has been a best-seller wherever it has appeared. Whether it retains its popularity, with the essential riddles solved and the prize claimed, has not yet been established.

MASQUERADE (1980; British edition, 1979)

Masquerade is a children's picture book that would certainly sell well in the normal way, on the strength of its illustrations if not of its rather crummy text. But the purchaser gets a sort of raffle-ticket too. . . .

Well, I wouldn't actually want that particular jewel, but no doubt it could be sold; so I, like everybody else into whose hands a copy will fall, have studied the volume with more than usual care. Ah, the cunning of the Williams plan! Not only do more people buy reproductions of his pictures but they look at them harder! And indeed they are admirably suited to their rôle, crowded with incident, symbolism, riddles, magic squares, double-vision, latent objects, all minutely and lovingly drawn with a high degree of technical skill. Some—for example, the opening, almost [Samuel] Palmer-like conjuration of nighted harvest-mice, a skeletal cratered moon and a hare-shaped hill—

are almost beautiful. But most are, to my mind, not pleasing at all.

Where the human figure enters, Kit Williams has as unfortunate a touch as [Walt] Disney in his different way. The almost trompe-l'oeil precision of figures anatomically unrealised, replete to every porcelain incisor and nylon hair, indeed even to every zip-tooth of the dandelion fairy's sexy rig, gives me that mal-de-mer in the presence of really bad art that corresponds to the notorious frisson in the presence of the good. There is a sort of glossy provincial satanism here, mish-mashed from [Arthur Rackham, Bernard Sleigh, Aleister Crowley, Randolph Caldecott, Richard] Doyle and the Birmingham School of Art, that turns the superficially sunny gemlike landscapes into frozen horrors—as if the pleasantness of this mortal veil was about to be twitched aside to reveal something really rather nasty, and really rather trivial too.

Anyway, I can see it won't be I who wins the golden hare. . . . It is not that I don't trust Mr. Williams's good faith: certainly that hare is buried somewhere. But I do distrust the quality of his mind, and hence the nature of the clues he has given. I don't know what astronomy one can expect of a "bright child of ten" but I suppose he might know that the heavenly twins were not of opposite sexes, and be disturbed at the moon plucking a jewel from 'a sea of clouds' on 'a perfect night, unclouded and still'. It is difficult, incidentally, to imagine how picture clues can identify a particular diggable square foot of British soil: my own considered suggestion is one yard down under the 18th hole at Sunningdale—and will the Greens Secretary please not write to me about that.

Hilary Corke, "Hare-Brained" (© British Broadcasting Corp. 1979; reprinted by permission of Hilary Corke), in The Listener, Vol. 102, No. 2642, December 20, 1979, p. 885.

The story of the journey is basically a traditional one, with characters such as the wise frog and the Penny-Pockets Lady. Some of the modern references—to early closing days and antique dealers—rather dilute the strength of it, but perhaps they play a part as clues? With this book one is never sure. The pictures, however, demonstrate why the author is a successful painter. They combine sharp, almost photographic realism with an undertone of horror. Even if this were all there is to Mr. Kit Williams's first children's book, it would be a fine effort.

But the clues scattered throughout the text and pictures belie the apparent simplicity of the story. Some are easy to solve (even a small child could find the hare hidden in each picture). A few are more difficult, but are clearly presented as riddles and number puzzles. And then there are others. But are they clues, or red herrings, or just part of the story? Each time one looks at a page more possibilities appear. (pp. 81-2)

Though definitely not a book for those who can't bear being teased, "Masquerade" could keep anyone else enjoyably puzzled for the whole 12 days of Christmas; with some healthy (and even profitable) exercise beyond. (p. 82)

JACK HARE JUMPS DOG ROSE BLUSHING PETALS TUMBLE UPON AIR IN HASTE TO CHASE

From Masquerade, *written and illustrated by Kit Williams.*

"Spadework," in The Economist *(© The Economist Newspaper Limited, 1979), Vol. 273, No. 7112, December 22, 1979, pp. 81-2.*

I am never likely to solve the puzzle in this extravagantly-praised book; it seems to me to need a Torquemada mind and an encyclopedic knowledge of myth and symbol. I must claim the right, then, to look at it as a picturebook, varied in style and provoking varied responses. The darkening landscape with which the book opens, with its exquisite gradation from foreground to background, its subtle twilight shades and rolling contours (one of them part of the conundrum, incidentally) is entirely satisfying to the eye. Move on to the next page, with its laboured triangular disposition of figures and elaborate deploying of zodiac symbol, and you find the eye obliged to work in a different way. A daffodil-girl as glossy as a lay-figure in a shop window is in one artistic manner: in another, a jointed wooden doll lies prone on a beach under a lurid setting sun in a chi-chi scene. If I deliberately ignore the artist's puzzle, I am intrigued by the puzzle of his artistry, with its odd mixture of almost vulgar magazine-illustration and serene traditional landscape. And what children will make of the book is the puzzle of the decade. (pp. 3660-61)

Margery Fisher, "Paper-Engineering: 'Masquerade'," in her Growing Point, *Vol. 18, No. 6, March, 1980, pp. 3660-61.*

[**Masquerade**] is not the ordinary children's book. . . . Kit Williams has risen from unsung painter to celebrity, and his book has replaced Scrabble as a family preoccupation.

This sudden popularity is partly due to the Britons' traditional interest in Lagomorpha, from the March Hare in [Lewis Carroll's] *Alice's Adventures in Wonderland* to the whole cast of [Richard Adams's] *Watership Down*. It may also be attributed to the book's Botticelliesque illustrations in which natural laws are suspended and the floating vistas of childhood are suffused with magic realism. But in the main, **Masquerade**'s phenomenal rise can be credited to that basic human characteristic: greed.

"Rabbit Run," in Time *(copyright 1980 Time Inc.; all rights reserved; reprinted by permission from* Time*), Vol. 115, No. 9, March 3, 1980, p. 83.*

If ever a book was predestined to sell out this is it.

Success in this case may have little to do with literature or even perhaps with art and everything to do with the universal lust for treasure. Behind all the publicity is a thin story told in enigmatic terms and crammed with riddles within riddles. The pictures are technically brilliant but they belong to a school of photo-realism which I find totally repellant. There never was a cleverer picture book; rarely have I seen one which I have been less inclined to love. (pp. 65-6)

"Picture Books: 'Masquerade'," in The Junior Bookshelf, *Vol. 44, No. 2, April, 1980, pp. 65-6.*

How can we explain such a *succès d'estime?* Plain, old-fashioned avariciousness is the obvious contender. . . . But I am inclined to think that there is more to it than mere cupidity, and that Kit Williams' . . . good fortune was to have hit on a way of harnessing an instinct more deeply innate even than gold lust. I refer, of course, to the remarkable appetite which humans appear to have for *puzzles* of all descriptions. . . .

John Naughton, "Pulling the Strings: 'Masquerade'," in Encounter *(© 1980 by Encounter Ltd.), Vol. LIV, No. 6, June, 1980, p. 54.*

Evaluation [of *Masquerade*] is difficult. The book's success is based on the pictures and the hidden amulet rather than on the text. Various adjectives spring to mind: pretentious, ingenious, nasty, fascinating, peculiar, brilliant, phoney, memorable. It is all these things, and should therefore be available in every school library where it will extend children's notions of what a picture book can be like.

Aidan Warlow, "For Younger Readers: 'Masquerade'," in The School Librarian, *Vol. 28, No. 2, June, 1980, p. 143.*

Lucky the parents who bring Britisher Kit Williams' fantasy to their children, because its appeal reaches to adults as well as to youngsters.

The fun of the book is its riddles and anagrams. . . .

Williams' illustrations are magnificent. The merry faces, whimsical details, and lush colors are clearly designed to captivate eyes of all ages. . . .

Perhaps the jewel has already been discovered. But the real treasure is Williams' ability to blend words and art to create a masterpiece for all readers.

Anne M. Flynn, "Young People's Books: "Masquerade'," in Best Sellers *(copyright © 1980 Helen Dwight Reid Educational Foundation), Vol. 40, No. 8, November, 1980, p. 304.*

Patricia Wrightson

1921-

Australian writer of fiction and fantasy for children and young adults, and editor. Wrightson is among the most respected Australian authors currently writing for children. Combining realistic characters and locale with native folklore and legends to present her image of Australia, she considers her land to be "a country as powerful and as magical as Earthsea or Middle Earth. It is the only one I know and the one I want to write about." Wrightson interweaves past and present to explore the child's significance in the universe while challenging her readers with such themes as the ownership and preservation of land and alternative ways of defining reality. Critics see her most unique contribution as the advancement of Australian fantasy literature through stories dealing with aboriginal spirits of water, rock, and tree. She is praised for blending fantasy and reality in a compelling way through her unusual plots and picturesque language.

Several of Wrightson's books reflect her concern with the land and its relation to time. School children disturb a legendary stone ax in *The Rocks of Honey* and reactivate an ancient power, while new machinery desecrates primitive land in *The Nargun and the Stars*, causing the spirits to rebel. *Down to Earth* explores the place of humanity in the cosmos as Martin the Martian views reality from a unique perspective. One of Wrightson's most notable books is her only work of realistic fiction, *A Racecourse for Andy*, which looks at reality through the eyes of a retarded boy. Reviewers note an uncommon perceptiveness and sensitivity in Wrightson's treatment of Andy, his situation, and the people who care about him. Wrightson has also received acclaim for her trilogy, *The Ice Is Coming, The Dark Bright Water*, and *Journey Behind the Wind*, which revolves around the young aborigine Wirrun, who represents the people, land, and spirits in their struggle for survival against other spirits who cause havoc in nature. Together with the Mimi, a rock spirit, he enlists the help of the spirits of sea, wind, and mountain in defeating the Ninya, who are bringing back the Ice Age. Wirrun also confronts the Yunggamurra, a troublesome water spirit who later becomes Murra, Wirrun's wife. A final battle pits Wirrun against the Wulgaru, a creature of death. These works appear to have the ingredients of a universal mythology—vivid characters, strong plots, and epic confrontations with evil.

Since the appearance of her first work, *The Crooked Snake*, Wrightson's books have been well received. Critics praise her graphic regional settings and realistic characters as well as her language and plots, even while finding her narratives too slowly paced or too specialized to be universally appealing. Wrightson's importance to children's literature is undisputed because she is felt to have remedied the need for a body of aboriginal folk literature and to write equally well in the genres of fantasy and realistic fiction. Wrightson won the Australian Children's Book of the Year Award in 1956 for *The Crooked Snake*, in 1974 for *The Nargun and the Stars*, and in 1978 for *The Ice Is Coming*. Other awards include Notable Books of the Year Award from the American Library Association in 1963 for *The Feather Star*; the Spring Award from *Book World* in 1968 and the Hans Christian Andersen Honor List award in 1970, both

for *A Racecourse for Andy;* and the Hans Christian Andersen Honor List award in 1976 for *The Nargun and the Stars*. (See also *Contemporary Authors New Revision Series*, Vol. 3, and *Something about the Author*, Vol. 8.)

AUTHOR'S COMMENTARY

Folklore is no amusing invention but the record of a long struggle with the strangenesses of life, and a new strangeness calls up a new speculation. And I think this authenticity, this lived and remembered experience, explains the lasting power of folklore. It is why fantasy, the exploring-outward-and-beyond branch of literature, clings like mistletoe to the root and branch of folklore. (p. 610)

It really was an accident that threw me into the folklore of Aboriginal Australia. I was just a writer with a need to explore, one who liked the kind of fantasy that draws on authentic experience in order to compel belief; and it seemed a worthwhile challenge to try to produce a fantasy of that kind. I already had written *Down to Earth* . . . which drew on the new folklore of science fiction, but that one—cheekily suggesting that the dreaded invasion from outer space had already happened while we were looking the other way—was pure fun. The genuine shivery conviction that comes from authenticity was not in it, for authenticity in the new folklore demands a background knowledge I don't have. For my one compelling fantasy I would have to draw on the older authenticity, of magic. And I tried. I really tried, reaching passionately for this fantasy, believing in it and wanting to do it. But whenever I tried to grasp it, the magic ran out between my fingers, and I couldn't understand why.

I began to look around, to question. For a small nation only two hundred years old Australians were doing well in developing a literature of their own. It was young enough to be still a vital and compelling adventure; yet in an outwardly exploring age when the rest of the world had slipped rightly and freely into fantasy, Australia was still notoriously poor in that literary form. (pp. 610-11)

I concluded that I must not be overambitious. I would try only a tradition that ought to be allowed anywhere: a magician, no more. But at my first try he became the keeper of a magic-shop, and the magic would not grow beyond stage-magic. At the second, he became a PR man, manipulating minds for the sake of sales. "That's it, then," I thought morosely, giving up. "I just can't believe in a modern magician of ancient power." And I named the story *A Shabby Kind of Magic* and pressed obstinately on with it.

And quickly it appeared that even this would not do. For if the ancient magician had degenerated into a shabby salesman, the point must be made. There must be a contrast to make it: something more real, more anciently and innocently dangerous, to put beside the shabby pretender and show him up. I still needed an older kind of magic. I was caught on the horns of a dilemma, and they pricked; but at least I knew why Australians failed at fantasy.

And with that the horns tossed me, and I tumbled into the solution. All people in all countries have had fairies; therefore, Australia must have had them too.

And these fairies would be as innocently dangerous, as shiveringly real, as all true fairies. They would be new and old like the country and would interpret its strangeness and its dangers, since that interpretation was the reason for their existence. . . . If I didn't see all of this clearly in the first head-bumping moment, I did feel certain that whatever bedevilment Australia turned against imported fairies would not be turned against fairies of its own. Those fairies would work, if only I could find them.

This need to find them was not as strange as it may seem, for at that time almost all white Australians knew Aboriginal folk-lore only, on the one hand, as a collection of sacred and sacrosanct myths and, on the other, as a series of stories industriously retold—fables like Aesop's or Cinderella or "how-and-why" tales similar to the *Just-So Stories* [by Rudyard Kipling]—immutable tales that would not nourish original fantasy but at best could be only retold. The high, free, ongoing life of fairyland was embedded in this mass, and only a glint or two here and there showed that it was there at all. (pp. 611-12)

The first time I went hunting fairies in the public library, I believed I had found them. They were fairies at least from the fantasy writer's point of view—spirits that anyone might meet at any time and that could therefore enter new stories; spirits not held to be secret or sacred, not involved in creation or preservation but only in the chanciness of daily life. I dug them out of the works of anthropologists and early field workers and of laymen who had lived in sympathetic friendship with Ab-

original Australians—not many, but enough to begin a small collection from which I would select. (p. 612)

So I'd found my authentic magic, old and innocently dangerous, to put my shabby magician in his place and allow me to finish his story, I had changed its title to *An Older Kind of Magic* . . . , and that changed title is the mark of my accident, which happened in the middle of the book. It was not the shivering fantasy I had wanted to do, but by now I had collected enough material to draw on. I started again with a monster of stone called a Nargun and landed myself in the thick of the problems.

For it is not enough to uncover a set of new shapes with new and difficult names and simply to apply these to a set of familiar concepts. If you are searching for an authentic magic with its own powers of conviction and interpretation, you must try to see it truly. . . . You will have to make decisions, not only on the touchy question of sacred-or-available but after that on questions of appearance, personality, turns of speech, and place in the scheme of life. To make those decisions for the living folklore of a hurt and sensitive people is, and should be, terrifying. Perhaps only a writer would be ruthless enough. And even the writer, surely, must also work for a comprehension of folklore and fantasy in general.

Luckily for me, the Nargun itself caught me and carried me off; and again the result was enormously encouraging. (pp. 613-14)

So now I had done my one fantasy with the shiver and strength of authentic magic. I was free—except that I couldn't feel free. My accident with the dilemma seemed to have produced complications.

For one thing, the country so poor in fantasy had warmed to one with indigenous roots, but still it did not recognize the roots. . . . Most of them saw only two possibilities—either the story was my own invention, in which case the Nargun, Nyols, and Pot-kurok were invented, too; or else the creatures were traditional, in which case the story was another, more extensive, retelling. And no one was going to use this rich material to enrich Australian fantasy until it had been shown that the material was there.

For another thing, there was my small collection of fairy types. By now I had about fifty and had learned how to find them. I knew there were traditions of Little People across the continent from northeast to southwest; that there were lovely and intransigent water-girls, poetic figures attached to desert mirages, giants, ghosts, and monsters of great variety, all waiting to be known. The folklore was adding its own demands to those of fantasy.

Again, there were the Aboriginal Australians themselves. All this richness came from them and was part of their creative thinking, so much of which is hidden from us by the secrecy of the sacred myths. What they could tell, they often told haltingly in a foreign tongue or with skilled techniques that could not be conveyed in print; and so it lay buried in scientific books or brief retellings. But how can you come to know and sympathize with a people unless you can know its poetic and creative thinking? The collection of this material is work for the anthropologist. Its right identification is for the folklorist. But to recognize story and drama in a halting phrase, to hear in a few broken words the poetry and terror of strangeness experienced, and to convey these things in the techniques of print—that is the writer's job. No one can take that responsibility from him. The folklore of this people is rich and strong, and for their sake as well as for its own, it should be known.

Whichever way I turned, from every point of view, it seemed that I must go on a little longer. And since the field was so large and there is a limit to every writer, and since a living folklore was at risk from lay fumblings, it seemed best to plan one large story that would cut right across the field—and then to stop. That is what I've been trying to do with the Wirrun stories; and now that the last of the three (*Journey Behind the Wind*) is finished, I can confess that I didn't mean to demand so much forbearance. (pp. 615-17)

The move away from very young readers is necessary, as the project could not be attempted on any other basis, for folklore at its source is fully adult; selection and watering-down can come only later. And surely it must have been puzzling to readers overseas, this determined whipping of what they must see as dead literary donkeys? It has delighted me that my publishers were ready to go with me along this unpromising path and that at least some readers in England and America have responded so warmly.

For probably only Australians can fully understand, and I have also to confess that ever since my accident, I've been working only for them. There was this door that had to be opened, and I do believe that for us it leads into more than simple fantasy. Surely it opens up other things that some of us have missed? The hero; legend in the grand style; an old and simple vision of the land. These are things we could never attempt in Australia based upon the European folklore we inherit. (p. 617)

> *Patricia Wrightson, "Ever Since My Accident: Aboriginal Folklore and Australian Fantasy" (reprinted by permission of the author), in* The Horn Book Magazine, *Vol. LVI, No. 6, December, 1980, pp. 609-17.*

GENERAL COMMENTARY

Patricia Wrightson's childhood in the 'rich North coast of New South Wales', where her grandfather settled in the pioneering period, is remembered in rocky hills and pastures of [*The Crooked Snake, The Bunyip Hole,* and *The Rocks of Honey*] . . . and the details of sand-dunes and mangrove-swamps in the estuarine settlement where the heroine of *The Feather Star* . . . spends a memorable holiday. Later, the author's explorations in the back streets of Sydney and its harbour environs gave her a habitation for the larrikins of *Down to Earth* . . . and *I Own the Racecourse!* . . .

Pelicans and lillipillies, the tracery of old ironwork, gullies and Domain and bush and quayside—yes, they do entrance the reader, but they do more. The setting of a story is important because of the people who exist in it and are conditioned by it. To offer us a motiveless piece of description is, obviously, to offer only paint and plywood as a setting. The scenery of *The Feather Star* is far more than background. We see the place through the eyes of an outsider, a girl of fifteen just arrived. Self-conscious and self-absorbed, Lindy Martin wants to be accepted, and at once, by the local young people. She must learn to fish, must wear the right clothes . . . , must learn the idiom of Bill and 'Fleece' and Ian and understand the ups and downs of their alliance. As the feather star in the cave alternately glows and shuts itself in darkness, so Lindy ingenuously advances, nervously retreats; and on a more secret level of understanding, she sees the frustrations which this holiday

place, so enthralling for her, has brought to those who know its shores too well. (pp. 22-3)

A symbolic object offers a clue to the theme of the book, as it does elsewhere with the 'bunyip' of Binty's fears or the ancient stone axe in *The Rocks of Honey*. Always it is an object that *belongs* to a place and is a part of the impact of that place upon one or more of the people in it.

That curious amalgam of young people, the gang, is one of the novelist's most useful devices; plot can stem from it, variety and colour. In her first book, *The Crooked Snake*, Patricia Wrightson was content to keep the members of the group more or less on equal terms. Born and bred in Turrawong, pupils at the local school, Peter and Jen and John and Roy and the little girls, Squeak and Spike, are almost part of the landscape. Their two-fold adventure rises out of it. They occupy holiday hours photographing local industries (dairy farm and beef yards, timber mill and coal-mine) to make a scrapbook, and their wandering plausibly involves them with older, less intelligent schoolfellows who prefer to spend their spare time destroying every animal they can find.

In the village of Magpie Creek, not far from Turrawong, the Collins children enjoy an expected holiday for 'the Gastric' in *The Bunyip Hole*. At first sight this is another story of the clash between dissimilar groups—the Collins children eager to explore, the two town boys staying nearby alleviating boredom through mischief. Here again is a significant landscape, narrowing to the creeper-filled gully, said to be haunted, where the climax of action rises. But there is a new element here. In this group of children one is different and his difference becomes the key to the story. Binty refuses to use his real name, Herbert, because it is 'pink', while the name Binty is 'dark red, nearly black'. Imagination is a good servant but a bad master; Binty discovers this when he ventures into the gully in search of his lost dog. . . . In all her books Patricia Wrightson is precise in her indication of social strata in a country which does not encourage class barriers but still certainly admits to class divisions. (pp. 23-4)

The suspicion of earnestness with which Patricia Wrightson made her points in earlier books has by now completely vanished. Comedy—racy, spontaneous, wild and slangy—takes you unawares throughout *Down to Earth*. You are rushed helter-skelter down the Steps, pushed on to the creaking balcony of the old house, crammed into a corner of the orphanage fence as George discusses with Martin his chance of escape. Everything is in movement—not least the moods of the children, for Martin is that catalyst who exists in every group, the boy who makes things happen, makes people change; the fact that he has come from outside Earth is simply the last and boldest stroke in a deliciously bold story.

What have Binty, Eustace, Martin and Andy Hoddel in common? Surely that they are different because they see things differently and because they make other people do the same. These are the characters Patricia Wrightson uses as yeast to convert several ingredients into a new whole. In *I Own the Racecourse!* . . . she suggests that Andy's deprived and shackled mind has a special power of sight. Not that she ever makes the mistake of telling the reader this. Sharp dialogue, significant detail, play their part in suggesting the theme and, as always, the setting actively contributes to the power of the whole book. . . . (p. 25)

Personality and accident play their parts in building the structure of event in this book. The layabout is more than a bit drunk when Andy meets him with his scraped-up three dollars: a box of discarded streamers and a tin of old paint are plausibly to hand to give the boy ideas which lead to disaster; the Committee's solution, in which Andy sells the racecourse back to them, is born naturally in a mixture of benevolence and social sense. The pyramid of characters narrows from the crowd to the boys' gang and thence to the single figure of Andy, whose wayward but often gentle affection keeps all heads turned to him.

In *I Own the Racecourse!* we have a selective, lively, authentic picture of a locality. Blunt Street with the boys swooping down on their skateboard; the yard which Mike's father turns into a car park on race nights; the course blazing with light or cluttered with rubbish in a grey morning; it is all effortlessly, utterly real. In this locality live people who are just as real—Joe the worrier, Andy's dressmaker mother, casual Mr. Hammond the course foreman—each of them altered because of the problem of Andy. Characters and district are inseparable and they are unmistakably Australian. Regional writing that is increasingly intuitive and skilful has put Patricia Wrightson among the best writers in the world of children's books. (p. 26)

> Margery Fisher, "Writers for Children: Patricia Wrightson," in The School Librarian, Vol. 17, No. 1, March, 1969, pp. 22-6.

Right from the beginning, Mrs. Wrightson's books have offered us the tried-and-true children's book formula of children on their own, fighting their battles in virtual isolation from the adults most closely related to them. It is only in . . . *The Nargun and the Stars,* that there is full understanding and unity of purpose between young Simon and his adult guardians, and in that instance the isolation of the setting and the seriousness of the threat posed by the Nargun could well account for the difference. For the rest, it would not be unfair to say that parents are primarily there when it's time to eat or sleep, and rarely occupy the centre of the stage. What, then, do the children do in this society of their own? Early in the Wrightson corpus, they have to cope with other children only, and the resulting antipathies and problems are low-keyed and unpretentiously realistic. . . . It takes only time and proximity to solve these problems. There is still something of the child-versus-child antagonism in *The Feather Star,* but here it has dwindled to friendly tiffs and general annoyance with Annie Tippett; the real conflict is with the soured old Bible-basher, Abel, and it is here, where the focus of conflict becomes an adult, that some uncertainty creeps into Mrs. Wrightson's treatment.

> "Spouting the Bible again, eh?" said Bill. "He thinks he owns it." Lindy giggled. This described exactly what she felt about aggressive Bible-quoting.

Bill's statement in itself is thoroughly believable. It is the author's comment which seems an unnecessary underscoring, further strengthened as it is by Mrs. Martin's analysis of Abel's behaviour and Lindy's pity for him (described by the omniscient narrator) in the final chapter. The heavy-handed treatment of Abel accords ill with the treatment of Lindy's tentative friendships, and we wonder whether Patricia Wrightson's dislike of Abel has upset her sense of proportion.

Similarly with the unpleasant Sir Mortimer Wyvern in *An Older Kind of Magic,* who has the misfortune to talk to a dog on a night of magically inspired topsy-turveydom and is in consequence transformed into stone. What is Mrs. Wrightson asking us to think here? That a man who has such a disregard for the

natural pleasures of the earth (wife and children, leisure and gardens are the pleasures we know he abjures) *ought* to be denied life? That he had a heart of stone and that it is fitting that he be utterly petrified? The fate of Sir Mortimer is the most drastic result of the comet magic, and it strikes a jarring note. It is not the disharmony which makes Sir Mortimer's end false, because we have all experienced the sudden accident which takes us unawares in the midst of gaiety; but the suspicious traces of *deus ex machina.*

We have, then, a situation in which Mrs. Wrightson seems happiest in envisaging minor conflicts among the inhabitants of an all-child society and least at ease when dealing with adults as the cause of conflict. What produces the sudden excess of authorial intrusion in the latter case? Let us say straightaway that a desire to impart information—if not actual didacticism— is an important element in many of Patricia Wrightson's books.

There is usually somewhere in each novel where Mrs. Wrightson's plot demands some knowledge in the child reader which she expects he will not have acquired and which she works into the story. In *The Bunyip Hole* an I.O.U. is used, as the younger boy has just discovered that this is the way to pay for something when you haven't got the money; in *The Rocks of Honey,* Eustace and Barney think that distilling eucalyptus oil will be a rapid source of income and find out later from their teacher how they should have gone about it. . . . [In] each case, Mrs. Wrightson feeds in her facts skilfully. Significantly, almost all this information comes from the author or from the children themselves, because her children are independent creatures who would rather manage with their own resources.

Apart from these examples of a consciously educational presence in the novels, we are treated to a good deal of less conscious local colour which shows an awareness of the range of Australian landscape and society as it is, rather than as it has so often been represented overseas. Here again, it is a matter of unpretentious realism, getting the details right. . . . (pp. 31-3)

[Mention of] descriptive accuracy brings us to a consideration of language in general, and here again one's feeling is that Mrs. Wrightson is working well within a tradition. The style of the earlier books is ready-made ("he glowed with pleasure" . . . "The green, smooth trees of the rain forest, reaching up for the sun") with humour being the main determinant of linguistic originality (witness a local illness called "The Gastric", where she gives her readers the chance to reconsider this particular colloquial term in an amusing context).

It is *The Feather Star* which marks a greater concentration on language. Why? Is it because, for the first time, a physical object becomes important for itself to her protagonists? When Lindy and Bill are captivated by the feather star, has the author's preoccupation with getting its details right spilled over into description of other things? It is probably not accidental that the novel which marks a greater emphasis on individual use of language is set by the sea, that phenomenon which baffles description but not would-be describers. (p. 34)

As with the sea, so with city lights—another "Romantic" subject that evokes a striving for effect, yet a failure to think through the implications of metaphor and evocative vocabulary. Buses "waddling among the lighter traffic like elephants" comes uncomfortably close to suggesting feet, and lights "winking" across the dark streets—surely the word is less appropriate when applied to electric lights than to candles or oil lamps? These are petty things, yet they point to an area of uneasiness that seems the result of too hard a striving on Mrs. Wrightson's part to produce "rich language". Nonliteral figures are her downfall. She can produce the absolute rightness of racecourse descriptions . . . and yet team it with "thunder cracked and crashed . . .", the sort of phrase known to every primary school composition.

Earlier we suggested that Mrs. Wrightson's basic sureness of touch in depicting child behaviour wavered when adults were the focus of conflict, and that the melodramatic adult villains opened up for her possibilities for heavy-handed didacticism. Similarly, we have just seen how pressure to enrich her language results in uneasiness of style. In both cases, one is aware of the author's conscious presence as artist-manipulator. Perhaps this could be related to her often-quoted statement that she tries to push each new novel in a different direction in order to avoid stagnating.

Certainly the new direction she attempts in *Down to Earth* poses some problems of its own. Here she wants us to grapple with the problem of a creature from outer space who can look like a child and go around without being noticed, but has the equivalent of a human adult consciousness so that he is able to verbalize clearly for the benefit of puzzled children. To this end she postulates a perceptual block which prevents the children from seeing the spaceman as he is, and vice versa. In addition there is a communication gap, or at least the spaceman claims there is, so that he refuses to explain to the children what his fellows look like, that is, what the children look like to him. To get this across to his helpers takes time, and Cathy Brimble for one never really does believe that Martin is what he claims to be. Any device which slows down the action with clumsy discussion at the level possible in a book for children ought to be carefully reconsidered.

The problem is worthy of our notice, but neither of her solutions to it is as neat as it should have been. Thus Martin has been given "treatment" which protects him for a limited stay on earth. If we are talking about an unknown civilization vastly superior to our own, we could surely grant such a civilization the skill to give Martin not only that treatment, but also a kind of temporary metamorphosis which would have taken only the same tiny amount of explanation as the treatment has been allotted. The boy's behaviour is otherwise interesting and consistent and he does show up the values of our own civilization, which is doubtless what Mrs. Wrightson primarily intended. Still, her book is flawed precisely in those areas where she is trying to establish a common ground between human and alien. (pp. 35-6)

I Own the Racecourse! postulates a situation ingenious in its simplicity: some children have a game in which they pretend to "own" various prominent Sydney buildings; but when Andy, a mentally retarded boy, has his claim to the racecourse bolstered by a derelict who "sells" it to him for three dollars, both his mates and the adults connected with the racecourse are drawn into a web of complicity in order to ensure that Andy's faith is not shattered. Almost a [William] Mayne plot in some ways, with a Mayne-like consciousness of the interpenetration of fantasy and reality. What, asks Mrs. Wrightson, is a racecourse? Is it the grounds? The dogs and horses that perform there? The atmosphere of the meet, with the glitter of lights, the extravagant colours, the movement and the giant voice of the loudspeaker? How exactly does one "own" anything? What is reality if it can be arbitrarily arranged to suit the mentality of a subnormal child? Without any need for pretentious sermonizing or contrivances, questions as substantial as these are

carried effortlessly by *I Own the Racecourse!* But it has struck many readers as an unrepeatable achievement and certainly the author herself has rightly chosen not to attempt anything similar.

If Andy Hoddle's story is a successor to, and culmination of, the early realistic tales, then *An Older Kind of Magic* and *The Nargun and the Stars* could be said to pick up a theme latent in *The Rocks of Honey*. *An Older Kind of Magic* is essentially a trial run, lighthearted and satirical, again with problems caused by the introduction of adult characters whose stereotyping is obvious in comparison with the naturalistic portrayal of children. But the Aboriginal nature spirits who in this novel creep out of unlikely places in city parks under the influence of comet light are to reappear on a lonelier and grander stage.

Most Australian fantasy has suffered from the influence of European imaginative writing, whether at the naive level of importing elves and gnomes direct from colder climates, or (more recently) at the subtler level of following too slavishly the time shifts and dualistic cosmic struggles that have characterized the recent English and American product. . . . But Mrs. Wrightson's nature spirits—the Potkoorok who dwells in the swamp, the Turongs glimpsed high up in the trees, and the Nyols of the caves—are triumphantly Other. Unconventionally, they are defined much less by their appearance, which we rarely get the chance to observe, than by their linguistic habits and their customs. Avoiding the problem of communication which caused the faltering we noticed in *Down to Earth,* the author elects this time for a straightforward approach. Simon can understand the Potkoorok—at least, up to a point, for the creature's vocabulary is limited by its conceptual framework. Either a grader or a bulldozer may thus be termed "the yellow machine", and "boy" is a term that denotes a different species from "man". Simon's puzzlement is our own; only gradually does he discover that the Potkoorok despite its vast age thinks of itself as akin to "boys" rather than adult humans. The implications are considerable, but Mrs. Wrightson resists the urge to spell them out. As in *I Own the Racecourse!* she seems totally sure of her ground; there is no sense of uneasiness or of striving to anticipate possible difficulties.

Even more important than the alienness of their language is the moral neutrality of the spirits. The Nargun itself, menacing though it appears, is not to be classed as evil. When questioned by Simon whether or not the Nargun is good, the Potkoorok rejects the question as irrelevant. Simon is frustrated to find that neither the Potkoorok nor the Turongs are automatic allies in a battle against the force he sees as malevolent. All they will concede of the Nargun is that "it doesn't belong here". The grand black-versus-white conflict of the [J.R.R.] Tolkien-[C. S.] Lewis tradition is simply out of place: this is a question of *territory*. The Nargun has come to a place that is not its own, and that is why things have gone wrong. The solution is not to destroy the Nargun, but to induce it to move. Horror—and there is genuine scalp-pricking stuff here of a kind Mrs. Wrightson has never essayed previously—has its origin not so much in the acts of an intrinsically evil being, but in a creature's natural response to threats to its own existence: when Simon stupidly shies a stick at the great rocky thing, the stick comes whipping back at him. For a generation raised on novels where nastiness is in no way the responsibility of the Powers of Light, this could come as a salutary corrective.

The build-up and the description of the Nargun are so compelling that the solution, not much more sophisticated than

Charlie's suggestion of fencing it in, seems somehow unworthy of the lonely, savage creature. The logic of Charlie's solution, however, is faultless, and Patricia Wrightson asks us to experience the vibration of the tractor and the bulldozer from the Nargun's angle, suspending our knowledge that they are bright yellow and man-made, and realizing that a beast which can make such a roar is a beast fit to challenge the Nargun, "a monster against a monster". Even so, the Nargun is not destroyed but walled in by a landslide, and we know that one day the Nargun may be freed by some natural accident and the whole struggle re-enacted.

It is not only in the assured way the fantasy elements are handled that *The Nargun* stands out, for it has avoided most of the other weaknesses of the earlier novels, and is both starker and funnier than any of them. Starker because of the loneliness of the setting and the knowledge that there is no human agency to appeal to if Charlie's plan goes astray; funnier because of Charlie, in the main. The language is vivid without striving for effect, and quite apart from its other virtues, *The Nargun* easily the most exciting of any of her books. Earlier in Mrs. Wrightson's work we noted instances where the intrusion of the adult world brought with it lack of credibility. But here, the sheer pragmatism of Charlie and Edie puts them, paradoxically, on the very same level as the child who sees and accepts the supernatural, a level on which it is possible to act rather than merely weigh probabilities. (pp. 35-9)

One is left feeling, after a survey of Patricia Wrightson's novels, that she has been quite a time in coming to a realization of where her own strengths lie, that she has felt the pressure to move forward without always being sure where it was she should be moving. But the conviction that there was a territory to be found has stayed with her, and her discovery of it has made the journey worthwhile. (p. 39)

Hugh Crago and Maureen Crago, "Patricia Wrightson" (copyright © 1976 Hugh and Maureen Crago; reprinted by permission of the author and The Thimble Press, Lockwood Station Road, South Woodchester, Glos. GL55EQ, England), in Signal, *No. 19, January, 1976, pp. 31-9.*

Dorothy Sayers once rejected the "Classic," "Romantic" division of poets and divided them instead into those who make a statement and those who invite their readers to participate with them in a search. Patricia Wrightson belongs to the latter category, and her books invite a variety of response. She uses symbols—an axe or a comet—which not only connect Time, but also are the key to an inner question. On one level, all her books except *The Nargun and the Stars* show a group of responsible children who cope with interesting situations without interference from their mainly authoritarian but absent parents. The story-telling is lively and humorous and compels the reader to keep the pages turning. At a deeper level, however, Mrs Wrightson looks at the whole cosmos—stars and outer space—and the way the world spins within it. . . . Like many Australian writers she is very aware of the different strata of time in Australia. She looks at the ancient land now being violated by machinery, the old legendary creatures, the tribes who came after and the final imposition of a new alien culture whose "false shabby city magic" hides the light of the stars. (p. 43)

Care for the land naturally leads to a strong feeling for conservation from her first book *The Crooked Snake* onward. One aspect of this is ownership—a particularly appropriate question for an Australian to explore, because traditionally aborigines thought that no one could "own" land. (p. 44)

[The] book mainly explores different kinds of magic, the false magic of the advertising copywriter who works on people's minds but then, as he says, "Only if somebody's paying me," the self-interested traditional magic of the magic shop and the effect of an older kind of magic of a comet which is seen only once in a thousand years. (p. 46)

An Older Kind of Magic is an interesting book, but perhaps less successful with many children than the previous novels because the ending, where Sir Mortimer Wyvern is turned into stone, is seen as unsatisfactory in much the same way that Father in the dogkennel in [Sir James M. Barrie's] "Peter Pan" is unsatisfactory. Children bred in the Northern tradition of fantasy are used to some distance between it and reality—either in a totally separate world, as in [J.R.R. Tolkien's] *The Hobbit* or in different Time levels as in many of the recent *Time* fantasy books. Here there is a confusion between the two. It is, however, a most significant novel both in the author's own development and in the emerging indigenous fantasy literature of Australia. (pp. 46-7)

Most writers who have achieved a high degree of success in their management of groups of children, lively dialogue, and crowded city scenes might be tempted to repeat the formula. Yet in *The Nargun and the Stars* Patricia Wrightson has taken a lonely boy, patient adults, the country, and fantasy creatures. She has abandoned much of the interaction of accurately recorded dialogue for a more poetic style. She has taken us with her on her own search for a meaning in the relationship between the individual, his environment, and the cosmos, and in the course of a search for the wider significance of human experience has made a statement that is specifically Australian. (p. 48)

Betty Gilderdale, "The Novels of Patricia Wrightson," in Children's literature in education *(© 1978, Agathon Press, Inc.; reprinted by permission of the publisher), Vol. 9, No. 1 (Spring), 1978, pp. 43-9.*

Patricia Wrightson published her first novel in 1955. She is not prolific, and twelve years later she had produced only four more books. By then she had built up a modest reputation as an intelligent and perceptive regional writer, but outside Australia her name was still not widely known. Then in 1968 came *'I Own the Racecourse!'* . . . It was highly successful, both with children and with adult reviewers, and Mrs Wrightson was suddenly recognized far beyond her own shores as a leading children's writer. In the ten years from *'I Own the Racecourse!'* to the present she has added only three more novels to her total, making nine in all over a period of twenty-four years; but the three have shown a remarkable extension of scope and have greatly increased her reputation. There has been no slack in her development.

'I Own the Racecourse!' now seems to mark her farthest advance in the direction indicated by her early work. *The Crooked Snake* . . . and *The Bunyip Hole* . . . had shown a talent for managing a cast of children, both as individuals and groups, and an unusually strong sense of place; her stories were, and continued to be, notable for the almost tangible solidity of their settings, whether in the bush, a little seaside resort, or the bustling and various city of Sydney. *The Rocks of Honey* . . . had demonstrated exceptional imaginative range and a willingness to tackle large and difficult themes. *The Feather Star* . . . was remarkable for the sensitivity and precision of its character-drawing and its grasp of the ways in which children change as they grow up, while *Down to Earth* . . . gave play

to a bold comic imagination and a gift for making ideas interesting. All these qualities came together in *'I Own the Racecourse!'*, which was one of the outstanding English-language children's books of its decade: a triumph in the mode of contemporary realism.

In the three books which have succeeded *'I Own the Racecourse!'*, Mrs Wrightson has moved into the exacting field of fantasy. She does not underrate its difficulty. She looks on fantasy as an extremely serious mode: a form of writing that needs to be powerful rather than pretty. . . . She abjures what she calls the Big Magics, the great creative myths which she regards as sacrosanct, unavailable to the modern writer, limited by their own authority. She sees the grass roots of fantasy in the traditional world of fairies, monsters and lesser magic. But she is convinced that in an Australian setting the traditional creatures of folktale from far-off countries are out of place. Instead she has introduced the folk-spirits of the Aborigines, inhabitants of an ancient land which is new only to its recent settlers. It can be seen with hindsight that *The Rocks of Honey* foreshadowed a later preoccupation with the land, its original People and their magic, and that *Down to Earth* was a fantasy which could have been described as 'thinking about reality but beyond the known facts'; but the nature and depth of Mrs Wrightson's involvement with the themes underlying her more recent books could not, I think, have been predicted. (pp. 194-96)

The sense of responsibility which children will accept—usually for younger or weaker children—is a recurrent Wrightson subtheme, one that comes straight from life and that is not overused in modern children's fiction. Joe and Mike, the friends of backward Andy in *'I Own the Racecourse!'*, care about him, stand up for him, and worry when everyone around him encourages his delusion. . . . (p. 199)

One wonders what way out there can be that will not deal a fearful psychological blow to Andy. But the author finds one; and it is the perfect and satisfying answer. A truly original plot is just about the rarest thing in fiction; *'I Own the Racecourse!'* has one. (p. 200)

The three books which followed *'I Own the Racecourse!'* could all be grouped together under the title of the first of them, *An Older Kind of Magic*. . . . Important parts are played in all of them by those indigenous spirits of Australia which Patricia Wrightson has adopted and adapted. There are the Nyols, small and stone-grey, 'simple creatures, not very clever, but bright with the happy mischief of children', who invite all their visitors to wrestle with them; the Potkooroks, golden-eyed froglike tricksters of the streams and swamps; the wispy elusive Turongs in the trees: these and a great many more emerge in the course of the three books.

The use of Aboriginal folklore does not of course alter the fact that the novel is a sophisticated product of the Western culture in which Mrs. Wrightson herself grew up: she has not actually created or re-created a native Australian form. But she has certainly tapped new sources and given an impressive new stimulus to her work. Each of the three novels is successively more ambitious; and the last, *The Ice is Coming* . . . , prompts and indeed appears to invite comparison with Tolkien or [Ursula K.] Le Guin. (pp. 200-01)

An Older Kind of Magic is a light, easily-readable story. It should not be underrated; there is a great deal in it that is original and stimulating. But the Nyols, Potkooroks and other creatures seem clearly to be out of place in the centre of Sydney;

they are more at home, more readily credible, in the less-populated settings of *The Nargun and the Stars* . . . and *The Ice is Coming*. . . .

In [*The Nargun and the Stars*] the accurate-seeming topography, the quiet firmness of the telling, the total believability of the down-to-earth old couple, carry great conviction; there is something more truly spine-chilling here than anywhere else in Mrs Wrightson's work. (p. 202)

[*The Ice Is Coming*] is a book of weight and substance, a major imaginative endeavour, whether successful or not. . . . (p. 203)

The story is on an epic scale, and is told in a style which is broadly appropriate (though Wirrun's own speech is a form of demotic English). It is a children's book to the extent to which [J.R.R. Tolkien's] *The Lord of the Rings* or [Ursula K. Le Guin's] *A Wizard of Earthsea* or [Richard Adams's] *Watership Down* is a children's book. I should be very surprised, however, if it were to achieve the reputation or popularity of any of these titles. The trouble does not, I think, lie with the Australian setting or with the author's sense of it, which is admirable. And although . . . the introduction of aboriginal folklore does not alter the fact that a novel is a sophisticated product of Western culture, that does not mean that it cannot be used successfully; on the contrary, it may well be that this is the only way to make an Australian epic fantasy viable. I suspect that what is lacking is something quite simple: the power of sheer compelling narrative. The story gives the impression of going on and on; it has its longueurs; it brings in more and more creatures, many of whom do not contribute anything very striking to the action; it builds up tension only occasionally, and then not for long. Disbelief is not always willingly suspended; one finds oneself asking why the Ninya should begin their campaign at this moment out of thousands of years, whether Wirrun would really have given up his job to embark on this unlikely-looking chase, and whether a few ice patches would be dramatic enough to create the stir they do. . . . *The Ice is Coming* does not, I think, quite come off; it is not so good a book as *The Nargun and the Stars*. I offer this judgement with respect and regret, with a willing acknowledgement that it is only the verdict of one person, and with the further thought that in any case one writer's failure may be much more interesting and valuable than another's success. Certainly the book does not diminish Mrs Wrightson's reputation. She remains an able, serious and courageous writer, with an invaluable readiness to attempt something new and difficult. (pp. 203-04)

One of the marks of a good novel is that it leaves one with the feeling that there is more to be discovered on further acquaintance. Patricia Wrightson has written several books of the kind that are worth coming back to, the kind that linger and echo in the reader's mind. (p. 205)

John Rowe Townsend, "Patricia Wrightson," in his A Sounding of Storytellers: New and Revised Essays on Contemporary Writers for Children *(copyright © 1971, 1979 by John Rowe Townsend; reprinted by permission of Harper & Row, Publishers, Inc.; in Canada by Penguin Books Limited), J. B. Lippincott, 1979, Kestrel Books, 1979, pp. 194-206.*

THE CROOKED SNAKE   (Australian edition, 1955)

[By] modern standards of the author and Australian children's literature it is lightweight, but it does show the promise which was later fulfilled. The title refers to the name of a gang of six children who plan a series of holiday expeditions and local research in their township and who run foul of a group of older boys intent on destruction and vandalism for which the gang is blamed. Their plans to trap and defeat the boys are ingenious and plausible, but the book is not of the same calibre as *I Own the Racecourse* although it makes a pleasant holiday adventure story. (pp. 359-60)

> Margaret Payne, "Eleven to Fifteen: 'The Crooked Snake'," in The School Librarian, Vol. 21, No. 4, December, 1973, pp. 359-60.

In comparison with the author's later work it seems unpretentious, almost naïve; the nice children who form the society are right-minded and constructive, reminding one slightly of Arthur Ransome's Swallows and Amazons; the baddies are consistently nasty and are duly defeated in the end. (p. 196)

> John Rowe Townsend, "Patricia Wrightson," in his A Sounding of Storytellers: New and Revised Essays on Contemporary Writers for Children (copyright © 1971, 1979 by John Rowe Townsend; reprinted by permission of Harper & Row, Publishers, Inc.; in Canada by Penguin Books Limited), J. B. Lippincott, 1979, Kestrel Books, 1979, pp. 194-206.

THE ROCKS OF HONEY   (Australian edition, 1960)

The Rocks of Honey [is] a delicately implied statement about the pitfalls and problems of a country where mixed races have not been altogether successful in living together. The understanding that comes to Eustace, a boy of mainly aboriginal stock, is clearly the author's own—"He knew that this old country would fashion its people, all of them, to its own shape in its own good time; and this slow growth of the country was the best hope of them all". The slightly didactic form of expression, heard elsewhere in the book as well, dates it a little, but there is nothing that is not immediately recognisable in the three children round whom the story is simply and neatly shaped. (p. 3183)

In one way this is a tale of domestic adventure, of holiday games and enterprises during which the children, vastly different in personality and background, find common ground in the search for what seems to them an exciting hidden treasure. In another, it is a particular illustration of a general thesis, couched in prose that is very direct and simple, quickened with humour and an observant eye for the behaviour of the young. The setting of bush and mountain lake, grassy plain and village street is unobtrusively built up, not in isolated passages of description but as and when the story demands it. Gum-trees, those clichés of Australian story, make their appearance when Eustace and Barney try to distil eucalyptus oil to make their fortunes. Life on the land is introduced piece-meal as the boys hurry through the chore of feeding pigs or joyously touch up Cooper's bull with a catapult. The hillside on which the Rocks of Honey stand is sharply visualised, with a superb sense of space, as the two boys help Winnie to scramble to shelter during a sudden storm. It is a measure of Patricia Wrightson's skill as a novelist that her story conveys a full and living picture of a small community which represents a wider land and wider issues. (pp. 3183-84)

> Margery Fisher, "An Old Favourite: 'The Rocks of Honey'," in her Growing Point, Vol. 16, No. 4, October, 1977, pp. 3182-84.

Compared with [*The Crooked Snake* and *The Bunyip Hole*,] *The Rocks of Honey* is ambitious. It begins in a matter-of-fact way, but goes on to open up some unexpected perspectives. The main characters are a trio of children. . . . The two boys become engaged in a quest for an ancient stone axe, reputed to lie hidden among the group of rocks now known as the Three Sisters but formerly as the Rocks of Honey. It is a pleasantly casual quest, the excuse for a good deal of exploring and picnicking and den-making; and then the story suddenly takes off, with the interpolation of a chapter telling how, long years ago, Warrimai the club-thrower made the axe, and how he came to put it, with a curse upon it, among these rocks. And when the axe comes directly into the story, tension rises and persists.

In the midst of a storm, Winnie finds the axe. Eustace and his uncle, as aboriginals, are convinced that it should be put back where it came from. [After three strange accidents] Barney and Winnie now agree that the axe should go back. And, replacing it among the Rocks of Honey, Eustace hears in the wind the Song of the Old King:

> . . . Oh, my country, the warm land of the Honey,
>   Have you broken and thrown away your own
>   brown people?

The underlying theme, it becomes clear, is a weighty one: the changing relationship of the land and the two peoples. And the author has sought to indicate the different ways of thought and feeling of the brown people and the white. Between Barney and Eustace, who have never felt any racial antipathy, the quest for the axe brings a believable strangeness. The different moods of the story reflect a similar duality. In the second half there is nothing explicitly supernatural, but there is a pervading sense of old magic, an awareness that there could be more in heaven and earth than practical farmers' sons normally think of. *The Rocks of Honey* is not entirely successful; its transitions are sometimes awkward, and the author may have reached out for more than she could grasp at that stage of her development; but it is an impressive story, and comes to seem more so at a second and third reading. (pp. 196-97)

> John Rowe Townsend, "Patricia Wrightson," in his A Sounding of Storytellers: New and Revised Essays on Contemporary Writers for Children (copyright © 1971, 1979 by John Rowe Townsend; reprinted by permission of Harper & Row, Publishers, Inc.; in Canada by Penguin Books Limited), J. B. Lippincott, 1979, Kestrel Books, 1979, pp. 194-206.

THE FEATHER STAR   (1963; Australian edition, 1962)

[*The Feather Star* is an] unusually satisfying and beautifully written story which will delight older girls because of the author's remarkable empathy with young adolescents. . . . The author has captured in a rare way the difficulties in the mother-daughter relationship, and in the Lindy-Bill and Lindy-Fleece variable states of friendliness. . . . A book any reader will remember.

> Virginia Haviland, "Late Spring Booklist: 'The Feather Star'," in The Horn Book Magazine (copyright © 1963, by The Horn Book, Inc., Boston), Vol. XXXIX, No. 3, June, 1963, p. 290.

The Feather Star has a familiar and apparently simple subject, though not an easy one to handle: the beginnings of a girl's growing up. Mrs Wrightson catches exactly the feeling, common in adolescence, of no longer knowing who or what one is. (p. 197)

With the girl who works in the shop . . . and two boys, [Lindy] forms a tentative foursome: shy, teasing, self-conscious, not knowing what to say to each other. The feather star of the title is a sea creature found by Lindy in a cave; broken, it will grow again two or threefold, and it symbolizes—one assumes—the breakup of childhood. Interestingly, Lindy's loss of childish innocence comes not in any of the obvious ways but through a series of encounters with a dreadful, censorious, all-hating old man. There is no reconciliation with him because he is lost, irredeemably lost, and the realization that this can happen is a fearful thing. 'She sobbed and sobbed, child and woman together, for the tragedy and wickedness of Abel. She sobbed for useless misery and bitterness; for age with its eyes on the ground refusing life, wasting all the adventure and beauty of a whirling planet in space.' (p. 198)

> *John Rowe Townsend, "Patricia Wrightson," in his* A Sounding of Storytellers: New and Revised Essays on Contemporary Writers for Children *(copyright © 1971, 1979 by John Rowe Townsend; reprinted by permission of Harper & Row, Publishers, Inc.; in Canada by Penguin Books Limited), J. B. Lippincott, 1979, Kestrel Books, 1979, pp. 194-206.*

DOWN TO EARTH   (1965; Australian edition, 1970)

The well-written, perceptive, highly original story has humor, excellent characterizations (especially Martin's), and an underlying irony that older boys and girls as well as adults will enjoy. The book will lend itself well to booktalks, and its audience should be among those who think they do not like fantasy, as well as among the readers who enjoy all unusual books. (p. 278)

> *Ruth Hill Viguers, "Late Spring Booklist: 'Down to Earth'," in* The Horn Book Magazine *(copyright © 1965, by The Horn Book, Inc., Boston), Vol. XLI, No. 3, June, 1965, pp. 277-78.*

Down to Earth . . . is, in its [quiet] way, most intelligent and well worked-out. . . .

The gradual growth of the children's belief in Martin's story, their unease at its implications and their totally differing attitudes towards him are quite impressively done; as is the polite puzzlement of Martin himself regarding most aspects of Sydney life. The story raises some interesting problems of communication between people from different planets which might equally well apply to people from the same street.

For the rest the atmosphere and background are exact here; the climax neat; the writing direct, vivid and often amusing. The story seems too long-drawn out at times and the occasional element of farce does not mix too well with the conviction of the rest. Otherwise this is an original and thoughtful book with some beautiful moments.

> *"Heirs of Tolkien, Nesbit and Carroll," in* The Times Literary Supplement *(© Times Newspapers Ltd. (London) 1965; reproduced from* The Times Literary Supplement *by permission), No. 3328, December 9, 1965, p. 1130.**

Patricia Wrightson has followed up the possibilities of her premise skilfully. Martin has taken on something of the character of the boy he is supposed to be. He is inquisitive, cocky and as friendly as a puppy. Other traits mark his difference from the children he meets. The gentle, considerate way he treats Cathy, his occasionally patronizing manner with his new

mates, his dislike of being treated as a child, all point to an intelligence developed outside our world as surely as the inconvenient fact that he glows with light when he is asleep. There are hints too, that his extra-terrestrial world is grey and inflexible; there is pathos in his excitement when he sees 'the wild, gay animals' in a child's picture lying in the old house where he shelters. . . .

[Martin's] descent to Earth allows the author to make a political point; he is shocked that the children should think that his planet might want to conquer theirs. Far more important to the general theme of the book is its sad indirect comment on the inept, inconclusive way humans communicate one with another and the consolation that children do, against odds, make friends outside their own little worlds. As Martin says, George's friendship is 'one coal from the fire of Earth, to take back home with me.' The remark can be expanded to include everything from colour-prejudice to the wider thought that no man, and every man, is an island.

> *Margery Fisher, "Who's Who in Children's Books: 'Down to Earth'," in her* Who's Who in Children's Books: A Treasury of the Familiar Characters of Childhood *(copyright © 1975 by Margery Fisher; reprinted by permission), Holt, Rinehart and Winston, Weidenfeld & Nicolson, 1975, p. 211.*

A RACECOURSE FOR ANDY   (1968; Australian and British editions as *I Own the Racecourse!*)

This outstanding story by an Australian author has no aura of sentimentality, no obtrusive message; it is poignant just because of the simple acceptance of Andy by both adults and children. They do not tolerate him, they like and protect him. A distinguished book.

> *Zena Sutherland, "A Note of Joy: 'A Racecourse for Andy," in* Saturday Review *(copyright © 1968 by Saturday Review; all rights reserved; reprinted by permission), Vol. LI, No. 19, May 11, 1968, p. 35.*

Here is a first-rate story, well worth buying for both primary and secondary school libraries. . . .

With remarkable skill and humanity Patricia Wrightson portrays the isolated twilight world of a simpleton within the framework of a lively, entertaining and often very funny story. Subtle characterization and a highly intriguing plot make this a book of rare interest and quality.

> *J.S.J., "Fiction: 'I Own the Racecourse'," in* Children's Book News *(copyright © 1968 by Baker Book Services, Ltd.), Vol. 3, No. 3, May-June, 1968, p. 153.*

In this very good story the character of Andy is beautifully but never mawkishly drawn and there is humour, strong feeling and an exciting story which holds the interest throughout. The descriptions, particularly of the racecourse itself "so cunningly, by daylight, hiding the shifting, glowing magic that fills it at night", of the greyhounds which Andy gets to know so well and of the trotting horses whose hooves "make a noise like silken drums" as they come round the course, are a joy. The only disturbing factor in this story is the involvement itself, which is dual. To be at one with Andy and share his outlook, sometimes so uncomfortably direct and at others so confused . . . , to share in his chuckling remarks to himself, gives one a feeling which is almost of vertigo; to identify with Joe, who knows that one can only live in the world with compromise, is to worry with him about what the future holds for Andy. Both identifications are uneasy, but if they can be accepted they will be immensely valuable.

"Deep Involvement," in The Times Literary Supplement *(© Times Newspapers Ltd. (London) 1968; reproduced from* The Times Literary Supplement *by permission), No. 3458, June 6, 1968, p. 583.*

[The] success of [*I Own the Racecourse*] depends to a large extent on the main character, how realistically he is drawn, whether or not children will be able to identify with him. . . . Miss Wrightson has to convey a mind partially removed from the ordinary world. Cleverly, she uses a window image. . . . (p. 12)

The key to the friendly response which Andy evokes from both children and adults throughout the book, despite his strangeness, is here. He is 'always warm and admiring', 'careful not to be a nuisance'. And so people accept him, feel protective towards him, try to help him. He is a sunny character. Child readers would probably identify with his friends, as well as with Andy, and so would share the gang's acceptance of him.

The group which Andy belongs to and the boyish world they inhabit are vividly drawn. It is being part of this gang which leads Andy into his fantasy about owning the racecourse. . . . (What is actually entailed in ownership is one of the book's themes.) (p. 14)

Two strands of the book are significant from this time onwards: the boys' attempts, thoughtful, tactful, direct, deeply concerned to try to persuade Andy that he is not the owner, and to disentangle him from the ownership mess without hurting him; and the way in which the adults, at the racecourse and elsewhere, amused at Andy's thinking he is the owner, treat him as the owner. (pp. 14-15)

Children's interest would be held particularly by a strong storyline with episodes in which they would delight: Andy allows a pack of stray dogs into the track to chase the hare; he paints some benches and the bandsmen sit on them while the paint is still wet; the owners of stalls in the racecourse pay him bags of chips as 'rent'. They would also enjoy the quiet humour which pervades the book.

On one level it is very amusing, but gradually the realization dawns that the fantasy is getting out of hand. One of the older boys, Joe, ponders deeply on the matter. . . .

Joe's concern for Andy shines through, and Patricia Wrightson has managed to explore a philosophical problem in words which an adolescent could use. Wider issues are raised as to whether the deception about ownership helps Andy or not, whether he will learn to distinguish between what is real and what is not if everyone keeps on pretending, and whether the story must end in dreadful disillusionment for Andy.

It is the adults who kid Andy along without really thinking of possible consequences. . . . (p. 15)

This book explores what can happen to a handicapped boy in a positive environment. The ways in which the gang care for him are admirable: they allow him to join in when he can; they protect him from activities which would be dangerous for him; they accept him as an individual and like him; they allow him to opt out of the gang's activities when he wants to and welcome him back afterwards; they realize the dangers of Andy carrying his fantasy to extremes; they understand that he must be allowed

to try things out on his own, to break things sometimes. They give him a chance to exist as an individual in his own right.

The book also raises the question of responsibility. Andy's mother's behaviour is questioned in that she tends to feed and clothe Andy and then hand him over to the group. . . . There is also a . . . questioning of when it is irresponsible to allow fantasy to continue. (pp. 16-17)

Compared with [Ivan Southall's] *Let the Balloon Go*, this book is lighter in tone, generally more cheerful and humorous, but Southall's book would probably provoke more thought about the problems of handicapped children. . . . Also, as a character, John Sumner has more depth than Andy, and one probably identifies more strongly with him. Although Miss Wrightson successfully creates Andy's world, it is a simpler, relatively undemanding place. And as a reader shares minds as well as environment, there is a difference in subtlety and satisfaction. (p. 17)

John Haynes, "No Child Is an Island: 'I Own the Racecourse'," in Children's literature in education *(©1974, Agathon Press, Inc.; reprinted by permission of the publisher), No. 15 (September), 1974, pp. 12-18.*

Patricia Wrightson marks Andy's difference from the other boys with subtle indications of his behaviour, his facial expressions, his mode of speech. As with Martin the Martian she uses the reactions of other people to extend her character-drawing. . . . Mike is sensitive enough to realize that Andy's simple outlook has its own value, and he is ready to support Andy's dream and to accept him as he is. When by a kind and cunning scheme Andy is persuaded to 'sell' the racecourse back to the Company and (with typical waywardness) wonders if he has enough money to buy a model 'plane, Mike puts his friends right once more: 'What does it matter if Andy gets a 'plane and breaks it? He's got to have things sometimes, even if he does bust them.' While the rest of the boys accept Andy for the residue of sense left in him, with pity and rough comradeship, it is Mike who sees something of the innocence which is Andy Hoddel's recompense; he sees that Andy does, in a way, really 'own' the racecourse through his vision of it. (p. 22)

Margery Fisher, "Who's Who in Children's Books: 'A Racecourse for Andy'," in her Who's Who in Children's Books: A Treasury of the Familiar Characters of Childhood *(copyright © 1975 by Margery Fisher; reprinted by permission), Holt, Rinehart and Winston, Weidenfeld & Nicolson, 1975, pp. 21-22.*

[*A Racecourse for Andy*] was published in this country . . . long before the terms *special needs, exceptional child,* or *mainstreaming* became part of our educational jargon. In the 1970s ideas about the education of children with disabilities, handicaps, or extraordinary gifts underwent scrutiny and change. . . . We have become more sophisticated in our understanding of such children and, we hope, more sensitive and responsible. . . . To read Patricia Wrightson, therefore, is a welcome delight. Not only does she have the sensitivity we are striving for, she also has the understanding and empathy of a gifted writer; moreover, she is neither stiff nor contrived. There is no hint of jargon. She does not write to be timely or to demonstrate proper attitudes. She writes a good story: tight, balanced, funny, suspenseful, and credible. It happens to be about a special child.

A Racecourse for Andy is, above all, Andy's story. Certainly other features help bring it to life: strong characters, young and old alike, and their relationships; a vivid setting, partly exotic and partly familiar; and a clever plot with humor and suspense. (p. 196)

The writing is energetic, detailed, concrete, and evocative. It creates moods, brings characters to life, conveys tension and emotion. Wrightson is precise, straightforward, and unsentimental. She describes Andy in a way that allows us to understand him and feel his frustration. Yet she avoids giving a label to his condition. . . . (pp. 197-98)

A Racecourse for Andy is a refreshing, optimistic book. It is about the best in people, their basic goodness. It is about friendship and the responsibility friends have for each other. It is about the "glowing, lively magic" of the racecourse and the gruff, kind people who work there. But most of all, it is about Andy, who sees life through the glass in the window, who trusts and smiles, who means well even in his most calamitous undertakings, who shares his laughter and his happiness. Andy is special, but his limitations can be seen as assets. Andy is innocent, and Patricia Wrightson shows us that innocence is a gift. (p. 199)

> *Christine McDonnell, "A Second Look: 'A Racecourse for Andy'," in* The Horn Book Magazine *(copyright © 1980 by The Horn Book, Inc., Boston), Vol. LVI, No. 2, April, 1980, pp. 196-99.*

AN OLDER KIND OF MAGIC (1972)

In a book blending realism and fantasy, the creatures of Australian folklore creep quietly about the edges of a story of urban conservation. At only one point do they impinge on the realistic, major narrative—and this aspect of the tale is not wholly convincing, yet the deft writing and strong characterization, the appeal of the setting and the contemporary interest of the plot carry the book. . . . [The] theme is conservation triumphant. The characterization of adults tends to be exaggerated, but the children are marvelously real.

> *Zena Sutherland, "New Titles for Children and Young People: 'An Older Kind of Magic'," in* Bulletin of the Center for Children's Books *(reprinted by permission of The University of Chicago Press; © 1972 by The University of Chicago), Vol. 26, No. 2, October, 1972, p. 35.*

Into a highly original story of "lovely and terrible" modern Sydney . . . , the author has drawn fascinating and mysterious magical elements. . . . The author has done a skillful job of tying together the mysteries of the comet and the aboriginal spirits; the delight of real children in the fanciful; and their discovery of a public relations man who believes that the advertising man is the only true magician left in the modern world. All of the fantastic matter is blended with a realistic controversy about turning the gardens into a parking lot. Along with Benny, the Potter children . . . are completely realized characters. . . . The author continues to be a superb storyteller; her graphic writing greatly enhances the suspense and sense of mystery, and sharpens character and scene. One rereads passages for the pleasure of their imagery. . . .

> *Virginia Haviland, "Early Fall Booklist: 'An Older Kind of Magic'," in* The Horn Book Magazine *(copyright © 1972 by The Horn Book, Inc., Boston), Vol. XLVIII, No. 5, October, 1972, p. 472.*

[*An Older Kind of Magic* is an] undistinguished fantasy. . . . Most children will not struggle through the confusing plot which

skips from the children to Ernest Hawke to the city's Minister to Sir Mortimer Wyvern, with occasional inserts about the Australian "folk magic" creatures. The author's attempt to integrate the modern magic of advertising and the "older kind of magic" to solve a contemporary problem is unsuccessful, and the book fails to fill the need for more Australian folklore.

> *Eileen K. Diercks, "Grades 3-6: 'An Older Kind of Magic'," in* School Library Journal, *an appendix to* Library Journal *(reprinted from the October, 1972 issue of* School Library Journal, *published by R. R. Bowker Co./A Xerox Corporation; copyright © 1972), Vol. 19, No. 2, October, 1972, p. 116.*

THE NARGUN AND THE STARS   (1974; Australian edition, 1973)

Patricia Wrightson's books have earned a special name for their originality, which *The Nargun and the Stars* will enhance. . . .

Simon's suffering at his parents' death is rapidly but accurately dealt with, something that children's writers seldom know how to do. The place-spirits are pleasingly matter-of-fact, with a touch of the Psammead about the complacent Potkoorok. The Nargun itself, described with passion, is a poetic creation, genuinely frightening and pitiful.

> *"Round the Bend," in* The Times Literary Supplement *(© Times Newspapers Ltd. (London) 1973; reproduced from* The Times Literary Supplement *by permission), No. 3742, November 23, 1973, p. 1434.**

Going more systematically into the hills of the Australian Dreamtime has become one of the most creatively-used features of modern fiction for children. . . . Patricia Wrightson captures this fine mixture of real landscape and of an older kind of magic underlying it, so that the fantasy-in-reality that is attributed automatically to books like [William Mayne's] *A Grass Rope* has the added texture in her books of Dreamtime mythology. At the centre of this, too, is how children look at the world, and Simon—in *The Nargun and the Stars*—can therefore be a creative dreamer and yet none-the-less retain all the reality of a real boy. (p. 180)

So many things have been successfully achieved here: landscape is no longer the excuse for plastic animation or for heroic survival; it is a reflection and extension of the imagination. (p. 181)

> *C. S. Hannabuss, "Reviews: 'The Nargun and the Stars'," in* Children's Book Review *(© 1973 Five Owls Press Ltd.; all rights reserved), Vol. 3, No. 6, December, 1973, pp. 180-81.*

Wrightson's considerable skill in managing texture and tension ensures that admirers of serious fantasy will breathe the air of Wongadill along with Simon, and to her credit the symbols and issues here represent a perspective more complex than is usual in fictional conflicts between technology and nature. But Simon's dreaded earth monster hardly justifies the author's overreaching attempt to make of him a timeless, literally star-shaking occasion for "naked pity" and "naked fear." (p. 303)

> *"Younger Fiction: 'The Nargun and the Stars'," in* Kirkus Reviews *(copyright © 1974 The Kirkus Service, Inc.), Vol. XLII, No. 6, March 15, 1974, pp. 302-03.*

The author, probably mixing primordial tribal legends with the driving force of her own imagination, has written a strong and memorable book. . . . The reader finds his senses sharpened by the precise images: "The wind was up again. . . . The sounds were blown away and came sweeping back like sheets on a clothesline"; and "daylight drained away like water from a tub." The characters, seemingly plain and uncomplicated people, subtly come to life as complex human beings; and the essentially simple plot is worked into the rich fabric of a story that begins serenely, arches up to a great crescendo of suspense, and then falls away at the end to "a whisper in the dark." (pp. 382-83)

> *Ethel L. Heins, "Summer Booklist: 'The Nargun and the Stars'," in* The Horn Book Magazine *(copyright © 1974 by The Horn Book, Inc., Boston), Vol. L, No. 4, August, 1974, pp. 382-83.*

The Nargun, a being evoked from a boulder, never humanized, allowed limited movement but the merest semblance of limb and eye, must be accounted one of the most remarkable myth-beings ever created—or recreated, if Patricia Wrightson found hints of it, as she did of the Potkoorok, the Bitarr and the Turongs, in aboriginal story. She offers as little description as possible, relying on effects of darkness or the surprise of sudden movement, on associative words (flank, muzzle, snout, lurch), to establish beyond any doubt the possibility that a boulder can have sentient being and, in a very primitive pattern, longings and desires that move it to dangerous activity.

> *Margery Fisher, "Who's Who in Children's Books: 'The Nargun'," in her* Who's Who in Children's Books: A Treasury of the Familiar Characters of Childhood *(copyright © 1975 by Margery Fisher; reprinted by permission), Holt, Rinehart and Winston, Weidenfeld & Nicolson, 1975, p. 256.*

THE ICE IS COMING (1977)

The Ice is coming is the tale of a journey from the interior down the eastern seaboard, through New South Wales to the south-west coast of Victoria. In its geographical sweep the book reminds me of Selma Lagerlof's two classic tales of Nils and his flight over Sweden with migrating geese [*The Wonderful Adventures of Nils* and *The Further Adventures of Nils*], books written with a specific educational purpose, to help school children to a better knowledge of their own country. I do not suggest that Patricia Wrightson had a didactic purpose but her book is, all the same, an expression of commitment to Australia—not the Australia of the Happy People, as she calls city-dwellers and beach players, but of the country settlers, the Inlanders, and still more the aborigines, the People, who have found names and attributes for spirits of wood and water, fire and air. (p. 3217)

Because this is a tale of Australian beings, its geographical structure and detail are vital. To each spirit its own place, weather and element. The relation of the various beings to the land, the central element in the complex folk-beliefs of the aboriginals, is consistently felt through the book, not superimposed but an integral part of its argument and its setting. Sometimes it is expressed in mysterious, ornate and enigmatic passages—as, for instance, in the fine description of the Bunyip as Wirrun first sees it. Sometimes the expression is direct and simple, as in a passage describing how the Wa-tha-gun-darl, a band of hill-spirits, first feel the approach of the dangerous cold. . . . (pp. 3217-18)

Patricia Wrightson handles her extra-human characters with the utmost ease and confidence. At the climax of the adventure,

when the Mimi, the People, an Inlander and a changing spirit, the Yabon, join Wirrun to hold the ice back, there is a unity of imagination so that it never matters how much any one person realises about the strange alliance. The Eldest Nargun, spoken of along Wirrun's route in such a way that he expects a massive, elemental rock shouldering the sea, is borne from the water by old Johnny Wuthergul, "a large pebble, the size of a teacup"; the Mimi rebukes the young man for his surprise with the words ". . . is not the rockpool a world among the stars? . . . Is a starfish smaller than a star?" It is because Wirrun has already unconsciously acknowledged a feeling for the whole of nature, not only for its impressive manifestations, that he is able at last to understand the Eldest Nargun's significance. Something of the intense reality of the folk-lore of the aborigines is suggested in this story, driving forward as it does through feeling and action in strong, flexible prose. More diffused in narrative and less concentrated than *The Nargun and the Stars,* it is an inevitable sequel to it, taking us more deeply into a unique, serious, considered interpretation of nature. (p. 3218)

> *Margery Fisher, "Special Review," in her* Growing Point, *Vol. 16, No. 6, December, 1977, pp. 3217-18.*

Patricia Wrightson gives a sentence a gentle shove and it seems to roll over the Australian landscape, echoing down the page in patterns of sound, transforming print into vistas of haunted rocky cliffs. . . .

Her story begins slowly, gathers momentum like a boulder, and pounds to a smashing finish in which all the scattered forces of the landscape, spirit and mortal, are mustered to turn back the deadly cold. Few books for young readers, East or West, convey so grand and sweeping a sense of the land, or are written with such majestic grace.

> *Jane Langton, "Children's Books: 'The Ice Is Coming'," in* The New York Times Book Review *(© 1978 by The New York Times Company; reprinted by permission), January 29, 1978, p. 26.*

Evocative in its description of landscape, sensitive to sounds and silences, and not without humor in its characterizations, the book—unlike its predecessor—presents difficulties. The reader must accommodate himself to a fantasy developed from a folklore not entirely dead, which is used in an original way to contrast the frivolity of modern life with the seriousness and depth of men in touch with nature. (p. 58)

> *Paul Heins, "Late Winter Booklist: 'The Ice is Coming'," in* The Horn Book Magazine *(copyright © 1978 by the Horn Book, Inc., Boston), Vol. LIV, No. 1, February, 1978, pp. 57-8.*

The Ice is Coming is a magnificent heroic novel. . . .

It is the story of how the Ninya, manlike spirits of ice, broke out of their caves in the heart of Australia and set out to create a new ice age, and how their enterprise was challenged by a young Aborigine and a Mimi, a frail spirit of the rocks. Of the many fine inventions in this book the Mimi is the most memorable. She is a prickly creature, proud of her independence, strong in the ability to survive in a world where the smallest puff of wind sends her spinning in the air. She is joint hero of the story with Wirrun, the black boy who speaks and acts for the land in its battle for survival. In their long travels these two meet many people, human and spirit, whose support they enlist in the fight against the ice. There are many unforgettable portraits, including George Morrow, the inland white man who gives his discreet support to the enterprise at a critical moment, and Old Johnny Wuthergul, the ancient aborigine who alone knows how to get in touch with the Eldest Nargun, the oldest of all the First Things and the arch-enemy of the ice. (p. 52)

The story opens slowly and develops pace and power as it goes. The reader's patience is called for in the first chapter or two, but thereafter there is no doubt. This is a major book, full of depth and compulsively readable. It is worth going back to the beginning to confirm with what architectural skill Miss Wrightson fits every small stone in place to support the main structure. Nothing is wasted. Every incident, each comment, humorous or ironic, is part of the wise, funny, exciting and moving whole. (p. 53)

> *"For Children from Ten to Fourteen: 'The Ice Is Coming',"* in The Junior Bookshelf, *Vol. 42, No. 1, February, 1978, pp. 52-3.*

With profound respect for those who live in the outlands of Australia, Patricia Wrightson has depicted the spirit world . . . of Aboriginal Australia. Her story has a feeling of the present with its trains and buses, its backpacks and petrol stations, and yet manages to evoke the spirits of the rocks, the mountains, and the sea, the ancient and eternal spirits of a people. This novel is both the present and the past, a remarkable combination of now and always. (p. 63)

Without inventing language of another fantasy culture, or creating another country beyond those we know, Wrightson beautifully sets up a system of spirits, all of them parts of the natural world and living in the elements of nature—the sea, the wind, the rocks, the mountains. These spirits are individual, different from each other, humanlike, and yet not human. They are willing and able to cooperate against their common enemy, the ice. Each must maintain its individuality, retain its system of allies, do only what is within that spirit group's capacities, and yet show respect for the human being who cares enough to come and help.

The reader is pulled into sympathy for creatures who fight a force that seems to be gaining control, creatures that have only a few characteristics like those of people. . . .

The theme of the novel is lyrically stated in a central paragraph; it is repeated without becoming didactic. And it is one of the essential themes of all literature. As the spirits Mimi and the Nyol watch Wirrun, they are aware that he is making great sacrifices and braving unknown dangers in order to save the continent from the return of the ice.

> This, they knew, was the curious thing that men were made for: to care. Spirits might care sometimes when something could be done. If they were the right kind they might help when help was needed. They might be and know and remember and do; but men cared even when they could not do.
>
> (p. 64)

Stylistically, Wrightson's novel also pleases. Her keen appreciation of the land, of its sounds, its wild animals and birds, its insects and its climate is apparent in the imagery rich with connotative meaning. Although the tone of *The Ice Is Coming* is serious, there is a section of delightful comment on the Happy Folk. . . . (pp. 64-5)

The Ice Is Coming is a rare book. It combines invention of a fantasy spirit world with suspenseful action leading to the saving of a continent and its people. A human hero, young, fallible, and dedicated, pulls us through to victory. (p. 65)

> Rebecca Lukens, *"Brief Review: 'The Ice is Coming',"* in The World of Children's Books *(© 1978 Jon C. Stott), Vol. III, No. 1, Fall, 1978, pp. 63-5.*

THE DARK BRIGHT WATER   (1979)

[While] there are times when one wishes Wrightson weren't saddled with all [the] elaborate plotting, the situations are independently convincing, even compelling. Can Ularra, once a beast, be wholly human again? "Can't ever be sure, can we?" he says at one point, with an unsteadiness, a tragic insight, that the old Ularra would never have known. Wirrun, too, begins to accept the role thrust upon him. . . . This ambitious enterprise—which will obviously continue—makes one glad at times that Wrightson has extended her reach into the perilous terrain of the aboriginal Beyond.

> *"Older Non-Fiction: 'The Dark Bright Water',"* in Kirkus Reviews *(copyright © 1979 The Kirkus Service, Inc.), Vol. XLVII, No. 6, March 15, 1979, p. 333.*

The book might be compared to the works of Tolkien, particularly in the interdependence of the People, the land, and the spirits except for the fact that the spirits are amoral rather than agents of good or evil. Although the customs and relationships of the People are somewhat alien to us, the author's magnificent style, her penetrating understanding of the minds of the People, and her characterization of Wirrun make an original, remarkable book.

> Ann A. Flowers, *"Early Spring Booklist: 'The Dark Bright Water',"* in The Horn Book Magazine *(copyright © 1979 by The Horn Book, Inc., Boston), Vol. LV, No. 2, April, 1979, p. 202.*

In *The Ice is Coming*—which, for my money, is one of the six best Australian novels of the century—Wirrun the young Aborigine won the titles of Hero and Ice-Fighter. Patricia Wrightson's new book takes up where the other left off and tells how Wirrun is again called to remedy a disorder in nature. . . .

All these stories of the elemental struggles which go on in modern Australia parallel with the activities of the Happy People . . . are concerned with disturbances of the natural order. In the earlier book the Ninya try to bring back the Ice Age. Now the disturbance is more fortuitous and individual. (p. 229)

It is typical of Mrs. Wrightson that the quest of elemental spirits starts with a plane flight halfway across the continent, followed by a journey in a broken-down van and another flight in the arms of the wind. Wherever he goes, whether to confer with his old friend the Mimi or fight a grim battle for the soul of Ularra, Wirrun has in his ears a strange and moving song. For the Yunggamurra who has upset the balance of the world woos her rescuer, Lorelei-like, in song. In the tremendous climax, which comes surprisingly early in the narrative, the water-spirit is discovered in all her beauty and Ularra dies trying to possess her.

A quarter of the story remains untold. Wirrun still has to fulfil his promise and get rid of this disturber of the underground world. In doing so he comes near to exorcising the ghost which has been haunting him, and the Yunggamurra nearly—but not quite—becomes Murra, a lovely girl who is not quite at ease in the water and who wears, with great reluctance, the shirt which Wirrun thrusts upon her. It is an intriguing conclusion, sufficiently open to give hope of yet another sequel.

Apart from her matchless powers as a story-teller, Mrs. Wrightson possesses two outstanding qualities. First there is her ability to evoke the spirit of the land. Whether seen from the air or at the close range of vulnerable men in the wild bush, here is the beauty and the harshness of a country hardly touched, except on the fringe, by the eager pursuits of the Happy Folk. It is a land where the People and the earth-spirits co-exist by an agreement based on mutual respect. Then there is Mrs. Wrightson's strength as a creator of character. There is only one major newcomer among the humans, Merv Bula, who sets his traps and works out his philosophy in the loneliness of the bush, but both Wirrun and Ularra grow in complexity as they move to full maturity. There is just a brief glimpse of the Mimi, and no other spirit character is her equal in subtlety. It is essential to Mrs. Wrightson's scheme that Murra should remain enigmatic to the end. But the gallery of earth-creatures is as fascinating and convincing as ever.

It should be added that, immensely readable as the book is, it is still not easy to digest. The earth retains enough of its secrets and we are left pleasurably mystified about many matters. No matter; the involvement is enough. These strange books are a deeply disturbing experience. No reader can ever be quite the same again. (p. 230)

> *"For Children from Ten to Fourteen: 'The Dark Bright Water',"* in The Junior Bookshelf, *Vol. 43, No. 4, August, 1979, pp. 229-30.*

Patricia Wrightson has devised a story built on the interdependence of the spirit-world and the landscape and city of today, a story whose conclusion rests in the integration of the two in the person of Wirrun, who becomes a legendary hero while remaining a man. In this sense, shape-changing and identity-change provide the underlying theme of this most challenging book, whose simple story-line is enriched with magnificently conceived scenes and settings.

> *Margery Fisher, "Spirits and Shape-Changers," in* her Growing Point, *Vol. 18, No. 3, September, 1979, pp. 3563-64.**

JOURNEY BEHIND THE WIND (1981)

In the last of an Australian myth-fantasy series about Wirrun and his struggles for the People and the spirits of the land, he is renowned as Hero but isolated, having lost first his friend Ularra in *The Dark Bright Water* and now his wife Murra to her Waterspirit sisters. Even old comrades back off in awe as he takes on the mission of defeating Wulgaru, a creature of death that has broken the law of its country. Wulgaru and its origins are hinted rather than clearly explained, but its effects are powerfully focused, as are the characterizations of Wirrun

and Murra. Younger readers will not be put off by their relationship, which appears more a friendship of playmates than a marriage, nor by the descriptive detail, which is offset by brisk pace. A surprise ending finds Wirrun undefeated but irretrievably changed, and Wrightson's fans can once again revel in her ingenuity of plot and her enveloping prose, speeded along here on the wings of dramatic action.

> *Betsy Hearne, "Children's Books: 'Journey Behind the Wind',"* in Booklist *(reprinted by permission of the American Library Association; copyright © 1981 by the American Library Association), Vol. 77, No. 14, March 15, 1981, p. 1036.*

Like the two earlier books, this is beautifully developed and paced, with vivid characters and with that smooth blending of realism and fantasy that marks the best in fanciful writing.

> *Zena Sutherland, "New Titles for Children and Young People: 'Journey Behind the Wind',"* in Bulletin of the Center for Children's Books *(reprinted by permission of The University of Chicago Press; © 1981 by The University of Chicago), Vol. 34, No. 8, April, 1981, p. 164.*

Journey . . . rustles with energy from beginning to end. Whether describing battles, spiritual travels, or love's laughter and sorrows, the prose is vibrant and evocative. The story moves from emotion to emotion, chronicling Wirrun's love for the waterspirit Murra, her capture and their joint failures that ultimately made them free. As in the best fantasy, the book is filled with perception. . . . Wrightson has so thoroughly assimilated the myths, she has made them her own and thus made her novel as universal as the mythology.

> *George Shannon, "Book Reviews: 'Journey Behind the Wind',"* in School Library Journal *(reprinted from the April, 1981 issue of School Library Journal, published by R. R. Bowker Co./A Xerox Corporation; copyright © 1981), Vol. 27, No. 8, April, 1981, p. 135.*

[This] is in every respect less successful than its predecessors—more amorphous (and less graphic), more fraught with portent (and less humanly appealing). In terms of characters, it's barely a story at all. . . . Via spirit-journeys—heavily dependent on references to the earlier books—Wurrin at last has his innings with the fearsome Wulgaru in the cave of the dead; and, in saying "I am, I am," he breaks free.

Even Wrightson's sonorous, emotive writing cannot make his more than a paper contest, however. In almost excluding the casual, pregnant exchanges that gave the other books their vitality, and virtually the whole element of personality (human or extra-human), she leaves readers in a ponderous fog of myth and elusive "meaningfulness." (pp. 1301-02)

> *"Older Fiction: 'Journey Behind the Wind',"* in Kirkus Reviews *(copyright © 1981 The Kirkus Service, Inc.), Vol. XLIX, No. 20, October 15, 1981, pp. 1301-02.*

Taro Yashima

1908-

(Real name Jun Atsushi Iwamatsu) Japanese author/illustrator for children, nonfiction for adults, and translator of children's fiction and adult nonfiction. Yashima's children's books are inspired by his special regard for children, his experiences with them, and his yearning for the small Japanese village of his youth. These quiet works are considered remarkable for their strong mood and atmosphere and for presenting depth of characterization and emotion within the picture book format. Critics also praise the originality and technical skill of Yashima's illustrations and the poetic quality of his texts.

Yashima and his wife Mitsu, with whom he collaborated on several books, came to America in 1939. They intended to return home after studying Western art, but when war began between the United States and Japan, Yashima joined the U.S. Office of Strategic Services to fight for Japanese democracy. He remained in the United States, writing two political autobiographical sketch books as Taro (fat boy, healthy boy) Yashima (eight islands, old Japan, peaceful Japan) to symbolize his longing for his home in Kyushu. According to many critics, his books for children retain much of the Japanese culture and the lifestyle of this village.

Yashima's special appreciation for the young began at an early age: even as a youth he saw the innocence of younger children as a unique and beautiful treasure. As an art teacher in Japan, Yashima was inspired by the creativity and imagination of his pupils, and he admired their vision and resilience. It was not until after the birth of his daughter Momo that Yashima began writing and illustrating children's books. He created his first picture book, *The Village Tree*, to give his American-born daughter a special gift—his memories of life as a child in Japan. Critics admire this book for its simplicity, its successful capturing of the child's sense of wonder, and its ability to relate to children. *Crow Boy* is set in the grade school of Yashima's youth and is based on the experiences of a fellow classmate. It is perhaps Yashima's most beloved work, and is especially credited for its purity and strength of character.

Yashima's books based on his daughter move away from a Japanese setting, but maintain the sense of Japanese culture and the childlike innocence of his other works. *Momo's Umbrella*, focuses on a child's anticipation as she waits to use her new umbrella and boots and shows how small incidents are a part of the things that children consider important. Yashima's ending was criticized for its abrupt switch from Momo as a tiny child to Momo as a much older child. *Momo's Kitten* also received negative reviews for the darker, less defined quality of its illustrations. Yashima is usually praised, however, for his work as an illustrator and a writer. He is considered successful at capturing the incidents and feelings that make up the essence of childhood, and several of his books are considered timeless classics. He was awarded a Caldecott honor book notation in 1956 for *Crow Boy* and in 1959 for *Momo's Umbrella*. He also received the Southern California Council on Literature for Young People Award in 1964 for Distinguished Contribution to the Fields of Illustration and Writing and was presented in the University of Southern Mississippi de Grum-

mond Collection Medallion in 1974. (See also *Contemporary Authors*, Vol. 74, and *Something about the Author*, Vol. 14.)

GENERAL COMMENTARY

The pictures by Yashima for *Crow Boy, Umbrella,* and *Village Tree* are as unusual as they are beautiful. Small details such as the design of a patch on a boy's shirt, the lines on the ceiling, or on a desk are all considered worthy of illustration. The pictures of the lovely sweeping pattern of the village tree and the far away countryside of Chibi's house, are not easily forgotten. (p. 109)

> *Charlotte S. Huck and Doris A. Young, "Children Read Pictures," in their* Children's Literature in the Elementary School *(copyright © 1961 by Holt, Rinehart and Winston; reprinted by permission of Holt, Rinehart and Winston, Publishers, CBS College Publishing), Holt, Rinehart and Winston, 1961, pp. 75-119.**

Yashima's technique is romantic and sentimental. An intimate quality is communicated to the viewer. This shared intimacy is achieved through the use of light and dark areas in his picture design. These contrasts contribute a subtle quality and a poetic mood to the drawing, often a gentle, quiet mood. At the same time, the light areas can be so bathed in artificial light that there is also a resulting sense of drama. It is almost as if the viewer held a bright flashlight, flooding the diorama. Yashima creates his forms by this illusion also, as in the people and animals stated as light against dark in *The Village Tree*. . . . Two children are built completely by light and dark areas, as well as the farmer, and the child and the goat in another illustration. The forms are sometimes actually broken and the color which would normally be assigned to the object replaced by a shape of white or light color. This creates depth in the object and differentiates the specific parts that make the whole image.

In *Umbrella* . . . he handles this technique deftly and creates a shimmering softness reminiscent of some of the Impressionists' work. The child's whimsical face and figure are delicately handled with dark and light contrasts, and an occasional sensitive line is added to delineate details such as the umbrella, the toes, or a straggle of hair. These line details are used on both the light and the dark areas and are treated with understatement and taste. They add to the sentimental aura of the book. The *sgrafitto* technique [paper covered in black crayon and etched with a sharp tool to reveal previously applied colors] is an interesting and successful addition to the surfaces of some of the pictures. The perspective device of looking over an object in the foreground to strikingly foreshortened background objects is used effectively in the pictures of figures in the rain.

In *The Seashore Story* . . . soft pastel colors are blended and smudged into fuzzy-edged shapes of landscape. Occasional line details appear in the large masses but are never obtrusive; one needs to search for them. Yashima's people are delineated similarly—fuzzy-edged, but with light and dark contrasts building the body structure. A giant turtle is developed in the same manner. The four large oval deep-water shapes tend to be monotonous. It seems as though Yashima might have detailed them variously or altered them in some way to add to their visual interest. The double-page spreads are, for the most part, nicely planned with the text at the bottom. Exceptions are the three double pages of figures at the beach which do not seem to be organically planned. One's eye does not carry visually from one side of the page to the other or from one figure to

From Umbrella, *written and illustrated by Taro Yashima.*

the other. These pages are more suggestive of the figures in an artist's sketchbook, done with no particular need for synthesis and lacking the appearance of a finished and planned arrangement of shapes. (pp. 66-8)

> *Donnarae MacCann and Olga Richard, "Outstanding Contemporary Illustrators," in their* The Child's First Books: A Critical Study of Pictures and Texts *(copyright © 1973 by Donnarae MacCann and Olga Richard; reprinted by permission of The H. W. Wilson Company), Wilson, 1973, pp. 47-72.**

[*The Village Tree*] has no story, no peg; and no young Taro. It is a chronicle in captioned pictures—cartoon sketches in tiers, sprawling landscapes, a still-life—as if Yashima had assembled some pages from [his illustrated adult autobiographies] *The New Sun* and *Horizon Is Calling* and some of the corresponding paintings of those years: an art-memoir. The same is true of *Plenty to Watch*. . . . Because the village is Japanese, we learn about a Japanese village, but one could in principle do likewise for Centreville or River Junction—or Bay Ridge, Brooklyn. What is personal to Yashima, and peculiar to his circumstance, is the intensity of vision.

The book that, on the same terms, became a picture-story is *Crow Boy*. The boy nicknamed Chibi, 'tiny boy' ("None of us knew him"), is found on the first day of school hiding under the schoolhouse, and remains odd and apart. . . . In defense he withdraws, draws inward; and how he feels, what he sees and what engrosses him, Yashima depicts. . . . Like the first, the pictures are vividly, vibrantly colored—Chibi's 'egg,' his nest, is red-orange-yellow—but the weight of the images is as evident in black and white, and the shimmer of the ceiling, the texture of the desk top: still-lifes of the searching eye. And it is all the more remarkable in that contours as such hardly exist; Yashima draws, like [Paul] Cézanne, from the interior outward. By chance, or perhaps not, a metaphor for his subject.

Chibi comes to school every day nonetheless; and in the sixth grade, the last in the school, the children have a new teacher. Mr. Isobe takes the class outdoors and admires Chibi's knowledge; he likes his drawings and tacks them on the wall with samples of his handwriting "which no one but Chibi could read." "And he often spent time talking with Chibi when no one was around." In the talent show of that year, to the children's amazement, Chibi appears on stage; he [imitates] the voice of crows. . . .

Thenceforward Chibi, coming to town to sell charcoal, will be Crow Boy, to his evident pleasure. . . . The artist showing to us Chibi bowing, Mr. Isobe's regardful stance, and the life of Chibi—the person, concern for him, the reason for that concern—and, opposite, the children's reaction, makes us see the story, within and without, as one experienced. (p. 446)

For [Yashima's daughter] Momo, then eight, came *Umbrella*, the story of Momo at three. A Japanese sign, *Haru (Spring)*; opposite, a tabletop and on it a few sprigs of blossoming peach and a glowing fruit: "Momo is the name of a little girl / who was born in New York. / The word *Momo* means 'the peach' in Japan / where her father and mother used to live." The serene sureness of that opening, the confidence it places in the small listener and looker, give the lie to all claims that children have to be cajoled or assaulted, as anyone who has read *Umbrella* to a rapt group can attest. . . .

The story is best presented verbatim because there is no simpler, more direct or succinct way of putting it: the narrative is an exact telling. We do have Momo's various expedients: on

Urashima climbed on the turtle's back. And the turtle swam away into the depths of the ocean, leaving the shore far behind.

From Seashore Story, *written and illustrated by Taro Yashima.*

a sunny day—"I need my umbrella. The sunshine bothers my eyes!" and on a windy one—"I certainly need my umbrella today! The wind must bother my eyes!" (One must know a child to write 'must.') (p. 449)

There is much misplaced sentimentalism about books done for or about artists' children; but Yashima has in his books—others besides—pictured his life, and his children's as an extension of it, with the same clear-eyed regard, as if to preserve were to commemorate, which it is. (p. 450)

> Barbara Bader, *"The Japanese Advent,"* in her American Picturebooks from Noah's Ark to the Beast Within *(reprinted with permission of Macmillan Publishing Co., Inc.; copyright © 1976 by Barbara Bader),* Macmillan, 1976, pp. 443-58.*

THE VILLAGE TREE (1953)

Momo, Mr. Yashima's small daughter, wanted to know what her father did when he was her age in Japan. This book is the answer. There could not be a nicer answer, whether in text or pictures. It is all very, very simple the way Yashima and his friends spent some of the days of their boyhood, yet it is brimful with a poetical sense of wonder, and though they played hard and had a wonderful time . . . it is beauty and peace which pervade this eloquent picture book.

> Claire Huchet Bishop, *"The World Today: 'The Village Tree',"* in The Saturday Review, *New York (copyright © 1953 by* Saturday Review; *all rights reserved; reprinted by permission), Vol. XXXVI, No. 46, November 14, 1953, p. 74.*

The color work is evidently lithographed from crayon plates made by the artist. It is made up of softly-shaped forms that suggest rather than define, with a special power to give sunlight and water and the fluid action of the children's almost naked bodies. It is unlike any other current illustrator's work, very interesting. There is a nice variety of broad, big scenes and small detailed action pictures. Probably it will appeal more to children of six to eight than to younger ones.

A village tree is a magical memory. Remember Mr. [Padraic] Colum's "Big Tree of Bunlahy," and the many banyan trees in Indian stories? The very brief text tells no story, just describes this memory, with a magic of happy, active childhood pervading the pages. . . .

These indeed might be lively children playing in any country.

> *"Windows on Foreign Lands: 'The Village Tree',"* in New York Herald Tribune Book Review, *November 15, 1953, p. 7.*

The work of Taro Yashima leaves this reviewer with a strong feeling that here is an artist-writer who knows children, respects

He was afraid of the children and could not make friends with them at all

From Crow Boy, *written and illustrated by Taro Yashima.*

and loves them deeply. With both words and pastel-and-ink strokes he has captured their simplicity, gaiety and sense of wonder.

Mr. Yashima recalls a huge tree on the river bank in the Japanese village of his childhood. . . . There, Taro and his friends gathered to climb, explore, observe, play games and swim. The story is as simple as that. Yet the strength of his pictures is more than likely to evoke self-identification whether the reader be in Tappan, N.Y., or Buntok, Borneo.

> *Pat Clark, "Japanese Boyhood," in* The New York Times Book Review *(© 1953 by The New York Times Company; reprinted by permission), November 15, 1953, p. 43.*

A strikingly beautiful interpretation in poetic prose and picture of the author's childhood in Japan. . . . The brief text and full-color sketches illustrate, in an atmosphere of great peace and happiness, the kind of tree-play, diving and underwater fun that boys anywhere might invent. Of ageless interest. (pp. 454-55)

> *Virginia Haviland, "Picture Storybooks: 'The Village Tree'," in* The Horn Book Magazine *(copyrighted, 1953, copyright renewed © 1981, by The Horn Book, Inc., Boston), Vol. XXIX, No. 6, December, 1953, pp. 454-55.*

CROW BOY   (1955)

Taro Yashima has created another sensitively evocative picture book out of the scenes of his childhood in Japan. This story about a shy and lonely mountain boy . . . unfolds through pictures and text of moving and harmonious simplicity.

From page to page it flows, revealing a deeper meaning to life as a child blossoms under the understanding eye of a true teacher. One is left refreshed at its close as though touched by the mountain air which is the source of Crow Boy's individuality.

> *Maria Cimino, "Picture Books: 'Crow Boy'," in* The Saturday Review, *New York (copyright © 1955 by Saturday Review; all rights reserved; reprinted by permission), Vol. XXXVIII, No. 46, November 12, 1955, p. 62.*

The simple, touching tale with its school setting, has story interest for children up to eight or nine. Whether they listen, or read themselves, they will be looking at these impressionistic, colorful pictures, whose art lies both in simplicity of form and in the fine use of blank spaces. It is a good companion book to [**"The Village Tree"** and **"Plenty to Watch"**], and because of its story, may live longest of the three.

> *Louise S. Bechtel, "New Picture Books Offer Unusual, Original Stories for Many Ages," in* New York Herald Tribune Book Review *(© I.H.T. Corporation; reprinted by permission), November 13, 1955, p. 2.**

Children will love [Chibi's] story; adults will be deeply moved by it; it is a remarkable accomplishment to have got so much into so few words. The beautiful pictures linger in one's memory as if one had been in the village and walked with little Chibi, morning and night, the long walk between his home and school.

> *Jennie D. Lindquist, "Christmas Booklist: 'Crow Boy'," in* The Horn Book Magazine *(copyrighted, 1955, by The Horn Book, Inc., Boston), Vol. XXI, No. 6, December, 1955, p. 447.*

A great many picture books are published each year. Among them are some good ones, but only a few that are excellent.

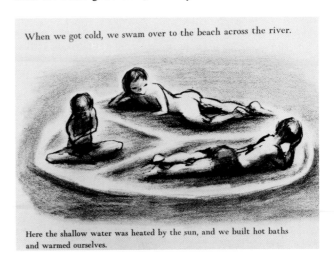

When we got cold, we swam over to the beach across the river.

Here the shallow water was heated by the sun, and we built hot baths and warmed ourselves.

From The Village Tree, *written and illustrated by Taro Yashima.*

One of the most striking published recently is **Crow Boy** by Taro Yashima. It does not belong in a class with painstakingly realistic representation or with sweet stereotyped stylizations. Neither could it be placed among the tasteful sophistications of the currently fashionable styles. It is therefore not altogether surprising that it did not attract more considerable attention.

The design is unusual. This large book seems even bigger than it is, yet not big enough for the colorful compositions that make the space surrounding them gleam magically more white than white. The sweeping rhythm of the pictures carries one through endless surprises; a page with one simple design will be followed by another filled with four or five small but well-composed pictures, sometimes suggesting no more than "a patch of cloth on a boy's shoulder," the wooden top of a desk with a knife or a pencil, streaks of rain on a window. The bold expressionism with a touch of humor, tempered by an oriental delicacy, blends in a rare poetic mood and carries through from the first to the last page—not to ignore the end papers, which are among the most beautiful designs.

Those who know the intricacies of the color separation technique for direct contact offset reproduction will be surprised by the ease with which Taro Yashima has mastered the medium. It is interesting to see the progress achieved since one of his earlier attempts in **The Village Tree.** Now the results are worthy of the best lithographers. With no more than the three basic colors, not counting the black, he fills his pictures with all the colors of the prism, combining the bright light of the Impressionists with a refined elegance reminiscent of Japanese paintings. The exuberance of his imagination held within the restraining limits of the technique is the mark of a draughtsman expressing himself with freedom and spontaneity and of an artist with a quality I praise above all—sincerity.

Since this has been an artist's choice, I have limited myself to the art work which, in a picture book, can by no means be considered independently, the essential quality being the unity of illustration, text and design. In this case we have a complete homogeneity, and if each picture can be enjoyed separately, so can the poetry of this simple story. . . . (pp. 429-30)

> *Nicolas Mordvinoff, "Artist's Choice," in* The Horn Book Magazine *(copyrighted, 1956, by The Horn Book, Inc., Boston), Vol. XXXII, No. 6, December, 1956, pp. 429-30.*

[A] teacher may be very much impressed by the visual beauty of Taro Yashima's **Crow Boy**—the highly controlled yet expressive brushwork, the visual unity of the whole little book— or by the vigor and tenderness of the narrative, or by the colorful and yet quite factual impression given of Japan, or by the honest illustration of how real worth may be hidden by superficial cultured differences, or by the book's suggestion that people can see much more than they ordinarily see in their environment. The teacher may respond to several or all of these qualities of **Crow Boy,** and she may use the book with any or all of these things in mind. She might read the book aloud (or have the students read it individually), for the drama and the color of the story itself and let it go at that. Or she might bring in the story when a question of differences in intelligence or clothes or habits came up in class or when the class was considering lands in the Pacific, or even crows. Or she might start with the story and then move in any of these directions. In such moving into, or away from, the story there would be no need to separate it from its content; the material is authentic, the story and illustrations are valuable aesthetic experiences,

and they harmonize. Indeed, Yashima's art is so casual and unpretentious that it is very easy to move between his story and the things it is about. Incidentally, the teacher could shift easily to the reading of fact-filled fiction or histories and geographies about Japan, in which Yashima's artistry was not present. Or she might read a few of the beautifully told Japanese folktales in *Tales of a Grandmother;* a child may sense in these, without being able to describe it or analyze it, something of the same restrained sensitivity, a kind of understatement that marks Yashima's art. (pp. 353-54)

> *James Steel Smith, "Children's Literature for Itself or 'In With'?" in his* A Critical Approach to Children's Literature *(copyright © 1967 by McGraw-Hill, Inc.; used with the permission of McGraw-Hill Book Company), McGraw-Hill, 1967, pp. 343-58.**

One of the few picture storybooks that portrays character development is **Crow Boy**. . . . In the very first picture of that wonderfully sensitive story, "Chibi" is shown hidden away in the dark space underneath the schoolhouse, afraid of the schoolmaster, afraid of the children. In subsequent pictures, he is always alone while the other children come to school in twos and threes. With the arrival of the friendly schoolmaster and his discovery of Chibi's talent to imitate crows, Chibi grows in stature and courage. . . . Chibi does not completely change with his new name of Crow Boy, for this story has the integrity of life itself. He remains aloof and independent as he assumes his increased adult responsibilities. He has lost the gnawing loneliness of Chibi, however, as the final pages of

Soon after that came graduation day.

Chibi was the only one in our class honored for perfect attendance through all the six years.

From Crow Boy, *written and illustrated by Taro Yashima.*

text and pictures combine to tell us of his character development. . . . (pp. 112-13)

> *Charlotte S. Huck and Doris Young Kuhn, "Picture Books," in their* Children's Literature in the Elementary School, *2nd ed. (copyright © 1961, 1968 by Holt, Rinehart and Winston, Inc.; reprinted by permission of Holt, Rinehart and Winston, Publishers, CBS College Publishing), second edition, Holt, Rinehart and Winston, 1968, pp. 95-155.**

There are many ways of making a psychological and social point. In a few direct, simple sentences [Yashima] shows the quiet endurance and determination a child can display and has made a firm statement about tolerance. In his words and his impressionistic pictures he shows a small boy who is at once an individual belonging to a particular background and a boy of all times and countries.

> *Margery Fisher, "Who's Who in Children's Books: 'Crow Boy'," in her* Who's Who in Children's Books: A Treasury of the Familiar Characters of Childhood *(copyright © 1975 by Margery Fisher; reprinted by permission), Holt, Rinehart and Winston, Weidenfeld & Nicolson, 1975, p. 75.*

UMBRELLA (1958)

With effective use of unusually brilliant color and simple singing text, Taro Yashima tells the story of a small Japanese girl in New York who wants to use her new umbrella. But the sun keeps shining. Mr. Yashima knows how to delight the eye and the ear and just what matters most to the 4-7's.

> *Pamela Marsh, "Books: 'Umbrella'," in* The Christian Science Monitor *(reprinted by permission from* The Christian Science Monitor; © 1958 The Christian Science Publishing Society; all rights reserved), May 8, 1958, p. 15.*

It seems to me that Taro Yashima makes his picture books live through the special gift of love with which he endows them. The simple charm and delicacy of his text and his impressionistic drawings always communicate more than is seen on the page. **"Umbrella"** was made for his daughter for her eighth birthday, but it is also a gift for every child—and grown-ups as well—so tenderly does it convey the excitement and pleasure of a small child with her first umbrella and red rubber boots, and the wonder of life itself.

> *Maria Cimino, "Spring Books for Young People: 'Umbrella'," in* The Saturday Review, New York *(copyright © 1958 by Saturday Review; all rights reserved; reprinted by permission), Vol. XLI, No. 19, May 10, 1958, p. 43.*

["**Umbrella**" is a] tender recollection of a little girl's impatience. . . . Granted, it relates only a small incident, but Mr. Yashima's talent as an artist is so considerable that he makes us clearly see that a child's life is composed of many such small episodes.

> *George A. Woods, "Pictures for Fun, Fact and Fancy," in* The New York Times Book Review *(©1958 by The New York Times Company; reprinted by permission), June 8, 1958, p. 42.*

Mr. Yashima's beautiful pictures and simple tale will be very appealing to young children. They will sympathize wholeheartedly with Momo's reasons for needing her umbrella. They

will be carried along by their identification with the actions of this very real little girl. It is only unfortunate that, at the end, the author swings forward, then backward again in time. Young children cannot make these rapid transitions and the adult reader will have a good deal of explaining to do. But the beauty of the book makes this worth while.

> *Elizabeth Doak, "Summer Booklist: 'Umbrella'," in* The Horn Book Magazine *(copyright, 1958, by the Horn Book, Inc., Boston), Vol. XXXIV, No. 4, August, 1958, p. 260.*

This is a sensitive, joyful story. . . . Colorful illustrations, done in a sophisticated and impressionistic style, will interest adults more than children.

It would have been helpful if the author had indicated that the raindrop sounds in the story are in Japanese and analogous to "pitter patter" in English.

> *Asian-American Task Force, "Book Reviews: 'Umbrella'," in* Interracial Books for Children Bulletin *(reprinted by permission of* Interracial Books for Children Bulletin, 1841 Broadway, New York, N.Y. 10023), Vol. 7, Nos. 2 & 3, 1976, p. 17.*

MOMO'S KITTEN (with Mitsu Yashima, 1961)

The artist's customary distinguished work is not as successful as in the earlier volumes; his blurred, subtle style results in the objects he is picturing being so indistinct as to be almost indistinguishable, and the warm appeal of the previous books is completely lacking.

> *Allie Beth Martin, "Preschool & Primary Grades: 'Momo's Kitten'," in* School Library Journal, *an appendix to* Library Journal *(reprinted from the November, 1961 issue of* School Library Journal, *published by R. R. Bowker Co./A Xerox Corporation; copyright ©1961), Vol. 8, No. 3, November, 1961, p. 48.*

Enchanting is the only possible word for this new picture book from the talented pen and brush of the Yashimas. . . . Illustrating this story—simple enough for a 3 year old—are striking pictures that make the book a must for every lover of cats.

> *E.C.L., "Fine Words, with Fine Pictures, for the 4 to 8s," in* Chicago Sunday Tribune Magazine of Books, *Part 4 (© 1961 Chicago Tribune), November 12, 1961, p. 10.**

A stray kitten adopted by a little girl and "growing cleaner and rounder every day" until "the most miserable kitten of a year ago was the most beautiful mother cat in the whole world" is a familiar and popular theme for small children. Taro Yashima's characteristic and unusual drawings with their sculptural feeling conveyed by many-colored crayon strokes make this a special study of mischievous kittens in a home and of a little girl's solicitous care of them. The simple text expresses the tender understanding of little Momo, who cherished the stray kitten, her concern for her charge, and her own progress towards growing up.

> *Margaret Sherwood Libby, "For Boys and Girls: 'Momo's Kitten'," in* Books—New York Herald Tribune *(© I.H.T. Corporation; reprinted by permission), December 17, 1961, p. 13.*

The drawings are typically Yashima, well done and lovely, but with a vague and unclear quality that is disconcerting. Because of the print and paper quality, some illustrations are very dark and difficult to interpret.

There is nothing in the story that would indicate that this family is Japanese American except for the names.

> *Asian-American Task Force, "Book Reviews: 'Momo's Kitten'," in* Interracial Books for Children Bulletin *(reprinted by permission of* Interracial Books for Children Bulletin, *1841 Broadway, New York, N.Y. 10023), Vol. 7, Nos. 2 & 3, 1976, p. 16.*

SEASHORE STORY   (1967)

The illustrations . . . in Taro Yashima's **Seashore Story** . . . are so lyrically lovely that one is apt to overlook the excellence of the text: a legend of years-ago Japan told for modern Japanese youngsters and for youngsters everywhere—and parents, teachers, all adults. Imaginative and tasteful. I hope the Caldecott jury is listening, as well as flower children, hippies, Tolkienites, all types.

> *Eve Merriam, "Children's Best Sellers: 'Seashore Story'," in* The New York Times Book Review *(© 1967 by The New York Times Company; reprinted by permission), November 5, 1967, p. 71.*

[This] unusual and beautiful book, the old tale of Urashima, the Japanese Rip Van Winkle, is retold using a story-within-a-story device. Japanese children from a ballet school visit a beach, and the stillness and remoteness of the place remind them of the familiar story of Urashima. The story is poetically told in a few words and dreamlike, melting illustrations which merely suggest images and convey the mystery and wonder of Urashima's experiences in the depths of the sea. The semi-abstract illustrations in rich but subtle opaque colors are strongly emotional and, with the evocative brief text, leave room for the imagination. Unfortunately, the book's ending is a return to the present-day seashore with a commentary on the story by the children and their teacher, which shatters the story's mood of haunting sadness, though the loveliness of the last glimpses of the seashore in the illustrations conveys a sense of time-lessness. The book is lovely to look at even though it tells a story awkwardly. (pp. 4607-08)

> *Nancy Young Orr, "Preschool and Primary Grades: 'Seashore Story'," in* School Library Journal, *an appendix to* Library Journal *(reprinted from the December, 1967 issue of* School Library Journal, *published by R. R. Bowker Co./A Xerox Corporation; copyright © 1967), Vol. 14, No. 4, December, 1967, pp. 4607-08.*

The legend is well-told, its framework about a ballet class at the beach inconclusive; what Taro Yashima does achieve is the awareness that important things endure (the legend, for example, is important enough for children today to discuss) but this is a concept too mature for the audience. The lovely illustrations, nebulous and shimmering, echo the quiet mood of the story.

> *Zena Sutherland, "New Titles for Children and Young People: 'Seashore Story'," in* Bulletin of the Center for Children's Books *(reprinted by permission of The University of Chicago Press; copyright 1968 by The University of Chicago), Vol. 21, No. 5, January, 1968, p. 88.*

This mysterious tale of Urashima . . . follows the adventures of a fisherman who is carried on a turtle's back to a palace under the sea, where he becomes unconscious of time. On his return home he is suddenly transformed into an old man. The subtle paintings, absorbing in their exquisitely muted but rich colors and their beautiful composition, will give the child much to think about. They present a commendable challenge, a contrast to the finished, the obvious, and the ordinary.

> *Virginia Haviland, "Picture-Book Editions of Folk Tales: 'Seashore Story'," in* The Horn Book Magazine *(copyright © 1968 by The Horn Book, Inc., Boston), Vol. XLIV, No. 1, February, 1968, p. 56.*

We might compare [the customary use of masculine pronouns in children's books] to Taro Yashima's treatment of a group of children in **Seashore Story,** where he uses such phrases as "One asked," "Another asked," and "A young teacher answered." For a writer to do what Yashima does rather than referring to everyone as *he*, takes both greater awareness and greater skill in writing. (p. 167)

> *Alleen Pace Nilsen, "Women in Children's Literature" (copyright © 1971 by the National Council of Teachers of English; reprinted by permission of the publisher and the author), in* College English, *Vol. 32, No. 8, May, 1971 (and reprinted in* Sexism and Youth, *edited by Diane Gersoni, R. R. Bowker Company, 1974, pp. 163-73).**

Jane Yolen

1939-

American author of folk and fairy tales, fiction, poetry, and plays for children and young adults, critic, essayist, and editor for adults. Descended from a line of writers and storytellers, Yolen is seen as carrying on the tradition with distinction. She is regarded as an outstanding prose stylist, and is perhaps best known for her literary folk and fairy tales. In these works Yolen combines familiar stories with modern twists or creates original stories which are reminiscent of the classic tales in structure and feeling. Yolen often writes metaphorically using symbols and allusions, and she believes strongly in the value of folklore to shape one's awareness of language, art, and culture.

Yolen's work is characterized by a diversity of subject matter and style. She often writes tales of transformation, a beast becomes human or a human a beast, and stories about youthful detectives set in present and future times. The history and characteristics of the Shaker movement appear in her fiction and nonfiction; Yolen's conversion to the Quaker religion led to her well-received biography *Friend: The Story of George Fox and the Quakers*. While much of her writing utilizes wit and puns, the struggle between opposing moral forces displays itself in numerous folk tales and in works with a religious theme such as *The Gift of Sarah Barker*.

Yolen strives to make her books read well both aloud and on the page, and critics note the lilt and rhythm in *The Seventh Mandarin* and *The Girl Who Loved the Wind*. Some reviewers find fault with the remoteness and shallowness of some of her plots and characters, but most praise Yolen's writing for its discipline, polish, insight, and beauty. In 1968 *The Emperor and the Kite* won the Lewis Carroll Shelf Award, was designated an American Library Association Notable Book, and chosen as one of the best books of the year by *The New York Times*, Yolen won the Lewis Carroll Shelf Award again in 1973 for *The Girl Who Loved the Wind*. She received the Golden Kite Award in 1974 for *The Girl Who Cried Flowers*, which was also a finalist for the National Book Award in 1975. She won the Golden Kite Honor Book Award for *The Transfigured Hart* in 1975 and in 1976 for *The Moon Ribbon and Others Tales*, and was given the Christopher Award in 1977 for *The Seeing Stick*. (See also *Contemporary Authors First Revision Series*, Vols. 13-16, and *Something about the Author*, Vol. 4.)

AUTHOR'S COMMENTARY

[There are] six whose names form the acronym SHAZAM: Solomon, Hercules, Atlas, Zeus, Achilles, Mercury. SHAZAM. It has become a mnemonic for instant change but, for most children, nothing more.

Mythology, legend, the lore of the folk, those tales were once as real to their believers as a sunrise. They do not even exist today as reference points. In our need to update the educational standards, we have done away with the old gods. And now we have names without faces, mnemonics without meaning. (p. 186)

Stories lean on stories, cultures on cultures. If our children can look at their own folklore, they will see some very surprising shadows indeed. Spiderman and the Incredible Hulk, Fonzie and the Bionic Woman do not spring from nothingness but from needs within our own culture. And those needs lean on past need. (p. 187)

And so, in Spiderman we see Prometheus and Anansi the Spider and Robin Hood. In the Incredible Hulk there is Atlas and Hercules and Paul Bunyan. Fonzie is both Loki and Achilles. And the Bionic Woman springs from Diana and the Amazons, propelled by the electronic revolution and feminist rage. (pp. 187-88)

[Four] functions of myth and legend and folklore make the listening to and learning of the old stories one of the most basic elements of our education: a landscape of allusion, the understanding of other cultures that leads to an understanding of our own, an adaptable tool of therapy, and the ability to express a symbolic or metaphoric statement of existence.

I draw on all those aspects of mythology and folklore when I write, for I write fantasy and fairy tales. I could even say that I am attempting to add to the growing body of such lore while working out my own belief system. Except, of course, it is all done subconsciously. What I am always trying to do is write a good story, tell a good tale. But obviously I think I have something serious to say about myself and my world. All writers write about themselves. We call it the world, but it is ourselves we portray. The world is only a reflecting mirror that shows the inside of our hearts, often more truly than we know.

So I write about myself, trying to make a serious statement. But I write in code, a symbolic language. That code can be read on many levels. The child reads it on one, the adult on another. The artist reads it differently from the analyst. My husband reads it differently from my father. And I read it another way still. Who is right? We are all right. For just as the writer writes about him/herself so the reader reads solipsistically. And this we call communication.

But a child, more open than the adult, is more changed by that reading. Just as the child is born with a literal hole in its head, where the bones slowly close underneath the fragile shield of skin and hair, just so the child is born with a figurative hole in its heart. Slowly it too is filled up. Slowly this wound of God heals. What slips in before it anneals creates the man or woman that child grows into. Literature, folklore, mythology—they surely must rank as some of the most important intrusions into the heart.

So a child reading my serious statement, my fairy tale, takes it—and me (for the story *is* me)—into his heart. There is a literary Eucharist: blood of my blood, heart of my heart. I am mother to all children who read my tales.

Yet in the back of my mind are all those children shouting SHAZAM without knowing its components; and the freshmen at Boston College who never heard of King David; and the senior at Smith who accused me of making up Lilith. And I worry.

Will we, instead of creating men and women who have a grasp of literary allusion, symbolic language, and a metaphorical tool for dealing with the serious problems of existence, only be forming boys and girls who develop their own truncated, allusion-free, barren language that reflects a truncated, allusion-free, barren way of life? Language reflects life just as language helps develop life. It is a most important part of the *human* condition. I deplore the loss of the word, of words. And I believe that language and myth are inextricably linked. (pp. 188-89)

What happens when we cut myth out of the child's life? We undercut, simultaneously, language and art. (p. 189)

> *Jane Yolen, "How Basic Is Shazam?" (adapted by permission of Philomel Books, a Division of The Putnam Publishing Group), in* Childhood Education, *Vol. 53, No. 4 (February, 1977), pp. 186-89 (and reprinted in a revised form in her* Touch Magic, *Philomel Books, 1981).*

THE WITCH WHO WASN'T (1964)

We found the text [of **"The Witch Who Wasn't"**] quite bland. [It] has a very amusing Spelling Bee at the end (the witch kind is for the making of spells, not for correct spelling) in which the little witch's harmless spell wins her surprising acclaim from her elders. [A] lighthearted Halloween trifle for 8 to 10-year-olds. . . .

> *Margaret Sherwood Libby, "Tricks As Well as Treats," in* Book Week—The Sunday Herald Tri-

bune (© *1964, The Washington Post), October 25, 1964, p. 16.***

[*The Witch Who Wasn't*] is a fairly common formula, the story of the sheep who cannot be black enough; Isabel cannot believe that she will pass the annual test for budding young sorceresses, because all her spells turn out too harmless and too nice. Her success depends on the exploitation of a well-known feminine weakness.

> *"Consumer Goods or Durables?: 'The Witch Who Wasn't'," in* The Times Literary Supplement (© *Times Newspapers Ltd. (London) 1967; reproduced from* The Times Literary Supplement *by permission), No. 3431, November 30, 1967, p. 1136.*

TRUST A CITY KID (with Anne Huston, 1966)

Trust A City Kid offers a peculiarly confused lesson in nonviolence to a deprived Negro city boy. . . . The pacifist Bradshaws and their son Frank claim to believe in the power of love, yet none of them seems to feel any real understanding of, or sympathy with, their visitor. On the contrary, they are superior and self-righteous and neglect Reg cruelly. Reg's sullen self-hatred is hardly more attractive, but his helplessness and loneliness make him mildly sympathetic. The plot, which hinges on his desire for a horse, is a series of humiliating misadventures in which Reg always does the worst possible thing and the Bradshaws show the most infuriating "tolerance." In the final crisis the reader can't help hoping that Frank Bradshaw will behave like the nasty fellow Reg thinks he is, but Frank turns the tables in true goodie-goodie fashion and teaches Reg the power of pacifism. It leaves a sour taste of contradictory morality. . . .

> *Elizabeth Tornquist, "Managing on Their Own," in* Book Week—World Journal Tribune (© *1967, The Washington Post), January 15, 1967, p. 12.***

The account of Reg's efforts to conceal and shelter the pathetic beast is quite moving. **"Trust a City Kid"** manages a satisfactory plot and several effective passages; Reg is a credible character—but the Bradshaws fail even as types.

> *Mary Louise Birmingham, "For the Young Reader: 'Trust a City Kid'," in* The New York Times Book Review (© *1967 by The New York Times Company; reprinted by permission), January 22, 1967, p. 26.*

Similar in theme, characters, and point of view to [Nan H. Agle's] *Joe Bean* . . . , this well-told story projects sharply a Harlem boy's attitudes during a summer spent with a Pennsylvania Quaker family. He comes to realize that the Friends' way of not striking back in anger is of more value in our society than is belligerent action. Reg's sympathy for a horse doomed to become mink food and his nighttime adventures on its behalf hold the interest of the reader. His inner development comes naturally enough to be credible, with the point clearly made here, as it is in *Joe Bean*, that a proud and intelligent child's ignorance or lack of understanding of common enough words and ways of behavior inevitably creates resistance and blind misbehavior.

> *Virginia Haviland, "Stories for the Middle Years: 'Trust a City Kid'," in* The Horn Book Magazine (*copyright © 1967, by The Horn Book, Inc., Boston), Vol. XLIII, No. 2, April, 1967, p. 206.*

ISABEL'S NOEL (1967)

The three hilariously caricatured witches and the frantic Santa make strange sled fellows as they all try desperately to get him off [to the North Pole.] . . . A zany fantasy with a MAD mag cast, equipped to tickle the reader as well as the read-to.

> *"Picture Books: 'Isabel's Noel',"* in Kirkus Service *(copyright © 1967 Virginia Kirkus' Service, Inc.), Vol. XXXV, No. 12, June 15, 1967, p. 693.*

Poor Isabel, too young to be an accomplished spell-caster; and she didn't even look like a witch, with her curly hair and blue eyes. One night to go, and she had nothing for her mother's or her grandmother's Christmas present, so she cast a spell; rather, she miscast a spell and Santa Claus magically appeared in her grandmother's cauldron of lizard soup. He had to get back, he announced, so Isabel tried her worst to conjure him home. . . . [The] story has the double appeals of the Christmas theme and the reversal-humor children enjoy, such as Mother's admonition to Isabel, as she gets ready to fly away, to "go inside and dirty up first."

> *Zena Sutherland, "New Titles for Children and Young People: 'Isabel's Noel',"* in Bulletin of the Center for Children's Books *(reprinted by permission of The University of Chicago Press; copyright 1967 by the University of Chicago), Vol. 21, No. 2, October, 1967, p. 36.*

["Isabel's Noel"] is a problem in itself. Labeled a fun and frolic book, it labors along mixing witches and Santa Claus, sleighs and broomsticks. . . . [Sometimes] just anticipating Christmas can be more fun than reading about it.

> *George A. Woods, "For Young Readers: 'Isabel's Noel',"* in The New York Times Book Review *(© 1967 by The New York Times Company; reprinted by permission), December 3, 1967, p. 68.*

THE EMPEROR AND THE KITE (1967)

This publishing season, the Far East seems to be getting nearer and nearer: there are countless books with Oriental backgrounds. This is easily one of the most distinguished—and distinguished proof that extravagance, intelligent, premeditated extravagance, always justifies itself. . . . It's a story with a theme to please small idealists—the triumph of loyalty, and with a feature to delight them—the heroine is *much* smaller than a breadbox.

> *"Children's Books: 'The Emperor and the Kite',"* in Publishers Weekly *(reprinted from the August 14, 1967 issue of* Publishers Weekly, *published by R. R. Bowker Company; copyright © 1967 by R. R. Bowker Company), Vol. 192, No. 7, August 14, 1967, p. 50.*

The story is told in a clear and supple prose, poetic yet simple, which is excellent for reading aloud. Here is a writer who delights in words and can use them in a controlled way to beautiful effect, and a style that accords well with the ancient Chinese setting. (p. 23)

> *J.A.C., "Picture Books: 'The Emperor and the Kite',"* in Children's Book News *(copyright © 1970 by Baker Book Services Ltd.), Vol. 5, No. 1, January-February, 1970, pp. 23-4.*

Djeow Seow manages to save her father, but she accomplishes this task only by being so tiny and inconspicuous that the evil men do not notice her. Although Djeow Seow is one of the two women central characters, the message conveyed to readers seems to be that a girl can only triumph by playing the traditional feminine role. Women who succeed are those who are unobtrusive and work quietly behind the scenes. Women who succeed are little and inconspicuous—as are most women in picture books. Even heroines remain "invisible" females. (p. 179)

> *Lenore J. Weitzman, Deborah Eifler, Elizabeth Hakada, and Catherine Ross, "Sex-Role Socialization in Picture Books for Preschool Children,"* in The American Journal of Sociology *(reprinted by permission of The University of Chicago Press; © 1972 by The University of Chicago), Vol. LXXVII, No. 6, May, 1972 (and reprinted in* Sexism and Youth, *edited by Diane Gersoni, R. R. Bowker Company, 1974, pp. 174-95).*

THE MINSTREL AND THE MOUNTAIN (1968)

If there is any quibble with this nicely rounded . . . little fable, it is that it is perhaps all too neat and sweet, occasionally even a trifle pompous in straining for the stature of a classic for our times. The world, however, could well use Miss Yolen's minstrel.

> *Selma G. Lanes, "Folk Tales and Fables for the Youngest: 'The Minstrel and the Mountain',"* in Book World—The Washington Post *(© 1967 Postrib Corp.; reprinted by permission of* Chicago Tribune *and The Washington Post), November 12, 1967, p. 26.*

An original fairy tale with an obvious moral . . . for the younger child. Children may enjoy the story . . . , but adults probably need the moralizing about how two warring kingdoms were brought to peace more than children do.

> *Flossie Perkins, "The Book Review: 'The Minstrel and the Mountain',"* in School Library Journal, *an appendix to* Library Journal *(reprinted from the February, 1968 issue of* School Library Journal, *published by R. R. Bowker Co./A Xerox Corporation; copyright © 1968), Vol. 14, No. 6, February, 1968, p. 86.*

GREYLING: A PICTURE STORY FROM THE ISLANDS OF SHETLAND (1968)

Life in the Shetland Islands, the most northerly part of Scotland, must be grim. You get that feeling from Jane Yolen's serious, gloomy **"Greyling."** . . . This legend stars a married couple who can't have children. He picks up a selchie—a seal who turns into a boy—and they raise him. One stormy day he dives into the ocean to save his "father" from drowning, regaining his old seal form forever. (He had to do it because the townsfolk refused to volunteer for a rescue mission.) The Shetland image suffers here.

> *Jerome Beatty, Jr., "Stories for 6 to 9: 'Greyling: A Picture Story from the Islands of Shetland',"* in The New York Times Book Review *(© 1968 by The New York Times Company; reprinted by permission), November 13, 1968, p. 67.*

Out of the legends of the Scottish isles comes a haunting story, bittersweet. . . . The style has the gentle, crooning quality of the seal songs of the islands, and [the story has] rugged simplicity. . . .

Zena Sutherland, "Books for Young People: 'Greyling: A Picture Story from the Islands of Shetland'," in Saturday Review (copyright © 1969 by Saturday Review; all rights reserved; reprinted by permission), Vol. LII, No. 12, March 22, 1969, pp. 62-3.

WORLD ON A STRING: THE STORY OF KITES (1968)

This is a book about kites that would be stylish *any* day, for in her text and in her choice of prints and photographs, Miss Yolen has told their glorious history with great style. And so persuasively that readers will be quick to recognize the validity of her statement, "the only way to discover if the kite is your 'contract of glory' is to make or buy a kite of your own and fly it."

"World on a String: The Story of Kites," in Publishers Weekly (reprinted from the February 3, 1969 issue of Publishers Weekly, published by R. R. Bowker Company, a Xerox company; copyright © 1969 by Xerox Corporation), Vol. 194, No. 5, February 3, 1969, p. 65.

[*World on a String: The Story of Kites*] gives an evocative account of the many practical and imaginative uses of kites from early times to the present, with hints of some future developments. The author's obvious enthusiasm is disciplined into a well organized presentation of kite flying in the Orient, Europe, and America, different types of kites, kite fighting, fishing, and swimming, etc. Numerous handsome photographs and reproductions, along with their excellent captions, add an important dimension to the text.

Mary Ann Wentroth, "The Book Review: 'World on a String: The Story of Kites'," in School Library Journal, an appendix to Library Journal (reprinted from the April, 1969 issue of School Library Journal, published by R. R. Bowker Co./A Xerox Corporation; copyright © 1969), Vol. 15, No. 8, April, 1969, p. 1787.

[Kiting] has become a popular pastime, and this book should enlist many a new recruit. The history of kites, which began at least 2,000 years ago in China, is given in vivid detail, with many a delightful anecdote. . . . How kites have contributed to weather watching, electricity, bridge building, the airplane, aerial photography, military operations, even rescues; how they have served as religious symbols, art objects, toys, and for sporting use, is told with style, enthusiasm and authority.

Polly Goodwin, "Children's Book World: 'World on a String: The Story of Kites'," in Book World— Chicago Tribune (© 1969 Postrib Corp.; reprinted by permission of Chicago Tribune and The Washington Post), April 20, 1969, p. 12.

This is an intriguing . . . volume, replete with legend, history and scientific data. It is intended for young people but any adult is sure to get caught up in its pages before passing it on.

Henry Gilfond, "For Young Readers: 'World on a String: The Story of Kites'," in The New York Times Book Review (© 1969 by The New York Times Company; reprinted by permission), July 13, 1969, p. 26.

THE INWAY INVESTIGATORS; OR, THE MYSTERY AT McCRACKEN'S PLACE (1969)

Memo from the president ("3-2. I voted for myself") of the Inway Investigators ("The two i's are always open—for trouble") . . . on the week's stakeout of the newly-walled McCracken Place: two ugly-looking bruisers (Joe and Sam? or Sam and Joe?) enter and leave daily in a truck . . . on the Great Watson Caper, or how to get dog Watson over the wall to lure the Dobermans away: no go . . . on the Br'er Rabbit Trick that prompts dognapping "Doctor" Payne ("Don't laugh") to put prying David where he wants to be—in the McCracken cellar . . . etc., etc. . . . all in a nine-year-old patter that's fresh, terse and funny—a capital new line in detection.

"Younger Fiction: 'The Inway Investigators; or, The Mystery at McCracken's Place'," in Kirkus Reviews (copyright © 1969 The Kirkus Service, Inc.), Vol. XXXVII, No. 9, May 1, 1969, p. 508.

The writing style is just a bit cute at times, but the book has plenty of action and not too many characters; the children's interest and their contribution are within the bounds of credibility, and the theme of pet-snatching is a serious matter that is handled just seriously enough. (p. 186)

Zena Sutherland, "New Titles for Children and Young People: 'The Inway Investigators; or, The Mystery at McCracken's Place'," in Bulletin of the Center for Children's Books (reprinted by permission of The University of Chicago Press; copyright 1969 by The University of Chicago), Vol. 22, No. 11, July-August, 1969, pp. 185-86.

THE WIZARD OF WASHINGTON SQUARE (1969)

As much fun as a white rabbit popping out of a magician's hat is this sprightly tale of a wizard who lives in Washington Square and who uses the silver sprayer from the fountain there as a periscope. He leads a native New York girl and a just-arrived-in-New-York boy and the boy's dog into antic and magical adventures. Young readers would do well to tag along.

"The Wizard of Washington Square," in Publishers Weekly (reprinted from the October 20, 1969 issue of Publishers Weekly, published by R. R. Bowker Company, a Xerox company; copyright © 1969 by Xerox Corporation), Vol. 196, No. 16, October 20, 1969, pp. 60-1.

Only in kooky Greenwich Village, where people plan "happenings" and sign petitions blindly, could a sniveling second-class wizard earn his return to the Old Country, i.e. away from America where only a few "*children* believe in magic." The first premise is very much a product of the premises and so, smugly, is the repeated insistence that this is a nation without imagination. Lonely newcomer David, an infantile eleven-year-old, has to be *shown*, too, before he believes Village veteran "dark as night" Leila. The wizard is a bore and the kids are a nuisance.

"Younger Fiction: 'The Wizard of Washington Square'," in Kirkus Reviews (copyright © 1969 The Kirkus Service, Inc.), Vol. XXXVII, No. 21, November 1, 1969, p. 1150.

[A few merry ploys] give the author a chance to poke fun at some of the Greenwich Village types and to exploit a few local legends. The bland style is a good foil for the gay extravagance of the fanciful plot.

Zena Sutherland, "New Titles for Children and Young People: 'The Wizard of Washington Square'," in Bulletin of the Center for Children's Books (reprinted by permission of The University of Chicago Press; © 1970 The University of Chicago), Vol. 23, No. 10, June, 1970, p. 170.

HOBO TOAD AND THE MOTORCYCLE GANG (1970)

Funny-punny or just a silly sally, depending on your sense of humor, or at least on how verbally precocious you are—and if you respond to a walking talking toad as gangbuster. *The Inway Investigators* . . . did what this does less anomalously since the people in question there were people; yet no less entertainingly, H.T. brings outlaws to justice.

"Younger Fiction: 'Hobo Toad and the Motorcycle Gang'," in Kirkus Reviews (copyright © 1970 The Kirkus Service, Inc.), Vol. XXXVIII, No. 8, April 15, 1970, p. 455.

There is some humor in the story and flashes of wild imagination in a few scenes. Miss Yolen likes to play with words—e.g., in conversations between Mac and H.T. and the Diner's signs. At best, it's a tale for the short haul.

Nancy Hyden Woodward, "For Young Readers: 'Hobo Toad and the Motorcycle Gang'," in The New York Times Book Review (© 1970 by The New York Times Company; reprinted by permission), May 17, 1970, p. 26.

There is an air of slapstick about the confrontation of Mac, the "'Tennyson of the Truckers,'" and H. T., his hitchhiking toad companion, with a gang of thugs. The latter are masterminded by the "Professor," who notes the word "inflammable" on the diesel truck outside Great Kate's Grate, a roadhouse where a famous variety of pies is served by button-bursting Kate. Taking the painted name to indicate contents that might be useful to the thieves in a bank holdup, they gag and bind the unsuspecting friends—but experience a hilarious upsetting of their calculations when the crashing vehicle spews out a load of marbles and the gang courts conviction by rolling straight to the Police Station. The narrative, with a high-flown style appropriate to the nonsense, will delight its audience. (pp. 391-92)

"Virginia Haviland, "Stories for the Middle Readers: 'Hobo Toad and the Motorcycle Gang'," in The Horn Book Magazine (copyright © 1970 by The Horn Book, Inc., Boston), Vol. 46, No. 4, August, 1970, pp. 391-92.

THE SEVENTH MANDARIN (1970)

In some phantasmal Eastern realm where only what is written in the books and scrolls is credited in the king's court and his soul is thought to fly into the sky each night on the wings of a dragon kite, the seventh and youngest mandarin, who has charge of the kite, loses it one night in a storm and, in recovering it, sees the hovels and hears the cries that are not in the books and scrolls. The king, awakening pale and shaken, has dreamed of such things, and the seventh mandarin confirms his vision; he should be punished for failing the king, for damaging the kite, for saying that what is *not* written is so,

but he will be excused "for discovering the truth and not fearing to reveal it." The walls around the palace will be taken down, and the king will listen and look as well as read. This is all pretty rarefied and remote. . . . A kind of hushed confidence that's not likely to get much of a hearing.

"Picture Books: 'The Seventh Mandarin'," in Kirkus Reviews (copyright © 1970 The Kirkus Service, Inc.), Vol. XXXVIII, No. 20, October 15, 1970, p. 1142.

Jane Yolen is a gifted writer whose style is economical yet sufficiently elaborated to give body and atmosphere to [this 'original' folk tale]. She conveys an eastern flavour through the cadence and rhythm of her sentences which read aloud exceptionally well.

Eleanor Von Schweinitz, "Reviews: 'The Seventh Mandarin'," in Children's Book Review (© 1971 by Five Owls Press Ltd.; all rights reserved), Vol. 1, No. 2, April, 1971, p. 48.

FRIEND: THE STORY OF GEORGE FOX AND THE QUAKERS (1972)

Anti-war sentiments . . . figure in **"Friend: The Story of George Fox and the Quakers."** . . . Jane Yolen makes Fox "relevant" by discussing his long hair and his support of women's rights, but the emphasis is largely unnecessary. For the most part Fox's story . . . is appealing enough to stand without such props. Because Miss Yolen does not let her own recent conversion interfere with her responsibilities as a biographer, her book should appeal to thoughtful teens of many denominations.

Marilyn Gardner, "Rebels Black and White," in The Christian Science Monitor (reprinted by permission from The Christian Science Monitor; © 1972 The Christian Science Publishing Society; all rights reserved), May 4, 1972, p. B5.*

Older readers are likely to appreciate the honesty with which [George Fox's] character is presented—as well as the vivid picture of England in his time. The author, a member of the Society of Friends herself, writes with fervor and clarity both of the founder of the Quaker movement and of the activities of Quakers today. Thoughtful readers of junior high and early high-school age should find this biography truly relevant and worth their while.

Margaret P. Sykes, "Worth Singing Out," in Book World—Chicago Tribune (© 1972 Postrib Corp.; reprinted by permission of Chicago Tribune and The Washington Post), May 7, 1972, p. 13.

[*Friend: The Story of George Fox and the Quakers* contains] a helpful final chapter on the history of Quakers and their present status, as well as a short but excellent bibliography. Although Jane Yolen writes dramatically of the physical life and adventures of George Fox and his followers, Fox's concern with the life of the mind and the spirit necessarily and appropriately dominate the book. Even where the subject is not in great demand, this beautifully written, valuable biography is an essential purchase.

Janet G. Polacheck, "The Book Review: 'Friend: The Story of George Fox and the Quakers'," in Library Journal (reprinted from Library Journal, June 15, 1972; published by R. R. Bowker Co. (a Xerox company); copyright © 1972 by Xerox Corporation), Vol. 97, No. 12, June 15, 1972, p. 2245.

Yolen's biography of George Fox, founder of the movement which came to be known as Quakerism, has at least some instructional value. It is possible to learn from it something of the religious turbulence of the 17th century, who George Fox was, how he lived, how the company of Friends was built into an international religious organization. It is helpful, no doubt, to be told how Quakers came to be called Quakers, why they wore funny clothes and why they said "thee" and "thou" instead of "you."

Miss Yolen's study of Fox also conveys some understanding of the mystical doctrine of the Inner Light, which Fox may not have originated but which he made the key to his religious teachings, and even some of the problems connected with belief in the infallibility of God's voice in the heart of every man. What happens, for example, when one man's infallible revelation is in conflict with another man's infallible revelation?

Nevertheless, no very deep understanding of Fox and the Quakers is made available in these pages. What the author presents, unfortunately, is not so much biography as hagiography, a simplistic recital of saintly virtue triumphing over vice. Even intellectually the perspective is narrow, with the perennial tension between religious enthusiasm, or the direct experience of God, and God apprehended through reason or scripture or tradition or church authority all but ignored. (pp. 8, 10)

But what is most disappointing here is the simplism. The picture of Fox as all-good, all-wise and all-kind, beset by vicious enemies but always victorious, is almost that of the American hero in an old war movie, miraculously overcoming brutal but stupid Nazis and maniacal Japanese. It ought to be possible to affirm the importance of George Fox in religious history and still to see him as a man among men, and to see Quakerism as a religion among religions. (p. 10)

Richard Horchler, "Friend: The Story of George Fox and the Quakers," in The New York Times Book Review *(© 1972 by The New York Times Company; reprinted by permission), September 10, 1972, pp. 8, 10.*

THE GIRL WHO LOVED THE WIND   (1972)

[Jane Yolen has] produced a treasure. The story has the grace and wisdom of a folk tale, the polish that usually comes from centuries of telling. A widowed merchant tries to protect his beautiful daughter from unhappiness and in so doing virtually makes her a prisoner. The wind visits her and sings her a song about life—how it is "sometimes happy, sometimes sad but always full of change and challenge." The princess is no longer content in her false, dull world and escapes with the wind "into the everchanging world." . . . This exotic creation will stimulate imaginations and linger in children's memories.

Marilyn R. Singer, "The Book Review: 'The Girl Who Loved the Wind'," in School Library Journal, *an appendix to* Library Journal *(reprinted from the March, 1973 issue of* School Library Journal, *published by R. R. Bowker Co./A Xerox Corporation; copyright © 1973), Vol. 19, No. 7, March, 1973, p. 102.*

Jane Yolen has an especial gift for the invention of traditional-type tales and this is complemented by her rare ability to use language creatively. Here she has used the simple rhythms of the storyteller to conjure up the distinctive flavour of an Eastern tale. (p. 172)

This is an original book which has a great deal to offer the discriminating child of seven upwards. (p. 173)

Eleanor Von Schweinitz, "Picture Books: 'The Girl Who Loved the Wind'," in Children's Book Review *(© 1973 Five Owls Press Ltd.; all rights reserved), Vol. 3, No. 6, December, 1973, pp. 172-73.*

THE WIZARD ISLANDS   (1973)

It would be hard to conceive of a more satisfactory way to spend an afternoon or an evening than in the company of Jane Yolen as she tells spellbinding stories of ghost islands, mystery islands and disappearing islands. A ghostly black dog is said to guard Castle Peel on the Isle of Man; no less than four ghosts haunt notorious Sable Island, the "graveyard of the Atlantic," and the wife of Blackbeard the pirate haunts Smuttynose Island. These legends are no less intriguing than the real mysteries which defy solution on Easter Island, the Galapagos and Surtsey.

"Children's Books: 'The Wizard Islands'," in Publishers Weekly *(reprinted from the December 31, 1973 issue of* Publishers Weekly, *published by R. R. Bowker Company, a Xerox company; copyright © 1973 by Xerox Corporation), Vol. 204, No. 26, December 31, 1973, p. 27.*

The ghost stories are adequately told but there is less conviction in the narration of these tales than in the sense of scientific excitement that is communicated in the sections on Surtsey or the Galapagos. A bibliography and an index are appended.

Zena Sutherland, "New Titles for Children and Young People: 'The Wizard Islands'," in Bulletin of the Center for Children's Books *(reprinted by permission of The University of Chicago Press; © 1974 by The University of Chicago), Vol. 27, No. 10, June, 1974, p. 167.*

THE GIRL WHO CRIED FLOWERS, AND OTHER TALES   (1974)

"The Girl Who Cried Flowers" is a collection of five carefully crafted stories which for all their style and elegance lack the insight into the human condition that so often distinguishes traditional material from its imitation. For those readers who honestly can't tell their folk-tale butter from margarine, these stories will doubtless be satisfying and even impressive; but one wishes that the author had taken the form she has chosen and used it more adventurously.

Three of the stories are just variations of tales that have been told over and over and over. Only **"Silent Bianca"** and **"The Weaver of Tomorrow"** show evidence of real ingenuity. . . .

Sidney Long, "Other Worlds, Other Times," in The New York Times Book Review *(© 1974 by The New York Times Company; reprinted by permission), May 15, 1974, p. 43.**

[In *The Girl Who Cried Flowers, and Other Tales* Yolen describes] **"Silent Bianca"** whose "face was like crystal with the features etched in" and "her words were formed soundlessly into tiny slivers of ice." In Bianca, Yolen might be describing her own glittering imagery and crystal prose. . . .

A showpiece, for those who can forgo the tough wisdom of traditional fairy tales for a masterful imitation of the manner.

> *"Books to Read Aloud: 'The Girl Who Cried Flowers, and Other Tales',"* in Kirkus Reviews *(copyright © 1974 The Kirkus Service, Inc.), Vol. XLII, No. 14, July 15, 1974, p. 741.*

Ms. Yolen's artistry with words . . . makes a striking book. These could be called modern folk- or fairy tales, since they boast all the usual ingredients—supernatural beings, inexplicable happenings, the struggle between good and evil forces. The title story concerns a foundling girl infant of ancient Greece. Instead of tears, blossoms drift down her cheeks when she cries. . . . Equally haunting (and an effective antiwar piece) is the story of Bianca who epitomizes the value of silent wisdom.

> *"Children's Books: 'The Girl Who Cried Flowers, and Other Tales',"* in Publishers Weekly *(reprinted from the July 22, 1974 issue of* Publishers Weekly, *published by R. R. Bowker Company, a Xerox company; copyright © 1974 by Xerox Corporation), Vol. 205, No. 4, July 22, 1974, p. 70.*

The title story follows a familiar pattern of the [fairytale] genre, the wife who comes from no known source, changes her ways when she weds, and goes back to her own milieu; another describes the fate of a girl with an insatiable curiosity about the future; a third heroine is silent Bianca, whose thoughts emerge as ice-slivers that must be thawed to be heard. A lonely giant befriended by a child becomes friendly, in another traditional pattern; the fifth tale is rather static, **"The Lad Who Stared Everyone Down."** Elements of other tales may be seen in the stories, but they are no more imitations than a new combination of old ingredients are an old dish. The recipes are inventive, and the writing style has a serious, polished grace.

> *Zena Sutherland, "New Titles for Children and Young People: 'The Girl Who Cried Flowers, and Other Tales',"* in Bulletin of the Center for Children's Books *(reprinted by permission of The University of Chicago Press; © 1975 by The University of Chicago), Vol. 28, No. 5, January, 1975, p. 88.*

RING OUT! A BOOK OF BELLS   (1974)

Remembering Jane Yolen's book of kites (**World on a String** . . .), one expects her to work some of her own ringing changes here. Certainly she has collected an intriguing amount of lore on special-purpose bells—Tocsin bell, Sermon bell, Pudding, and Doom; anecdotal explanations of their use in religion, medieval town government, war and death rites; the most famous bell legends; a history of carillons and inscriptions; even a selection of bell poems. The material is inherently intriguing, and here and there Yolen allows herself to have some fun with the reverberating names of famous bells or the permutations of change ringing. Nevertheless, the organization—by use, with a little vignette prefacing each chapter—makes the whole business more sober and slow-moving than it need be. . . . [In] any case, enterprising kids will be able to dig out the aspects of campanology that strike their fanciers.

> *"Young Adult Non-Fiction: 'Ring Out! A Book of Bells',"* in Kirkus Reviews *(copyright © 1974 The Kirkus Service, Inc.), Vol. XLII, No. 21, November 1, 1974, p. 1166.*

The structure of this discursive book from America seems likely to confuse some young readers, since anecdotes and history are given equal weight and are loosely held together by section headings like town and country bells, war and peace, and music; a few poems and songs are included as a kind of coda. Marginal notes or captions are used to extend the text and these tend to interrupt the reader, who has to stop and correlate them with the main text. . . . Readers may browse pleasurably through a series of interesting facts but they are likely to be wearied after a time by the lack of emphasis in what is really a running list of examples.

> *Margery Fisher, "How It Works: 'Ring Out! A Book of Bells',"* in her Growing Point, *Vol. 18, No. 1, May, 1979, p. 3528.*

THE LITTLE SPOTTED FISH   (1975)

Drawing upon the poetry and folklore of the British Isles, Ms. Yolen has written an exciting tale of enchantment. Dylan, a "fisherlad," sees a coracle (a wicker boat used by ancient Britons) adrift near the shore of a lake. He climbs aboard and the magic boat rows itself to a spot where a little spotted fish with a human face leaps out of the water. She sings, "Dylan, Dylan, son of the wave / The spotted fish thy life shall save." The fish is transformed into a lovely girl but only when the boy has conquered evil forces. This is terrific storytelling. . . . Note humorous anachronism as Dylan's fish-girl pours him tea from a bone china teapot—veddy British!

> *"Picture Books: 'The Little Spotted Fish',"* in Publishers Weekly *(reprinted from the February 24, 1975 issue of* Publishers Weekly, *published by R. R. Bowker Company, a Xerox company; copyright © 1975 by Xerox Corporation), Vol. 207, No. 8, February 24, 1975, p. 114.*

Fisherboy Dylan relies on his own pluck instead of lucky charms and so saves the human-faced little spotted fish who then turns into a girl with "silver-gray hair and silver-gray eyes." . . . [Yolen's] moral—that it's better to trust one's own skill than magic in dealing with the unknown—is not so different from all those traditional tales about three wishes that go wrong. And the juggling of folk motifs (most obviously the Irish singing trout legend) and archaic language most often seems pointless and sterile. (pp. 237-38)

> *"Picture Books: 'The Little Spotted Fish',"* in Kirkus Reviews *(copyright © 1975 The Kirkus Service, Inc.), Vol. XLIII, No. 5, March 1, 1975, pp. 237-38.*

THE TRANSFIGURED HART   (1975)

When loner Richard Plante, a sickly, bookish orphan of twelve, first sees the white hart "by the shimmering pool," he knows it's a unicorn. Heather Fielding, an "enjoyer," is less romantic: "'An albino,' she breathed, and then was still." But when the two children meet "by the shimmering pool" (the phrase occurs over a dozen times) Richard talks Heather into believing his version. . . . As each had already determined to tame the deer, they agree that she, as a pure maid, must lure it to her lap. Meanwhile of course the children discover each other—both, it seems, read Gerard Manley Hopkins—and Richard opens up. Then after an uncomfortable dinner when Heather inadvertently betrays their secret to her family and Richard spills Mr. Fielding's wine as he dashes off distressed, each is again convinced that (s)he alone must seek out the animal. But they meet again at midnight by that shimmering pool and the unicorn arrives on cue . . . and submits to the maiden. . . . But then the hunters' horns signal the dawning of deer season and to save the hart Heather must untie the golden bridle (a yellow ribbon from her nightgown) and send the animal away . . . to a protected reserve. When Richard and Heather are awakened in the woods hours later, the wine-stained dinner napkin, tucked all the while in Heather's bodice, is white and fresh and fragrant. The relevance of this inescapably sexual symbolism however is less clear than the napkin, and the featured ideals of faith and purity even solo responsibility and shared awakening, remain bloodless and archaic abstractions. To recognize this for the fluttery, self-consciously poetical fabrication it is, only compare the spring-in-November midnight miracle with the similar kitchen blooming in [D. Manus] Pinkwater's *Blue Moose*. . . .

> *"Younger Fiction: 'The Transfigured Hart',"* in Kirkus Reviews *(copyright © 1975 The Kirkus Service, Inc.), Vol. XLIII, No. 12, June 15, 1975, p. 662.*

[Richard Plante] is an introverted love-starved orphan and the most erudite 12-year-old you'll ever meet. His bearing the name of Richard is no accident, but a signal that his heart, though damaged by rheumatic fever, is rich. And people who are rich in heart see a unicorn where others see only a deer—at least, so the author is trying to tell us. . . .

When Heather and Richard meet he introduces himself. Heather replies that she knows who he is: "The boy with the broken heart"—a phrase so stilted and improbable, I strongly doubt any real 13-year-old girl would say it. Despite a few such instances of awkwardness, the author tells with empathy how their isolation crumbles as each discovers a kindred spirit in the other. Their developing friendship is touchingly rendered and constitutes the kind of miracle any reader would accept.

But Miss Yolen has another, more exalted, miracle in mind: to make Richard's vision of the albino deer-as-unicorn literally happen. She brings narrative skill, considerable daring and her own avowed "passion for unicorns" to the attempt. Even so, it fails. Perhaps the choice of genre—realism blended with allegory and fantasy—is wrong. Perhaps the underlying assumptions about the nature and power of belief are too large. In any case, the "midnight transfiguration," much as one would like it to be true, remains merely willed.

> *Doris Orgel, "For Young Readers: 'The Transfigured Hart',"* in The New York Times Book Review *(© 1975 by The New York Times Company; reprinted by permission), September 14, 1975, p. 10.*

Jane Yolen, with **"The Transfigured Hart"** . . . , almost succeeds in creating an authentic modern fairy tale. I think she does not quite bring it off, because, fearful of making a false step, she divests her characters of the colloquial and leaves them in literary nudity. . . . I want very much to like this book altogether, but I have serious reservations. For one thing (and by no means an unimportant thing), I wish that Heather's dappled horse were not named Hop, short for Gerard Manley Hopkins. You know—"Glory be to God for dappled things"? (pp. 187-88)

> *Jean Stafford, "Children's Books for Christmas: 'The Transfigured Hart',"* in The New Yorker *(© 1975 by The New Yorker Magazine, Inc.), Vol. 51, No. 41, December 1, 1975, pp. 187-88.*

THE MOON RIBBON: AND OTHER TALES (1976)

Six more exquisite fabrications in the author's familiar self-infatuated cadences. In **"Moon Ribbon,"** the first, a Cinderella type is carried off on a river/ribbon woven from the gray hairs of her dead mother . . . with whom she then exchanges hearts in the form of rubies and crystal. Elsewhere an old couple who fashion a longed-for son of sticks and honey are taught a lesson by the Spirit of the Hive; another old woman who finds a tiny "rosechild" ("though she was neither widow nor wed") learns that what it needs to grow is her own love; just as platitudinously, a young man spends his life seeking **"Somewhen"**—to illustrate that it's the journey that matters; and the only spunky character—Viga, a sun-fearing prince's bride ("the two talked and kissed far into the night as befits a couple who are but newly wed")—loses him as a result of her iconoclasm. The last story, about a "Moon Child" born into a sun-worshipping society, is a smug and pointless fable of ignorance and persecution. Artificial as we found the elegance of *The Girl Who Cried Flowers* . . . , this is weaker and sillier. (pp. 792-93)

> *"Books to Read Aloud: 'The Moon Ribbon: and Other Tales',"* in Kirkus Reviews *(copyright © 1976 The Kirkus Service, Inc.), Vol. XLIV, No. 14, July 15, 1976, pp. 792-93.*

Jane Yolen has written some fine children's books (**"The Seventh Mandarin"** and **"The Girl Who Loved the Wind,"** among others). Her prose is often quite beautiful. Here are six new parables of some wondrous worlds and an age gone by, written in that characteristically fine style, yet with seemingly borrowed characters and contrived situations. Why would she need to recycle Cinderella (Sylva in **"The Moon Ribbon"**)? Or reconstitute Thumbellina without adventure (**"Rosechild"**)? Why would Miss Yolen, a master of the woven theme-into-story, give us pallid characters and pretentious, almost overwritten and over-moralistic tales? It just doesn't make sense.

In **"The Moon Ribbon,"** Sylva, to escape her cruel stepmother and two stepsisters, floats away to her chance for freedom on a river that has been magically made from a silver ribbon woven of her dead mother's gray hair. In so doing, Sylva learns that she does have choices, must give of her heart and "once given, twice gained."

The old woman who finds the tiny infant "nestled in the petals of a wild rose" puts her in a walnut bed and dubs her "Rosechild." The great problem is how to feed the tiny babe. "If it were a real child, I would feed it pieces of bread sopped in honey and milk. . . . But as it is a Rosechild, goodness alone knows what I must do, for I do not." This seems an arbitrary rejection of food to me, but without this rejection there would have been no story, no chance for her to discover that her Rosechild would grow if fed only on love.

The sun worshippers of Solin hated and feared Mona (in **"The Moon Child"**) because she was born at night and dared to enter the dark forest. This is the strongest of the stories, perhaps because the theme does have some contemporary application, or would have in witch-burning days, and there are beautiful moments when lonely Mona is discovering the natural treasures of the forest. Yet this, too, seems removed and detached and not quite convincing.

With the exception of **"Somewhen,"** which is neither parable nor adventure but a play on words without passion or conviction, all of these stories are about love, misguided or fitting, its absence as well as its presence. And if taken together, each tries to explore a different aspect of love. That, as an aim, is lofty enough and might explain why Yolen chose to borrow from other tales. The trouble is they don't quite come off, and too often I felt a lack of logic, was too conscious of the author manipulating events to suit a one-liner or moral that she had decided would be the stem of the story.

> *Cynthia King, "For Young Readers: 'The Moon Ribbon: and Other Tales'," in* The New York Times Book Review *(©1976 by The New York Times Company; reprinted by permission), September 19, 1976, p. 16.*

SIMPLE GIFTS: THE STORY OF THE SHAKERS   (1976)

Yolen's interesting historical account of the Shaker movement is presented in the context of American and English social history of the 18th and 19th Centuries. The lives of Mother Ann Lee and other Shaker leaders are chronicled with sympathy and good humor as are the elaborate rituals and religious ecstasies of the sect.

> *Phyllis Ingram, "Book Reviews: 'Simple Gifts: The Story of the Shakers'," in* School Library Journal *(reprinted from the October, 1976 issue of* School Library Journal, *published by R. R. Bowker Co./A Xerox Corporation; copyright © 1976), Vol. 23, No. 2, October, 1976, p. 121.*

Shakerism has become such a familiar presence on the juvenile scene, that it's hard to imagine what Jane Yolen's slight history could add to the record. Yolen does stress a few points that others have slighted—tracing connections between the origin of Shakerism and the French Camisards, and concentrating on the development of Shaker dance and songs along with the changing atmosphere of the order under successive leaders. Otherwise, she offers less history of the movement and less insight into its mystical worship than either [Doris] Faber's *The Perfect Life* (1974) or [Nardi Reeder] Campion's *Ann the Word* . . . and little of the background found in the handful of books on communal societies. Yet her short, uncluttered text does make the essence of the Shaker experience available to younger or less ambitious readers, and in this case the "gift to be simple" is both an appropriate and a useful contribution. (pp. 1106-07)

> *"Young Adult Non-Fiction: 'Simple Gifts: The Story of the Shakers'," in* Kirkus Reviews *(copyright © 1976 The Kirkus Service, Inc.), Vol. XLIV, No. 19, October 1, 1976, pp. 1106-07.*

THE SULTAN'S PERFECT TREE   (1977)

The latest of Yolen's remote, complacent fables concerns a sultan who decrees perfection everywhere. When a real tree isn't perfect he has a symmetrical, unblemished one painted on his window. But this of course must be redone for every season, and when in summer the artist can't make one that will "bend and sway with the weight of its ripe fruit," a servant girl bares the window to reveal the imperfect but beautiful real tree. Thus the sultan learns what Yolen has yet to realize— that living and growing and changing is better than being perfect. Like the painted tree, the moral is unassailable but sterile.

> *"Younger Fiction: 'The Sultan's Perfect Tree'," in* Kirkus Reviews *(copyright © 1977 The Kirkus Ser-*

vice, Inc.), Vol. XLV, No. 6, March 15, 1977, p. 287.

One name I always look for among recent children's fiction is Jane Yolen. Amid much of the lightweight children's literature today, one is always assured of a quality book from Miss Yolen. **"The Sultan's Perfect Tree,"** a book aimed at a young audience, does not disappoint.

This is a tale about an age-old problem: the quest for perfection at the expense of life itself. . . .

The tale [has] elegant simplicity. . . .

> *Alexandra Johnson, "Caldecott Winners Paint African Tribal Alphabet," in* The Christian Science Monitor *(reprinted by permission from* The Christian Science Monitor; © 1977 The Christian Science Publishing Society; all rights reserved), May 4, 1977, p. B2.**

The whole is quite lovely and yet, like the sultan's philosophy, it is a little too refined. Some asymmetrical touches, a bit more . . . verbal drama, would lighten the going. Then it might be perfect.

> *Karla Kuskin, "Children's Books: 'The Sultan's Perfect Tree'," in* The New York Times Book Review *(© 1977 by The New York Times Company; reprinted by permission), July 3, 1977, p. 11.*

THE GIANTS' FARM   (1977)

Yolen's easy-to-read storybook is easy to take, an infectiously giggly collection of five tales about five giants. . . . [The] book is a natural to seduce beginners into the world of books.

> *"Fiction: 'The Giants' Farm'," in* Publishers Weekly *(reprinted from the August 29, 1977 issue of* Publishers Weekly, *published by R. R. Bowker Company, a Xerox company; copyright © 1977 by Xerox Corporation), Vol. 212, No. 9, August 29, 1977, p. 367.*

Jane Yolen's **"The Giants' Farm"** . . . has a faint air of derivativeness hanging over it. Neither traditional fairy tales nor modern lessons in manners, the adventures of a commune of amiable giants are so gently plotted that this "easy to read" book seems more a bedtime cuddling story than one a child would curl up with on his own. And Little Dab, the wise youngest giant, must be one of the most saccharine heroes since Tiny Tim. But a giants' crumbling song and a recipe for Giant No-Cook Bon-bons make this a decent rainy-day activity book. . . .

> *Jennifer Dunning, "Children's Books: 'The Giants' Farm'," in* The New York Times Book Review *(© 1977 by The New York Times Comapny; reprinted by permission), November 13, 1977, p. 45.*

[*The Giants' Farm*] is a collection of five vignettes, in each of which the problems of a group of giants are solved, as might be expected, by the smallest and smartest of the group. Only Chapter Four, **"Grizzle's Grumble,"** which tells how the biggest giant is taught to accept and appreciate his size, qualifies as a true story. It alone has a meaningful conflict, a significant arrangement of details to display the conflict, and a structure which terminates in an expected but satisfying conclusion. The chief difficulty with the book is that none of the other chapters contain problems which are as significant and the characters never really come to life through action. (p. 8)

Raymond E. Jones, "Easy Reader: Literature and Reading Matter for the Beginning Reader," in The World of Children's Books *(© 1978 Jon C. Stott), Vol. III, No. 1, Spring, 1978, pp. 7-8.**

THE HUNDREDTH DOVE AND OTHER TALES (1977)

Jane Yolen's fables are told with sober strength and native wit. They are simple and perfect, with not a word too much. One could search in them for hidden psychological symbolism, but I am content to let them be, rather than ask what they mean. As in the best folk tales, a pressure wells up in the first paragraph of each of these stories, sweeps to its release in a predestined ending that is satisfying, whether it is happy or sad, so that the reader smiles and says, Yes, yes that is the way it has to be. . . .

[Jane Yolen's text displays] gravity and felicity. . . .

Jane Langton, "Children's Books: 'The Hundredth Dove and Other Tales'," in The New York Times Book Review *(© 1977 by The New York Times Company; reprinted by permission), November 20, 1977, p. 30.*

These imitations of folk narratives do not possess the archetypal power toward which they aspire. The title piece and **"The White Seal Maid"** are metamorphosis tales, while **"The Wind Cap"** is about that familiar figure, the poor but honest boy who makes good. **"The Maiden Made of Fire"** and **"The Lady and the Merman"** are melancholy stories of demon lovers. **"Once a Good Man"** concerns a female Chief Angel who traipses about doing the Lord's bidding and conducting a miniature Dantesque tour through Heaven and Hell. Several of the above are momentarily fetching, capably capturing the loneliness and longing for love so characteristic of the superior fantasy of [Hans Christian] Andersen, George MacDonald, or C. S. Lewis. . . .

Allene Stuart Phy, "Book Reviews: 'The Hundredth Dove and Other Tales'," in School Library Journal *(reprinted from the January, 1978 issue of* School Library Journal, *published by R. R. Bowker Co./A Xerox Corporation; copyright © 1978), Vol. 24, No. 5, January, 1978, p. 83.*

Death and judgment, in Jane Yolen's vision, are endowed with melancholy grace, held at a distance in the conscious poise of dignified formality. Beside forests, mountains or the sea, king and fowler, charcoal-burner and fire-maiden, lady and merman, love and lose, yearn and pine, aspire and surrender, haunt and are haunted, in an archaizing mode which was originally directed, in North America, towards fantasy buffs of mature years. Such exquisitely mannered magic does not work for everyone; the rare British 10-year-old who responds to it will probably remain forever spellbound.

Marion Glastonbury, "Stories in Season: 'The Hundredth Dove and Other Tales'," in The Times Educational Supplement *(© Times Newspapers Ltd. (London) 1980; reproduced from* The Times Educational Supplement *by permission), No. 3327, March 14, 1980, p. 27.*

All [the tales here] are ambiguous and painful. The pain is that which exists between men and women, and between women

and men; it is chiefly the pain of separation. The writing is lean enough to carry this weight of ambiguity without it ever growing clogged. (p. 271)

Ralph Lavender, "Seven to Eleven: 'The Hundredth Dove and Other Tales'," in The School Librarian, *Vol. 28, No. 3, September, 1980, pp. 271-72.*

THE SEEING STICK (1977)

Jane Yolen has written numerous successful fairytales. They all have much in common: a dreamy sweetness that echoes Oscar Wilde. This gentle story is no exception. It tells of a blind Chinese Princess whose father, the Emperor, promises a fortune to anyone who can help her. Along comes an old man with a walking stick on which he records, in tiny carvings, the things he encounters on his journeys. With this kind of pictorial Braille he trains the fingers of the Princess to see the world around her, adding new carvings as new things arise, and taking her out of the Palace into the city to touch the things themselves. And so she grows "eyes on the tips of her fingers" and teaches other blind children to do the same. . . .

Classic fairytale forms have rules of their own—rather rigid rules that govern their own fragile brand of credibility. **"The Seeing Stick"** violates those rules by dealing in miracles rather than magic. This makes it a parable rather than a fairytale, in spite of other clues to the contrary, but its genuine kindliness probably renders such distinctions unimportant.

Natalie Babbitt, "Children's Books: 'The Seeing Stick'," in The New York Times Book Review *(© 1978 by The New York Times Company; reprinted by permission), January 1, 1978, p. 20.*

THE SIMPLE PRINCE (1978)

Merrily mocking wealthy people's conception of the virtues of "a simple life" is the amusing tale of **The Simple Prince**. (p. 16)

[The story is] funny on an adult, as well as a child's, level, which is a bonus for a book one reads to a young child. This critical reader was hoping the servants would not so "rejoice" at their belated polite treatment. Like Ann McGovern's recent effort to mold benevolent, sharing rulers in *Half a Kingdom* . . ., the book is definitely more humanistic than most tales of royalty, but it is hardly the approach I keep hoping for. Shouldn't children be led to question *anyone's* right to rule over others, however benevolently? (pp. 16-17)

Lyla Hoffman, "Bookshelf: 'The Simple Prince'," in Interracial Books for Children Bulletin *(reprinted by permission of* Interracial Books for Children Bulletin, *1841 Broadway, New York, N.Y. 10023), Vol. 9, No. 7, 1978, pp. 16-17.*

A spoiled prince . . . looks for the simple life and thinks he has found it at the door of a hard-working peasant's cottage. What he finds, however, is that some people have to work for what they eat, a simple fact that is hard to take. He returns to his palace, not to give up his privileges and work, but to be more courteous to those who work for him. An appended "moral" asserts the efficacy of saying "please" and "thank you"—a gratuitous lesson in courtesy that evades the not-so-simple issue of privilege and makes this "simple" tale border on the simplistic.

Stephen D. Roxburgh, "Book Reviews: 'The Simple Prince'," in School Library Journal *(reprinted from the January, 1979 issue of* School Library Journal, *published by R. R. Bowker Co./A Xerox Corporation; copyright © 1979), Vol. 25, No. 5, January, 1979, p. 49.*

NO BATH TONIGHT (1978)

Some people must think kids are dumb. Here's a boy who, on Monday, hurts his foot stepping on a king in the sand (a figurine—if you can figure that out); on Tuesday, hurts his backside sitting on a "pricker bush"; on Wednesday, hurts his nose sliding into first base—and on these and like pretexts, gets out of taking a bath for a week. Then his grandmother capitalizes on his interest in tea leaves by proposing that they make "kid tea"—that is, put him in a bathtub and, from what appears in the water, see what he's been doing all week. It's ingenious, you can say that, but the relation to real children in real life is imperceptible.

"Picture Books: 'No Bath Tonight'," in Kirkus Reviews *(copyright © 1979 The Kirkus Service, Inc.), Vol. XLVII, No. 1, January 1, 1979, p. 4.*

The grandmother-child relationship is pleasant, the round of daily minor calamities should amuse the lap audience, but listeners may wonder why Jeremy's parents accept his nightly dictum in so docile a fashion.

Zena Sutherland, "New Titles for Children and Young People: 'No Bath Tonight'," in Bulletin of the Center for Children's Books *(reprinted by permission of The University of Chicago Press; © 1979 by The University of Chicago), Vol. 32, No. 9, May, 1979, p. 167.*

THE GIANTS GO CAMPING (1979)

Yolen relates . . . five flimsy bits in jerky easy-readerese and, as in *The Giants' Farm* . . . , she relies on the turnabout trick of the little giant's superior wisdom to give them a needed twist—but Dab is no more engaging than he was before, which is to say no more than any other know-it-all kid.

"Easy Reading: 'The Giants Go Camping'," in Kirkus Reviews *(copyright © 1979 The Kirkus Service, Inc.), Vol. XLVII, No. 7, April 1, 1979, p. 387.*

This sequel to the *Giants' Farm* . . . succeeds in retaining the original's lively sense of fun. . . . The funniest episode concerns the largest giant, Grizzle, who brings home a bear he names Spot, vowing it's a dog. . . . Though the format suggests an easy-reading book, the sentences are long and some words difficult for truly-beginning readers.

Anne McKeithen-Boes, "Book Reviews: 'The Giants Go Camping'," in School Library Journal *(reprinted from the September, 1979 issue of* School Library Journal, *published by R. R. Bowker Co./A Xerox Corporation; copyright © 1979), Vol. 26, No. 1, September, 1979, p. 125.*

DREAM WEAVER (1979)

[*Dream Weaver* is a collection] of Yolen's surrealistic tales. Her Dream Weaver is an old blind gypsy who sells fantasies symbolic of the inner worlds of seven purchasers. The collec-

tion shows the influence of classic literature, but each story bears the author's hallmarks: deep insights, unhampered imagination and graceful telling. **"The Tree's Wife"** is Drusilla, married to a rich man and widowed at age 15. Scorning suitors avid for her gold, youths who had ignored her when she was poor, Drusilla declares she would sooner wed the sturdy birch in a nearby wood. Their eerie marriage and the child of their love make a parable echoing the Grimm Brothers. Yolen also makes inimitable use of Greek myth and finishes with an impressive glimpse into the driven worlds of creative people.

"Fiction: 'Dream Weaver'," in Publishers Weekly *(reprinted from the May 7, 1979 issue of* Publishers Weekly, *published by R. R. Bowker Company, a Xerox company; copyright © 1979 by Xerox Corporation), Vol. 215, No. 19, May 7, 1979, p. 84.*

This is a collection of tales which combines threads of classic folklore with modern strains of psychological insight into a rich tapestry of fantasy. . . . [These are] bittersweet stories. . . . Death, love, faith, and greed are the themes woven through these sensitively drawn portraits of human sorrow and joy. Adult readers will probably enjoy the truths in them as they share them with their children.

Violet H. Harada, "Older Readers: 'The Dream Weaver'," in Children's Book Review Service *(copyright © 1979 Children's Book Review Service Inc.), Vol. 8, No. 1, September, 1979, p. 10.*

On one level, Jane Yolen's seven tales are a love affair with language. The author delights in sonorous words like "obeisance," "pullulation" and "soughing." Sometimes she seems to be almost carried away by the lilt of it all. In one story of this septet, a stone image kills its creator. "With a silent shout it brought the hammer down," the author writes. Good as the opening phrase sounds, it has no meaning. There is a seductive quality to Miss Yolen's writing, but too often her tales ingratiate the reader rather than carry him or her along by their narrative strength.

On another level, the author is uncommonly skilled at using elements from other storytellers and folklorists, transforming them into new and different tales. In this book, her first story, **"Brother Hart,"** takes the characters and situation from the Grimms' "Brother and Sister," but Miss Yolen—in tune with our times—makes the vague sexual undercurrent explicit. She dwells on the degree of intimacy between the siblings in what the jacket blurb characterizes as the author's "exploring the Jungian shadow-world of the subconscious."

Holding these stories together is a blind gypsy, the Dream Weaver of the title, who fashions each story-dream to suit the needs and interests of a particular passer-by. Fans of Miss Yolen's romantic prose will not be disappointed in this latest work. (pp. 18-19)

Selma G. Lanes, "Children's Book: 'Dream Weaver'," in The New York Times Book Review *(© 1979 by The New York Times Company; reprinted by permission), October 28, 1979, pp. 18-19.*

ALL IN THE WOODLAND EARLY (1979)

An outstanding alphabet book features merry verses and music composed by Yolen. . . . Progressing from the meeting between a pert little girl and a brisk boy, the rhymes go on from his declaration that he's going a-hunting, through the letters of the alphabet. "I saw an ANT running / I saw a black BEAR, / All in the woodland early; / I saw a small CHIPMUNK, / I saw a brown DEER, / All in the woodland early." How gratifying to find such oddities as an URBANUS, a VOLE, an XYLEBORUS and a ZEMMI representing letters that most authors fudge, and even better, to find that the young hunter is gathering animals to play with him and the little girl—not to capture or kill.

> *"Picture Books: 'All in the Woodland Early',"* in Publishers Weekly *(reprinted from the January 11, 1980 issue of* Publishers Weekly, *published by R. R. Bowker Company, a Xerox company; copyright © 1980 by Xerox Corporation), Vol. 217, No. 1, January 11, 1980, p. 88.*

Jane Yolen tries a different approach in **All in the Woodland Early:** a pseudo Child ballad featuring an alphabetical list of animals in bold-face type and a musical score that turns the poetry into song. . . . One wonders . . . whether the choice of such animals as urbanus, vole, xyleborus and zemmi are really an aid to learning the alphabet.

> *Kristi L. Thomas, "Book Reviews: 'All in the Woodland Early',"* in School Library Journal *(reprinted from the February, 1980 issue of* School Library Journal, *published by R. R. Bowker Co./A Xerox Corporation; copyright © 1980), Vol. 26, No. 6, February, 1980, p. 42.*

Count on versatile Jane Yolen to invent something special and intriguing. For her alphabet book, **All in the Woodland Early,** she has written not only words but music to go with them. The verses feature birds, animals and insects from ant to zemmi (whatever that is!), concluding with a page of music alongside a page with all the lyrics repeated. That means a grown-up and child can place the book on the piano, like sheet music, and sing "All in the Woodland Early." So clever! It adds another dimension to a lesson in the ABCs, does it not?

> *Jerome Beatty, Jr., "Herds of Hungry Hogs Hurrying Home,"* in Book World—The Washington Post *(© 1980, The Washington Post), April 13, 1980, p. 10.**

HOW BEASTLY! (1980)

A dash of imaginative poetry informs Jane Yolen's **"How Beastly!"** a rhymed nonsense menagerie. . . . Some of its word play may need explaining ("The Taughtus is a Bahston beast / That climbs up Beacon Hill"), but there are memorable creatures such as the Edgehog that "nests in tippy places, like / A jutting rock or ledge / And never lives life to the full / But always on the edge."

> *X. J. Kennedy, "Children's Verse: 'How Beastly',"* in The New York Times Book Review *(© 1980 by The New York Times Company; reprinted by permission), April 27, 1980, p. 47.*

Many poets have made a literary sport of inventing and describing strange and marvelous animals; one recalls Countee Cullen's memorable absurdities in *The Lost Zoo* (Follett) and James Reeves's mock horrors in *Prefabulous Animiles* (Dutton). Jane Yolen's brief rhymes about creatures of her imagination have less poetic splendor, but they are written with honest humor and skill.

> *Ethel L. Heins, "Poetry and Songs: 'How Beastly',"* in The Horn Book Magazine *(copyright © 1980 by The Horn Book, Inc., Boston), Vol. 56, No. 4, August, 1980, p. 425.*

THE ROBOT AND REBECCA: THE MYSTERY OF THE CODE-CARRYING KIDS (1980)

In this fun-to-read science-fiction story, which takes place in 2121 in Bosyork, biggest metroplex on the East Coast, Rebecca receives a robot for her ninth birthday. Dubbing herself Sherlock Holmes and the robot Watson II, the two set out to find a mystery and solve one involving lost twins carrying codes with rollicking success. Liberally sprinkled with forecasts of 22nd century life, this makes a satisfying read.

> *Janice P. Patterson, "Older Readers: 'The Robot and Rebecca: The Mystery of the Code-Carrying Kids',"* in Children's Book Review Service *(copyright © 1980 Children's Book Review Service Inc.), Vol. 8, No. 14, August, 1980, p. 140.*

The Robot and Rebecca: the Mystery of the Code-Carrying Kids . . . is a tongue-in-cheek mystery. . . . The mystery itself takes a back seat to all the aliens met along the way, Venusian swamp people, huge Efflerumps and four-foot-high insectoids called Sizzlegridions.

> *"Book Reviews: 'The Robot and Rebecca: The Mystery of the Code-Carrying Kids',"* in School Library Journal *(reprinted from the December, 1980 issue of* School Library Journal, *published by R. R. Bowker Co./A Xerox Corporation; copyright © 1980), Vol. 27, No. 4, December, 1980, p. 74.*

DRAGON NIGHT AND OTHER LULLABIES (1980)

The title poem's verses include lines representative of the tenderness in all: "Night is coming, / Bank your fire. / Time for dragons / To retire. / Hiss. / Hush. / Sleep." To some adults, the mother owl's song may be too lurid an evocation . . . of predatory dreams: "the faltering heartbeat beneath your claws," the blood and screams of the owl's prey. But the descriptions are accurate and also convey what is meant, an idea of parental love and concern.

> *"Nonfiction: 'Dragon Night and Other Lullabies',"* in Publishers Weekly *(reprinted from the January 2, 1981 issue of* Publishers Weekly, *published by R. R. Bowker Company, a Xerox company; copyright © 1981 by Xerox Corporation), Vol. 219, No. 1, January 2, 1981, p. 51.*

The concept is original, . . . but the poems are sometimes tedious, sometimes frightening. Better poems and songs with more imaginative themes and language are available to help engender a love of poetry in the young child.

> *Renee Queen, "Younger Readers: 'Dragon Night and Other Lullabies',"* in Children's Book Review Service *(copyright © 1981 Children's Book Review Service Inc.), Vol. 9, No. 7, February, 1981, p. 55.*

Sixteen simple unrhymed verses, small in size (four-to-ten lines) and sensibility, cast as lullabies or night songs sung by animal mothers or others (a giant, a troll, a mermaid, a shepherd). The opening **"Whale's Lullaby"** shows us we can't expect anything fresh and new: "Asleep in the deep, / Lullabied by the ocean, / Rest, calf, on my back. / I am your crib and your cradle. / I am both rocker and rock.'' Boldest perhaps is **"Mother Owl's Song,"** not the stuff of conventional lullabies. . . . Like the owl's, all the lullabies are matched to their subjects—the bear's deals with hibernation, the wolf's with a midnight hunt, . . .—which might help focus a small child's interest where the generally mild imagery does not.

> *"Picture Books: 'Dragon Night and Other Lulla-bies',"* in Kirkus Reviews *(copyright © 1981 The Kirkus Service, Inc.), Vol. XLIX, No. 8, February 15, 1981, p. 211.*

SHIRLICK HOLMES AND THE CASE OF THE WANDERING WARDROBE (1981)

The Jane Yolen of the precious fairy tales tries her hand here at the kid detective story and turns out the standard, fast-reading product she apparently intended. . . . There's a bit of feminist fun-making when George must agree to become an ''honorary girl'' in order to join the detectives. This, like the rest of the story, goes down painlessly.

> *"Younger Fiction: 'Shirlick Holmes and the Case of the Wandering Wardrobe',"* in Kirkus Reviews *(copyright © 1981 The Kirkus Service, Inc.), Vol. XLIX, No. 5, March 1, 1981, p. 284.*

Shirli has a problem. No one takes her seriously as a detective. . . . On a dare, she tries to solve a real crime. It seems there are thieves breaking into summer homes and stealing antique furniture. Shirlick Holmes (her nickname) and her girl-friends, the ''Seekers,'' set out to catch the crooks. What they find is that, along with the thrill of solving the case, comes a real danger when tangling with people outside the law. Fun reading for mystery and detective lovers of early years. Fast-paced and cleverly handled, this will keep readers turning pages to the end.

> *Patt Parsells Kent, "Younger Readers: 'Shirlick Holmes and the Case of the Wandering Wardrobe',"* in Children's Book Review Service *(copyright © 1981 Children's Book Review Service Inc.), Vol. 9, No. 9, April, 1981, p. 76.*

UNCLE LEMON'S SPRING (1981)

This is another of Yolen's recent departures from her characteristic precious fairy tales, and here she tries to match her prose to the sort of hill country shenanigans more closely associated with [her illustrator Glen] Rounds. . . . But despite all the peepin' and snufflin' and the stomach jumpin' like a sack of hoptoads, Yolen hasn't the earthy wit and outrageous imagination to give this the zip of Sid Fleischman's tall tales— or those of Rounds himself.

> *"Younger Fiction: 'Uncle Lemon's Spring',"* in Kirkus Reviews *(copyright © 1981 The Kirkus Service, Inc.), Vol. XLIX, No. 10, May 15, 1981, p. 634.*

This rousing tall tale is full of action and rich in unusual turns of phrase (e.g., "If pigs had wings, they'd built nests in trees."). . . . The outrageous happenings and the warm sense of fun put this on a part with Mr. Yowder and McBroom.

> *Holly Sanhuber, "Book Reviews: 'Uncle Lemon's Spring',"* in School Library Journal *(reprinted from the September, 1981 issue of* School Library Journal,

published by R. R. Bowker Co./A Xerox Corporation; copyright ©1981), Vol. 28, No. 1, September, 1981, p. 132.

In a congenial bit of yarn spinning that departs from her usual storytelling mode, Yolen relates how Uncle Lemon and his niece Letty outwit the nasty Preacher Morton in a battle over Lemon's new blue-white mountain spring. The text's broad rustic dialect is humorous and colorful: Letty's characterization of Preacher Morton as ''so almighty took up with God and money that he keeps the Sabbath and everythin' else he can get his hands on'' is typical of the book's arch country wit. The story reads aloud well and has a structure suitable for classroom chapter sessions. . . . It's a rich slice of Americana.

> *Denise M. Wilms, "Children's Books: 'Uncle Lem-on's Spring',"* in Booklist *(reprinted by permission of the American Library Association; copyright © 1981 by the American Library Association), Vol. 78, No. 2, September 15, 1981, p. 113.*

THE GIFT OF SARAH BARKER (1981)

[Yolen] portrays the contradictions of Shakerism through the perspectives of her characters in [this] bittersweet novel. . . . While the personal dynamics of the story could have been more fully developed, Yolen effectively individualizes her characters and evokes a vivid image, rich in fact-based detail, of a tightly structured Shaker haven. Into the fabric of a teenage romance she also weaves complicated and disturbing—at times violent—undercurrents that add a dimension both powerful and provocative.

> *Stephanie Zvirin, "Books for Young Adults: 'The Gift of Sarah Baker',"* in Booklist *(reprinted by permission of the American Library Association; copyright © 1981 by the American Library Association), Vol. 77, No. 18, May 15, 1981, p. 1250.*

This is an absorbing tale. . . . Yolen uses the contradiction between the religious ecstasy of the community and its total celibacy to heighten the tension in her novel. Even the minor characters are rounded personalities! A jewel of a historical romance.

> *Barbara Baker, "Older Readers: 'The Gift of Sarah Baker',"* in Children's Book Review Service *(copyright © 1981 Children's Book Review Service Inc.), Vol. 9, No. 11, June, 1981, p. 100.*

A predictable novel about two young people raised as Shakers and their inner struggles in breaking away from that strict, celibate life. . . . Yolen conveys the community's repressive atmosphere and extensive thought-control in a stiff, prim style that's as leaden as their imposed serenity. For balance, she shows us some Shaker dances and ecstatic celebrations (but without much change in her sober style); and her community includes joyful singers and a compassionate woman leader as well as petty conformists, the unforgiving, self-righteous prig who's the male leader, and the self-punishing Sister Agatha— but the range is as stereotypical as the individual responses. (pp. 1166-67)

> *"Older Fiction: 'The Gift of Sarah Barker',"* in Kirkus Reviews *(copyright © 1981 The Kirkus Service, Inc.), Vol. XLIX, No. 18, September 15, 1981, pp. 1166-67.*

Adolescents looking for a steamy tale of about-to-be-requited love will not find it here, although Abel's feelings of discontent are described as sexual urges (he notices a "burning . . . between his legs"), and the plot is too meager to draw more mature readers. The Shaker setting lends intrigue, and the dances and postures that gave the Society of Believers their popular name are effectively described. The concepts of having a "gift" (as in the title) and "Shakering" a plate, however, are neither defined nor made altogether clear in the text. Sister Agatha, Sarah's natural mother who beats and abuses the girl after every small disobedience, is the most vivid character. It is Agatha's suicide that generates the dramatic climax: Sarah and Abel's leave-taking is only a weak conclusion. (p. 155)

> *Karen Stang Hanley, "Book Reviews: 'The Gift of Sarah Barker'," in* School Library Journal *(reprinted from the October, 1981 issue of* School Library Journal, *published by R. R. Bowker Co./A Xerox Corporation; copyright ©1981), Vol. 28, No. 2, October, 1981, pp. 154-55.*

THE BOY WHO SPOKE CHIMP (1981)

[The struggle of Kriss, the old hermit, and the chimp] for survival is courageous and exciting (if somewhat farfetched), and Yolen relates the adventure in short, manageable sentences and a lively style. Horrors and problems encountered are balanced with humor, while Kriss' leaving the chimp behind to save its life results in a bittersweet ending that tugs at the heart.

> *Barbara Elleman, "Children's Books: 'The Boy Who Spoke Chimp'," in* Booklist *(reprinted by permission of the American Library Association; copyright © 1981 by the American Library Association), Vol. 77, No. 21, July 1, 1981, p. 1397.*

[Considered] "a walking woodland disaster" by [his] father, 12-year-old Kriss Pelleser is portrayed in the most unbecoming stereotyped way: bespectacled, skinny, having a cowlick, carrying Kleenex in his pocket. Kriss departs from his namby-pamby ways by leaving home and hitchhiking with a trucker and two chimps from the UCLA Language Lab. Inept Kriss manages to use a compass, ration his food and water, even forgets to brush his teeth one night—all of this just to prove himself a hero. Kriss has not planned on an earthquake, however. After a tremor overturns the truck, Kriss shows little compassion for the dead (?) trucker but does cry when one of the chimps falls to its death. Rescued after the quake, Kriss nonchalantly leaves the surviving chimps in the woods—research forgotten/friendships dissolved. What a split personality! The only unusual aspect of this forgettable book is that Kriss "Crusoe" and his monkey "Friday" communicate through sign language.

> *Lynette Tandy, "Book Reviews: 'The Boy Who Spoke Chimp'," in* School Library Journal *(reprinted from the August, 1981 issue of* School Library Journal, *published by R. R. Bowker Co./A Xerox Corporation; copyright © 1981), Vol. 27, No. 10, August, 1981, p. 61.*

BROTHERS OF THE WIND (1981)

Beautifully descriptive with a lilting flow of words, this is a mythical, sensitive tale of an orphan slave boy and a horse born with wings. The dreams of the ruler, the role of Allah, and the boy's faith in the horse are a bit abstract for young readers. The realization that the "palace of the wind" is life after death should instigate a challenging discussion for gifted children.

> *Renee Queen, "Older Readers: 'Brothers of the Wind'," in* Children's Book Review Service *(copyright © 1981 Children's Book Review Service Inc.), Vol. 10, No. 1, September, 1981, p. 10.*

This is one of Yolen's frail, fluttery tales that asks readers to marvel at an escapist miracle. When a foal is born with wings, the sheik who owns it calls it "Allah's jest" and orders the young slave Lateef, "the tender one," to dump it in the desert. Instead, Lateef, who thinks the foal might be "Allah's test," takes it across the desert to the city of Akbor . . . where the Caliph, he discovers, lies dying from an unfulfilled dream of riding a winged horse. So Lateef and his "little brother" the foal move into the stable, and when the foal has grown enough to be mounted, slave, caliph, and mount go flying off to dwell as brothers somewhere that Yolen's last words refer to as "the palace of the winds." Trite and anemic.

> *"Younger Fiction: 'Brothers of the Wind'," in* Kirkus Reviews *(copyright © 1981 The Kirkus Service, Inc.), Vol. XLIX, No. 18, September 15, 1981, p. 1162.*

THE ROBOT AND REBECCA AND THE MISSING OWSER (1981)

Rebecca, who longs to be a detective, is not one to give up easily. With her sleuthing techniques and Watson II's computer mind, the mystery eventually gets solved. Lightweight and fast-paced, this will find high appeal with futuristic fans looking for a good, quick story.

> *Barbara Elleman, "Children's Books: 'The Robot and Rebecca and the Missing Owser'," in* Booklist *(reprinted by permission of the American Library Association; copyright © 1981 by the American Library Association), Vol. 78, No. 1, September, 1, 1981, p. 52.*

An owser is a fuzzy dog-like creature with three legs that understands and feels what its best friend feels and understands. Someone is stealing people's owsers in . . . ***The Robot and Rebecca and the Missing Owser***. . . . Rebecca Jasons, junior detective in the year 2121, and her robot pal Watson II must first find out what an owser is before they can track down the owsernapper. Along the way they meet all kinds of futuristic creatures like a snakeman, Canterloopers and a being from the planet Chameleon III, who can change his shape. Like Rebecca's previous . . . adventure . . . , this is light, brisk entertainment. Large print, simple sentences and short chapters make this a good pick for younger and reluctant readers as well as for read-aloud sessions.

> *"Book Reviews: 'The Robot and Rebecca and the Missing Owser'," in* School Library Journal *(reprinted from the December, 1981 issue of* School Library Journal, *published by R. R. Bowker Co./A Xerox Corporation; copyright © 1981), Vol. 28, No. 4, December, 1981, p. 83.*

THE ACORN QUEST (1981)

Yolen's play on the quest tradition sets five small animals off to find the golden acorn that can save their starving Woodland kingdom. . . . Altogether the Fellowship endures a Perilous, a Dolorous, and a Very Queer adventure, none of them taken seriously by Yolen, who plays the whole as a homey little spoof. As such it is well-turned, and pleasingly light-footed.

"Younger Fiction: 'The Acorn Quest'," in Kirkus Reviews *(copyright © 1981 The Kirkus Service, Inc.), Vol. XLIX, No. 21, November 1, 1981, p. 1346.*

Humor arises from absurd incidents in [the knights'] travels (trying to skirt a dragon by hiding under a brown blanket and pretending to be a bog, for example), and there's a touch of pathos in the way the knights find more strength in themselves than they thought. A funny spoof for those not minding Arthur done up lightly. (p. 445)

Denise M. Wilms, "Children's Books: 'The Acorn Quest'," in Booklist *(reprinted by permission of the American Library Association; copyright © 1981 by the American Library Association), Vol. 78, No. 6, November 15, 1981, pp. 444-45.*

Cute animals have almost destroyed the Arthurian stories in the last 50 years, but Yolen's parody of quest narratives, in which *all* the knights are cute animals, avoids the temptations rampant in this idea. . . . Yolen has produced a hilarious story, full of monomaniacal characters and archetypal but silly incidents. The story will stand by itself without any knowledge of Arthur or medieval romances. . . . [The tale has] wit and simplicity. . . .

Donald K. Fry, "Book Reviews: 'The Acorn Quest'," in School Library Journal *(reprinted from the December, 1981 issue of* School Library Journal, *published by R. R. Bowker Co./A Xerox Corporation; copyright © 1981), Vol. 28, No. 4, December, 1981, p. 58.*

APPENDIX

THE EXCERPTS IN CLR, VOLUME 4, WERE REPRINTED FROM THE FOLLOWING PERIODICALS:

American Artist
The American Journal of Sociology
American Libraries
Appraisal
The Atlantic Monthly
Best Sellers
The Black Scholar
Book Week—Chicago-Sun Times
Book Week—New York Herald Tribune
Book Week—The Sunday Herald Tribune
Book Week—The Washington Post
Book Week—World Journal Tribune
Book World—Chicago Tribune
Book World—The Washington Post
Booklist
The Booklist
The Booklist and Subscription Books
  Bulletin
The Bookman (New York)
Books—New York Herald Tribune
Books and Bookmen
Books for Your Children
Bulletin of the Center for Children's Books
Canadian Children's Literature
Chicago Sunday Tribune Magazine of
  Books
Chicago Tribune
Chicago Tribune Books Today
Childhood Education
Children's Book News
Children's Book Review
Children's Book Review Service
Children's literature in education
The Christian Science Monitor

College English
Curriculum Review
Dance Magazine
The Economist
Elementary English
Encounter
English Journal
The German Quarterly
Growing Point
The Horn Book Magazine
In Review
Interracial Books for Children Bulletin
The Journal of Negro Education
The Junior Bookshelf
Junior Libraries
Kirkus Reviews
Kirkus Service
Kliatt Young Adult Paperback Book Guides
Language Arts
Library Journal
The Lion and the Unicorn
The Listener
Lively Arts and Book Review
Minnesota History
The Nation
Natural History
The Negro History Bulletin
The New Republic
New Society
New Statesman
The New Statesman & Nation
New York Herald Tribune
New York Herald Tribune Book Review
New York Herald Tribune Books

New York Herald Tribune Weekly Book
  Review
The New York Review of Books
The New York Times
The New York Times Book Review
The New Yorker
PNLA Quarterly
Publishers Weekly
The Reading Teacher
Reference Services Review
Saturday Review
Saturday Review of Education
The Saturday Review of Literature
School Arts
The School Librarian
The School Librarian and School Library
  Review
School Library Journal
Science Books
Science Books & Films
Scientific American
The Spectator
Teacher
Time
The Times Educational Supplement
The Times Literary Supplement
Top of the News
The Use of English
Virginia Kirkus' Bookshop Service
Virginia Kirkus' Service
The World of Children's Books
Young Readers Review

THE EXCERPTS IN CLR, VOLUME 4, WERE REPRINTED FROM THE FOLLOWING BOOKS:

Arbuthnot, *May Hill*. Children's Reading in the Home. *Scott, Foresman, 1969.*

Arbuthnot, *May Hill, and Sutherland, Zena*. Children and Books. *4th ed. Scott, Foresman, 1972.*

Bader, *Barbara*. American Picturebooks from Noah's Ark to the Beast Within. *Macmillan, 1976.*

Bader, *Barbara; Binns, Betty; and Eisenman, Alvin, eds.* Children's Book Showcase 1977. *Children's Book Council, 1977.*

Blount, *Margaret*. Animal Land: The Creatures of Children's Fiction. *Morrow, 1975.*

Books for Children: 1960-65. *American Library Association, 1966.*

Cameron, *Eleanor*. The Green and Burning Tree: On the Writing and Enjoyment of Children's Books. *Atlantic-Little, Brown, 1969.*

Crouch, *Marcus*. Treasure Seekers and Borrowers: Children's Books in Britain 1900-1960. *The Library Association, 1962.*

Egoff, *Sheila*. The Republic of Childhood: A Critical Guide to Canadian Children's Literature in English. *Oxford University Press, 1975.*

Fisher, *Margery*. Intent Upon Reading: A Critical Appraisal of Modern Fiction for Children. *Hodder & Stoughton Children's Books, 1961.*

Fisher, *Margery*. Who's Who in Children's Books: A Treasury of the Familiar Characters of Childhood. *Holt, Rinehart and Winston, Weidenfeld & Nicolson, 1975.*

Fraser, *James H., ed.* Society & Children's Literature. *David R. Godine, Publisher, Inc., 1978.*

Georgiou, *Constantine*. Children and Their Literature. *Prentice-Hall, 1969.*

Gersoni-Stavn, *Diane*. Sexism and Youth. *R. R. Bowker Company, 1974.*

Hearne, *Betsy, and Kaye, Marilyn, eds.* Celebrating Children's Books: Essays on Children's Literature in Honor of Zena Sutherland. *Lothrop, Lee, & Shepard Books, 1981.*

Huck, *Charlotte, and Kuhn, Doris Young*. Children's Literature in the Elementary School. *2d ed. Holt, Rinehart and Winston, 1968.*

Huck, *Charlotte S., and Young, Doris A*. Children's Literature in the Elementary School. *Holt, Rinehart and Winston, 1961.*

Hürlimann, *Bettina*. Three Centuries of Children's Books in Europe. *Edited and translated by Brian W. Alderson. Oxford University Press, 1967.*

Jan, *Isabelle*. On Children's Literature. *Edited by Catherine Storr. Schocken, 1974.*

Kingston, *Carolyn T*. The Tragic Mode in Children's Literature. *Teachers College Press, 1974.*

Kirkland, *Winifred, and Kirkland, Frances*. Girls Who Became Artists. *Harper & Row, 1934, Books for Libraries Press, 1967.*

Larrick, *Nancy, ed.* Somebody Turned a Tap in These Kids: Poetry and Young People Today. *Delacorte Press, 1971.*

Last, *R. W.* Erich Kastner. *Oswald Wolff, 1974.*

Lonsdale, *Bernard J., and Mackintosh, Helen K*. Children Experience Literature. *Random House, 1973.*

MacCann, *Donnarae, and Richard, Olga*. The Child's First Books: A Critical Study of Pictures and Texts. *Wilson, 1973.*

Meigs, *Cornelia; Eaton, Anne Thaxter; Nesbitt, Elizabeth; and Viguers, Ruth Hill*. A Critical History of Children's Literature. *Edited by Cornelia Meigs. Rev. ed. Macmillan, 1969.*

Miller, *Bertha Mahoney, and Field, Elinor Whitney, eds.* Newbery Medal Books: 1922-1955. *Horn Book, 1955.*

Milne, A. A. Introduction to The Travels of Babar, *by Jean de Brunhoff. H. Smith & R. Has, 1934.*

Sendak, Maurice. Introduction to Babar's Anniversary Album: 6 Favorite Stories, *by Jean and Laurent de Brunhoff. Random House, 1981.*

Smith, James Steel. A Critical Approach to Children's Literature. *McGraw-Hill, 1967.*

Smith, Lillian H. The Unreluctant Years: A Critical Approach to Children's Literature. *American Library Association, 1953.*

Spirt, Diana L. Introducing More Books: A Guide for the Middle Grades. *R. R. Bowker Company, 1978.*

Sutherland, Zena; Monson, Dianne L.; and Arbuthnot, May Hill. Children and Books. *6th ed. Scott, Foresman, 1981.*

Townsend, John Rowe. A Sounding of Storytellers: New and Revised Essays on Contemporary Writers for Children. *J. B. Lippincott, 1979.*

Wintle, Justin, and Fisher, Emma. The Pied Pipers: Interviews with the Influential Creators of Children's Literature. *Paddington Press Ltd, 1974.*

CUMULATIVE INDEX TO AUTHORS

AUTHOR INDEX

CUMULATIVE INDEX TO TITLES

TITLE INDEX

TITLE INDEX

TITLE INDEX

TITLE INDEX

TITLE INDEX

TITLE INDEX

CUMULATIVE INDEX TO CRITICS

CRITIC INDEX

CRITIC INDEX

CRITIC INDEX

CRITIC INDEX

CRITIC INDEX

CRITIC INDEX

CRITIC INDEX